Hands-On
Systematic
Innovation

for Business and Management

IFR Press

Library of Congress Cataloging-in-Publication Data
Mann, Darrell L
        Hands-On Systematic Innovation for Business & Management
    Darrell L Mann

ISBN 1-898546 -73-8

First Edition printed 2004. Re-printed 2006.
Second Edition printed 2007. Re-printed 2009.

Printed in the UK by Lazarus Press.
Unit 7 Caddsdown Business Park
Bideford
Devon, EX39 3DX
www.lazaruspress.com

F²

Foreword

The capacity to originate has become the most sought after talent of our time. There is growing consensus that human creativity has replaced **scale** as the defining feature of the 21st century corporation. This shift raises new challenges and opportunities. Recall how the Total Quality Management (TQM) movement built reliable and repeatable systems for ever greater productivity. Today, we need the same kind of systematic capability for driving creativity. Organizations that learn how to manage for creativity will have a crucial competitive advantage. But unlike the transparent process of TQM, the thought processes involved in producing breakthrough innovations are hidden, and even mysterious -- not just to the awestruck admirers, but often to the innovators themselves.

This lack of transparency has lead to the common belief that creativity, whatever it is, is something special. But is it? Is it really a rare gift of a select few (DaVinci, Mozart), or is it an egalitarian skill we all possess to some degree, like athletics, that can be improved with practice? These are critical business questions. Their answers determine whether we as managers can substantially improve the creative process that drives Innovation.

If game-changing ideas arise mainly through inspired, unpredictable flashes of a maverick genius, then the role of the manager is very limited. Your job is reduced to cheerleader. Round up all the gifted people and then get out of their while they work their magic. If, on the other hand, creativity turns out to be a trainable skill, then the manager's role is significant.

Nicknamed "The Fuzzy Front- End", Industry has tended to treat creativity as more Alchemy than Chemistry – a seemingly magical process that has the power to turn lead into gold, a small idea into a gigantic discontinuity. The alchemists were attempting to investigate nature before basic scientific tools and practices were available, relying instead on traditions, basic observations, and mysticism to fill in the gaps. However, when new technology allowed scientists to see more deeply into the core of molecules, Alchemy began to fall apart. Thanks in no small part to the work of Darrell Mann, we are at this point in the study of creativity.

In *Hands-On Systematic Innovation*, Darrell Mann provides compelling evidence that creativity can be a predictable and controllable process. Despite the fact that many innovators quip their Big Idea "just seemed to pop into my head", Mann shows us that such originality simply cannot be produced out of thin air. This means that, paradoxically, even the most radical new concept must, by definition, be firmly rooted in "old knowledge".

With the benefit of hindsight, all "revolutionary" innovations can be described in terms of an evolutionary extension of some existing technology -- "somebody, some where, has already solved your problem." This claim holds true for everything from the jet engine to the jet ski.

In the following pages, Mann gives example after example that convincingly demonstrates the emergence and implementation of innovation is neither mysterious, random, nor haphazard. The thesis for *Hands-On Systematic Innovation* is grounded in this insight. It is jammed full with the knowledge and tools necessary to make the creative process genuinely systematic.

February - 2007
Craig B. Wynett
Chief Creative Officer
The Procter & Gamble Company

Warning I

This is not a typical 'management' book. It is a book built on ideas distilled from areas of human endeavour beyond the traditional management sciences. Going beyond traditional boundaries means venturing outside zones of comfort. It also means we need to think about whether the journey might be worth the effort.

Time is a precious commodity for any manager. Lack of time is one of the things that encourages us to stay within our own comfort zones.

We think the ability to innovate systematically – to genuinely and reliably be able to generate successful innovations that will make a positive difference to the bottom-line of a company – is worth the time to dip a toe or two into the contents. We have structured the book on this basis.

Nevertheless, we assume that those time pressures and comfort zones may cause some to end their interest in the book right here.

Warning II

This book assumes that readers already recognise the importance of creativity and innovation. It does not try to justify why anyone should be creative, nor why any organisation needs to be innovative. If you don't know why innovation is important then you don't need this book. Yet.

Warning III

This book is a companion to the technical version of the systematic innovation story. That book was configured for engineers, scientists and designers. This one is configured for managers and leaders.

Clearly, in our highly segmented and specialised world there is a need to separate the technical from the non-technical. Clearly also, in the large majority of organisations, the separation between 'technical' and 'business' is almost complete. This is unfortunate. Very often we see that the best solution to a technical problem is a business one. Similarly, very often the best solution to a business problem is a technical one. In the real world, there is no separation between technical and business – they are simply two aspects of a unified whole.

In the future, we hope that it will be possible to combine the two disciplines into one coherent whole. For now, we have assumed that it is still necessary to separate the two sides. This book consequently requires no knowledge of science, engineering, mathematics or anything that managers and business people might describe as 'technical'.

Warning IV

"The average man would rather face death or torture than think."
Bertrand Russell

This warning is only for those readers that know about TRIZ. If you have never heard of TRIZ, you can skip to the next section. Finding out that this book is built on some TRIZ ideas and that TRIZ was a product of the former Soviet Union and built on the study of technical patents can only look like, a big pair of negatives from a business standpoint, so best to ignore both.

People familiar with TRIZ, of course, will have at least an inkling that it can be applied to business situations. For those people, the health warning is that we have strayed – sometimes considerably – from the traditional versions of TRIZ. It is very difficult to convince a busy, stressed manager that applying a simple one word Inventive Principle is the solution to his or her problem. Business problems involve people. People are fuzzy, inconsistent and often downright awkward. In a word, people are complex. The tools and methods we present here seek to take into account that complexity. Every complex problem can be solved by a simple solution. Just not very well. Our aim here is to provide means of generating real and effective solutions; where we see TRIZ fails, we have developed new tools.

Foreword II

Some time in 1998, we sat down and wrote out a list of the books we would like to read on TRIZ. Top of that list was a 'good' book to help apply TRIZ in technical applications. Second was one on business and management applications. While it is too early to say whether our previous book, 'Hands-On Systematic Innovation', qualifies for the 'good' description in the first case, it was decided that the growing interest in the second meant that it was necessary to proceed with trying to meet the need in any event. And so 'write book on business application of TRIZ' was duly added to the collective job catalogue. Friends, partners and all those around us no doubt groaned in anticipation of the late nights, and all around grumpy behaviour that would inevitably follow.

The book that you see before you is the end result. To our surprise, however, this time, although the late nights certainly came true, the grumpiness didn't. I'm not sure I have ever seen the process of writing 'pleasurable', but that is certainly the way it has felt for all but a tiny number of the chapters in this book (I'll leave it to you to guess which ones!). Part of the reason for this is that all the hard work trying to work out theme and structure has carried across almost directly from the first book. The other part is the combined feeling that we are doing something that hasn't been done before, and the knowledge – based on our ever expanding list of clients in the business and management sector – that what we're describing actually works.

With respect to this second point, although we have spent time working in industry and have been responsible for strategies, budgets and people the size and breadth of small towns, we have never considered ourselves to be 'management consultants'. In the same breath, we find the description both overwhelming and profoundly depressing. Overwhelming, because during the course of distilling best practice for some of the Systematic Innovation principles described in the book, we have found ourselves in the company of some truly great thinkers, for whom the Wayne's World originated exhortation 'we're not worthy' springs instantly to mind. Profoundly depressing because our own personal experiences with 'management consultants' have often been frustrating and a to a significant extent a poor use of our time. Put simply, it seems to us that a very large proportion of it is boundary-condition-ignoring, fashion-following, 'here's one I did earlier, no need to think, just do it' corporate dogma. In any event, it all seemed to be saying things that were almost the opposite of what we know to be the important philosophical constructs of what we now refer to as Systematic Innovation. Whether these turn out to be 'right' of course is a matter of some debate. Our money is on the fact that they are (they work literally everywhere else – including that biggest system of all 'nature' – so why not here?). You, as the reader – provided you got past the raft of health warnings that appeared before you even arrived at this Foreword – have a similar choice to make.

With regard to theme and structure, things have changed little from the companion 'technical' book. The theme, in fact, is almost identical – starting from a focus on benefits rather than features, and going on to recognize that it's not just the 'what' of Systematic Innovation but the 'how' and 'why' that are necessary to properly communicate the subject matter. Related to this theme and the consequent need for the tools, methods and strategies being discussed to be applicable to any problem or opportunity situation we may care to throw at them, it is also worth noting that where the TRIZ philosophy which formed a significant part of the foundation contained holes (and although it is undoubtedly the most comprehensive creativity and innovation system in existence, it undoubtedly does contain holes at this point in time), we have sought to plug them with the best alternatives we could find.

In terms of structure, a cursory glance at the chapter listing for this book and the previous technical book will show there to be almost no difference. What that means in the context of this book, is that things are arranged in such a way that after four general introductory chapters describing the overall Systematic Innovation picture, the book is arranged such that there is a different chapter for each of the definition, selection, solution or evaluation tools and that things will be read on an 'as required' basis.

The most significant variations in structure involve the shifting balance between overview and detailed process. One of the golden rules of management texts (based on the analysis of several hundred during the process of distilling best practice) seems to be 75,000 words is about what is expected – too many more and 'busy' managers will never have the will to pick it up; too many less and it obviously can't be serious. The technical book was over 150,000 words because that's how much content we felt there needed to be to adequately communicate the message. Here we have slightly more. The best way to think about this potentially daunting number is that there is around 30,000 words (or half of a trans-Atlantic plane journey) worth of 'reading matter', and another 140,000 worth of how-to for when you get back to the office, and, if we've done anything like a half decent job, you want to get your hands dirty and actually use Systematic Innovation to make a difference.

Darrell Mann
Clevedon,
April 2004.

Foreword to the Second Edition.
The contents of parts of this book have been taught to over 1500 people since 2004. This second edition emerges from some of the dialogues with those people on how things could be made clearer. This new version also benefits from the output of our ongoing research programme and the analysis of as many of the management texts we have been able to access during the period between the publication of the first edition and the present day.
Darrell Mann
Bradford
February 2007.

Contents

1.
Introduction

"Ours is not so much an age of vulgarity as of vulgarization; everything is tampered with or touched up, or adulterated or watered down, in an effort to make it palatable, in an effort to make it pay."
Louis Kronenberger

and

"Whether you believe you can, or whether you believe you can't, you're absolutely right."
Henry Ford

There are approximately 1800 management texts published every year, 1800 and rising. Whichever way you look at it, that is a large number. The choice of titles is almost as overwhelming as the variation in quality. As a consequence, very often the decision to purchase a given book veers towards 'random'. But then what is the alternative? No-one – least of all a busy manager – has the time to look at even a fraction of what is available.

This lack of time versus quantity of information conflict is the basic dilemma central to the theme of this book. The subject matter of the book is systematic innovation. The foundations of the methods we will describe go back to 1946, when someone sat down and thought wouldn't it be great if we could analyse successful solutions from every area of human endeavour and distill the results into a form that would be useful to individuals irrespective of which area they were working. What if, we thought to ourselves back in the mid 1990s when we started applying the systematic innovation techniques to business situations, what if we could distill all of the useful stuff from those 1800 management texts per year and present the results in a coherent and integrated manner.

It is our belief that we have now done exactly that. We realize that that might sound rather difficult to believe. 1800 books per year – not to mention all of the other sources of learned business knowledge – is a considerable number to have to analyse. Plus, who on earth are we to determine what is 'successful' and what is not? In many respect we are in exactly the same position as the original 1946 researchers. Except they were looking at patents rather than business texts. When we look at patents, that 1800 number looks like an even more overwhelming 200,000 per year. However, two important things happen when you start looking at mankind's inventive capabilities. The first thing you discover is that there is an awful lot of low quality stuff out there. Typically, when we are looking at patents, we are able to reject over 90% almost immediately since they contribute nothing to the furtherance of human knowledge. The second thing you discover is that there is an awful lot of re-inventing the wheel takes place. Different industries and disciplines tend not to communicate with one another, and consequently, they all devote sometimes massive resources to solving what turn out to be problems that someone in a completely different field already solved. In part this happens because we all have a tendency to think that our problems and situations are unique. Well, of course, in many ways they are. But in many other ways they absolutely are not. After you have examined close to three million examples of successful innovation, you begin to see that there are some very definite patterns, strategies and techniques that emerge time and time again across disciplines that appear to be at completely different ends of a spectrum. How could it possibly be, for example, that aircraft designers, teachers, computer scientists, chemical process engineers, and (to take a very broad extreme) termites are all working on the 'same problems'? And – even more surprising – using the same inventive strategies to derive successful solutions.

Yet this is what the systematic innovation research has uncovered. The findings when we look at what managers, strategists and business leaders do when they are successful are remarkably similar to what those same aircraft designers, teachers, computer scientists, chemical engineers and even termites have done. Likewise, the findings show us that a very high proportion of management texts and management solutions have little or nothing to contribute to the furtherance of knowledge. There are an awful lot of bad management textbooks in the same way that there are an awful lot of bad patents.

In effect what the systematic innovation research – now running at several thousand person years of effort – has done is to define a knowledge framework based on success. According to us that framework is 'universal'. Recognising that such a statement can be quite inflammatory, especially to those of an academic persuasion, let us qualify it by saying that it has applied so far to everything that is currently known. What is 'currently known' and what is 'knowable, but not yet known' are two different things. Every day that we continue to extend the method – and currently the family of full-time researchers numbers over 30 – we are constantly testing the bounds of that framework. Every day we try to disprove the framework. Occasionally we find things that cause us to extend or modify it – not, as it happens, in the last two years of activity – but 'occasionally'. One day we might even succeed in showing that it is the wrong framework, but at this point in time we have failed in our attempts to do that.

So, what you will find in this book is a description of this framework, and the tools that emerge from it to help us to solve problems and create opportunities in a systematically reproducible way. The remainder of this chapter is divided into four main sections. In the first of these sections we take a helicopter ride high over the whole systematic innovation terrain in order to present a 'big picture' overview. The aim of this section is to provide a means of seeing the whole thing in the smallest space possible in order to act as a navigation aid later on.

In the second section we examine what is meant by 'success' and 'successful solutions'. Here the aim is to show what we mean when we say that there are an awful lot of bad management texts. Specifically within this section we will examine a series of tests that we will routinely apply whenever we are considering whether a solution we find is one that has something to contribute to the advancement of the management discipline or not.

In the third section we look at the important issue of context. Context is the thing that transforms knowledge into wisdom. Too many management texts fall into our 'low quality' category because they recommend strategies that, although they applied in the context being used by the author, they may well not apply in yours. In this section we will examine different innovation contexts in order to begin to make sense of the who, when and where parts of the story.

Finally, in the fourth section we briefly explore some of the time implications of learning the systematic innovation tools. The toolkit is the result of the biggest study of creativity and innovation ever conducted, and consequently to learn every part of the toolkit is going to take some months to achieve. Very few managers have a 'few hours' never mind a 'few months' to devote to learning new things, hence we spend our time in this section examining what we can do to get the maximum innovation benefit from the minimum investment of time.

In putting together the specification for this book, we set ourselves some interesting challenges. We wanted a book that focused on benefits (i.e. that it enabled the reader to successfully tackle any problem or opportunity situation they were working on), rather than being just another collection of features. We also decided we wanted a book that could be read from start to finish, or could use as a quick-dip reference; and we wanted it to be both academically rigorous and at the same time not the crushingly dull experience most academic books tend to be. In other words, we identified a number of contradictory requirements and decided we wanted to avoid compromising on any of them. How successful we have been remains to be seen.

In keeping with all of the above aims, the book has been structured and sequenced in such a way that anyone working on a problem (in the most general terms that word implies) could begin at the beginning of the book and be taken on a journey through only those chapters necessary to solve the problem.

The main method of achieving this feat of navigation is the small figure appearing at the top right hand corner of each page of the book. A larger version of that figure is shown in Figure 1.1 below.

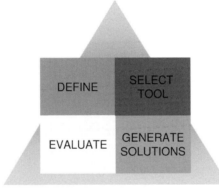

Figure 1.1 Hands-On Systematic Innovation Navigation Aid

Three of the four steps contained in the box at the center of the figure are like any generic problem definition and solving process; it being necessary to define what the problem is, to generate some solutions and to then evaluate those solutions. We add in a fourth step – 'select tool' because of the richness and breadth of the problem solving tools available to us through all of the tools, techniques and methods we have found it necessary to include. We examine this four-step process in more detail in the next chapter, and follow this by a chapter on each of the elements of each box in turn. As you will see there, some of the boxes – most notably the problem definition and generate solutions boxes – contain a host of other boxes.

The aim of this section is to discuss the triangle drawn behind the four boxes (hence the reason the top right hand corner of this page emphasizes the triangle to indicate that this is what we're talking about at this point in the book). The triangle is there to denote the existence of an underlying philosophy behind the process being discussed in future chapters.

If you're already familiar with systematic innovation and its application in a business or management context, you may wish to delve straight into the other Chapters. If you're not, we recommend that you read this chapter and the following two – 'process overview' and 'psychology' in order to obtain the maximum benefit from subsequent chapters.

1) Systematic Innovation – Helicopter View

As illustrated in Figure 1.2, systematic innovation can be thought of on three basic levels. At the first level it is a collection of tools. These tools can be used individually, or they can be coupled together to form a comprehensive start-to-finish method. The basic idea behind this method is that it will take us through a systematic procedure that will progressively help us to define what our situation is and what we should do to improve it, until we reach a point where we have a 'best' solution to the situation we have defined. Beyond that, then, is a third level on which systematic innovation works. We have labeled this third level 'philosophy'. 'Philosophy' perhaps sounds like a very grand word. What we mean when we use the term is that there are high level concepts and ideas that should influence how we utilize the method and tools.

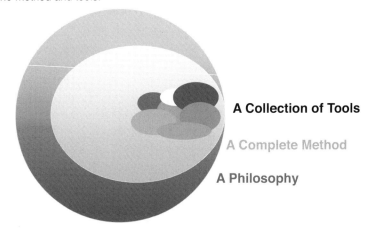

A Collection of Tools

A Complete Method

A Philosophy

Figure 1.2: Hierarchical View of Systematic Innovation

Our main emphasis for the remainder of this chapter is to focus on those philosophical elements. Before doing that, however, it is worth setting the scene for them by reviewing some of the main findings of the systematic innovation research. These are:-

- that there are only a small number of fundamentally different types of problem
- that someone, somewhere, therefore, has already solved a problem something like the one you wish to solve
- that there are only a small number of possible strategies for generating inventive solutions
- that system evolution trends are highly predictable
- that the strongest solutions transform the unwanted or harmful elements of a system into useful resources.
- that the strongest solutions also actively seek out and destroy the conflicts and trade-offs most design practices assume to be fundamental.

In allowing us access to these findings, systematic innovation has incorporated the knowledge and experiences of the world's finest inventive minds. It effectively strips away all boundaries between different business disciplines.

The tools can be used in a number of different ways. The overall process enables users to systematically define and then solve any given problem or opportunity situation. Some users will rigorously apply this process. Others are happier extracting individual elements from the overall structure and using those. This book has been configured in such a way as to allow users significant flexibility, offering both an over-riding structure and access to individual problem definition and solving tools. An over-riding aim of the book has been to construct a problem definition and solving process that works for any situation users may care to throw at it – whether that be technical or business, simple or complex, highly constrained or clean-sheet, step change innovation or incremental improvement, or focused on products, processes or services. In that sense, even though we focus here on business and management issues, it is worth noting that the basic philosophy, method and toolkit is conceptually almost identical to the companion technical version of the book.

Systematic innovation is both simple and complex. To learn and gather a working knowledge of the whole structure will probably take several months. Some people are prepared to make this investment, and others are not. Those that are not usually take great comfort from the fact that they will be able to learn and realise significant benefit from just a short exposure to individual elements of the overall structure. In many instances these benefits are enough. We've tried to design the book to suit every individual requirement. The basic idea here is that the process and tools should, as far as possible, adapt to your way of working and your requirements, rather than the other way around. One thing that is clear, however, is that it is not a 'creativity replacement' kit. It absolutely demands the users creative input in order to get the best out of it. Best to think of the whole as a creativity turbo-charger. A turbocharger is a great power booster, but is useless without the engine.

Systematic innovation is different to most other creativity aids, and may appear a little unnatural at first. Here are some of the high-level philosophical elements that we hope will to guide your overall perception and use of the method and tools:

Firstly regarding the big idea that 'someone, somewhere already solved your problem' is the way by which problem solvers become able to access the good solutions obtained by the world's finest creative business minds. The basic process by which this occurs is illustrated in Figure 1.3 below.

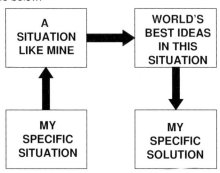

Figure 1.3: Systematic Innovation Abstraction Philosophy

Essentially, the systematic innovation researchers have encapsulated the principles of good practice and set them into a generic problem-solving framework. The task of problem definers and problem solvers using the large majority of the systematic innovation tools thus becomes one in which they have to map their specific problems and solutions to and from this generic framework. The main tasks here are, first of all being able to abstract your situation in such a way that it begins to look like a situation that someone else has already generated solutions for, and then secondly, transforming the generalized solutions into things specifically relevant to your context.

Seven Pillars

Beyond the abstraction requirement, there are seven other philosophical pillars upon which the systematic innovation framework rests. These pillars are illustrated in Figure 1.4.

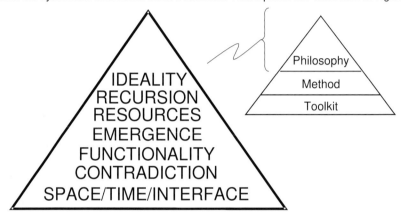

Figure 1.4: Systematic Innovation Pillars

Let us now look at each of these seven pillars in turn in order to examine the influence they should exert on the way in which we deploy the systematic innovation tools and processes. Thus, in no particular order, we have:-

Ideality

One of the first tests of a successful innovation uncovered by systematic innovation researchers was that they gave customers a more ideal solution than what had previously been available. 'Ideal' in this sense is defined as the (perceived) benefits that the customer receives divided by the costs and harms that are also present. The fact that successful innovations deliver more ideality implies that there is an overall direction of success. Hopefully this direction – give customers more of the things they want and less of the things they don't – may be seen as a fairly obvious one. While this direction is fairly obvious, what is less obvious, is that this evolution process takes place through a series of discontinuous evolutionary jumps. We usually think of these jumps as steps from one way of doing things to another, or, more formally, jumping from one s-curve to another. As we shall see in a later chapter, the s-curve characteristics that determine how all systems evolve are a central aspect of the innovation dynamic. A key finding of the systematic researchers beyond this is that the steps denoting a shift from one s-curve to the next are predictable. This fact emerges from the study of large numbers of business and technology system evolutions, and the analysis of what jumps take place as systems shift from one way of doing things to another. The overall dynamic of evolution – with systems making discontinuous jumps from one s-curve to another all the time heading in a direction of increasing ideality is summarized in Figure 1.5 below:

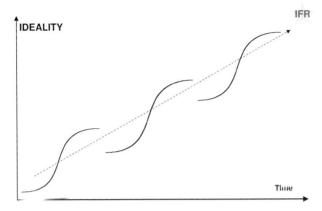

Figure 1.5: Evolution Dynamics – Systems Jump From One S-Curve To Another In The Direction of Ideal Final Result Outcomes

The figure actually takes the story a step further by suggesting that the evolutionary direction towards increasing ideality is driven by a destination – called 'Ideal Final Result (IFR) – where the customer has received all of the benefits they require and none of the costs and harms. In most senses the Ideal Final Result is a theoretical rather than a practical limit (although we shall see examples of systems that have achieved this goal in later chapters). Practical use of the idea demands also that we take into account the fact that different customers, as well as different parts of a value network may have very different interpretations of what 'ideal' means to them. Nevertheless, there are certain common themes (e.g. 'free, perfect and now' – Reference 1.1) that make the IFR a useful thing to think about when trying to determine a strategic direction.

A rather more surprising aspect of the IFR idea has been that as systems get closer and closer to their Ideal Final Result destination, the number of possible solutions capable of delivering the desired outcome reduces. Figure 1.6 illustrates this convergent evolution idea. It is not clear whether it will ever be possible to definitively prove that evolution is convergent.

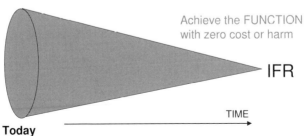

Figure 1.6: Evolution Is A Convergent Process

We used to spend inordinate amounts of time trying to convince audiences that it was so, before realizing that it saved a lot of pain and argument by simply stating that a) ever system we have so far examined has followed such a characteristic, and – more importantly – b) if you merely think of the image as a 'useful image' it will have served enough of a purpose.

Used as a problem definition aid, the ideality part of the toolkit encourages problem solvers to break out of the traditional 'start from the current situation' type of thinking, and start instead from what is described as the Ideal Final Result (IFR). Generally speaking IFR-focused solutions incorporate the concept of systems solving problems 'by themselves'. The key word is 'self'; things that achieve functions by themselves – self-regulating, self-organising, self-correcting, etc – all represent, when incorporated in a true systematic innovation fashion, very powerful and resource-efficient solutions.

Contradictions
Taking the Figure 1.5 image of evolution taking place through a sequence of discontinuous shifts a step further, the systematic innovation researchers further identified the fact that what causes the flattened profile at the top of an s-curve is the emergence of a conflict or contradiction. The s-curve flattens at the top, not because we stop trying to improve a system, but because something comes along and stops us. One of the most important findings, then, of the research has been that the world's strongest solutions have emerged from situations in which a problem solver has successfully sought to avoid the conventional trade-offs that everyone else has taken for granted. Having uncovered a number of strategies whereby problems solvers have successfully eliminated compromises and trade-offs, systematic innovation offers tools through which problem solvers can tap into and use the strategies employed by such people. The most commonly applied tool in this regard is a business conflict/trade-off elimination Matrix – a 31x31 matrix containing the four or five most likely strategies for solving design problems involving the most common business trade-off and conflict situation types. Probably the most important philosophical aspect of the contradiction part of systematic innovation is that, given there are ways of 'eliminating' contradictions', managers and business leaders should actively look for them. Instead of being seen as a threat, systematic innovation tells us that every unresolved trade-off and compromise we can find is an opportunity. This is a subtle but often profound shift in thinking for many managers.

Functionality
Although the functionality aspects of systematic innovation owe a significant debt to the pioneering work on Value Analysis, the method of defining and using functionality data is markedly different; sufficient at the very least to merit discussion as a distinct paradigm shift in thinking relative to traditional occidental thought processes. Three aspects are worthy of particular note:-
1) The idea that a system possesses a Main Useful Function (MUF) and that any part of the system which does not contribute towards the achievement of this function is ultimately harmful. In a banking insitution, for example, the MUF is to manage the flow of money; everything else in the system – like personnel, sales or marketing departments are there solely because we don't yet know how to achieve the MUF without the support of the ancillary components. (Systems may of course perform several additional useful functions according to the requirements of the customer.)
2) In traditional function mapping, the emphasis is very much on the establishment of positive functional relationships between components. Systematic innovation places considerable emphasis on plotting both the positive and the negative relationships contained in a system, and, more importantly, on using the function

analysis as a means of identifying the conflicts, contradictions, in-effective, excessive, harmful and missing relationships in and around a system. Function and attribute analysis thus becomes a very powerful problem definition and 'complexity management' tool.

3) Functionality is the common thread by which it becomes possible to share knowledge between widely differing business sectors. A matrix management structure is a specific solution to the generic function 'organise people', just as a training department is a specific solution to the generic function 'disseminate knowledge'. By classifying and arranging knowledge by function, it becomes possible for organisations to examine how other businesses in very different disciplines have achieved the same basic 'organise' function. *'Solutions change, functions stay the same'* is a message forming a central thread in the systematic innovation methodology: People want a hole not a drill; benefits not features.

Resources

The Resources pillar of systematic innovation relates to the unprecedented emphasis placed on the maximisation of use of everything contained within a system. In systematic innovation terms, a resource is *anything in the system which is not being used to its maximum potential*. The method demands an aggressive and seemingly relentless pursuit of things in (and around) a system which are not being used to their absolute maximum potential. Discovery of such resources then reveals opportunities through which the design of a system may be improved. In addition to this relentless pursuit of resources, systematic innovation demands that the search for resources also take due account of negative as well as the traditionally positive resources in a system. Thus the competitors, subcontractors and forces we typically attempt to fight when we are designing and running systems, are actually resources. Systematic innovation, as we shall later see contains a number of strategies to help us to perform this 'turning lemons into lemonade' switch in the way we think about things that we currently think of as harmful in a system.

Space, Time And Interface

Psychological research clearly shows that the human brain is not designed to be creative. It undoubtedly *can be* creative, but that is not one of its main functions. Its main function is to develop and store patterns so that we know how to react in a given situation. Hence, we don't have to think when we get dressed in the morning, or when we drive to work, because we have performed both actions so many times that we have a pre-stored 'program'. Only when something out of the ordinary happens do we have to jump out of these patterns. One such time when the patterns don't help is when we are trying to be creative. This is one of the reasons for the cliché expression 'thinking out of the box'. And it is undoubtedly not an easy thing to do. In particular, our brain very quickly makes assumptions about what a problem is. Very often we only discover later on that we have been solving the wrong thing. An important finding of the systematic innovation research has been that the strongest problem solvers have found ways of overcoming this type of assumption-making phenomenon. The effect is known as 'psychological inertia' or 'paradigm paralysis', and the tools for overcoming the effect involve techniques for forcing problem solvers to shift their perspective on situations. As suggested in the title of this section, there are three dimensions to these perspective-shifting techniques. Experienced systematic innovation users are continuously changing their perspective on problems – zooming in to look at the fine details, zooming out to see the bigger picture, thinking about how the situation is affected by changing time – whether that be nano-seconds or decades – in both the past and future – and also thinking about how different parts of systems interface and relate to one another. This is not a natural process for most people – our brains aren't wired that way – and so we introduce and discuss tools to help in the process of thinking in time, space and interface as we work our way through the book.

Recursion

Related in some ways to the space-time-interface viewing perspective pillar, the concept of recursion relates to the phenomenon of self-similarity in systems. Specifically, recursion encapsulates the idea that many systems repeat as we switch our focus from the macro scale to the micro-scale and vice versa. By 'repeat', we mean that features that are present at one scale, will also exist at other scales. We will see recursion in action at several points during our exploration of systematic innovation. Two specific instances are worth mentioning here as a way of explaining the implications of recursions.

The first relates to the cybernetics work of Stafford Beer (Reference 1.2). Stafford Beer's Viable System Model emerged from the study of organisation structures and resulted in two very important conceptual findings. The first involved the identification of five essential elements that a system had to contain if it were to be 'viable'. The second involved the idea of recursiveness – and the discovery that the five-element viability test still applied at different hierarchical levels of consideration of a system organisation structure. There are, in other words, certain elements that will determine the viability of a section, a department, a division, a company, a corporation, and so on.

The second involves the recognition that as systems evolve through successive disruptive shifts from one system (s-curve) to another, the complexity of the respective systems recursively passes through a characteristic increasing-decreasing profile – Figure 1.7. This particular recursive effect allows us to utilise the parts of the systematic innovation toolkit most relevant to a given phase in the complexity cycle.

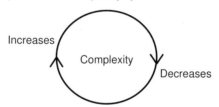

Figure 1.7: Recursion In System Complexity Evolution

Emergence

To reduce the entire scientific and mathematical base of complexity theory to a single philosophical foundation is probably a little unfair given the breadth and depth of work being devoted to the subject. Nevertheless, there is at least some justification for suggesting that the whole field emerged as a result of a very simple idea; that enormously complex systems emerge from what may be extremely simple base rules and principles. The interaction of individually simple elements, in other words, can produce some highly unexpected outcomes.

Businesses and organisations are fundamentally complex systems. Take two people and you have the makings of a system acting on the edge of chaos. Although we shall not see complexity theory discussed explicitly anywhere except in the trends of evolution part of the systematic innovation discussion, its presence is everywhere. The great implication of emergent systems on organisation design is that the success or failure of that system will ultimately depend on the 'DNA' that makes up that organisation. In the organisational context, 'DNA' consists of things like the mission and vision statements, value systems –

both formal and informal – and the beliefs of the individuals present. Many business problems occur due to conflicts between what managers wish the system to deliver and what the corporate-DNA says it is capable of delivering. A key idea that emerges from this in the context of innovation is that it is much easier to achieve success if the innovation comes *from* the DNA rather than *despite* it.

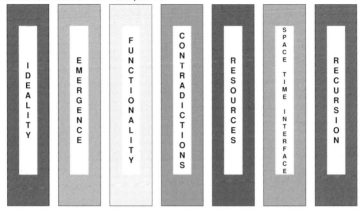

Figure 1.8: Seven Pillars Summary

2) Defining 'Success'

One of the important assumptions made at the beginning of the chapter was that the systematic innovation research was somehow able to discern what defined a 'successful' innovation. In this section we examine some of the main criteria used to distinguish success from failure.

An obvious test of success is financial. A successful innovation, by definition, must offer paying customers a value proposition that they will pay sufficient for that it not only pays all of the direct and indirect costs of providing it, but also allows the provider to obtain a profit.

Financial success, however, is a very poor means of determining success in any sense that allows us to transfer any useful knowledge to others wishing to create a success of their own. Financial reward is merely the manifestation of success. It has nothing to do with the mechanics of what has *actually* made something successful.

Nevertheless, during the early stages of the systematic innovation research it was important to correlate financial performance to the underlying mechanisms of success. One of the main objectives of the research has been to identify the mechanics of success in such a way that we can usefully use them to transfer that success to other applications. The way that this has happened is that the researchers have systematically studied known financially successful innovations with the aim of identifying any common factors that they may possess.

Any financially successful innovation inevitably becomes clouded in ego, mythology, the whims of the media, and in a significant number of cases, plain luck. It is absolutely in the interests of anyone involved in an innovation to present that innovation in the best possible light. Consequently, any analysis of a financially successful innovation can only obtain, at best, a partial perspective on what actually enabled the success to take place. Analyse enough cases, however, and gradually consistent patterns begin to emerge.

It is these patterns that we now use as a means of determining whether an innovation can be classified as successful or not. We believe that these patterns offer a series of tests that are much more reliable as an indicator of success than mere finance.

Many innovations that can be classified as 'successful' under the terms of these tests, we now see, have 'failed' in a business context. This doesn't necessarily mean that we have eliminated them from our analysis. In the same way that financially successful innovations become the subject of myth-building, so those involved in innovations that failed have it in their interests to cover what has happened in a cloud of smoke and mirrors. Trying to blow these clouds away, we see that in a great number of such cases, there were many elements of the innovation that were indeed 'successful'. In many cases innovators get almost everything right. 'Almost', however is not good enough to deliver financial success. But just because an innovator failed to get the timing right, or failed to market to the right audience, does not mean that we should ignore all of the good things that happened.

That, then, is the way that the research has been conducted. Almost every attempted innovation has something to commend it. Our job has been to find those 'somethings' and to put them together into a package that allows us to distill out a series of success factors that are generically applicable.

The following is what we have so far come up with. Perhaps not surprisingly, the list connects strongly to the philosophical pillars detailed in the previous section.

i) Essential Elements

Successful innovation emerges from the interaction of five essential elements. These are illustrated in Figure 1.9.

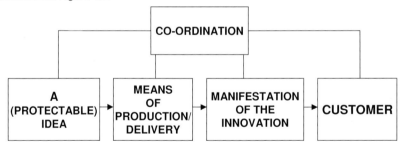

Figure 1.9: Essential Elements Of A Successful Innovation

In more detail, the five elements comprise the following:-

    a) An Idea. The most obvious part of the list; without the idea, there will be no innovation. The figure includes the word 'protectable' in parentheses. There have certainly been successful innovations that have not had any kind of copyright or patent protection, but they are few and far between. Even fewer are the cases of unprotected ideas that allow a company to sustain their presence. Unprotected ideas are easy to copy. The only sustainably successful innovations where there is no formal protection are either narrow niches or (more likely) situations where one or more of the means, manifestation or co-ordination are so good that they preclude the successful entry of a competitor.

    b) A Customer. The next most obvious element of the five is the customer. Without a customer demand for the innovation – whether that demand be a stated need or one that is 'hidden' – there will be no success. We will talk a lot more about identifying customer needs in future chapters. The large majority of organizations are very bad at anticipating the future needs of their customers (and non-customers). Likewise, the vast majority of customers are very bad at being able to describe what their future needs and desires are. Systematic innovation will allow us to do a much better job of anticipating those spoken and unspoken needs.

c) A Manifestation. Whether it is a product or a service, there has to be a manifestation of the idea. The manifestation may be physical or virtual.

d) A Means. Very many innovations fail because the idea is not produce-able in an economic manner. The problem may be lack of ability to manufacture or deliver, or it may simply not be possible to produce at a sufficiently low cost.

e) Co-ordination. If the other four elements are not managed and co-ordinated then again the innovation will fail. The co-ordination part of the story is largely about timing, and making sure all of the other elements are in the right place at the right time.

The next series of tests all relate primarily to the 'Idea' element, and what makes an idea into one capable of delivering a successful innovation:

ii) Function

Successful innovations recognize that customers buy functions. People don't buy a watch they buy the ability to tell the time. Either that or they are buying a statement about their wealth or fashion consciousness. Functions, in other words, can be tangible or intangible. In both cases, function is king.

iii) Ideality

As already discussed, successful innovations travel in the direction of increasing (customer) ideality. (Perceived) benefits divided by the sum of cost and harm. One test of a successful innovation, therefore, is that at least one customer segment receives a more ideal solution than the one they already have. Broadly speaking, the more segments that perceive your innovation as 'more ideal', the more successful it will be.

iv) Resources

A slightly more subtle test of a successful innovation is that the problem identifies and makes use of a resource that no-one has previously recognized as a resource. This is particularly so, if the 'resource' is seen or has previously been viewed as a negative thing. Turning lemons into lemonade breeds innovation success.

v) Contradiction

Probably the single most important test of a successful innovation. Success happens when conflicts, trade-offs and contradictions are 'eliminated' (Reference 1.3). While it is not always the case that a contradiction is completely eliminated, what is important is that it is challenged to such an extent that a step-change jump in the direction of the Ideal Final Result takes place.

vi) Trend Jumps

The final test of successful innovation involves the discontinuous trend jumps uncovered during the research. A product or service that makes such at least one advance along one of the trends is likely to be a successful one.

3) Context

A commonly asked question is 'when should I use systematic innovation?' It is easier to answer this question by examining situations in which it is *not* going to be helpful. There are two such situations:-

a) if we are simply looking to replicate something that we have already done before. This 'here's one I did earlier' situation, frankly does not need a systematic innovation methodology to help achieve it.

b) if we are looking to 'optimize' a system. Systematic innovation contains virtually no mathematics and so if we are trying to answer questions like 'what is the optimum batch size?' or 'what is the best interest rate?' or 'what bonuses should everyone get this year?' then systematic innovation is not going to help.

Both of these situations are rare in our view. Or rather they ought to be. In the first case, it is our belief that there is no such thing in reality as an 'identical' situation in a management context. Anything that involves people has to recognize that every one of us is different, and that every one is different at different times. 'You can never step in the same river twice' as the old adage goes. Systematic innovation can play a significant part in identifying and doing something about the differences between last time and this.

In the case of optimization problems, systematic innovation adopts a somewhat different view. 'Optimum' is a dangerous word in systematic innovation because it implies the presence of trade-offs and compromises. Any manager that has faced the onerous task of allocating staff bonuses will know that there is no way to satisfy everyone. This is a characteristic common to all 'optimum' or 'best' calculations since what is best for one situation is anything but for another. Whenever a systematic innovation user sees the word 'optimum', they immediately visualize the existence of a conflict or a contradiction. As we saw earlier, eliminating contradictions will always be preferred to finding an optimum average.

Of the remaining situations where we believe systematic innovation is the most beneficial, it is worth discussing two here. Both relate to s-curves again (we will see many more instances too as we progress through the book). Figure 1.10 illustrates a very common situation in many businesses.

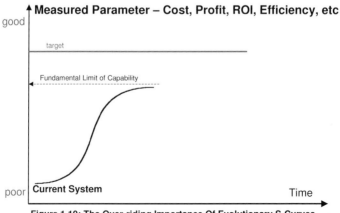

Figure 1.10: The Over-riding Importance Of Evolutionary S-Curves

In the figure we see the setting of a target that lies beyond the fundamental capability of the system expected to deliver it. All systems will eventually find themselves in this situation irrespective of what parameter we are interested in improving. The more competitive the industry, the quicker it will tend to happen. When we find ourselves in this position then all of the normal things we would do to improve will no longer work. We could optimize and optimize the system from now until the end of time and still fail to bridge the gap between capability and target. 'Fundamental Limit', unfortunately, means exactly that.

When we find ourselves in this position, we are basically faced with two choices; change the target or change the system. One of the two is undoubtedly easier to achieve than the other. Changing the target, however, tends not to offer a recipe for long term business success – unless we can convince our competitors to change the target too. That, then, leaves the option of changing the system. This is undoubtedly the more difficult of the two options. This also happens to be an area where systematic innovation excels. As suggested in Figure 1.11, systematic innovation offers three mechanisms for enabling us to identify the relevant system change that will permit the target to be achieved. Each of the three is covered in detail in separate chapters later in the book. For the moment it remains sufficient to say that we will be able to identify the required jumps in a systematically reproducible manner. Moreover - and an important final word on this topic – what the method will also tell us is which part of a system it is that needs to be changed. When a system hits a fundamental limit, in other words, it is usually one element within that system that has hit its limit. Hence we don't have to completely scrap our current way of doing things in order to 'change the system' – merely find the limiting element and change that.

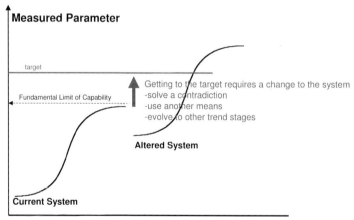

Figure 1.11: Systematic Innovation Tools Bridging The Gap Between Limit And Target

The second major application scenario for systematic innovation occurs when there is currently no system. Here the method can help us to conceive what systems should look like when we are starting from a clean sheet of paper. When we are using the methods in this role we will be guided by the Ideal Final Result concept. Figure 1.12 reproduces a version of the conical evolution image from Figure 1.6. The figure is here modified to outline the main evolution directions available to us in any innovation situation.

The first (and most commonly applied) direction involves starting from today's system and using the relevant tools to change to become more ideal. The second involves the 'use another means' idea from Figure 1.11. This is another strategy that allows us to change to another s-curve by shifting to a solution that exists somewhere and which we can import into our situation. The third direction is the one more attuned to the blank piece of paper start point. This is the direction that tells us to forget about today's system, and to think instead about the Ideal Final Result.

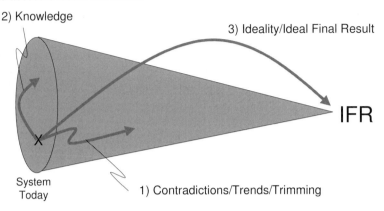

Figure 1.12: Three Main Innovation Directions

All three routes are relevant. Which one we will choose will depend on our context. If we are bound to starting from what we already have, then we are most likely to choose route 1; if we have the ability to look outside and start again using proven capabilities from elsewhere, then we are more likely to explore route 2. Finally, if we have the freedom to completely start again, or are looking to get into a new market, then route 3 is the most appropriate direction.

The overall process should ultimately act as our guide. Chapter 10 in particular is designed to help identify which tools are most appropriate in which contexts. In the meantime, the Figure 1.12 image is, we think, a useful one to keep in mind when thinking at the big-picture, helicopter-view level.

4) Time Implications

Systematic innovation is not and never has been designed as a recipe to be followed blindly. It requires you to think about what is happening, and it requires you to do some work. We are reminded here of the Toyota lean production system and the following quote from the Head of Toyota Consulting *"The Toyota production system has been studied by the West over the past 20 years. Many books and videos are available. The book, 'The Machine that Changed the World', provides all you need to know to implement the Toyota production system. Yet everywhere I go in the west I see no evidence of its implementation. What do we see that you do not see?"* And a comment by Konosuke Matsushita, Founder of Matsushita Electric Industrial Co., Ltd & PHP Institute from 1979: *"We are going to win and the industrial West is going to lose out; there is not much you can do about it because the root of your failure is in yourselves. Your firms are built on the Taylor model. Even worse, so are your heads. With your bosses doing the thinking while the workers wield the screwdrivers, you're convinced deep down that this is the right way to run a business. For you the essence of management is getting the ideas out of the heads of the bosses and into the hands of labour. We are beyond the Taylor Model.*

16

Business we know, is now so complex and difficult, the survival of firms so hazardous in an environment increasingly unpredictable, competitive and fraught with danger, that their continued existence depends on the day-to-day mobilisation of every ounce of intelligence."

In other words, sure, you can follow a recipe, but don't forget there are some underlying 'why's' behind it, and that it is a good idea to think about them. In another old adage, a surgeon can be trained to remove an appendix in about an hour, but it takes several years to work out what to do when something not in the basic recipe happens. Same thing here, albeit, if you don't start getting some immediate benefit, we have failed in our main goal.

If that hasn't put you off, we need to talk a little bit more about the underlying 'why's' of systematic innovation in its business context:

The essence of its philosophy is distillation of large quantities of knowledge and experience into a small, manageable entity. It might take users a considerable amount of time to appreciate the significance of the seven philosophical pillars of systematic innovation, but they can at least be remembered in a few minutes.

At the other end of the hierarchy pyramid, the toolkit contains a series of tools that, to varying degrees can be learned and applied also in a relatively short space of time. There Is a deal of variation, but as an average, a half-day of learning and doing is usually enough to give a newcomer the will, confidence and ability to use a given tool.

In between toolkit and philosophy, the learning curve for the complete systematic innovation method and processes (with or without software 'support') is probably measurable in weeks.

'Weeks' unfortunately is then at the heart of a big problem for the large majority of newcomers. A week is a serious investment of time for anyone in these busy times; there is simply too much else needing to be done, and not enough time to do it. Does this mean we should give up? Or does it mean that it might be better to think about alternative ways of doing things? The latter would appear to make the most senses.

Different User Profiles
Figure 1.13 illustrates a graph compiled from the experiences of watching several hundred students, strategists and managers go through at least two-days worth of systematic innovation 'training'. (Two days is a typical figure since most managers tend to think a one-day event will be too trivial, and they are too busy to be away for any longer than two. It is however a very short period of time in relation to the total amount of content – which is equivalent to an MBA in many respects.)

The first category of user types is the 'not for me' variety. This is the individual who, for whatever reason (with bad teaching and instinctive aversion because people have been instructed to attend by their boss being probably the top two reasons), decides they do not like systematic innovation or do not want to commit the time necessary to learn it.

The second category involves those who discover a part of systematic innovation that they like and chose to adopt it into their way of doing things. This 'part' might be a tool like the Business Conflict Matrix or the Trends of Evolution, or it might simply be one or two of the Inventive Principles. At the end of their initial exposure to the toolkit, this category of user has achieved some success using the particular tool or element of, is 'satisfied' by that success, and shows no desire to expand their knowledge further. In some small way, however, this category of user has been changed by their experience.

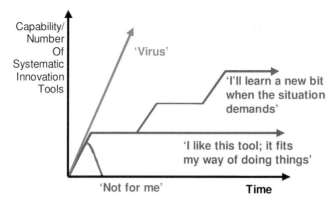

Figure 1.13: Typical Systematic Innovation User Profiles

The third category of user might be seen as the pragmatist. They usually start as users of the second category, but find that there are certain types of problem – or more usually a specific problem – that the tool they know has failed to solve. They therefore look at other elements of the toolkit until they find something that does solve the problem. The success with the new tool then prompts the incorporation of that tool into that persons 'way of doing things'. (The importance of 'success' in determining whether someone picks up a part of systematic innovation or not cannot be under-estimated.)

The fourth category of user profile is what is commonly described amongst long-time systematic innovation users as 'having the virus' or 'being infected'. This type of user typically reads all of the books, papers and articles they can find on the subject, and it changes the way that they do things.

The Folly of 'I Am Right; You Are Wrong' (Reference 1.4)
Everyone has their own way of doing things. Some of these ways are demonstrably more effective than others, but nevertheless those embedded ways are present and they are constraints that will dictate how much and which parts of systematic innovation people will be attracted to and which they will reject. So which are the most important parts of systematic innovation? The simple answer to the question is that it depends. It depends on the circumstances of the problem or opportunity under consideration, it depends on the user, and it depends on how the tools are presented to them.

To take a cooking analogy; there are definitely right and wrong ways of using the various tools contained in the kitchen. There is a right and a wrong way of holding a whisk, in the same way that once we have picked the whisk up by the handle instead of the blades, there is then a considerable degree of flexibility in how we can use the tool to achieve the desired function; we can stir clockwise or anti-clockwise, with or without a vertical component of motion, we can stop and start, we can change speed, we can change direction, we can do pretty much anything so long as the whisk is in the product and moving it.

At a higher level, we can then use a recipe to help us sequence ingredients and the things we do to them in order to eventually get me to a finished product. If we are trying to make soup, we could probably find several hundred recipes to help us do it. Some will say put the stock in first, and some will say don't. Assuming that the different authors are all trying to help me make soup that is edible, we can probably safely assume that each of them has created a recipe that will work. Some recipes will produce better (to us!) soup than others, but they will all provide us an output that looks and functions like soup.

The point is to find something that fits your way of doing things (whether it be one individual principle or a complete problem solving method/recipe). As far as this book is concerned, one of the major underlying aims has been to present things in a way that enables this pick-and-choose flexibility to happen.

Self-Adapting Systems

A large proportion of users will only ever know and use one or two tools from the toolkit. Chapter 18 later in the book suggests the importance of 'self' in the drive towards increased ideality; self-regulating, self-organising, etc, and any system that works out 'for itself' what is right are all good solution directions. If systematic innovation is about encouraging people to think, perhaps a useful goal would be to offer them a structure that allows them to – as much as is feasibly practical – mix and match tools (both within and beyond the current bounds of the method) to suit their particular individual circumstances. In other words, that they are able to adapt what tools and methods they use, how and when they use them to suit themSELVEs.

If we choose to ignore a recipe that is our decision. If we're making soup it doesn't matter- we may get a thin soup or a thick one or even a stew, but it will be edible. If we're making bread, and stray too far from the recipe, we will end up with something that isn't bread, and might not even be edible, or we might end up with something exciting and new. The former is usually more likely than the latter however, so in future, we might be well advised to follow some form of structure. We also know that we each have our own tastes and that if we take a bit of this recipe and add a bit of that and then add this bit of our own, then we will end up with our ideal bread. 'Our' being the important word.

If we ask ourselves the question is it better for us to adapt to systematic innovation or for it to adapt to us, for the most part, many of us (especially those working in a time-constrained environment) would choose the latter. This again represents an important underlying theme of the book and its layout.

Overview of Other Chapters

Beyond the first three chapters, this book has been designed as a working reference rather than a start-to-finish read. The first three chapters represent the part describing the big picture in more detail than has been relevant in this helicopter-level view; the following chapters are then divided so that each describes and shows you how to use each of the different parts of the toolkit. The different tools, then, are:-

Chapter 4 – System Operator (9-Windows) – detailing a specific tool to assist in the process of thinking in terms of space, time and relationship. This chapter forms a bridge between the overview chapters and the other specific tools – the 9-Windows representing a tool in their own right, but the underlying concepts are used extensively in every other aspect of systematic innovation.

Chapter 5 – Problem Definition (Problem/Opportunity Explorer) – the first of five chapters describing problem definition tools. This first one is the most general in nature; setting the scene for defining where we are trying to get to, what is stopping us, and what resources we have available to help us get there.

Chapter 6 – Problem Definition (Function/Attribute Analysis) – detailing the process of managing problem complexity by modelling the positive and negative functional relationships between the different components, people or other elements of a system.

Chapter 7 – Problem Definition (S-Curve Analysis) – the evolutionary s-curve concept plays an important role in systematic innovation. This chapter details that role and how it impacts on the overall problem definition process.

Chapter 8 – Problem Definition (Ideal Final Result) – closely allied to the ideality concept, is a tool called 'Ideal Final Result'. The Ideal Final Result tool actually has two forms. In Chapter 8 it is discussed in the context of its role as a problem definition aid. The main idea of the tool is that it encourages users to define a somewhat different situation to the one they might otherwise.

Chapter 9 – Problem Definition (Perception Mapping) – the Perception Mapping tool has been designed specifically for problem settings involving people. Every one of us sees the world around us through different eyes. This results in perceptions of reality that may be different from one another. This tool allows us to manage the inevitable complexity that arises when we try to make sense of the different views and perceptions that different people possess.

Chapter 10 – Select Tool – as stated earlier, the systematic innovation toolkit is very richly populated with solution generation tools. Chapter 10 acts as the transition between problem definition and problem solving; offering users a road map that directs them to the most appropriate solving tool for any given problem or opportunity situation.

Chapter 11 – Problem Solving Tools (Conflict & Trade-Off Elimination/Inventive Principles) – a chapter where we detail the mechanics whereby the successful trade-off eliminating business solutions of others can be legitimately transferred to our situations. Of specific interest in this chapter are trade-offs in which, as we try and improve one aspect of a system, some other aspect gets worse or prevents us. The chapter also includes a reference detailing the 40 currently known strategies for eliminating trade-off solutions.

Chapter 12 – Problem Solving Tools (Contradiction Elimination) – related to the previous chapter, but this time focusing on problem situations which contain a contradiction – for example, where we want something to be 'present and absent' or 'big and small', 'independent and attached', etc – and detailing strategies for its elimination.

Chapter 13 – Problem Solving Tools (Measurement Standards) – measurement problems form a specific class within the systematic innovation toolkit. In this chapter we examine the best practices of other managers and problems solvers when they have successfully solved measurement problems.

Chapter 14 – Problem Solving Tools (Linear and Non-Linear Trends of Evolution) – detailing a host of linear trend directions and over 30 discontinuous trends of business evolution and how they apply in both strategic and problem solving situations. This chapter also introduces the concept of evolutionary potential – defined as the distance that a system is able to evolve from its current state to known evolutionary limits.

Chapter 15 – Problem Solving Tools (Resources) – detailing strategies for identifying and utilising system resources, and putting them to best use. The chapter shows how most organisations not only make poor use of most of their resources, but often don't recognise their existence.

Chapter 16 – Problem Solving Tools (Knowledge) – in which we discuss the importance of context in the search for existing knowledge from other areas, and detail strategies for effective knowledge searching.

Chapter 17 – Problem Solving Tools (Re-Focus/Re-Frame) – The Re-Focus/Re-Frame (RF^2) tool is primarily designed and used as a back-up if other tools within the systematic innovation portfolio are not producing adequate results.

Chapter 18 – Problem Solving Tools (Trimming) – detailing a simple a tool that can help in reducing the complexity of systems. Closely related to business process re-engineering in many senses, the 'trimming' tool is accompanied by a set of rules that determine when it is and isn't possible to remove elements from a system.

Chapter 19 – Problem Solving Tools (Ideal Final Result) – detailing the problem solving side of the Ideal Final Result tool.

Chapter 20 – Problem Solving Tools (Psychological Inertia Tools) – another set of 'back-up' tools that are intended to help users 'think out of the box' in those situations where this is required and other tools are not providing the necessary shifts.

Chapter 21 – Problem Solving Tools (Subversion Analysis) – detailing one of the more specialised systematic innovation tools – this one being used in situations where we are trying to improve the robustness of a business model, strategy, organisation structure or other system elements.

Chapter 22 – Solution Evaluation – shifting from problem solving to solution evaluation, this chapter details strategies for making legitimate apples-versus-oranges comparisons between different solutions in order to identify the one that best meets the problem boundary conditions.

Chapter 23 – Into The Future – a short summary chapter examining where systematic innovation itself may be expected to evolve in the future in its business and management contexts.

Each chapter is divided into a number of different sections. Each chapter possesses a similar structure; firstly combining descriptions of the tool under consideration and a series of case study examples of the tool in action. Then, where relevant, subsequent sections describe possible alternative means of actually using the tool; a summary containing 'what do I do' hints, and then finally, a reference section in which the tool content is shown in detail. The latter two parts are there primarily for the use of practitioners. Readers who are simply interested in obtaining a snapshot overview of a given tool, may like to read just the first parts of each chapter.

What Do I Do?

The book has been designed as something that can be read from start to finish, and also be dipped into as a working reference. The general hope is that you will find a way if using the book to fit whatever style of working you personally prefer; there is a complete process we have called 'systematic innovation' for those that want it, or you may prefer to just concentrate on one or two individual tools. Either way, the main aim is to get the reader to a point of delivering tangible success in the shortest possible space of time.

If you are new to systematic innovation, we recommend you read the next two chapters to get a broader feel for what the bigger picture looks like and how it matches to the ways in which our brains function.

Whatever happens, you should keep in mind the seven pillars of the method – CONTRADICTIONS, IDEALITY, FUNCTIONALITY, RESOURCES, RECURSION, EMERGENCE and SPACE/TIME/INTERFACE – in everything you do with TRIZ.

References

1) Rodin, R., 'Free, Perfect And Now', Simon & Schuster; 1999.
2) Beer, S. 'The Brain Of The Firm: The Managerial Cybernetics of Organization', The Professional library, Allen Lane, The Penguin Press, London, 1972.
3) Mann, D.L., 'Design For Wow', TRIZ Journal, October 2002.
4) De Bono, E., 'I Am Right; You Are Wrong', Penguin Books, 1991.

2.
Process Overview

*"It is best to do things systematically, since we are only human,
and disorder is our worst enemy."*
Hesiod

Being the output of the biggest piece of creativity research ever conducted, it may not be surprising to learn that obtaining a working knowledge of all of the parts of the toolkit, and knowing which tool in which situation will require a significant commitment of time and effort. The idea behind the structure of this book is that it will help navigate us through a large part of the complexity of the overall method. The specific aim of this chapter is to outline what that structure is and therefore to help us to see the bigger picture from an overall process perspective.

Recognising that one of the main functions of the book is to help the reader to solve problems and deliver tangible benefit, and that not everyone is going to want to go through the rigours of learning the overall process, a final section of the chapter presents a pair of useful 'short-cuts'. We have included this section as we have found that people obtaining a quick-hit, success from the method are much more likely to want to go on and learn about other parts of the toolkit. Those readers may wish to jump to the end of this chapter now. For those interested in investing a few minutes to explore the full process and to see what they might be missing by going directly to the short-cuts, the next section is where to begin:

A Complete Process

If it is what we want, systematic innovation offers us a complete start to finish process, which – as shown in Figure 2.1 –will take us from whatever vague start point we might be at, through a series of steps that will first help us to define what the right thing to be focusing on is, and then help us to identify the best solution to that situation. While it might be said (often with good cause) that 99% of the problem comes in the implementation, we hope that the 1% we are covering is of value. In any event, the other 99% will be full of other issues and problems to solve – all of which will benefit from the use of this process.

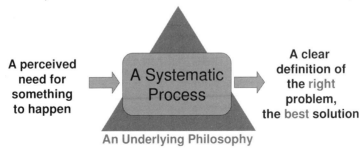

Figure 2.1: Systematic Innovation Process Overview

The start point for the process has been that we should literally be able to begin from any place. We have included inside that wide-ranging ambition the desire to look at business, political, social science, architecture, software and even what might be loosely termed 'the arts' in this start point. While the focus throughout this book will be the application of systematic innovation in business and management centred situations (check out the other books in the series for examples of other application areas), it is worth noting that it is more or less exactly the same process that we can apply to any of these other problem types. Hence the steps the process will take you through will be largely the same as those that someone solving a technical problem will also go through. We hope that this common approach will help to break down some of the barriers that still exist between different disciplines. At the very least, we hope to plant the suggestion that by studying success from literally all forms of human endeavour and distilling them into a unified whole, we have devised a problem solving structure that is 'universal' (the research goes on, of course, and so we are always actively exploring the possibility of extending and revising the structure – that being said, it has remained stable now for the last two years).

Any problem situation start points we could possibly imagine have to be amenable to treatment if the process is to be of generic use. We have tried to validate the process on as many situations as possible, and always present the challenge to problem solvers to try and come up with a scenario the process cannot handle. The sorts of start points we see emerging on a regular basis, and which the process has been validated against include the following sorts of 'perceived need for something to happen' start point:

- How do I improve sales?
- How do I reduce my costs?
- What might the new markets for product X be?
- What is the best way to re-invigorate sales of service Y?
- What is the best strategy for exploiting solution Z?
- Where should we be going next?
- What are the things that might come along in the future and threaten my business? When are they going to arrive?
- How do I reduce waste?
- How do I improve efficiency by B%?
- How do I improve morale?
- How do I prevent change programmes from losing momentum?
- How do I encourage employees to remain in the organisation? What is the best way to do my succession planning?
- How do I get better buy-in to improvement initiatives?

And so on ad infinitum. Note in particular that the process has been designed to cope with the things we normally view as 'problems' ('challenges', or whatever politically correct terminology happens to be fashionable at the moment), but also the other side of the coin, the 'opportunities' – those situations where we think we have a solution, but we don't know what to do with it, or how to exploit it. In this latter case, we need to re-cast our thinking a little (we will do this in the next section of the chapter), but for now all we need to know is that the same generic process will apply to both scenarios.

Some, of course, will argue against both the need for a truly generic process, and whether, even if such a thing is possible, whether it is ethically or morally right to 'inflict' a rigorous structure to something (creativity) that is often fundamentally about doing things differently. We have some sympathy with this view – and the systematic innovation method itself, as discussed in the last chapter, makes great play on the need for 'self-organizing'/'self-adapting' systems. On the other hand, there are two reasons which have prompted us to include and detail a generic process:-

1) some people like the structure it provides, and
2) whether we like a structure or not, the framework provided by a systematic process makes it far easier to communicate our problem or opportunity situation to others in a recognizable and reproducible form.

Like many other problem/opportunity definition/solution (from now on, we'll stick to the abbreviation 'problem solving') processes, the one used in this book contains three basic steps; things start with a part of the process called 'define', then there is a step called 'generate solutions', and finally, a step called 'evaluate solutions'. One of the most challenging aspects of the overall method is that it is far richer than any other process we've ever seen in terms of the options available during the 'generate solutions' part of the process. We usually describe this part of the process when it appears in other methods as the 'insert miracle here' part, because if you check out these processes (we don't need to name them), they all rely very heavily on brainstorming as the means of generating solutions. This is not to denigrate brainstorming (we will use many of the underlying principles in the systematic creativity process), merely to say that systematic innovation provides a substantially higher level of generative richness. So much so in fact that the process we describe here includes a fourth step into the three basic 'define', 'solve', 'evaluate' ones you will find everywhere. That fourth step sits between 'define' and 'solve' and is called 'select'. The basic idea behind the 'select' part of the process is that, having defined a problem situation, and seeing the broad array of possible systematic innovation solution generation tools, how do we know which ones are the ones we should use to tackle the problem? This is an area that seems to confound many newcomers to the method. We hope that Chapter 10 describes a tool selection process that will lift the fog.

To continue describing the overall process then, we now have a four step process – 'Define', 'Select', 'Solve' and 'Evaluate' as illustrated in Figure 2.2.

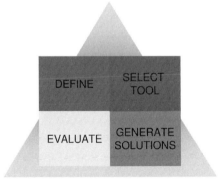

Figure 2.2: Four Basic Steps of the Systematic Innovation Process

Let us now zoom in a little to examine each of these steps in a little more detail:

DEFINE
It is often said that 90% of a problem is defining what the problem actually is. Systematic innovation concurs with this view. It also goes further. It recognises that the average human brain is much happier in 'solve' mode than it is in 'define' mode. A very typical scenario seems to involve the obligatory 10 minutes thinking about the problem, followed

by an hour or so of the enjoyable creative 'solving' part, followed by a race to implement the solution to see how good we were at solving it. The usual outcome of this race is we discover that if we'd just spent a few more minutes thinking about exactly what problem it was that we should have been looking at, we would have saved ourselves an awful lot of time and energy racing to the right answer to the wrong problem. Systematic innovation tries to encourage us to stay in 'define' mode for as long as possible. It does this in ways that are both explicit and subtle. Taken as a whole, the 'define' part of the overall four-step process itself involves five groups of activities. Three of these five – the 'problem explorer', some kind of function and attribute analysis, and some kind of s-curve analysis - are as close to 'fundamental' to defining a problem situation adequately as makes any difference. The recommended 'define' process will **always** encourage problem solvers to go through these three activities. We would also highly recommend that a fourth 'define' activity – involving the consideration of ideality – is also carried out. We don't include this fourth step in the 'fundamental' category, because, frankly, the social and business constraints present in a given situation may dis-allow its use. We will discuss the potential implications of this in Chapter 8. As far as this overview is concerned, the overall process of defining a problem situation should involve the three compulsory plus one highly recommended activity. There is then a fifth definition tool, 'perception mapping'. This tool acts in a rather more specialised role and hence falls into the category 'use if appropriate'. Appropriate in this context means 'does the situation under evaluation involve 'people issues'? The perception mapping tool exists to help us to unravel the inevitable complexities present when different people perceive situations in different ways. The Perception Mapping tool and the specifics of when and where we will use it are detailed in Chapter 9. Meanwhile, the complete problem definition part of the process now contains three essential, one highly-recommended and one context specific parts. Figure 2.3 reflects how these five groups of activities will be displayed in the book.

Figure 2.3: Five Basic Steps of the DEFINE part of the Systematic Innovation Process

Each of the groups is discussed in its own chapter. For ease of reference, the navigator icon at the top right hand corner of each page in the book lets you flick through to view the chapter relevant to the part of the process you are involved in at any point in time.

Staying in overview mode for the moment, however, it is worth recording a few comments here about how these four groups of 'define' activities should be approached:

First, it is worth noting that although there are three compulsory define activities, it doesn't matter what order we tackle them. The default chapter sequence that we recommend is:

   5 – Problem/Opportunity Explorer

6 – Function and Attribute Analysis
7 – S-Curve Analysis
8 – Ideality/Ideal Final Result, and
9 – Perception Mapping

If you prefer a different way of doing things, then great. A cursory examination of past studies that we have conducted would show that we actually change the sequence in which we do things quite considerably according to the type of problem, the mood we are in, and the dynamics of the different members if we are working in a team.

Second on the list of important things to note is that it is highly possible that when we exit any of the five activities, we leave with nothing. This is particularly common, for example, if we are in that very fortunate position of having a blank sheet of paper start to a problem – 'think of a new marketing campaign that will make lots of money' to take an extreme example. It is not possible to conduct a function analysis of a system that doesn't exist yet, and so the answer when we ask the function analysis questions is 'we don't know yet'. The main point in each of the five groups, though, is that although the answer we come out with might be a blank, it is vitally important that we at least enter and ask the question.

Each of the five groups of define activities has a distinct purpose:

- The **Problem/Opportunity Explorer** – is the foundation of the problem definition activity. It is the part of the process that gets us to record things like where we are now, where we are trying to get to, how will we know when we've got there, what resources have we got available to us, and, perhaps most significant for any 'real' problem, what constraints have we got to work within. This is the part of the process where we define the boundaries of the problem/opportunity setting.
- **Function & Attribute Analysis** (FAA) – is where we will gain our appreciation of the functionality of an existing system. It is where we will delve into the details of a system in order to examine and record what is supposed to be happening within and around it, and also what is happening that we don't want to happen. FAA is the place where we will usually find ourselves doing the majority of the problem definition detail. If we do this task correctly, we will often find that the problem suddenly becomes 'obvious'; this is particularly so in the business and management contexts. If systematic innovation is about 'managing complexity', function analysis is where an awful lot of that management happens.
- **S-Curve Analysis** – is where we conduct some kind of assessment of the relative maturity of the different parts of an existing system. This part of the define process is vital as it forces us to obtain a better understanding of the evolutionary mechanics that dictate so much of the how, why, when and where's of problem solving. It will also play a significant role in helping us to determine how we should proceed after the define stage is completed. This part of the define process is often the most qualitative in nature. Fortunately, as we will see in Chapter 7, such qualitative output is in most cases sufficient to allow us to proceed to subsequent stages with confidence.
- **Ideal Final Result** – the fourth activity in the 'define' process involves an analysis of where we are, and where we're trying to get to in the context of 'where could we be ultimately'. It is an extremely powerful tool for helping us to think 'out of the box'. As stated above, the process will always recommend that this activity be carried out – you can be pretty sure your current and future competitors are going to be doing it even if you're not – if only to obtain a gauge of how far along the line of evolution you and your problem currently are. On a more profound level, the thinking provoked by this activity can often lead to the

definition of a much better problem than the one you started with. It is also an extremely good way to help identify conflicts and contradictions.

- **Perception Mapping** – as already hinted, this tool exists to help us to make sense of situations in which different people are involved. We all see the world through our own unique perspectives, and very often these perspectives are different from those of the people around us. This may mean that we are right and they are wrong; or they may be right; or neither of us may be right; or we both may be right. The Perception Mapping tool is a way of helping us to map and understand the issues that often arise in these kinds of situations – even, in fact, those ones where people are not necessarily telling the truth, or are not willing to divulge the truth.

Appendix 2 at the back of the book provides a series of blank sheets to help structure your thinking as you progress through these five problem definition steps. Please feel free to photo-copy and use them on any problem or opportunity situation you are involved in. For anyone preferring to use an electronic version, you will find a free downloadable version at the www.systematic-innovation.com website.

SELECT

Having completed the 'Define' part of the systematic innovation process, we progress to the second major stage, 'Select'. This is where the method guides us through a series of steps aimed at helping us to identify what sort of problem situation we have, and what the most appropriate tools to help us solve it are. The 'select' process is described in detail in Chapter 10. While we are still sitting in our helicopter looking down at an overview of the whole process, it is worth recording here that this part of the process has been designed in such a way that we recognise that not everyone reading the book will be equally skilled in all aspects of all of the different tools. As discussed in the previous overview chapter, systematic innovation contains, and we have deliberately configured, an amount of overlap between the different tools in the kit. This means that, except for very specialised cases, the Select process will give us more than one recommendation on possible routes to generate solutions to a given problem. In actual fact, for the majority of cases, we will be able to access a menu of three or four possible routes. This menu is ranked, to reflect the fact that some tools will take you to 'good' answers more directly than others. The general idea is that as your working armoury of tools expands (assuming you want that to happen!), you will increasingly find yourself heading straight to the tool recommended at the top of the menu. We believe also that this 'Select' navigation tool is a useful addition to what can look like an overwhelming level of complexity when trying to transition from defined problem to best solve tool.

SOLVE

Given the richness of the systematic innovation solve tool-kit, the number of possibilities once a problem enters the third 'Solve' or 'generate solutions' stage is extensive. For the purposes of this book, we have provided eleven basic clusters of solve tools. These are shown in the navigation icon reproduced in Figure 2.4 below.

The general idea is that the 'Select' process tells us exactly which of the chapters – one for each of the eleven tool clusters – we should be heading towards for any given problem. Thus Chapters 11 to 21 inclusive describe the different tools as follows:

Chapter 11 – Conflict & Trade-Off Elimination/Inventive Principles
Chapter 12 – Contradiction Elimination
Chapter 13 – Measurement Standards

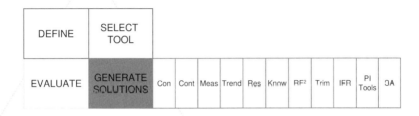

DEFINE	SELECT TOOL											
EVALUATE	GENERATE SOLUTIONS	Con	Cont	Meas	Trend	Res	Know	RF²	Trim	IFR	PI Tools	OA

Figure 2.4: Eleven Basic Tools of the SOLVE part of the Systematic Innovation Process

Generally speaking, the 'Select' tool will manage the process of navigating between and around the different tools, while the above chapters concentrate on the detailed mechanics of the specific tool in question. A couple of general points about navigation are worth making here from this overview perspective, however:

1) The process is always trying to offer the user 'back-up' possibilities in case things should go wrong. The first of these involves the possibility that we may go through all of the various definition steps of the process and still not know which tools to use to help us generate solutions. In this case, the Re-Focus/Re-Frame tool (Chapter 17) comes in to play. This is a tool designed for specifically this kind of 'don't know what to do' situation. It is designed to take the user back to the beginning of the problem definition process and work them through a series of questions asked from a slightly different perspective – hence the 're-frame' aspect of the title – trying to help guide things towards an 'aha, now I know what to do' moment.

2) It is, of course, also possible that we emerge from the 'Define' part of the process with what turns out to be a wrong or fundamentally unsolvable problem definition. In this regard it is worth noting that while many experienced systematic innovation users will tell you there is no such thing as an 'unsolvable' problem, they will also tell you that there are very definitely constraints that can make the problem unsolvable. We believe this is a useful output from the solve part of the process – 'knowing' that your problem plus your constraints means you will *fundamentally* not be able to generate a viable solution offers good justification to go around and re-challenge the constraints. We also believe that – and have tried to structure the solve tools in such a way that – they become self-correcting. In other words, if your constraints have taken you into a cul-de-sac, or if it turns out you have defined a problem situation incorrectly, the tools will first try and tell you, and then second, try and tell you which directions to travel in order to rectify the situation. You will experience this most commonly in solution triggers that suggest you try and solve a problem at a higher or lower hierarchical level (the most common kind of required

re-direction), or that you should re-challenge a given constraint. This 'self-correcting' nature will initially require a little faith on your part – the tendency is often to fight the direction being suggested – but experience tells us that the benefits of following the re-directions being offered are there to be taken.

3) By way of offering a final back-stop, it is worth noting as a final point that, on the rare occasions when we have been through all of the tools recommended as relevant to a problem and not generated any solutions, there is a specific set of tools (the Psychological Inertia tools – Chapter 20) that can help us to work out why we aren't generating solutions, and what to do about it. (They feature amongst the eleven solve tool clusters because they are also commonly used in precisely the 'solve' role.)

EVALUATE

The last of the four major parts of the overall systematic innovation process is 'Evaluate'. This is the part of the process where we identify the 'best' solution from the ones generated during the preceding 'solve' part. The 'evaluate' process is described in detail in Chapter 22. The real essence of it involves the mechanics of transforming the uncertainties commonly involved in making 'apples versus oranges' comparisons between different solutions.

And so there is the overall process. Except not quite. At several points in the book you will see the four-stage process being drawn as a repeating loop – Figure 2.5.

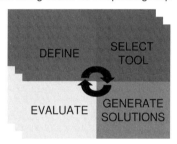

Figure 2.5: The Cyclic Nature of the Systematic Innovation Process

This is an extremely important point in the context of ensuring we *really* achieve the 'best' solution to a given problem. Again the point stems from one of the cruel tricks our brains often play on us. The trick in this case is similar to the one where our brain is over-eager to jump from problem definition mode to problem solution mode, except in this case, having generated a solution we like, our brain is over-eager to jump into what we might call 'satisfied' mode. In other words, we come up with a solution we like and our brain switches out of creative mode, out of critical mode and into a mode that says ' look what a great job we did'. We will see several examples of this in action in case studies throughout the book – solutions where the problem solver came up with a good idea, which they sought to exploit without stepping back to wonder whether they could make it better.

We include the looping process image as a way of reminding ourselves of the dangers of this 'satisfied mode' thinking. The general message we should draw from it is that we should always look to go around the loop at least once more after we have derived a good solution.

Innovation Chains

The 'going around the loop again' idea should provide us with a very useful image of what systematic innovation is trying to do in terms of helping us to evolve a system in the direction of increasing ideality. We will discuss this 'chain' idea further in Chapter 11 in the context of how the contradiction elimination process in particular will produce the chaining effect.

Overall Summary Of The Process

Figure 2.6 takes the four basic stages of the overall process in a way that details the various routes and fallback options available. This is a picture that you will also find reproduced on the back of the book. As such, it is intended to act as a quick reference navigation aid.

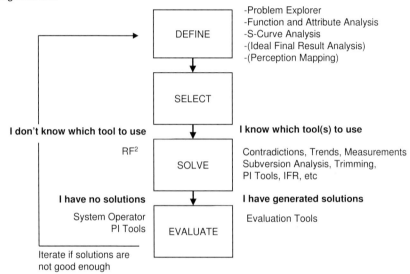

Figure 2.6: Overall Systematic Innovation Process Map

Convergent and Divergent Thinking

A further point to mention at this stage in the description of the overall process is the connection with 'convergent' and 'divergent' thinking. The convergent and divergent ideas are found in many areas of creativity research and are intended to represent two fundamentally different modes of thinking. 'Convergent' thinking occurs when we are trying to reduce the number of options. It is essentially analytical thinking. 'Divergent' thinking on the other hand is the mode we use when we are trying to increase the number of available options. Brainstorming sessions are a prime example of divergent thinking. One of the rules of brainstorming is that we don't criticise ideas. This rule exists because when we are criticising something we are using 'convergent' thinking, and the two types need to be separated from one another. The separation is necessary because each uses a different part of the brain. By trying to do both things together, we flood the brain with chemicals sending opposite signals. It is not always easy to achieve the separation because most people are happier in one situation rather than the other. One of the reasons that the Six

Thinking Hats concept (Reference 2.1) works is that it deliberately forces people to recognise what thinking mode they should be in at any given point during a problem solving process. More on this in the next chapter. For the moment, it is sufficient to record the big difference between convergent and divergent and to register the idea that there are two divergent-convergent cycles that fundamentally occur during the course of an application of the systematic innovation process. These two cycles are illustrated in Figure 2.7.

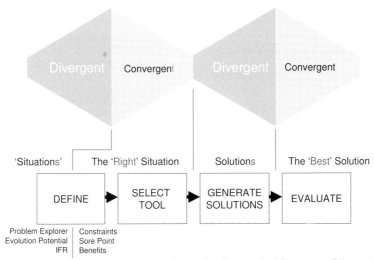

Figure 2.7: Connection Between Systematic Innovation Process And Convergent/Divergent Thinking

The second divergent-convergent cycle is the easier to explain as it directly correlates to the use of the solution generation and solution evaluation parts of the process. The first cycle is a little more complicated. This cycle relates to the part of the process where we are trying to get to the definition of the 'right' situation. The initial divergent activity, therefore, occurs when we are trying to scope a situation. It is where we are trying to explore all of the different avenues that might have something to do with our situation. The problem explorer, evolution potential resource identification and Ideal Final Result tools are all trying to force us to see situations from different perspectives and generate as many possible scenarios as possible. When we have done this, we will use the convergent parts of the process – constraint management, sore-point analysis and benefit description – as a means of homing in on the 'right' situation.

The Figure 2.7 image and the general convergent/divergent idea is worth keeping in mind at all times during systematic innovation sessions. Especially when we are working in a team environment.

Problems and Opportunities

Questions along the lines of 'I can see that systematic innovation is useful for solving problems, but can it do anything to help me identify opportunities for exploiting my existing solutions' seem to appear increasingly frequently. The question of identifying opportunities is, of course, not a new one – Edward DeBono's important book on the subject, for example, dates back to 1978 (Reference 2.2). The book offers much advice that remains relevant and is still to be highly recommended some 25 years after its initial publication. The simple answer to the question, though is 'yes, systematic innovation can help you to identify opportunities for exploiting existing solutions'.

Here we overview some of the most common 'opportunity identification' and 'opportunity exploitation' strategies available from within the armoury of systematic innovation tools. Never wishing to pass up the chance of a rant about problems versus opportunities, however, we begin with a short section on possible ways of thinking about and articulating the differences and similarities between the two definitions:

Problems And Opportunities

One of the most useful things an academic ever said to us was that in management, everything has to be distilled down to a maximum of 4-boxes – plan-do-study-act, strengths-weaknesses-opportunities-threats, important/not-important versus urgent/not-urgent, being just three examples that spring immediately to mind from the days we were forced to attend these kinds of management 'training' event. The 4-box limit obviously presents some serious problems when trying to establish systematic innovation as a standard part of the manager's toolkit, but should not, however, stop us presenting a new 2x2 matrix to help structuring our thinking for problems and opportunities – Figure 2.8.

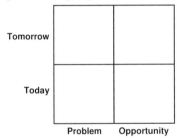

Figure 2.8: Problem/Opportunity versus Time Matrix

Even in this crude form, we think the picture offers a useful image, in that if we see the 4 boxes together as a way of plotting the 'whole world', we can quickly see that the large majority of organizations spend the large majority of their efforts working in just one of the four. Surprise, surprise, this turns out to be the near-term, problem box, we probably all know as 'fire-fighting'. The other three boxes give us some useful additional generalizations – as illustrated in Figure 2.9.

Figure 2.9: Useful Interpretations of the Matrix Segments

Both axes, of course, actually represent a continuum rather than a segmented 2x2 box. This is probably more obvious for the time axis than the problem/opportunity axis, but a very useful image to hold – one that will help considerably in guiding how we think about problems and opportunities – is that the problem-opportunity axis extends from sub-system to system to super-system. In other words, the problem/opportunity axis can usefully be seen as a SPACE axis. Figure 2.10 illustrates the idea.

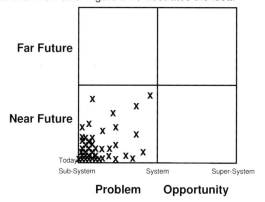

Problem   Opportunity

Figure 2.10: Space-Time Version of Problem/Opportunity Matrix

Thinking of the problem/opportunity axis as space like this, we think, provides a very useful image and a good way of discriminating between 'problems' and 'opportunities'. Thus, in our picture, a 'problem' becomes defined as something focused on the internal issues – we are looking at the system level and smaller. An 'opportunity' on the other hand becomes those situations where we lift our heads to look at the outside world; the times when we start thinking about how our system and its sub-systems and how they might be applied in other situations. Thus, if we have a situation where a customer order (i.e. a component deep into the detail of the sub-system) is lost or acted upon incorrectly, then we have a problem. If we have a situation where we have a fully automated, fool-proofed order processing which never goes wrong, we might lift our heads to the super-system and ask the question 'who else might want such a system?' In this situation, we have identified an opportunity. Likewise, when we lift our heads and look outside and see how other people have solved the order-processing problem, and find something better than our way of doing things then we have also found an opportunity; there is nothing wrong with our system, but there is an opportunity to create a better system.

Coming back to the figure for a final moment, and seeing the two axes as continuous variables, we should be able to imagine plotting an X for each 'thing' a hypothetical organization might be working on at any one time, and where/when it is focused, we gain another image of how the business is being managed. Again in our hypothetically drawn figure, we see a strong clustering towards the very near-term, fine detail fire-fighting work.

We make no judgment on whether this is right or not – priority one in business is to stay in business – merely that the figure usefully defines a way of seeing the bigger picture as well as allowing us to offer a useful way of seeing problems and opportunities.

So now let us now overview the opportunity side of the picture and how we can deploy the systematic innovation tools to help take maximum advantage of opportunities. We can split this story into two parts, the first looking at opportunity identification (i.e. the equivalent of 'problem definition'), and the second looking at opportunity exploitation (i.e. the equivalent of 'problem solving'). As with 'problem definition', 'opportunity identification' is probably 90% of the solution, and so we will concentrate our discussion on that focus.

Opportunity Identification

Opportunity identification is essentially about two things. The first is about working out which of the things an organisation knows how to do, that they do better than other people (maybe some, maybe all) outside the organisation. These things might be 'core competencies' or, more interestingly, things that are merely taken for granted in the way the company does business. The second is about what happens when we find things that outsiders are better able to do than the current inside capability and wish to import those ideas.

The key to identifying possible opportunities in both cases, is understanding FUNCTION: What functions do we deliver, what functions would we like to deliver, and how do others deliver the same functions represent the core questions.

An important concept to introduce at this stage is that of 'functional benchmarking'. Everyone is aware of the term 'benchmarking', but few have thus far made the connection with the idea of classifying knowledge in terms of function. This kind of functional benchmarking is more mature in a technical sense rather than a business one. The technical capability that now exists is already beginning to have a profound affect on the way that companies conduct their business and think about their future and hence we can't afford to ignore it here. It is in fact a topic we will return to in more detail in Chapter 16, and it also plays a significant role in the technical version of this Hands-On book.

In simple terms what functional benchmarking permits is easy comparison between different ways of delivering useful functions to customers. The importance of being able to make such comparisons is that we are able to identify ways of doing things that we know about that are better than other people's solutions. In which case, we have found opportunities. Conversely, of course, if we find solutions out there that are more effective than ours then we have found a potential threat... which, using true systematic innovation thinking, is really still just an opportunity we have the chance to exploit before those with the solution do.

Trends and Opportunity Identification

The linear and non-linear trends of evolution described in Chapter 14 also provide powerful means of identifying opportunities. The most important connection here comes with the concept of evolutionary potential. The concept is based on the idea that all systems and system components have the potential to evolve through all of the stages identified in each of the evolution trends that have been uncovered by looking across different industries. A system that has evolved all the way along all of the trends may be said to have used up all of its evolutionary potential; a system that has not, has some remaining untapped potential still left to exploit. We introduce here the image of an evolutionary radar plot as illustrated in Figure 2.11.

The plot is drawn by comparing the system under evaluation with each of the known trends in order to establish first whether the trend is relevant, and second, assuming it is, to establish how far along the trend the system has evolved. Thus, in the above example 10 relevant trends have been identified – these make up the spokes of the radar plot – and in the case of the first trend, the component has used two of the possible 5 evolution stages.

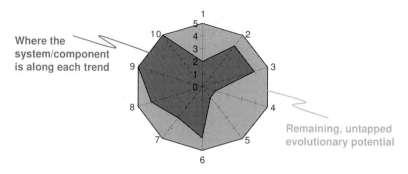

Where the
system/component
is along each trend

Remaining, untapped
evolutionary potential

Figure 2.11: Evolutionary Potential Radar Plot

Again in simple terms, this type of plot enables users to begin to identify opportunities. This works in both inward and outward directions; in the above example, it may be speculated that the component has hit the limits of its evolutionary potential for trends 9 and 10. In both of these cases, the component may be presenting opportunities for outside exploitation if equivalent systems elsewhere have not evolved so far. Conversely, the example radar plot suggests that trends 4 and 5 have hardly been exploited at all, and as such may be amenable to the introduction of a more evolved solution from outside.

We examine this whole trend and opportunity finding subject in more detail in Chapter 14 – including the critical parallel issue of opportunity timing – and how we can use systematic innovation tools to help us get both right.

In summary, then, opportunities exist outside the current system. There are several different means of identifying opportunities. In the most random sense, opportunity finding depends on the connection-making capabilities of the human brain, and the chance connections made by individuals as they experience life outside the system and capabilities within the system. Some organizations maximize such opportunity finding chances by encouraging and empowering everyone within the organization to look for and exploit such connections rather than just specifically tasked individuals (Reference 2.3). The systematic innovation toolkit provides a much more systematic way of identifying opportunities. In the first instance, it recognizes and classifies knowledge in terms of function delivery. In the simplest sense, then, we might view 'opportunity finding' as the successful connection of either a function someone else is capable of delivering that might be imported into an organization, or that a function currently delivered by the organization is more effective than other known ways of delivering the same function outside the organization. At a more detailed level, the trends of evolution tools and the concept of evolutionary potential, and the resources part of the method offer even more structured ways of identifying opportunities.

Finally in this section, we re-emphasise the point that, whether we are looking at a problem or an opportunity situation, the same basic four stage process overviewed in this chapter has been designed to cater for both. We will find that the main differences between problem and opportunity strategies will emerge during the 'Solve' parts of the overall process. We will also find that Chapter 10, which describes the 'Select' part of the process, will take on the management of those differences should we so desire.

Before closing this Chapter, however, it is worthwhile spending a few moments describing a pair of short-cuts that may be of interest to new systematic innovation users, and also those people that wish to avoid some of the rigours of the full process. Any short-cut carries with it a number of dangers. Foremost among those dangers here is that we don't spend enough time working out what the 'right' thing to be working on is, and consequently waste time generating solutions to the wrong problem. That being said, the two short-cuts have their place, and this author certainly uses them on a regular basis. The first relates to the identification and resolution of conflicts, and the second relates to the identification of resources. Let us look at each one separately:-

Conflicts
If it is true – as our problem solving consultancy activities suggest – that 80% of problems exist because a system (or one of its constituent elements) has hit a fundamental limit, then a very effective short-cut involves looking for conflicts and then using the conflict and contradiction elimination tools to directly challenge them. In workshops, we very often do an exercise in which we examine a system – a bank, or an HR department, or B2C relationship, for example – and ask delegates to think about a pair of questions; a) what would you like to improve about this system, and b) what is stopping you from making that improvement. This is a very quick way of creating out a long list of conflict pairs. Having generated such a list, the short-cut then says to use the conflict elimination tools to begin challenging some of the pairs on the list. This rapid transition to the solution generation mode can be further accelerated it we chose to avoid the use of the conflict elimination Matrix and go straight to the 40 Inventive Principles. This is the simplest (and most effective) approach to take when working with people with no background in the systematic innovation subject, since the Inventive Principles can be used as brainstorming aids with little introduction. A common phenomenon in most traditional brainstorming sessions is that the number of ideas being generated peaks quickly and then falls to zero after 15 to 20 minutes. What the Inventive Principles offer is a way to re-invigorate these sessions by adding a new attention focus each time idea generation begins to drop. As suggested by Figure 2.12, using the Principles in this way can often result in brainstorming sessions that are still generating new ideas several hours later.

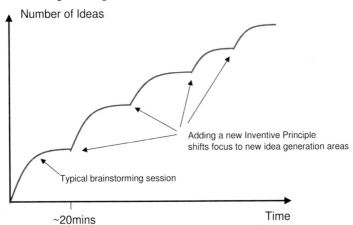

Figure 2.12: Use Of Inventive Principles As A Way Of Re-Energising Brainstorming Sessions

Having too many ideas can be as big a problem as not having enough of course, but one of the big underlying ideas behind the Inventive Principles is that they act as sign-posts towards good solution directions. Hence a large proportion of the ideas we generate will tend to be 'good' ones. The next trick, then, is to set about distilling and combining ideas into more manageable numbers. As we will see later in Chapter 11, there is a very strong correlation between the strength of a solution and the number of Principles that were combined to generate it.

As a final thought on the conflict elimination short-cut, it is worth noting that even though we have not spent enough time in problem definition mode and hence may not be solving the 'right' problem, one of the very nice side-effects of eliminating conflicts is that they often solve problems above and beyond the one that we were focusing on. Solve a contradiction and nice things tend to happen.

Resources
In the same way that finding a good unsolved contradiction acts as a good short-cut to effective solutions, finding a 'resource' – i.e. 'something in or around the system that is not being used to its maximum potential' – is another. One of the common factors of just about every problem we work on is that we will conduct some kind of evolutionary potential analysis in the early stages. We do this because we know that if we can find something fitting that 'not being used to its maximum potential' definition, we have identified an opportunity. That opportunity, and finding ways to utilise the untapped potential makes for a very effective short-cut in many situations. In addition to the use of the evolution potential tool, the use of resource check-lists (Chapter 15) can also serve as a quick way of identifying things that might help us to solve our problem. A good untapped resource is almost guaranteed to send your brain into solution generation mode ('How could I use this? How could it help me to solve my problem?'). The short-cut says to let your brain follow this instinct. After all, you can always come back to the process afterwards.

What Do I Do?

As we've stated previously, systematic innovation is a very big and rich thing. We readily accept that some people will use the full process being espoused here, while others will just want to delve into the parts that they are interested. Still others will wish to mix and match parts of the process to suit the way they do things. As we will discuss later in the chapter on the Re-Focus/Re-Frame tool, this is absolutely fine. Ultimately, any process you might use has to belong to you. Systematic innovation, in other words, should adapt to you and not the other way around.

That being said, if you are looking for 'a process' this is the one we recommend. We recommend it not because we defined it, but because we defined it to be flexible enough to accommodate a wide range of personal tastes. Thus, to take a specific example, the process suggests that there are five distinct activities that should be carried out if we are to be confident that we have defined the 'right' problem, but it doesn't dictate what order you do them in. The limitations of a hardbound book have meant that we have had to present a certain order, but our suggestion to you is that if you'd rather conduct things in a different order, by all means do so.

If you decide to try the whole process, we suggest you first read all of the first four Chapters of the book, then let this chapter be your guide through the ones in the rest of the book relevant to defining and solving your problem or opportunity.

Case Studies

Because the possible variety of problem types and application routes is so large, and the space in this book so limited, we have not included any complete start-to-finish case studies – although you will find many examples of parts of the process in action. It is planned to publish a book of complete case studies in the not too distant future.

References

1) DeBono, E., 'Six Thinking Hats', Viking, 1986.
2) DeBono, E., 'Opportunities', Penguin Books, 1978.
3) Fradette, M., Michaud, S., 'The Power of Corporate Kinetics', Simon & Schuster, New York, 1998.

3.
Psychology

The human brain is a wonderful instrument, but, as the above Edward DeBono quotation suggests, its function in life is not to be creative. Let us be clear, this does not mean that it is *incapable* of being creative, but merely that this is not its natural state. For 99.9% of our lives, not being creative is a good state to be in. Being creative about crossing a busy road, or using a chainsaw is more likely to leave us in hospital than picking up a Nobel prize. The brain is designed to remember how we do things so that next time we have to do them, we don't have to think about it. Great for the 99.9% occasions, but unfortunately not so good when we are looking to generate new ways of doing things. Then we have a problem. Indeed, the more time we have spent doing something the more difficult it becomes to break out of the patterns that we have learned. Widen this characteristic to a whole organisation of people and it doesn't take long to see why so few companies are able to innovate successfully. It also helps to explain why nearly all major innovations emerge from people outside an industry If history repeats itself in this way, the thing that is going to come along and put you out of business is not going to come from you or one of your competitors, it is going to come from someone completely outside your field.

A large part of the systematic innovation methodology is about that 0.1% situation where we are trying to do things differently. Or, in the words of the cliché, 'think out of the box'. This chapter is about setting the creative context within which the systematic innovation tools will work to their best effect. Some people mistakenly think that 'systematic innovation' is all about automated answers, 'invention machines' and replacing individual human creativity. This view actually couldn't be much further from the truth if it tried. Systematic innovation absolutely demands us to use our creative skills; the more we put in the more we will get out. This chapter offers an overview of human psychology and the impact that it has on the way we define situations and generate the best possible solutions.

One of the first things we will see is that systematic innovation operates at a considerably different level to other creativity tools and aids. The large majority of other creativity tools are built on the belief that our brains are highly inefficient and that most of us use a very small proportion of its capacity (every time we read a text in this area, the proportion of our brain capacity that gets used seems to be reported as an ever smaller percentage – 5%, then 1%, now about 0.1%, and so on). Hence the main task of traditional 'creativity tools' is to help us to think more effectively, to 'unblock' us, to help us get all the great ideas trapped inside us out into the world.

One of the key findings of the research that has fed the systematic innovation method on the other hand is that 'someone, somewhere has already solved a problem something like ours'. In other words, it takes as its start point the belief that we should be looking outside for solutions to our problems.

The contrast between these internal 'unblocking' and external 'someone-already-solved-my-problem' approaches can be clearly elicited with a problem like asking a group of people to think of ways of, say, 'improving customer service'. The best creativity tools will help a group tasked with generating solutions to 'unblock' and be able to suggest many ways of achieving a solution. None of these techniques, however, will be able to elicit ideas which do not exist in any of the heads present. Access to the systematic innovation toolkit, on the other hand, will allow the group to, in generic terms at least, access all of the good solutions of everyone in the world. Clearly, no amount of 'unblocking' is going to allow us to develop ideas which do not exist inside our heads. This global knowledge outlook is a definite advantage that systematic innovation has over other creativity tools.

The idea that 'someone, somewhere already solved my problem' can be one that is very threatening to some people, however. How could it be conceivably possible that a manager with decades of experience cannot know about it if someone has already solved their problem? What would people think if they knew that we'd spent those same decades not finding a solution that might have been sitting there waiting for us the whole time? This is another psychological effect that we need to take serious heed of if we are to make best use of systematic innovation. The simple answer is to recognize that being a successful manager in a particular discipline is a full time job. To know what your competitors, your customers, and your suppliers are doing is more than a full-time job. In this situation, there is simply not enough time to look at what other industries and disciplines are doing. Okay, so you may get to go to a conference once a year, or meet someone interesting on a plane, but this is a mere drop in the ocean as far as seeing what is 'out there' is concerned. And so this is the job that the systematic innovation researchers have taken on on your behalf. To allow you to combine all of the good stuff you know with all of the stuff that you never get the chance to find out about. The purpose of this chapter, therefore, is not to suggest that the external perspective is 'better' or that there is a need to make any kind of choice between internal or external creativity strategies, but that – in line with the philosophical importance of eliminating contradictions and an 'A and B' rather than 'A or B' perspective – we should be looking to combine the strengths of your domain specialist knowledge plus the general world-view perspective that systematic innovation offers. Thus, the view taken throughout this book is the one illustrated in Figure 3.1 – the best creativity approach involves combining the best of the internal and external perspectives.

So all of those 'traditional' creativity methods designed to unblock the countless great ideas swimming around your head are going to be extremely useful to us. Any tool with such capabilities is to be embraced with open arms. Someone, somewhere already solved your problem, and so, consequently, if a particular tool, method or strategy has something to offer in helping us to define and solve problems more effectively, you can be pretty certain that it will feature somewhere in the toolkit, the method or the overall philosophy.

It is our clear and distinct belief that in order to create effectively it is absolutely essential to combine the internal and the external. It also appears clear that we need to do this in as coherent and jargon-free manner as possible. Consequently, this chapter aside, the rest of the book will not make any distinction between 'internal' or 'external' approaches. More specifically, when we are describing or demonstrating the use of a particular tool or part of the systematic innovation process, we will attempt to integrate 'internal' and external invisibly in a way that allows us to focus on benefits rather than features.

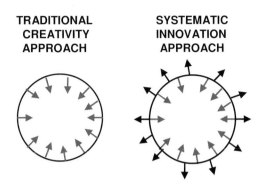

TRADITIONAL CREATIVITY APPROACH

SYSTEMATIC INNOVATION APPROACH

Figure 3.1: Combined 'Internal' and 'External' Systematic Creativity Strategy

That being said, there are a number of points that are worth making here in order to set a scene for the 'internal' elements of the creative process, in order that we can see what is expected or desirable when we come to the job of defining and solving actual problems.

In all, we will make five points. The first relates discusses the meaning of the important systematic innovation term 'psychological inertia. In this section we examine why psychological inertia is a bad thing, and how we can overcome the problems it causes. In the second section we go one to discuss the mechanisms by which our brains interpret and use the solution 'triggers' that the systematic innovation tools provide. The third relates to the higher-level physiology that dictates the manner in which our brains operate during 'problem solving' in its most general context. Fourthly we look at mechanisms to help us to better sequence and structure our creative thinking. Then in the fifth and final section we briefly outline the importance of psychology during group problem solving sessions. It is not our intention to be comprehensive – the list of references at the end of the chapter should provide a number of useful links for anyone wanting to find out more – but merely to give us enough awareness of psychological effects so that we can get the maximum possible benefit from using the systematic innovation toolkit.

1) Psychological Inertia

Much of Edward de Bono's pioneering study on lateral thinking stemmed from the hole-digging analogy he developed in his very earliest work (Reference 3.1). In the analogy, we are trying to solve a problem, the solution to which is a seam of gold buried at some unknown location in a field.

If the problem we're trying to solve is 'similar' to one we've already solved, we are likely to attempt to solve it using what he described as 'vertical' or 'logical' thinking. In such a scenario, we have already started digging a hole, we've already found some gold in it, and we are expecting to find the solution to our new problem simply by digging – vertically, logically – deeper. Whole industries are built on this very principle. The next car tyre to enter the market is almost guaranteed to emerge from a hole labelled 'moulded rubber, radial wound re-enforcement'. The next driver protection system from one labelled 'steering-wheel mounted, inflating bag'. And so on, and so on, at each and every level - from the macro to the micro - of whatever problem it is we're looking at. Each of the products or solutions that emerges will generally have been obtained by digging an existing hole a little deeper.

Unfortunately, once we've started digging a hole, it doesn't take long for our competitors to find us. In a mature industry like the automobile one, we've probably dug a quarry-sized hole, all the other manufacturers are in there with us, and we're all desperately scratching around for some nugget or other which will discriminate our product from everyone else's for a year or two.

Unfortunately also, we all suffer from what systematic innovation calls 'psychological inertia' (PI). In the context of the hole-digging analogy, this is the thing that tells us to stay in the hole we've been digging. It is the thing that tells us that if we just keep on digging a bit deeper, we're bound to eventually come across the solution we're looking for. It is the thing that tells us 'look how much time and energy we've expended digging this hole; how could we possibly let it go to waste?' It is the thing that gives us a quite potent image of industries digging deeper and deeper holes that they are progressively less likely to be able to get out of.

De Bono used the term 'lateral thinking' to denote a different kind of thinking to the vertical/logical variant. Lateral thinking is the thinking that prompts us to set about looking somewhere else in the field in search of a better solution. Lateral thinking is the thing which got us out of a hole labelled 'horse-drawn carriage' into our current '4-wheeled, internal combustion engine driven' one. It will also be the thing that gets us into the next hole, whatever that might turn out to be.

Of course, the difficult part here is knowing where to dig our new hole. In the past, we probably did it to a large extent by accident or hunch or guesswork. Today, few if any organisations can afford either the time or money to embark on this type of random digging exercise. Economic and competitive necessities demand that if we're going to dig a new hole, we'd better have a pretty good idea **where** we're going to start before we pick up a shovel.

De Bono recommends a number of techniques to help locate worthwhile places to start digging new holes – for example PMI or 'Po' or word-association ('pick a random word from a dictionary…') – some more useful than others. None however appear to be as powerful as the opportunities that have emerged through the systematic innovation methodology.

In the context of the finding the right place to begin digging a new hole analogy, there is probably no single technique in existence more powerful than the solution generation tools detailed in this book. What systematic innovation is in effect saying is that actually there are only very few places where we might profitably dig a new hole.

Some applied innovation researchers have suggested that problem definition – determining what it is we're digging for – should be given rather more of our attention than the then comparatively simple tasks of location finding and hole digging. Unfortunately, another depressing human psychological trait – our apparent need to be seen to be 'getting on with the job', to show some shovel-wielding sweat - often means we don't give problem definition nearly enough of the attention it in fact merits. Psychological Inertia, however, also comes into the problem definition equation. Psychological inertia is the thing in this context which says to us 'I've been digging for gold, I'm good at it, people have always bought the gold I find, I'm going to keep right on doing it'. It's the thing which tells us not to even think about the fact that people might one day decide what they actually want is something other than gold.

So, what's this hole-digging analogy stuff all about anyway? What has it got to do with Psychological Inertia? And what is there we can usefully learn from it? We submit three thoughts for your consideration:-

1) Effective gold seam location requires a map. The systematic innovation solution generation tools are probably the best mapping tools available anywhere. Awareness that there are 40 Inventive Principles, for example, and that **any** might be useful to solve a problem gives us 40 extremely effective means of defeating PI.

2) The image of seeing ourselves stuck at the bottom of a mile-deep, vertically sided quarry is the very best way we know of telling ourselves that, perhaps, maybe we've been caught out by the PI thing again, and that perhaps, maybe we had better start thinking about finding a better hole to dig. There is always a better way.

3) Not only does Psychological Inertia try and prevent us from getting out of the holes we dig, it also tells us to assume that what we started out digging for remains constant. It often doesn't, and we therefore need to be aware of **both** problem definition **and** problem solution aspects of the PI problem.

2) The Space Between 'Generic' and 'Specific' Solutions

As discussed in the previous chapter, a large part of the systematic innovation process is built on the concept of abstraction. Abstraction is the process that allows us to connect our supposedly unique situation to a generalized situation that someone has already found solutions for. As detailed in the previous chapter, the overall abstraction process is illustrated in Figure 3.2.

Once we are able to overcome the hurdle of accepting that it may be possible that someone has already found a solution to our situation, the next biggest problem is usually one of translating the abstracted solutions that the method will offer into something that is applicable to our specific setting. Hopefully the case studies contained throughout the book will offer convincing evidence that it really is true that someone has already solved our problem. The second problem is one that requires a rather more focused discussion here.

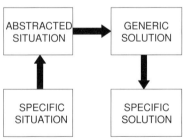

Figure 3.2: The General Systematic Innovation Abstraction Model

Unfortunately, the systematic part of the process effectively ends at the delivery of the Generic Solutions. These 'generic solutions' include the 40 Business Principles, the Measurement Standards, and the Trends of Evolution that will be covered in later chapters of the book. Although highly valuable, many problem solvers still find there is a considerable gap between these generic solution triggers and the desired specific solution. This gap is illustrated in Figure 3.3.

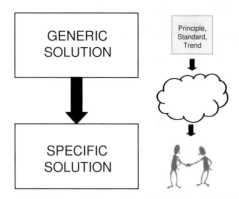

Figure 3.3: The Space Between Generic And Specific Solution

Systematic innovation is being used successfully in a wide and widening variety of fields. The space – this 'gap' – between generic and specific solutions is obviously therefore not a vacuum. Whatever it is, however, is at present obscured by clouds. The question is what is behind those clouds, and whatever it is, is it in any way mappable?

The Irreversible Nature of Good Ideas

The best if not only way of usefully looking beyond the clouds is through examination of case study examples. Every successful business innovation offers potential data. There is thus an awful lot of case study material from which to choose. Unfortunately there is a problem, and it is a fairly fundamental problem associated with each and every case. It is a problem of irreversibility: Moving forwards from problem to solution – in effect the process hidden behind the cloud – is a highly nebulous, highly intractable path. Before that moment when the light-bulb finally lights, the problem owner is often literally as well as metaphorically in the dark. Figure 3.4 summarises the irreversibility problem.

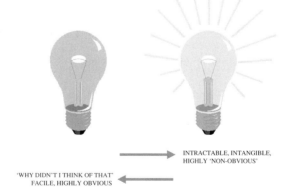

INTRACTABLE, INTANGIBLE, HIGHLY 'NON-OBVIOUS'

'WHY DIDN'T I THINK OF THAT' FACILE, HIGHLY OBVIOUS

Figure 3.4: The Irreversible Nature Of Creative Ideas

Looking back at the problem after the solution has been discovered, on the other hand, is a completely different matter. Now the solution is viewed as 'obvious', often to the point of being almost facile. It's the 'why didn't I think of that' experience. In fact the very 'obviousness' of a solution is very often used as a test of how 'right' the solution is. The more 'obvious' the answer, the better the solution

Think, for example, of how obvious a solution the wheel is. Then think how non-obvious it was for the first 98% of human existence. Or think of how 'obvious' it is now that business is about processes; whereas 50 years ago it had never been thought about in that way at all.

This 'obviousness' irreversibility and the speed with which the light gets turned on once the switch is found makes it extremely difficult to establish what the turning on process actually was. Without direct access to the problem solver – which is likely to be the case in most instances – the problem will be even greater.

In trying to get 'behind the cloud', the irreversibility problem can be expected to be a fairly major one.

First, however, let us have a look at a number of case studies in order to gain a more specific feel for the size of the unknown behind the cloud:-

Case Study 1: The Patriarch
In this first scenario – an actual case study that will be described in more detail in Chapter 12 – a pre-prepared food products company has recently lost two major clients and net sales have fallen by 20% relative to projected targets. The company is run by X. He is a self-made man, setting up the company and has nurturing its growth over a period of 20 years. X has been the source of nearly all of the sales made by the company to the extent that the company does not possess a sales team. The basis of X's success has been the personal relationships he has built up with the client base over the life of the company. Six months ago, X decided to retire, and he is in the process of handing over the running of the company to his oldest son. He has stated that he still wants to help in the sales area during the transition. One of the first things the son does, however, is to appoint a sales manager. He does this because a) he is not interested in the sales side of the business, and b) because he wants to help his father transition to a happy retirement as soon as possible. Within two months of the appointment of the sales manager, the lost client and reduced sales symptoms have begun to appear.

The key to finding good solutions to the problem can be shown to depend on the definition of the 'present and not present' contradiction shown above. This is turn leads to the idea of placing X's picture on each of the products produced by the company as a means of re-enforcing his importance (and perceived importance in the eyes of the customers who have been lost since his departure) – Figure 3.5.

X should be present
AND
not present

Figure 3.5: One Of The Solutions To The 'Patriarch' Contradiction

The Inventive Principle used to derive this elegant and simple solution was Inventive Principle 27, 'Cheap Disposable'. Case Study 1 then leaves us with 'Cheap Disposable' and the idea of putting a picture of X on the food jars as the entry and exit points respectively of any process that may exist behind the cloud.

Case Study 2: Virgin Brides

For most couples, the process of arranging a marriage ceremony requires a considerable amount of logistical skill and effort to organize all of the different elements that need to be brought together to make a successful event. Virgin Brides in the UK was set up to overcome this problem. In effect it is a one-stop shop for wedding ceremonies –Figure 3.6 – enabling a couple to organize everything via a single interface.

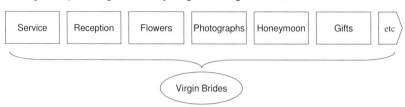

Figure 3.6: A One-Stop Shop for Marriage

In this case study, systematic innovation solution generation tools offered the suggestion 'Merging' (Inventive Principle 5), and so we have 'Merging' and one-stop shop as the respective start and end points of the process behind the cloud.

Case Study 3: One Quarter or Two

A third example is an adaptation of a story first told in one of Edward DeBono's books (Reference 3.2). The story involves an onlooker watching a group of children teasing a small boy. The leader of the group has three quarters, two in one hand and one in the other. He shuffles the coins in such a way that it is quite obvious even to the distant onlooker which of the hands holds the two quarters. The onlooker watches as the group ask the small boy to pick a hand. The boy thinks for a minute before picking the hand with one quarter in it. The group laugh at his choice. The boy pockets the quarter and the group run off, still laughing. The following day the same thing happens again, only this time the hand containing the two quarters is made even more obvious. Again the boy picks the hand with one quarter in it, and the group runs off laughing at his even greater stupidity. After the third repeat of the incident, the onlooker, unable to stand watching the teasing any longer goes over to the small boy after the group has left. 'They're making fun of you', the onlooker says, 'why do you keep picking the wrong hand?'. The small boy looks at the onlooker, confused, and replies 'do you think they'd still be giving me quarters if I picked the hand with two?'

In this case, the relevant systematic innovation tool would have suggested Inventive Principle 13 'The Other Way Around' ('turn the process upside down or the other way around') to get us to the inventive solution derived by the small boy.

Mechanisms of Mind: Pattern Recognition

To solve the mystery of what lies behind the cloud in the gap between generic and specific, would be to solve a problem that has confounded many hundreds of man-years of effort. To suggest that a solution exists here, therefore, would be an action of extreme folly. That being said, it is apparent that the systematic innovation researchers have already done much to de-mystify the creative process. The Inventive Principles, for example, provide 40 very good start points from which to search for problem solutions.

Systematic innovation provides a powerful foundation point. A pointer to how the steps between Inventive Principle and design solution might then be plotted perhaps comes from some of the research on how the human brain functions and, particularly, on its pattern recognition capabilities.

By way of demonstration, the 'Connect-Up' idea first written about by Edward de Bono (Reference 3.2 again) offers a helpful start. In 'connect-up', if any two words are picked at random, the brain will almost without fail manage to come up with another word which connects them. The process is often expressed in a manner like that shown in Figure 3.7. Here the two chosen random words are BANANA and PENCIL – at first glance neither word has anything at all to do with the other, but the brain will almost inevitably make some kind of connection. Indeed, given a couple of minutes, most people will be able to make associations with ten or more connecting words.

BANANA   PENCIL

Figure 3.7: Connecting Words

This association making capability is an undoubtedly powerful one. Even more exciting, however is the fact that if a number of people are asked to perform the same exercise, the level of duplication of words between individuals would be very small (Reference 3.3). On average, the number of duplicated words would be around 5%. In other words, ten people writing down ten connecting words each would tend to produce a total of over 90 different connecting words. (Try it as an exercise sometime and watch it happen.) This phenomenon occurs because every one of us has very different experiences stored in our brains, and we will all therefore tend to make very different types of connections.

So what does this mean from the perspective of systematic innovation and the need to solve problems?

On the positive side, it means that given a problem and an Inventive Principle – for example the Case Study 1 scenario as re-drawn in Connect-Up form (Figure 3.8) – the brain **will** make interesting connections.

Figure 3.8: Case Study 1 Connections

Knowing the eventual solution to Case Study 1 and seeing this picture, it is already extremely easy to see how the solution came about. Recognising the Irreversibility phenomenon described in the previous section, perhaps it is too easy to be believable?

Perhaps Case Study 2 even more so. The historical facts, however, show that the world had not even contemplated the one-stop shop wedding service until very recently.

The same may be seen to apply to the other Case Study example.

So what about another case study? One where the 'answer' may not previously been seen? Your turn to have a go!

desired outcome:
competitive advantage

Figure 3.9: Connecting Inventive Principle and Desired Business Outcome

The (an?) answer to this one can be found in Reference 3.4.

So, what are we to make of all of this? What is it that fills the gap between generic and specific solution? Unfortunately there is still no definitive theory to answer the question. Nor is it clear that there ever will be. On the other hand, we then have to wonder, is a theory relevant? If something works in practice, do we also have to prove that it works in theory too? For some people the answer to that question is yes. For the rest of us, fortunately, there are some important messages in Edward DeBono's 'connect-up' research; take two random words and the brain will find ways of connecting them together. Sometimes the connections that we make will prove to be invaluable, but mostly they will be closer to its opposite. The 'Connect-Up' idea is still some considerable distance from offering us a systematic procedure. But it does give us a direction. If we then combine that direction with the systematic innovation idea that there are only a small number of solution strategies that will prove to be productive, then we end up with the possibility that in actual fact we don't require a whole dictionary of random words to connect to our problem, but a considerably smaller set. According to the research reported in Reference 3.5, all of the useful solution directions generated from a random-word start point map to solutions that would have come from the systematic innovation solution generation trigger list. Our dictionary of useful solution generation start points, in other words need only contain the 40 Principles, the Trends, the Measurement Standards. While still not theoretically precise, it does mean that there is a finite list of useful solution connect words. We like to think of the words as signposts. These words tell us 'good solutions will happen if you connect to this word'. In the absence of a theoretically precise, we think the signpost connector idea is at the very least an extremely effective start towards one. Moreover, it is a strategy that has shown itself to be effective in generating breakthrough solutions on countless occasions.

3) Thinking Hats

Edward De Bono's 'Six Thinking Hats'™ concept (Reference 3.6) is one area where a great deal of synergy exists with systematic innovation. This section describes how the Six Thinking Hats™ concept has been integrated into the generic systematic innovation problem definition and solving process described in this book.

The Thinking Hats concept is built on the fact that the human brain works in physiologically different modes depending on the sort of task it is being asked to perform. Thus, to take two extremes, the mechanisms used by the brain when generating new ideas is significantly different to those present when we are calculating the pros and cons of an existing idea. In all, De Bono has identified six different important modes of thought that are relevant across the range of actions taking place during the problem solving process (Figure 3.10).

Figure 3.10: Six Thinking Hats – Schematic Representation

Each mode has been identified by a different coloured hat, such that:-

A WHITE hat – denotes a mode of thinking during which an objective look at data and information is required.

A RED hat – denotes the mode of thinking associated with feelings, hunches, and intuition.

A BLACK hat – denotes the mode of thinking associated with caution, judgement, and looking logically at the negative aspects of a problem – often described as the 'devil's advocate' mode of thinking.

A YELLOW hat - denotes the mode of thinking associated with examining the feasibility and benefits of a given situation, and looking logically at the positive aspects.

A GREEN hat – denotes the mode of thinking associated with the generation of new ideas, creative and 'lateral' thinking.

A BLUE hat – denotes the mode of thinking associated with the overall control and organisation of the thinking processes.

We describe here how the Hats concept can be integrated into the systematic innovation process, covering the complete spectrum of activities to be found in a facilitated inventive problem solving session – from initial situation assessment, to problem definition, to problem solution. We begin, however, with an examination of the different Hat modes, and the times we might chose to wear them when using different elements of the systematic innovation toolkit:

White Hat
We wear the white hat when we are seeking to take a non-emotional, objective look at data and information. We are most likely to require use of White Hat thinking strategies at the following points during use of the systematic innovation problem definition and problem solving process:

- During the initial problem assessment and definition phase. Specifically, when conducting the first stages of a function analysis – in which we are seeking to describe the actual functioning of the existing system – but also when examining statements describing the desired end point for the problem, and understanding the present level of maturity of the system in terms of it (and its sub-systems') position on their respective evolutionary S-curves.
- During the phase in which, having completed an initial problem definition, the problem owner is looking to select the most appropriate of the solution generation tools.
- Defining the Ideal Final Result, and using the Ideality problem solving tool concept of working back from this IFR to a physically realisable solution.
- Conducting a perception mapping analysis – constructing and interpreting the perception map.
- When defining contradictions, and when translating specific problems into the generic terms of either the Business Conflict Matrix or the contradiction-elimination separation strategies.
- When recording generated solutions.
- When assessing and ranking the quality of solutions during the Select part of the overall process.
- In conjunction with the 9 Windows tool, throughout the overall problem definition and solving process in order to ensure that space and time dimensions are given appropriate attention.

Given the 'systematic' nature of the methods present in this book, it should not come as a great surprise to learn that the White Hat is worn most during a systematic innovation session. The other 5 Hats, however, are still vital at certain points during the process:

Red Hat
The red hat is worn when we are using our intuition and relying on our feelings and emotions. The red hat mode of thinking may at first sight appear to be the complete antithesis of a systematic creativity process, but it has its uses, and – most importantly – we need to recognise that the way our brains operate means that many of us spend a large proportion of our time naturally thinking in a Red Hat mode. At the very least, therefore, we need to be aware of Red Hat thinking modes, if only to recognise that we need to step out of it for much of the time. We are most likely to wish to use Red Hat thinking strategies positively, though, at the following points during the systematic innovation definition and solution generation processes:

- Almost inevitably, given the way our brains are wired and the way we have been thought to problem solve traditionally, when someone gives us a problem, we shift immediately into Red Hat 'problem solving' mode. We should recognise this phenomenon and try to use it to positive effect. It is common, therefore, to include a five or ten minute period of traditional brainstorming either right at the beginning of a session, or immediately after the initial problem definition phase. The output from such a brainstorming session is commonly recorded and placed in a 'car-park'. This is a place where all participants can see that their input has been registered and hence will not be forgotten.
- Red Hat thinking mode can also be useful as a psychological inertia-breaking tool if use of the available solution generation tools has not produced any viable results.
- Red Hat thinking mode can also be used to good effect at times during a problem solving session to break out of the rut that can sometimes occur if participants have been kept in other thinking modes – particularly White Hat –

for extended periods. Provocations like 'spend five minutes thinking about the worst possible means of solving the problem' (see also the PI Tools in Chapter 20) have relatively frequently generated some interesting and subsequently viable solution options.

Nevertheless, these points aside, Red Hat thinking mode should be deployed only sparingly when using systematic innovation methods.

Black Hat
We wear the black hat when we employing caution and judgement, and looking logically at the negative aspects of a given situation. We are most likely to require use of Black Hat thinking modes at the following points during the problem definition and solution generation parts of the overall systematic innovation process:

- During the initial problem definition phase, where we are attempting to identify all of the constraints that exist in and around our problem.
- During the conducting of a function and attribute analysis of the problem situation, when we are looking to identify the harmful, insufficient, excessive and missing functions that exist in the current system. (NB it is very important to recognise that Black Hat thinking and White Hat thinking are two significantly different modes, and that a proper function analysis requires both. The most effective function analysis sessions occur when the White Hat and the Black Hat modes are conducted sequentially, with White Hat first, and Black Hat being allowed to commence only after a specific instruction from a problem facilitator that modes should now be shifted.)
- During a 'how could we destroy this system?' subversion analysis.
- During assessment of solution options when trying to gauge the relative weaknesses of the solutions under consideration.
- When answering the question 'is the chosen solution good enough?' at the end of a session. Another common human trait is that we are highly inclined towards accepting and settling on a solution that we think is novel. This is particularly evident when we have successfully broken a conflict or contradiction.

Yellow Hat
We wear the yellow hat when we are examining the feasibility and benefits of a potential solution, or are seeking to logically assess the positive aspects of a given situation. We are most likely to require use of Yellow Hat thinking strategies at the following points during a systematic innovation session:

- During the initial definition stage of a problem when we are examining the resources that exist in and around the current system.
- During assessment of solution options when trying to gauge the relative strengths of the solutions under consideration.
- When seeking to challenge the validity of the initially defined problem constraints.
- When using the Trimming part of the solution generation toolkit – particularly when asking the questions 'do I need this function?' or 'can an existing element within the system perform the function for me?' or 'can a resource perform the function?' (NB some users find that Trimming works more successfully in White Hat mode; the author has generally had more success getting groups to wear a Yellow Hat.)
- When using the Measurement Standard solutions of Chapter 13, and trying to relate them to the problem situation. Solution triggers like 'eliminate the need to

make the measurement' can be a little too obtuse for some people; this is less of a problem if such people are specifically asked to be in Yellow Hat mode.

Green Hat

We wear the green hat when we are looking to generate new ideas or are seeking to 'be creative'. We are most likely to require use of Green Hat thinking strategies at the following points during use of the systematic innovation problem definition and solution generation processes:

- During the initial definition stage, a short period of Green Hat thinking immediately after the Yellow Hat search for resources often sees the realisation of a considerable number of additional ideas that did not arise previously. (NB the preceding Yellow Hat mode is important and should not be replaced by Green.)
- When we are exploring 'what else?' type questions during the use of the Ideal Final Result tool in its definition mode, or when using the re-definition tool in the Problem/Opportunity Explorer. Very often in traditional problem solving sessions, 'the right problem' only becomes apparent some time after we start thinking about a situation. Employing some generative thinking during these parts of the systematic innovation process can prove to be very constructive.
- During a Perception Mapping exercise in the part of the process in which we are trying to a) list perceptions, and then, b) answer the 'leads to?' question for each perception.
- During any point when using the solution generation tools when we are seeking to translate generic solution triggers – e.g. Inventive Principles, Trends of evolution, translation of conceptual solutions from the Ideality tool, use of Omega Life View, Size-Time-Interface-Cost, etc – into specific solutions. The importance of Green Hat thinking here cannot be over-estimated. This will be the place where the systematic innovation process succeeds or fails.

Blue Hat

We wear the blue hat when looking to provide a controlling function, or when organising the overall thinking process. The Blue Hat is the hat that we wear when judging when and where to put on the other Hats. The Blue Hat is the overall process organising Hat. It is the one worn almost continuously by the facilitator of a systematic innovation problem solving session rather than specifically by all members of a problem solving team. That being said, there are times when the team may benefit through collective donning of the Blue Hat:

- During post-session recording of events.
- Periodically during subversion analysis when trying to ensure that all failure modes are being adequately traced and recorded.
- When a problem solving team is getting bogged down in the detail of a particular part of a process, it is often useful for the facilitator to get the rest of the team to shift into Blue Hat thinking mode in order to zoom out of the details and to re-datum or re-orient themselves to see where they are in the overall process.

Putting It All Together

There is no one definitive version of 'the' systematic innovation process. In many senses, such a thing can only exist in the mind of an individual. On the other hand, in order to examine how a 'typical' problem definition and solving session might require us to shift from one Hat to another, a number of generic steps are present in the vast majority of situations. These generic steps will be described below alongside a description of how we might shift from one Hat to another as we progress through the steps.

At the very broadest level, as we described in the previous chapter, the systematic innovation process consists of four major steps – starting with Problem **Definition**, then **Select**ing the most appropriate solution routes, then generating **Solution**s, and finally **Evaluat**ing and down-selecting. We might see these steps as a looping process which repeats until we obtain a solution with which we are happy – Figure 3.11.

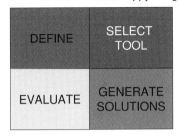

Figure 3.11: Four Major Steps Of The Systematic Innovation Process

Looking at each of these in turn:

DEFINE
- What benefits are we looking to achieve, how will we know when we've got there? (White Hat)
- Are we solving the right problem (Green Hat)
- What are the constraints? (**Black** Hat, possibly followed by Yellow)
- What resources are available? (Yellow Hat, possibly followed by Green)
- Where is the 'sore point'? (White Hat)
- What are the functions and attributes contained in the current system? (White Hat to define intended functions, then specifically followed by **Black** Hat to identify the harmful, insufficient, excessive and missing functions)
- How mature is the current system (where does it and its sub-systems sit on their current evolutionary S-curves?) (White Hat)
- (Optional) Ideality and Ideal Final Result analysis (Green Hat)
- (Optional) Perception Mapping analysis (White and Green Hat)
- (Optional) Brainstorm and 'Car-Park' initial solution thoughts (**Red** Hat)

SELECT
- Determine the most appropriate solution generation tools for the particular problem (White Hat)

SOLVE
A variety of options here, depending on which of the TRIZ tools are relevant:
- (Ideality) (White Hat)
- (Knowledge) (White Hat)
- (Conflicts/Contradictions) (White Hat to generate and look up contradictions; Green Hat to translate the generic triggers into specific solutions)
- (Trends) (Yellow Hat followed by Green)
- (Trimming) (Yellow Hat, probably followed by Green)
- (Measurement Standards) (Preferably Yellow; probably followed by Green)
- OLV/STIC/9-Windows Psychological Inertia Tools (Green Hat)

- Re-Focus/Re-Frame (mostly White with periods of Green Hat during solution generation phases)
- (Subversion Analysis) (**Black** Hat; probably interspersed with periods of **Blue**)

EVALUATE
- Have solutions been generated? If no, then the problem needs to be re-cast (**Black** Hat, possibly followed by **Red**, Green, or maybe **Blue**, probably in that order)
- If yes, then solutions need to be ranked (Yellow Hat, systematically followed by **Black** Hat)
- Deciding where to go next (i.e. around the loop again or to finish) (White Hat, but the facilitator should definitely encourage participants to go into **Black** Hat mode one more time if possible)

Of course, the above does not claim to be in any way definitive, rather that it should be judged as a measure of the need for us to shift our mode of thinking both systematically and regularly during a problem session.

Whether or not you chose to incorporate any of these ideas into the way in which you use any of the systematic innovation tools, successful use demands that we recognise that the human brain works in distinctly different modes. Edward DeBono's Six Thinking Hats™ show us the six main modes of operation. Awareness of the different modes, will massively increase the likelihood that the outcome of the process will be a successful one.

4) Information Structuring – Systematic Innovation and Mind-Maps™

Have you ever found yourself in the situation where you have to write a letter or report; you have done all of the information searching you need, and have successfully filled your head with facts, but when it comes to getting started, you suddenly find yourself at a complete loss? You wouldn't be alone if you had.

Ask the majority of people to write a report and typically they will attempt to sit down and write it in a linear fashion – starting at the beginning and finishing at the end. A common symptom of this kind of method of tackling the task is that we spend an age trying to work out where to start. Another is that we will get part the way through writing a report and realise we have missed something out. What is happening in both cases is that we are asking our brain to carry out two functions simultaneously – 1) identifying what to write and 2) putting it in the right hierarchical structure and sequence. Most of us find it difficult to conduct both activities in parallel, and rapidly become saturated by complexity as a result. Mind-mapping™ is a means of enabling us to manage this complexity. It seeks to achieve separation between the 'identify' and 'sequence' functions. It has a particular relevance to the way we define and solve problems within the systematic innovation process. It is not essential to our success, but is certainly recommended.

Tony Buzan (Reference 3.3) developed Mind Maps as an efficient way of using the brain's ability for structuring information and making associations between different ideas and concepts. Association plays a dominant role in nearly every mental function, and especially creativity.

To make a MindMap, we typically start in the centre of a page by focusing on the overall theme of a problem. As illustrated in the generic mind-map in Figure 3.12, we then work outwards in all directions in a branching manner to produce a tree like structure around that central theme. We can develop a hierarchical structure from main branches, to sub-branches to twigs and eventually leaves – each representing different levels of a problem or solution situation.

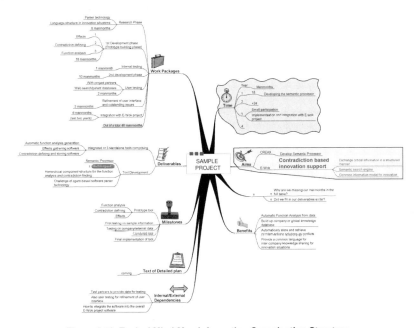

Figure 3.12: Typical Mind-Map Information Organisation Structure

MindMaps can be usefully applied at a number of stages in the problem definition, problem solving and solution evaluation phases of a problem. We typically use them to help define a problem, analyse resources and constraints, and then provide a structure during the generation of problem solutions.

Those wishing to find more details about the combined use of Mind-mapping in the systematic innovation context may wish to refer to Reference 3.7.

5) Group Psychology

If the problems of harnessing individual creativity are still largely intractable, issues concerning the effectiveness or otherwise of individuals working together can be an order of magnitude more so.

The Six Hats™ idea is an attempt to ensure alignment of thinking modes during a group session ("everybody switch to green hat mode"), and as such offers a way of segmenting highly complex phenomena into a commonly understood framework. Anyone who has tried to facilitate a group session, however, is likely to be acutely aware that some people are happier wearing certain colour hats relative to other ones.

In other words, as much as it might be desirable to force someone into green hat thinking mode, if that person is not used to or does not like that type of thinking, no amount of pressure will make that person don the hat. Different character types appear to be happiest wearing just a small number of the available thinking hats.

In the same way that there are an infinite number of ways of segmenting the world, the creativity literature describes a near infinite number of ways of defining personality traits and how those traits mix or don't mix with one another.

The only practical remedies to this type of group dynamic problem are firstly to try and select teams with an appropriate clustering of personality types during the relevant parts of the problem solving process, and secondly – more pragmatically in situations where we have no control over who is or isn't a member of the team – to segment that team such that different personality types are tasked with different parts of the overall process. For example, thinking about the thinking hat requirements at different stages in the definition-selection-solving-evaluating, it is a good idea to place 'innovators' in green hat tasks and 'adaptors' in black and white tasks and not vice versa. Likewise it is often a good idea to conduct certain parts of the overall process (or at least the first iterations thereof) outside of the group setting. Function analysis (Chapter 6), for example is very difficult to conduct in a group setting as it is difficult to keep everyone actively involved.

Try to encourage people to experience modes different to the ones they instinctively migrate towards. In the short term you might not be thanked; in the longer term you will probably be rewarded with a more rounded team producing higher quality results.

The next issue then is how we establish which personality types will and won't work well in combination with others. This is another complex issue. We do not attempt to be in any way comprehensive in reviewing the range of personality measurement tools, but instead merely seek to record three methods and tools that have been shown to have a significant effect on group dynamics in creative problem solving situations.

The first is the classic Meyers-Briggs (Reference 3.8) personality profiling method, and a second is the Kirton Adaptor-Innovator (Reference 3.9) method. Both serve to highlight that groups featuring individuals with personalities at different extremes of the profile types (e.g. a group of extreme innovator types combined with extreme adaptor types) are highly prone to failure during jointly conducted creativity sessions.

More recently, we have introduced a creativity self-assessment tool of our own. In common with one of the big systematic innovation methodology themes, the idea behind this tool has been to distill best practices from wherever they can be found. The resulting tool is an on-line questionnaire (found at www.systematic-innovation.com) that allows users to compare their strengths and weaknesses against a comprehensive range of factors found to be relevant in a creativity context. Figure 3.13 illustrates the output that a user will receive at the end of the questionnaire.

The first thing to note about the output is that it divides the problem of measuring creativity into the eight key parameters that we think determine what creativity is, and what skills people will require if they are to create effectively. The eight parameters are:-

Abstraction - the ability to abstract concepts from ideas.

Connection - the ability to make connections between things that don't logically appear to have any connection with one another.

Perspective - the ability to shift ones perspective on a situation – in terms of space and time, and interfaces with other people. In many ways, the perspective skill is about ability to empathise with the views of others.

Curiosity - the desire to change or improve things that everyone else accepts as the norm.

Boldness   —   the confidence to push boundaries beyond accepted conventions. Also the ability to eliminate fear of what others think of you.

Paradox   —   the ability to simultaneously accept and work with statements that are in conflict or contradictory to one another.

Complexity —   the ability to carry large quantities of information and be able to manipulate and manage the relationships between such information.

Persistence —   the ability to force oneself to keep trying to derive more and stronger solutions even when good ones have already been generated.

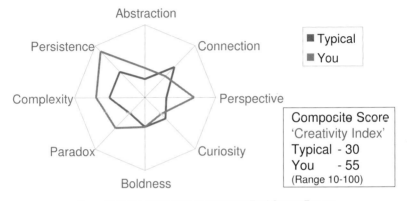

Figure 3.13: Creativity Self-Assessment Tool Output Format

The database of people taking the questionnaire is now measured in the tens of thousands. Some of the things that we have learned that can have a significant impact on the success or otherwise of a creative problem solving session are the following:-

Low-performing teams:-
- are generally low in Persistence, Abstraction and Curiosity across the whole team
- feature strong polarisation between high and low Paradox scores
- feature strong polarisation between high and low Connection scores
- possess lots of high Boldness scores, and no high Complexity scores
- possesses generally high Curiosity scores, and generally low Perspective
- possess a very 'distorted' radar plot profile when the profiles of everyone involved are over-laid, one on top of the other

High performing teams, on the other hand are likely to possess some or all of the following characteristics:-
- generally high in Persistence, Abstraction and Curiosity across the whole team
- good overall Paradox scores – with everyone close to or above average, quite possibly with one or two people with very high scores
- good consistency across Connection scores, again with some advantages if there are one or two people with very high scores
- at least one member with a high Complexity score
- a very 'circular' radar plot profile when the profiles of everyone involved are over-laid, one on top of the other

What Do I Do?

1) Awareness of how the brain works is highly beneficial in maximizing the benefits of using the systematic innovation method; obtain this awareness and (more importantly) experience it.

2) Recognise that different parts of the process demand physiologically different modes of thinking, and take account of these differences.

3) Understand your personally preferred thinking modes and those of the people around you. Try to match the different preferences to the different requirements of the process.

4) Keep psychological issues in mind whenever possible during the systematic innovation process. This is especially so with respect to the issue of psychological inertia. Psychological inertia is the thing that will tell you that you have spent enough time defining the problem, that there are no other possible solutions, and that the solution you just generated is good enough. In the large majority of occasions, what it is telling you is wrong.

Final Point – 'Yes, But....'

Everyone knows that one of the all-time great ways of killing off creative ideas is to deliver a sentence starting with the words 'yes, but'. Three great 'yes, but' sentences:-

....something else gets worse
....I don't know how to....
....someone already owns the solution

Systematic innovation provides a very good rebuttal to each of these questions; 'someone, somewhere already solved your 'yes, but' problem'. 'Yes, but' very simply means that you have found the next contradiction your system has to solve. Don't let this phrase kill any idea too soon. Whatever you think might be stopping you from solving a problem, whatever that next contradiction is, it has already been solved by someone else. The method will help you find that someone.

References

1) De Bono, E., 'The Use of Lateral Thinking', Penguin, London, 1967.
2) De Bono, E., 'The Mechanism Of Mind', Penguin, London, 1969.
3) Buzan, A, 'The Mind Map Book', BBC Books, London, 1993.
4) Mann, D.L., 'Systematic Win-Win Problem Solving In A Business Environment', TRIZCON2002, St Louis, April 2002.
5) Mann, D.L., 'Klondike Versus Homing Search Strategies', TRIZ Journal, February 2002.
6) DeBono, E., 'Six Thinking Hats'. Penguin, 1988.
7) Care, I., Mann, D.L., 'Mind-mapping and TRIZ', TRIZ Journal, www.triz-journal.com, January 2001.
8) Bayne, R., 'The Myers-Briggs Type Indicator', Nelson Thornes, 1997.
9) Kirton, M.J., 'Adaptors and Innovators: The Way People Approach Problems', Planned Innovation, 3, pp51-54, 1980.

Creativity text bibliography:

10) Boden, M., 'The Creative Mind: Myths and Mechanisms', Basic, New York, 1991.
11) Cooper, L., Shepard, R.N., 'Turning Something Over in the Mind', Scientific American, December 1984, pp106.
12) Regis, E., 'Who Got Einstein's Office?: Eccentricity and Genius at the Institute for Advanced Study', Addison, Reading, MA, 1987.
13) http://www.buffalostate.edu/~cbir/ cbirgenb.htm
14) Hofstadter, D., 'Fluid Concepts and Creative Analogies', Harvester Wheatsheaf, London, 1995.
15) Mitchell, M., 'Analogy-Making as Perception', MIT Press, Cambridge, MA, 1993.
16) Dasgupta, S., 'Creativity In Invention And Design', Cambridge University Press, 1994.
17) Claxton, G., 'Hare Brain, Tortoise Mind', 4th Estate, London, 1997.
18) Hudson, L., 'Frames Of Mind', Methuen, 1968.
19) Root-Bernstein, R. & M., 'Sparks of Genius', Houghton Mifflin, Boston, 1999.
20) Gelb, M., 'How To Think Like Leonardo Da Vinci', Thorsons, London, 1998.
21) Levesque, L.C., 'Breakthrough Creativity: Achieving Top Performance Using the Eight Creative Talents', Davies-Black Publishing, April 2001.
22) Ramachandran, V.S., 'Phantoms In The Brain', 4th Estate, London, 1998.

4.
System Operator/9-Windows

"We don't see things as they are, we see things as we are"
Anaïs Nin

Although the concept of thinking in time and space and its importance in the overall context of systematic innovation has already been described in previous chapters, the existence of the System Operator or '9-Windows' tool warrants a chapter of its own. The chapter is placed here, before delving into the details of any of the individual elements of the systematic innovation process, as it is something that we should be aware of and using at all stages of that process if we are to achieve any significant degree of success.

The chapter is split into five main segments. The first examines and describes the system operator in its standard form; the second examines the tool in a globally holistic sense; the third examines different ways of interpreting and using the classic tool; the fourth examines extensions to this tool that are often necessary in certain problem settings; and the fifth examines how the system operator can be further extended using other existing perspective-based creativity tools.

1) System Operator Concept

The System Operator 'tool' is a simple means of helping users to think in terms of TIME and SPACE. The basic principle of operation divides 'the world' into nine segments as shown in Figure 4.1.

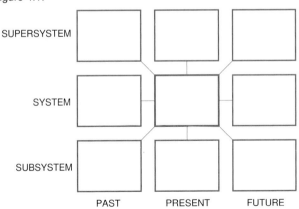

Figure 4.1: '9-Windows' of the System Operator

The central box of the nine – system, present – is the one our brains naturally migrate to whenever we are given a problem situation. In other words, asked to think about 'designing a better sales model', our brains are likely to immediately conjure up the image

63

of our current model ('the system') being used to sell whatever it is we sell to a customer that we currently already know ('the present'). What the system operator tool is trying to get us to do is also think about the sales model in the bigger ('super-system') context – the position of the sales force in the context of the organisation, *all* customers, people who are not yet customers, possible outside channels, complementors, etc. It is also trying to get us to zoom-in and look at the finer details. These finer details represent the 'sub-system' context – the sales personnel, the forms the have to complete, the means of communication, the agreed discounts, etc. It is also about the sales model in the future – what happens to the model if we provide a new web-site (i.e. the very near term future), or if a new competitor appears, or a new channel, or market trends drift over the edge of a cliff that changes the whole market dynamic (i.e. the longer term future). Figure 4.2 illustrates some of the main time and space features that we might like to consider when thinking more completely about the design of our sales model. The point of this exercise is to help us overcome the psychological inertia of present and system level only thinking.

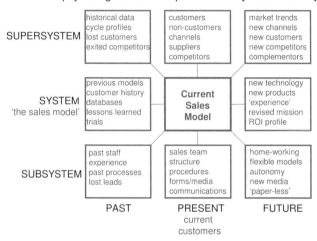

Figure 4.2: Example System Operator Picture For 'Sales Model Design'

We will see this aspect of the tool covered in more detail in Chapter 20. For now, it is important only to be aware of this cruel 'present and system level box' trick our brain often plays on us when we are thinking about a problem situation, and how the 9-Windows tool can help us to overcome the adverse effects of that trick.

In order to use the 9-Windows effectively, the first thing we need to do is define what we mean by 'SYSTEM' and 'PRESENT'. In the sales model example we defined the model 'system' in the context of our organisation and its customer/supplier base, and the way we sell to our current customer base as the present.

These definitions then allow us to define what we mean by super-system, sub-system, past and future. It is often a good idea to label these things on a 9-Windows picture – as illustrated in Figure 4.2. Not only does this allow our brains to see how we have chosen to segment a given problem, it also allows us to define the situation for others who may be able to help us. In the final analysis, it does not matter how we define the borders of what we mean by 'system' and 'present'; the only important thing is that we remain consistent with the definition throughout a problem solving session.

From a 'sales model design' perspective, the system operator is trying to encourage us to think in a much more holistic way about our task; thus improving the way we design the model is not just about what happens when a current customer is experiencing it, but about **all** of the other aspects shown in Figure 4.2 (and others we might also be able to think of if we were really in the business of designing sales models).

The system operator concept is – as we probably won't be able to state often enough – used throughout the problem solving process (note: as per convention elsewhere in the book, we are using 'problem solving' as a short-hand for the whole problem definition, problem solving, opportunity finding, opportunity exploiting creativity spectrum). We should be using it when we are looking for resources, identifying constraints, specifying the design requirements during the problem definition process (see the problem explorer in the next chapter), we should be using it during idea generation, and we should also be using it when evaluating our solutions.

An Alternative Perspective

The 9-windows of the system operator offer a simple and effective way of encouraging problem solvers to see their problem situation from different perspectives. The tool in its 9-windows form is, however, relatively crude in many senses. This is acutely evident when, for example, using the 'past' or 'future' triggers to prompt the problem owner to think about the problem in terms of time. Thus in the sales model context from above, 'future' might mean a few days or it might mean several years. A simple way of encapsulating this kind of breadth of consideration is the expanded system operator idea shown in Figure 4.3.

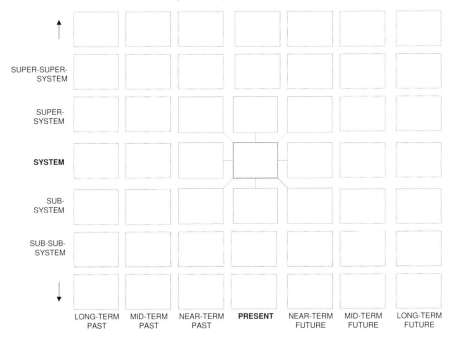

Figure 4.3: Expanded Multi-Screen System Operator

This increasing number of windows can be further expanded into an infinite number in both time and space dimensions. In terms of 'space' segmenting sub-system, system and super-system into potentially many more different perspectives is analogous to a movie camera 'zooming in and zooming out' on the problem. In terms of 'time', this author has come across several highly creative individuals who segment the number of time windows to such a degree that they in effect 'run a movie' in their minds; tracking the problem situation from its very beginning through to its final end. In fact the movie image seems to be quite an effective one for combined thinking in space and time – with the film running through time and the camera image focusing in or out on micro detail or macro scenery.

2) 9-Windows On The World

In this second section we attempt to relate the system operator to a global space and time framework. Rather than this being an attempt to draw any all-embracing philosophical conclusions, our theme is merely to highlight the changing perspectives obtainable during application of the system operator tool.

A considerable problem that managers of multi-disciplinary teams face is that everyone in that team sees the world differently to everyone else. Some of these differences may simply be ones of perception – an issue that we will return to in Chapter 8 – but then others are rather more fundamental and relate to the whole educational background of the different disciplines of human endeavour.

Taking the above 'movie' expanded segmentation idea a little further takes us towards a much more holistic map of the world. A 'complete' (as we know it today anyway) map of space and time might look something like the picture drawn in Figure 4.4. Sticking with the idea of space being represented up and down a vertical axis and time progressing along a horizontal axis with the past disappearing off to the left, and the future progressing across to the right, as with the 9-Windows, but now expanding those axes to their limits, the figure shows a big time-space framework. The borders of our framework have been drawn to start with the big bang about 10 billion years ago, and an assumption that the future will last as long if not longer (no-one said the thing had to be symmetrical, right?), and, in terms of SPACE, to zoom in to the structure of a proton or electron, and right out to the size of the whole mass of galaxies spawned by the big bang.

The idea takes at least a part of its inspiration from the work of Charles and Ray Eames (Reference 4.1) and their seminal images of how our perspectives change when we zoom in and out from our very human level perspective of the world around us. Like the Eames' model, a logarithmic scale has been used, although this is a detail that need not bother us unduly – it simply makes it possible to fit the whole of Earth's history and future on a single side of paper.

Besides the overall global space and time scale, what the figure shows is an approximation of where different people with different skills will typically define the boundaries of their world. Thus – and here is the main point of this section – other scientific, engineering or management disciplines are likely to have different time and space definitions of what super-system, system, sub-system, past, present and future might mean to them. Thus a physicist conceptualizing future computer chips is increasingly interested in time measurements of 10^{-9} or less – and so to them the line denoting the difference between 'present' and 'future' might be drawn much closer to the central axis, and the idea of thinking of 'past' or 'future' in terms of years might seem ridiculous.

Likewise, the map drawn by a cosmologist or an archeologist or a biologist or a chemist or a physicist, or a manager running a department in an organisation will be coloured by different perspectives. This is not to say that any of them are wrong, merely that a) they are different, and that b) in each case they are likely to define their 9 (or however many) window boundaries at different places. Vive la difference.

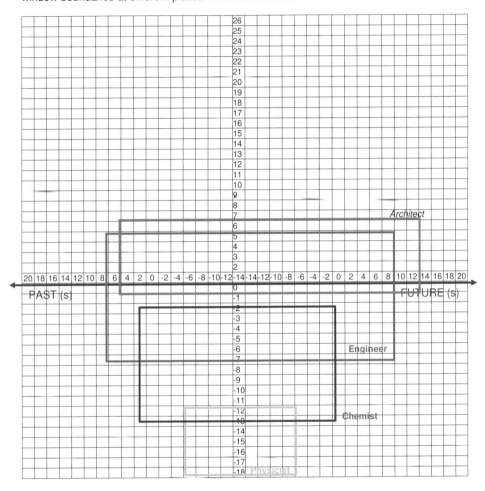

PHYSICAL DIMENSION (m)

Figure 4.4: Typical 9-Windows Perspectives Map of the Space-Time Territory

Furthermore, we are not saying either, of course, that we should all be thinking about the big bang when we're trying to design a new sales model. Far from it. What such a time-space map it is trying to do is get us to recognise that a) the actual world is much bigger than our personal perspectives on it, and, b) more importantly, that each of us has a potentially different way of thinking about where the boundaries are, and that someone else's perspective may very well help us to solve our problem. As we will see in the next section, this is particularly relevant as our knowledge heads further and further into the sub-system.

3) Between The Boxes – Changing Perspectives

One of the problems commonly associated with the use of the system operator tool emerges from the way we draw it or see it presented to us. Almost inherently in either situation, we are separate from the 9-Windows; we sit above them, looking down on them from a third dimension; we are outside, separate from the windows, looking in. While this can sometimes be a very useful stance to take (indeed in the fourth section, we will be examining this vital three dimensional aspect in some detail), it can also inhibit our understanding of the reality of a problem situation, and –we will hopefully see here – seriously impair our ability to solve a problem in the most effective way.

This second section is thus aimed at examining the consequences of us looking at the 9 windows as outside observers versus what happens when we are able to 'enter' the windows and look at the problem situation from within.

One way to look at this is that we place ourselves 'in' each window and view the other windows from this new perspective. Something like the 9-windows picture shown in Figure 4.5.

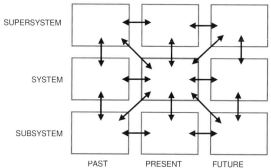

Figure 4.5: Using The 9-Windows To Change Our Viewing Perspective

If this picture is difficult to imagine (we do after all live in a three-dimensional world), some people find it useful to recast the windows as 'rooms' they become a part of, and from which they can see each of the other rooms – Figure 4.6.

Figure 4.6: Turning The 9-Windows Into 9 Rooms

In any given problem or opportunity situation, any or all of the viewing directions shown in Figure 4.5 may provide a valuable new insight into a solution. Rather than look at all 16 of the viewing perspective possibilities, we examine some of the ones most likely to be useful in the greatest number of cases:

Empathy Views

Putting ourselves in the position of other people is an excellent way to better understand their perspective on situations. Too many managers ride roughshod over the views of subordinates. Too many also fail to appreciate what their customers and suppliers are experiencing. For problems associated with subordinates, putting ourselves in the box marked 'sub-system, present' and looking upwards to the system is a good empathy-based viewing perspective. Likewise, if we are experiencing a problem with external people or systems, then putting ourselves into the 'super-system, present' window and looking down onto the system can also help us to better appreciate their outsider perspective. Chapter 20 talks about this latter situation through a description of a tool called 'Omega Life Views' (OLV). This is a tool that deliberately forces us not only to shift our perspective to a 'typical' someone in a different window, but to examine someone sitting at the extreme limits.

The 'super-system, present' view is the 'becoming part of the super-system looking in at the system' view. Or, 'what does the system look like, when we view it from the perspective of the outsider?' In crude terms, this perspective might be seen as that of a customer looking at a product. More importantly, from a problem solving perspective, it is not just about encouraging the problem solver to recognize that the super-system exists (which is what the classic 9-Windows tool is trying to do), but encouraging them to adopt the position of that customer and to see the system from their perspective. To many the concept sounds so trite it shouldn't require mentioning. Unfortunately the plethora of 'bad' business models in the world suggests that managers and strategists (or more likely the system they are constrained to work within) do not adopt this position as a matter of normal or even occasional practice.

Airports perhaps provide a good example. Most of the systems known as 'airport' appear to have little to do with empathy with the customer. This is especially unfortunate when thinking about airports we might visit in other countries for that establishment gives us our first and last impression of the country. Anyone unfortunate enough to have to use airports a lot will probably feel that as 'customers' they are a tiny, apparently inconvenient part of a super-system which has, first and foremost, been designed to satisfy the smooth running requirements of the airport managers and the fragile egos of the architects that designed them.

What if there was a better way? What if the architects and managers saw things from the perspectives of the super-system?

- Would they think it was a good use of passengers' time to have them sitting doing nothing in a departure lounge and then moving them on to an aeroplane to do more nothing for several hours and then force them to endure another possibly several hours passing through immigration?
- Would they recognize that passenger consumption of electrical power – for laptops, phones, personal stereos, etc – has risen phenomenally in the past five years but that battery power hasn't matched the change? There are a host of passengers who would be willing to pay for plug-in or recharging facilities.

- Would they recognize that more and more passengers are more and more likely to use carry-on luggage and are therefore less and less likely to want to check their baggage if they can possibly help it?
- Would they recognize that many business travellers travel to get to meetings and that these travellers would be as happy to have that meeting at the airport as locating appropriate ground transportation (in an unfamiliar location) to get them to a meeting somewhere else?

And so on. Not to mention the 'empathy' discussions we might get into if we refocused on the system ('instrument of torture'?) known as the airliner.

Standing In The Future And Looking To The Present

A second altered viewing perspective involves placing ourselves in one of the 'future' windows and looking back to the 'present'. Examples of benefits accruable from problem solvers taking this stance include just about every recycling issue currently known ("your customers are your grandchildren"), changing demographics (what will I think about the pension system in twenty years time when I might actually become the recipient?), maintenance issues (this author has direct personal experience of designing solutions in a conventional environment only to find out when actually out in the field that that 'conventional environment' becomes totally irrelevant after a short period of use), and, thinking about future super-system, a whole host of contradictions that emerge as different parts of society evolve at different rates. We will return specifically to the issue of emerging trends of evolution and how they should affect the way we think about the design and management of business systems in Chapter 14.

4) Another Dimension

In the last section we discussed some of the problems that can occur when we place ourselves 'outside' the 9 windows of the system operator, and how we can overcome those problems. In this one, we look at why this separation takes place and how our understanding of this 'why' can influence a range of problem and opportunity situations. In examining this situation, we will also see how systematic innovation has benefited by integrating similar but in many ways more fully developed tools from Neuro-Linguistic Programming (NLP), and how this integration can, in turn, influence how we define and solve problems.

We use an isometric view of the classical 9 Windows – as illustrated in Figure 4.7 – to begin examining what might happen when we follow the advice of the TRIZ geometric evolution trend, and move out of the two-dimensional model perspective and begin to actively use the third dimension.

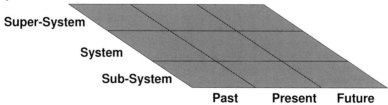

Figure 4.7: Isometric View Of The Classic 9-Windows

A useful first question, then, might be, what can we usefully use this third dimension to express? A very good answer comes from NLP and the work of Robert Dilts (Reference 4.2 and 4.3) who first drew a version of the picture reproduced in Figure 4.8. If the classical 9 windows describe a SPACE – TIME plane, then Dilts suggested that the third plane should describe the different levels of human awareness. The first plane represents physical actuality. Successive planes then represent a hierarchy of awareness of the way we perceive and are affected by that physical reality, from first the way we behave in response to the actuality, right up to how our identity is affected by the actuality.

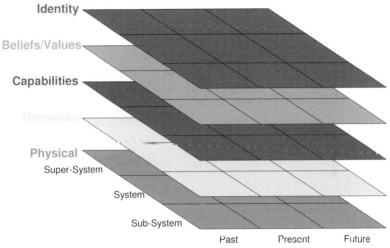

Figure 4.8: Turning The 9-Windows Into 45 Windows

A detailed discussion of the deep philosophical issues potentially raised by this picture is somewhat beyond the scope of this book however; the reference is a far better next step for anyone interested. We, on the other hand will see what we might extract from the image that might help us in a practical problem solving sense.

(By way of a short intrusion, however, Dilts actually uses first, second and third person to represent what the system operator defines as sub-system, system and super-system respectively. This too can add an interesting perspective to the way we use the 9-Windows, albeit one also beyond the scope of this article.)

Many managers are instinctively comfortable with the 9-windows, 'thinking in time and space' idea. Indeed, the design and management of physical organisations is highly amenable to this kind of world-view. Many management and 'people' problems, on the other hand are not so amenable to successful treatment by such a two-dimensional perspective. Such 'people' related problems demand that all of the issues associated with human behaviour have to be considered if we are going to successfully define and solve the real problem. In the NLP view, this means looking at all five levels. In terms of management type problems, just using the bottom two would represent a significant advance on the way most problems are viewed and dealt with today.

The Map and The Territory
Using the bottom two of the five system operator 'levels' – the 'physical' plane and the 'behaviour' plane (Figure 4.9) – should straightaway get us to recognize that potential for differences between the 'actual' and our perception of that actual. In more common

71

parlance, the two planes represent the 'territory' and a 'map'; the territory is what actually exists, while the map represents an opinion of what the territory looks like. Sometimes these two things are closely aligned, and sometimes they are not. When they are not, we have the basis of a contradiction. And once we have a contradiction, we have the ability to use the relevant contradiction elimination tools (Chapters 11 and 12) to help improve the situation.

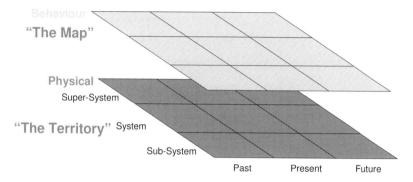

Figure 4.9: The Map Is Not The Territory – Difference Between Physical Plane And Our Perception Of It

Common 'Map versus Territory' Differences

The literature is literally full to brimming with examples of contradictions emerging as a result of differences between map and territory. A particularly fine collection of examples may be found in the 'decoding the corporate culture' chapter in Reference 4.4. Author Eileen Shapiro describes the 'internal game':

Espoused Rule ('the Map')	Real Rule ('the Territory')
'Quality comes First'	'Ship product no matter what'
'Never sell the customer something they don't need'	'Get the order; whoever gets most sales gets the biggest bonus'
'We take the long-term view of our businesses'	'Miss your quarterly budget and you're dead meat'
'We have an open environment speak up if you have a concern'	'Accentuate the positive, hide the negative (unless you have a death wish)'
'Developing people is one of our top priorities'	'Managers who spend time developing their people are weaklings and aren't tough enough to be in the job'
'Improve efficiency...'	'...and then we can cut jobs'

Awareness of the 'internal game' contradictions is not the same thing as a solution of course; but recognition of the map-territory contradictions is at least a start.

Marks and Spencer

Retailer M&S has traditionally positioned itself at the high-end of the high street chain store market. The map of their customer base has traditionally consisted of the aspirant middle-class family, and their competitors are other high street chains. In terms of the classic benefits versus price trade-off of the retail sector, they hold a solid middle-ground position.

Unfortunately in recent times, it has become apparent that the benefits-versus-price map for high-street stores – the map drawn by M&S – is somewhat different from the substantially bigger retailing benefit versus price territory. The difference is highlighted in Figure 4.10.

By no means uniquely – in fact we can observe very similar maps drawn by companies in a variety of markets from household to body-care, from automobiles to airlines – the territory turns out to be a threat to the middle ground business. In the case of M&S, the territory actually also contains private-label goods at the low-price end of the benefits-price spectrum, and a number of niches, but most notably 'little luxuries' at the other end (see Reference 4.5 for more detailed discussion of this trend). In this bigger picture context, M&S is actually a rather small player, and, unless it recognizes the difference between its map and the territory, it will continue to get smaller as the private label and 'little-luxury' players gradually encroach further and further onto the M&S map as all associated trends say they will.

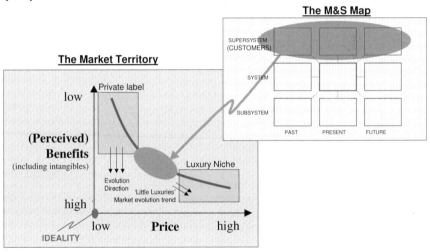

Figure 4.10: M&S - The Map Versus The Territory

(A simple yet surprisingly effective remedy to the type of situation M&S now finds itself in is to use Principle 13 (Chapter 11) and ask the question 'who doesn't buy our products?' The roots of increased market share usually exist outside the existing customer base.)

John – The Insensitive Line Manager

By way of another example of the problems that can be caused by the differences between map and territory, we look again at a well-known TRIZ case study – the insensitive line manager problem first discussed in Reference 4.6. Essentially the problem comes about as a result of the causal map described in Figure 4.11.

The core conflict is that John channels all resources under his control towards meeting the group's goals but he does this in a style that demoralises and renders ineffective other organisational goals. The previous analysis detailed in Reference 4.6 presents a rather crude application of Inventive Principles to try and solve the contradiction 'John should be present and not-present'.

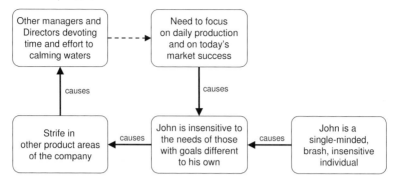

Figure 4.11: The Insensitive Line Manager

As subsequently discussed in Reference 4.7, stronger solutions will emerge by obtaining a better understanding of the root causes underlying the contradiction. It is suggested here that understanding of the problem can be further improved by recognising the differences between not just 'map' and 'territory', but also that different participants draw different maps. The point is illustrated in Figure 4.12 below.

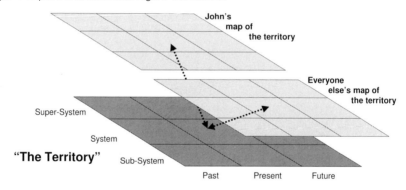

Figure 4.12: The Insensitive Line Manager – Multiple Maps of One Territory

Given this picture, it should become possible to provide a basis for allowing everyone involved in the problem to see what is happening. It also helps us to identify not just the 'John should be present and not-present' contradiction, but also other – perhaps more appropriately tackled – contradictions like John's map versus the territory, and everyone else's map(s) versus the territory. We will return to this specific problem situation in more detail in Chapter 12.

5) Integrating Other Perspectives

Following on from the previous section examining the introduction of a third dimension dealing with aspects of perception, personal belief and relationships, the start point here assumes that this three dimensional space-time-'interface' (Figure 4.13) viewing system applies to all of the aspects here. For the sake of clarity of illustration, however, we will focus primarily on the conventional space-time plane.

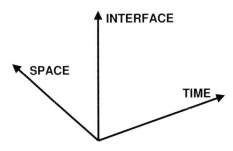

Figure 4.13: Three-Dimensional Space-Time-Interface System Operator Axes

Co-opetition

The Co opetition idea of a 'value net' previously discussed in Reference 4.8 provides a first example of the 9-Windows being used In conjunction with other ways of scoping and framing a given problem or opportunity situation. The 'value net' idea discussed in Co-opetition (Reference 4.9) is of significant interest when thinking about a holistic approach to business oriented problems – offering a much more broad reaching view than would normally be the case. In effect the 'value net' appears in each of the windows of the system operator tool – Figure 4.14.

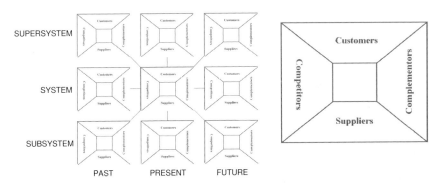

Figure 4.14: Combined 9-Windows and Value-Net Concepts

The importance of integrating the Co-opetition Customer-Supplier-Competitor-Complementor model with the 9-Windows emerges because, as Reference 4.8 suggested, the value net may well change with respect to both SPACE and TIME.

Strengths, Weaknesses, Opportunities, Threats (SWOT) Analysis

By way of a first extension to the co-opetition extension to the 9-Windows, Figure 4.15 illustrates a similar integration of the classic Strengths-Weaknesses-Opportunities-Threats (SWOT) analysis into the system operator space-time framework.

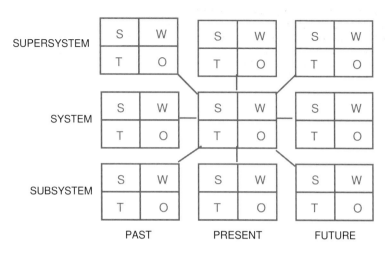

| | PAST | PRESENT | FUTURE |

Figure 4.15: Combining 9-Windows And SWOT Analysis

The SWOT analysis idea is used widely across a range of business areas as a means of scoping a given problem, opportunity or innovation situation. It attempts to get the person or team involved in the analysis to look at their situation from a number of different perspectives – namely, what are we good at, what are we not so good at, what are the things that could help us to become good, and what are the things that could stop us from becoming good.

Combining this thinking approach with the 9-Windows offers a number of additional useful perspectives. Of particular interest in many situations are the idea of repeating the SWOT analysis in the 9-Windows 'future' positions and 'super-system' positions. With regard to the 'future' perspective, the idea of re-thinking the questions on opportunities and threats can be very important because it forces the team to think about not just what they think will happen in the future, but also what they think their competitors and the market will do. In a related manner, asking the same questions from a super-system perspective opens the eyes of the team to other industries beyond their own.

By way of example of both, if we put ourselves in the position of a hypothetical car manufacturer struggling with the idea of developing a commercially viable electric car then, thinking about 'threats' at the system level present (as a conventional SWOT analysis would), is likely to get us to think about what other car manufacturers are doing. This is likely to put us into a psychological inertia hole (Chapter 3) that will focus our thinking onto the same hybrid vehicles and fuel cell technologies that ever other player is exploring. While this is undoubtedly necessary, it is far from certain that it is sufficient. Conducting the same SWOT analysis from the perspective of the super-system ought to point us at already viable electric transport systems like golf carts and postal delivery vans. According to Reference 4.10, it is more likely that these things will evolve and improve to take over the electric car market than anything developed by Ford or General Motors. Conducting the SWOT analysis from the 'future' perspective would further force the inclusion of solar energy and battery technology evolution (and, probably as likely, evolutionary limits), and, at the future-super-system level, global warming, choking of road systems and development of better public transport systems.

Thinking about the third 'interface' dimension illustrated in Figure 4.13, it is interesting to note that the idea of integrating the SWOT analysis into the different hierarchical levels of 'interfaces' (environment, behaviour, capability, belief, identity) and seeing how the analysis changes between different viewing perspectives ('the map is not the territory'), is already established practice in certain forms of Neuro-Linguistic Programming (NLP) – see Reference 4.11 for example.

Association/Dissociation

NLP gives us yet another means of using the 9-Windows to better effect when we consider the strategy of association and dissociation. Reference 4.11 discusses the importance and benefits of being able to control whether we examine situations from either an internal (i.e. we are a part of the situation and are emotionally connected to it), associated state, or whether we chose to view the situation from an external, dissociated state (we are outside the situation and are non-emotionally looking in). In some ways this idea is similar to the 9-rooms idea discussed in the third part of this chapter, although there in an increased emphasis here on comparing the detached and attached perspectives. Figure 4.16 presents the basic idea more explicitly in the context of the 9-Windows tool.

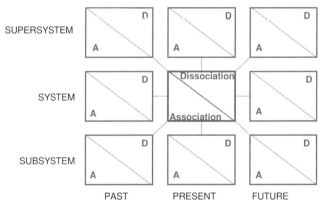

Figure 4.16: Combining Association/Dissociation And The 9-Windows

As described in the reference, the ability to associate and dissociate from any chosen situation is one of the cornerstones of NLP. The model already makes use of the space-time axes by, for example, helping people to solve (primarily) human-relations type problems by anchoring to past successes, and transplanting those anchors into future situations.

VAKOG

VAKOG stands for visual, auditory, kinesthetic, olfactory and gustatory. The acronym is a means of enhancing our ability to remember the five main human senses. The point is that, in a problem-solving context at least, we are often prone to not only forget any of the senses that are not already being used in the system. The use of all senses is important in many problem situations. The inclusion of a specific reference to increasing senses in the Inventive Principles (Principle 28, 'Another Sense' – Chapter 11) should further suggest the importance of solving problems by increasing interaction with more of the human senses. The point in the 9-Windows context is that if we recognize the five senses in not just the context of the current system, but also in the other 8 windows, we can often create new problem definition and solution opportunities.

The basic idea is illustrated in Figure 4.17 – which hopefully also serves to reinforce the overall theme of this chapter – that just about any of the problem situation framing tools available to us can be re-framed 9 times into the system operator. 45 times if we chose to use the fully three-dimensional space-time-interface window structure.

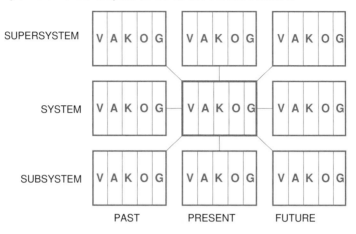

Figure 4.17: Combining VAKOG and the 9-Windows

Too Many Windows?

Anyone that has struggled through a SWOT analysis or an Association/Dissociation or any other analysis, will know that it can be very difficult to maintain concentration (will to live?) through all segments of the process. So what, therefore, are the chances of maintaining concentration over potentially nine times the number of segments as is being advocated by the system operator? Answer; it depends. If done in a single brainstorming session, the answer is probably as close to zero as makes any difference. If done in several sessions, or by splitting groups so that each covers different segments, the chances will increase markedly. The unfortunate truth according to a variant on Murphy's Law is that you can probably bet that the ones you chose not to analyse are the ones that contain the inventive spark that makes the biggest positive difference.

Summary

1) The '9-Windows' System Operator tool is a very effective way of encouraging problem solvers to recognise the importance of and to think in terms of TIME and SPACE. It should be there in our minds throughout our use of all of the different parts of the systematic innovation toolkit if we are to get the most out it.

2) It is, however, a relatively crude segmentation of what is in reality a continuous situation. Some people seem to think naturally in this continuous 'zooming-in, zooming-out' film-like kind of way, the rest of us still need some help.

3) The tool explicitly exists to help us avoid the trick our brain plays on us in which we tend to see situations from solely a 'system' level, in the 'present' context.

4) 'The map is not the territory' is a commonly described statement in the context of our frequent failure to effectively solve problems. The difference between the actuality of a situation and our personal perception of that actuality is often significant. We have seen here, however, how the 9-windows concept is a very effective tool for getting us to think in terms of time and space, but that it is also a way, if we're not careful, of also altering our map of the territory; the 'territory' is continuous in both time and space; it is not a series of window segments; the 'territory' is usually also much bigger than even our 9-windows perspective.

5) Different people will draw different maps of the territory. 'Different maps' represent the root of disagreement and contradiction. Awareness of these differences – through awareness of a third 'interface' dimension in the system operator – offers at least the potential of better understanding of how conflicts arise, and thus how we might apply systematic innovation tools to resolve them.

6) Our brains seem to work naturally over only a small number of orders of magnitude of either size or time at a given time. The 9-Windows idea is useful in helping us to jump deliberately from one mind-set to another, and, moreover, allow us to construct a mental map that allows us to position ourselves at any moment in time relative to an all-encompassing total.

7) In its original form, the 9-Windows system operator, whether intentionally or otherwise, separates us from the problem; we are encouraged to see it from 'outside' each of the windows; we look into the windows. On some occasions this can be a very useful position to hold. On others, however, it can separate us from the problem in a harmful way. Awareness of this phenomenon is hopefully over half of the solution.

Final Thought

The system operator in whatever form we chose to use it is an important element within the overall systematic innovation philosophy. Its presence is (or should be) felt in just about everything we do with the toolkit – hence the reason its image features on every page of this book. The idea of thinking in space and time is commonly mentioned and applied in many management texts. The addition of a third dimension called 'interface' or 'relationship' offers an important additional thinking direction. Whether we divide things into 9-windows or 45 or even more, we are simply using the idea of segmentation to help us manage complexity more effectively than we otherwise would. What we have hopefully hinted at in this chapter is that there are many more ways of applying segmentation than just segmenting in space or time. Someone out there has already solved your problem; different people like to segment things in different ways. Some will be more helpful in certain situations than others, but ultimately, the best ones will be those that fit into *your* way of doing things.

The following chapters will demonstrate places where the concept of thinking in time, space and interface are important, and will make suggestions – usually based on the 9-Windows tool – as to how to incorporate the thinking being sought by the tool into the problem definition and solving process.

What Do I Do?

1) Think about your problem/opportunity situation. Define 'the system'. Define what you mean by 'present' (these definitions can be largely arbitrary, so long as you remain consistent after you have defined what each is).

2) Draw the 9-Windows. Based on your definitions of 'system' and 'present', define what 'past' and 'future' mean, and what 'super-system' and 'sub-system' contain. In terms of the time elements, it is useful to think in terms of 'before the problem' and 'after the problem'. In the case of process-type problem situations, this may require several time segments as opposed to simply 'past, present and future' as shown in Figure 4.1.

3) Proceed to Chapter 5.

References

1) Eames, C. and R., 'Powers of Ten Interactive' CD-Rom, http://www.eamesoffice.com/
2) Dilts, Grindler, 'Neuro-Linguistic Programming Volume 1', Meta Publications, November 1989.
3) Dilts, R., *et al*, 'Tools For Dreamers', Meta Publications, 1991.
4) Shapiro, E.C., 'Fad Surfing In The Boardroom – Reclaiming The Courage To Manage In The Age Of Instant Answers', Addison-Wesley Publishing Company, 1995.
5) Popcorn, F., 'EVEolution', Harper-Collins, 2000.
6) Kowalick, J., 'THE TRIZ APPROACH Case Study: Creative Solutions to a Human Relations Problem', TRIZ Journal, November 1997.
7) Mann, D.L., Stratton, R., 'Physical Contradictions and Evaporating Clouds', TRIZ Journal, July 1999.
8) Mann, D.L., 'Laws Of System Completeness', TRIZ Journal, May 2001.
9) Nalebuff, B.J., Brandenburger, A.M., 'Co-opetition', Harper Collins Business, 1996.
10) Christensen, C.M., 'The Innovator's Dilemma', Harvard Business School Press, 1995.
11) Merleverde, P.E., Bridoux, D., Vandamme, R., 'Seven Steps To Emotional Intelligence', Crown House Publishing Ltd, 2001.

5.
Problem Definition – Problem Explorer

"If I had asked the public what they wanted, they would have asked for a faster horse"
Henry Ford.

and

"If I had asked the public how they wanted their coffee, I doubt they would have requested a double short caramel skim cappuccino"
Modern day equivalent, J.M. Dru

In this chapter, we examine one of the essential parts of the problem definition process. We will use the word 'problem' here as a short-hand for any kind of situation where we are looking to change something. This might literally mean that we have a problem ('sales are down') or it may mean that everything is fine, but we'd like to see if there is something we could do that is new or better ('what will the next killer application in banking be?'). The 'problem explorer' is where we will set the context for the problem or opportunity under consideration and lay down the ground rules for what we can and can't do when we start to generate possible solutions. The problem explorer contains four basic parts:-

1) Benefits Analysis
2) Identification of Resources
3) Identification of Constraints
4) Identification of 'Sore Point'

The four parts can be done in any sequence, although it is useful to begin with a Benefits Analysis as this helps set the appropriate context for everything that follows.

Appendix 2 at the back of the book contains an example pro forma usable for all types of problem and opportunity situation. Feel free to photocopy this pro forma for every problem you intend to work on. The pro forma also contains elements of Function and Attribute Analysis (Chapter 6), S-Curve Analysis (Chapter 7), Ideality Analysis (Chapter 8) and Perception Mapping (Chapter 9). In this chapter we will just examine those elements of the pro forma relevant to problem exploration and scene setting. For those with a preference for things electronic, there is a downloadable version available at www.creax.com in the 'free downloads' page.

We will detail each of the four parts of problem exploration in turn, before examining a typical example of a completed problem explorer analysis:-

Benefits Analysis

In this first part of the problem exploration process, we are primarily setting the scene for a problem situation. As may be seen from the front page of the pro forma (Figure 5.1), this activity requires us to ask a series of questions:

Firstly, it is often useful to clarify who is involved in the problem – who is the customer, who is the sponsor and who are the people working on the problem. The distinction between customer and sponsor is not always obvious unless explicitly stated. In most circumstances, the customer is the person (or persons) who will receive the output of the problem solving process, while the sponsor is the person paying to have the problem solved. Normally, one is internal and the other external, although, of course, there may be situations where they are both the same. It is important to note the differences that do exist because their motives might be quite different.

We will see whether this is the case when we look at the next groups of questions – 'where are we trying to get to?' and 'how will we know when we've got there?' It is recommended that you begin by answering these questions from the perspective of the customer, before re-asking them from the perspective of sponsor and the team working on the problem.

Project Title		Date	
Project Sponsor			
Project Customer			
Project Team			

Benefits	Where are we trying to get to (what are the goals)?	How will we know when we've got there (measures of success)?
Sponsor		
Customer		
Team		

Figure 5.1: Benefit Analysis Pro Forma

It is recommended (but not essential – hence it doesn't feature on the standard pro forma) that we also think about the 'where are we trying to get to from a 9-Windows perspective. In particular, it is sometimes useful to ask the question 'where will the (customer/sponsor/team) want to get to in the future?' This is really just a means of checking the stability of the problem – and to find out if the solution is likely to change in the future. If the answer to the question implies that the problem and its answer *will* change in the future, we should contemplate re-answering the 'where are we trying to get to?' question accordingly.

Problem Hierarchy Explorer

'The customer is always right, except when it comes to defining the problem' is a common saying. While intended to be flippant, it nevertheless makes the important general point that the human brain has a very strong tendency to believe the *first* defined problem is the *right* problem. The world is full of stories of companies and individuals spending inordinate amounts of both time and money solving what turns out to be the wrong problem. The problem hierarchy explorer is a way of clarifying the space around the originally stated problem definition. The tool framework is based on the work of Min Basadur (Reference 5.1) and the ubiquitous 'ask why 5 times' philosophy of root cause analysis. A schematic of the tool is illustrated in Figure 5.2.

The basic idea underlying the tool is the use of two questions 'why?' and 'what's stopping?' to respectively broaden and narrow the initially stated problem. The outcome of repeating these questions several times is a hierarchical list of problem definitions, from which the problem owner is able to select.

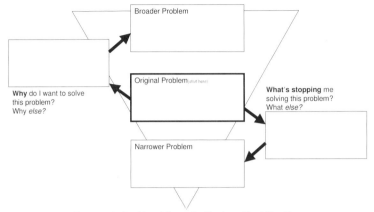

Figure 5.2: Problem Hierarchy Explorer Tool Pro Forma

A simple example should serve to illustrate the mechanics of the tool. Suppose someone approaches us with the problem that they have a problem of low staff morale. This becomes our 'original problem'. We then use the pro forma to broaden and narrow the problem. An example is illustrated in Figure 5.3.

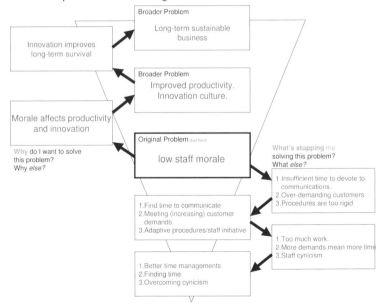

Figure 5.3: Problem Hierarchy Explorer For 'Low Morale' Problem

Thus we see the tool gathering a much more complete understanding of the problem situation and the problem we should eventually be tackling – is it about building an innovation culture, or is it about sending the management on a time-management workshop so that they can learn how to communicate more effectively and realise the true costs of not communicating enough?

We can of course extrapolate further in both directions, and force ourselves to ask the 'why else?' and 'what else?' questions at each hierarchical level in order to broaden the space even further. The higher we go, the more we will approach the main useful function of what we're trying to achieve (in this case 'long-term sustainable business', which is pretty much as far as we can go if we stay within the organizational context. If we choose to go beyond this – which is what the 'why?' question is asking us to think about – we may get into issues of regional or national sustainability). Conversely, the lower we go, the closer we will head towards the micro-scale understanding of the way things work (e.g. next level down from the 'overcoming cynicism' problem would be something like 'find ways of breaking link with past management history' or 'identify and convince the main influencers among the staff', or whatever else may be appropriate to our specific situation.

The main thing we will use to determine which of the problems the tool eventually ends up helping us define is the 'right' one will usually be determined by the constraints imposed upon us (for example, if in this problem we decide we only have a small amount of money to spend, we are more likely to solve the problem at the 'finding more time to meet customer demands' level than at the re-building corporate culture level). We will get to the constraint definition part of the problem explorer shortly. In the meantime, our job at this stage is merely to explore the problem space.

(Final thought; The 'Why-What's-Stopping' tool is also useful from a more general psychological inertia eliminating perspective at other times in the systematic innovation process. An example of the tool in action in this role may be found in Chapter 20.)

Identification of Resources

The next part of the problem explorer involves identification of resources in and around the current system or situation. The general identification of a resource is 'anything in or around the system that is not being used to its maximum potential'; which, especially when thinking about the discontinuous trends of evolution and the concept of 'evolutionary potential (Chapter 14), means there are usually a rather large list of resources locatable.

The main idea at this point in the systematic innovation process is to adopt a systematic approach to help look for resources. As illustrated in the sample resource identification pro formas in Figures 5.3 and 5.4, the search space is best segmented using firstly the 9-Windows tool, and then to look at tangible (the things) and intangible (the knowledge, the people) resources.

As a general rule, it is easiest to conduct this resource identification activity as a brainstorming session. It is also useful to treat the pro forma as a living document – something that lives alongside the problem and which is continuously added to as new resources are identified. In this way, it becomes a document that everyone in a problem team, for example, can use to share the problem in a coherent and consistent fashion.

There are no rules concerning what order to fill the boxes in, or that all boxes have to have something written inside them. What is required is that we at least *ask the question* for each.

It is useful to refer to the resource trigger lists in Chapter 15 to make sure you have considered all of the different types of resource available. Some find that it is also useful to examine the trends of evolution and to conduct an evolutionary potential assessment at this stage in the process. Again, there are no rules to say this is right or wrong. What is worth saying, as a final thought on this resource identification activity is that finding something in or around the system that *really* isn't being used to its maximum effect, is an often very important step towards solving the problem. Resources solve problems.

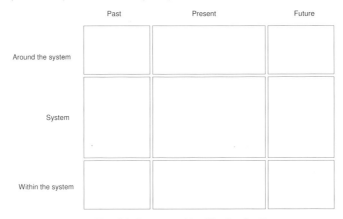

Figure 5.3: Tangible Resources Identification Pro Forma

In the search for knowledge resources (Figure below), the main questions to be asking are 'has anybody already solved this problem before?' and 'who knows the real background to this problem?' This examination of people and knowledge around us is often useful in getting us out of another psychological inertia effect in which our brains sometimes trick us into thinking we have to separate ourselves from the outside world when we are problem solving. Someone, somewhere has already solved something like your problem. This part of the process is to help register the existence of both external knowledge bases and the local experts that may be able to help.

	Past	Present	Future
Around the system (SPONSOR)			
System (including CUSTOMER)			
Within the system (TEAM)			

Figure 5.4: Knowledge Resources Identification Pro Forma

Identification of Constraints

Identification of the constraints on a problem situation form the next cluster of things we need to consider in exploring the problem space. All real problems come attached to constraints. These are the things telling us don't touch this, don't touch that, don't move this, only move that when, only use these people, cost less than that, and have the implemented solution by then. Some of them will be real and some perceived. Whatever, any viable, real-world systematic innovation process has to take account of them.

The form of the constraint analysis is similar to that for resources; again the 9-Windows plays an important role, and again it is useful to distinguish between technical and other (in this case 'business') types of constraint. Figures 5.5 and 5.6 illustrate the recommended pro formas. In the case of technical constraint identification, we are primarily interested in things like components we are not able to change, functions that must remain unchanged, processes that cannot be changed and tools and equipment that cannot be replaced.

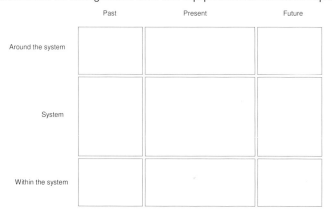

Figure 5.5: Tangible/Technical Constraints Identification Pro Forma

In terms of definition of business constraints, we are primarily interested in the classic time, cost, risk and specification issues central to successful project management. We should also take due account of any constraints imposed by the availability (or absence) of skills. As with the identification of resources, there may be some constraint boxes that remain empty after the analysis has been completed; the point is that we have at least asked the question for each one.

One very important point concerning all constraints is that very often psychological inertia rears its ugly head and we identify things that, upon further analysis, turn out to not be constraints at all. It is crucial that the constraint pro formas, once completed, are used as a living document by a problem solving team, and that each constraint is periodically challenged for its validity. 'Why is this a constraint?' is very often a useful question to ask. Many classic problem solving texts will talk about phrases that kill creativity. One of the most common and most destructive is 'yes, but...', where the but is some perceived constraint like we already tried it, or it will cost too much, or we don't know how to do it. A vital, vital message that the systematic innovation method will always try and tell us is that no matter what the 'but' is, someone, somewhere will already have found a solution to it. A 'yes, but..' is a perceived constraint and not a real one.

Prolonged exposure to the systematic innovation philosophy and methodology tends to make people believe there is no such thing as an unsolvable problem. The truth or otherwise of this belief could be argued for an eternity. What is clear, whether it is true or not, is that there are most definitely problems that *become* unsolvable due to the constraints we impose upon them. We should always challenge the constraints we define.

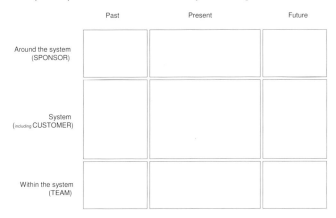

	Past	Present	Future
Around the system (SPONSOR)			
System (including CUSTOMER)			
Within the system (TEAM)			

Figure 5.6: Business Constraints Identification Pro Forma

Identification of 'Sore Point'

The 'sore point' of a system is that element which prevents it from delivering the required benefits. The idea is analogous to 'bottlenecks' in manufacture and other processes. According to the Theory of Constraints (Reference 5.2), if we are looking to improve the throughput of a process there is no point in addressing anything other than the bottleneck. The same thing applies with the 'sore-point' in problem solving in general. According to TOC again, there is likely to be only one bottleneck in a process at any one time. It is not clear that this holds true for problems more generally, but it is nevertheless a useful model to help focus thinking on the crux of a problem and why we can't get to where we want to go. There are a number of techniques to help us to identify what the sore point of a system is. The ones that need concern us here are:-

- Efficiency Auditing – for problems associated with system performance or efficiency issues
- The Theory of Constraints – for process related problem situations
- Subversion Analysis – for reliability centred problems
- Root Contradiction Analysis/Limiting Contradictions

Efficiency Auditing – is the process of analyzing the value flows within and around a system. If the problem we are tackling is of the nature 'improve efficiency by x%', it is precisely this kind of audit we need to conduct in order to identify where the inefficiencies occur and thus where we should be focusing our improvement actions. By way of example, thinking of the problem of solar-powered cars, we can construct an energy trail as follows:-

> Energy from sun
> Conversion by solar cells
> Energy store
> Drive motors

Transmission losses
Bearing losses
Tyre losses
Vehicle drag
etc

and by supplying quantified data quickly learn that a commercially viable solar-car needs better everything, but most significantly, better solar energy conversion, and better bearings – one perhaps more surprising than the other.

This example is one of an essentially sequential energy flow chain. This is one in which whatever we improve will have a net benefit on the overall outcome. Many systems, on the other hand – particularly manufacturing operations – often feature many parallel flow paths. In these situations improvements to some parts of the system will not result in a net benefit. In these situations, we require a different approach:

Theory of Constraints – includes a variety of tools and strategies for identifying the bottlenecks in a system. Often a simple critical path analysis will help to identify where the bottlenecks are, and hence what the sore point is.

Subversion Analysis – if we are dealing with what appears to be a robustness problem, our equivalent of the efficiency audit or critical path analysis is a 'how could this system go wrong?' subversion analysis (Chapter 21). Again this type of analysis will contain both sequential and parallel routes to vulnerability and non-robustness in and around business systems and so we need to obtain a view of the big picture to ensure we pick out the issues that are limiting the current level of robustness the most. If the robustness of a sales and marketing model, for example, is deemed to be threatened by lack of customer feedback, inflationary economics and lack of competitor intelligence, then subversion analysis will help us to understand the links and connections between the three and hence point us towards which elements are more significant than others.

Root Contradiction Analysis – many readers will be familiar with root cause analysis. There are various available tools and techniques available to purportedly help problem solvers to ascertain root causes. Simplest of the techniques is probably the 'ask why five times' idea. Why did the failure occur? Why did the system not prevent it? Why did the system not anticipate it?

The main underlying idea of root cause analysis is to ascertain why things went wrong so that we can both correct them and, more importantly, prevent them from happening again.

So much for the theory. When we actually get down to the mechanics of root cause analysis, on the other hand, things have a tendency to get out of hand very quickly. Quite simply, root cause analysis requires data. Asking 'why' means we have to understand the system. To understand the system requires data. Very often the cost and time involved in capturing that data can be prohibitive.

The problem with root cause analysis in general, is that it only stops when the root cause has been found. If this takes a few hours, this is not a problem. But if it means a year of conducting surveys, doing experiments, running simulations and still no answer, we should start to ask whether there is a better way.

An even more serious concern of root cause analysis – one that is particularly evident in the business and management context – is that even though we are often able to find what we think is the 'root cause' of our problem, it turns out there is nothing we can do about it. What do we do then? What do we do if the root cause of a problem is government legislation? Or bank interest rates? Or that solving our problem requires someone else to change what they are doing when it is not in their interests to do it? Most managers have control over the people that work for them, they have a group of peers that they can hope to influence, and possibly a boss that is willing to listen to reason. If the root cause to a problem lies within this range, then there may be a chance to resolve it. But what if the root cause is a policy decision two or three layers higher up the organization tree? Are we going to be able to influence things at that level? Or, more importantly, is it worth the time, energy and career risk that may be entailed in tackling such a root cause? The answer in the majority of cases is that the (career) risk makes the challenge too great. Now we're in a situation where knowing the root cause is of no practical use to us at all.

Whether the situation involves not being able to find a root cause, or not being able to do anything about a root cause that we can identify, the suggestion here is that there is indeed a better way. We call it 'root contradiction analysis'. The key similarity between this method and root cause analysis is that both are built on the question 'WHY?' The first key difference is that, while root cause analysis has a voracious appetite for analysis and data, root contradiction analysis requires only that we gain a qualitative understanding of what is happening in a system.

The second key difference – one even more important than the first – is that root cause analysis is a method closely allied to optimization of processes, while root contradiction analysis is about recognising systems hit fundamental limits, beyond which no amount of optimization will take them. In other words, you could spend an infinite amount of time gathering data to help optimize something that refuses to be optimized any further.

In our experience – which now covers several thousand technical and business problem situations – the 'root cause' of **over 80%** of the problems we see is that the system has been optimized to a fundamental limit. Think about it. What is the job of every one of us working in an organization – it is to get the maximum benefit out of the minimum amount of resource. Our job is to squeeze the last drop out of the systems we design and operate. If it may be true that over 80% of problems are in this situation, then clearly we need a different approach than root cause analysis.

The conflict elimination part of the systematic innovation toolkit is the only systematic way in existence for helping us to jump from one optimized system to a better way of doing things. Root Contradiction Analysis is about helping us to find the key contradictions we need to solve if we are to make the jump to that new system.

This is not to say that Root Contradiction Analysis works miracles. We still have to do a lot of thinking – 'why' is often the most difficult of the 5Ws – but at least we don't have to accompany it with a warehouse full of expensive-to-acquire data, and we know that solving contradictions is fundamentally good direction to travel in any event.

'The most important numbers are unknown and unknowable.' So said W.E. Deming. The quote is particularly relevant to traditional root cause analysis – which often has a seemingly never-ending appetite for data. Finding root contradictions is generally easier, cheaper and quicker than finding root causes. This is not to try and completely dismiss root-cause analysis, however, but merely to say that if you have spent more than a week trying to ascertain root-causes and are not at 'the answer' yet, then maybe it is time to try looking for root contradictions instead. At the very least, root contradiction analysis can be tried on a quick-and-dirty basis in a few hours.

Root cause analysis is sometimes great for optimizing systems. If the system has been optimized to the limits of its capability (as many manufacturing processes have – thanks to years of 'continuous improvement' initiatives), no amount of additional optimization will improve the result. The only way to improve a fully optimized system is to change the system. Solving contradictions is a good way to achieve this. Root Contradiction Analysis is a good way to find the right contradictions to solve. More on this subject in a case study in Chapter 11.

Figure 5.7 presents a pro forma designed to help structure our thinking when it comes to finding root contradictions within a system. The fifth example problem in the chapter on Trade-off and conflict elimination demonstrates the process in action.

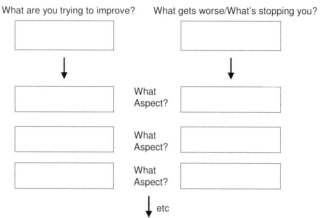

Figure 5.7: Problem Sore-Point Identification Pro Forma

When conducting this kind of root contradiction analysis it is useful to keep the 31 parameters of the business conflict Matrix in mind in order to help speed the transition from specific problem to generic problem.

Two Final Points

Cruel tricks the human brain plays, part 67; most of us possess brains that long to get to the solving part of the creativity process. Problem definition might be 90% of the problem, but typically (in true Pareto style), we spend 10% of the available time on it. From a psychological perspective we feel like we are making progress when we are generating solutions. Perhaps more importantly, we *look like* we are making progress (or at least we look busy) when we are generating solutions and trying things out. Problem definition often feels like we are travelling in the worn direction – we may be getting further from our solution, or we may turn up something that *really* sets us back. As a consequence, we are all prone to convincing ourselves that we have gone far enough into the problem definition hole and can thus start thinking about 'making progress' again. The problem explorer part of the systematic innovation process is probably the place where our brains feel the longing to switch to problem solving mode most acutely. You are strongly recommended to fight this urge. You may hate doing it, and your brain will do all that it can to convince you that you have done enough, but all of our evidence clearly shows that those that are prepared to stick with the definition task even after they have uncovered things they really wish they hadn't, that the benefits are well worth the pain and frustration. If necessary, do the definition job in stages, or allocate different parts to different participants. Please stick with it. Think about all of the time you have spent fire fighting through your career and try and balance that against spending another 15 minutes trying to make sure you are working the truly 'right' problem.

A second common experience having reached the end of the problem explorer is that your brain (or collective brains) are bursting with problem solving ideas. It is usually pointless to ask people to ignore these ideas, and to get back to the process. The best strategy in this situation is to add another part to the pro forma called 'car-park'. This is a place where all the initial ideas can be written down so that everyone knows they have been registered and can be returned to later. A short – 10 minute – 'idea dump' session at the end of the problem explorer is highly recommended. If only to demonstrate how many more and how many better ideas will emerge when we do get back to the rest of the systematic innovation process.

And Then?

Having completed each of these problem explorer steps, we should continue to examine the other parts of the problem definition process contained in Chapters 6, 7, possibly (hopefully!) 8 and possibly (if it is a people-related situation) 9. After that, it is time to head towards Chapter 10 in order to find out which problem solving tools are best able to help us solve the problems we have defined.

Before any of those activities, here is an example of the problem explorer in action:

Worked Example

Rather than try to explain the background to a problem and then try and show how that background expands into the problem explorer format, we will now simply provide an example of how the pro-forma's have been completed for a hypothetical situation in order to illustrate the mechanics of the process and likely depth of analysis. (Note; the problem is one that we return to in Chapter 12 when we try and generate some effective solutions.)

Sheet 1 - Benefits

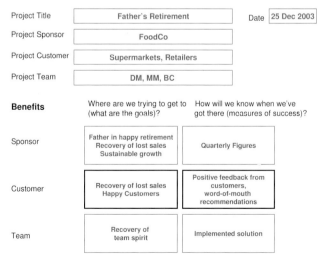

(Note the importance of discrimination between 'customer' and 'sponsor' – both of whom are likely to have different goals and different measures of success. The project should be aiming to satisfy not just these two but also the 'team' benefit goals.)

Sheet 2 – Problem Hierarchy

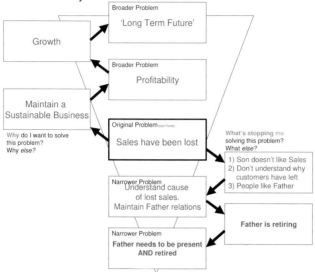

In this instance, the hierarchy model has helped to transform a vague start point – 'lost sales' into something more tangible. The problem 'father needs to be present and retired' appears to be at least an intriguing one to explore further. It is in fact this start point that we use when we chose to employ the contradiction elimination part of the solutions generation toolkit in Chapter 12.

Sheet 3 – Tangible Resources

	Past Successful Company-Client, Sales Model	Present 20% sales reduction	Future Sustainable Business
Around the system	Client Base	80% remaining customers	
System 'Company sales model'	Father-Client Relationships	Father, Son, Sales Manager	Sales Manager Son
Within the system		Father-Son relationship Son-Sales Manager relationship Father-Sales Manager relationship	

Note that we decided to label what exactly we meant by 'system', 'past', 'present' and 'future' in order that everyone had the same mental image of what was what as everyone else. As is often the case during this stage of the problem definition process, we decided to conduct an evolutionary potential assessment of the system. Two evolution potential radar plots have been included in the resource identification exercise – one looking at the internal organisation of the company (the plot shown in the 'system, present' window), and one looking at the company's relationship with its external customers (the plot shown in the 'around-the-system, present' window). See Chapter 14 for a detailed description of the content and method of construction of these plots.

Sheet 4 – Knowledge Resources

	Past	Present	Future
Around the system (SPONSOR)		Competitors/competitor strategies	Sales projections, Competitor scenario planning
System (including CUSTOMER)	Previous business models	Business model	Market trends – e-commerce mass-customization, little luxuries, selbstverwirklichung aging population
Within the system (TEAM)	Father knowledge of customers	Son's knowledge of business Sales Manager background	

Sheet 5 – Business Constraints

	Past	Present	Future
Around the system		Lost customers will not tell us why	
System		Father is definitely retiring	Cash Flow means sales recovery required in next three months
Within the system		Sales Manager contract	

Thinking about 'future' constraints can be difficult, but is generally an extremely valuable thing to try and anticipate. When scoping the problem and defining what 'future' means in all of the 9-Windows sheets it is important to be clear what the event horizon we wish to include is. When thinking about future constraints, think particularly about possible changes in legislation, standards, emerging technologies, competitors and likely future scarcity of resources, etc. Note here that we have integrated the two constraint sheets from the problem explorer pro forma into one sheet as there are no real technical issues present in this problem scenario.

Sheet 6 – Sore Point

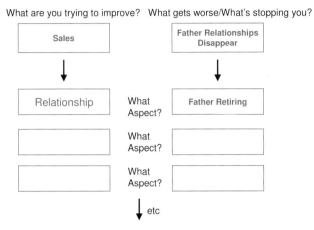

Straight away, examination of the sore-points in the existing system clearly highlighted the fact that the father in the problem is retiring and yet we need him because of the relationships he has built with his customers. This sore point analysis confirms the suggestion of the earlier Problem Hierarchy analysis that this problem contains a contradiction. As mentioned earlier, we will return to this father retirement example in a solution generation context in Chapter 12 when we examine this contradiction in more detail.

What Do I Do?

The sequence in which we do all of the definition tasks that the systematic innovation process would like us to complete is not important, and is left to the personal preferences of the reader. Many people, however, chose to begin by filling in the Problem Explorer pro forma.

The pro forma can be photocopied from the Appendix at the back of the book. An electronic version of the pro forma can be found at www.creax.com via the 'free downloads' page.

The complete problem explorer questionnaire can generally be completed in an hour or two. If you spend less than 30 minutes filling it out then either you have a very simple problem or (far more likely!) you haven't thought hard enough about your situation.

References

1) Basadur, M., 'The Power of Innovation', Pitman Publishing, 1996.
2) Scheinkopf, L.J., 'Thinking For A Change – Putting The TOC Thinking Processes To Use', St Lucie Press/APICS Series on Constraints Management, Boca Raton, 1999.

6.
Problem Definition – Function and Attribute Analysis

*"The organism is not a static system closed to the outside and always containing the
identical components; it is an open system in a (quasi-) steady state.. in which material
enters from, and leaves into, the outside environment."*
Ludwig von Bertalanffy

or

*"Because you understand one, you think that you also understand two,
because one and one make two, but you must also understand 'and'"*
Sufi teaching

Function and attribute analysis (FAA) is one of the three essential elements of the problem
definition process. It represents a systematic method through which it is possible to
analyse the detailed workings of a system. In this chapter we examine an analysis method
designed specifically to help manage the often enormous complexities found in
organizations and business systems. The chapter is divided into seven main parts:-

1) a brief history
2) description of the basic FAA method
3) extension to cover the effect that *intangibles* have on FAA models
4) extension to cover the effect that *time* has on FAA models
5) extension to cover *attribute* modeling issues
6) optional enhancements to the tool
7) an examination of complexity theory issues affecting the interpretation and use
of the FAA models

Those readers not interested in the historical evolution of function analysis may wish to
proceed directly to the second part. This second part is an essential precursor to parts
three, four, five, six and seven. The basic principle guiding the structure of these parts of
the chapter is that of a progression to increasing levels of modeling sophistication; some
problem situations will require the construction of just a simple model, while other
situations will require additional features and capabilities.

1) A Brief History

Function analysis has its roots in the pioneering work by Larry Miles (Reference 6.1) at
General Electric in the late 1950s/early 1960s. The original Miles-based method
recognizes the importance of function and functionality in the design of systems, and
undoubtedly, offers benefits to users who are registering this importance for the first time.
This version of function analysis can be seen as very much a first generation of capability
– it is undoubtedly useful, but its use has not become widespread, because the benefits
offered by the method are relatively small beyond the initial function comprehension
capability. In this Miles-ian first generation function analysis method, the application
process is principally about identification of the constituent elements within a system, and
the definition of the functional relationships that exist between each pair of those elements.

What can be viewed as a second generation of function analysis (Figure 6.1), emerged
when the basic ideas contained in Miles' work were integrated into a TRIZ-based way of

thinking. The major innovation to occur in this second generation is that as well as describing the useful functional relationships that exist between components within a system the user is encouraged to also describe negative (harmful, insufficient, excessive and missing) functional relationships. This simple but profound addition transforms a tool that is 'useful' into one that plays a very big role in the problem definition process.

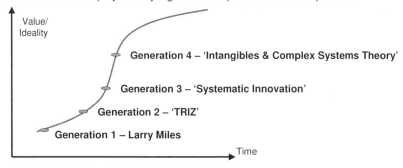

Figure 6.1: Evolution of Function Analysis Methods

What may be thought of as a third generation of function analysis capability emerged when the ability to model time and attribute aspects were incorporated. These two additions enable users to model changes in relationships between different elements of a system that might occur over time. If we were to construct function analysis models for a supermarket check-out operation, for example, we may well observe that the functioning of the system for a customer purchasing very few items is different to that for a customer with a full trolley, or that the functional requirements are different for late night shoppers and lunch-time shoppers. The third generation modeling capability would allow us to fully model these situations.

The modeling capability we present here is what may be considered to be a fourth generation. This generation integrates tools to help model and therefore 'manage' the highly complex systems that emerge when the foibles of human nature are taken into consideration. The main additions in this case have involved integrating the ability to model intangibles, and aspects of complex systems theory. Intangibles such as knowledge, skills, communications, or brand recognition are often a vitally important factor determining business success. In developing a method of modeling intangibles, we have drawn on the pioneering work of Verna Allee (Reference 6.2). As is often the case in these situations, when we combine Allee's 'value mapping' method with some of the systematic innovation ideas (in this case the modeling of positive and negative intangibles), what emerges is a method greater than the sum of its parts.

Also included in this latest version of function modeling are elements taken from complex systems theory. Complex systems theory is having a profound impact on the way that we see the world. It is one of the pillars of systematic innovation and an area discussed in more detail in the Chapter on Trends of Evolution (14). For the purposes of this chapter, our primary concern is the subject of emergence and the belief that the functioning or otherwise of a system is ultimately determined by the ratio of positive to negative relationships that it contains. Systems, in other words, emerge from the sum of the individual relationships they contain; too many negative relationships and the system will fail. In the final section of the chapter we will examine the subject of 'too many' and attempt to distill some guidelines that will help us to design systems with the maximum likelihood of being successful.

Before that, however, we need to describe the mechanics of the basic function analysis process. This we do in the second part of the chapter below.

2) Basic Function Analysis Method

At the risk of suggesting that function analysis modeling is only relevant to simple systems, we shall use the example of a simple customer-supplier relationship as a means of describing the process. While it is not entirely clear that there is ever such a thing as a 'simple' relationship involving humans, we hope that the reader will bear with us and recognize that the process is the important message. It has been designed to apply to all types of system. The model illustrated here contains only a few elements. Real-life models may – and frequently have – taken up most of the space available on a whole wall.

The basic function analysis process is conducted in three main stages. It is important that these stages are conducted sequentially. The three stages are:-
a) definition of the elements of the system. 'Elements' here is used as a generic term encapsulating people, departments, physical components or any other thing that may be found within a system.
b) Identification of the useful relationships that exist between the various different elements defined in the first stage.
c) Identification of the negative relationships that exist between the various different elements defined in the first stage.

For our example customer-supplier operation, we shall very simply define the elements as the customer and the supplier. In our modeling convention, each element of the system is described as a rectangular box. As we increase the sophistication of our models, we may introduce other shapes and colours to represent different things. For the moment, we will stay with just the rectangular format.

Figure 6.2: Elements of the Customer-Supplier Relationship

In the second part of the modeling process then involves describing the useful relationships contained within the system. The main idea here is to examine each pair of elements in turn and ask the question 'is there a useful relationship that exists between these two elements?' Every pair should eventually be considered, even though some pairs may turn out not to have a connection. For those pairs where a relationship is present, we will draw an arrow connecting the two elements at each end of the relationship, and describe as simply as possible what the relationship between the two elements is. The main purpose of this part of the process is to construct a picture of what happens (or at least what we think is happening) within the system. Although there is a considerable degree of flexibility in terms of how we describe the relationships, it is most helpful to use active verbs such that we obtain expressions of the form 'element X does something to element Y'. So, for our simple two-element model, we will have relationships like 'Customer orders from Supplier'.

Having described all of these positive relationships, we can move on to the third stage of the function modeling process. This is where we identify and record the negative relationships present in the system. There are four basic categories of negative relationships that are recognised in the FAA context. These are:-

- **harmful** relationships – this is where something happens that we don't want to happen
- **insufficient** relationships – this is where we have a relationship that is essentially a positive one, but when we ask the question 'would I like there to be more of this relationship?' the answer has been yes
- **excessive** relationships – like the insufficient relationship, excessive is an essentially positive one, but when we ask the question 'would I like there to be less of this relationship?' the answer has been yes.
- **missing** relationships – this is the most difficult of the four types of negative relationship to uncover. A missing relationship is a positive relationship that we would like to be present, but is currently not. The main question that will help us to identify missing relationships will be something along the line 'would I like there to be a relationship between these two elements that is currently not present?'

A good first way of recording the positive and negative relationships is to use the sort of tabular structure presented in Figure 6.3. As can be seen, we have completed the tables – one for each direction of the relationship – with the positive and negative relationships that we have identified are present in our (hypothetical) customer-supplier example.

Customer to Supplier

Positive Relationship	Type	Negative Relationship
checks (references)	E	delays payment
orders from		
confirms	I	
pays	E	

Supplier to Customer

Positive Relationship	Type	Negative Relationship
responds	I	delays
clarifies	I	
delivers to		
confirms payment		

Figure 6.3: Tabular Presentation of Positive and Negative Functional Relationships

The 'type' column in the tables is used to record whether a particular positive relationship is insufficient (I), excessive (E) or missing (M).

An alternative way of presenting the information is a function analysis model. The function analysis model corresponding to the customer-supplier relationships described in Figure 6.3 is drawn in Figure 6.4. As we shall shortly see, the flexibility that this method of presenting what is happening in a system becomes very important as we start adding progressively more elements into our model; our customer-supplier example has two elements, but many systems may contain several thousand elements.

Something else that is very important to note at this stage is that we need to think very carefully about the functions present in a system. The function analysis tool is there in no small part to encourage us to think about the interfaces between things rather than the things themselves. This is important from a psychological inertia perspective because our brains are usually configured to think more about the things than the things-between the things.

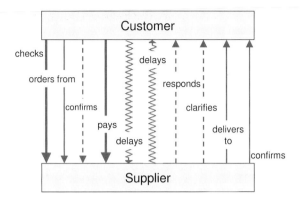

Figure 6.4: Positive And Negative Relationships Between Different Elements In The Customer-Supplier Example

The different types of possible relationship between the two elements are represented slightly differently in the function analysis model. Figure 6.5 illustrates the line convention used to describe each of the possible different relationship types.

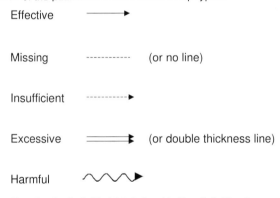

Figure 6.5: Function Analysis Model Relationship Type Labelling Conventions

If we think about the functions present in the Figure 6.4 system (particularly if we combine our thinking with the 9-Windows idea of zooming in and out of a problem), we should register the fact that the system is actually more complicated than the way it has currently been drawn. If we focus, for example, on the Supplier for example, we may observe that they will actually comprise many different parts – customer interface, finance department, shipping, support, etc – and that each of those parts has different functions. Sometimes, it will be necessary for us to expand our model to include these elements as separate entities. We will explore how we decide how much detail to go into in the next part of the story. For the moment it is sufficient to reflect on what we have done in Figure 6.4 and note that by the time we have mapped all of the necessary elements in a system and all of the positive and negative relationships that exist between them, we are well on the way to understanding how we are going to make improvements to the system.

The decision to dissect models into ever more and smaller constituent parts is often one that is hard fought. Unfortunately there are no absolute rules on exactly how far to segment a model. Generally speaking the systematic innovation method tries to be self-correcting, in that it will guide us towards zooming-in to look at finer detail or zooming-out to look at the bigger picture if we are having difficulty in generating solutions to improve the system. That being said, one thing that is close to being an absolute rule – let's call it a 'good rule of thumb' – is that *the analysis should record all of the functions present.* We have chosen to draw Figure 6.4 retaining just the two elements as it is merely our intention to detail the mechanics of the process. Also, as you may notice from the figure, even with just two components, the model can become very complex, very quickly.

Another useful rule to apply when conducting a function analysis, is to define the Main Useful Function (MUF) of the system and to record this somehow on the FAA picture. This will be shown to be important because it encourages us to focus on the main purpose of the system. In the system under consideration here, the MUF is the 'supplier delivers to customer' function. Figure 6.6 records this fact. It is important because, if we think about systems evolving towards ideality, we will see all of the functions around the MUF gradually disappearing. As long as there is a need for the system to deliver products or services to customers, there will be evolutionary pressure to eliminate the secondary functions and components to leave behind just the MUF-delivering components.

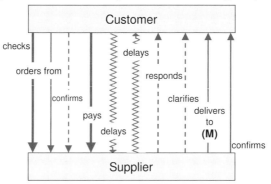

Figure 6.6: Recording Of Main Useful Function (MUF)

As we will see later, this picture has helped us to perform a lot of problem definition work. It has done it by segmenting a potentially large problem space into a series of relationships between pairs of components – first positive relationships and then negative relationships.

3) Adding Intangible Elements To The Model

Modeling of functional relationships is an important step towards obtaining a better understanding of the workings of organizational and business systems, but it is by no means complete. It is increasingly the intangible elements that will discriminate one system from another. Intangibles, according to the Brookings Institution are "...non-physical factors that contribute to or are used in producing goods or providing services, or that are expected to generate future productive benefits for the individuals or firms that control the use of those factors." Figure 6.7 provides a check-list of intangibles that should be considered when thinking about intangible function relationships.

Although thinking about intangibles adds a new layer of complexity in the function analysis models, fortunately, adding them can be done using exactly the same procedures as has been described in the previous section. This means that we need to examine each pair of elements in a system and ask the question 'are there any intangible function links between these two elements?' Again as before, this activity needs to be performed separately for both positive and then negative perspectives.

Positive
- knowledge/know-how
- skills
- experience
- authority/responsibility
- judgment
- alliances
- relationships
- commitment
- brand recognition
- trust
- status/reputation

- motivation
- morale
- culture
- contacts/access (to others)
- attraction/emotion
- processes

Negative
- (inversion of the positives)
- fear
- envy/jealousy
- distraction/deceit
- wastes time

Figure 6.7: Check-List Of Different Types Of 'Intangible' Relationship

As far as our example customer-supplier relationship from the previous section is concerned, when we start to explicitly think about the intangibles present, then we can begin to coo a whole host of additional relationships that are present. Some of these are recorded in Figure 6.8. The figure expands the basic relationship tables shown in Figure 6.3 and adds to them a new row focusing on intangible relationships.

Customer to Supplier

	Positive Relationship	**Type**	**Negative Relationship**
Tangible	checks (references)	E	delays payment
	orders from		
	confirms	I	
	pays	E	
Intangible	recommendation (to friends)		lack of trust
	knowledge (future design)	M	

Supplier to Customer

	Positive Relationship	**Type**	**Negative Relationship**
Tangible	responds	I	delays
	clarifies	I	
	delivers to		
	confirms payment		
Intangible	brand image	I	-
	status		
	know-how (use)	I	

Figure 6.8: Tabular Presentation of Positive/Negative and Tangible/Intangible Functional Relationships

There may be situations – as in the supplier-to-customer negative intangibles box in the Figure 6.8 example – where we cannot identify any connections. The important point here is that each box in the table represents a question. If the box remains empty after we have asked that question, at least we have asked it.

As we saw in the previous section, it is also possible to translate the contents of the tables into a function analysis model. The model for the customer-supplier example information in

Figure 6.8 is presented in Figure 6.9. Something that becomes evident when we glance at this model is that our simple two-element model has suddenly taken on an even more complex appearance. This is a very common phenomenon when we are constructing these types of model. When we start to draw models with more elements in them, the level of complexity will tend to grow significantly. There is a tendency when this happens to concede defeat. It is important to fight this desire if at all possible. Try to remember that every negative relationship that can be identified represents an opportunity to improve the system; hence the more negatives we can identify, the more improvement opportunities we have found.

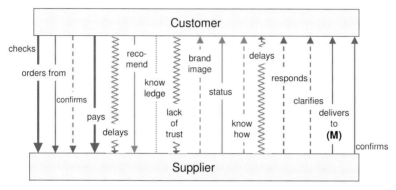

Figure 6.9: Positive/Negative And Tangible/Intangible Relationships Between Different Elements In The Customer-Supplier Example

Procedurally, this is the end of the intangibles story. Before we leave the specific subject of intangibles, however, it is worth making a brief comment about their emotional context. The systematic innovation pillar idea that 'customers buy functions' is a compelling one, and yet also one that is deemed to be incomplete by several people working in the world of innovation. Perhaps the most relevant of the 'incomplete' arguments comes from the work of designer, Donald Norman. Norman is the author of at least two important books on the design process and what makes customers select one offering relative to another one – 'The Psychology Of Everyday Things' and 'Emotional Design' (Reference 6.3). In Emotional Design, Norman identifies three basic levels on which the brain processes information. These are the visceral, behavioral and reflective. The visceral part is the rapid judgment part of the brain. This is the part that 'instinctively' tells us whether to fight or flea, or whether we like something or not. The behavioral part is the part that controls our everyday actions, and is the part most closely connected to the function of things. Finally, there is the 'reflective' level of brain activity. This is where we contemplate and reflect on sensory information coming in to the brain and use it to affect our behaviour. One of Norman's arguments is that the functionality of an artifact (something that we can relatively safely extend to also include services) is only one aspect of what causes us to prefer it to another, and that there are higher processes in place that will also influence our decision. Thus, whether something is aesthetically pleasing to us, or makes us feel better about ourselves, or whether it improves our status in the eyes of our friends must also play a part in our purchase/no-purchase decision. One of the main points of the 'intangibles' element of the FAA tool is to allow us to include such things into the models that we construct. We continue to call it a 'function analysis' model, but to aesthetically please, or increase status, or increase perceived status are all functions too in the way the tool works. Intangibles, in other words, are functions too. At least in the way that we will apply later tools to improve the negative things that we have found in our function analysis models.

4) Adding Time Elements To The Model

Sometimes it is possible to simply construct one function analysis model to describe a system. If it transpires that the functioning of a system changes with time, then this single model approach will cease to adequately describe what is happening. This next level of sophistication in the overall FAA modeling process, then, looks at time issues. Before we start the description of the process, it is worth remembering that at all stages in the FAA process that our aim is to define a situation well enough to be able to improve it and not simply to produce a model for the sake of producing a model. Thus when we begin to consider how time might affect a problem definition, we should be interested in at least three scenarios:

1) the system before any problem occurs
2) the system during a problem, and,
3) the system after any problems

Not all need to be relevant, of course, and by the same token three time points may be insufficient. This is especially so when we are trying to model a process, in which different things are inherently happening at different stages. Many of us – thanks to the ubiquity of the Gantt Chart – are probably much more familiar with the construction of process maps than we are with function analysis models.

Fortunately, the basic FAA modeling approach described in the previous two sections applies to process based problem situations as well as time-independent scenarios. The method requires one or two additions however in order to achieve optimum management between defining the system and transitioning it to the downstream problem-solving parts of the systematic innovation process.

We will examine a typical process-based problem situation in order to illustrate these additions. The process in question is a hypothetical representation of the initial stages of a typical new product development operation. A schematic of the process is illustrated in Figure 6.10.

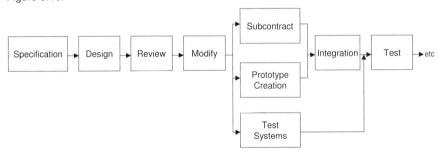

Figure 6.10: Schematic of Hypothetical Order Processing Operation

The general idea, then, when defining the FAA model is to construct a different model for each of the key time steps in the process. At each step, we will use exactly the same function analysis process described in the two preceding sections. We will illustrate only the most important ones here. For any real problem, it may be necessary to construct an FAA model for each step. The FAA model for the first key step – the specification task – is shown in Figure 6.11.

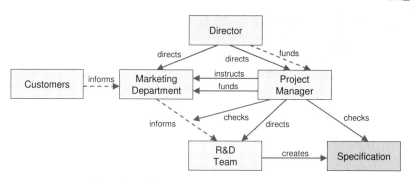

Figure 6.11: FAA Model at Specification Part of Process

This figure indicates the first of the additional things we need to be aware of when modeling process-based systems:-

1) The product of this first part of the overall process is the 'specification'. This is included in the model as an element. This is the thing that will be carried forward from this model into the model that will be drawn for the next (design) stage in the Figure 6.10 process. Sometimes we will give the 'output' or 'product' of a process stage in a different colour to indicate that it is different from the other elements.

2) You may note that the Project Manager is indicated as performing an action to check that the marketing department informs the R&D Team. In this function model, we have indicated this action as an arrow connecting from the Project Manager element to the 'informs' function relationship arrow rather than to an element. The need to connect arrows to other arrows rather than boxes is a common occurrence and is a perfectly legitimate method of describing what is happening in a system. Some software tools will not permit this kind of arrow-connects-to-arrow convention. Readers intending to model such relationships in these software tools would need to add a new element in order to capture the functional relationships accurately. For this particular case, the required modification would probably look something like the model shown in Figure 6.12.

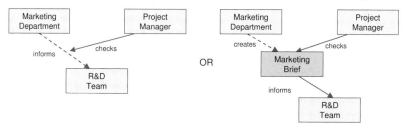

Figure 6.12: Alternative Methods Of Representing Arrow-To-Arrow Relationships

The simple general rule we can extract from this example is that we can re-frame an arrow-to-arrow relationship by adding a new element – which may be a piece of information (as in this case), or a tangible thing.

Figure 6.13 illustrates another important step in the Figure 6.10 process – this time at a point towards the end of the process, when we are looking to conduct a test of the prototype. Remember that in an actual modeling situation, the times at which FAA models should be driven by when we can identify negative things happening in the system – i.e. if there is nothing apparently negative in the test stage of the process, then we may choose not to model it. In our hypothetical example, we have determined that there are some negative aspects (as there frequently will be if we force ourselves to identify things that we would like to do better), and hence have decided to draw the model.

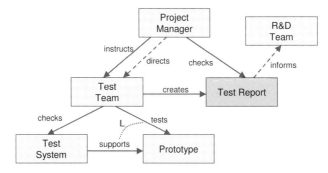

Figure 6.13: FAA Model During The Test Stage Of The Process

As can be seen from the initial process flow chart, the Test phase requires that both the test system and the integrated prototype be present. Both are represented in Figure 6.13. Since neither function is valid without the other, the FAA model illustrates the linked nature of the two actions by the joining line labeled with an 'L'. This line is there to remind us that we cannot have one function without the other.

Also worth noting in Figure 6.13 is that the Project Manager and the R&D Team are present again. As we construct FAA models for progressively more stages of the process, we will see some elements (like the Project Manager) who may be present in all, while others may only be present at one or two stages (the Test team possibly). When we see elements appearing and disappearing, like this it is often prudent to think about whether there is any value in them being present at all stages – especially when we start thinking about the negative relationships question 'are there any relationships that are missing?'

Beyond the basic time-based guidelines presented here, the problem solver would continue to construct other FAA models to represent other parts of the process. We, having made the necessary points about the recommended conventions defining what happens when elements combine or separate, or when elements interact with functions (as opposed to other elements). Next we need to examine another phenomenon that can occur when we are constructing the models; what happens when functions don't act on the elements themselves, but rather act to change only certain aspects of those elements. This gets us into the 'Attribute' part of Function and Attribute Modeling:

5) Adding Attribute Elements To The Model

Every element that we might choose to include in a function model will contain attributes. If the element is a physical object, then these attributes will be things like size, weight, volume, etc., if the element is a person or a team of people, then the attributes will be things like skills, perseverance, creativity, etc. Very often when elements have a functional relationship with other elements, it is one of these attributes that is affected rather than the element itself. A good way to think about attributes and their relation to system elements is to picture the idea of double clicking on an element in order to open up a new layer of information. Figure 6.14 provides an example where some of the attributes of the R&D team from the preceding example have been highlighted. This attribute listing capability becomes useful when we have a functional relationship like 'Project Manager increases stress level in R&D Team'. We can, of course, record this relationship in the previously discussed 'something does something to something' fashion although in this kind of situation the 'does something' part is a rather long description. Figure 6.14 provides an often more elegant means of describing the relationship.

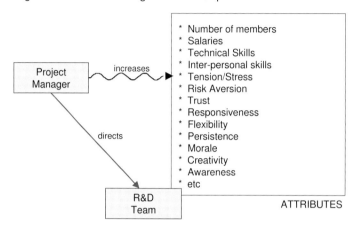

Figure 6.14: Function Relationship Acting On Attributes Rather Than Elements

As it happens, the distinction between the two ways of representing relationships that affect attributes of an element is not massively important. Certainly when it comes to using the FAA model as a means of transitioning to the appropriate solution generation tools, the Select tool is primarily interested in the types and combinations of lines present (i.e. insufficient, excessive, harmful, etc) rather than the words that they contain. That being said, we mention the attribute modeling side of the FAA story because whenever we have function relationships like increases, decreases, changes or measures, those functions are almost certainly acting on an attribute of an element rather than the element itself. It is also worth making the connection between attributes and the parameters present in the conflict elimination Matrix in Chapter 11 since this list is primarily also concerned with attributes. Hence, by explicitly recording relationships concerning attributes in the FAA model we are able to accelerate the translation from our specific situation to the general situation. In the Figure 6.14 model, for example, we see that the Project Manager does something useful ('directs') and harmful ('increases stress'). As we shall see in Chapter 10, whenever this combination of positive and negative relationships occurs, we know we have a conflict and that the conflict-elimination tools will help us to generate a strong solution. In order to then use this tool, we need to map the positive and negative function descriptions onto words contained in the Matrix – so, in this case, we may well see the Figure 6.14 situation as an R&D Interface versus Tension/Stress conflict. As soon as we have made such a link (don't worry, Chapter 11 will show us how to do that), we are well on the way to seeing how other people have already solved such a conflict.

Taken together the basic, intangible-based, time-based and attribute-based examples described in the previous four sections should provide a sufficient description of the mechanics of FAA analysis to allow us to construct models for any type of problem situation. Let us now take a look at some of the optional things we might also do to help improve the problem definition information the FAA tool can provide:

6) Optional Enhancements

a) Functional Hierarchies

A simple thought to enhance the information within an FAA is that instead of placing components at random on the page ('screen' if we are using a software version of the tool), there are advantages in arranging things in such a way that they communicate more useful information. Little if any extra effort is required, and quite possibly the modification offers even greater structure to the way in which the function analysis process is conducted.

A 'normal' FAA picture might look something like the one shown in the second case study example (Figure 6.13). That picture was constructed using the usual sequence of 1) define elements, 2) define the positive functional relationships existing between each pair of elements, and, 3) define the negative functional relationships.

A revised function analysis illustrating exactly the same information is reproduced below. The only difference between this picture and the previous one is that this new analysis has been conducted after taking into account the idea of functional hierarchy.

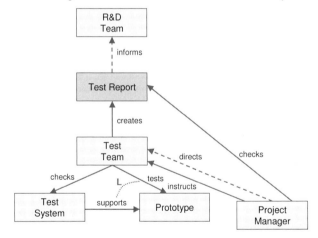

Figure 6.16: Hierarchical Component Structure For FAA Model

The hierarchy idea encourages the user to think more carefully about the functionality of a system. It begins this process by asking what the Main Useful Function (MUF) is. In the case of this test example, the MUF is 'test report informs R&D department'. This becomes the start-point for the functional hierarchy – every other function contained in the system existing to serve this one. At the next level down, for example, it is clear that the MUF requires 'test team creates test report' to be performed.

The completed hierarchical function analysis is useful from several perspectives: At a first most basic level, it has provided more structure to the way the analysis has been conducted, and will consequently offer ease of reading benefits because fewer lines will intersect one another. At a more important level, the functional hierarchy presents a likely sequence for trimming of components from the system – those at the bottom end of the hierarchy being much more likely to be 'Trimmable' (Chapter 18) than those at the top.

The conclusions we can draw from this hierarchical method of constructing FAA models allow us to structure our thinking better, and offers us a picture that communicates more information for little or no extra effort.

b) Relationship Matrix

In situations where the number of elements and functions within a system is large, it can very quickly become apparent that it is difficult to maintain a track on which pairs of components have been analysed and which have not. A simple remedy to this problem involves the definition of a function relationship matrix. An example – for the Test process case of earlier – is presented in Figure 6.17. While it is not clear that this system is complex enough to justify constructing the matrix, at least it illustrates the necessary construction method.

From \ To	R&D Team	Test Report	Test Team	Test System	Proto-type	Project Manager
R&D Team	X					
Test Report	informs (i)	X				
Test Team		creates	X	checks	tests	
Test System				X	supports	
Prototype					X	
Project Manager		checks	directs (i) instructs			X

Figure 6.17: Functional Relationship Matrix For Test Process Example

In addition to offering a checklist ensuring that every pair of components is considered (in both directions between each), this kind of relationship matrix offers the additional benefit of simplifying the process of seeing how many functions any given component delivers (count the number of entries along the row for the component of interest) or receives (count down the column).

c) Cause-Effect Mapping

A frequent criticism of FAA models is that it doesn't provide any definition of *why* things are the way they are. This has greatest relevance when we are considering the negative functional relationships within a system – why they are there, and what are the causes. The importance of this kind of cause-effect thinking is fundamental to the Theory of Constraints (TOC) (Reference 6.4) which has specific tools and conventions to help structure thinking in this regard. Interested readers may care to check out the Current Reality Tree tool contained in TOC. This tool is discussed in its systematic innovation context in Reference 6.5.

For the purposes of this brief discussion, we will make just two points. The first concerns TOC's recognition of the importance of identifying all of the relevant contributory factors to an effect or outcome produced by a component or system. The method talks about necessary and sufficient condition relationships. It is basically a mechanism for increasing understanding of a system, and particularly the relationships between components. Every adverse relationship in a system is caused by something. There may be several things. The necessary and sufficient thinking tool is a way of ensuring all are mapped and the inter-relationship between them are understood. To take a crude example, suppose we examine the insufficient 'Project Manager directs the Test Team' relationship from the earlier test process function analysis model. A conventional root cause analysis of this harmful relationship might (hypothetically!) tell us that the Project Manager provides insufficient direction because his/her time is over-committed elsewhere or that there is little understanding of what the test team's job is and what it is that they actually do. Although we can see these things as the causes of the insufficient relationship, they alone may not be sufficient to explain the situation fully. The key question in such a situation is '*if just these things are present, is the insufficient effect present?*' If the answer to this question based on the causes we have thus far identified is no, then TOC will tell us that we should identify what is missing from our list. We are trying to find a necessary *and* sufficient list of reasons to explain the insufficient relationship. In this case – again hypothetically – we may determine that the Project Manager also fails to fully understand what it is that the R&D Team actually want from the testing. While this is an almost facile example, it does hopefully serve to illustrate the point that our normal, traditional way of situation definition does not naturally encapsulate necessary and sufficient cause thinking. By explicitly forcing ourselves to think about necessary and sufficient in this case, we now have three solution focus aspects to work with rather than just one.

The second point of this short section is to suggest that it is often useful to draw this kind of necessary/sufficient cause model either onto the FAA model, or by extracting and expanding segments, or, if you have access to a software tool, to incorporate the model in an additional screen connectable to each functional relationship in the system. In all of these cases, the model could look something like the image in Figure 6.18.

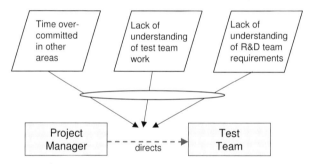

Figure 6.18: Necessary And Sufficient Causes Connected To A Functional Relationship

(The oval shape borrows from the TOC convention and defines that all three of the conditions identified are necessary for the insufficient direction problem to occur.)

Finally in this chapter, let us explore another optional extension to the FAA method. This time, however, the subject matter (complexity) is broad enough and the importance is high enough to merit a more detailed discussion.

7) Seven and the Downward Spiral – Complexity Theory Effects

"If someone thinks they are being mistreated by us, they won't tell 5 people, they will tell 5000."
Jeff Bezos, Amazon (Wall Street Journal, May 1996)

We've all heard stories about how bad news seems to travel faster than good news; about how customers are much more likely to tell their friends about their bad experiences than

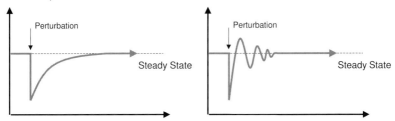

their good ones; about in-company communications being corrupted by a negative minority. We've probably had direct experience of the phenomenon at some time or another. It seems to be another of those fundamental characteristics of the human brain. At least the evolved, modern-day version. This article tries to draw some sense from the phenomenon and tries to define ways of identifying when it is about to happen and what we might then be able to do to prevent the negative from turning into a self-re-enforcing downward spiral.

Special Cause/Common Cause?

One of the first things we need to do when thinking about self-re-enforcing spirals – whether they be upward or downward – is to think about common and special causes. The two terms were first popularised by W.E. Deming (Reference 6.6 gives the probably best description) when thinking about statistical process control and the desire to improve manufacturing systems. A common cause problem is one associated with the 'normal' functioning of a system, while a 'special' cause is typically a one-off event that by definition is not attributable to the 'normal' functioning of a system. Variation in sales of, say, greetings cards due to the changing seasons (Christmas, New Year, etc) may be seen to be 'common cause'. A lull in sales due to a postal strike on the other had, would represent a 'special cause' variation.

The point of mentioning special and common causes here is that most commonly, only the latter will result in the creation of spirals. When a system is disturbed in some way by a special cause perturbation, the most likely result –assuming the system is in control prior to the disturbance – is that after the perturbation has disappeared, the system will return to normal. Figure 6.19 presents two possible graphical representations of this special cause perturbation phenomenon.

Figure 6.19: System Returning to Steady State Following a Special Cause Perturbation

In the left hand picture, we observe the system (green-line) gradually return to the steady-state following the perturbation. In the right hand picture, the return to steady-state is more oscillatory. The difference between the two pictures is indicative of the amount of damping in the system. The left-hand system may be said to be heavily damped, while the right hand picture shows the characteristics of a system with much less damping. The former may be seen to represent, for example, the recovery of the stock-market after a global incident. Here the damping comes from the large inertia of a large population of investors. Smaller, more localized systems are less likely to have the same levels of inertia, and are thus more likely to exhibit the less damped behaviour shown in the right-hand picture.

Neither of these two situations is of particular interest to us in the context of self-re-enforcing systems since both eventually return to the steady-state. There is a third kind of response to a special cause perturbation, however, that should be of interest. This third kind may be thought of as the 'un-damped' response to the perturbation. Graphically it will look something like the image shown in Figure 6.20.

In this third system the oscillations following the perturbation become progressively bigger and bigger and the system swings more and more out of control. If left unchecked, this third response will ultimately destroy the system altogether. Conflicts very often result from this kind of un-damped system – a neighbour holds a noisy party without informing the people next door, which subsequently provokes them to submit a complaint to the police, which then results in the neighbours letting down the tyres on the complainants car, and so on until something really bad happens.

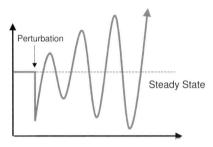

Figure 6.20: Undamped System After Perturbation

This kind of un-damped, oscillatory behaviour results from classic win-lose responses. If someone has kept you awake all night with their party, your first reaction is very often to seek some kind of revenge.

So, the situation where a special cause event is followed by win-lose reaction, which in turn is followed by a succession of tit-for-tat reactions can be (and often is) the source of downward spirals. In the next section, we examine common causes situations and see how spirals can (and often do) emerge from this type of situation too.

Self-Re-enforcing Loops?

One of the key contributions to the process of Function Analysis made by TRIZ was the incorporation of negative functional relationships – harmful, excessive, insufficient or missing elements. The recent re-framing of the method into a business and management context has seen the additional segmentation of functional relationships into tangible and intangible elements. 'Intangible' again means all those relationships that are not traditionally written down in procedures – things like personal relationships, knowledge transfer, branding aspects, ego, etc as defined in Figure 6.7 earlier in the chapter.

The combined positive plus negative, tangible plus intangible method of constructing function analysis models gives four different types of relationship – positive tangible, positive intangible, negative tangible and negative intangible. A typical function analysis model produced from these parts might look something like that shown in Figure 6.21. Many of the relationships that would be present in the actual situation have been eliminated for clarity – in real life modeling of even this simple four-element system can often result in function analysis maps with several dozen relationships of different sorts present.

The idea behind function analysis models of this type is that they describe the steady state version of a system. True, as we saw in section 4), the model may change as a function of time as the relationship between customer and consultant evolves, but essentially the model is intended to represent the system in its current 'normal' state.

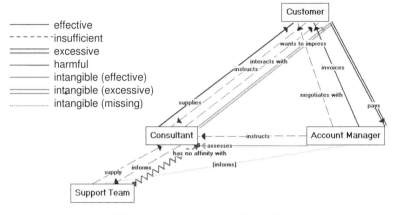

Figure 6.21: Function Analysis For A Typical People System

If we now examine just a part of this system – say the part involved with internal relationships (Figure 6.22) – we may be able to identify loops containing a series of negative relationships. In this (admittedly hypothetical) case, we may see two particular negative sets of relationships involving loops – firstly a pair of insufficient relationships between the consultant and support team, and secondly a missing connection between account manager and support team that results in the absence of a working loop between the three different parts of the internal system.

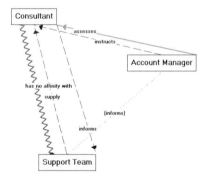

Figure 6.22: Partial Function Analysis Model Illustrating Negative Relationship Loops

The presence of either of these situations – or indeed any other form of negative loops or missing loops represents the potential for a self re-enforcing downward spiral. Similarly, loops which feature positive relationships represent the possibility of self-re-enforcing loops that are positive in nature.

Thus we see the function analysis model existing as a means of plotting relations between different parts of a system in its 'in control' normal state, and the idea that wherever there are loops of negative or positive relationships there exists the potential for self-re-enforcing loops to be created. The function analysis model, therefore, becomes a useful means of identifying the presence of either upward or downward spirals.

Seven?

One of the weaknesses of the function analysis method is that it is very difficult to provide a visual indication of the relative importances and weights of the different functional relationships. So, wherever we observe a combination of positive and negative relationships in a given loop, it is difficult to know which are more important than others. Or indeed whether there is the potential for the creation of the self-re-enforcing upward or downward spirals suggested by Figure 6.23 below.

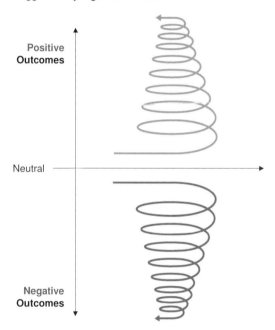

Figure 6.23: Virtuous And Destructive Spirals

It is not clear at this time how or whether this shortcoming might be overcome. What we can say quite clearly from empirical evidence is that the downward spiral effect of negative loops tends to be greater than the equivalent upward effect of positive loops. This is the time when we might think about the psychology of the human brain and our frequent preference for bad news over good. It is frequently stated, as in the Jeff Bezos quotation at the start of this section for example, that bad news travels many times faster than good news – take any given news bulletin and compare the ratio of 'good' news stories to 'bad'. Consumer research will tell us that people are up to ten times more likely to write a letter of complaint following a bad experience with a product or service than they are to write a letter of thanks if things went better than expected. It is not clear from any of this research what the precise ratio of good-to-bad transmission likelihood is. In all probability, the answer is likely to be either unknowable or inconsistent as we look across different situations. For the sake of specifying a convenient label only, we have used the number 7 in this article to give an impression of the average difference between good and bad transmission likelihood. Bad news is seven times more likely to spread than good news; a negative self-re-enforcing loop is seven times more likely to become a downward spiral than a positive self-re-enforcing loop is to become an upward spiral.

Thus, when we look at our function analysis models, we should take into account the existence of a significant difference in the importance of negative loops relative to the positive loops – Figure 6.24.

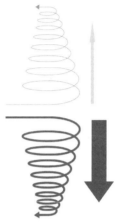

Figure 6.24: Downward Spirals Seven Times More Likely Than Upward Spirals For An Equivalent Magnitude of Positive and Negative Self-Re-Enforcing Loops

We often experience this kind of self-re-enforcing downward spiral when we are stuck in a traffic jam for a very long time – suddenly our brain shifts into a mode where the frustration of the wait becomes so bad that our only remaining response is to laugh. Possibly we might also begin to hope that the jam will last for an even longer time so that we will be able to tell our friends how bad it was (here we make the subconscious realization that if the jam is only moderately bad then it will not be interesting to anyone, but, if it lasts for several hours, on the other hand, then we *really* have a story to tell). A similar thing happens with the long-suffering fans of some football clubs. Watching your side go three or four goals down is bad, but when the total get to five or six goals then we start to wish for a seventh goal. And an eighth. And so on; because only when things get *really* bad do we have some news. Or do we feel that the team will become shocked out of their downward spiral and do better next time. (See Chapter 19 for an explanation of why this self-compensating action takes place.) More seriously, we may see how many regional and national conflicts appear to grow in very similar sets of circumstances.

The main point of this 'seven and the downward spiral' section is to reflect on the relative importance of positive and negative relationships between the different elements of a system. Although the number seven is primarily there as a banner headline rather than scientific fact, empirical evidence clearly shows that humans respond much more to the negative than they do to the positive. This phenomenon appears to be part of human nature. What it tells us is that when we observe loops of negative relationships within a system we should be very careful to make sure they don't turn into self-re-enforcing downward spirals that will eventually serve to destroy the system.

Function and attribute analysis enables us to model systems that are 'in control'. Downward spirals can also emerge through special cause disturbances or perturbations to an in-control system. Destructive downward spirals often grow in systems where the participants approach events with a win-lose mindset. The smart player reacts to any negative special cause disturbance with a win-win response. This can be a very difficult thing to do. Especially if you perceive that someone has done something bad to you. The normal reaction in these types of circumstance – as evidenced by the large bulk of governmental and industrial experience – is to fight back. When we chose to fight back with traditional you-do-something-bad-I-do-something-bad-back-again strategies we plant the seeds of a downward spiral. The key word here is 'chose'. To start or halt a downward spiral is always within the realms of our choice.

Whenever we can find negative loops in a function analysis model, we should pay particular attention as we transition to the solution generation parts of the systematic innovation process. Negative relationships forming a closed loop should be at the top of our priority list when it comes to choosing which aspects of a model to tackle first.

What Do I Do?

Function and attribute analysis (FAA) is one of the three essential parts of the problem definition process. In terms of managing complexity, it is the most comprehensive of the three. A completed FAA model presents an important lead into knowing how to approach the improvement of systems.

Successful function analysis modelling demands a process in which components are defined and then relationships between those components are established. In terms of defining the positive relationships, the method is useful because in many situations this will be the first time people have viewed the system under evaluation from such a functional perspective. In terms of the subsequent identification of negative - harmful, insufficient, excessive or missing – relationships in the system, this is where the user is identifying where problems exist. Forced questions like 'would I like to perform this function better?', 'would I like less of this function?', 'is it possible to identify anything harmful in the system?' and 'is there any missing relationship?' for each pair of components in the system, and taking due account of the place time takes in affecting these components, are extremely important from a problem and opportunity definition perspective.

Follow the steps detailed in the case studies for simple, complex and time-based process systems in order to construct the FAA model. The general sequence is:-
1) Identify the system elements
2) Identify the positive tangible relationships between the different element pairs
3) Identify the positive intangible relationships between the different element pairs
4) Identify the negative (harmful, insufficient, excessive, missing) tangible relationships
5) Identify the negative intangible relationships

A completed FAA model offers a link into the Select part of the systematic innovation process in Chapter 10. The Select tool will permit us to examine the combinations of relationship types and connect us to the most appropriate solution generation tools to help eliminate the negative relationships present. It is also a document that should live with the system as it evolves over time, so even though for many people it is the most tedious part of the whole process, at least we know that the bulk of the work only has to happen once.

Health Warning

By far and away the biggest place where group systematic innovation sessions fail is during the FAA modeling stage. This is because it is an activity that is very difficult to actively engage multiple people in. Net result; one person is doing all of the work, while everyone else has spent the time convincing themselves that systematic innovation is 'boring' and has no interest to them. Therefore, it is highly recommend that you do not try to construct function analysis models in groups. There are two basic strategies that are recommended to prevent the boredom/engagement problem from occurring:-

    a) segment the system to be modeled in such a way that everyone has taken responsibility for their part, or

    b) (usually easier) have someone construct an initial attempt at the model before bringing the group together. This model may not be 'correct' per se, but experience clearly shows that it is much easier to engage a group in critiquing something that is already there, rather than asking them to start from scratch.

References

1) Miles, L.D., 'Techniques of Value Analysis and Engineering', McGraw-Hill Book Company, New York, NY, 1961.
2) Allee, V., 'The Future of Knowledge – Increasing Prosperity Through Value Networks', Butterworth-Heinemann, 2003.
3) Norman, D.A., 'Emotional Design: Why We Love (Or Hate) Everyday Things', Basic Books, Perseus, New York, 2004.
4) Scheinkopf, L.J., 'Thinking for a Change: Putting the TOC Thinking Processes to Use', St Lucie Press, Boca Raton, 1999.
5) Mann, D.L., Stratton, R., 'Physical Contradictions and Evaporating Clouds' TRIZ Journal, April 2000.
6) Neave, H., 'The Deming Dimension', SPC Press, Knoxville, TN, 1990.

7.
Problem Definition – S-Curve Analysis

*"Doing the things we do now and doing them better, cheaper and faster will take us so far.
But it will not take us far enough. We are going to have to do new things in new ways."*
Peter Bonfield

and

"To understand is to perceive patterns."
Yoko Ono

The characteristic manner in which systems of all descriptions evolve has been observed by researchers from many fields of endeavour. Biologists (Reference 7.1), organisational analysts (Reference 7.2), engineers (Reference 7.3), economists (Reference 7.4, 7.5) have all recorded the existence of distinctly s-shaped evolution profiles when some measure of 'goodness' of a system is plotted as a function of time. The generic s-curve characteristic illustrated in Figure 7.1 is seemingly ubiquitous these days.

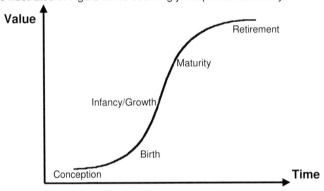

Figure 7.1: Generic S-Curve Characteristic

This s-curve profile is often described in subtly different ways, but all tend to indicate the existence of at least four of the 'conception', 'birth', 'infancy/growth', 'maturity' and 'retirement' stages shown on the figure. These subtle differences are really just symptoms of different researchers segmenting the same space in different ways. For the most part, these differences have little effect on what we actually do with the s-curves for a system once we have defined them.

The s-shaped curve is a characteristic that the original TRIZ researchers also observed (Reference 7.6), and not surprisingly the s-curve features prominently throughout the systematic innovation methodology.

The s-curve in any event is interpreted and used in a much more detailed manner in systematic innovation than in any other known application. This chapter examines how the s-curve and families of s-curves operate. This overall description is followed by a rationale on why s-curves are important – particularly in the context of problem or opportunity definition. Finally, we will examine methods of establishing where a system is positioned within a given s-curve and a given s-curve family.

S-Curves and System Evolution

In the majority of applications outside of systematic innovation, the 's-curve' is usually seen to exist as a singular entity – such that any system has 'an' s-curve. In systematic innovation, the concept is rather more multi-dimensional. Five dimensions in particular are important in the context of system s-curves and s-curve dynamics. The five dimensions are:-

1) Labelling of the X-axis
2) Labelling of the Y-axis
3) Relative positioning of s-curves on the Y-axis
4) S-curve system-sub-system hierarchy
5) S-curve system-function hierarchy

Labelling of X-Axis

The x-axis on an s-curve graph is almost always 'time'. Certainly this is the parameter we will always use when drawing s-curves in this book. The main reason for mentioning the x-axis definition at all is simply to remind readers that the actual time involved for a given s-curve and hence system may be a few minutes or a few thousand years, the timescale could be plotted linearly or (occasionally) logarithmically. Overall, time is not a good indicator of how mature a system is, because market forces drive so much of the dynamic of the s-curve with relation to time. By way of example, the filtration system used on most swimming pools has changed little since Roman times in terms of technology, but this should not be interpreted as meaning the system is 'mature' (it is in actual fact some considerable distance short of mature), merely that the market has not been demanding a better system for the last 2000 years.

Labelling of Y-Axis

There are various forms of defining what is used to define the y-co-ordinates on the s-curve graph. Within systematic innovation, they are usually plotted as measures of ideality. Actually, the image of 'plotting' points on the s-curve is not really an accurate description of the mechanics of constructing s-curves, because only in very special circumstances will they be 'plotted' in terms of quantified values. Far more common is that the curves are drawn qualitatively. The definition of ideality used in this book is:

$$\text{Ideality} = \frac{\text{(Perceived) Benefits}}{\text{(Cost + Harm)}}$$

Other equivalent forms of the equation (most commonly; benefits/cost) will also result in curves featuring the same basic characteristic shape. As will the plotting of other forms of s-curve. The most common alternative y-axis labels involve extraction of elements of the ideality equation – most usually measures of 'benefit', but also 'cost' or 'harm' (actually 1/cost or 'cost reduction' or 1/harm or 'harm reduction' to ensure the important characteristics of the s-curve are retained).

As illustrated in Figure 7.2, it can be useful to think of the composite 'ideality' s-curve as a clustering of the elements of the ideality equation. Most importantly with respect to the plotting of s-curves of elements of the 'benefit' side of the ideality equation, it is common to plot the y-axis featuring just elements of the possible array of benefits in a system, and especially parameters concerned with the Main Useful Function (MUF) of the system. We will see this in the form of curves plotting market share, or ROI or whatever other business performance metrics we might be interested in.

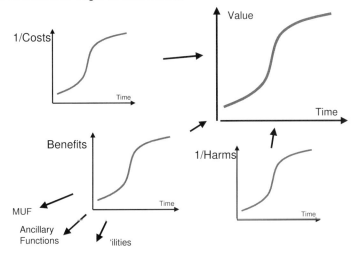

Figure 7.2: Different Forms Of Y-Axis Labelling

Now, looking across all of the analyses done on s-curves, it is clear that there is insufficient evidence to justify the claim that any form of y-axis definition will give a precisely s-shaped curve. For a start, in many instances it is simply not possible to extract accurate enough numerical information. Fortunately, this will turn out to be unimportant from the perspective of us actually being able to use the s-curve concept to do something useful in the systematic innovation process.

One thing that is clear, having made the above admission, is that the common feature of all the forms of y-axis is that we do obtain the characteristic flattening at the top of the curve. This flattening is characteristic of the emergence of contradictions within a system, and its presence is one of the first indications during any s-curve analysis which problem solving tools are going to be relevant to improving the system.

In summary – for the purposes of conceptualising s-curve dynamics, the idea that different ways of plotting the y-axis of the s-curve will all result in the same basic s-curve shape is a useful one to keep in mind. While this may turn out to be an over-simplification in some instances, what is clear is that the flattening of the top of the s-curve is generic. This flattening will help guide us during the transition from problem definition to best solution route.

Relative positioning of s-curves on Y-axis
The third dimension of s-curve complexity concerns the positioning – or more specifically the relative positioning of s-curves in relation to one another. In very simple terms, every different customer of a system could well have a different perception of its overall ideality. Actually, we could take this a step further and say that every changing mood of every individual customer could change their perception of ideality. In other words, the positioning of an s-curve relative to any scale defining its y-axis is often extremely dynamic in nature – Figure 7.3.

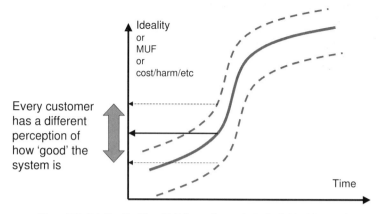

Figure 7.3: Relative Position Of S-Curve Depends On Individual Perception

This dynamic curve-positioning phenomenon is of greatest relevance when we are considering the relative position of two different s-curves. How an individual views the relative ideality of two different s-curves will dictate their selection decision. In terms of large numbers of customers, the shifting relative positions of different s-curves will be the principle factor determining the timing of disruptive shifts from one to another.

Given an existing system A at a given time, t (Figure 7.4) any individual customer seeing an alternative system – s-curve B – may perceive that alternative as a relatively more or relatively less ideal option. Different customers will have different perceptions of relative ideality – so that to some customers, option B looks better, while to others, option B appears inferior.

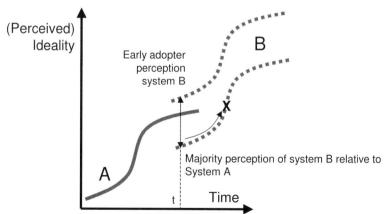

Figure 7.4: Relative Position Of Different S-Curves Depends On Individual Perception

The basic mechanics of discontinuous shifts from one system to the next are then largely driven by the customers who think the new system is superior and go on to buy it. These 'early adopter' purchases then provide the funds to support the R&D required to improve system B to a point (X) where its ideality is higher than the maximum level achievable by system A in the eyes of all customers.

By way of example, if we consider the relative positions of the s-curves for washing powder and, say, the emerging re-usable washing-balls (Reference 7.7), we might see that the inferior washing capability of the washing-balls means that for the majority of customers, this product has a lower ideality than washing powder. For those customers valuing environmental issues and who wash clothes to freshen them rather than because they are dirty, on the other hand, the washing ball may well have a higher overall ideality. If the washing-ball company gets their strategy right, the income they receive from those early adopter purchases will fund the R&D necessary to improve the washing performance of the product to a point where the cleaning performance improves to the same level as the washing powder and hence relative ideality balance shifts from the washing powder to the washing ball. They will then present customers with a fundamentally better ideality offer than can be achieved by the washing powder.

S-Curve System/Sub-System Hierarchies

One of the most important aspects of s-curve analysis from the systematic innovation perspective is that, unlike conventional ways of looking at s-curves where we normally think of there being 'an' s-curve, every element within a system has its own family of s-curves. Thus we should not just consider 'the' s-curve for, say, the business model for a bank, but recognise that the bank is made up of M&A, retail, insurance, HR, etc – each of which has its own s-curve. This idea is illustrated schematically in Figure 7.5.

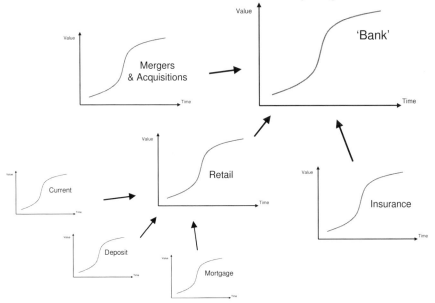

Figure 7.5: Basic System/Sub-System S-Curve Hierarchy Model
(Note: Each hierarchical level is actually representable by a chain of s-curves –
only one – the 'current s-curve' – has been drawn at each level for the purposes of clarity)

The figure (simplified for clarity) basically suggests the fact that s-curves have a hierarchical structure, with the s-curve for the overall system emerging from the s-curves for different assemblies, which in turn emerge from the s-curves for their sub-assemblies; which in turn emerge from the s-curves for their constituent elements; and so on for as many hierarchical layers as are necessary to draw a representative picture of the overall structure. This ever-repeating hierarchy of s-curve families represents another example of recursion in action.

The same basic idea of s-curve hierarchy also applies when we add a time dimension to a problem. This is particularly useful when we are conducting an s-curve analysis for a process. Figure 7.6 illustrates how a hypothetical customer order processing operation has been segmented into different constituent manufacture stages, and how each stage can be analysed in terms of position on its current s-curve.

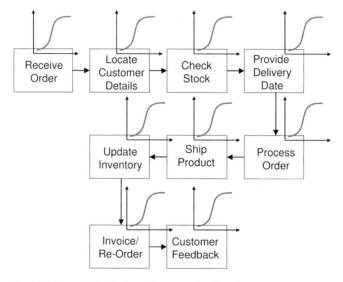

Figure 7.6: Hypothetical S-Curve Segmentation For a Process-Based System

S-Curve System-Function Hierarchy

The other important hierarchical aspect of s-curves worth noting is the distinction between an s-curve for a system and the higher-level s-curve describing the function that that system delivers. This is an important distinction to make because our perception of where we are on an s-curve (which we need to help guide us to the right systematic innovation tool to help improve our system) can vary considerably between the two definitions.

The issue is most simply illustrated by means of an example. Say we are in the business of supplying domestic land-line telephone services and are looking to see how to improve our current offering. Asked the question 'where are we on the telephone service s-curve?' we are likely to conclude (rightly) that the current system is at the mature end of the curve. If we make the shift from 'telephone' to the function the service delivers ('verbal communication') and ask the question 'where are we on the 'verbal communication' s-curve we are much more likely (rightly again) to conclude that we are some considerable distance away from its mature end.

A schematic representation of the difference between solution s-curve and the higher-level 'function' s-curve is provided in Figure 7.7.

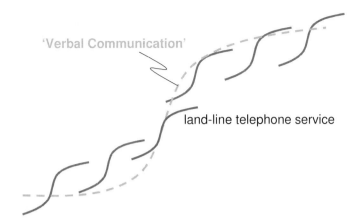

'Verbal Communication'

land-line telephone service

Figure 7.7: Distinguishing Between Solution And Function In Terms Of S-Curves

The question being posed by this solution s-curve versus function s-curve distinction is quite simply 'are we interested in improving tho ourront solution, or looking for other ways to deliver the function?' The two approaches will require fundamentally different solution generation tools in order to help us generate the strongest possible solutions.

Final Thoughts
If, during this description, any readers have been troubled by the lack of a 'decline' phase – i.e. a downturn after the highest value of the s-curve (Figure 7.8 over the page), the answer lies in two further basic mechanisms that can be useful in helping our understanding of the s-curve phenomenon:

1) It is actually very rare for an actual s-curve to produce a genuinely marked decline, because few producers will wilfully degrade the benefits produced by a system or increase cost or increase harm – and certainly not when the system is really at the mature end of the s-curve (see 2) below though). What is very common, however, is that customers' *perception*s (the fourth element contained in our ideality equation) of the system can change. In fact they can change quite dramatically; and so the curve can, if we are plotting 'perceived' elements exhibit this downward curve trajectory. A good example here may be seen with the mobile phone when the public were told about the potentially harmful effect of microwaves from the antennae – nothing had changed about the *actual* ideality of the system (it was the same design as it was before the news broke); but there had been a marked drop in net *perceived* ideality.

2) There are, on the other hand, fairly rare instances when the curve trajectory does genuinely head downwards. These are usually instances where the s-curve that is in the process of replacing the existing system is seen to have an effect on the first s-curve. A good example of this in action can be seen in cases where the new system causes sales of the old system to drop; which in turn causes the unit cost of the original system to fundamentally rise (manufacture cost and quantity produced being strongly correlated in the large majority of cases). As a specific example think of vinyl records being replaced by CDs – the now much lower volumes of vinyl meaning that that the unit cost of records is forced upwards so that those customers who still wish to buy vinyl records are forced to pay more for them – i.e. they have experienced a genuine reduction in ideality of their purchase. Fortunately for the

vinyl producers, this actual fall in ideality is such that their overall ideality is still greater than that for CDs for a certain customer niche.

As the two reasons (and particularly the first) have little to do with the actual form or content of the system under examination, we will plot all s-curves without the drooping 'decline' characteristic. Quite simply, from the perspective of creating a better system (which is the main benefit targeted by the book after all), the decline characteristic is a red-herring.

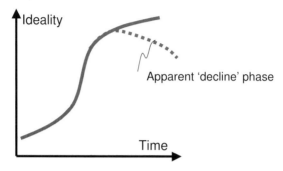

Figure 7.8: Plotting 'Decline' On The S-Curve

S-Curves and Problem Definition

Before examining the mechanisms through which we are able to establish where a system or sub-system is on its current s-curve, it is worth spending a few moments examining why we need this information and what we will do with it once we have got it.

As already stated, the principle purpose of conducting an s-curve analysis during a problem definition exercise is to enable us to better select which of the systematic innovation solution generation tools are going to be of most help to us. (There are also secondary reasons; better understanding of the s-curve family for the system will help us to better prioritise which problems to tackle, and will help bridge the gap between our solutions and market requirements.)

As far as linking problem definition to 'right' solution generation tool(s) is concerned, it turns out there are three areas of an s-curve that we can use to help determine what 'right' is:

1) If the system is at the beginning of the s-curve
2) If the system is at the mature end of the s-curve
3) Whether the system is before or after a 'point of maximum complexity'

None of the three require us to acquire precisely quantified definitions of how far up an s-curve we are, merely to identify whether we are close to certain characteristics. Conducting a 'serious' s-curve analysis of a system and all of its components can take several hours or possibly days. Fortunately, this is not the kind of depth or duration of analysis we require, and in fact, for the great majority of cases, what we need to answer the 'right' solve tool question should be acquirable in minutes.

The details of what we will do with the s-curve analysis information is covered in Chapter 10 – which describes the mechanics of the systematic innovation 'Select' process. For now, we will simply register the need to identify the above three regions of the s-curves.

System at Beginning of S-Curve

Generally speaking, if a system is at the beginning of its s-curve we are likely to be solving problems involving *improvements* to the system. At the sub-system or component levels it may well be that there is simply no system present to deliver a function, or we may be in the position of looking to add functions. Identifying the need to add functions is an important element of the analysis at this end of the s-curve. An example of this type of identification, picked up later in Chapter 13, comes if we look at the our land-line telephone service again, this time from the perspective of how we measure something like customer satisfaction. If we ask the question 'how mature is the sub-system responsible for understanding how satisfied customers are?' we are likely to rapidly conclude that, actually, no such sub-system exists at the moment – i.e. the sub-system tasked with the function 'find out how happy customers are' is right at the beginning (if not before the beginning) of its s-curve.

System at Mature End of S-Curve

By far and away the most important aspect of s-curves from the systematic innovation perspective is the inherent flattening of the top of the curve as a system approaches fundamental ideality limits. The key word here is 'fundamental' – the limits of any system are indeed fundamental, and the only way to exceed them is to change the system in some way. Identifying that we are at the top end of an s-curve is a sure way of telling ourselves that we need to adopt solution generation strategies that enable us to make these system-changing leaps. Business processes (which also have their own family of s-curves) are particularly prone to be at this mature end of the s-curve – usually being the object of 'continuous improvement' initiatives that tend to optimize the system performance to the nth degree (see Six-Sigma comment in Chapter 23). Use of an s-curve analysis to justify the belief that further optimization will not produce increases in ideality can offer very powerful arguments for the need for different approaches; at the mature ends of an s-curve, 'optimization' is rarely if ever the right problem solving strategy.

Point of Maximum Complexity

As will be detailed later in the chapter on trends of evolution (14), all systems evolve along a path that sees complexity first increase and then decrease again. We need to know whether our system (and its sub-system components) are in the 'increasing' or 'decreasing' phase of their development, as the two phases require different problem solving strategies, some of which are contradictory and will fundamentally not work if we try and deploy them at the wrong time. A common scenario is that people will try and apply a systematic innovation tool like Trimming (which is all about reducing the number of elements in a system) at a time in the evolution of the system when complexity is still in the 'has to rise' phase.

Finding Where A System Is On Its Current S-Curve

Systematic innovation describes four characteristics that enable problem solvers to establish whereabouts a system 'is' on its current s-curve. These three characteristics are the result of analysis of thousands of business systems from all sectors of human endeavour. The first characteristic relates to those businesses and industries where intellectual property plays a role. It emerges through correlating the number and rate of patenting that occurs through the life of a system. The other three are then:

1) Business Attention Focus
2) Management Processes
3) Market and Competition Dynamics

For the first of the four – rate of intellectual property generation - Figure 7.9 illustrates the established characteristic:

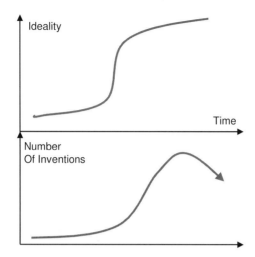

Figure 7.9: Generic Correlation Between S-Curve Position And Number Of Inventions

Basically, the finding uncovered during the systematic innovation research was that the number of inventions filed by an industry increase markedly during the maturity phase of the evolution of a system. A simple search of on-line patent databases is often sufficient to confirm the validity of the correlation for anyone wishing to observe it for themselves. The most useful correlation point to be gathered from the characteristic occurs when the number of inventions characteristic begins to decline – which is a sure sign that the retirement phase of the s-curve has been reached.

The curve characteristic is usually driven by competing companies within the industry attempting to squeeze the last few increments of improvement out of a system that is beginning to approach and hit some fundamental limits. The rise in number of inventions can also be driven by the emergence of a disruptive new system, and the resulting (ultimately futile) attempts of the incumbent industry to prolong the life of the original system. Chapter 14 will talk in a lot more detail about the dynamics of discontinuous and disruptive innovations in both business and technological situations.

The health warning carried by the curve is that as the world of intellectual property changes (some companies/industries choosing to not patent, others to saturate the arena with large quantities of 'smoke-screen' patents for example), this characteristic may begin to shift. The likelihood that this will happen is one of the reasons why the systematic innovation research is actively continuing – when any shifts do occur, we want to be the first to know about them.

Business Attention Focus
The simplest means of identifying where a system is on its current s-curve is to examine the general focus of the management of a business. Research conducted during the preparation of this book has highlighted the sometimes subtle, often pronounced shifts in the strategic focus of a business over the course of its evolutionary life. The summarized form of these focus shifts is illustrated in Figure 7.10 below.

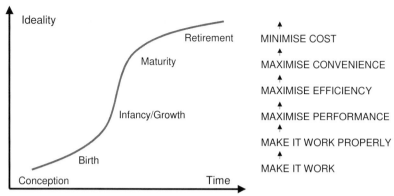

Figure 7.10: Correlation Between S-Curve Position And Strategic Focus Of A Business

The stages shown heading up the right hand side of the figure describe a progression from first getting the system to deliver its main useful function at all, and then adequately ('make it work' and 'make it work properly' respectively). Then when customers are receiving enough of the function, the focus shifts towards maximizing performance and then efficiency, and then, when the customer appetite for these has been sated, the focus is seen to shift again to convenience (including reliability and robustness) issues. Finally, when the system has delivered all of the benefits that it can, and efficiency and convenience foci have minimized the harm aspects of the system, the only remaining focus is cost.

Thus, by tracking these progressions (see also the related 'Customer Focus' trend in Chapter 14), we are able to obtain an appropriately reliable estimate of overall system maturity. Things that can help us to identify the different stages are things like the shifting focus of improvement initiatives (starting with things like 'the customer is always right', through 'need for speed', through to a plethora of campaigns at the mature end all seemingly more desperate than the last to deliver 'zero defects', right-first-time', 'total quality', and so on).

Improvement initiatives relating to cost reduction are often also a sign that the s-curve for the system in question has reached a point of maximum complexity, which, as described in the previous section will have an important role to play in our choice of problem solving strategy.

Figure 7.11 – also derived from recent research (Reference 7.8) – highlights the presence of considerable variability in the position of the point of maximum complexity relative to the s-curve. The position does appear to correlate to the relative complexity of the system – such that for complex systems featuring several hundred or more elements, the point of maximum complexity will be towards the center of the s-curve, whereas, for a relative simple system, the maximum complexity point may be pushed well over to the right of the s-curve. This variation means that when we have obtained a reliable estimate of the position of the system on its current s-curve, we haven't necessarily answered the question about whether this point has been reached or not. Consequently the focus of improvement initiatives on 'Design for Manufacture' or part-count reduction or 'business process re-engineering' or 'right-sizing' offer the surest sign that the point of maximum complexity has been passed.

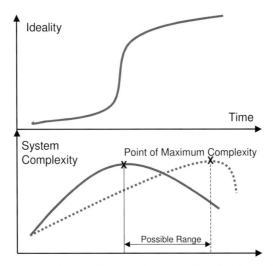

Figure 7.11: Variation In Maximum Complexity Point Relative To S-Curve.

Management Processes

Although not an absolute rule, a thought that is well worth keeping in mind when analyzing s-curves – particularly the curves for the sub-elements within a system – is the role of the manager in the definition of those elements. The job of the manager is very often one of pushing a component to the limits of its capability. By way of example, think of a manager managing a system to deliver a certain quantity and quality of service to customers. The very job of that manager is to maximize both outputs while at the same time minimizing the cost and therefore effort required to achieve the desired output. This kind of limit pushing happens throughout the world of business – often driven by the fight that takes place between the top half (benefits) and the bottom half (costs and harms) of the ideality equation.

The simple image that emerges from this business process optimization motivation scenario is that managers will tend to push the systems that they are responsible for to the top end of their s-curve (Figure 7.12). In other words, they will design to the edges of a contradiction – try to get the very most out of a system without allowing anything to go 'bang'. This is particularly evident at a departmental or sectional level. When asking the question 'where is this element on its current s-curve?' therefore, it is always worth connecting the question back to the motives of the responsible manager – who, more likely than not, will have pushed the system to a limit that is fundamental, and which will only be exceed-able by changing to a new way of doing things. In our experience working with companies on business and strategic issues in the last eight years, it is our estimate that well **over 80%** of businesses or elements within businesses have been driven to the limits of their current capability. There is nothing wrong in this, of course – if anything we would find ourselves being critical of any manager who had not spent their time trying to get the most out of the resources available to them – merely that all of the wonderful mathematical models and optimization techniques that we have all had drummed into our heads throughout our education are no longer appropriate. There is simply no way to incrementally optimize your way across a chasm.

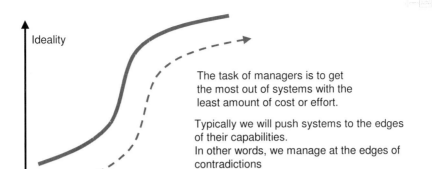

The task of managers is to get the most out of systems with the least amount of cost or effort.

Typically we will push systems to the edges of their capabilities.
In other words, we manage at the edges of contradictions

Figure 7.12: Managers Push Systems Towards The Limit Of Capability

Market and Competition Dynamics

Reference 7.4 contains the fruits of a considerable programme of analysis into what the underlying principles of innovation are. One of the findings described in the book can be modified to give us yet another indicator to help us identify where a system (this time at the 'system' as opposed to sub-system or individual element levels) is on its current s-curve. That modified finding is illustrated in Figure 7.13 below.

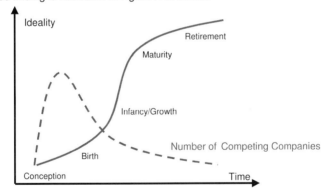

Figure 7.13: Correlation Between S-Curve Position And Number Of Competitors

What this characteristic shows is that during the initial stages of evolution of a market, there is a tendency for many players to try and enter. Then as the market gradually matures, a small number of 'winners' will emerge – either because the weaker companies fail, or because the ones with most money buy others. At the 'mature' end of the s-curve, the market is usually dominated by a 'big-3'. Reference 7.9 in fact is full of examples of industries that have reached or are in the process of reaching this magic 'three' number. At this point in time, we can see industries as diverse as aerospace, cosmetics and consumer electronics very much in this final phase on a global scale. In other industries – from athletics shoes to airlines to carpets – the shift to a big 3 has taken place on a national or continental level. e-Business and the Internet, on the other hand, are very much still in the explosion of companies phase – suggesting that current consumer electronics and e-Business paradigms are at opposite ends of their respective s-curves.

What Do I Do?

This chapter is primarily about using s-curves to guide the choice of tools to help solve a given problem. Position of a system, sub-system or component on its current s-curve will affect solution strategy. There are three main positions we need to be aware of – is the system at the beginning, end or before or after its point of maximum complexity?

We do not need to be quantifiably precise when identifying these positions. The chapter describes a number of simple ways of determining s-curve position – either from a) number of patents/time period, b) business attention focus, c) the management processes being employed, and d) the number of players involved in producing the system under consideration.

A secondary purpose of the chapter is to encourage the reader to become familiar with the concept of s-curves as they play an important linking role across the whole of systematic innovation.

If you are looking to use the chapter simply as a means of structuring an s-curve analysis and then identify current position on s-curve, we recommend you construct an s-curve hierarchy like that shown in Figures 7.5 and/or 7.6, and then use Figures 7.10, 7.12 and 7.13 to help identify the position of your system.

If you are looking to gain a broader understanding of s-curves and s-curve dynamics, you may care to peruse the whole chapter and check out the quoted references.

References

1) Hofbauer, J., Sigmund, K., 'Evolutionary Games and Population Dynamics', Cambridge University Press, 1998.
2) Handy, C., 'The Empty Raincoat, Making Sense of the Future', Hutchinson, London, 1994.
3) Burgelman, R.A., Maidique, M.A., Wheelright, S.C., 'Strategic Management of Technology and Innovation', Richard D Irwin Inc., Burr Ride, IL, 2000.
4) Utterback, J., 'Mastering The Dynamics of Innovation', Harvard Business School Press, 1993.
5) Nelson, R.R., Winter, S.G., 'An Evolutionary Theory of Economic Change', Harvard University Press, 1990.
6) Altshuller, G., 'Creativity As An Exact Science', Gordon & Breach, New York, 1984.
7) Re-usable washing ball – www.ecozone.co.uk
8) Mann, D.L., 'Trimming Evolution Trends in Complex Technical Systems', TRIZ Journal, June 1999.
9) Sheth, J., Sisordia, R., 'The Rule Of Three: Surviving And Thriving In Competitive Markets', The Free Press, New York, 2002.

8.
Problem Definition – Ideality/Ideal Final Result

"I am not anti-research but I like to have the big idea first and then test it
as opposed to using testing, testing, testing to try to come up with the big idea...
over reliance on research is like trying to drive by looking in the rear-view mirror"
Robert Lutz, Dodge.

or

" ... The leader is the one who climbs the tallest tree, surveys the entire situation and yells, 'Wrong Jungle!'"
Stephen Covey, Seven Habits of Highly Effective People

The twin concepts of increasing ideality as an evolutionary direction, and an 'Ideal Final Result' (IFR) destination point are very important philosophical elements of systematic innovation. We discuss both in this chapter in the context of their applicability during the problem definition process. In Chapter 2, where we overviewed the complete systematic innovation process, we identified ideality and IFR as 'recommended' rather than compulsory elements of the problem definition process. Strictly speaking, of course, this 'not-compulsory' position is forced by the pragmatic demands a given problem situation; put simply, many problems do not permit us the freedom to throw away all that has gone before in order to pursue what, inconveniently, turns out to be a more ideal solution route. As you can probably imagine, such a pragmatic stance carries with it considerable dangers – as we will see later, history says that organizations that don't tackle the issues arising from ideality thinking tend to go out of business. At least a part of this chapter, therefore, will seek to convince the reader of the importance of at least considering what an ideality-based thought process does for the problem they end up defining.

The chapter itself is divided into three main sections. The first section details the mechanics of an ideality/IFR based problem definition tool. The second section then works through a series of case study examples showing how others have successfully defined 'better' problems using the tool. A shorter third section then offers some additional thoughts on how the concept of ideality links to other systematic innovation tools, and how we might use the concept to enhance the way we deploy those tools.

The chapter is very much about the use of ideality in the context of problem definition. Certain elements contained within the concept also make it amenable to application in a solution generating context. Such applications are detailed in Chapter 19.

1) Ideality/IFR as a Problem Definition Tool

The basis of ideality as a problem definition tool begins from a logic that works something like the following: Increasing ideality is the overriding trend of evolution of systems of all descriptions. We can define ideality in several ways, but the most useful one tends to be:-

$$\text{Ideality} = \frac{(\text{Perceived}) \text{ Benefits}}{(\text{Cost} + \text{Harm})}$$

And so, if we accept increasing ideality as an evolutionary direction, it is basically saying that as a system evolves, it will progressively deliver more of the benefits (the top half of the equation), and progressively less of the bad things – the costs and harms (the bottom half of the equation). If we evolve a system to its furthest limits, the thinking goes, the system would deliver *all* of the good stuff we require and literally *none* of the bad stuff. Such an evolutionary state becomes our Ideal Final Result. The next part of the thinking then says, 'okay, if everything is evolving in this direction, why don't I start by thinking about that end-point rather than from the baggage of today?' This simple thought process represents a subtle but actually rather profound shift in the way most organizations (and many individuals) think. Most organizations actually think in the direction illustrated in Figure 8.1. This is the direction that uses the 'current system' as its start point. All improvement effort is then based on this starting model. The 'continuous improvement' phrase most of us have drummed into us is a direct consequence of this kind of 'start from the present' thinking. As we probably know, the law of diminishing returns (but actually the fundamental dynamics of evolutionary s-curves) says that as time progresses, we will achieve lower and lower levels of improvement in a system for ever greater levels of effort.

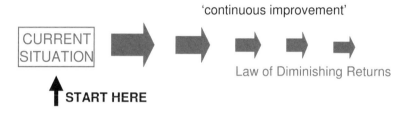

Figure 8.1: The Way Most Organisations Think

The next thing that tends to happen is that someone then finds a better way of doing things. This new way of doing things is, in systematic innovation terms, the emergence of a new s-curve – Figure 8.2.

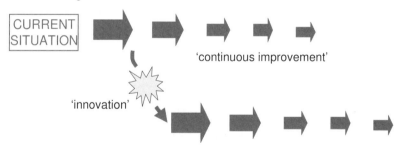

Figure 8.2: The 'Flash Of Inspiration'

The interesting fact found by systematic innovation researchers looking at these major flashes of inspiration was that they almost always came from someone outside the existing range of current providers of a product or service. The finding has also been observed and independently reported by James Utterback in the seminal book 'Mastering The Dynamics Of Evolution (Reference 8.1). Utterback records that for major product innovations (things at the level of jet-engines, carpets, refrigerators, ice manufacture, radial tyres, ball-point pens, diesel locomotives, incandescent lamps, transistors, celluloid film, calculators, parallel super-computers, etc) it was always an outsider who made the innovative jump. Put another way, based on history, the likelihood that your current organization will develop the product that puts your current product out of business is **zero**.

The ideality and IFR concept is a systematic way of at least seeing what these yellow innovation flashes are going to be.

There is an interesting paradox in the shift in thinking provoked by ideality. Practical constraints and convention say we should solve problems by starting from the current situation. That is in fact the way most people seem to think. But at the same time ask a manager or anyone for that matter how to solve the puzzle illustrated in Figure 8.3 and the almost immediate answer that comes back is 'start from the prize and work back'.

Figure 8.3: 'Which Line Leads To The Prize' Ideality Analogy

This simple model turns out to offer an extremely simple analogy of what the Ideal Final Result problem definition tool is trying to achieve; if we equate IFR to prize, then start from the prize and work back to the answer, we have a much more efficient way of doing things.

Of course, the actual tool is not quite that simple. But almost. The basic idea contained in the tool is illustrated in Figure 8.4.

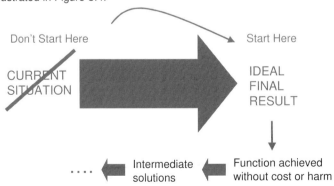

Figure 8.4: Ideal Final Result Problem Definition Strategy

The additional requirement when using the tool is that, having started by defining the IFR, the process then works back through a series of conceptual steps. The basic thinking required to make this work goes something along the lines 'if I can't achieve the IFR specification then what is the smallest step back I could make?', followed by 'if I can't achieve a solution from that small step back, what is the next smallest step back I could take?', and so on until a conceptual solution that is realisable is obtained.

One final important point before examining the mechanics of the actual IFR problem definition tool is the image illustrated in Figure 8.5.

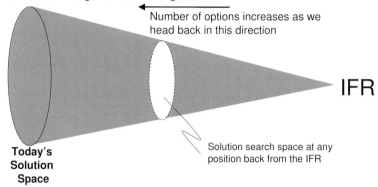

Figure 8.5: Conical Search Space When Using IFR

This figure illustrates the almost inevitable widening of the search space as we head back from the IFR (which is – conceptually at least – a very definite end point). In practical terms, the implications of this broadening are that as we step back from IFR to other conceptual solutions, we will tend to create an ever increasing number of conceptual directions the more steps back from IFR we take. We will see this phenomenon in action in some of the examples in the next section.

As a small aside, it is also worth considering the cone idea in the context of the problem-solving-as-hole-digging analogy in the chapter on psychological aspects of systematic innovation (3). In this analogy, it is necessary to re-draw the cone so that it points in a vertically downward direction (Figure 8.6) – to symbolise the search for buried treasure, with the deepest hole being the location of the ideal treasure.

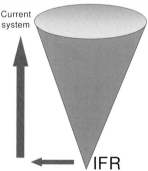

Figure 8.6: Vertical Cone/Digging-For-Treasure IFR Image

In either image, the main point is the widening of the search space as we retreat away from IFR to the current situation.

So let us now examine a simple tool to show how the IFR concept can help guide our problem definition thinking. The tool is based on a simple questionnaire designed as a way of structuring thinking. The questionnaire is illustrated in Figure 8.7.

1) What is the final aim of the system?

2) What is the Ideal Final Result outcome?

3) What is stopping you from achieving this IFR?

4) Why is it stopping you?

5) How could you make the thing(s) stopping you disappear?

6) What resources are available to help create these circumstances?

7) Has anyone else been able to solve this problem?

Figure 8.7: Ideal Final Result Problem Definition Questionnaire

The sequence of questions is important. The first question represents the first challenge. This question demands that the problem definer thinks about the FUNCTION(s) required to be delivered by the system – functionality being the key to why systems exist, and so the 'final aim' should accurately reflect that.

The second question – what is the IFR – is something of a no-brainer, certainly on the first iteration through a problem definition exercise. The answer to this question will be something along the lines of 'deliver the function/final-aim/benefit with zero cost or harm.

The third question is the first of what may be seen as the big challenge questions. The answers to this question may be both non-obvious and multitudinous. The main point of the questionnaire at this stage is to provoke 'strong thinking'. Be sure to record all of the answers found.

The fourth – why? – and fifth – how? – questions are equally challenging from the required thinking quality perspective. The underlying provocation provided by the question is to challenge the answer of the previous – what? – question. Sometimes the answers generated by these questions can appear to give an argument that becomes somewhat circular, but don't let this detract from the overall purpose of the tool – which is to help you explore the problem space as fully as possible.

The sixth question seeks to make an explicit link between ideality and the resources that should have been identified during the problem explorer part of the overall problem definition process. Ideality and resources are very closely linked; if there is something already around a system that can perform the function of the system instead of the system, it will provide us with a very good route to achieving our desired IFR. This ideality-resources link is discussed in more detail in Chapter 19 – where we examine the use of ideality in its problem-solving role.

The final question in the questionnaire is there to provide a connecting link to downstream solving tools. The very large majority of all ideality-centred problem definition thinking will lead to either a 'knowledge' problem ('I want to do this, but I don't know how to do it') or a conflict/contradiction ('I want to do this, but this other thing stops me'). This final question is intended to help formulate which. It is also there to begin the transition from the specific towards the generic.

Having answered all of the questions, the general idea is that the problem situation has become much clearer. It is by no means a one-off activity however. The ideality problem definition process described here offers two possible exploration routes should the first time through the questionnaire result in the definition of a problem that cannot be solved:-

1) we cannot achieve the stated IFR and wish to explore other problem definitions with a less challenging IFR definition, or
2) there are more than one things stopping you from achieving the IFR and you wish to explore each one in more detail.

The first instance, is equivalent to us stepping back towards the current situation to the 'intermediate solutions' denoted in Figure 8.4. The second is equivalent to the broadening of the cone as we seek to explore the search space at a given IFR definition.

The net result of the two different exploration directions is that we may end up with several questionnaires, each with its own position on the conical search space – as illustrated in Figure 8.8.

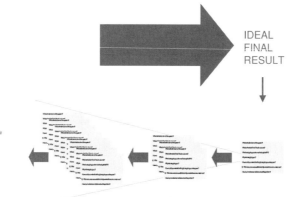

IDEAL
FINAL
RESULT

Figure 8.8: How The IFR Questionnaire Fits With The Conical Search Space

The general idea then is that we use the resulting collection of questionnaires as a way of mapping the available solution space for a given problem, and use the triggers provided by the questions at the end of the list of questions as the means by which we tap into the solution parts of the systematic innovation toolkit.

The next section illustrates examples of this process in action.

2) Case Study Examples

a) Washing Clothes

There has been a noticeable shift in the thinking of certain forward thinking washing powder manufacturers in recent times from a business strategy built on 'sell more washing powder' to one built on 'sell more clean clothes' (although the connection was first made in

1975 – Reference 8.2 – which probably tells us a lot about how long ideas can take to catch on). The simple but profoundly important difference between the first and second objectives being that the first represents a solution and the second a function. The distinction is important because, solutions change and functions stay the same. In other words, any organisation that thinks it is in the washing powder business is likely to find themselves out of business when someone works out a more ideal (again; 'benefits divided by the sum of cost and harm') way of delivering the same function as their washing powder.

This 'solutions change, functions stay the same' phenomenon applies across all industries not just washing powder – people want a hole not a drill, 'communication' not a mobile phone, 'thrust' not a jet engine, and so on. This shift to building business strategy around function fits in very neatly with the first question of the IFR problem definition tool; 'what is the final aim?'

In the case of the washing powder business, the final aim (the function being delivered) is 'clean clothes'. A good IFR definition having made this solution-to-function connection is then 'clothes clean themselves' or 'clothes don't get dirty'. Running this definition through the IFR questionnaire for the first time should give us something like:-

1) **What is the final aim of the system?**
   Clean clothes
2) **What is the Ideal Final Result outcome?**
   Clothes that clean themselves
3) **What is stopping you from achieving this IFR?**
   Textile fibres are not able to perform this function
4) **Why is it stopping you?**
   If the fibres can't perform the function, the clothes aren't cleaned
5) **How could you make the thing(s) stopping you disappear?**
   If there was a fibre or fibre structure that was able to clean 'itself'
6) **What resources are available to help create these circumstances?**
   Fibre, atmosphere, wearer, wardrobe, sunlight,
7) **Has anyone else been able to solve this problem?**
   The 'self-clean' function is possible in nature (Lotus Plant), but the only man-made self-clean structures (e.g. ovens, glass) use resources that are not present in this case. Alternative; disposable clothes.

Figure 8.9: Example IFR Questionnaire For 'Clothes That Clean Themselves' Definition

The net result of going through the questionnaire this first time is that, while we might have a few leads on how to achieve self-cleaning clothes, at this point in time we do not know how to achieve a practical solution. When this happens, the IFR definition process asks us to take a small step back from our ideal, and to define an alternative – as illustrated in Figure 8.10.

As suggested by the figure, there may be several possibilities to be considered when we make this step back. Essentially, if we are unable to achieve 'self-cleaning' clothes then the step back we take must involve some external cleaning mechanism. We could pick various different concepts – 'clean clothes without washing machine', 'clean clothes without water', and so on. As we are (for the moment) examining the problem from the perspective of the washing powder manufacturer, we will select from the possible options, 'clean clothes without a powder', or, more formally, 'clean clothes without external agent'. If we were seriously in the 'cleaned clothes' business, however, it would be strategically prudent to explore all of the different perspectives. The real key to making the 'smallest possible' steps backwards from the IFR is to recognise that with several possible options, it is important to establish which require bigger compromises than others. As we will discuss later, the size of the backward steps is also likely to depend on the perspective of different parts of the value chain.

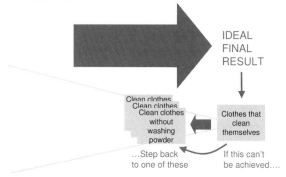

Figure 8.10: IFR Definition Space For 'Washing Clothes'

The washing machine manufacturers might well pick the 'without machine' option initially. Meanwhile, we will stay with 'clean clothes without external agent' for the purposes of illustration. This new IFR definition thus forms the basis of a new questionnaire:

1) **What is the final aim of the system?**
   Clean clothes
2) **What is the new Ideal Final Result outcome?**
   Clean clothes without the need for an external agent
3) **What is stopping you from achieving this IFR?**
   The external agent is required to break down the bond between the dirt from the clothes
4) **Why is it stopping you?**
   If the bond isn't broken, the clothes aren't cleaned
5) **How could you make the thing(s) stopping you disappear?**
   If there was some other way of breaking the bond between dirt and clothes
6) **What resources are available to help create these circumstances?**
   Water, clothes, dirt, washing machine, other household products, electricity, etc
7) **Has anyone else been able to solve this problem?**
   Only the washing powder industry has to solve the 'clean clothes' problem, but many industries have to solve the more general 'clean' or 'remove dirt' problem.

Figure 8.11: Example IFR Questionnaire For 'Clean Clothes Without External Agent' Definition

This time the questionnaire has taken us to a point where we have identified a 'knowledge problem'. We know that other industries are able to perform the 'clean' function, but as yet we don't know how. This kind of end to the questionnaire should be the prompt that takes us to a version of the systematic innovation technical knowledge/effects database (Reference 8.3). If we do this, we are likely to find that there are several ways of delivering the required 'clean clothes without external agent' function – not least of which would be ultrasound. Now, we might not like this finding, but at least we now know the threat is there, and that if ultrasound (say) turns out to be a better way of delivering the 'clean clothes' function than a washing powder, we are in trouble. Hence the reason some organisations don't like using the IFR approach during problem definition; it is never good news when you find that someone may come along and supersede all of your invested time, effort and money. Interested readers may like to note that Sanyo recently launched such an ultrasound based washing machine. Note that it is Sanyo and not one of the major established white-goods organisations.

The story doesn't end quite at this point, however. Although this IFR definition has realised possible future options, for the moment, that is exactly what they are; future options. What happens if we need a better solution more quickly than is achievable through any of the 'clean clothes without external agent' options? The Sanyo ultrasound machine, for example, is still at the relatively early stages of its evolution, and is hence unlikely to be superior to conventional machines in all of the parameters of the ideality equation for some time yet. And yet, the fast-moving consumer goods sector operates on having something 'new' on the supermarket shelves typically every six months. The answer if we are in this situation is to take another step back along the IFR definition space – Figure 8.12.

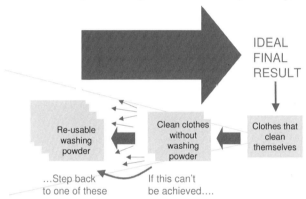

Figure 8.12: IFR Definition Space For 'Washing Clothes' – New Iteration

(Note again how each of the conceptual stages can and usually does branch out into a multitude of options as we head back closer to the current situation. This is why the solution search space is drawn as a cone.)

Stepping back from 'clean clothes without external agent' can result in several conceptual definitions. The figure highlights 're-usable washing powder' as this is one that certain sectors of the industry appear to be working towards, but other options might well include 'concentrated powders', 'concentrated liquids', 'field-based additives', 'hybrids' and so on.

Taking another step back from any of these options is likely to get us back to the current situation. At which point, we may be seen to have fully mapped, if not the breadth of conceptual definitions, at least their depth from ultimate IFR back to the present.

Another interesting aspect of the IFR definition space is that we can use it to identify a potent strategic road-map in which we not only identify where we should be traveling, but also gain an important insight into the enabling technologies that will be required and the contradictions that will need to be solved.

(As a hopefully interesting aside to this case study, the switch from selling solutions to selling 'functions' is also beginning to happen in the washing machine industry. Again, the theory goes, customers want clean clothes, not a washing machine. Find more on this 'functional sales' story at Reference 8.4.

b) Retail Banking

The retail banking sector is an industry ripe for some ideal final result oriented thinking. The following is an example of application of the IFR questionnaire to re-examine the way one of the services offered to customers are defined. As is the convention when using the questionnaire, it is best to put ourselves in the position of the customer.

1) **What is the final aim of the system?**
   Manage funds
2) **What is the Ideal Final Result outcome?**
   Funds manage themselves
3) **What is stopping you from achieving this IFR?**
   Bank will lose revenue since customer pays to have funds managed
4) **Why is it stopping you?**
   Without revenue, bank is unable to sustainably compete with other banks
5) **How could you make the thing(s) stopping you disappear?**
   If there was no loss of revenue; if revenues could be generated in other ways
6) **What resources are available to help create these circumstances?**
   Customers, Internet, mobile-phone/SMS, interactive-TV, banks, ATMs
7) **Has anyone else been able to solve this problem?**
   Several Internet-based services (e.g. Amazon) have self-organizing properties. Revenues are maintained in these solutions since the system builds a knowledge of the customer that makes life easier for the customer

Figure 8.13: Example IFR Questionnaire For Retail Banking Operation

As happens in many situations, the questionnaire encourages us to answer some questions that, when we answer them, offer some fairly obvious solution directions. Many banks are indeed beginning to experiment with Internet-based services. A few – like Virgin Direct – have automated systems so that, for example, funds will automatically move themselves from current to deposit to mortgage, etc accounts in order to guarantee the customer that their money is always being used in the most effective manner. Because the system is run by software, the bank's costs are reduced and hence revenues are maintained (by integrating mortgages into the package, however, the bank has the opportunity to actually increase revenues since it encourages customers to integrate all of their finances into one package).

Many banks also use intelligent software to monitor usage patterns of an individual customer in order that if a pattern suddenly changes they are able to hypothesise that a credit card has been stolen and contact the owner to make sure. No banks to date have sought to integrate this kind of intelligent, learning software algorithm to the fund management task. There is technically no reason why they could not do this, and indeed, given the highly competitive nature of the industry it will probably not be too long before intelligent software agents will be introduced to act on behalf of customers, helping to not only manage funds but learn the habits of the customer and anticipate future transactions.

The banking sector – like many that are able to take advantage of the virtual world of the Internet – is evolving at an ever-increasing rate in many parts of the world. It is consequently more and more difficult for one bank to discriminate itself relative to another. Any kind of competitive edge is likely to be a short-lived one. As the banks get closer and closer to the customer IFR definition, it may well transpire that the Reference 8.5 'free, perfect and now' definition may have to be revised. Perfect is perfect (provided it recognises that everyone potentially has a different definition of the word (that might change as a function of time)), just as now is now. Which then only leaves 'free' – how long, therefore, before this definition heads not just to zero cost, but to negative values? Why, indeed, don't banks pay us for the privilege of managing our funds?

3) Links to Other Tools and Additional Thoughts

Who's Ideal Final Result?

One of the biggest challenges during use of the ideality/IFR tool as a problem definition mechanism is discriminating between what the customer wants and what the manufacturer/supplier is willing to offer. In the large majority of instances, the difference between these two perceptions of what Ideal Final Result means can be widely different between each of the different parties involved in the value chain. The most extreme difference usually occurs when we consider the IFR definitions that a customer might write down versus those that a supplier might wish for – Figure 8.14.

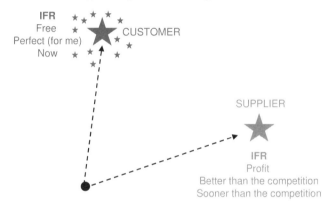

Figure 8.14: Difference Between Customer And Supplier IFR Definitions

The cluster of stars representing the customer IFR are intended to reflect the idea that every individual customer may have their own personal definition of what is ideal to them. The big star at the centre of the cluster is there to indicate that, although there will be differences in the definitions, there will also be some strong common factors – like for example 'free' and 'now'.

To take a simple example of the conflicts that arise when we take this dual customer/supplier perspective, think about the different elements of the value chain involved in the manufacture, supply and use of lawnmowers. The following is a hypothetical ideal final result definitions from the respective stakeholders:-

Lawnmower manufacturer	-	A machine that cuts grass effectively, that is aesthetically pleasing, is silent, requires no user-maintenance, no user effort, burns no fuel, profitable, and (in the short term at least) needs replacing the day after the guarantee runs out.
Lawnmower dealer	-	A product that sells itself, has excellent profit margin, and requires servicing or replacing the day after the guarantee runs out

141

| Energy supplier | - | A machine that uses lots of fuel or electricity, and oil |
| The lawn owner | - | An attractive, no maintenance lawn |

The point being that while companies have one set of goals, the ultimate customer quite often has a very different set. The mind-set of the lawnmower manufacturer is that one day, given enough R&D effort, they will produce their ideal machine – one that makes no noise, is 100% efficient, makes no mess and weighs nothing. Unfortunately, their idea of 'ideal machine' is some considerable distance away from the ideal desired by the customer; the customers ideal machine is the one that delivers the required function without cost or harm (in other words, it doesn't exist). From another perspective, what the customer probably wants is grass that knows how to make itself attractive, and maintains itself (okay, so some customers love mowing their lawn, which is why we need to consider a multitude of different IFR definitions).

The reason this customer IFR concept is important (if it is not already obvious) is that whereas in the past the poor old customer was generally at the mercy of the manufacturer, and basically got what they were told to have, the increasingly globally market means it is increasingly likely that someone, somewhere will supply those customers with exactly what they want. Historically, as stated earlier, that someone else has been a newcomer with no vested interest in maintaining the status quo. As companies become more enlightened, it will be increasingly the case that the organization that delivers the customer the customer's IFR will be the forward looking one. A smart, forward thinking lawnmower company will be the one that recognizes that it is likely to become an 'attractive, self-maintaining grass seed' company in the future.

In summary; the customer is always right; the customer's IFR is always right. It is increasingly likely someone will offer it to them.

As a general customer IFR direction, the phrase 'free, perfect and now' (Reference 8.5) makes an excellent, customer-friendly statement of what ideal final result means. What do customers want? They want something that fits their personal needs perfectly, they don't want it to cost anything, and they want it now. Simple.

We can add considerable rigour to the IFR problem definition process by using the template illustrated in Figure 8.15. The template prompts the user to examine each of the attributes that are relevant to the stakeholders in any current or planned system. It then requires the user to define what 'ideal' looks like for each of those stakeholders.

Figure 8.15: Stakeholder Attribute IFR Definition Template

A closer examination of the lawnmower example should serve to illustrate how the template is used and what it is useful for. Figure 8.16 shows a partially completed template showing some of the main attributes that may be relevant to a lawnmower business. The first attribute in the template is noise. Having defined this as an attribute we now investigate what the ideal noise value is for the customer. Here we are likely to answer 'zero', since noise is generally perceived as a harmful attribute of the system.

Next we should ask the question 'is there any customer who does not want zero noise? This question should be explored in as much detail as possible. Two scenarios are likely as we come to answer the question:

- we realize that a reason that zero noise might be a bad thing in that it may affect safety – a silent lawnmower being one that we may accidentally run over our foot because we don't know it is switched on. What we have found here is that noise and safety are coupled attributes of the system. What we do now is de-couple them and say 'if I know I will still be safe, do I want zero noise?' If the answer is yes, then we have identified all of the coupling effects. We can record each coupling effect we have found by shading the relevant box in the 'attribute conflict' triangle on the left hand side of the template.
- we realize that not every customer wants zero noise – some, for example, may want some noise so that the neighbour's can hear; or they may want the sound of a radio. Whatever the reason, what we are trying to do here is identify in the 'Customer A' and 'Customer B' columns of the template, what are the two extreme customer requirements. In the template we have summarized the 'noise' attribute extremes as zero at one extreme and 80dB on the other.

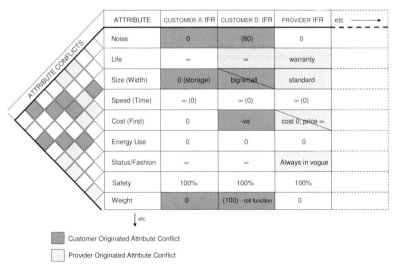

Figure 8.16: Example Completed Template For Lawnmower Problem

By the time we have completed the template – assuming we have been comprehensive – we have identified all of the contradictions that exist between today's system and the Ideal Final Result. Actually, we have identified three types of contradictions – ones where different customer want different things (possibly at different times – e.g. we ideally want a variable size lawnmower during use, but then the ideal will head towards zero when it comes to storing the machine); ones where what the customer wants and what the provider wants are different; and conflicts between different attributes. In general, the latter type tend to be the easiest, the middle type the most difficult, and the first type the most important.

A really important strategic idea stemming from this template and the idea of 'finding all the contradictions', is that we create a menu of possible directions. As discussed in Reference 8.6, a very simple and effective business model is one that says we should 'stay one contradiction ahead of our competition'. Establishing which is the best contradiction is a task discussed in Chapter 14 (Figure 14.8). In many ways, since evolution to the Ideal Final Result is convergent, it tends not to be so important which contradiction we pick. One of the reasons this seemingly un-systematic strategy works is that very often when we solve one contradiction it dissolves several other ones.

As far as we can tell from all of our research, there are only two sure ways to create a breakthrough business innovation; one is to solve one of these contradictions. The other is to identify and add a new attribute that none of your competitors has thought about. This latter idea in fact is one of the core concepts of Blue Ocean Strategy (Reference 8.7). The only real problem with the latter strategy (and therefore Blue Ocean Strategy) is that the resulting idea is far more difficult to protect than ideas generated from eliminating contradiction. Nevertheless, both strategies are worth considering.

IFR as a Function of Time

An often useful extensive to the basic ideality/ideal final result concept is to incorporate an element of time into the IFR definition process. This achieves two things; first of all it encourages a more holistic view of the ideality picture, and second it recognise that our definitions of ideality can (and often do) change as a function of time. The ideality equation

$$\text{Ideality} \quad = \quad \text{(Perceived)} \frac{\text{Benefits}}{\text{(Cost + Harm)}}$$

can be a very dynamic one. The 'perceived' word is very important in this context, with the fickle customer frequently seeming to change their perspective on what's 'good' and what isn't at the turn of an eye. This is not to say that they are wrong of course (the customer is always right, right?), merely that we should wherever and whenever possible try to anticipate how their views will change. Fortunately the focus on FUNCTION, provides some stability to this process – function being the thing that stays the same.

A good example of how the balance of the ideality equation can shift comes with the mobile phone. Initial drives towards increase in ideality came in the form of phones that were ever smaller, weighed less, had increased talk-time, and increasing numbers of features. That dynamic was shifted significantly for a while when people became aware of the potential harm caused by radio-waves heating the brain, and more recently it has shifted again towards added functionality and integration with other systems.

Although this one is a difficult one to predict (although having said that, the ideality equation does specifically prompt the problem definer to think about what 'harm' might mean), a simple lesson we can draw from it, and a simple tool we can employ to help structure our thinking on IFR definition, is a combination with the 9-Windows tool.

Figure 8.17 outlines how we can use the 9-Windows to force us to define what the Ideal Final Result might be from the perspective of each of the windows in turn. Sometimes we will find that the IFR definition stays the same as we look at it from each box, but often we will find it changes significantly. The most likely windows within which we will experience this type of definition change are:-

- Sub-System Future – from the perspective of individual components within a system, the future will see them increasingly evolve to their IFR and hence disappear from the system – i.e. have their function delivered by something else in the system. Conducting an IFR assessment of each component in a system can thus be useful in seeing which components will continue to be present in the future and which ones won't.

- Super-System Future – how things around the system will evolve can have a profound influence on how we define the IFR of the system under evaluation. The big questions are 'is something at the super-system level going to make the system redundant?' and (more difficult) 'is some change in the super-system going to change how we define our IFR?'

- System-Future – the big issue here is whether the IFR definition for the system under evaluation would be different at different times in the future.

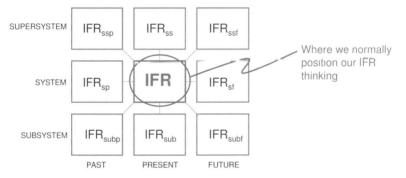

Figure 8.17: IFR In Relation To The 9-Windows

Expanding on this last point a little, it is also worth remembering that the 9-Windows tool is a way of segmenting what is actually a time-space continuum. An additional level of sophistication in IFR thinking is to position yourself at various points along a time-line into the future, and see if your perspective of IFR changes at those different points – Figure 8.18.

Figure 8.18: Does IFR Change As A Function of Time?

Another way of looking at this image involves mimicking the back-to-front thinking shift at the center of the ideality thinking paradigm shift. First imagine the ultimate Ideal Final Result definition; then put some kind of estimated timescale on this (remember we're trying to think at a conceptual rather than definitive detail level), and gradually step back from this point in the future to the present in order to see how the IFR can be redefined at each time point to fit with the prevailing constraints.

Example; Whilst I might have an ultimate IFR definition of a mobile phone that goes something along the lines of 'I want to be able to speak to anyone, anywhere, from anywhere, at any time without having to carry around a phone', and be working towards this, it is often essential in a business context at least to have some more tangible, realizable goals in the interim – like for example a fourth generation phone in 5 years, a third generation phone in the next year. IFR-based milestone setting in other words.

Links To Trends of Evolution
Some users find it difficult to imagine what the different conceptual steps back from ideal final result might be for a given system. This would not be without good reason – as the available solution space can often be very large. We recommend two strategies if this type of thinking does not come naturally (and it almost certainly won't for most people at first).

The first strategy links to the 'Trimming' trend to be found in Chapter 18. The trend suggests that systems will eventually evolve to achieve the same or greater levels of functionality with progressively fewer system elements. We can turn this phenomenon the other way around when we are thinking about IFR and working back from it – in that the number of elements in the systems will gradually increase as we return from IFR to the current system. A crude, but nevertheless useful way, therefore, of thinking about conceptual solutions is the image illustrated in Figure 8.19.

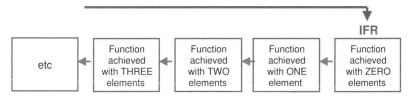

Figure 8.19: Connection Between IFR Problem Definition Strategy and Trimming Trend

An example of this model in action may be seen if we take our retail banking example from earlier and explore it in a bigger context. 'Elements' of the system in this bigger picture might be the range of different financial products that the bank offers. At this point in time, the range of products available to customers is extensive – there being a whole range of different products, all fulfilling functional requirements that are only subtly different from one another (e.g. instant-access deposit, 30-day notice, 60-day notice, etc accounts). The Figure 8.19 trend would suggest to us that over time, these different products are likely to be merged or eliminated. Absolutely crucial in the thinking that accompanies this trend is that we do not add compromises when we reduce the number of available elements. By way of an example, we might imagine a single deposit account system that automatically calculates interest rates based on how long since a customer made a withdrawal – in this way the customer receives all the advantages of higher interest the less withdrawals they make, while the bank gets to eliminate the overhead and complexity of having to manage a whole range of different products.

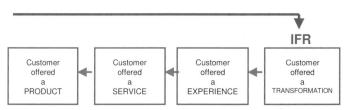

Figure 8.20: Customer Expectation Trend As An IFR Definition Guide

The idea of using the trends to help guide the IFR problem definition space can also be applied to some of the other trends. The customer expectation trend in particular (Chapter 14) can act as a very useful guide. The evolution from commodity to product to service to experience and beyond described within the trend offer very useful conceptual maps, as may be seen in Figure 8.20

What Do I Do?

Although conducting an Ideal Final Result analysis is not a compulsory part of the problem definition process, it is nevertheless very strongly recommended that one is carried out.

The concept of defining an ideal final result (especially one as far-reaching as achieving the desired benefits with zero cost or harm) and then working back from it to something that is achievable does not come naturally to most people. It is nevertheless a very potent strategy for achieving the oft sought goal of 'thinking out of the box'.

In order to make most effective use of IFR as a problem definition tool, the basic questionnaire illustrated in Figure 8.7 is recommended as a start point. Use this questionnaire multiple times as you gradually step back and broaden outlook (Figure 8.8) coming back in conceptual design stages to the current situation.

It is important to do all IFR thinking from the perspective of the customer. The customer will ultimately get what they want; if you're not prepared to provide it, then someone else increasingly is. Apart from the uncomfortable feeling that often comes when comparing our own IFR with those of the customer, it is a useful comparison to make since the conflicts we identify ultimately represent opportunities to utilise the conflict elimination tools and deliver outcomes where not only does the customer win, but we do too.

Every customer is different from every other one. Hence there may be a whole host of different customer IFR definitions that we should define and think about. As with customer/supplier conflicts, customer/customer conflicts also represent opportunities to deploy the conflict elimination part of the systematic innovation toolkit. It is often helpful to construct a table in which customer and supplier perspectives can be mapped against each other. If we do this for all of the key attributes that will define the IFR (cost, efficiency, life, etc), we can obtain a clear understanding of where the conflicts and contradictions that need to be resolved will occur.

Think about a 'one contradiction ahead of the competition' strategy for your business. Here is a useful image to keep in mind:

The cheese is the Ideal Final Result (as defined by the customer). The walls between us and that Ideal Final Result represent each of the contradictions and conflicts that haven't been solved yet.

This kind of conceptual thinking can be guided by the trends of evolution found within the systematic innovation toolkit – particularly the segmentation and trimming trends.

References

1) Utterback, J., 'Mastering The Dynamics of Innovation', Harvard Business School Press, 1993.
2) Ohmae, K., 'The Mind Of The Strategist', McGraw-Hill Inc, New York, 1982 (first published in Japanese in 1975).
3) Mann, D.L., 'Hands-On Systematic Innovation', CREAX Press, April 2002, Chapter 15.
4) Electrolux - functional sales web-site, http://www.corporate.electrolux.com/
5) Rodin, R., 'Free, Perfect and Now', Simon & Schuster, New York, 1999.
6) Systematic Innovation e-zine, 'Staying One Contradiction Ahead Of The Competition', Issue 16, May 2003.
7) Kim, W.C., Mauborgne, R., 'Blue Ocean Strategy: How To Create Uncontested Market Space And Make The Competition Irrelevant', Harvard Business School Press, 2006.

9.
Problem Definition – Perception Mapping

"From the crooked timber of humanity, no straight thing was ever made"
Immanuel Kant.

Problem situations that involve the presence of different parties with different perceptions of a given reality can very often benefit from techniques that seek to unravel the different perspectives. This chapter is about such techniques. The tools described in this chapter have been designed to manage the emotional and perceptual complexities present in business problem situations involving people. The techniques are aimed at managing those complexities in a way that seeks to obtain mutual understanding and appreciation between parties with potentially conflicting views. The techniques do not seek to prove 'right or wrong' or partition blame, but merely to elicit the facts and allow all sides of a situation to see and appreciate those facts. Experiences using the tools in anger have demonstrated that in over half of cases the 'solution' to a given problem becomes obvious during use of the tools. In the other cases, we will demonstrate how the tools can be used to identify which of the systematic innovation solution generation tools should be brought into play in order to resolve the problem, and on what aspects of a situation they should be focused.

The chapter is divided into five main sections. The first section provides a description of the main tool in this part of the problem definition process – the 'perception mapping' tool. The second, third and fourth parts then detail a trio of worked examples of the process in action. The fifth part then identifies optional extensions to the basic method that users may wish to experiment with once they have seen some success using the basic methodology.

The three cases represent different extremes which are intended to span the range of applicability of the tools. The first problem situation examines the impact of ethical elements on the manner in which problem situations are tackled. Although the case study appears to be relatively simple, we demonstrate that firstly there is nothing simple about dealing with ethical issues, and then how the perception-mapping tool can help us to manage that complexity. The second problem situation involves the mapping of perceptions of four different parts operating within an organization structure and facing a conflict situation. The aim in this case study is to demonstrate how we can take the perspectives of multiple parties in a way that allows them to come together and work together to resolve a situation in an emotionally neutral atmosphere, even when the realities of the situation will prevent people communicating the 'real' reasons why they hold a particular perspective. The third case study examines the situation in which we are trying to model the different perceptions of a wide range of people – in this case 'customers' – when we don't have direct access to any of them. In this situation, the purpose of the case study is to demonstrate how we can use the perception mapping process to tackle situations where the available data is sparse and incomplete and where there is no possibility to acquire additional data. The intention again in this case is to generically reproduce a situation that occurs frequently in the world of business.

Perception Mapping

The Perception Mapping tool is a derivation of a tool known as a 'flowscape'. A flowscape is a tool developed by Edward de Bono during the early 1990s (Reference 9.1). Both it and the perception-mapping tool that has grown from it represent a way of looking at the features and characteristics of a complex problem or opportunity situation. The tool uses the way the human brain works in order to develop lists of our *perceptions* about the situation under evaluation, and then progresses to examine how each of these connects to the others. Perception mapping diagrams thus represent perceptions of certain situations. They offer a brain-compatible means of managing complexity. Perception maps can be used to analyse situations as they are or propose solutions in order to identify what you would like them to be. In many senses the method operates in the opposite way to root cause analysis; in root cause analysis we are looking to identify what causes things to happen. The key question during a perception mapping exercise is to ask the questions 'what does this lead to?' While this might appear to be a rather subtle distinction, the truth of the implementation is often profoundly different. This is because the former encourages negative, analytical, convergent thinking, while the latter requires us to think in a much more positive, divergent frame of mind. Hence, perception mapping enables us to use the creative parts of our brain rather than the analytical part that is inevitably called for during root cause analysis. The perception mapping method operates in four basic stages; the first stage involves recording the perceptions about a given situation. The second stage then involves asking the question 'what does this lead to? for each of the perceptions identified. The idea is that the user draws a line from the perception under consideration to the perception that is most likely to be the thing that the first perception leads to. In each case, it is important that each perception in the map has one and only one 'leads to' arrow pointing from it. The third stage involves an examination of all of the perceptions and trying to identify pairs that represent contradictory or conflicting perceptions. The fourth stage then involves interpretation of the resulting perception map.

In summary, the method comprises:-

a) List down as many perceptions as you like about a situation you are facing. Label them A, B, C etc. Typically you should aim for a minimum of ten perception statements.

b) for each perception, pick one (and only one) of the others on the list that you feel it 'leads to' or 'flows to'. Put the letter of this second perception after the first. For a simple example:

A I feel happy *B*
B Life is full of contradictions *A*

c) identify a pair or pairs of perceptions representing any statements that are contradictory or in conflict with one another

d) the fourth stage of the process involves mapping how the different perceptions relate to one another. In the above (trivial) example, we see the perceptions feeding back to each other in a 'loop' – A leads to B leads to A. By definition, if each perception possesses one and only one arrow, there must be at least one loop. This loop may comprise just two perceptions – as above – or it could contain many. There may also be several different loops. Another possibility is that several different perceptions may all 'lead-to' the same perception. Where this occurs, we have what is known as a 'collector point'. Lastly, any perceptions that form a 'chain' between the conflict pairs identified in the previous stage, should also be noted. When we come to draw the map, these loops, chains and collector points are the areas that the process is trying to tell us are the most significant. Thus, by making a diagram of the perceptions and how they relate to each other, we can see more clearly what the 'central issues' are. In this fourth stage, it is far easier to examine specific examples in order to see how the perception map is able to identify what these central issues are. This is what we will do in the three case studies.

The formation of at least one loop and emergence of chains and collector points are the three most important outputs from the perception mapping analysis. The appearance of any or all features will help us to identify which of the listed perceptions are more important than others, and thus will provide us with a means of managing the complexity in situations where different perceptions are at play. Let us now try to demonstrate the power of the method with the first of the three case studies:

Case Study 1 – Pressure from the Boss

This first study is an adapted version of a case first described in Reference 9.2. In that reference, the problem was primarily dealt with as a situation resolved by means of compromise. The case contained little if any analysis of the underlying perceptions governing the dynamics of the situation. We interpret those dynamics somewhat in the description here. In the interpretation, we have attempted to model the situation in as realistic a setting as possible. Whether our perceptions of the situation are 'right' or not in this case is irrelevant since our aim is primarily to demonstrate the process. In picking a situation that occurs in related forms quite regularly, our hope is that readers will be able to mimic the structure of the analysis, replacing our perceptions with their own. All that being said, we hope also that the insights offered by the process for this specific problem are seen to be realistic and relevant to any number of similar real-life situations.

The case study centres around Alice. Alice has recently been promoted to the position of manager of a successful branch of a large banking operation. Very shortly after moving in to the post, Alice is phoned from the company headquarters by the boss of her direct boss, a company vice-president. During the phone call she is given the advice that one of her employees – Janice – was 'trouble' and that Alice would be well advised to force her to quit somehow. Although the words were supposedly offered as suggestion, Alice believed that they had in fact been presented as an order, and that the VP would be checking up on her in future weeks to see that it had been carried out. After the phone conversation, Alice was troubled. In the next few days she decided to make some discrete enquiries about Janice. These revealed that Janice's performance in recent months had indeed been poor, although at an earlier point in time it had been okay. Upon further investigation, she found out that Janice was a recently divorced parent of two children. Both of the children had learning difficulties. Alice immediately felt some personal empathy with the situation, having been raised alone by her mother following a messy divorce.

Alice's problem is typical in a number of important regards, but probably most notably, that the situation appears complicated and is essentially driven by perceptions of a situation where the available data contains many holes. Although it may transpire that more data would be helpful, the perception mapping tool offers a means of trying to draw some sense from the situation as it currently stands. As it happens, the case study is also fairly typical in that there is only a relatively small likelihood that Alice could physically acquire more data to fill in her gaps since involved parties are often reluctant to reveal the real motivation behind their actions.

So, the first stage of the Perception Mapping process then involves writing down a series of concise statements relating to the problem situation as we might perceive it. Our list is reproduced below:-

•VP wants Alice to force Janice to quit
•Janice's performance is poor
•Janice's performance adversely affects the morale of others
•Janice is a single parent
•Alice can empathise with Janice's domestic situation
•Janice's children have learning difficulties
•Alice needs to demonstrate success
•Alice needs to gain the respect of the VP
•Alice needs to gain the respect of the other people in the department
•Janice's performance has been okay in the past
•Alice wants to give Janice a chance to succeed
•Alice wants to build a long-term career at the company

After reviewing the list, it was felt that although we were happy that all the available information and perceptions had been captured, the way forward to resolving the problem was no clearer. This is a typical reaction at this stage.

The second step of the process then involved assignment of a unique identifier to each perception and, for each in turn, asking the question, 'which out of the other perceptions is this one most likely to lead?' The results of the analysis are recorded in Table 9.1 below.

Identifier	Perception	Leads To
A	VP wants Alice to force Janice to quit	H
B	Janice's performance is poor	C
C	Janice's performance adversely affects the morale of others	I
D	Janice is a single parent	B
E	Alice can empathise with Janice's domestic situation	K
F	Janice's children have learning difficulties	B
G	Alice needs to demonstrate success	H
H	Alice needs to gain the respect of the VP	L
I	Alice needs to gain the respect of other people in the department	G
J	Janice's performance has been okay in the past	K
K	Alice wants to give Janice a chance to succeed	G
L	Alice wants to build a long term career at the company	I

Table 9.1: Perception Statements Plus Result Of 'What Does This Lead To?' Analysis

Again, at the end of this exercise, it was felt that we had merely revealed that the problem was indeed a complex one. We felt no nearer to any kind of resolution. This feeling turns out to be both general, and, more importantly, a characteristic that has much to do with the ultimate success of the method. Although there is a knowledge that the end result is going to be some kind of diagram with loops and collector points, the form of the picture does not become apparent during the questioning process. Because this is so, it is very difficult to try and manipulate the answers to any kind of 'desired' pattern. The result is therefore an honest evaluation of how different perceptions lead from one to another.

In looking for contradictory perceptions from the list, during the third stage of the process, perceptions A and K were identified as the two that seemed best to define a contradiction: in perception A, Janice has to go, while in perception K Janice stays.

The fourth stage of the process is the one in which the complexity of the situation begins to be 'managed' by the process. It involves mapping the connections between the different perceptions. This is usually a process that requires a little trial and error in order to position perceptions so that lines don't get crossed. Hence, it is often preferable to use a presentation media that permits some kind of re-arrangement and manipulation of the individual perceptions. Post-Its or MagNotes offer good options. Especially since both allow users to interact physically with the perceptions.

The resulting Perception Map for this particular problem is reproduced in Figure 9.1 below. As we will see when looking at the perception maps for the other two case studies, every map has the possibility to be different from every other map. This adaptiveness is in fact one of the strengths of the method. The only common factor of any Perception Map in fact is that it must contain at least one loop. As can be seen from the figure, in this case, that is precisely what has happened. There is a single loop made of from four of the twelve perception statements – G-H-L-I-G. We know from our general description of the Perception Mapping technique that these loops are significant. We also know that 'collector points' – perceptions which have several other perceptions pointing to them – are also of importance. In this case, perceptions B and K both have two other perceptions leading to them, but none has what we might interpret as a 'lot' of connector points.

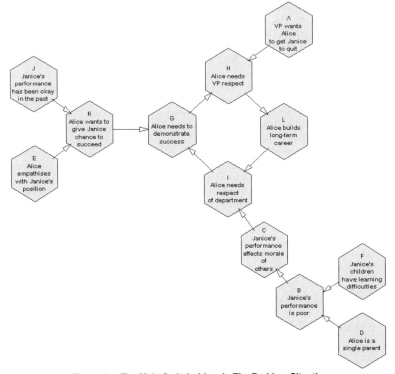

Figure 9.1: The Main Stakeholders In The Problem Situation

Immediately after the construction of this Map, the two conflicting perceptions A and K were highlighted. A segment of the thus modified Map featuring the chain of perceptions connecting each side of the conflict is reproduced in Figure 9.2.

The perception map illustrated in Figure 9.1 and the excerpt shown in Figure 9.2 when taken together offer the opportunity to construct some order from the chaos of the individual perceptions. The loop observed in Figure 9.1 for example, may be seen to represent a self-re-enforcing loop relating to the role of department staff members and the VP in the creation of a Alice's long term success in the organization. This alone is felt to offer useful insight. In terms of Alice's ethical dilemma, on the other hand, it is the two sides of the conflict illustrated in Figure 9.2 that are likely to be helpful in understanding what to do to solve the problem.

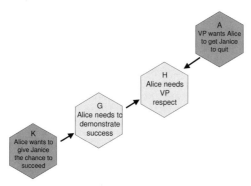

Figure 9.2: Perception Chain Connecting The Two Conflicting Perceptions

The perceptions contained within the chain connecting one conflict perception to the other are very often the ones that hold the key to successful resolution of the conflict. In this instance we notice the presence of perception H 'Alice needs the respect of the VP' on the chain. This perception is also present in the main loop of the map, further emphasizing its overall importance. If we then focus on this part of the chain it becomes apparent that the two conflicting perceptions both ultimately lead to the same end point; if Alice forces Janice to quit it will lead to her respect from the VP, and similarly, if she demonstrates success in the job, that will also lead to the respect of the VP. With this insight, it would seem that there is the possibility of a win-win successful outcome if Alice gives Janice another chance to succeed. Indeed, if she presents the situation to Janice in an appropriate manner, it ought to be possible to generate a number of wins – Janice produces more, the morale in the department goes up and thence forward, the self-re-enforcing loop is charged up and operational. Managing the complexity enables better understanding enables delivery of win-win outcomes may be seen as the overall message of the case study.

The case illustrates the mechanics of the Perception Mapping method on an ethical problem which, although complex, is something that Alice alone was capable of constructing. In the next case study, we examine a more intricate problem situation in which several parties are involved and where none is apparently willing to talk openly and frankly with the others.

Case Study 2 – Trying To Reduce Defects

Case Study 2 relates to the operation of a bottling plant. The plant fills, labels and packs bottled food products for a variety of different customers. The plant has been operating for several years. Profitability has been good despite an average defect rate of 7% across its full range of output. Overall downtime averages around 5%. Competition has gradually been catching up with the plant, and the projections for this year suggest that profit will disappear. In addition to a renewed marketing initiative, the management has decided that it needs to significantly reduce the defect rate and overall downtime.

The plant operates a 2-shift production system. Operators on both shifts are expected to record defects and their sources. The plant has a specific maintenance department responsible for setting machines and correcting problems. In order to begin tackling the situation, the four principle areas connected to the problem – Management, the Operators of the machines, members of the Maintenance Department and the trade union (Figure 9.3) - were brought together. Although it appeared clear that everyone present was expressing a willingness to address the defect reduction issue, it very quickly became clear that not everyone was speaking as frankly as would have been expected in a truly impartial setting. It was decided that the four parties would examine the problem separately for a short while, recording their perceptions about the problem. Each party was thus asked to go and work on answers to the question 'How do we reduce downtime and defect rates?'. Each group was asked to agree and record their thoughts and opinions. MagNotes (Reference 9.3) were used.

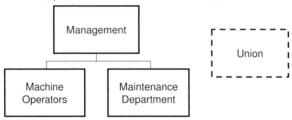

Figure 9.3: The Main Stakeholders In The Problem Situation

The perceptions recorded by the management team were as follows:-
•*Obtain better understanding of root causes*
•*Stronger ownership of processes by operators*
•*Accelerate response time of Maintenance Department*
•*Avoid repeating same mistakes/Introduce 'lessons learned' database*
•*Introduce formal spc computer monitoring system*
•*Commonalise design of different bottles*
•*Introduce fully automated system*
• *Tie operator wages to defect and downtime*
•*Introduce formal quality training to operators*

For the machine operators, the recorded responses were as follows:-
•*Productivity demands push the system too hard and need to be reduced*
•*Replace ageing machines*
•*Improve response time of Maintenance Department*
•*Change design of bottles*
•*Automate machine setting adjustments between batches*
•*Increase shift handover overlap time- better communication between shifts*
•*Introduce 'lessons learned' system*

For the members of the maintenance department, the recorded responses were:-
•*Allow Maintenance to influence the design of the bottles*
•*Improve spares supply turnaround from machine manufacturers*
•*Replace ageing machines*
•*Reduce bureaucracy*
•*Give Maintenance authority to purchase spares*

The trade union representatives were less forthcoming than the other three parties. Their recorded responses, however, were:-
•*Better working environment*
•*Benchmark against comparable plants (to establish whether performance is normal)*
•*Replace ageing machines*
•*Disconnect productivity and jobs*

For the next stage of the perception mapping process, all of the responses were collated and the four parties came back together to review what had been produced. The following Table 9.2 was produced as a means of highlighting which ideas were common to which groups:

Perception	Mgrs	Optrs	Mntce	Union
Obtain better understanding of root causes	X			
Stronger ownership of processes by operators	X			
Improve response time of Maintenance Department	X	X		
Introduce 'lessons learned' database	X	X		
Introduce formal spc computer monitoring system	X			
Commonalise design of different bottles	X			
Introduce fully automated system	X			
Tie operator wages to defect and downtime	X			
Introduce formal quality training to operators	X			
Reduce productivity demands – stop over-pushing system		X		
Replace ageing machines		X	X	X
Change design of bottles		X	X	
Automate machine setting adjustments between batches		X		
Increase shift handover overlap time		X		
Improve spares supply turnaround from machine manfctrs			X	
Reduce bureaucracy			X	
Give Maintenance authority to purchase spares			X	
Better working environment				X
Benchmark against comparable plants				X
Disconnect productivity and jobs				X

Table 9.2: Perception Statements Of The Four Parties

Tensions during the bringing together of the ideas were reduced by explaining that the recorded ideas were only perceptions and not decisions. The next part of the process then sought to highlight which of the perceptions were in conflict with one another. The group in fact identified two pairs of perceptions that were out of line with one another:-
   a) the management perception that response time by the maintenance department was poor versus the maintenance department perception that bureaucracy was high
   b) the management perception that the defect rate problem would be solved by automation versus the Union perception that any productivity improvement would result in loss of jobs.

Of the two, the group agreed that the second was the most serious. At this point in the perception mapping process, the group was asked to record the conflict and move on to the next phase. It was made clear that this step did not mean the conflict was being ignored, on the contrary, it was emphasized, the next part of the process would help later efforts to explore and hopefully resolve the conflict to the satisfaction of all.

The next part of the process involved providing a unique identifier to each of the recorded perceptions. An A-to-V code structure was used as shown in Table 9.3 below. Also shown in this table is the result of the most important part of the process; the results of the group being asked the question 'what does this perception lead to?' for each of the perceptions in turn. Importantly, this task was performed collectively, with appropriate discussions taking place to ensure consensus in the opinions recorded. As it happens there was little disagreement over the answers obtained. If there had been (which seems to be the exception rather than the rule based on the evidence of many other real problem settings), then all of the different answers would have been recorded and discussed until a consensus selection was reached.

Identifier	Perception	Leads To
A	*Obtain better understanding of root causes*	D
B	*Stronger ownership of processes by operators*	K
C	*Improve response time of Maintenance Department*	T
D	*Introduce 'lessons learned' database*	A
E	*Introduce formal spc computer monitoring system*	A
F	*Commonalise design of different bottles*	G
G	*Introduce fully automated system*	R
H	*Tie operator wages to defect and downtime*	B
J	*Introduce formal quality training to operators*	E
K	*Reduce productivity demands – stop over-pushing system*	T
L	*Replace ageing machines*	G
M	*Change design of bottles*	K
N	*Automate machine setting adjustments between batches*	C
P	*Increase shift handover overlap time*	K
Q	*Improve spares supply turnaround from machine manfctrs*	C
R	*Reduce bureaucracy*	C
S	*Give Maintenance authority to purchase spares*	C
T	*Better working environment*	B
U	*Benchmark against comparable plants*	K
V	*Disconnect productivity and jobs*	T

Table 9.3: Mapping Connections For Each Perception

Identifiers G and V record the previously recorded conflict between the management perception that the defect rate problem would be solved by automation versus the Union perception that any productivity improvement would result in loss of jobs.

Having completed the table, the resulting perception map was constructed. As is sometimes the case, two separate self re-enforcing loops emerged from the analysis. One of the loops (Figure 9.4) was seen to relate to what could be seen as 'data' issues:-

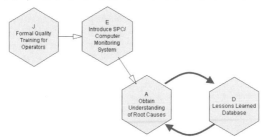

Figure 9.4: Integrated Perception Map of the Individual Perception Statements
I – Data Loop

The team for the most part agreed with both the logic of the model and the need for a system of not only recording defects, but also which fixes worked and which didn't. The main source of disagreement came from the Maintenance department. No one from the Maintenance team was prepared to discuss why they disagreed.

The second loop system was rather more complicated. This loop was more connected to what the group saw as the people issues of the problem situation. The perception map for this second loop is reproduced in Figure 9.5 below:-

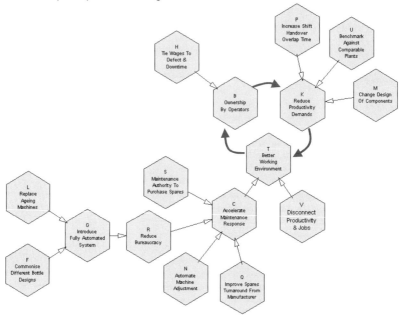

Figure 9.5: Integrated Perception Map of the Individual Perception Statements
II – People Loop

The perception map revealed a very interesting self-re-enforcing loop. The loop centred around the benefits of management giving more control of the manufacture process to the operators. It also revealed perception C 'accelerate maintenance response' as the perception that acted as the most significant collector.

Management was immediately concerned that the loop contained the perception (stated by the operators) that the current system was being pushed too hard. In fact they found it very difficult to accept the truth of the system. The loop, in fact appeared to them to suggest a downward spiral of operators improving their working environment by setting themselves easier targets. The operators, in contrast, saw the situation the other way around – that by giving them ownership of the process (that after all only they properly understood), they would generate increases in productivity. They pointed to perception H 'tie wages to defect and downtime' as the mechanism through which the management would ensure they got what they wanted.

The significance of the loop was further emphasized when the two sides of the G/V conflict were identified within the map – Figure 9.6. Also felt to be significant in the chain of perceptions connecting the two ends of the G/V contradiction was the presence of the collector point C.

When interpreting the perception maps in general, the situation where two sides of a conflict both lead to the same perception – as was present here – it is usually the case that the win-win solutions will emerge by breaking the chain of connections in some way. In many senses this breaking of connections is similar to the strategies used by the Theory of Constraints (TOC, Reference 9.4). The main difference between the two approaches, however, is that the TOC 'Evaporating Cloud' tool simplifies conflicts to just two different connection paths, whereas the perception mapping tool provides a much more flexible means of mapping all of the perceptions relating to a situation.

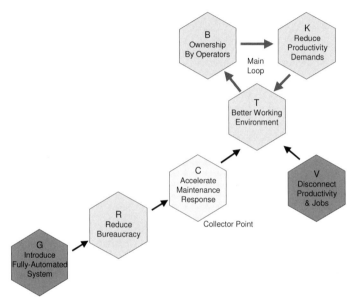

Figure 9.6: Key Re-enforcing Loop Of The Integrated Perception Map And Relation To Identified Conflict

The eventual key to the resolution of the overall problem came through examining Figure 9.6 and focusing on the presence of the collector point C 'accelerate maintenance response' in the conflict chain. The conflict between C and V 'disconnect productivity and jobs' immediately put the spotlight on the Maintenance department and their reluctance to agree to the need for recording lessons learned in the earlier (Figure 9.4) data loop discussion.

As is often the case in these situations, when the 'real' problem emerges, the solution becomes almost self-evident. In this case, it became apparent to everyone that that real problem was that by reducing defects the Maintenance department believed they were putting themselves out of a job. Prior to the perception mapping sessions, this connection was something that they had been extremely unwilling to admit or discuss. In fact, it was never even something they felt willing to write down while recording their perceptions during the idea generation phase of the analysis. But now the analysis had brought the issue clearly to light for all to see; eliminate defects and Maintenance disappears. Or rather Maintenance perceive that they will disappear.

Now that the cat was out of the bag, the Maintenance people also revealed that not only were they afraid about their jobs, but that they were also in the shorter term worried about losing their overtime.

In emotive situations like this, it was decided that a win-win solution was the only way of proceeding with the agreement of everyone. This is the point where we may well shift to the 'solution generation' parts of the systematic innovation process, and specifically – since the perception mapping analysis has highlighted the existence of a conflict – to the conflict elimination tool found in Chapter 11. The conflict-elimination problem defined here is discussed in more detail in that chapter. For those that don't wish to see that process in action yet, the end result was that instead of rewarding the Maintenance Department for maintaining the plant, they should be rewarded for *not* having to conduct any maintenance. In other words, the lower the defect rate, the more the 'Maintenance' Department would be remunerated. With this simple shift in thinking, the Maintenance Department was suddenly highly motivated to have lessons learned records and to pro-actively seek to improve the system.

In fact this solution and the perception map permitted everyone to win; the Maintenance Department had the opportunity to earn more; the operators got the opportunity to earn more because lower defects meant higher productivity for them; the managers won because they were getting better productivity and were no longer effectively paying twice for defects (once for the defect, and once again to pay the Maintenance department to fix them); and the trade union won because jobs were stable and likely to become more stable as productivity and hence the effectiveness of the business improved.

Case Study 3 - If TRIZ Is So Good, Why Isn't Everyone Using It

This case study is an adapted version of an article that first appeared in the Systematic innovation e-zine. The problem involves the spread – or at the time of writing – lack of spread of the TRIZ methodology. While attempting to tackle a real problem, the main purpose of the case study is to demonstrate new ways of managing the enormous complexity present in problems like this in order to hopefully allow users to look at other types of problems of their own. In this sense, the name of just about any other method or technique or company initiative could be substituted in place of TRIZ in this example. The main factor concerning this type of problem is how, when we have a situation dominated by many different perceptions involving many different and inaccessible people, do we establish which ones are more important than others.

The perception mapping exercise was performed on the 'why isn't TRIZ...' problem as a group of three people. In order to help manage the generation, collation and organisation of perceptions we used the MagNotes within the LVT for TRIZ kit (Reference 9.5).

The first thing that had to be done in trying to understand the current TRIZ situation was to write down the group's perceptions about why everyone isn't using TRIZ. Initially this was done individually, with each person writing each of their perceptions down on a single MagNote hexagon. It is important to only record one perception on each MagNote. After spending about 15 minutes writing down our perceptions, all of the MagNotes were brought together and all of the ideas that were similar to one another were clustered. Also, as people saw some of the perceptions written down by others, it prompted them to think about new ideas. These were also recorded on MagNotes and added to the total. Once we had a complete list we were happy with we had agreed 27 perceptions related to why everyone isn't using TRIZ. Those perceptions were (in no particular order): -

A   In-fighting amongst TRIZ providers
B   Lack of easy to follow products/books
C   Fear of the unknown/Ostrich Effect
D   'Cult'ism
E   'Me versus TRIZ' Effect
F   Too mechanical/technical
G   Not enough real case studies
H   Most people have never heard of TRIZ
I ·   Lack of integration into company cultures
J   'Simple solutions make me look dumb'
K   Lack of credibility/validation
L   'Doesn't apply to my problems'
M   Bandwagon jumping consultants
N   Expensive consultants
O   'It didn't work'
P   No 'official' journals/publications
Q   'What have the Russians ever done…'
R   Over-selling TRIZ
S   'Sleeping with someone else's partner'
T   TRIZ is 'too complicated'
U   TRIZ 'produces too many ideas'
V   'Its not the ideas, it's what you do with them that counts'
W   Bad experiences with other methods
X   'It didn't work'
Y   TRIZ providers 'don't understand my way of doing things'
Z   Western academic community is not teaching/researching TRIZ
ZZ   'Lack of managed implementation process after training'

The perceptions in quotes are ones that had been heard directly (often many times) from people in and around the TRIZ world. Hopefully the perceptions are self-explanatory. Perhaps one or two are not:-

'Me versus TRIZ' – those situations where new users think they are in a competition to prove that they are 'better' than TRIZ, or can 'beat' TRIZ. The only certain outcome in these situations is that if someone is determined to compete with TRIZ, they will win!

'Sleeping with someone else's partner' – a (deliberately) very emotive analogy for a sometimes very serious issue. The story behind this idea places the TRIZ consultant in front of a client with the problem that he and his partner are unable to have children. The TRIZ consultant solves the problem by sleeping with the partner. While this act might achieve the desired pregnancy, it is highly unlikely to engender satisfaction in the eyes of the client. Substitute the pregnancy for the solution to a problem, and the analogy describes the resentment and lack of ownership that often results when an outsider tries to present their own solution. This is a perception about solution ownership issues.

Ostrich Effect – the tendency of some people to deliberately avoid looking at TRIZ in case it might do something to change their outlook or way of doing things.

'It didn't work' – a common complaint, which should more accurately be described as 'we tried consultant X, and he/she didn't work'. Unfortunately, TRIZ often seems to take the rap for the failures (or perceived failures) of individuals.

'What have the Russians ever done...' – horribly inaccurate perceptions held by some parts of the population. These are usually people unable to see beyond the failure and fall of communism in the Soviet Union.

Next up, we had to go through each of the perceptions in turn asking the question 'which of the other perceptions does this one lead to?' In each case, we individually found a 'best' connection, and then pooled them in order to arrive at a consensus view. For most of the perceptions, agreement came surprisingly naturally. On others there was more of a debate. A large part of the power of the method – and the requirement to only permit one connection – comes through this debating activity.

With respect to the third 'identify the conflicts' stage of the process, it was decided that none of the 27 perceptions was particularly in conflict with any other. Hence this part of the process resulted in no additions to the data to be plotted on the map.

Then it was possible to construct a map detailing how all of the perceptions related to one another. The power of the MagNotes at this stage was its ability to allow the perceptions to be moved relative to one another until we could see a coherent picture. The results of those manipulations are reproduced (via the Visual Concept software (Reference 9.5) that accompanies the MagNotes) in the figure below. The reader may care to spend a little time reflecting on some of the connections that were made.

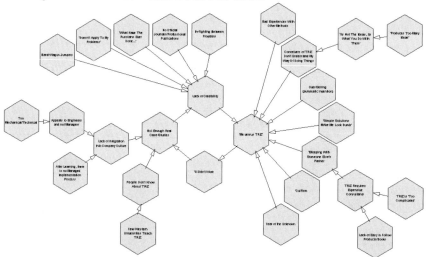

Figure 9.7: Final Perception Map For The 'Why Isn't Everyone Using TRIZ?' Problem

What the perception mapping activity is doing is identifying patterns and structure from the unsorted mass of initial ideas. As previously demonstrated, collector points (perceptions that have a large number of other parameters leading to them) and loops are the main points of interest. The loops are especially important because they represent self-re-enforcing systems – in which one thing leads to another, which in turn leads to another, which in turn... etc until everything leads back to the first thing, at which point the loop starts again.

The map for this problem highlighted the presence of a closed loop of four perceptions in which three of the four also acted as strong collection points for all of the other perceptions – Figure 9.8.

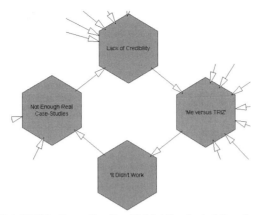

Figure 9.8: Detail Of The Perception Map Highlighting Central Re-enforcing Loop

The downstream analytical part of the perception mapping process clearly indicates the importance of breaking these self-re-enforcing loops when trying to solve a problem. Breaking down loops eliminates the downward spirals present in typical lose-lose situations, and – according to flow-scape experience – make the other non-critical perceptions either disappear or become much less significant. The self-re-enforcing destructive loop in the 'Why isn't everyone using TRIZ' situation it became apparent may just be the critical factor in solving the problem. This loop of lack of case studies leads to lack of credibility leads to 'me versus TRIZ' phenomena leads to 'it didn't work' leads back to lack of case studies, etc may just be the downward spiral causing the current lack of spread of TRIZ.

By way of testing whether the loop was 'real', we repeated the perception mapping exercise individually substituting personal opinions for group decisions in the areas where we had disagreed about what a given perception lead to. The outcome of this exercise were a number of markedly different maps featuring three common factors – the self-re-enforcing harmful loop always had 'me versus TRIZ', 'it didn't work' and 'lack of credibility' in it, suggesting a significant level of stability in the map.

Recognising the existence of this loop, of course, is not the same thing as solving the problem. The perception mapping exercise raised awareness of it for the first time, however, and was hence useful. Also, the group later convinced themselves, no form of root cause analysis would have delivered the same level of understanding of such an undoubtedly complex situation.

Thinking afterwards about what can actually be done about breaking the loop, just to take the story a little further, it was decided that only two of the four perceptions in the loop were amenable to challenge. The first was the 'lack of case studies' perception. Here, it seemed clear that the present strategy of the TRIZ community is (slowly) addressing this issue. The second, was the 'Me versus TRIZ' effect. This is something that, although awareness had been present for some time, prior to doing the perception mapping exercise, there was no clue that it played such a crucial role in affecting the whole problem of spreading TRIZ.

The more the group thought (and continue to think!) about it, the more they saw that if TRIZ newcomers can be brought to a state where they are wanting to use it, and not to be competing with it, the more likely it is they will produce good results, the more it 'will work', the more real case studies we'll get, the greater the credibility and validation of the method, the more likely that others will want to use it.... and so on. Successfully tackling the 'me versus TRIZ' problem turns a destructive lose-lose loop into a self-re-enforcing virtuous loop in which everyone wins.

We conducted this exercise for TRIZ. Looking back on it now, it seems clear that we could have substituted just about any other name and obtained the same result. If QFD is so good, why isn't everyone using it? If Theory of Constraints is so good, why isn't everyone using it? If Axiomatic Design is so good, why isn't everyone using it?

Solving the 'Me versus X' problem perhaps holds an important key in many areas.

Case Study 3a - What Would Make TRIZ *Really* Take-Off

The second part of this third case study takes the theme of the first part and turns it on it's head. The question this time around is 'what would make everyone use TRIZ?' The purpose of posing the question is to demonstrate that the perception mapping tool also works when we use it in a wholly positive as opposed to negative sense – trying to identify and develop possible opportunities as opposed to the originally conceived use as a problem solving methodology.

The first part of the process, like the 'conventional' problem-solving use of the technique, involves listing as many possible answers to the posed question. That question in this case was the 'what would make TRIZ really take-off' one that forms the title of this case study. In thinking about possible answers to the question, it would be fair to say that we derived far fewer than in the earlier 'If TRIZ is so good why isn't everyone using it?' attempt to look at what was stopping TRIZ from taking off. As it happens, in this case, we were able to identify just 10 possible strategies. These were as follows (in no particular order):-

- Produce a 'good' introduction book
- Introduce certification an/or a recognized qualification (a la 'black-belt' from Six Sigma)
- Political support
- Solve a major problem
- Get TRIZ into school/college curricula
- Produce a mass-media/popular film/programme
- Celebrity endorsement
- Find the 'tipping point' (see Reference 9.6 – basically, the tipping point is an event – often quite peripheral to the actual issue at hand at the time it happens – that prompts something to turn from a cult into a popular phenomenon)
- Press support
- 'Guarantee' success to users

Of interest when comparing this list to the 'opposite' list of items preventing TRIZ from taking off from the earlier 'negative' list, was the fact that considering the positive aspects of the situation produced almost completely different results than might have been expected. Considering the positive, in other words, was not the same thing as negation of the original negative elements. This seems to be an important consequence of specifically approaching the situation from a very different start point.

The next part of the process, then, involved asking the question 'what does this lead to?' for each of the ten listed opportunity generating strategies. The rules of this exercise were as before; each of the ten had to be connected to one (and only one) of the remaining nine strategies. The result of this analysis are reproduced in Figure 9.9 below. As in the previous exercise, we used the Visual Concept software to produce the picture.

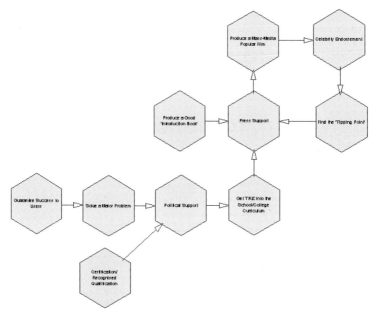

Figure 9.9: Perception Map Of The 'What Would Make TRIZ Really Take-Off?' Exercise

As with the perception mapping procedure used in the earlier case studies, the significant elements of the resulting picture are the loops and the collector points (points that several other points 'lead to'). That being the case, the key elements of the picture this time appear to be the achievement of press support (the strongest collector point), which in turn forms part of a self-re-enforcing loop along with the production of a mass-media outlet for TRIZ, celebrity endorsement and finding the tipping point. With the possible exception of the press support element (although even this has only ever been at best sporadic and temporary so far), it seems that few if any of the attempts to engineer a bigger place for TRIZ in the world have made use of any of these elements. Rather they have tended to focus on some of the things that at first sight appear to be rather more 'obvious' strategies – like for example the French emphasis on getting TRIZ into the school/college curriculum (Reference 9.7) or attempts to introduce certification and recognized levels of qualification.

As far as actually answering the 'what would make TRIZ really take-off' question is concerned, the analysis seems to suggest a somewhat different strategy to the ones currently being deployed. Of the four elements contained in the self re-enforcing loop, it seems to us that only the celebrity endorsement one seems like a relatively 'easy hit'. There have been one or two previous attempts at this in the recent past (perhaps most notably (or notoriously depending on whether you think he is an asset or liability in terms of defining what an inventor is – insert mental image of scatter-brained man in garden shed here to achieve the relevant effect) the endorsement of inventor Trevor Bayliss in the UK – Reference 9.8. The trick (if there is one) seems rather to be one of finding the 'right' celebrity to give TRIZ its due credibility. Finding Mr or Ms 'Right' needs some of the inventive thinking found in, for example, the Absolut vodka advertising campaign – where

Andy Warhol or David Bowie (neither person expected to be associated with vodka necessarily) turns out to set exactly the right context for giving the brand the reputation it now holds.

More generally, we believe the positive-thinking version of the perception mapping tool holds significant potential for managing the complex and differing perceptions typically found in situations like the TRIZ one. In fact, it seems clear again that the name of several other tools and techniques could very easily have been substituted into the question used in this exercise with little impact on the findings. At this generic level, we encourage readers to give the method a try when they find themselves in need of a simple, easy to use tool for managing complex opportunity finding or problem solving situations.

Extensions To The Basic Perception Mapping Method

The simple, four-step perception mapping process described in this chapter describes a technique still at the early stages of its ultimate evolution potential. In its current form, we believe it offers users an effective complexity management tool with a minimal learning curve.

Without complicating the technique significantly (especially if users are already familiar with some of the ideas presented below), we briefly outline a series of simple enhancements that can be used to give more power to the method.

9 Windows
It is often very useful to derive perceptions by placing oneself in a variety of different perspectives. The most commonly used systematic innovation tool for ensuring that problems are viewed from all possible perspectives is the 9-Windows concept discussed at length in Chapter 4. From this specific Perception Mapping enhancement perspective, the 9-Windows offers a useful framework from which to produce the different perceptions of a situation. Typical questions when combining 9-Windows and Perception Mapping will be 'what does the situation look like from the super-system, future?', 'what does the situation look like when we look at the system from the past?', etc. In this way, the 9-Windows provides a structure for generating a holistic spectrum of perceptions.

SWOT
The well-known Strengths-Weaknesses-Opportunities-Threats analysis structure is another way of generating a broad range of different perceptions pertaining to a given problem situation. In this case, we will typically generate perceptions from a perspective in which we are focused on strengths. Then separately, we will repeat this perception generation exercise by successively shifting our perspective to the W, O and T parts of the framework.

Six Thinking Hats
One of the reasons the SWOT method will enable us to generate more perception statements to include in the Perception Map is that it forces us to use different parts of our brain. Edward DeBono's Six Thinking Hats™ method (Reference 9.9) is another well known method that forces users to engage different parts of their brain. In this case, we will be asking questions like, 'what perceptions do we have when we examine the situation from an intuitive/emotional (red-hat) perspective?' 'what perceptions do we have when we examine the situation from a very cautious, negatively-focused (black-hat) perspective?'

Association/Empathy

Without going in to the complexities of Neuro-Linguistic Programming, the Association/Dissociation idea in this Perception Mapping context is about forcing us to place ourselves in the minds of other people involved in a situation. In Case Study 1 for example, if Alice was conducting the analysis, the Association (i.e. 'empathy') model would have encouraged her to generate perceptions from the VP and from Janice's perspective as well as just her own. Typical questions for her to think about would then be 'how does the VP see the situation?', 'what is Janice's perspective?'

Spiral Dynamics

Taking the above association/empathy idea a step further, the pioneering work of Beck and Cowan on Spiral Dynamics (Reference 9.10) presents another way of focusing a perception mapping exercise. Spiral Dynamics presents a number of different levels of consciousness (or 'thinking modes') that humans pass along over the course of their lives. The basic pattern can be found in the Trend reference section in Chapter 14. By positioning ourselves in each of the different modes and asking what the perceptions of a situation look like from that perspective is a very good way of finding the conflicts that exist between different people's perspectives of the system under investigation.

Contradiction/Problem Hierarchies

Another emerging use of the perception-mapping tool occurs when we have a situation where it has been possible to define a number of different problems and/or conflicts and are unsure which is more important than another. Listing the different problems and asking the question 'if I solve this one, which of the others does it also lead to solving?' is a very good way of gaining an understanding of the relationships between different problems.

What Do I Do?

Use the perception-mapping tool for those problem situations that involve different people with potentially different perceptions of a situation.

The process is essentially quite simple, comprising the following basic steps:-

a) identify a question that you wish to answer
b) identify a list of perceptions relating to the possible answers to this question
c) for each perception ask the question 'which of the other perceptions is this one most likely to lead to?
d) identify any perceptions that are in conflict with one another
e) construct the perception map and highlight any loops, collector points and conflict chains since these will represent the areas where solution generation activities should occur.

From here we can transition to the downstream parts of the systematic innovation knowing that we have at the very least identified the key areas of a problem that we should focus our solution generation activities on.

The variety of different question types amenable to the process is wide and varied. It is often a good idea to formulate questions as the first half of a sentence. The subsequently produced list of perceptions will then represent the second half of the sentence. Typical questions:

•Staff become de-motivated **because**....

- People don't buy-in to ERP (a surprisingly common one!) **because**.....
- People don't buy-in to change **because**....
- We would be more successful **if**.....
- Communications would be more effective **if**.....
- Quality improvements could be achieved **by**...
- In order to solve problems more effectively **we should**...

References

1) DeBono, E., 'Water Logic', Viking, 1993.
2) Badaracco, J.L., 'Leading Quietly; An Unorthodox Guide To Doing The Right Thing', Harvard Business School Press, 2002.
3) Blake, A., Mann, D.L., 'Making Knowledge Tangible', TRIZ Journal, December 2000.
4) Scheinkopf, L., 'Thinking for a Change', St Lucie Press, January 1999.
5) LVT for TRIZ product, www.changeandinnovation.com, 2003.
6) Gladwell, M., 'The Tipping Point', Little Brown, London, 2000.
7) Cavallucci, D., 'The Role of TRIZ in Technology Development', keynote address at TRIZCON2003, Philadelphia, March 2003.
8) 'A Breakout for British Invention?' article in Eureka magazine, March 2003.
9) DeBono, E., 'Six Thinking Hats', Penguin, 1988
10) Beck, D.E., Cowan, C.C., 'Spiral Dynamics: Mastering Values, Leadership And Change', Blackwell Publishers, 1996.

10.
Select Solve Tool

The purpose of this chapter is to bridge the gap between the situations we have defined and tools that are most appropriate for generating ideas to improve those situations. For many users, this gap is the most difficult part of the systematic innovation process to master. The aim in this chapter, therefore, is to make the links between definition and solution as seamless as possible.

The systematic innovation solution generation toolkit contains a wide variety of different tools and techniques. Each has been designed with a specific purpose in mind. Hence, for any given type of situation there is a 'best' tool. Not every systematic innovation user, however, is likely to have a full working knowledge of all of the different tools (at least not in the early stages). Each tool operates in a different manner. Each of them also possesses a degree of overlap with other tools, not so much in the way that they work, but in the sorts of directions that they will point the users to look for solutions. That there should be some overlap between different tools in this way should not be such a big surprise given that one of the big ideas contained within systematic innovation is that the evolution of systems is convergent rather than divergent. While this overlap can be frustrating to some, to most users – and particularly those that are unlikely to ever learn how to use all of the tools – it is a benefit. The main benefit probably centres around the idea that even if we don't know all of the tools, there is likely to be one that we know that will be able to help us to generate useful solutions. The chapter, therefore, presents tool selections in the form of ranked menus. In other words, the intention of the chapter is to provide you with the sort of route map that says, 'for situation type X, first try tool Y, then if that doesn't work, try Z, and if that doesn't work, try A' etc. The general idea behind this strategy is that if you happen not to be familiar with tool Y, you should still be able to generate good answers from tools, Z, A and any of the other recommendations.

There are many types of problem and opportunity situations, and so the menu of options is quite large. The chapter is structured in such a way that each problem type is described individually, followed by a matrix that then summarises the whole tool selection strategy into a compact, easy to read form. Some readers may prefer to head straight for this summary table. For everyone else, what follows is a hopefully logically ordered sequence of questions and answers we should go through when we are seeking to select the most appropriate solution generation tool for the situation we are in the process of tackling.

Regarding the next section, it should be noted that there is no absolutely unique logical involved in the sequence of the questions presented; if you are happier adjusting the sequence to fit better into your way of doing things, then please feel free to do so.

One final point before delving into the details of the tool selection process is a reminder that even though this book is about business and management situations, neither can be dealt with in total isolation from the technologies and technological problems that surround them. Often times, the solution to a business problem is a technical one, and conversely, the solution to a technical problem is a business one. Unfortunately, if we determine that our 'business' problem is actually a technical one, then we will have to use the technical version of this book to help us (or someone else) to generate solutions. Fortunately, on the other hand, one of the nice outcomes of trying to define a systematic innovation process applicable to both technical and business problems is that the rules for determining whether a particular problem situation is a 'contradiction problem' or a 'knowledge problem' or whatever type of problem are almost identical in both arenas. Hence, if we find ourselves in the position where our definition of a business situation suggests the use of a certain array of solution generation tools, then we can be reasonably certain that the technical versions of exactly the same tools will help us with the technical problem.

So, putting those thoughts onto one side, we will start here with the first big solve tool selection discriminator; the s-curve. Figure 10.1 illustrates the typical s-curve characteristic discussed in detail in Chapter 7. As detailed in that chapter, the relative position of the system (or sub-system or component) at the heart of the problem on its current s-curve will have an influence on both the type and sequence of problem solving tools employed. The main characteristics to examine are whether the system under investigation is at the conception/birth/growth or mature/retirement end of its s-curve and whether the point of maximum complexity has been passed.

One of the first questions we should therefore be asking when transitioning from situation definition to solution generation tool is where is the system under consideration – or, more specifically, the part of the system which we are specifically trying to improve – is on its current s-curve.

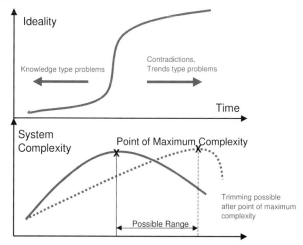

Figure 10.1: How Position on S-Curve Influences Problem Solving Tool Selection

Limiting Contradiction?

If either your s-curve analysis or your assessment of the sore point in the system has revealed the existence of a limiting contradiction, you should head directly towards the contradiction resolution solution generation tools. Your route could take you to either the conflict or contradiction elimination parts of the method. Let your definition of how different aspects of a system conflict with one another determine which route you take. If you are in a position where you can identify both conflicts and contradictions, you are advised to start by looking at the conflict and trade-off elimination toolkit in Chapter 11.

If the conflict/contradiction route proves fruitless, your next best option is to head towards the Trends of Evolution (Chapter 14) in order to establish whether there is some unused evolutionary potential in your system that might reveal means of overcoming the limiting contradiction.

A third option is to examine the chapter on Knowledge (Chapter 16) to see if anyone has already solved your problem directly. Some people will instinctively head down this route before the other two. While this is certainly not 'wrong' it does present significant potential for becoming embroiled in psychological inertia issues – if you find something that might be relevant, the very specific nature of a solution that already exists can often cause our brains to jump into its 'this will be good-enough', satisfied mode. Hence, the process recommends you try Conflicts, Contradictions and Trends first.

Other Trade-Offs and Conflicts

As Figure 10.1 suggests, systems that have evolved to the top half of their current s-curve are highly likely to contain contradictions. If you have developed function and attribute analysis models while defining the situation under investigation then it too will help to identify the existence of these contradictions in the system. Contradictions can be identified by the existence of things within a system that feature both positive and negative interactions with other things. The FAA model excerpt illustrated in Figure 10.2, for example, should suggest that there is a conflict associated with the Department Manager – in that he/she performs a useful 'co-ordinates' function, but also creates a *different* harmful (intangible) function 'de-motivates'.

There are many combinations of possibilities here, but the real key lies with arrow direction (where we should focus on arrows directed out of a component) and the presence of 'good' and 'bad' functions. Any combination of outgoing arrows featuring at least one positive and at least one negative function is an indication that a trade-off is present.

Figure 10.2: Manifestation of Trade-Off/Conflict in FAA Model

Contradictions

Function analysis models can also help to identify the presence of contradictions in a system. There are two main characteristics that can be used to signify the presence of a contradiction. These are shown in Figure 10.3. In the first situation, we have a case of John informing and not informing at the same time (i.e. he informs some people and not others), while in the second, John performs the inform function as we would like at Time X, but fails to inform at Time Y. A good first indication that a contradiction exists is that the same function ('informs' in this case) is involved in both a positive and negative sense.

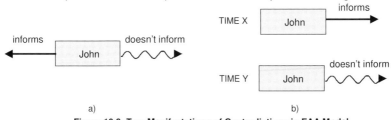

Figure 10.3: Two Manifestations of Contradictions in FAA Model

The two scenarios in the figure also help us to identify the types of solution strategy we might apply to the contradiction. In Figure 10.3b), the fact that a problem exists at one time and not at another should indicate that we can use the separation by time contradiction elimination strategies. In Figure 10.3a), John informs one part of the system and doesn't inform another, but time is not involved. This should suggest that a physical separation solution strategy would be appropriate.

Insufficient Actions

Wherever an FAA model indicates the existence of insufficient actions in a system, there are two primary options to help increase the action – Knowledge and the Trends of evolution. Selecting between the two will largely depend on the constraints attached to the problem; if there are no constraints to prevent you from looking to alternative means of delivering the function, you should start with the Knowledge chapter in order to scope the range of possible other available ways and to see if any are capable of delivering the function to better effect. If the constraints imposed on the problem situation are such that it is not permissible to fundamentally change the means of function delivery, the Trends of evolution should be used to establish means of enhancing the capability of the current function delivery means.

Insufficient actions can also be symptomatic of the presence of conflicts and contradictions. A simple test whenever we see an insufficient action is to ask the question 'what is stopping me from increasing this action?' If the answer is that you don't know, then stick to the above recommendations. If you are able to identify what is stopping the increase, then we suggest that you add Conflicts and Contradictions to the list of possible solution generation tools.

Excessive Actions

The presence of excessive actions in an FAA model suggests similar solution strategies to those recommended for insufficient actions. We recommend that the Trends should be the first port of call, followed by Knowledge (if the constraints of the problem present the freedom to consider other ways of delivering the function). The appropriate conflict-finding question for excessive actions is 'what is stopping me from reducing this action?'

Missing Actions

Indications of a missing action suggest the use of the Resources tool in order to identify whether there may be something already within or around the system under consideration that may be capable of delivering the missing action. If no resources are available, then it may well be inevitable that something will have to be added to the system in order to deliver the missing function. Use the Trends of Evolution (and particularly the Mono-Bi-Poly trends), IFR and possibly also Knowledge in order to identify possible things that could be added.

The above list of problem types all build from s-curve analysis or an FAA model. There may be situations where the problem we are looking to tackle is more general:

System and/or Function Doesn't Currently Exist

If your FAA model is a blank piece of paper, and the problem explorer full of blanks, chances are that the function you are looking to deliver is not yet present. Alternatively, a system may already exist, but it doesn't deliver the function you require from it. In either of these situations, the recommended problem solving strategy is to first try the IFR tool to help define and scope the situation. Beyond this, use the Resources check-list in order to identify whether there is anything that can be harnessed to deliver the function, or possibly try the Knowledge part of the method in order to identify whether someone, somewhere has already successfully found a way of delivering the function you are trying to achieve.

No Problem?

If you have constructed a function and attribute analysis model and it contains no harmful, insufficient or excessive relationships, or you find it difficult to picture that your current system could or should be improved, the best suggestion would be to don a black hat, think explicitly about the 9-Windows and try harder. Are you sure you wouldn't like more of the Main Useful Function of the system? If you still can't see a way forward, you should definitely take a(nother) look at using the IFR tool to re-define the problem. If that reveals nothing, Trimming (Chapter 18) should be your next port of call (check first that the system is at an evolutionary state where trimming is a viable option – Figure 10.1).

Measurement Problems

Measurement problems form a special category of problems within the systematic innovation toolkit. The first port of call for any type of measurement problem, therefore, should be Chapter 13. You might complement this with a look at Ideality (Chapter 19). If neither of these offers anything useful, your next port of call should be the chapter on Knowledge (16) to see if anyone has already thought of a way of solving your problem. If none of these approaches bears any fruit, it is likely to be that your measurement problem is a technical one rather than a management one, and you should therefore look to the strategies suggested for solving technical measurement problems.

Reliability or Robustness Related Problems

Statistics describing the durability of organizations clearly shows that very few that are sustainably robust. Employ the strategies recommended in Chapter 21 when you wish to build more robustness into business and organizational systems. See also the Trends section, and particularly the trends relating to design of business processes and the design of robust business models. A reasonable proportion of robustness problems have an element of conflict and contradiction present. If you are able to identify things that are preventing you from improving the robustness of a system, then you may wish to explore the conflict and trade-off elimination tool – paying particular attention to the 'risk' and 'adaptability' parameters.

Reduce Costs?

If the problem definition part of the process confirms that the requirement of the problem is to reduce first cost, the most obvious place to start is the Trimming tool. It will certainly provide some initial provocations consistent with movement in the right – cost reducing – direction. You might also consider combining the 'self' idea from the solving version of the Ideal Final Result tool (Chapter 19) in with the Trimming tool. Either from the trimming provocations – which will often introduce a conflict or contradiction that something gets worse if we take out a certain element – or because it is simply a good thing to do, application of the Conflict or Contradiction Elimination tools are also recommended in this type of problem. Provided the system in question is beyond its point of maximum complexity, you might like to consider focusing on the Inventive Principles specifically targeted at reducing part count within a system – see Chapter 11, part 2) of the section on 'what to do when the Matrix doesn't work'.

Specifically Searching for a Discontinuous Shift

There are occasions when we are specifically looking to jump from a current way of doing something (one s-curve) to a new one. This may be at the system level, or for a sub-system or individual person. In the case where we are looking to evolve at the system level, we should first of all examine the main useful function delivered by the current system and then examine the Knowledge part of the toolkit to establish whether there are alternative means of delivering that function. If the answer is yes, then these should act as the start of an exercise to determine how the particular knowledge could be translated into the specific requirements of the system being replaced – this may well necessitate another complete cycle of the systematic innovation process. If no suitable alternative means of delivering the function can be found, the next best strategy is to examine the Trends of evolution in the reference section at the end of Chapter 14 in order to see if any of these offers new insight.

If we are looking to find new s-curves at the sub-system or component level, it is usually preferable to begin the search by exploring the evolutionary potential of the existing sub-system or component, rather than starting from knowledge. A search of knowledge can be conducted as a secondary route – but care needs to be taken if there are significant integration issues regarding other components within the overall system.

Specifically Searching for a Disruptive Shift

Clayton Christensen in his seminal Innovator's Dilemma and new Innovator's Solution (Reference 10.1) books discusses three main innovation directions. The most common is what he labels a 'sustaining innovation'. This is the situation where we wish to advance our current capability in a direction that delivers greater functionality and benefits to existing customers. It is the situation corresponding to the 'discontinuous shift' situation type discussed in the preceding category, and we should deal with it accordingly. The second innovation strategy is what Christensen describes as 'disruptive'. This is the situation where – as discussed in more detail in Chapter 14 – customers (or a proportion of them) already have 'enough' functionality and benefits. These 'over-supplied' customers may well be amenable to an innovation that actually delivers inferior performance, but instead delivers other advantages. These advantages may consist of any number of things, but are likely to include things like delivery of different functions, convenience or price. When we believe ourselves to be in this situation where we are looking for a 'downward' disruptive innovation, then the first port of call in the systematic innovation toolkit should be to the Trends of evolution chapter (14). Once there, we may wish to use the trends slightly differently to the manner in which we would normally use them. Although it is possible to achieve a disruptive innovation by making an advance along the trends, it becomes highly likely that the disruption opportunity emerges by 'going backwards'. Hence, when we are using the trends to help us to find disruption opportunities, we should be looking at them from a backwards as well as forwards perspective.

A second tool that is particularly useful when looking for disruption opportunities is the Omega Life View (OLV) tool found in Chapter 20. This has been designed to specifically help find those customers that may be over-supplied by our current offering, and are looking for different functions. Whether using this tool or the Trends, we should always have one eye clearly focused on the *functions* that customers of our disruptive offering might be looking for.

The third innovation direction identified by Christensen is what he describes as the 'new-market' direction; find a customer – quite possibly someone who is currently not a customer at all at the moment (a 'non-consumer') – and find a way of satisfying them better than they are at present. This is the direction the systematic innovation method knows as 'opportunity finding':

Opportunity Finding

If the situation you are working through is of the 'opportunity' type ('where is the best place for me to exploit solution X?' for example) the comments at the end of Chapter 2 are worth re-reading. The key to successful opportunity identification is the recognition of the useful functions and attributes being delivered by your solution. Customers buy functions – the things that our products and services *do*. When we are in opportunity finding mode, we should be looking for customers who are currently having the functions they want delivered in a way that is inferior to the way in which we are able to offer it.

Our first port of call when we are looking at this kind of situation is the Knowledge/Effects part of the toolkit (Chapter 16). It is highly likely that we will also have to examine the technical as well as the business versions of this tool – particularly if we are in a product-based industry.

The Trends part of the toolkit can also be helpful in trying to identify opportunities in that any system that is at an earlier evolution stage on any of the trends than our solution is potentially threatened by the advance we offer. The key to successful deployment of the Trends in this opportunity-finding role is working out 'why' the evolutionary advance in our system offers a benefit to the users of the other system. See the 'reasons for jumps' reference section in Chapter 14. This 'why' provides the reason why a customer might contemplate shifting from their current method of doing something to ours.

Marketing And Advertising

Questions like 'how can I do a better job of marketing my product/service?' arise frequently in the systematic innovation context. The toolkit contains a number of tools that can help to answer this question. Reference 10.2 describes a programme of research that examined differences between conventional advertisements and those judged most successful. The most striking difference between the two (6% versus 85%) was that the most successful advertisements had identified and sought to resolve a conflict. With this in mind, the conflict and trade-off elimination tool will be helpful in generating breakthrough concepts. Definition of what the conflicts and trade-offs might actually be between product or service and the customer that we are trying to encourage to buy it is not always easy (see Reference 10.3 to see how the industry typically fails to do it). The advice if this is your situation is to focus specifically on the functions rather than the attributes delivered by the offering you are trying to promote. If it is still not possible to identify conflicts, we suggest that the 40 Inventive Principles are used as a way of systematically brainstorming breakthrough ideas. The Trends tool – and specifically the trends reference section at the end of Chapter 14 – can also be useful in finding breakthrough jumps.

Self-Re-Enforcing Loops

Either a function analysis model or a perception map may highlight the existence of self-re-enforcing loops within systems. These loops may act in destructive as well as positive directions. The removal of destructive loops should be a high priority during any activity to try and improve a system. The conflict and trade-off elimination and contradiction tools are a good place to start when looking to eliminate the harmful relationships contained within a loop, or one of the perceptions contained in the loop of a perception map. The IFR (Chapter 19) and Subversion Analysis (Chapter 21) tools can also be used to beneficial effect in many instances.

Zero Risk

There are certain occasions where the innovation requirement demands a 'zero risk', right-first-time approach. To some, the combination of 'innovation' and 'zero risk' might sound like an oxymoron. Whether it does or not, the most effective strategy if the imposed constraints really do necessitate zero risk, inevitably have to involve some kind of 'here's one I prepared earlier' solution search. Knowledge/Effects is the most appropriate start-point in such cases. Preferably using an in-house knowledge source. A sometimes valid subsequent option is to conduct a resource analysis to establish whether there is something already in the system that can be used to better effect than at present. As a third possibility, the conflict elimination tool can be used with some success by examining the strategies used by others who have been focused on the 'risk' parameters.

Optimization

There are situations where 'optimization' is an appropriate solution strategy. We might define optimization as the task of finding the absolutely best balance between the conflicting parameters within a system in order to achieve the best possible output. A useful way of visualizing the optimization process is connects back to the 'problem solving as digging for treasure' analogy described in Chapter 3: Optimization is the technique that helps us to find the deepest possible hole. Figure 10.4 illustrates the idea, while also showing the potential dangers if it turns out there are 'better' solutions in another direction.

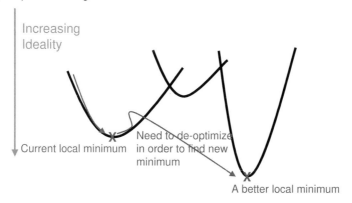

Figure 10.4: Schematic Difference Between 'Innovation' and 'Optimization'

(Read more about this analogy in Reference 10.4). Another potentially useful image relates to the fluid-filled bag model used in the next chapter to describe the importance of trade-off and conflict elimination in the innovation process. In this model, innovation is about changing the size of the bag, while optimization is about massaging the bag to get it to the best possible shape.

Drawing a line between what is optimization and what is innovation is probably a pointless exercise, nevertheless it is clear that the systematic innovation method in general is not well suited to the bag-massaging, move-the-trade-off-from-one-place-to-another optimization role. Optimization is largely about mathematics, and these days some undoubtedly sophisticated mathematics geared towards taking the human out of the optimization process altogether (another distinction with creativity and innovation – where we are not as yet able to automate the process).

The advice here is to seriously ask yourself whether the problem you are tackling is *really* about optimization, or whether you might not be better thinking about changing the size of the bag. If you genuinely believe the answer to be that optimization is what is required, the world is full of better techniques than those in the systematic innovation toolkit. Some of the places we suggest you look for help are listed in the optimization bibliography at the end of this chapter. Reference 10.5 deserves a special mention thanks to the recognition that business systems are complex adaptive systems, and that, therefore, optimization is far more effectively done using 'bottom-up' rather than 'top-down' solution strategies. The discussion on software-agent based optimization strategies and particularly the benefits achieved at the GM Fort Wayne paint shop are well worth detailed investigation.

Don't Know

If, having been through the preceding problem definition steps, you cannot make a connection to the problem types listed in this chapter, head in the direction of Chapter 17 and the Re-Focus/Re-Frame tool.

No Solutions?

If you have tried all of the recommended strategies for your given problem situation, consider using the Psychological Inertia tools (Chapter 20) to first help clarify that you are solving the right problem, and then to explore alternative solving routes. These tools will help to push you towards seeing your situation from some more radically 'out-of-the-box' perspectives.

Prioritisation of Problems

It is possible – likely even – that having been through the situation definition part of the systematic innovation process a large number of problems and opportunities for improvement have been identified. Although there are no absolute rules for prioritising problems, this section examines some general strategies for helping us to prioritise which problems we should tackle in what order.

For existing systems, generally speaking, contradictions should receive the highest priority. Eliminating contradictions generally gives more powerful solutions than conflicts and trade-offs – with a strong likelihood that un-anticipated benefits will emerge if the contradiction can be successfully challenged (on the down-side, contradictions can be more difficult to solve). After this, the priority should usually shift to the elimination of harmful functions, then insufficient and excessive. It is a good idea to begin by focusing on main useful functions, and gradually working away to the ancillary functions.

If the system doesn't currently exist, or we are looking to exploit one in a new role, the priority should generally begin with recognition of the useful functions required, application of the IFR tool, and the use of functional-benchmarking that will determine what we do next and in what order.

Ultimately, it will be the marriage of defined problem and the constraints that have to be accommodated that will determine which solution routes will be tackled in what sequence. See Chapter 5 for a more detailed description of the constraint management process.

One of the emerging uses of the Perception Mapping tool (Chapter 9) is in helping to prioritise problems in those situations where we are really not certain which ones are more important than others. A good way to think about using the tool in this context is to begin with a list of the different problems identified and to build a hierarchy using the perception mapping question 'if I solve this problem, which of the others will it eliminate, prevent or make irrelevant?' in the 'leads to' part of the analysis. The resulting perception map can then be used to understand the relationships between different problems, and also – by examining problems forming self-re-enforcing loops, and collector points – to help identify where to focus problem solving efforts.

We end the chapter with an overall summary table. The general idea here is that you work your way down the problem/opportunity situation column until you meet a description matching your situation:

Tool Selection Summary Table (relevant Chapter Numbers in parentheses)

Problem/Opportunity Situation	1st Choice Solve Tool	2nd Choice Solve Tool	3rd Choice Solve Tool	4th Choice Solve Tool
Limiting Contradiction	Contradictions (12)	Conflicts (11)	Trends (14)	Knowledge/ Effects (16)
Other Contradictions	Conflicts (11)	Contradictions (12)	Trends (14)	
Harmful Actions	Trimming (18)	Contradictions (12)	Resources (15)	
Insufficient Actions	Knowledge/ Effects (16)	Trends (14)	Conflicts/ Contradictions (11/12)	Resources (15)
Excessive Actions	Trends (14)	Knowledge/ Effects (16)	Conflicts/ Contradictions (11/12)	
Missing Actions	Resources (15)	Trends (14)	IFR (19)	Knowledge/ Effects (16)
System Doesn't Exist	IFR (19)	Resources (15)	Knowledge/ Effects (16)	
System Improvement/ 'No Problem'	IFR (19)	Trimming (18)	Conflicts/ Contradictions (11/12)	
Measurement Problem	Measurement Problems (13)	IFR (19)	Knowledge/ Effects (16)	Conflicts (11)
Reliability/Robustness Problem	Subversion Analysis (21)	Trends (14)	Conflicts (11)	
Cost Reduction	Trimming (18)	IFR (19)	Conflicts/ Contradictions (11/12)	
'Discontinuous Shift' (system level)	IFR (19)	Knowledge/ Effects (16)	Trends (14)	
'Discontinuous Shift' (sub-system level)	IFR (19)	Trends (14)	Knowledge/ Effects (16)	Conflicts (11)
Disruptive Shift	Trends (14) (forwards and backwards)	Omega Life Views (20)		
Opportunity Finding	Knowledge/ Effects (16)	Trends (14)		
Marketing/Advertising	Conflicts (11)	Trends (14)		
Self-Re-Enforcing Loops	Conflicts/ Contradictions (11/12)	IFR (19)		
'Zero Risk'	Knowledge/ Effects (16)	Resources (15)	Conflicts (11)	
'Optimization'	Optimization Methods			
'Don't Know'	Re-Focus/ Re-Frame (17)			
'No Solutions'	PI Tools (20)			

What Do I Do?

Start with the above summary table in order to identify a logical sequence of problem solving strategy options. Use the preceding text as support if you require it.

Remember above all that the general idea behind this selection part of the systematic innovation process is to guide thinking, and not to replace it. The more you put into thinking – as in really thinking – about problems/opportunities, the more you will get out of both the process and the solutions you generate. 'Process' does not mean 'panacea'. It does mean that there should be a structured framework if we are to problem solve effectively and systematically. We hope that is the part we have succeeded in delivering.

References

1) Christensen, C.M., Raynor, M.E., 'The Innovator's Solution', Harvard Business School Press, 2003.
2) Mann, D.L., 'Disruptive Advertising: TRIZ And The Advertisement', TRIZ Journal, October 2002.
3) Dru, J.M., 'Beyond Disruption: Changing the Rules in the Marketplace', John Wiley & Sons, New York, 'Adweek' Series, 2002.
4) Mann, D.L., 'Klondike versus Homing Solution Searches', TRIZ Journal, February 2002.
5) Moody, P.E., Morley, R.E. 'The Technology Machine: How Manufacturing Will Work In The Year 2020', Free Press, Simon & Schuster, New York, 1999.

Optimization Bibliography

• Ahuja, R.K., T.L. Magnanti and J. B. Orlin, 'Network Flows. Theory, Algorithms and Applications', Prentice Hall, Englewood Cliffs, NJ, 1993.
• Avriel, M., 'Nonlinear Programming: Analysis and Methods', Prentice-Hall, Englewood Cliffs, NJ, 1976.
• Bazaraa, M.S., Sherali, H.D., Shetty, C.M., 'Nonlinear Programming', John Wiley, New York, NY, 1993.
• Bertsekas, D.P., 'Nonlinear Programming', Athena Scientific, Boston, MA, 1995.
• Birge, J.R., Louveaux, F., 'Introduction to Stochastic Programming', Springer, New York, NY, 1997.
• Chvatal, V., 'Linear Programming', W. H. Freeman and Company, New York, NY, 1983.
• Duff, I.S., Erisman, A.M., Reid, J.K., 'Direct Methods for Sparse Matrices', Oxford University Press, Oxford, 1986.
• Gill, P.E., Murray, W., Wright, M.H., 'Practical Optimization', Academic Press, London, 1989.
• Gondran, M., Minoux, M., 'Graphs and Algorithms', Wiley-Interscience, Norwich, UK, 1986.
• Horst, R., Pardalos, P.M., Thoai, N.V., 'Introduction to Global Optimization', Kluwer Academic Publishers, Dordrecht, 1995.

- Horst, R., Tuy, H., 'Global Optimization: Deterministic Approaches', Springer Verlag, Heidelberg, 1996.
- IBM Corporation, 'IBM Optimization Solutions and Library', QP Solutions user guide, 1998.
- Kall, P., Wallace, S.W., 'Stochastic Programming', John Wiley & Sons, Chichester, England, 1994.
- Minoux, M., 'Mathematical Programming. Theory and Algorithms', Wiley, New York, 1986.
- Nemhauser, G. L., Wolsey, L.A., 'Integer and Combinatorial Optimization', Wiley, New York, NY, 1988.
- Nesterov, Y. Nemirovskii, A., 'Interior-Point Polynomial Algorithms in Convex Programming', SIAM, Philadelphia, PA, 1994.
- Papadimitriou, C. H., Steiglitz, K., 'Combinatorial Optimization. Algorithms and Complexity', Prentice Hall, Englewood Cliffs, NJ, 1982.
- Rockafellar, R.T., Wets, R.J.-B., 'Variational Analysis', Springer-Verlag, Berlin, Germany, 1998.
- Schrage, L., 'Optimization Modeling with LINDO', Duxbury Press, Pacific Grove, CA, 1997.

11.
Problem Solving Tools -
Conflict And Trade-Off Elimination/Inventive Principles

"From a narrow either/or society with a limited range of personal choices,
we are exploding into a free-wheeling multiple option society."
John Naisbitt, Megatrends.

or

"I'm an optimist, but I always carry an umbrella"
Norman Blake, Teenage Fanclub.

Conflicts – or rather the elimination of conflicts, paradox, trade-off, or whatever we prefer to label them as – are a central part of the systematic innovation philosophy. While many authors have begun to recognise and report the importance of not accepting the contradictions we normally take for granted, systematic innovation is unique in that it offers problem solvers tangible tools to help to actually 'eliminate compromise'.

The toolkit has two parts; one for dealing with what we might like to think of as trade-offs – situations where there are two different things in conflict with one another (for example cost-versus-quality, or risk-versus-revenue) – and the other where there are contradictory requirements concerning a single parameter (where, for example, we may see a requirement for interest rates to be both high and low). We will use the terminology 'trade-off' and 'contradiction' to discriminate between the two. Later on we will see how they are connected to one another, but for now we will treat them as separate entities, beginning with trade-offs.

Before we delve into the detail of trade-off definition and 'elimination', it is worth spending a few moments examining the expressions 'eliminate trade-offs' or 'eliminate compromise', which are used often in and around the systematic innovation community. The expressions are both useful and dangerous. They are useful because they are deliberately trying to get us to think about doing things differently than the ways most business schools teach. It is dangerous because they carry the implication that we can literally eliminate trade-offs. While there are indeed many instances where this can be shown to be the case, the concept of 'no-compromise' should be viewed as a good **direction** to travel rather than as a test of whether a solution is successful or not; a solution which significantly reduces a trade-off (without having anything else becoming worse) can very often be sufficient to deliver a paradigm-shifting innovation.

The point is worth exploring a little further, because there are important philosophical elements at play here which will have a significant impact on the way we use this part of the systematic innovation toolkit. A useful analogy is the fluid filled bag concept illustrated in Figure 11.1.

In the analogy, the bag is filled with an incompressible fluid representing all of the parameters we are typically expected to think about when we are managing a business;

classic things like time, costs, quality and risk, plus other more specific things like relationships with employees, peers and customers, communication channels, stresses, stability, and all of those other things we have to worry about if we are to run the business, or our part of it, successfully and sustainably.

The vast majority of the things we are taught about organizations and businesses and business-systems tell us that the size or amount of fluid contained in this bag is pretty well fixed. Thus, if we are tasked with improving one aspect of a system, something else 'must' get worse. Or, in the analogy, if we squeeze the bag in one place – say to reduce the cost – then it must bulge out somewhere else – the quality gets worse, or morale drops, or whatever. Business schools do a very good job of providing us with the mathematical tools that will allow us to make the trade-offs between all these battling parameters; they are very good at enabling us to 'optimise' the shape of the bag we eventually present to the customer or the shareholders.

What the trade-off elimination part of systematic innovation is about, on the other hand, is 'wouldn't it be great if we could change the size of the bag?' If the amount of fluid in the bag is a measure of 'bad'ness or non-idealness, wouldn't it be great if we could reduce that amount.

This is the real essence, then, of 'eliminating compromise'. The trade-off elimination tools are there to enable us to reduce the amount of fluid in the bag. If we are literally able to 'eliminate compromise', this is equivalent to removing all of the fluid in the bag. We probably won't be able to achieve this, at least not straight away (but see Chapter 18 on Ideality and Ideal Final Result), but, again, it is the direction of removing fluid that is important.

Figure 11.1: The Management Process As A Fluid-Filled Bag

The trade-off elimination tool is about using the successful strategies of other business leaders and problem solvers who have not followed the normal route of massaging the shape of the bag, but have instead found ways of reducing the amount of bad stuff.

As we will see, it may not be easy – the process of 'eliminating compromise' almost inevitably means inventing something new – but the benefits if we can promise to be substantial. An early discussion of the bottom-line benefits attributable to the elimination of compromises may be found in Reference 11.1. The fact that this paper was originally published in 1998 should tell us that the subject of 'compromise elimination' is still a relatively new one. At least in a business context. Essentially, the paper was an analysis of three mature companies (Charles Schwab, South-West Airlines and Wal-Mart) operating in three mature markets over a seven-year period. Figure 11.2 illustrates the performance of these three companies relative to the corresponding industry average

	(%) Industry average growth '88-'95	(%) Industry -leader growth in same period
Securities Brokerage	90	520
US Domestic Airlines	80	370
Home Improvement Retailing	40	1500

Figure 11.2: Benefits Of Compromise-Elimination Business Strategies

The clear evidence from the paper and from these three companies was that it is clearly possible to 'eliminate compromise'. If we accept for the moment, then, that if some companies can do it, then so can we – that it is in fact possible to change the size of the bag – to in effect have your cake and eat it, then this should encourage us to think about our own business in a very different way. If the size of the bag can be changed, if conflicts and compromises can be eliminated then surely we should be looking to find those compromises. In systematic innovation terms, if the system exists; it contains trade-offs and compromises. Every trade-off and compromise we can identify, in other words, is an opportunity to do a better job.

This is quite a big shift in thinking. One might even say a profound shift in thinking. Compare this 'compromises are opportunities' philosophy with what normally happens: Compromises are typically either not recognized, or are assumed to be 'fundamental', so what's the point in looking at them, or – worse – are casually brushed under the carpet and hidden from the view of others.

One final point on the compromise-elimination theme and the reducing-bag analogy before we actually look at how the toolkit enables us to achieve this compromise 'elimination' feat, is that we may well have to think about *successive application* of the tools. This means that one application of the tools might allow us to squeeze the bag in one area (solve one problem), but at the same time introduce another (smaller) bulge in another area. We should then look to use the tools again to tackle this new bulge, and so on until the size of the bag has been reduced sufficiently. We will see several instances of this 'compromise chain' idea in the following case study examples.

In graphical terms, conflicts – the fight between two different parameters can be seen as the curve illustrated in Figure 11.3.

The hyperbolic curve on the graph is not usually drawn explicitly, but most of our business mathematics and calculations exist to help us to find the point on this line where we achieve an 'acceptable' value of the two conflicting parameters. We might see this as a line of constant design capability, or designing to the established rules.

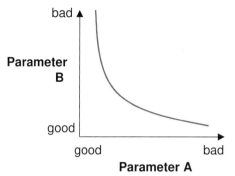

Figure 11.3: Graphical Representation Of A Trade-Off

What the trade-off elimination part of the systematic innovation toolkit is trying to do is get us to alter and shift the line towards the origin of the graph; the point where, again, the trade-offs have been eliminated. The basic line shifting idea is illustrated in Figure 11.4. For those that prefer a graphical image of what trade-off elimination is about, this is the thing to keep in mind.

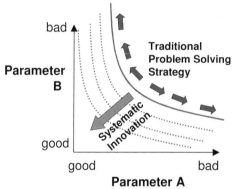

Figure 11.4: Graphical Representation Of The Trade-Off Elimination Process

So now let us have a look at exactly how the systematic innovation toolkit allows us to conduct the trade-off elimination process:

The remainder of the chapter is divided into four main sections. In the next part, we examine the main tool; secondly we provide a number of case study examples of the tool in action; thirdly we explore some fall-back options and alternative strategies just in case the main tool either 'doesn't work' or doesn't fit with your particular mindset or preferred way of doing things. The last part of the chapter – the longest part – is then the reference section. This is the part where the whole of the trade-off elimination tool kit is presented. We introduce the tool now in the first of the four sections:

1) The Business Conflict Matrix

Thinking about the fluid filled bag from Figure 11.1, it should be possible to see that the parameters contained in the bag are the ones that every manager or business leader has to think about when designing or improving a system.

In broad terms, they are the collection of parameters we used when they were formulating a systematic way of classifying problem types. The forerunner of the tool – and the thing that defined the architecture for it – was the two-dimensional Matrix configured by the original systematic innovation researchers during their search for a way to map solutions to technical problems. Given the importance of eliminating compromises, the basic form for the tool generated was a two-dimensional matrix. Parameters of interest were then listed along the top and down the side of the Matrix and so by identifying what it was that you were trying to improve, and what it was that was stopping you (or was getting worse) it was possible to browse down to the appropriate row, and across to the appropriate column and at the intersection of the two, find a place where the successful solution strategies of other problem solvers tackling the same conflicting pair could be stored. The original Matrix for technical problems had 39 such improving and worsening parameters (Reference 11.2). It has subsequently been expanded and updated to include 48 Parameters (Reference 11.3). The Matrix configured for business problems has been designed with 31 different improving and worsening parameters. These parameters divide 'business' into five main areas – R&D (the stuff that happens before a product or service is offered to a customer), Production, Supply, Support, and then a big cluster of things relating to the 'Customer'. Then, within each sector are the parameters – risk, cost, time, relationships, etc – that managers and leaders are most likely to be interested in. The general idea is that, taken, together, the Matrix makes it possible to map any business trade-off or conflict situation into the terms of parameter. The process of selecting these parameters and creating the Business Conflict Matrix is described in more detail in Reference 11.4 for those that are interested.

The manner in which the Matrix is used involves selection of a pair of parameters in conflict with one another (we will show several examples in the next section); firstly a parameter we are trying to improve, and then a second parameter which either gets worse as we try and improve the first, or somehow stops us from making the desired improvement. The first (improving) parameter we look up in the left hand column down the side of the Matrix; the conflicting parameter then being taken from the list across the top of the Matrix. The selection process is summarized in Figure 11.5.

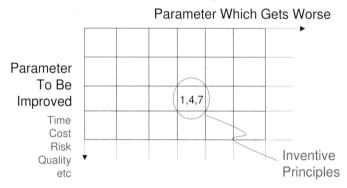

Figure 11.5: Segment of Matrix Illustrating Principles of Operation

As it happens, at this point in time, the Matrix is symmetrical in such a way that it doesn't matter if the improving and worsening parameters are interchanged – the same solution suggestions will emerge in both the row-column or column-row search method.

The box then denoting the intersection of the improving and conflicting parameters we pick contains the numbers of the Inventive Principles that other problem solvers have used most successfully to tackle the conflict in question. A quick scan around the Matrix will soon highlight the fact that there are very few such Principles; in fact, as far as this business Matrix is concerned, just 40. This is not to say that there aren't other Principles out there waiting to be discovered, simply that so far – from all the patents, scientific discoveries, business concept innovations and inventive solutions studied (approaching three million now, from all fields of human endeavour) – only these Principles have been observed. The reference section at the end of this chapter lists each of the 40 Principles along with details of how they have been interpreted by business problem solvers, and a list of examples of the Principle being used.

In the same way that there may be more Principles (actually some people prefer the words 'strategies' or 'triggers'), the ones contained inside each box of the Matrix should in no way be considered to be the *only* ones potentially relevant to a given problem – see the section on 'what happens when the Matrix doesn't work' in the third section of the chapter. Experience across a wide variety of problems, on the other hand, justifies use of the Matrix as an excellent start point.

Though conceptually quite simple, the actual mechanics of using the Matrix can appear a little unnatural at first. This can be particularly so with respect to the process of mapping your specific problem onto the 31x31 framework of the Matrix. The best advice here is to write the thing you're trying to improve and the thing stopping you, or that gets worse as succinctly as possible and then try and make connections to the 31 possible links to the Matrix. Comprehensive definitions of the parameters can be found in the first part of the reference section of this chapter. Sometimes the links will be obvious, but other times you may find that several 'may' be relevant to your problem. The simple advice in this scenario is to not try too hard to pin the conflict down to one pair; if you're not sure whether your desire to improve 'efficiency' maps better to 'time' or 'cost' or 'revenue' or even 'stability', look them all up. (You will often find if you do this that the uncertainty you have experienced is resolved by the Matrix by having some of the suggested Principles occurring several times.)

So much for the mechanics of how to use the Matrix. The reference section has been configured in such a way that each row of the Matrix is represented by two pages in the book. Hence, to use the Matrix it is necessary, first, to identify the thing that you are trying to improve, map that thing into the best match(es) with parameters in the Matrix, and then go to the pairs of pages featuring those particular improving parameters. The table of data will then suggest the Inventive Principles most relevant to each of the 'worsening' parameters. Don't worry, it will be obvious when you see the thing in action.

Let us, in fact, do that right now by looking at a number of case study examples of solving conflicts and compromises using the Matrix.

2) Conflict Elimination Case Studies

There are several different aspects of the conflict-elimination process that are worth exploring. We shall explore several different case studies, each one of which is intended to highlight a certain specific point. Let's begin with a simple case study aimed at describing the basic mechanics of the process:

a) The Maintenance Department Problem

The background to this case study comes from the Perception Mapping tool case study described in Chapter 8. This, in fact, will be a very typical means of arriving at the definition of a conflict – some part of the problem definition process helps us to identify where a problem exists, and will then send us here to establish ways of solving it.

To briefly summarise the background to the problem; production at a factory is hampered by a high rate of defects and down-time. Various people around the organization (managers, machine operators, maintenance department and trade-union) have been asked how they think the problems might be solved, and it has emerged that the Maintenance Department feels that their jobs would be under threat if there was no maintenance for them to do.

This then becomes the start point for a conflict elimination exercise; we have a broad definition of our specific situation, and can see the existence of a conflict – there is something we would like to improve (defect rate) and something preventing us from making the improvement (the Maintenance Department jobs are threatened). Under normal circumstances, management may choose to solve such a problem using the usual route of trade-off and compromise. A very simple one in this case, apparently, would be to make the Maintenance Department staff (or the troublesome ones at least) redundant. The big compromise with this kind of philosophy is that it takes into account none of the surrounding issues – like the morale of the remaining workers to take just one significant example. The conflict elimination process is aimed at getting us to do things differently. Specifically, to try and achieve a win-win outcome.

The underlying idea behind the Business Conflict Matrix is that someone, somewhere has already found a good solution to our problem. The next thing we need to do if we are to test this hypothesis, is to translate the specific terms of our problem into the general terms of the Matrix. Essentially, here we are following the problem abstraction scheme used in several of the other tools in the systematic innovation toolkit. Figure 11.6 reviews the process in the context of the conflict elimination tool.

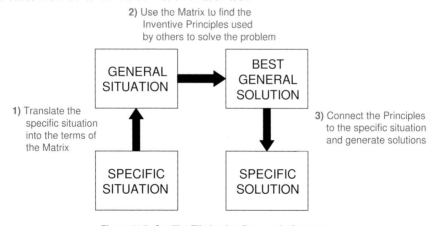

Figure 11.6: Conflict Elimination Process In Summary

In terms of the Maintenance Department problem, we have already defined our specific situation. The next thing we need to do then is to translate it into a pair of parameters found in the Business Conflict Matrix.

The key to the specific-to-general mapping task is to look for connections in which the parameters in the Matrix *'mean the same as'* the specific parameters of our problem.

The mapping process usually works something like this:-

The thing we would like to improve: *reduce defect rates*
Corresponding best match to a parameter in the Matrix: *Production Quality*

Thing that prevents us: *Maintenance Department will lose jobs*
Corresponding best match to a parameter in the Matrix: *Harmful Factors Affecting System*

We might wonder at this stage whether these are the best matches. The improving parameter seems like a close fit, but the other one is perhaps less clear. Why isn't 'Stability' a better match? Or 'Production Interfaces'? There are two answers to this query; firstly there is no such thing as a single 'right' match, and so if we make a connection to any of the parameters, then we could very simply look up all of them in the Matrix. The only downside in this case is a small time penalty, in which case we might like to review the 'means the same as' question to try and focus our connections. Secondly, and more importantly, the Matrix tries to be self-correcting and so uncertainty we might have in mapping this problem to the Matrix is exactly the same sort of uncertainty that occurs every time a new solution is added to the database. In this case for example, if we look up Production Quality versus Harmful Factors Affecting System and Stability and Production Interfaces we will see that Principles 13 and 35 appear in all three places, and several other parameters appear in two places. This is the process of 'self-correcting' in action. When we are looking up multiple conflict pairs in the Matrix and we see the same Principles emerging again and again as solutions, we can be reasonably certain that these Principles are going to be very effective ones when it comes to generating our own 'good' solutions.

As far as this case study is concerned, and our desire to examine the mechanics of the process, we will chose to simply look up the Production Quality versus Harmful Factors Affecting System conflict pair in the Matrix. If we do this, according to the Figure 11.6 process summary, we are identifying the best known general solutions to that conflict pair. Figure 11.7 illustrates the Matrix search process and the resulting Inventive Principle suggestions.

6
Parameter We Want to Improve – Production Spec/Quality/Means

List of Principles relevant to each specific worsening parameter:

Worsening Parameter	Description	List of Relevant Inventive Principles (decreasing order of frequency)
4	R&D Quality/Capability M...	22 29 35 1 19 5
23	Communication Flow	6 2 19 29 16
24	Harmful Factors Affecting System	22 24 35 13 24 2
25	System Generated Harmful Factors	35 22 18 39

Figure 11.7: Business Conflict Matrix Suggestions for Maintenance Problem

188

The Matrix shows us that the most commonly used Inventive Principles used to resolve Production Quality versus 'Harmful Factors Affecting System' are:-

22, 24, 35, 13, 24 and 2

The sequence of the numbers is indicative of the frequency with which each Principle has been used in the particular conflict pair. In this case, Principle 22 is the most commonly used, Principle 24 the second most commonly used, and so on.

Having obtained these Principle recommendations, the third and final stage of the process of Figure 11.6 requires them to be converted into specific solutions to the problem at hand. This process can be done in a number of ways – either individually or in a group setting, by working through them in a rigid sequence, or, most simply, by using them as a focus for brainstorming-type solution generation strategies. In this instance – an actual case study – there was a group of people involved, none of who had received any prior training in the method. The only impact this had on the session was that it had to be preceded by a short description of the Principles. The group working on the problem then used the recommended Inventive Principles as a focus for brainstorming possible solutions to the situation. After around an hour of idea generation – with over 50 idea suggestions recorded – and evaluation, the group collectively agreed that Principle 13, The Other Way Around' had been the one that offered the best overall solution direction. Ideas generated from other Principles also had something to contribute to the detailed implementation, but the main idea resulting from the Inventive Principle 13 suggestion 'invert the action used to solve the problem' was that instead of rewarding the Maintenance Department for maintaining the plant, they should be rewarded for not having to conduct any maintenance. In other words, the lower the defect rate, the more the 'Maintenance' Department would be remunerated. With this simple shift in thinking, the Maintenance Department was suddenly highly motivated to have lessons learned records and to pro-actively seek to improve the system.

In fact this solution and the perception map permitted everyone to win; the Maintenance Department had the opportunity to earn more; the operators got the opportunity to earn more because lower defects meant higher productivity for them; the managers won because they were getting better productivity and were no longer effectively paying twice for defects (once for the defect, and once again to pay the Maintenance department to fix them); and the Union won because jobs were stable and likely to become more stable as productivity and hence the effectiveness of the business improved.

As far as we are concerned here, the case study is intended merely to illustrate the mechanics of the Matrix problem solving process. The next example seeks to explore the translation of Inventive Principles solution suggestions into specific solution opportunities in a little more detail. As with the first example, we will begin by showing the process up to the point where we arrive at the Inventive Principle solution suggestions.

b) Load/Capacity Balancing

The second case study examines a common problem in a wide variety of business settings; the balancing of load and capacity. The details of the business involved in the case are unimportant as far as explaining the process is concerned. As illustrated in Figure 11.8, the important aspect of the problem is that the company has a fixed number of employees and hence a fixed capacity, while the demand from customers, and hence load on the system, has a degree of seasonal variation.

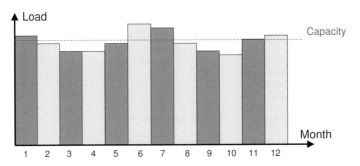

Figure 11.8: Typical Load/Capacity Balance Situation

The factory has traditionally matched load and capacity using contract workers. A recent analysis has shown that, unfortunately, the output of these workers is not to the same high standard as that produced by permanent staff and that this has lead to a series of customer complaints and lost revenues. In order to achieve the desired quality levels, therefore, the company has decided that in the future it wishes to use only permanent staff since they are more likely to have a long-standing commitment to the success of the company. The inevitable (and uncontrollable) variations in the load at the factory, however means that there are times when not all of these workers are required to work.

The start point for exploring this situation in more detail is to then identify possible conflicts that exist. A good way of starting this process is to identify what it is that we would like to improve. Well, since we have called this a load/capacity problem, it seems logical to say that this is the thing we would like to improve. The next question is 'what is stopping us from solving this problem? The answer to this one is a little less clear, and perhaps all we can say at this point in time is that it is our current method of working – with the permanent-worker-only decision as a potentially significant factor.

Next we have to translate these (admittedly vague) descriptions into the terms of the Matrix. We know that we are in a production environment so it looks like the 'production' related cluster of the Matrix parameters looks like a good start point. Looking then at the 'load/capacity balance' improving factor and recognizing that the balance problem exists due to seasonal (i.e. time) variation, the best means-the-same-as match in the Matrix then looks like Production Time. On the other side of the conflict pair, then, is 'our current way of working'. The best match to this description looks like Production Means. And so we now have established a conflict pair:

Thing we wish to improve : *Production Time*
Thing stopping us : *Production Means*

The Matrix then tells us that others have resolved this type of conflict using Principles

1 35 21 15 4 10

It is now up to us to translate these suggestions into specific solution possibilities for our problem situation. Let us explore that translation process in a little more detail than in the last example. We will focus on Principle 15, Dynamics, as this is the one that eventually lead to the solution that was actually implemented, but in doing so we recognize that exactly the same strategy would be applicable if we looked at each of the other suggested Principles (in fact, there may turn out to be solutions that turn out to be stronger in amongst the Principles we haven't looked at – consider that a challenge to find them for yourself).

If we look at the additional information that the list of Principles at the end of the Chapter gives us, we will see that Principle 15 includes the following:-

Principle 15. Dynamization
A. *Allow (or design) the characteristics of a system, object, external environment, or process to change to be optimal or to find an optimal operating condition.*
B. *Divide a system or object into parts capable of movement relative to each other.*
C. *If a system, object or process is rigid or inflexible, make it movable or adaptive.*

This is now all the detail that is available to us. If we are to make further progress with the problem it is going to be up to us to translate these solution suggestions into some we can apply to our specific situation. This means that we need to make some connections to our situation. Example: Principle 15B asks us to divide a system into parts. The first connection we can perhaps make, therefore, is that our factory is a 'system'. As soon as we have made this connection, we can begin to apply the direction suggested by the Principle – in this case 'divide the factory into parts'. Similarly, we might also connect the idea of a calendar year to the word 'object'. If we make this link, then again, the Principle offers the suggestion to 'divide the year into parts', and also – more intriguingly – 'allow those parts to move relative to each other'. So move February to October? Or Spring to Summer? It is not particularly clear that either might offer any kind of solution, but here lies an important aspect of how the conflict elimination tool works. The Principles are in many ways dumb; they merely say that other people have found that good things happen if you move in a certain direction. In this sense, they can be thought of as ways of getting us to think out of our box. If this sounds somewhat random, remember that, the evidence of nearly three million solutions has said that the directions are signposts to 'more ideal' systems; 'good things happen if you move in this direction'.

Let's try a different part of Principle 15 and see what effect it might have. 15C says 'if a system is rigid, make it movable'. If we are going to be able to use this suggestion then again we need to make some connections to our specific situation. In this case we might ask ourselves what are the things in the current system that are 'rigid'? Possible answers:

- the number of workers
- the product we manufacture
- the capacity
- the number of working days in the week
- the number of hours in a shift
- the number of shifts
- ...and so on

As soon as we have made any of these connections, the Principle is able to give us suggestions about what to do to solve the problem. In this case 'make the rigid thing movable or adaptive'. Again, some of the resulting solution directions perhaps don't make much immediate sense – an 'adaptive product' for example? – but others may immediately set us on course to success. Like the idea of a movable or adaptive number of working days per week? Or shift? Again, the method doesn't know which of these is any better or worse than any other, merely that 'somewhere' the concept of 'adaptive' is going to help solve problems. As it happens in this specific case, the idea of adaptive days-per-working week did not fit the constraint that the times when the greatest number of people was required, were the ones where workers were most likely to be going away for the weekend. The idea of flexible shifts (i.e. some days 7 hours; others 8 or 9 or 6), on the other hand, has delivered a very effective, and now deployed, win-win solution – the management get better load/capacity matching, and the workers, through a system that allows the length of a given working day to be altered, to better plan their life outside work. The improved business performance also ensures that the workers jobs will be secure in the long term.

c) Richness versus Reach At Charles Schwab

The case of security brokerage Charles Schwab's transition to leading e-based share dealer has been discussed on several occasions (References 11.5, 11.6). As discussed in Reference 11.6, the company has successfully challenged the richness (quality of information or service) versus reach (number of customers reached) conflict present in many walks of modern life. Figure 11.9 illustrates how they introduced first telephone brokerage and then touch-tone dialling as means of increasing reach. In both of these instances, the Figure shows, the increased reach was achieved at the expense of reductions in 'richness': a full-service dealer builds a relationship with a client which no telephone operator, and certainly no automatic telephone exchange can hope to match. The figure also illustrates how, when they introduced on-line dealing in 1998 (www.schwab.com), the company was successfully able to finally break the richness-reach conflict and became able to reach a very wide customer base with a service they now claim to offer higher richness than that achievable via a full service broker. The conflict is 'eliminated' here since the on-line service is able to provide large amounts of information that would previously have only been available through a dealer. Clearly there is no dealer directly involved in the on-line service, but if we imagine that the information of many dealers becomes integrated rather than just having access to the knowledge of one, then we can see that in many ways the on-line service offers greater richness than any individual dealer can offer.

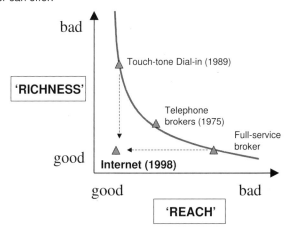

Figure 11.9: Richness versus Reach Conflict Broken by the Internet

In terms of the Business Conflict Matrix, the 'richness versus reach' conflict was judged to most closely match the Matrix parameters 'Supply Specification' and 'Supply Interface'. The use of an Internet solution to the conflict reflects the recommendation of Principle 35 ('shift from a physical to a virtual state') from the 'always consider these Principles' section of the Supply Specification part of the Matrix, Principle 6, 'Universality' (i.e. the Internet provides a universal communication protocol) and Principle 40 'Composite Structures' – which leads to the idea of combining the knowledge from multiple sources.

The Figure 11.9 image provides a further useful illustration of the difference between solutions that merely move a trade-off from one place to another, and those that genuinely seek to move the paradigm towards the no-compromise end-state. The case also provides additional demonstration of the conflict-elimination process. The main point of the case, however, is still ahead of us.

The use of an on-line solution to a business problem is used so commonly these days that it hardly seems worth going through the process of finding Inventive Principle 35 to get us to the idea. As effective as the on-line solution can be (if it is implemented correctly), it is ultimately just one (disruptive) step closer to an ideal final result end point. The real trick to the compromise elimination game – we think – is managing to stay one conflict ahead of the competition.

Remember the statement 'if the system exists, it contains compromises' from the beginning of the chapter? It implies that, if we're smart, we should be actively looking for some of the trade-offs and conflicts that still exist in the system, go around the process again and see if we can create an even more ideal solution.

For many people, the new conflict that emerges in relation to the richness-versus-reach problem is the one illustrated in Figure 11.10

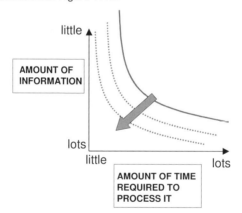

Figure 11.10: Richness versus Reach – The New Conflict

The big new conflict many of us face is that there are massive amounts of information available to us, but the time we have available to process that information is fixed (or in fact is reducing). Just as the process says that someone, somewhere already solved the richness-versus-reach problem, this time it will again tell us that someone (else), somewhere (else) has already solved the new problem. And so we go around the loop again – mapping the new problem to the Matrix (Loss of Information versus (Research) Time), and obtaining recommendations to use Inventive Principles 7, 2, 37, 20 and 25. We won't dwell too much on the use of these Principles to generate new solutions – although even a cursory examination of Principle 2 will quickly get us to the idea of emerging semantic processor technologies – but rather make the point that the whole dynamic of conflict elimination involves the successive emergence and resolution of trade-offs and compromises. In summary, thinking back to the fluid bag analogy at the start of the chapter, our aim is to use the Inventive Principles to progressively reduce the size of the bag – as illustrated in Figure 11.11:

Figure 11.11: Successive Conflict Elimination and the Fluid Filled Bag

d) Root Cause Analysis Paralysis

The final case study in this chapter perhaps gets us into more controversial territory. An article we published in 2002 (Reference 11.7) served to make us very unpopular with experts and devotees of root-cause analysis methods of problem solving. Our aim in both that article and here is to be provocative of course. But provocative with strong justification, we believe, since we seem to spend far too much of our time being asked to solve problems where the thirst for data in trying to locate root causes has caused all perspective on the economics of the situation to be lost. This last case-study – actually a more general discussion than the previous examples – tries to clarify our position for any of those people we have inadvertently offended in the recent past.

Let us begin by thinking about problems. Two basic scenarios should suffice to cover the relevant spectrum of possibilities. In the first we have a situation in which a problem has always been there, but we only just had to start worrying about it (nobody cared about defect rates at the start of the computer chip industry for example because everyone was making so much money from the good chips). In this case there is a clear need to acquire some data to find out what is happening. We need to ask 'why?' Why does the problem exist? We might conduct some experiments on the system to try and establish the conditions that make the problem disappear. This is the data we need in order that we might make some kind of reasoned decision on how to solve the problem. There is little getting around this need other than to make un-reasoned decisions. Which does happen, but not generally in organizations that stick around for very long. So, if we have **no** data, then we need to get some.

In the second scenario, a problem emerges because something has changed. In this situation we already have some data – we know that we have crossed some kind of a boundary; on one side of which there is no problem and on the other there is. In this kind of scenario there is usually a very strong desire to collect or acquire a bunch of data to explore the problem/no-problem boundary more completely – to understand how all of the possible system variables affect the whether the problem occurs or not.

The two scenarios define opposite sides of the root-cause-analysis versus root-cause-analysis-paralysis coin. Sensible problem solving requires the presence of data. The new problem then becomes one of balancing the cost of acquiring the data versus the benefit that solving the problem might bring. No data is bad, but too much data can be equally bad. Root cause analysis recognizes the first statement, but rarely the second.

Root cause analysis likes data. Lots of it. The more the better. There is little concept of 'enough' in root cause analysis.

This often unquenchable thirst for more data is the result of some very deeply engrained psychological inertia effects. Usually two that are significant:

1) The more data we have acquired, the more it looks and feels like we understand the system. Psychological inertia here is particularly cruel. It tells us that if we have acquired all this data and still don't get to solve the problem, it *must* be because we haven't acquired enough yet. Data breeds data breeds data. Often way beyond the bounds of common sense.

2) The more data we have acquired, the more we will have to discard if (when) the system changes. Discarding large quantities of expensive data is not something that comes easily to us. Consequently, the data encourages us to stick with the current system, and the more data we have, the more we 'lose' if we shift to a new system. Sticking with the current system and not being able to solve the problem sends us around a new vicious circle that says we just haven't found the 'right' data yet, and should therefore keep looking until we find it.

Simple economics should tell us that there is definitely such a thing as 'too much data'.

So in the first scenario we could see there was too little data, and in the second there is a tendency to get too much. Too much data? Too little data? Hmm. Perhaps this could suggest the presence of a conflict?

Should we try and work out, therefore, what the 'right' amount of data is? Do the trade-off calculations? Or should we try and eliminate the conflict?

The systematic innovation method would encourage us to think about the second option. In fact, it would further suggest that in this kind of too-little versus too-much trade-off situation, it is actually not the data we should be focusing on at all. Or at least not the type of data root cause analysis asks us to acquire. Use of Inventive Principle 35 – Parameter Changes – to challenge the conflict may suggest the need for some *different type* of data.

Root cause analysis is a tool of trade-off and optimization. It requires us to acquire data that will enable us to make the trade-off and optimization decisions as effectively as possible. It will enable us to plot the boundaries between problem and no-problem. What if this is the 'wrong sort of data'?

So What Is The Alternative?

Very simply, consider the possibility that the 'root cause' of any problem you are facing is that your system has hit a fundamental limit.

Difficult as it might be to believe, it is our experience that 80-90% of all the problem solving cases we come up against are precisely in this situation. If we take a moment to think about why this might be so, we might start to think about how the role of managers and leaders is to get as much as possible out of a system, to push systems as hard as possible, and that therefore, they are inherently driving them towards the limits of their capability - to the top of their s-curve -right from day one. Figure 11.12 provides a useful illustration of the potential consequences of this scenario.

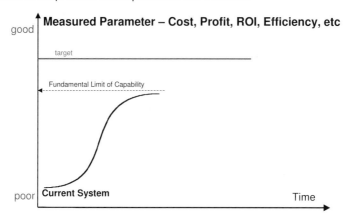

Figure 11.12: System At Fundamental Limit As A Problem Root Cause

When a system has reached this top-of-the-s-curve state, there is simply no point in investing money to acquire more trade-off and optimization data. Fundamental, in system evolution terms, unfortunately means fundamental. You would like to improve some aspect of a system and something is now stopping you from doing it. Hey, you have found a conflict. It applies to both of the problem scenarios at the beginning of this section. In the first scenario, the thing you want to improve is the problem; and you need to identify the 'what's stopping' part. In the second scenario, you already know what has changed in your system, and so already have a good idea of what is in conflict with what else. In both situations, we say save your root-cause analysis data acquisition time and money and invest it instead in resolving the conflicts. Resolving conflicts breaks us out of the trade-off and optimization mindset. It enables us to find new s-curves.

This limit-finding activity is something we call 'root conflict analysis' (Reference 11.8). In the first instance it involves asking a pair of questions. 1) What is it that we would like to improve? 2) What is it that is stopping us (or gets worse)? While answering these questions – or the second one at least – may not be immediately obvious (in which case, that's where we need to focus our data finding activities), overwhelming evidence suggests that it is a much more effective use of time than setting up a programme of experiments to 'acquire more data' to feed root cause analysis methods.

Its not about data, it's about the right kind of data.

Root cause analysis encourages us to find trade-off and optimisation data. Numbers. Root conflict analysis encourages us to find out what is stopping the system from improving. Parameters. Parameters tend to be easier to identify than numbers. They are also very much cheaper. Even more important, the benefits of solving the root conflict are very often many times greater than a trade-off and optimization solution. Take the earlier Maintenance Department problem and look in Chapter 8 at the solution strategy suggestions made by the managers; set up a database, install a statistical process control system. Measurements, measurements. 'If in doubt, measure something' seems to be a very commonly applied management strategy. It is certainly easier than thinking. In actual fact, the 'real' problem in the Maintenance Department situation turns out to be that the system (or the Maintenance Department part of the system) has hit a limit. SPC could have been applied to the defect rate problem from now until the end of time and the problem would still have existed. Again, trade-off and optimization is sometimes not the right thing to be doing.

Less money and a better solution? Does that sound like a more ideal solution? We think so. Root-cause analysis has its place. If 80-90% of business and management problems are really ones where a system or one of its elements has hit a limit, though, that should suggest that the usefulness of root-cause analysis is highly likely to be limited or non-existent. Even if you don't believe that root-conflict analysis is a serious alternative (yet!), at the very least accept that it is quick and cheap to give it a try.

3) What Happens When The Conflict Matrix Doesn't Work?

The Business Conflict Matrix was never intended to be infallible; merely a useful start point for addressing a business or management problem situation in a win-win manner. The Matrix has been constructed through a combination of distilling best win-win practice from as many published business success stories as possible (a very high proportion of the, currently, several hundred have been included in the analysis) and through synthesis of best solutions to generic business conflict situations as judged by a panel of experts. Readers interested in seeing more details of the strategy and process of constructing and populating the Matrix may care to examine Reference 11.4. The Matrix published here, therefore, is very much a distillation of past and current best practice. It is highly likely – as we have observed with the technical version of the Matrix (Reference 11.3) that the content can shift significantly over a period of years as problem solvers uncover new ways of doing things. There are two consequences of this evolving state of affairs. The first is that we are continually seeking out new case studies and adding them to the Matrix database. The second – the one of direct relevance here – is that occasionally it is advisable to adopt alternative or supplementary strategies to the Matrix method.

One very simple such strategy is to simply apply all 40 of the Inventive Principles to a problem. One thing that appears to be highly stable regarding possible strategies for eliminating business conflicts is the number of possible ways of doing it. Although we spend our days looking for solutions that result from the application of strategies outside the current list of 40, as yet we haven't found any. The last addition to the list, in fact, when we look across all areas of human endeavour, was over twenty years ago. This is not to say that there isn't a 41st or a 42nd Principle out there somewhere; merely that wherever we look, we can't find them. So, unless you are in the business of re-inventing the planet, it is extremely highly likely that if there is a win-win solution to your problem, it is going to come from one or more of the existing 40 Principles. What we can perfectly legitimately do, therefore, is use all 40; trying to connect each one to our given problem situation and using those connections to generate hopefully useful solution ideas. (Ideally, if we are going to adopt this strategy, we should use a random and shifting sequence of Principles so that we don't eventually get bored fall into a rut.) This 'use all 40' strategy is a perfectly valid course of action. The only real problem with it, in fact, is that there is a strong tendency to lose momentum when trying to investigate all 40 routes; and that consequently some will be given less than adequate consideration.

We present here four alternative routes to the 'use all 40' option, with the recommendation that none of them, like the Matrix, are intended to be in any way the definitive 'right' way. The general idea, then, is that you find one or more of the available strategies that fits the

way your brain, or the collective brain of your team, works the best and use that one. Alternatively, of course, you could develop your own strategies. The four alternatives discussed here are:-
  a) Basing selection on a 'most commonly used' sequence
  b) Basing selection on what parameters you are trying to improve
  c) Basing selection on the complexity of the system you are dealing with
  d) Looking at the Principles from a completely different perspective.

a) Principle Selection Based on 'Most Commonly Used' Sequence

A slightly less random approach than simply working through all 40 Inventive Principles emerges by examining which of the Principles have been responsible for delivering the greatest number of successful solutions. Extracting this information from the data that enabled the Matrix to be constructed gives the following sequence. Principles are listed in descending order of frequency of successful application. Hence, we see that Inventive Principle 35 is the most commonly used; Principle 2, the second most common, and so on through to Principle 36 down in 40th place.

	1st	2nd	3rd	4th	5th	6th	7th	8th	9th	10th
0	35	2	25	10	13	3	1	15	5	24
+10	6	37	28	7	29	40	19	26	17	27
+20	4	23	11	22	30	12	32	9	31	38
+30	16	14	39	18	20	34	33	8	21	36

Thus, if we find that the time available to generate possible solutions to a problem is limited, and we do not have a clear definition of the situation that we are trying to improve, this table offers some suggestions on which Principles are – on a global average basis – most likely to point us in the right direction.

To add a little more detail to the picture, it is also worth noting that there are big gaps in likelihood between the 4th and 5th place (i.e. the first four Principles are significantly more likely to deliver results than the next four), between the 7th and 8th places, and between 26th and 27th.

b) Principle Selection Based on Improving Parameter

Some users find it difficult to formulate the conflicts present in the systems they are evaluating. The problem usually relates to identification of the worsening parameters – the things stopping the desired improvement from occurring. Most users, on the other hand, find it relatively simple to work out what it is they wish to improve.

Although we always recommend that people try to formulate complete conflict pairs – reason; because it is often profoundly important to understanding what is happening in a system – some will always wish to take a short-cut.

We have provided means of making such short-cuts in the way in which the Matrix is presented in the reference section. There, for each of the 'Improving Parameters', you will find two section headings:
  • Inventive Principles that should always be considered for problems where we wish to improve this parameter

- Averaged list of other Principles that should be considered where we wish to improve this parameter (decreasing order of frequency)

These categories offer two short-cut opportunities. The first category – parameters that should always be considered – are the ones that provoke questions that are always worth asking whenever we are looking to improve an aspect of a business. We might not be able to generate anything specifically useful from them for every specific instance, but it is important that we at least ask the question.

The second –averaged list – category is the part where the globally averaged list of most likely Principles for each of the improving parameters has been calculated and presented. This information results from an exercise to integrate the solution contents of each of the conflict-pairs for the given improving parameter. Thus, if you know that you wish to improve, say, Stability, but you don't know what it is that is stopping you, it is possible to obtain a list of most likely Principles to help you generate win-win solution ideas.

c) Principle Selection Based on System Complexity

One of the trends of evolution identified during the systematic innovation research (Chapter 14) highlights the manner in which systems evolve in a way that means their overall complexity (usually correlated at least in part to the number of elements in a system) increases and then decreases over the span of a given s-curve. With this increasing-then-decreasing element count idea in mind, examination of the Inventive Principles suggests that certain of the complexity or number of elements:

Principles Associated With Increasing Number of Elements
(In numerical order)

Principle 1 – Segmentation – usually implies increased number of elements or re-distribution or re-organisation of existing resources rather than necessarily addition of new resources

Principle 7 – Nested Doll

Principle 8 – Counterbalance – implies addition of something to counter the out of balance elements of a problem.

Principle 9 – Preliminary Anti-Action – as 10 below

Principle 10 – Preliminary Action – implies supply of additional things to perform the preliminary action

Principle 11 – Beforehand Cushioning – addition of something to counter non-desirable affect in current system.

Principle 15 – Dynamics – transition from immobile to mobile system generally implies addition of elements to permit relative movement of different sub-components

Principle 23 – Feedback – addition of elements or communication links required to first sense and then relay feedback messages

Principle 24 – Intermediary

Principle 27 – Cheap Short-Living Objects ('replace an expensive object with a multiple of inexpensive objects, compromising certain qualities')

Principle 38 – Enriched Atmosphere – addition of active elements plus possible need for additional elements to contain or control the active element.

Principle 39 – Inert Atmosphere – similar to Principle 38; addition of inert elements may also prompt addition of other elements to contain or control the inert elements.

Principles Associated With Decreasing Number of Elements
(In numerical order)

Principle 2 – Taking Out

Principle 3 – Local Quality – implies making existing elements be modified to achieve the functions of several.

Principle 5 – Merging

Principle 6 – Universality ('make an object or system perform multiple functions')

Principle 20 – Continuity of Useful Action ('B: eliminate all idle or intermittent actions or work')

Principle 25 – Self-Service

Principle 40 – Composite Structures – combining multiple structures/functions into a coherent composite structure.

Bringing the 'increasing' and 'decreasing' Principles together onto one picture (also showing the system complexity evolution trend) gives the reference image shown in Figure 11.13. It is hoped that this picture will be of some value to problem owners working in areas where the Matrix does not fit with working methods or is not effective.

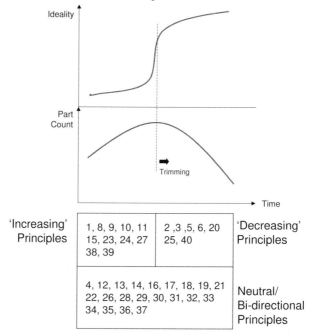

Figure 11.13: Influence of Problem Type on Inventive Principle Selection

Note that some of the Principles cannot be categorised into either 'increasing' or 'decreasing' part count usage because they are either part-count neutral ('Colour Changes') or may cause part count to change in either direction depending on the particular circumstances of the system.

These patterns can often be useful in reducing the number of Inventive Principles that might be relevant to a given problem type: There is little point in looking at Principles that will increase system complexity at a time in the evolution of a system where the trend indicates the need for a reducing strategy for example.

d) Different Perspectives

For many users, the 40 Inventive Principles are a very effective series of solution triggers. Used at this fairly basic level, they may be seen as a more comprehensive version of the SCAMMPERR model developed by Osborn (Reference 11.9). The problem with the 40 Principles for many newcomers, however is that 40 is a lot of triggers to remember. Most people keep a list with them, but there is the bigger issue that our brains are wired with a short-term memory store capable of storing only around about 7 different pieces of information. Actually 7 ± 2. We wondered, therefore whether it would be possible to re-configure the 40 Principles into a structure that would ease our ability to remember them. As we progressed, incorporating NLP thinking and the SCAMMPERR model, we believe that it has been possible to not only achieve this, but also enrich the overall quality of the Principles.

In the first instance, we saw the space-time-interface dimensional thinking concept discussed in Chapter 2 as an important start point. Many will notice how some of the Principles can be related to all three dimensions – Segmentation for example can be applied as a conflict eliminating strategy with respect to physical segmentation, segmentation of time (see also 'Periodic Action' – which might specifically be seen as 'segmentation of time') and segmentation of the interfaces between things. We also noted that some Principles had analogues that reversed the Principle – e.g. 'Segmentation' and 'Merging' are often interpreted as two opposites. Some on the other hand didn't – Asymmetry being one such example. When asking the question 'would it be possible to challenge a conflict by making something symmetrical instead of asymmetrical, we answered with a definitive yes. The opposite can also occur, balance and proportion then becoming important factors. The same happened with many other Principles.

Next we looked at our space-time-and interface entities and saw that within each category, all of the Principles grouped into just five different strategies for modifying a system :-
1) segment or merge (i.e. change the number of entities)
2) make the entities bigger or smaller
3) change the external form
4) change the internal structure
5) substitute the existing structure for something else.

We then found that the existing Principles fitted very neatly into a 5x3 matrix as illustrated in Figure 11.14.

The figure diagonally divides each box to illustrate that every one has both its positive and negative sense. It also illustrates the relative position of each of the 40 Principles within the structure. Thus Principle 13 – the other way around – now features implicitly in each element of the Principle Matrix.

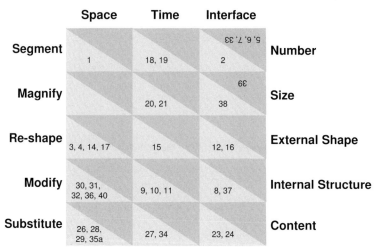

	Space	Time	Interface	
Segment	1	18, 19	5, 6, 7, 33 2	**Number**
Magnify		20, 21	39 38	**Size**
Re-shape	3, 4, 14, 17	15	12, 16	**External Shape**
Modify	30, 31, 32, 36, 40	9, 10, 11	8, 37	**Internal Structure**
Substitute	26, 28, 29, 35a	27, 34	23, 24	**Content**

Figure 11.14: Revised Inventive Principles Structure

Actually, we found two other special case Principles that did not fit into the Matrix, but fitted instead into the higher order philosophical level. These were:-

> 25 Self-Service – This is a Principle that is highly connected to the Ideality concept.

> 22 Blessing in Disguise – in a similar vein, this Principle encourages users to think about the resources element of the systematic innovation philosophy.

In examining the SCAMMPERR model in more detail, we found that while 8 of the 9 strategies in the model were covered by the Inventive Principles and by the 5x3 matrix framework above, the 'P' – 'put to another use' was not. In SCAMMPERR, this trigger encourages users to solve problems by changing function. This is not normal systematic innovation practice, but, again, when we asked the question 'would it be possible to challenge a conflict by changing function, the answer was an unqualified 'yes'. For example, here is a quote from Reference 11.10:

"Not long ago, Pfizer invested considerable energy and resources in a drug for treating hypertension. Tests indicated that its effects in hypertension were not all we had anticipated. This disappointment was offset by tests indicating that it would prove a much better treatment for arrhythmia – irregular heartbeat – than any other available medication. Another medicine, which was slated to treat anxiety, seems to be a very effective headache remedy."

"On another occasion, our researchers were dissatisfied with the performance of a new medication we had developed to treat angina; it failed to alleviate angina's paroxysmal chest pains. Serendipity intervened, however, and defeat emerged as opportunity. By chance we discovered the medication's extraordinary side effect: It restores sexual vigor to the impotent. The US market for such a drug is significant. Impotence afflicts some 20 million men in this country alone."

Taken together with the above Principles 22 and 25, we believe this 'change function' Principle forms a useful third entry in a trio of special Principles linked directly to five of the philosophical strands of systematic innovation. I.e.

Functionality	-	Change Function
Resources	-	Blessing in Disguise
Ideality	-	Self-Service
Space/Time	-	New 5x3 Matrix
Conflicts	-	New 5x3 Matrix

So, we found it was not possible to quite achieve the 7 ± 2 model – having 3 special Principles plus 8 labels for the Matrix. But what we did have was a system that featured significantly greater richness than the 40 Principles. The 40 Principles for example do not explicitly suggest that making a system or object physically bigger or smaller is a way of solving a conflict (although Principle 21 – Hurrying does do in the time dimension – see figure). Similarly, some of the 40 Principles (e.g. Local Quality and Asymmetry) are traditionally directed towards a physical interpretation – whereas in each case there are very definite time and interface analogies of the Principle.

Thus (SPACE-TIME-INTERFACE) + (SEGMENT, SIZE, SHAPE, STRUCTURE, SUBSTITUTE) + (FUNCTION-IDEALITY-RESOURCES) – SIT-5S-FIR – provides a means of remembering a richer, more structured version of the 40 Principles.

Or (more closely related to a start-point at the main philosophical elements of systematic innovation):

FUNCTIONALITY-IDEALITY-RESOURCES-(SPACE-TIME-INTERFACE)-CONTRADICTIONS
|
5S

(Read more about this re-framing of the Inventive Principles in Reference 11.11.)

Final Thought

The concept of trade-off or compromise or conflict elimination as the primary driving force of the evolution of systems means that it is very difficult to justify ignoring the content of this chapter. We have hopefully written it in a way that everyone takes away at least something that they can and want to try out on some real problems. Whether you liked the Matrix or the Principles, or one of the short cuts, or maybe even just one or two of the Principles, there is a final important point to make about the strength of the solutions we are able to generate.

Extensive research aimed at correlating the very best solutions to the strategies that problem solvers have used to achieve them has resulted in one consistent conclusion;

**The stronger the solution,
the greater the
number of Principles
that have been deployed
to achieve it.**

Net consequence; as we try and evolve systems in the direction of literally eliminating all of the conflicts – as per Figure 11.4 (reproduced below) – it is advisable to use several

Principles to generate ideas, and to then explore ways of combining the various ideas emerging from each Principle into a single coherent, integrated solution.

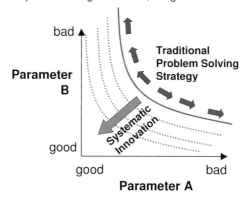

What Do I Do?

The conflict elimination tool is quite possibly the first thing that many systematic innovation newcomers will be exposed to. Often, unfortunately, the concept of compromise elimination is often quite difficult to achieve – hey, something that has delivered several billion dollars of added value in other companies ought not to be too easy, right? – but at least we can claim here that there is a systematic process to help us get to where we want to be.

The conflict elimination tools are a very important part of the overall systematic innovation philosophy. In the first instance, we therefore suggest that users familiarise themselves with the form and content of the Business Conflict Matrix and Inventive Principles listings in the following reference section. Specifically, it is a good idea to become familiar with the parameters contained in the Matrix and the Principles.

As stated earlier, 'if a system exists, it contains conflicts and compromises'. The next stage of the process of using this part of the conflict elimination tool then requires that we are able to identify some of those conflicts. If we have entered this chapter following a recommendation from Chapter 9, it probably means that we have already identified good conflicts from either an FAA analysis or from an s-curve analysis. Alternatively, it is very often possible to begin to compile a list of conflicts and compromises very simply by writing a two-column list; writing down all the things you would like to improve about your system in the first column, and then all the things that are stopping you from making the improvement in the second.

How we then actually use the tool depends largely on preferred ways of working. Some people prefer to just use the Inventive Principles; others like the idea that the Matrix will reduce the number of possible Principles to be evaluated, while still others will prefer some of the alternative strategies related in the latter part of the chapter. The main message here, is to find strategies that best suit your way of doing things.

The Inventive Principles suggested by the method are quite generic in nature. Effective use demands familiarity with the way in which the human brain works as an effective connector of ideas. In this regard, we recommend that you examine the content of Chapter 3.

References

1) Stalk, G., Pecaut, D.K., Burnett, B., 'Breaking Compromises, Breakaway Growth', paper in 'Markets of One', Harvard Business School Press, 2000.
2) Altshuller, G., 'Creativity As An Exact Science', Gordon & Breach, New York, 1985.
3) Mann, D.L., Dewulf, S., Zlotin, B., Zusman, A., 'Matrix 2003: Updating The TRIZ Contradiction Matrix', CREAX Press, Belgium, July 2003.
4) Mann, D.L., 'Systematic Win-Win Problem Solving In A Business Environment', paper presented at TRIZCON2002, St Louis, March 2002.
5) Mann, D.L., Domb, E., 'Using TRIZ to Analyse and Solve Mass Customization Contradictions', European TRIZ Association 'TRIZ Future 2001' conference, Bath, November 2001.
6) Evans, P., Wurster, T.S., 'Blown To Bits: How The New Economics of Information Transforms Strategy", Harvard Business School Press, 2000.
7) Mann, D.L., 'Root Cause Analysis Paralysis', TRIZ Journal, May 2002
8) Mann, D.L., 'Hands-On Systematic Innovation', CREAX Press, 2002.
9) Osborn, A.F., 'Applied Imagination: Principles and Procedures of Creative Problem-Solving', Scribners, 1963.
10) Kanter, R.M., Kao, J., Wiersma, F., 'Innovation: Breakthrough Thinking at 3M, DuPont, GE, Pfizer and Rubbermaid', Harper Business, 1997.
11) Mann, D.L., 'Evolving The Inventive Principles', TRIZ Journal, August 2002.

4) Conflict Elimination Reference Section

This section is divided into two different parts. The first part provides the content of the Business Conflict Matrix. The Matrix contains a two-page segment for each of the 31 improving parameters. In each of these segments you will find a description of what each parameter means and a list of related words and meanings, followed by lists of the Inventive Principles most likely to help the given parameter to be improved under a series of different situations. Here, there are three main ways in which this Inventive Principle information is presented;

1) a list of Inventive Principles that should always be considered when trying to improve the parameter at hand
2) a prioritized list of Principles that other people have, on average, found to be most useful in helping to improve the parameter at hand, and
3) a table containing Inventive Principle suggestions for each of the other parameters that may be in conflict with the parameter which we are trying to improve.

We have left some space in these segments for you to add your own notes and discoveries as you become more familiar with the Matrix and begin to use it to generate your own successful win-win solutions.

The second part of the reference section contains a listing of the 40 Inventive Principles. Here we list detailed interpretations of each Principle and a series of illustrative examples of the Principle in action. Again, we invite readers to add their own examples to this list as they observe or discover other applications.

1

Parameter We Want to Improve – R&D Spec/Capability/Means

Meanings: 'R&D' perhaps implies a bias towards high technology manufacturing industry – where the term is most frequently used. The meaning here, however is intended to be much more general; referring to all of those activities that occur in conceptualising, trialing, beta-testing, verifying and validating any kind of novel product, process or service before it is finalised and offered as a final entity to customers.

'Specification/Capability/Means' relate to quality related aspects of a product, process or service. Again intended to be general, the terms relate to the quality of what is produced, and the means by which we achieve it. The term should be interpreted to include both tangible and intangible elements – i.e. knowledge, emotional qualities, etc as well as physical artefacts or functional services.

Synonyms, Antonyms and Equivalent Meanings: business concept innovation, new product development, proof-of-concept, pre-production, trial version, alpha, beta, experimental, novel, advanced, early adopter products/services, bread-board, Quality, output, defects, concessions, rapid-prototyping and other advanced one-off manufacture methods, certification standards, qualification activities.

Inventive Principles that should always be considered for problems where we wish to improve this parameter:

2, 10, 22, 25

Averaged list of other Principles that should be considered where we wish to improve this parameter (decreasing order of frequency):

25, 2, 35, 15, 3, 13, 5, 11, 6, 10, 23, 38

List of Principles relevant to each specific worsening parameter:

Worsening Parameter	Description	List of Relevant Inventive Principles (decreasing order of frequency)
1	R&D Spec/Capability/Means	(see Physical Contradictions section)
2	R&D Cost	2 4 15 38
3	R&D Time	21 38 35 23 15
4	R&D Risk	3 9 24 23 36 11
5	R&D Interfaces	3 13 24 33 38 25
6	Production Spec/Capability/Means	23 29 35 4 13 5
7	Production Cost	37 35 10 3 6
8	Production Time	35 6 10 2 20

9	Production Risk	3 5 10 2 23 12
10	Production Interfaces	5 7 37 1 4
11	Supply Spec/Capability/Means	6 2 35 25 3
12	Supply Cost	15 6 1 5 13
13	Supply Time	2 3 12 26 19 38
14	Supply Risk	11 39 30 31
15	Supply Interfaces	11 26 2 5 13
16	Support Spec/Capability/Means	36 11 2 35 27
17	Support Cost	15 35 28 25 29
18	Support Time	5 2 6 27 25
19	Support Risk	15 27 40 12 27
20	Support Interfaces	11 2 5 9 26
21	Customer Revenue/Demand/Feedback	14 13 22 7 10
22	Amount Of Information	37 13 25 10 39
23	Communication Flow	6 25 31 29 7 23
24	Harmful Factors Affecting System	11 25 2 26 3
25	System Generated Harmful Factors	25 29 2 37 13
26	Convenience	15 35 25 16 28
27	Adaptability/Versatility	30 25 29 1 35
28	System Complexity	17 25 1 19 35
29	Control Complexity	25 15 19 35
30	Tension/Stress	3 2 25 35 9
31	Stability	25 2 15 36 29

Notes:

Combination of Principles 25 and 38 - autonomous creatives working in a suitably enriched environment (e.g. Lockheed Skunkworks) – delivers a highly effective R&D solution.

2
Parameter We Want to Improve – R&D Cost

Meaning: 'R&D' perhaps implies a bias towards high technology manufacturing industry – where the term is most frequently used. The meaning here, however is intended to be much more general; referring to all of those activities that occur in conceptualising, trialing, beta-testing, verifying and validating any kind of novel product, process or service before it is finalised and offered as a final entity to customers.

Cost: anything relating to financial matters. Costs can be direct or indirect, visible or invisible, tangible or intangible. In the context of this parameter, 'cost' can also mean waste of money or other forms of financial resource.

Synonyms, Antonyms and Equivalent Meanings: price, subcontract cost, contingency, redundant costs, cost of unused fall-back solutions, investment cost, opportunity cost, risk capital, overhead, IP costs, value, seed-money, venture capital, government support funding.

Inventive Principles that should always be considered for problems where we wish to improve this parameter:

6, 10, 22, 25

Averaged list of other Principles that should be considered where we wish to improve this parameter (decreasing order of frequency):

10, 2, 1, 6, 25, 35, 27, 13, 26, 28, 15, 19, 37

List of Principles relevant to each specific worsening parameter:

Worsening Parameter	Description	List of Relevant Inventive Principles (decreasing order of frequency)
1	R&D Spec/Capability/Means	2 4 15 38
2	R&D Cost	(see Physical Contradictions section)
3	R&D Time	26 34 1 10 3
4	R&D Risk	27 9 34 16 37
5	R&D Interfaces	13 26 35 10 1
6	Production Spec/Capability/Means	5 2 27 1
7	Production Cost	26 35 1 7 27 34 3
8	Production Time	10 2 6 15
9	Production Risk	6 7 23 26 13
10	Production Interfaces	15 35 10 25 24
11	Supply Spec/Capability/Means	23 6 11 28

12	Supply Cost	10 5 35
13	Supply Time	10 19 35 22
14	Supply Risk	11 13 2 16
15	Supply Interfaces	10 38 13
16	Support Spec/Capability/Means	27 6 1 10
17	Support Cost	6 1 10 25 13
18	Support Time	6 1 25 10 27
19	Support Risk	10 25 22 2
20	Support Interfaces	6 10 1 7 20
21	Customer Revenue/Demand/Feedback	7 25 30 21 10 9 2
22	Amount Of Information	37 25 28 2 32
23	Communication Flow	6 18 37 13 25 22
24	Harmful Factors Affecting System	35 27 3 28 2
25	System Generated Harmful Factors	28 26 2 22 8 35
26	Convenience	25 2 6 5 40
27	Adaptability/Versatility	35 28 19 1 8
28	System Complexity	5 2 35 1 29
29	Control Complexity	25 19 2 37 32
30	Tension/Stress	1 19 35 27 2 18
31	Stability	11 25 27 15 2

Notes:

3
Parameter We Want to Improve – R&D Time

Meaning: 'R&D' perhaps implies a bias towards high technology manufacturing industry – where the term is most frequently used. The meaning here, however is intended to be much more general; referring to all of those activities that occur in conceptualising, trialing, beta-testing, verifying and validating any kind of novel product, process or service before it is finalised and offered as a final entity to customers.

'Time'; anything relating to temporal issues. This includes the time and level of effort required to do something, both visible and invisible, tangible and intangible. The emphasis here is on issues where time is the specific focus (in line with the axiom 'time is money', if we are interested in financial implications rather than the actual time itself, the 'Cost' parameter should be used in preference to this on).

Synonyms, Antonyms and Equivalent Meanings: critical path, parallel activities, sequential activities, waiting time, overtime, working hours, shift length, shift pattern, lost time, meeting time, standard hours, meetings, approval delay, launch-date, late, overdue, insufficient time, late-start, early-start, race-to-market, first-to-market.

Inventive Principles that should always be considered for problems where we wish to improve this parameter:

6, 10, 38

Averaged list of other Principles that should be considered where we wish to improve this parameter (decreasing order of frequency):

2, 35, 15, 7, 10, 6, 40, 26, 25, 37, 24

List of Principles relevant to each specific worsening parameter:

Worsening Parameter	Description	List of Relevant Inventive Principles (decreasing order of frequency)
1	R&D Spec/Capability/Means	21 38 35 23 15
2	R&D Cost	26 34 1 10 3
3	R&D Time	(see Physical Contradictions section)
4	R&D Risk	1 29 10 40 11
5	R&D Interfaces	15 25 35 1 40
6	Production Spec/Capability/Means	5 6 20 35 2
7	Production Cost	5 29 35 2
8	Production Time	7 26 10 15 3
9	Production Risk	6 15 7 37 13 9
10	Production Interfaces	25 23 35 29 2 13

11	Supply Spec/Capability/Means	11 6 23 19 18 2
12	Supply Cost	5 13 23 25
13	Supply Time	10 25 7 2
14	Supply Risk	23 7 29 2 24 37
15	Supply Interfaces	11 7 40 38 24 2
16	Support Spec/Capability/Means	6 10 3 35 20
17	Support Cost	7 15 40 26 5
18	Support Time	7 40 1 26 15
19	Support Risk	23 24 2 37 7
20	Support Interfaces	6 10 26 24 2 38
21	Customer Revenue/Demand/Feedback	7 19 21 29 30
22	Amount Of Information	7 2 37 20 25
23	Communication Flow	6 26 18 19 40
24	Harmful Factors Affecting System	26 2 35 24 11
25	System Generated Harmful Factors	26 2 15 19 35 40
26	Convenience	1 2 15 19 25 28
27	Adaptability/Versatility	15 1 35 14 4
28	System Complexity	5 6 25 10 2 37
29	Control Complexity	25 28 15 2 6 37
30	Tension/Stress	2 39 24 10 4 13
31	Stability	10 3 35 22 27

Notes:

Use of Principle 37, 'Relative Change' is particularly important from a data gathering perspective – suggesting the need, often, for relative rather than absolute data for decision making purposes.

4
Parameter We Want to Improve – R&D Risk

Meaning: 'R&D' perhaps implies a bias towards high technology manufacturing industry – where the term is most frequently used. The meaning here, however is intended to be much more general; referring to all of those activities that occur in conceptualising, trialing, beta-testing, verifying and validating any kind of novel product, process or service before it is finalised and offered as a final entity to customers.

'Risk'; matters associated with likelihood and consequences of things happening that will cause a deviation from established plans. Risk can, of course, be manifested in terms of quality, specification, time or cost. This parameter seeks to encourage users to focus on risk in its most general sense. Where a risk could apply to any or all of the cost, time or quality parameters, this is the one that should be used.

Synonyms, Antonyms and Equivalent Meanings: likelihood, consequence, probability of failure, contingency, fall-back, alternative, tipping point, moving goal-posts, back-up, reserve, liability, infringement (IP), 'design-for-Murphy', robust design, stability, vulnerability, sensitivity.

Inventive Principles that should always be considered for problems where we wish to improve this parameter:

6, 10, 15, 35, 36

Averaged list of other Principles that should be considered where we wish to improve this parameter (decreasing order of frequency):

1, 13, 35, 11, 9, 26, 2, 7, 3, 40, 25

List of Principles relevant to each specific worsening parameter:

Worsening Parameter	Description	List of Relevant Inventive Principles (decreasing order of frequency)
1	R&D Spec/Capability/Means	3 9 24 23 36 11
2	R&D Cost	27 9 34 16 37
3	R&D Time	1 29 10 40 11
4	R&D Risk	(see Physical Contradictions section)
5	R&D Interfaces	6 29 15 14 17 25
6	Production Spec/Capability/Means	24 35 10 3 13 11
7	Production Cost	5 35 40 23 1 12
8	Production Time	5 40 20 15
9	Production Risk	11 23 39 7 9 33
10	Production Interfaces	7 3 17 23 24

11	Supply Spec/Capability/Means	5 35 13 26 6
12	Supply Cost	1 11 2 34
13	Supply Time	1 2 11 38 15
14	Supply Risk	13 7 9 37 12
15	Supply Interfaces	13 22 25 9 35 26
16	Support Spec/Capability/Means	6 1 26 37 15
17	Support Cost	11 7 28 35
18	Support Time	1 2 32 28 7
19	Support Risk	40 36 6 10 26 13
20	Support Interfaces	6 10 7 26 13
21	Customer Revenue/Demand/Feedback	36 13 25 22 37 3
22	Amount Of Information	1 3 10 26 25 4 37
23	Communication Flow	30 6 31 4 9 13 22
24	Harmful Factors Affecting System	35 2 15 26 3
25	System Generated Harmful Factors	2 3 35 15 12 9
26	Convenience	26 3 11 24 5 13 40
27	Adaptability/Versatility	2 40 31 28 35 29 7
28	System Complexity	28 30 35 1 17
29	Control Complexity	25 1 3 37 40 12 24
30	Tension/Stress	1 23 2 25 13 39
31	Stability	9 14 1 12 4

Notes:

5
Parameter We Want to Improve – R&D Interfaces

Meaning: 'R&D' perhaps implies a bias towards high technology manufacturing industry – where the term is most frequently used. The meaning here, however is intended to be much more general; referring to all of those activities that occur in conceptualising, trialing, beta-testing, verifying and validating any kind of novel product, process or service before it is finalised and offered as a final entity to customers.

'Interfaces'; issues relating to the connections that exist (or don't exist but should) between different parts of a system. This may be interpreted as person-to-person, peer-to-peer, department-to-department, division-to-division, B2B, B2C or any other relationship between one entity and another. Interfaces can be internal or external, formal or formal, and there will always be elements of tangible and intangible interfaces. Interfaces can be verbal, written, legal, visual, etc.

If there is an interface issue relating to two different parts of an organisation – say between R&D and production' then this should be modelled as a conflict between the 'R&D Interfaces' and 'Production Interfaces' parameters.

Synonyms, Antonyms and Equivalent Meanings: relationship, interaction, communication links, command structure, network, authority, peer, spoken, hand-shake, 'old-pals act', not-invented-here, commanders intent, edict, buy-in, people, perceptions, 'the map is not the territory', perspective, fear, authority, rights, responsibilities, friendship, rivalry, respect, trust, dependence, independence, dispute, argument, consensus, agreement, protocol.

Inventive Principles that should always be considered for problems where we wish to improve this parameter:

2, 12, 22, 27, 35

Averaged list of other Principles that should be considered where we wish to improve this parameter (decreasing order of frequency):

3, 35, 40, 6, 13, 25, 28, 15, 10, 1, 37

List of Principles relevant to each specific worsening parameter:

Worsening Parameter	Description	List of Relevant Inventive Principles (decreasing order of frequency)
1	R&D Spec/Capability/Means	3 13 24 33 38 25
2	R&D Cost	13 26 35 10 1
3	R&D Time	15 25 35 1 40

4	R&D Risk	6 29 15 14 17 25
5	R&D Interfaces	(see Physical Contradictions section)
6	Production Spec/Capability/Means	5 6 17 40 33 10 26
7	Production Cost	15 23 29 5 13
8	Production Time	15 40 23 3 24 13
9	Production Risk	7 5 3 37 10
10	Production Interfaces	28 40 6 29 13 31 30
11	Supply Spec/Capability/Means	6 35 15 13 14
12	Supply Cost	2 33 3 15 10
13	Supply Time	5 2 35 10 12
14	Supply Risk	5 35 13 40 3 9
15	Supply Interfaces	28 40 6 15 29
16	Support Spec/Capability/Means	6 1 3 35 21 12
17	Support Cost	6 7 40 38 13
18	Support Time	6 38 20 10 37
19	Support Risk	5 35 40 13
20	Support Interfaces	28 40 6 7 30
21	Customer Revenue/Demand/Feedback	4 7 25 40 13 35 28
22	Amount Of Information	1 6 3 40 25
23	Communication Flow	2 6 35 3 25 18
24	Harmful Factors Affecting System	3 26 35 28 24
25	System Generated Harmful Factors	3 26 35 37 2 40
26	Convenience	16 13 25 28 37
27	Adaptability/Versatility	29 37 40 1 35 17 30
28	System Complexity	25 28 1 3 10
29	Control Complexity	6 28 1 3 40 25 13 9
30	Tension/Stress	35 3 37 32 9 18
31	Stability	15 17 25 3 4 36

Notes:

6
Parameter We Want to Improve – Production Spec/Quality/Means

Meaning: 'Production' – any activities involved in the production of goods or services. In the case of manufactured articles, the meaning relates to all of those activities required to translate the designer's intent into the product that the customer will eventually receive. In the service sector, the meaning is perhaps better interpreted as that collection of activities that are required to translate a customer's wishes into the output they receive. In a retail banking transaction, for example, 'production' in this context involves all of the actions that take place immediately after the customer gives the teller an instruction, until the moment when that instruction has been successfully carried out (e.g. entry into system, confirmation, clearing, entry into account).

'Specification/Capability/Means' relate to quality related aspects of a product, process or service. Again intended to be general, the terms relate to the quality of what is produced, and the means by which we achieve it. The term should be interpreted to include both tangible and intangible elements – i.e. knowledge, emotional qualities, etc as well as physical artefacts or functional services.

Synonyms, Antonyms and Equivalent Meanings: manufacture, transaction, assembly, preparation, package, consistency, standard, output, defects, concessions, customer satisfaction, process, repeatability, standard deviation, sigma, mean, datum, variation, bespoke, customized, function, attributes, experience, iconic, load, capacity, bottleneck, constraint, 'drum-buffer-rope', inspection, subcontractor quality, tolerance.

Inventive Principles that should always be considered for problems where we wish to improve this parameter:

2, 6, 10, 25, 35

Averaged list of other Principles that should be considered where we wish to improve this parameter (decreasing order of frequency):

35, 13, 10, 2, 5, 1, 6, 15, 25, 24, 12

List of Principles relevant to each specific worsening parameter:

Worsening Parameter	Description	List of Relevant Inventive Principles (decreasing order of frequency)
1	R&D Spec/Capability/Means	23 29 35 4 13 5
2	R&D Cost	5 2 27 1
3	R&D Time	5 6 20 35 2
4	R&D Risk	24 35 10 3 13 11

218

5	R&D Interfaces	5 6 17 40 33 10 26
6	Production Spec/Capability/Means	(see Physical Contradictions section)
7	Production Cost	15 25 3 10 5 8
8	Production Time	1 35 21 15 4 10
9	Production Risk	6 27 35 22 12 37
10	Production Interfaces	3 25 17 35 12 13
11	Supply Spec/Capability/Means	7 13 22 6 35
12	Supply Cost	15 35 13 22
13	Supply Time	35 5 13 22
14	Supply Risk	15 16 3 2 24 6
15	Supply Interfaces	10 25 3 33 12
16	Support Spec/Capability/Means	35 23 1 24
17	Support Cost	13 10 17 2 27 34
18	Support Time	5 6 10 12 27 25
19	Support Risk	6 10 2 27 12
20	Support Interfaces	6 40 10 2 7
21	Customer Revenue/Demand/Feedback	5 15 35 25 33
22	Amount Of Information	13 32 15 23 24 18 16
23	Communication Flow	6 2 13 25 10
24	Harmful Factors Affecting System	22 24 35 13 2
25	System Generated Harmful Factors	35 22 18 39
26	Convenience	2 15 1 5 28 7 10 13 16 12
27	Adaptability/Versatility	1 15 17 2 28 38
28	System Complexity	12 17 27 26 1 28 24 13
29	Control Complexity	28 1 13 16 25 37
30	Tension/Stress	35 1 3 10 16
31	Stability	35 1 23 3 19 13 5 39 40

Notes:

7
Parameter We Want to Improve – Production Cost

Meaning: 'Production' – any activities involved in the production of goods or services. In the case of manufactured articles, the meaning relates to all of those activities required to translate the designer's intent into the product that the customer will eventually receive. In the service sector, the meaning is perhaps better interpreted as that collection of activities that are required to translate a customer's wishes into the output they receive. In a retail banking transaction, for example, 'production' in this context involves all of the actions that take place immediately after the customer gives the teller an instruction, until the moment when that instruction has been successfully carried out (e.g. entry into system, confirmation, clearing, entry into account).

Cost: anything relating to financial matters. Costs can be direct or indirect, visible or invisible, tangible or intangible. In the context of this parameter, 'cost' can also mean waste of money or other forms of financial resource.

Synonyms, Antonyms and Equivalent Meanings: manufacture, transaction, assembly, preparation, package, output, defects, concessions, customer satisfaction, variation, (selling) price, overhead, value, discount, inventory, stock, assets, capital expenditure, operational expenditure, cost-of-defects, cost-of-lost-sales, invisible earnings, gross/net profit, return-on-investment, spent-cost, recoverables, non-recoverables, tax, liabilities, balance, profit-and-loss.

Inventive Principles that should always be considered for problems where we wish to improve this parameter:

10, 15, 25, 26, 27, 35

Averaged list of other Principles that should be considered where we wish to improve this parameter (decreasing order of frequency):

35, 10, 25, 1, 2, 27, 3, 5, 29, 24

List of Principles relevant to each specific worsening parameter:

Worsening Parameter	Description	List of Relevant Inventive Principles (decreasing order of frequency)
1	R&D Spec/Capability/Means	37 35 10 3 6
2	R&D Cost	26 35 1 7 27 34 3
3	R&D Time	5 29 35 2
4	R&D Risk	5 35 40 23 1 12
5	R&D Interfaces	15 23 29 5 13
6	Production Spec/Capability/Means	15 25 3 10 5 8

7	Production Cost	(see Physical Contradictions section)
8	Production Time	1 24 19 10 27 3 14
9	Production Risk	26 10 1 3 25 12
10	Production Interfaces	26 1 37 25 2 28
11	Supply Spec/Capability/Means	5 2 30 35 17 8 25
12	Supply Cost	5 35 31 2 17 24
13	Supply Time	2 35 24 10 13 5
14	Supply Risk	2 13 10 26 29
15	Supply Interfaces	12 3 35 5 10 7
16	Support Spec/Capability/Means	1 35 10 29 27
17	Support Cost	3 2 35 10 27
18	Support Time	27 3 10 25 24
19	Support Risk	10 25 27 3 35
20	Support Interfaces	10 35 7 24 25
21	Customer Revenue/Demand/Feedback	7 13 1 24 25
22	Amount Of Information	26 27 25 34 37
23	Communication Flow	6 35 37 18
24	Harmful Factors Affecting System	2 35 5 34 15
25	System Generated Harmful Factors	1 35 27 10 2
26	Convenience	1 25 2 27 29
27	Adaptability/Versatility	1 30 10 38 29 35
28	System Complexity	35 5 1 2 29 25
29	Control Complexity	6 3 25 10 32 37
30	Tension/Stress	1 35 2 25 13 17
31	Stability	10 1 35 27

Notes:

8
Parameter We Want to Improve – Production Time

Meaning: 'Production' – any activities involved in the production of goods or services. In the case of manufactured articles, the meaning relates to all of those activities required to translate the designer's intent into the product that the customer will eventually receive. In the service sector, the meaning is perhaps better interpreted as that collection of activities that are required to translate a customer's wishes into the output they receive. In a retail banking transaction, for example, 'production' in this context involves all of the actions that take place immediately after the customer gives the teller an instruction, until the moment when that instruction has been successfully carried out (e.g. entry into system, confirmation, clearing, entry into account).

'Time'; anything relating to temporal issues. This includes the time and level of effort required to do something, both visible and invisible, tangible and intangible. The emphasis here is on issues where time is the specific focus (in line with the axiom 'time is money', if we are interested in financial implications rather than the actual time itself, the 'Cost' parameter should be used in preference to this on).

Synonyms, Antonyms and Equivalent Meanings: manufacture, transaction, transaction rate, calls-per-hour, throughput, assembly-time, preparation-time, defect-identification-time, critical path, parallel activities, sequential activities, waiting time, overtime, working hours, shift length, shift pattern, lost time, meeting time, standard hours, meetings, approval delay, late, overdue, over-promise.

Inventive Principles that should always be considered for problems where we wish to improve this parameter:

5, 10, 15, 25

Averaged list of other Principles that should be considered where we wish to improve this parameter (decreasing order of frequency):

13, 10, 3, 35, 2, 15, 25, 29, 24

List of Principles relevant to each specific worsening parameter:

Worsening Parameter	Description	List of Relevant Inventive Principles (decreasing order of frequency)
1	R&D Spec/Capability/Means	35 6 10 2 20
2	R&D Cost	10 2 6 15
3	R&D Time	7 26 10 15 3
4	R&D Risk	5 40 20 15
5	R&D Interfaces	15 40 23 3 24 13

6	Production Spec/Capability/Means	1 35 21 15 4 10
7	Production Cost	1 24 19 10 27 3 14
8	Production Time	(see Physical Contradictions section)
9	Production Risk	10 27 15 6 3 22 29
10	Production Interfaces	10 15 38 20 27 6 3
11	Supply Spec/Capability/Means	5 17 16 3 10
12	Supply Cost	5 2 35 13 25
13	Supply Time	3 10 23 40 13 4
14	Supply Risk	13 2 35 10 24
15	Supply Interfaces	23 12 3 24 13 7
16	Support Spec/Capability/Means	1 35 10 38 29 25 13
17	Support Cost	3 13 25 5 35
18	Support Time	35 25 5 4 19
19	Support Risk	35 29 13 25 2 31
20	Support Interfaces	13 9 26 23 7
21	Customer Revenue/Demand/Feedback	13 1 37 17 31 29
22	Amount Of Information	13 15 23 25 3 37
23	Communication Flow	2 37 18 19 25
24	Harmful Factors Affecting System	22 35 3 13 24
25	System Generated Harmful Factors	35 22 18 10 24 2
26	Convenience	19 2 35 26 13 30
27	Adaptability/Versatility	10 15 30 7 2 29 25 13
28	System Complexity	25 28 2 35 10 15
29	Control Complexity	25 37 3 13 28
30	Tension/Stress	2 20 12 25 3 13 14
31	Stability	10 15 29 2 19 7

Notes:

9
Parameter We Want to Improve – Production Risk

Meaning: 'Production' – any activities involved in the production of goods or services. In the case of manufactured articles, the meaning relates to all of those activities required to translate the designer's intent into the product that the customer will eventually receive. In the service sector, the meaning is perhaps better interpreted as that collection of activities that are required to translate a customer's wishes into the output they receive. . In a retail banking transaction, for example, 'production' in this context involves all of the actions that take place immediately after the customer gives the teller an instruction, until the moment when that instruction has been successfully carried out (e.g. entry into system, confirmation, clearing, entry into account).

'Risk'; matters associated with likelihood and consequences of things happening that will cause a deviation from established plans. Risk can, of course, be manifested in terms of quality, specification, time or cost. This parameter seeks to encourage users to focus on risk in its most general sense. Where a risk could apply to any or all of the cost, time or quality parameters, this is the one that should be used.

Synonyms, Antonyms and Equivalent Meanings: manufacture, transaction, throughput, critical path, likelihood, consequence, contingency, fall-back, alternative, back-up, reserve, liability, 'design-for-Murphy', robust systems, stability, vulnerability, sensitivity, complexity, priority-clash, emergency back-up, liability, disruption, patent infringement.

Inventive Principles that should always be considered for problems where we wish to improve this parameter:

9, 10, 25, 37

Averaged list of other Principles that should be considered where we wish to improve this parameter (decreasing order of frequency):

25, 10, 35, 2, 3, 5, 7, 13, 24, 37, 26, 6

List of Principles relevant to each specific worsening parameter:

Worsening Parameter	Description	List of Relevant Inventive Principles (decreasing order of frequency)
1	R&D Spec/Capability/Means	3 5 10 2 23 12
2	R&D Cost	6 7 23 26 13
3	R&D Time	6 15 7 37 13 9
4	R&D Risk	11 23 39 7 9 33
5	R&D Interfaces	7 5 3 37 10
6	Production Spec/Capability/Means	6 27 35 22 12 37

7	Production Cost	26 10 1 3 25 12
8	Production Time	10 27 15 6 3 22 29
9	Production Risk	(see Physical Contradictions section)
10	Production Interfaces	5 6 23 20 7 10 25
11	Supply Spec/Capability/Means	5 25 3 35 2 10
12	Supply Cost	5 35 23 25 2
13	Supply Time	13 22 25 1 10
14	Supply Risk	5 26 35 2 25
15	Supply Interfaces	5 10 40 2 4 25
16	Support Spec/Capability/Means	13 35 2 15 24
17	Support Cost	3 35 19 24
18	Support Time	24 14 13 35 2
19	Support Risk	7 5 3 10 25
20	Support Interfaces	5 35 33 7 25 10
21	Customer Revenue/Demand/Feedback	13 22 7 13 24 39
22	Amount Of Information	5 25 3 37 32 28 13
23	Communication Flow	25 38 3 26 10 13
24	Harmful Factors Affecting System	35 2 26 34 25
25	System Generated Harmful Factors	25 10 39 24 29
26	Convenience	3 26 6 11 35
27	Adaptability/Versatility	2 40 38 30 35 29
28	System Complexity	25 2 26 5 29 35
29	Control Complexity	30 12 25 40 2 37
30	Tension/Stress	25 9 24 39 7 19
31	Stability	9 1 37 3 19

Notes:

Inventive Principle 3, Localisation of risk often used in combination with Principle 39, Inert Atmosphere – i.e. the risky elements of a system are managed in a localised inert setting.

Inventive Principle 7, Nesting is indicative of a large number of solutions seeking to reduce risk by cocooning a high-risk element inside something else.

10
Parameter We Want to Improve – Production Interfaces

Meaning: 'Production' – any activities involved in the production of goods or services. In the case of manufactured articles, the meaning relates to all of those activities required to translate the designer's intent into the product that the customer will eventually receive. In the service sector, the meaning is perhaps better interpreted as that collection of activities that are required to translate a customer's wishes into the output they receive. In a retail banking transaction, for example, 'production' in this context involves all of the actions that take place immediately after the customer gives the teller an instruction, until the moment when that instruction has been successfully carried out (e.g. entry into system, confirmation, clearing, entry into account).

'Interfaces'; issues relating to the connections that exist (or don't exist but should) between different parts of a system. This may be interpreted as person-to-person, peer-to-peer, department-to-department, division-to-division, B2B, B2C or any other relationship between one entity and another. Interfaces can be internal or external, formal or formal, and there will always be elements of tangible and intangible interfaces. Interfaces can be verbal, written, legal, visual, etc.

If there is an interface issue relating to two different parts of an organisation – say between R&D and production' then this should be modelled as a conflict between the 'R&D Interfaces' and 'Production Interfaces' parameters.

Synonyms, Antonyms and Equivalent Meanings: manufacture, transaction, throughput, goodwill, relationship, interaction, communication links, command structure, network, authority, peer, spoken, hand-shake, 'old-pals act', edict, buy-in, people, perceptions, perspective, fear, authority, rights, responsibilities, friendship, rivalry, respect, trust, dependence, independence, dispute, argument, consensus, agreement, protocol.

Inventive Principles that should always be considered for problems where we wish to improve this parameter:

12, 20, 35

Averaged list of other Principles that should be considered where we wish to improve this parameter (decreasing order of frequency):

10, 2, 25, 3, 40, 5, 23, 28, 35

List of Principles relevant to each specific worsening parameter:

Worsening Parameter	Description	List of Relevant Inventive Principles (decreasing order of frequency)
1	R&D Spec/Capability/Means	5 7 37 1 4

2	R&D Cost	15 35 10 25 24
3	R&D Time	25 23 35 29 2 13
4	R&D Risk	7 3 17 23 24
5	R&D Interfaces	28 40 6 29 13 31 30
6	Production Spec/Capability/Means	3 25 17 35 12
7	Production Cost	26 1 37 25 2 28
8	Production Time	10 15 38 20 27 6 3
9	Production Risk	5 6 23 20 7 10 25
10	Production Interfaces	(see Physical Contradictions section)
11	Supply Spec/Capability/Means	6 2 37 40 10
12	Supply Cost	5 30 10 15 2 12
13	Supply Time	5 35 6 13 17 10 24
14	Supply Risk	23 33 5 26 2
15	Supply Interfaces	33 5 2 26 10
16	Support Spec/Capability/Means	23 11 40 2 32 29
17	Support Cost	23 10 3 13 22
18	Support Time	23 13 10 1 2
19	Support Risk	10 14 2 25 29
20	Support Interfaces	40 33 6 10 26 2
21	Customer Revenue/Demand/Feedback	7 5 10 40 4 2 25
22	Amount Of Information	2 37 4 13 37 25
23	Communication Flow	2 28 3 37 32 25 10
24	Harmful Factors Affecting System	3 26 35 28 10 24
25	System Generated Harmful Factors	3 26 35 29 24
26	Convenience	5 19 28 32 2 10
27	Adaptability/Versatility	29 1 17 40 38
28	System Complexity	10 18 28 2 35
29	Control Complexity	10 28 19 15 40 2 25
30	Tension/Stress	3 40 19 1 24
31	Stability	11 25 1 3 4

Notes:

Mention of Inventive Principle 40, Composite Structures, frequently means the use of multi-disciplinary teams.

11
Parameter We Want to Improve – Supply Spec/Quality/Means

Meaning: 'Supply' – any activities associated with the delivery or supply of a finished product or service to the intended customer. In the product context the parameter should be interpreted as including all of the logistical elements associated with the packaging, transport, receipt, unpacking and confirmation of delivery of the thing that a customer has ordered. In the service sector, the meaning is perhaps better interpreted as that collection of activities that are required to supply or deliver the required service to the customer. In a retail banking transaction, for example, 'supply' in this context involves all of the actions that take place when the teller provides the customer with confirmation that an instruction has been successfully acted upon (e.g. through the arrival of a monthly bank statement). 'Supply' also includes the manner in which an organisation presents itself to its customers – in the form of branding, advertising, appearance of store, etc.

'Specification/Capability/Means' relate to quality related aspects of a product, process or service. Again intended to be general, the terms relate to the quality of what is produced, and the means by which we achieve it. The term should be interpreted to include both tangible and intangible elements – i.e. knowledge, emotional qualities, etc as well as physical artefacts or functional services.

Synonyms, Antonyms and Equivalent Meanings: shipping, goods-in, receiving, shipping damage, error, invoice, check-out, sales assistant, appearance, brand image, advertising, customer satisfaction, loyalty, process, repeatability, standard deviation, sigma, mean, datum, bench-mark, variation, bespoke, customized, experience, bottleneck, constraint, relationship management, promotional activities.

Inventive Principles that should always be considered for problems where we wish to improve this parameter:

5, 35

Averaged list of other Principles that should be considered where we wish to improve this parameter (decreasing order of frequency):

35, 2, 10, 6, 13, 23, 5, 25, 17, 15, 11, 3

List of Principles relevant to each specific worsening parameter:

Worsening Parameter	Description	List of Relevant Inventive Principles (decreasing order of frequency)
1	R&D Spec/Capability/Means	6 2 35 25 3
2	R&D Cost	23 6 11 28
3	R&D Time	11 6 23 19 18 2

4	R&D Risk	5 35 13 26 6
5	R&D Interfaces	6 35 15 13 14
6	Production Spec/Capability/Means	7 13 22 6 35
7	Production Cost	5 2 30 35 17 8 25
8	Production Time	5 17 16 3 10
9	Production Risk	5 25 3 35 2 10
10	Production Interfaces	6 2 37 40 10
11	Supply Spec/Capability/Means	(see Physical Contradictions section)
12	Supply Cost	7 35 19 1 10 29
13	Supply Time	35 1 13 2 24
14	Supply Risk	7 8 11 10 24 12 25
15	Supply Interfaces	6 30 15 40 12 2
16	Support Spec/Capability/Means	11 23 35 1 29 17
17	Support Cost	23 11 2 6 26
18	Support Time	23 11 26 2 7
19	Support Risk	11 23 24 2 9 17
20	Support Interfaces	23 11 2 25 35 32
21	Customer Revenue/Demand/Feedback	10 3 25 5 15
22	Amount Of Information	13 4 28 37 17 7
23	Communication Flow	5 25 23 10 35 28
24	Harmful Factors Affecting System	13 17 29 2 35 15
25	System Generated Harmful Factors	10 1 34 35 15 13
26	Convenience	35 3 13 2 15
27	Adaptability/Versatility	13 17 7 15 19
28	System Complexity	29 30 35 17 3
29	Control Complexity	6 5 28 37 3 25
30	Tension/Stress	2 23 5 30 10 13 35
31	Stability	15 5 25 10 35

Notes:

For some reason applications where this parameter is required to be improved currently appear to be missing feedback loops in several areas, hence the frequent recommendation and use of Inventive Principle 23 as a solution strategy.

12
Parameter We Want to Improve – Supply Cost

Meaning: 'Supply' – any activities associated with the delivery or supply of a finished product or service to the intended customer. In the product context the parameter should be interpreted as including all of the logistical elements associated with the packaging, transport, receipt, unpacking and confirmation of delivery of the thing that a customer has ordered. In the service sector, the meaning is perhaps better interpreted as that collection of activities that are required to supply or deliver the required service to the customer. In a retail banking transaction, for example, 'supply' in this context involves all of the actions that take place when the teller provides the customer with confirmation that an instruction has been successfully acted upon (e.g. through the arrival of a monthly bank statement). 'Supply' also includes the manner in which an organisation presents itself to its customers – in the form of branding, advertising, appearance of store, etc.

Cost: anything relating to financial matters. Costs can be direct or indirect, visible or invisible, tangible or intangible. In the context of this parameter, 'cost' can also mean waste of money or other forms of financial resource.

Synonyms, Antonyms and Equivalent Meanings: shipping, goods-in, receiving, cost of shipping damage, error, invoicing mistakes, etc, cost-of-sales, import duty, export duty, cost of advertising, (supply) price, overhead, value, discount, inventory, stock, capital expenditure, operational expenditure, cost-of-lost-sales, invisible earnings, cost of intangibles.

Inventive Principles that should always be considered for problems where we wish to improve this parameter:

5, 13, 35

Averaged list of other Principles that should be considered where we wish to improve this parameter (decreasing order of frequency):

2, 35, 5, 10, 25, 3, 1, 13, 19

List of Principles relevant to each specific worsening parameter:

Worsening Parameter	Description	List of Relevant Inventive Principles (decreasing order of frequency)
1	R&D Spec/Capability/Means	15 6 1 5 13
2	R&D Cost	10 5 35
3	R&D Time	5 13 23 25
4	R&D Risk	1 11 2 34
5	R&D Interfaces	2 33 3 15 10

6	Production Spec/Capability/Means	15 35 13 22
7	Production Cost	5 35 31 2 17 24
8	Production Time	5 2 35 13 25
9	Production Risk	5 35 23 25 2
10	Production Interfaces	5 30 10 15 2 12
11	Supply Spec/Capability/Means	7 35 19 1 10 29
12	Supply Cost	(see Physical Contradictions section)
13	Supply Time	3 24 38 10 19
14	Supply Risk	27 3 19 24 8
15	Supply Interfaces	1 28 6 38 4
16	Support Spec/Capability/Means	35 24 5 13 27 17
17	Support Cost	27 5 35 25 10 2
18	Support Time	10 27 30 35 2 5
19	Support Risk	10 12 2 27 7 5
20	Support Interfaces	10 24 25 1 6
21	Customer Revenue/Demand/Feedback	2 35 13 25 26 16
22	Amount Of Information	28 35 2 37 34 7
23	Communication Flow	35 6 1 27 25 12 28
24	Harmful Factors Affecting System	11 35 2 3 39 19
25	System Generated Harmful Factors	10 35 2 12 31 30
26	Convenience	30 2 15 3 5 13
27	Adaptability/Versatility	1 17 40 3 29
28	System Complexity	35 19 1 25 2
29	Control Complexity	22 2 37 4 32 25
30	Tension/Stress	10 3 25 7 40
31	Stability	19 3 35 10 4

Notes:

13
Parameter We Want to Improve – Supply Time

Meaning: 'Supply' – any activities associated with the delivery or supply of a finished product or service to the intended customer. In the product context the parameter should be interpreted as including all of the logistical elements associated with the packaging, transport, receipt, unpacking and confirmation of delivery of the thing that a customer has ordered. In the service sector, the meaning is perhaps better interpreted as that collection of activities that are required to supply or deliver the required service to the customer. In a retail banking transaction, for example, 'supply' in this context involves all of the actions that take place when the teller provides the customer with confirmation that an instruction has been successfully acted upon (e.g. through the arrival of a monthly bank statement). 'Supply' also includes the manner in which an organisation presents itself to its customers – in the form of branding, advertising, appearance of store, etc.

'Time'; anything relating to temporal issues. This includes the time and level of effort required to do something, both visible and invisible, tangible and intangible. The emphasis here is on issues where time is the specific focus (in line with the axiom 'time is money', if we are interested in financial implications rather than the actual time itself, the 'Cost' parameter should be used in preference to this on).

Synonyms, Antonyms and Equivalent Meanings: shipping, goods-in, receiving, calls-per-hour, throughput, preparation-time, shipping delay, late, on-time performance, instant access, overdue, over-promise/under-deliver, waiting-list, tipping point, 'stickiness', reservation, schedule, timetable, distraction.

Inventive Principles that should always be considered for problems where we wish to improve this parameter:

10, 24, 35

Averaged list of other Principles that should be considered where we wish to improve this parameter (decreasing order of frequency):

10, 35, 2, 13, 25, 3, 24, 5, 1, 15

List of Principles relevant to each specific worsening parameter:

Worsening Parameter	Description	List of Relevant Inventive Principles (decreasing order of frequency)
1	R&D Spec/Capability/Means	2 3 12 26 19 38
2	R&D Cost	10 19 35 22
3	R&D Time	10 25 7 2
4	R&D Risk	1 2 11 38 15

5	R&D Interfaces	5 2 35 10 12
6	Production Spec/Capability/Means	35 5 13 22
7	Production Cost	2 35 24 10 13 5
8	Production Time	3 10 23 40 13 4
9	Production Risk	13 22 25 1 10
10	Production Interfaces	5 35 6 13 17 10 24
11	Supply Spec/Capability/Means	35 1 13 2 24
12	Supply Cost	3 24 38 10 19
13	Supply Time	(see Physical Contradictions section)
14	Supply Risk	10 29 15 13 2 3
15	Supply Interfaces	5 19 3 15 10 18
16	Support Spec/Capability/Means	25 10 29 19 4
17	Support Cost	25 27 10 2
18	Support Time	27 2 13 35 10
19	Support Risk	10 25 35 6 13
20	Support Interfaces	24 5 35 25 7 10
21	Customer Revenue/Demand/Feedback	35 13 25 1 22 26
22	Amount Of Information	28 2 37 32 35 7
23	Communication Flow	6 31 25 35 37 16
24	Harmful Factors Affecting System	35 3 29 2 10 12
25	System Generated Harmful Factors	25 10 29 13 12 21
26	Convenience	24 35 28 1 29
27	Adaptability/Versatility	15 1 10 27 7
28	System Complexity	38 24 16 15 3
29	Control Complexity	28 32 25 2 37
30	Tension/Stress	1 10 15 25 24 2 19
31	Stability	35 3 5 27 20 18

Notes:

14
Parameter We Want to Improve – Supply Risk

Meaning: 'Supply' – any activities associated with the delivery or supply of a finished product or service to the intended customer. In the product context the parameter should be interpreted as including all of the logistical elements associated with the packaging, transport, receipt, unpacking and confirmation of delivery of the thing that a customer has ordered. In the service sector, the meaning is perhaps better interpreted as that collection of activities that are required to supply or deliver the required service to the customer. In a retail banking transaction, for example, 'supply' in this context involves all of the actions that take place when the teller provides the customer with confirmation that an instruction has been successfully acted upon (e.g. through the arrival of a monthly bank statement). 'Supply' also includes the manner in which an organisation presents itself to its customers – in the form of branding, advertising, appearance of store, etc.

'Risk'; matters associated with likelihood and consequences of things happening that will cause a deviation from established plans. Risk can, of course, be manifested in terms of quality, specification, time or cost. This parameter seeks to encourage users to focus on risk in its most general sense. Where a risk could apply to any or all of the cost, time or quality parameters, this is the one that should be used.

Synonyms, Antonyms and Equivalent Meanings: shipping, goods-in, receiving, likelihood, consequence, contingency, fall-back, alternative, back-up, reserve, liability, 'Murphy's Law', robust systems, stability, vulnerability, sensitivity, priority-clash, emergency back-up, liability, disruption.

Inventive Principles that should always be considered for problems where we wish to improve this parameter:

2, 11, 16, 24, 39

Averaged list of other Principles that should be considered where we wish to improve this parameter (decreasing order of frequency):

2, 13, 10, 24, 35, 25, 5, 15, 37

List of Principles relevant to each specific worsening parameter:

Worsening Parameter	Description	List of Relevant Inventive Principles (decreasing order of frequency)
1	R&D Spec/Capability/Means	11 39 30 31
2	R&D Cost	11 13 2 16
3	R&D Time	23 7 29 2 24 37
4	R&D Risk	13 7 9 37 12

5	R&D Interfaces	5 35 13 40 3 9
6	Production Spec/Capability/Means	15 16 3 2 24 6
7	Production Cost	2 13 10 26 29
8	Production Time	13 2 35 10 24
9	Production Risk	5 26 35 2 25
10	Production Interfaces	23 33 5 26 2
11	Supply Spec/Capability/Means	7 8 11 10 24 12 25
12	Supply Cost	27 3 19 24 8
13	Supply Time	10 29 15 13 2 3
14	Supply Risk	(see Physical Contradictions section)
15	Supply Interfaces	5 10 25 37 2 14 38
16	Support Spec/Capability/Means	1 35 6 24 25
17	Support Cost	19 10 5 27 2
18	Support Time	2 27 10 5 25
19	Support Risk	24 25 10 7 1
20	Support Interfaces	5 35 2 13 19
21	Customer Revenue/Demand/Feedback	25 22 2 35 10 17
22	Amount Of Information	5 37 15 6 32
23	Communication Flow	6 16 13 35 7 2
24	Harmful Factors Affecting System	2 13 35 31 24 12
25	System Generated Harmful Factors	2 15 19 23 40 24
26	Convenience	5 16 10 13 25 2
27	Adaptability/Versatility	15 17 40 3 29 25
28	System Complexity	2 4 15 28 35 32
29	Control Complexity	2 28 15 24 37
30	Tension/Stress	1 19 13 10 39
31	Stability	9 13 1 25 14

Notes:

15
Parameter We Want to Improve – Supply Interface

Meaning: 'Supply' – any activities associated with the delivery or supply of a finished product or service to the intended customer. In the product context the parameter should be interpreted as including all of the logistical elements associated with the packaging, transport, receipt, unpacking and confirmation of delivery of the thing that a customer has ordered. In the service sector, the meaning is perhaps better interpreted as that collection of activities that are required to supply or deliver the required service to the customer. In a retail banking transaction, for example, 'supply' in this context involves all of the actions that take place when the teller provides the customer with confirmation that an instruction has been successfully acted upon (e.g. through the arrival of a monthly bank statement). 'Supply' also includes the manner in which an organisation presents itself to its customers – in the form of branding, advertising, appearance of store, etc.

'Interfaces'; issues relating to the connections that exist (or don't exist but should) between different parts of a system. This may be interpreted as person-to-person, peer-to-peer, department-to-department, division-to-division, B2B, B2C or any other relationship between one entity and another. Interfaces can be internal or external, formal or formal, and there will always be elements of tangible and intangible interfaces. Interfaces can be verbal, written, legal, visual, etc.

If there is an interface issue relating to two different parts of an organisation – say between supply and production' then this should be modelled as a conflict between the 'Supply Interfaces' and 'Production Interfaces' parameters.

Synonyms, Antonyms and Equivalent Meanings: shipping, goods-in, receiving, goodwill, intangibles, relationship, interaction, connection, empathy, richness, reach, media, multi-media, inspirational, aspirational, communication links, command structure, network, spoken, face-to-face, remote, distance, hand-shake, 'old pals act', edict, people, perceptions, perspective, authority, rights, responsibilities, friendship, complementor, competitor, respect, trust, dependence, independence, dispute, argument, consensus, agreement, protocol.

Inventive Principles that should always be considered for problems where we wish to improve this parameter:

1, 12, 20, 24

Averaged list of other Principles that should be considered where we wish to improve this parameter (decreasing order of frequency):

5, 25, 3, 2, 10, 13, 40, 28, 35, 12

List of Principles relevant to each specific worsening parameter:

Worsening Parameter	Description	List of Relevant Inventive Principles (decreasing order of frequency)
1	R&D Spec/Capability/Means	11 26 2 5 13
2	R&D Cost	10 38 13
3	R&D Time	11 7 40 38 24 2
4	R&D Risk	13 22 25 9 35 26
5	R&D Interfaces	28 40 6 15 29
6	Production Spec/Capability/Means	10 25 3 33 12
7	Production Cost	12 3 35 5 10 7
8	Production Time	23 12 3 24 13 7
9	Production Risk	5 10 40 2 4 25
10	Production Interfaces	33 5 2 26 10
11	Supply Spec/Capability/Means	6 30 15 40 12 2
12	Supply Cost	1 28 6 38 4
13	Supply Time	5 19 3 15 10 18
14	Supply Risk	5 10 25 37 2 14 38
15	Supply Interfaces	(see Physical Contradictions section)
16	Support Spec/Capability/Means	10 31 24 35 3
17	Support Cost	5 10 26 1 13 25
18	Support Time	29 30 2 25 5 32
19	Support Risk	5 25 10 9 2 35
20	Support Interfaces	5 6 38 40 25 10
21	Customer Revenue/Demand/Feedback	13 25 39 24 7 17
22	Amount Of Information	3 6 37 28 32 35
23	Communication Flow	2 3 13 4 12 25
24	Harmful Factors Affecting System	3 35 13 14 39
25	System Generated Harmful Factors	2 30 40 22 26
26	Convenience	5 25 3 40 20
27	Adaptability/Versatility	29 28 30 3 15
28	System Complexity	28 5 3 25 37 40
29	Control Complexity	25 8 22 28 32 37
30	Tension/Stress	5 3 17 29 13 35 2
31	Stability	33 15 23 17 7

Notes:

Use of an external specialist supply interface is a commonly applied strategy – hence the high profile of Inventive Principle 24, Intermediary.

16
Parameter We Want to Improve – Support Spec/Quality/Means

Meaning: 'Support' – all of those activities after the customer has purchased and received the product or service they have ordered. In the case of products, this is likely to include things like maintenance, reliability, life and after-life (recycling for example) of that product. In the case of services –which tend to feature a multitude of contacts with the customer, the 'support' parameter should be used for all of those after-sales activities that occur following the first contact after customer commitment has been received. The period over which the support activities may last can be minutes to decades depending on the different market. As more and more organisations shift to service, function or 'experience' based business models, the 'support' timeframe becomes increasingly important.

'Specification/Capability/Means' relate to quality related aspects of a product, process or service. Again intended to be general, the terms relate to the quality of what is produced, and the means by which we achieve it. The term should be interpreted to include both tangible and intangible elements – i.e. knowledge, emotional qualities, etc as well as physical artifacts or functional services.

Synonyms, Antonyms and Equivalent Meanings: after-sale, customer relationship, customer-care, package, process, function, reliability, durability, longevity, life-cycle design, robust design, 'design-for-Murphy', accidental damage, through-life design, warranty, extended-warranty, lifetime guarantee, maintenance-contract, replace-with-new, lease, lend-lease, buy-back, re-usable, recyclable, environmental impact, sustainability, life-brand, customer satisfaction, loyalty, repeatability, standard deviation, sigma, mean, datum, bench-mark, variation, bespoke, partnership, customized, experience, feedback, 'working-together', clinic, update, upgrade, loyalty scheme, spin-off, end-game, iconic, collectable.

Inventive Principles that should always be considered for problems where we wish to improve this parameter:

2, 3, 15, 23, 25

Averaged list of other Principles that should be considered where we wish to improve this parameter (decreasing order of frequency):

35, 25, 10, 2, 1, 24, 13, 3, 29, 27

List of Principles relevant to each specific worsening parameter:

Worsening Parameter	Description	List of Relevant Inventive Principles (decreasing order of frequency)
1	R&D Spec/Capability/Means	36 11 2 35 27

2	R&D Cost	27 6 1 10
3	R&D Time	6 10 3 35 20
4	R&D Risk	6 1 26 37 15
5	R&D Interfaces	6 1 3 35 21 12
6	Production Spec/Capability/Means	35 23 1 24
7	Production Cost	1 35 10 29 27
8	Production Time	1 35 10 38 29 25 13
9	Production Risk	13 35 2 15 24
10	Production Interfaces	23 11 40 2 32 29
11	Supply Spec/Capability/Means	11 23 35 1 29 17
12	Supply Cost	35 24 5 13 27 17
13	Supply Time	25 10 29 19 4
14	Supply Risk	1 35 6 24 25
15	Supply Interfaces	10 31 24 35 3
16	Support Spec/Capability/Means	(see Physical Contradictions section)
17	Support Cost	2 25 10 35 15
18	Support Time	22 25 15 3 32
19	Support Risk	13 22 10 35 4 6
20	Support Interfaces	28 25 5 7 2 24
21	Customer Revenue/Demand/Feedback	28 25 7 22 5 13
22	Amount Of Information	10 28 3 25 37 4
23	Communication Flow	10 28 37 3 7
24	Harmful Factors Affecting System	27 35 34 2 40
25	System Generated Harmful Factors	2 35 40 24 26 39
26	Convenience	27 17 40 3 8
27	Adaptability/Versatility	35 13 8 24 29
28	System Complexity	13 35 1 2 9
29	Control Complexity	11 13 2 35 25
30	Tension/Stress	11 35 24 19 2 25
31	Stability	25 26 1 10 12

Notes:

17
Parameter We Want to Improve – Support Cost

Meaning: 'Support' – all of those activities after the customer has purchased and received the product or service they have ordered. In the case of products, this is likely to include things like maintenance, reliability, life and after-life (recycling for example) of that product. In the case of services –which tend to feature a multitude of contacts with the customer, the 'support' parameter should be used for all of those after-sales activities that occur following the first contact after customer commitment has been received. The period over which the support activities may last can be minutes to decades depending on the different market. As more and more organisations shift to service, function or 'experience' based business models, the 'support' timeframe becomes increasingly important.

Cost: anything relating to financial matters. Costs can be direct or indirect, visible or invisible, tangible or intangible. In the context of this parameter, 'cost' can also mean waste of money or other forms of financial resource.

Synonyms, Antonyms and Equivalent Meanings: after-sale, customer-care, reliability-cost, life-cycle-cost, through-life cost, operating expenses, disposal cost, environmental cost, social cost, offset, retirement cost, pension, warranty costs, maintenance-contract, lease, lend-lease, buy back, re-use, repeat business cost, follow-on sale revenue, mass-customization, liability cost, insurance, pension, intangibles, brand-value, bankruptcy, asset depreciation, appreciation.

Inventive Principles that should always be considered for problems where we wish to improve this parameter:

5, 10, 12, 16, 25

Averaged list of other Principles that should be considered where we wish to improve this parameter (decreasing order of frequency):

25, 35, 10, 2, 1, 3, 13, 15, 17, 28, 5

List of Principles relevant to each specific worsening parameter:

Worsening Parameter	Description	List of Relevant Inventive Principles (decreasing order of frequency)
1	R&D Spec/Capability/Means	15 35 28 25 29
2	R&D Cost	6 1 10 25 13
3	R&D Time	7 15 40 26 5
4	R&D Risk	11 7 28 35
5	R&D Interfaces	6 7 40 38 13
6	Production Spec/Capability/Means	13 10 17 2 27 34

7	Production Cost	3 2 35 10 27
8	Production Time	3 13 25 5 35
9	Production Risk	3 35 19 24
10	Production Interfaces	23 10 3 13 22
11	Supply Spec/Capability/Means	23 11 2 6 26
12	Supply Cost	27 5 35 25 10 2
13	Supply Time	25 27 10 2
14	Supply Risk	19 10 5 27 2
15	Supply Interfaces	5 10 26 1 13 25
16	Support Spec/Capability/Means	2 25 10 35 15
17	Support Cost	(see Physical Contradictions section)
18	Support Time	5 4 25 10 17 14 13
19	Support Risk	27 35 25 14 1 31
20	Support Interfaces	26 25 37 3 24 2
21	Customer Revenue/Demand/Feedback	24 25 37 3 7 28 18
22	Amount Of Information	28 3 17 37 32 4
23	Communication Flow	25 1 28 32 20 35
24	Harmful Factors Affecting System	1 35 22 25 17
25	System Generated Harmful Factors	2 24 35 22 13 31 10
26	Convenience	25 1 12 26 10 15
27	Adaptability/Versatility	17 35 15 1 3 2
28	System Complexity	35 1 25 2 17
29	Control Complexity	15 25 19 28 37
30	Tension/Stress	35 24 10 2 25 31 19
31	Stability	1 35 2 29 10

Notes:

18
Parameter We Want to Improve – Support Time

Meaning: 'Support' – all of those activities after the customer has purchased and received the product or service they have ordered. In the case of products, this is likely to include things like maintenance, reliability, life and after-life (recycling for example) of that product. In the case of services –which tend to feature a multitude of contacts with the customer, the 'support' parameter should be used for all of those after-sales activities that occur following the first contact after customer commitment has been received. The period over which the support activities may last can be minutes to decades depending on the different market. As more and more organisations shift to service, function or 'experience' based business models, the 'support' timeframe becomes increasingly important.

'Time'; anything relating to temporal issues. This includes the time and level of effort required to do something, both visible and invisible, tangible and intangible. The emphasis here is on issues where time is the specific focus (in line with the axiom 'time is money', if we are interested in financial implications rather than the actual time itself, the 'Cost' parameter should be used in preference to this on).

Synonyms, Antonyms and Equivalent Meanings: after-sale, customer relationship, customer-care, package, process, reliability, durability, longevity, life-cycle, meant-time-between-overhaul, meant-time-between-failure, through-life design, warranty period, lifetime guarantee, lease period, loyalty-effect, memory, long-term partnership, retirement, post-retirement, recovery-time, time-to-maturity, incubation-period, time-limit.

Inventive Principles that should always be considered for problems where we wish to improve this parameter:

2, 5, 10, 20

Averaged list of other Principles that should be considered where we wish to improve this parameter (decreasing order of frequency):

2, 25, 10, 35, 15, 1, 5, 27, 29, 37

List of Principles relevant to each specific worsening parameter:

Worsening Parameter	Description	List of Relevant Inventive Principles (decreasing order of frequency)
1	R&D Spec/Capability/Means	5 2 6 27 25
2	R&D Cost	6 1 25 10 27
3	R&D Time	7 40 1 26 15
4	R&D Risk	1 2 32 28 7
5	R&D Interfaces	6 38 20 10 37

6	Production Spec/Capability/Means	5 6 10 12 27 25
7	Production Cost	27 3 10 25 24
8	Production Time	35 25 5 4 19
9	Production Risk	24 14 13 35 2
10	Production Interfaces	23 13 10 1 2
11	Supply Spec/Capability/Means	23 11 26 2 7
12	Supply Cost	10 27 30 35 2 5
13	Supply Time	27 2 13 35 10
14	Supply Risk	2 27 10 5 25
15	Supply Interfaces	29 30 2 25 5 32
16	Support Spec/Capability/Means	22 25 15 3 32
17	Support Cost	5 4 25 10 17 14 13
18	Support Time	(see Physical Contradictions section)
19	Support Risk	15 29 9 19 1 18 35 31
20	Support Interfaces	15 29 10 1 35 30
21	Customer Revenue/Demand/Feedback	7 20 24 35 25 26
22	Amount Of Information	1 2 15 35 25 4 37
23	Communication Flow	6 31 2 35 28 37
24	Harmful Factors Affecting System	35 15 1 3 10
25	System Generated Harmful Factors	35 15 29 3 1 19
26	Convenience	5 25 13 2 10
27	Adaptability/Versatility	3 30 40 29 17
28	System Complexity	28 15 17 32 37
29	Control Complexity	28 25 37 15 3 1 4
30	Tension/Stress	2 24 10 40 25 8
31	Stability	10 15 2 30 29 12

Notes:

19
Parameter We Want to Improve – Support Risk

Meaning: 'Support' – all of those activities after the customer has purchased and received the product or service they have ordered. In the case of products, this is likely to include things like maintenance, reliability, life and after-life (recycling for example) of that product. In the case of services –which tend to feature a multitude of contacts with the customer, the 'support' parameter should be used for all of those after-sales activities that occur following the first contact after customer commitment has been received. The period over which the support activities may last can be minutes to decades depending on the different market. As more and more organisations shift to service, function or 'experience' based business models, the 'support' timeframe becomes increasingly important.

'Risk'; matters associated with likelihood and consequences of things happening that will cause a deviation from established plans. Risk can, of course, be manifested in terms of quality, specification, time or cost. This parameter seeks to encourage users to focus on risk in its most general sense. Where a risk could apply to any or all of the cost, time or quality parameters, this is the one that should be used.

Synonyms, Antonyms and Equivalent Meanings: after-sale, risk-share partnership, longevity, liability, insurance, assurance, terms of warranty/guarantee, amortisation, 'Murphy's Law', accidental damage, environmental impact, retrospective damages, indemnity, robustness, stability, vulnerability, sensitivity, emergency back-up, disruption, bankruptcy, investigation.

Inventive Principles that should always be considered for problems where we wish to improve this parameter:

10, 24, 25

Averaged list of other Principles that should be considered where we wish to improve this parameter (decreasing order of frequency):

10, 35, 25, 2, 1, 13, 7, 15, 6, 5, 24

List of Principles relevant to each specific worsening parameter:

Worsening Parameter	Description	List of Relevant Inventive Principles (decreasing order of frequency)
1	R&D Spec/Capability/Means	15 27 40 12 2
2	R&D Cost	10 25 22 2
3	R&D Time	23 24 2 37 7
4	R&D Risk	40 36 6 10 26 13
5	R&D Interfaces	5 35 40 13

6	Production Spec/Capability/Means	6 10 2 27 12
7	Production Cost	10 25 27 3 35
8	Production Time	35 29 13 25 2 31
9	Production Risk	7 5 3 10 25
10	Production Interfaces	10 14 2 25 29
11	Supply Spec/Capability/Means	11 23 24 2 9 17
12	Supply Cost	10 12 2 27 7 5
13	Supply Time	10 25 35 6 13
14	Supply Risk	24 25 10 7 1
15	Supply Interfaces	5 25 10 9 2 35
16	Support Spec/Capability/Means	13 22 10 35 4 6
17	Support Cost	27 35 25 14 1 31
18	Support Time	15 29 9 19 1 18 35 31
19	Support Risk	(see Physical Contradictions section)
20	Support Interfaces	5 6 40 33 7 24
21	Customer Revenue/Demand/Feedback	20 7 4 13 35 25 24
22	Amount Of Information	25 3 28 35 37 10
23	Communication Flow	29 31 6 2 30 15 10
24	Harmful Factors Affecting System	25 35 11 15 19 1
25	System Generated Harmful Factors	25 3 4 35 15 19
26	Convenience	2 3 25 10 16 5
27	Adaptability/Versatility	1 30 40 17 14 15
28	System Complexity	13 35 4 2 37
29	Control Complexity	10 15 1 34 37
30	Tension/Stress	10 11 39 1 24 35
31	Stability	10 35 7 9 19 1

Notes:

20
Parameter We Want to Improve – Support Interfaces

Meaning: 'Support' – all of those activities after the customer has purchased and received the product or service they have ordered. In the case of products, this is likely to include things like maintenance, reliability, life and after-life (recycling for example) of that product. In the case of services –which tend to feature a multitude of contacts with the customer, the 'support' parameter should be used for all of those after-sales activities that occur following the first contact after customer commitment has been received. The period over which the support activities may last can be minutes to decades depending on the different market. As more and more organisations shift to service, function or 'experience' based business models, the 'support' timeframe becomes increasingly important.

'Interfaces'; issues relating to the connections that exist (or don't exist but should) between different parts of a system. This may be interpreted as person-to-person, peer-to-peer, department-to-department, division-to-division, B2B, B2C or any other relationship between one entity and another. Interfaces can be internal or external, formal or formal, and there will always be elements of tangible and intangible interfaces. Interfaces can be verbal, written, legal, visual, etc.

If there is an interface issue relating to two different parts of an organisation – say between support and production' then this should be modelled as a conflict between the 'Support Interfaces' and 'Production Interfaces' parameters.

Synonyms, Antonyms and Equivalent Meanings: after-sale, customer relationship, customer-care, package, maintenance-contract, life-style, life-brand, customer satisfaction, loyalty, repeat business, partnership, experience, feedback, 'working-together', transformation, loyalty, iconic, trust, collaboration, social impact, user-group, special-interest-group, user network, committee, family, cluster, complementors.

Inventive Principles that should always be considered for problems where we wish to improve this parameter:

10, 20, 24

Averaged list of other Principles that should be considered where we wish to improve this parameter (decreasing order of frequency):

10, 2, 7, 25, 6, 24, 5, 13, 40, 26, 35

List of Principles relevant to each specific worsening parameter:

Worsening Parameter	Description	List of Relevant Inventive Principles (decreasing order of frequency)
1	R&D Spec/Capability/Means	11 2 5 9 26

2	R&D Cost	6 10 1 7 20
3	R&D Time	6 10 26 24 2 38
4	R&D Risk	6 10 7 26 13
5	R&D Interfaces	28 40 6 7 30
6	Production Spec/Capability/Means	6 40 10 2 7
7	Production Cost	10 35 7 24 25
8	Production Time	13 9 26 23 7
9	Production Risk	5 35 33 7 25 10
10	Production Interfaces	40 33 6 10 26 2
11	Supply Spec/Capability/Means	23 11 2 25 35 32
12	Supply Cost	10 24 25 1 6
13	Supply Time	24 5 35 25 7 10
14	Supply Risk	5 35 2 13 19
15	Supply Interfaces	5 6 38 40 25 10
16	Support Spec/Capability/Means	28 25 5 7 2 24
17	Support Cost	26 25 37 3 24 2
18	Support Time	15 29 10 1 35 30
19	Support Risk	5 6 40 33 7 24
20	Support Interfaces	(see Physical Contradictions section)
21	Customer Revenue/Demand/Feedback	16 17 40 13 10 25
22	Amount Of Information	1 3 37 2 28 7 4
23	Communication Flow	2 3 15 18 25
24	Harmful Factors Affecting System	11 24 35 5 21 14
25	System Generated Harmful Factors	25 13 22 10 17
26	Convenience	7 5 6 20 26 2 31
27	Adaptability/Versatility	29 30 17 14 18 1
28	System Complexity	28 17 29 37 10 4 13
29	Control Complexity	25 15 10 30 29
30	Tension/Stress	10 8 2 24 6 21 13
31	Stability	11 1 40 13 22 23

Notes:

21

Parameter We Want to Improve – Customer Revenue/Demand/ Feedback

Meaning: Those *things that come back to the supplier from the customer.* Although it may seem that this parameter is rather general, the research that derived this Matrix clearly showed that there are very definite similarities in the strategies used to achieve win-win outcomes when the parameter being improved is the desire or demand of the customer for a product or service, the revenue they are prepared to offer to receive it, and the information they will give back to the supplier. The key concept of this parameter, then, is that of closing the loop back from the customer to the supplier. Includes tangibles and intangibles, subconscious or conscious, explicit and implicit, one-off or recurring, scheduled or random.

Communication issues where a problem exists between the customer and a part of an organisation is best modelled by matching this parameter with the relevant 'Interface' element in parameters 5, 10, 15 and 20.

Synonyms, Antonyms and Equivalent Meanings: order, purchase order, income, payment, feedback, thanks, advice, complaint, recommendations, desire, wish, aspiration, request, survey, questionnaire, relevance, empathy, trust, relationship, emotion, involvement, brand-awareness, lifestyle involvement, commitment.

Inventive Principles that should always be considered for problems where we wish to improve this parameter:

2, 10, 23, 25, 26

Averaged list of other Principles that should be considered where we wish to improve this parameter (decreasing order of frequency):

25, 13, 7, 35, 10, 2, 24, 17, 1, 40

List of Principles relevant to each specific worsening parameter:

Worsening Parameter	Description	List of Relevant Inventive Principles (decreasing order of frequency)
1	R&D Spec/Capability/Means	14 13 22 7 10
2	R&D Cost	7 25 30 21 10 9 2
3	R&D Time	7 19 21 29 30
4	R&D Risk	36 13 25 22 37 3
5	R&D Interfaces	4 7 25 40 13 35 28
6	Production Spec/Capability/Means	5 15 35 25 33
7	Production Cost	7 13 1 24 25

8	Production Time	13 1 37 17 31 29
9	Production Risk	13 22 7 13 24 39
10	Production Interfaces	7 5 10 40 4 2 25
11	Supply Spec/Capability/Means	10 3 25 5 15
12	Supply Cost	2 35 13 25 26 16
13	Supply Time	35 13 25 1 22 26
14	Supply Risk	25 22 2 35 10 17
15	Supply Interfaces	13 25 39 24 7 17
16	Support Spec/Capability/Means	28 25 7 22 5 13
17	Support Cost	24 25 37 3 7 28 18
18	Support Time	7 20 24 35 25 26
19	Support Risk	20 7 4 13 35 25 24
20	Support Interfaces	16 17 40 13 10 25
21	Customer Revenue/Demand/Feedback	(see Physical Contradictions section)
22	Amount Of Information	2 29 3 35 13 1 37 28 4
23	Communication Flow	29 31 30 7 13 17 38
24	Harmful Factors Affecting System	39 3 5 17 26 35
25	System Generated Harmful Factors	38 10 6 5 35 24
26	Convenience	28 27 35 40 1 30
27	Adaptability/Versatility	40 17 16 14 15 1
28	System Complexity	25 1 2 19 10 4
29	Control Complexity	25 2 7 37 6 4 19
30	Tension/Stress	2 10 12 24 25
31	Stability	10 40 29 30 28 26

Notes:

22

Parameter We Want to Improve – Amount of Information

Meaning: The amount, quantity or number of a system's informational resources. 'Information' should be interpreted in its most generic form to include any form of information that might be passed between two or more people, departments, divisions or systems in general, whether it be tangible or intangible, explicit or implicit. Also includes instances in which information is lost or is in danger of being lost.

Synonyms, Antonyms and Equivalent Meanings: data, knowledge, wisdom, memory, properties, richness, accuracy, credibility, validity, message, volume, capacity, excess, absence, missing, forgotten, archive, library, repository, summary, detection, search, identification, unlearning.

Inventive Principles that should always be considered for problems where we wish to improve this parameter:

35

Averaged list of other Principles that should be considered where we wish to improve this parameter (decreasing order of frequency):

37, 25, 2, 28, 3, 13, 4, 10, 35, 32, 7, 1

List of Principles relevant to each specific worsening parameter:

Worsening Parameter	Description	List of Relevant Inventive Principles (decreasing order of frequency)
1	R&D Spec/Capability/Means	37 13 25 10 39
2	R&D Cost	37 25 28 2 32
3	R&D Time	7 2 37 20 25
4	R&D Risk	1 3 10 26 25 4 37
5	R&D Interfaces	1 6 3 40 25
6	Production Spec/Capability/Means	13 32 15 23 24 18 16
7	Production Cost	26 27 25 34 37
8	Production Time	13 15 23 25 3 37
9	Production Risk	5 25 3 37 32 28 13
10	Production Interfaces	2 37 4 13 25
11	Supply Spec/Capability/Means	13 4 28 37 17 7
12	Supply Cost	28 35 2 37 34 7
13	Supply Time	28 2 37 32 35 7
14	Supply Risk	5 37 15 6 32
15	Supply Interfaces	3 6 37 28 32 35
16	Support Spec/Capability/Means	10 28 3 25 37 4

17	Support Cost	28 3 17 37 32 4
18	Support Time	1 2 15 35 25 4 37
19	Support Risk	25 3 28 35 37 10
20	Support Interfaces	1 3 37 2 28 7 4
21	Customer Revenue/Demand/Feedback	2 29 3 4 13 1 37 28 35
22	Amount Of Information	(see Physical Contradictions section)
23	Communication Flow	2 37 3 4 31 28 7
24	Harmful Factors Affecting System	22 10 1 2 35
25	System Generated Harmful Factors	10 21 22 29 19
26	Convenience	27 25 4 10 22 13 6 19
27	Adaptability/Versatility	15 10 2 13 29 3 4
28	System Complexity	10 25 13 40 2
29	Control Complexity	2 7 25 19 1 40 37
30	Tension/Stress	2 28 35 10 24 31
31	Stability	11 13 25 2 24

Notes:

Extensive presence of Principle 37, Relative Change reflects widespread use of rate-of-change data when assessing data.

Principle 4, Asymmetry reflects widespread use of skew on normal curve data.

23

Parameter We Want to Improve – Communication Flow

Meaning: Aspects relating to the flow of communication. Other parameters like the various versions of 'interface' or 'customer feedback are intended to deal with the interpretation and use of whatever it is that is being communicated; this parameter is specifically focused on the ability and means by which the communication moves. Strategies for solving communication flow problems are often considerably different from the ones used when that communication is generated or interpreted, and hence the inclusion of 'flow' as a separate parameter in the Matrix.

Synonyms, Antonyms and Equivalent Meanings: flow, transmission, channels, networks, links, nodes, inertia, resistance, delay, lag, noise, corruption, interference, integrity, resolution, intensity, modulation, amplification, attenuation, bandwidth, speed, media, public, underground, whisper, buzz, 'word-on-the-street', tangible, intangible, medium.

Inventive Principles that should always be considered for problems where we wish to improve this parameter:

2, 4, 20, 35, 40

Averaged list of other Principles that should be considered where we wish to improve this parameter (decreasing order of frequency):

6, 25, 37, 35, 13, 2, 3, 28, 31, 10, 7

List of Principles relevant to each specific worsening parameter:

Worsening Parameter	Description	List of Relevant Inventive Principles (decreasing order of frequency)
1	R&D Spec/Capability/Means	6 25 31 29 7 23
2	R&D Cost	6 18 37 13 25 22
3	R&D Time	6 26 18 19 40
4	R&D Risk	30 6 31 4 9 13 22
5	R&D Interfaces	2 6 35 3 25 18
6	Production Spec/Capability/Means	6 2 13 25 10
7	Production Cost	6 35 37 18
8	Production Time	2 37 18 19 25
9	Production Risk	25 38 3 26 10 13
10	Production Interfaces	2 28 3 37 32 25 10
11	Supply Spec/Capability/Means	5 25 23 10 35 28
12	Supply Cost	35 6 1 27 25 12 28
13	Supply Time	6 31 25 35 37 16

14	Supply Risk	6 16 13 35 7 2
15	Supply Interfaces	2 3 13 4 12 25
16	Support Spec/Capability/Means	10 28 37 3 7
17	Support Cost	25 1 28 32 20 35
18	Support Time	6 31 2 35 25 37
19	Support Risk	29 31 6 2 30 15 10
20	Support Interfaces	2 3 15 18 25
21	Customer Revenue/Demand/Feedback	29 31 30 7 13 17 38
22	Amount Of Information	2 37 3 4 31 28 7
23	Communication Flow	(see Physical Contradictions section)
24	Harmful Factors Affecting System	6 30 15 28 13 36 2
25	System Generated Harmful Factors	1 28 4 35 7 24
26	Convenience	25 1 19 29 35 28
27	Adaptability/Versatility	25 6 37 40 15 19
28	System Complexity	1 25 4 37 6 18
29	Control Complexity	25 1 19 37 10
30	Tension/Stress	3 4 6 7 13 36
31	Stability	37 1 39 40 9 31

Notes:

24
Parameter We Want to Improve – Harmful Factors Affecting System

Meaning: This parameter is designed as a catch-all for any form of action or phenomenon in or around a system that manifests itself as a harmful effect on something *in* the system.

Synonyms, Antonyms and Equivalent Meanings: undesirable effect, security, threats, allegations, compatibility, contamination, safety, noise, dispute, competitive threat, (hostile) take-over, debt, legal challenge, change in the law, law-suit, job-cut, redundancy, act-of-God, down-turn, recession, quarantine, siege, espionage, breach of confidentiality, bad-press.

Inventive Principles that should always be considered for problems where we wish to improve this parameter:

2, 10, 35

Averaged list of other Principles that should be considered where we wish to improve this parameter (decreasing order of frequency):

35, 2, 3, 15, 24, 26, 25, 28, 22, 13, 10

List of Principles relevant to each specific worsening parameter:

Worsening Parameter	Description	List of Relevant Inventive Principles (decreasing order of frequency)
1	R&D Spec/Capability/Means	11 25 2 26 3
2	R&D Cost	35 27 3 28 2
3	R&D Time	26 2 35 24 11
4	R&D Risk	35 2 15 26 3 15
5	R&D Interfaces	3 26 35 28 24
6	Production Spec/Capability/Means	22 24 35 13 2
7	Production Cost	2 35 5 34 15
8	Production Time	22 35 3 13 24
9	Production Risk	35 2 26 34 25
10	Production Interfaces	3 26 35 28 10 24
11	Supply Spec/Capability/Means	13 17 29 2 35 15
12	Supply Cost	11 35 2 3 39 19
13	Supply Time	35 3 29 2 10 12
14	Supply Risk	2 13 35 31 24 12
15	Supply Interfaces	3 35 13 14 39
16	Support Spec/Capability/Means	27 35 34 2 40

17	Support Cost	1 35 22 25 17
18	Support Time	35 15 1 3 10
19	Support Risk	25 35 11 15 19 1
20	Support Interfaces	11 24 35 5 21 14
21	Customer Revenue/Demand/Feedback	39 3 5 17 26 35
22	Amount Of Information	22 10 1 2 35
23	Communication Flow	6 30 15 28 13 36 2
24	Harmful Factors Affecting System	(see Physical Contradictions section)
25	System Generated Harmful Factors	35 3 24 4 13 31 15
26	Convenience	2 25 28 39 15 10
27	Adaptability/Versatility	35 11 22 32 31
28	System Complexity	22 19 29 40 35 15 10
29	Control Complexity	3 15 2 22 25 9 28 26
30	Tension/Stress	11 25 30 2 35 28
31	Stability	35 24 30 18 33

Notes:

25
Parameter We Want to Improve – System Generated Harmful Factors

Meaning: This parameter is designed as a catch-all for any form of inefficiency or negative effect internal to or immediately around a system that manifests itself as a harmful effect *on* something *around* the system.

Synonyms, Antonyms and Equivalent Meanings: environmental damage, adverse social consequence, adverse political consequence, adverse effects on health, addiction, litter, noise, pollution, contamination, safety hazard, short-term, long-term, side-effect, consequence, precedent, incitement, chaos, co-lateral damage, dispute.

Inventive Principles that should always be considered for problems where we wish to improve this parameter:

2, 10, 12, 16, 35

Averaged list of other Principles that should be considered where we wish to improve this parameter (decreasing order of frequency):

35, 10, 2, 15, 24, 3, 13, 22, 1, 25, 40

List of Principles relevant to each specific worsening parameter:

Worsening Parameter	Description	List of Relevant Inventive Principles (decreasing order of frequency)
1	R&D Spec/Capability/Means	25 29 2 37 13
2	R&D Cost	28 26 2 22 8 35
3	R&D Time	26 2 15 19 35 40
4	R&D Risk	2 3 35 15 12 9
5	R&D Interfaces	3 26 35 37 2 40
6	Production Spec/Capability/Means	35 22 18 39
7	Production Cost	1 35 27 10 2
8	Production Time	35 22 18 10 24 2
9	Production Risk	25 10 39 24 29
10	Production Interfaces	3 26 35 29 24
11	Supply Spec/Capability/Means	10 1 34 35 15 13
12	Supply Cost	10 35 2 12 31 30
13	Supply Time	25 10 29 13 12 21
14	Supply Risk	2 15 19 23 40 24
15	Supply Interfaces	2 30 40 22 26
16	Support Spec/Capability/Means	2 35 40 24 26 39

17	Support Cost	2 24 35 22 13 31 10
18	Support Time	35 15 29 3 1 19
19	Support Risk	25 3 4 35 15 19
20	Support Interfaces	25 13 22 10 17
21	Customer Revenue/Demand/Feedback	38 10 6 5 35 24
22	Amount Of Information	10 21 22 29 19
23	Communication Flow	1 28 4 35 7 24
24	Harmful Factors Affecting System	35 3 24 4 13 31 15
25	System Generated Harmful Factors	(see Physical Contradictions section)
26	Convenience	1 15 13 34 31 16
27	Adaptability/Versatility	3 1 29 15 10 24
28	System Complexity	19 1 31 3 35 10
29	Control Complexity	25 3 15 22 10 23 13
30	Tension/Stress	11 25 12 8 37 35
31	Stability	35 40 27 39 2

Notes:

26
Parameter We Want to Improve – Convenience

Meaning: The extent and ease with which people are able to learn how to learn, operate or control a system whether it be a product, process or service. Convenience of use.

Synonyms, Antonyms and Equivalent Meanings: simplicity, complexity, learnability, operability, training, education, usability, user guide, manual, help-file, help-line, call-centre, learning-curve, self-learning, familiarisation-time, ease-of-use, labour-saving, effort, intelligence (of system), smart, instinctive, anticipatory, consistency, predictability, transferability.

Inventive Principles that should always be considered for problems where we wish to improve this parameter:

2, 5, 13, 27

Averaged list of other Principles that should be considered where we wish to improve this parameter (decreasing order of frequency):

25, 2, 13, 5, 28, 10, 35, 3, 15, 1, 19, 16, 26

List of Principles relevant to each specific worsening parameter:

Worsening Parameter	Description	List of Relevant Inventive Principles (decreasing order of frequency)
1	R&D Spec/Capability/Means	15 35 25 16 28
2	R&D Cost	25 2 6 5 40
3	R&D Time	1 2 15 19 25 28
4	R&D Risk	26 3 11 24 5 13 40
5	R&D Interfaces	16 13 25 28 37
6	Production Spec/Capability/Means	2 15 1 5 28 7 10 13 16 12
7	Production Cost	1 25 2 27 29
8	Production Time	19 2 35 26 13 30
9	Production Risk	3 26 6 11 35
10	Production Interfaces	5 19 28 32 2 10
11	Supply Spec/Capability/Means	35 3 13 2 15
12	Supply Cost	30 2 15 3 5 13
13	Supply Time	24 35 28 1 29
14	Supply Risk	5 16 10 13 25 2
15	Supply Interfaces	5 25 3 40 20
16	Support Spec/Capability/Means	27 17 40 3 8
17	Support Cost	25 1 12 26 10 15
18	Support Time	5 25 13 2 10

19	Support Risk	2 3 25 10 16 5
20	Support Interfaces	7 5 6 20 26 2 31
21	Customer Revenue/Demand/Feedback	28 27 35 40 1 30
22	Amount Of Information	27 25 4 10 22 13 6 19
23	Communication Flow	25 1 19 29 35 28
24	Harmful Factors Affecting System	2 25 28 39 15 10
25	System Generated Harmful Factors	1 15 13 34 31 16
26	Convenience	(see Physical Contradictions section)
27	Adaptability/Versatility	15 34 1 16 29 36 19
28	System Complexity	26 27 32 9 12 24 17
29	Control Complexity	25 5 10 12 24 28 3
30	Tension/Stress	10 5 14 12 13 35
31	Stability	32 35 30 25 13 19 3

Notes:

27
Parameter We Want to Improve – Adaptability/Versatility

Meaning: The extent to which a system, an organisation or person is able to respond to external changes. Also, relates to a system capable of being used in multiple ways or under a variety of circumstances. Flexibility of operation or use. Customizability

Synonyms, Antonyms and Equivalent Meanings: adaptive, dynamic, variation, compliance, rigidity, tolerance, smart-systems, genetic algorithms, universality, switchable, tunable, configurable, user-configurable, re-configurable, one-size-fits-all, template, slot-in solutions, modularity, bespoke, individual, time-variant, seasonal, two-in-one, all-in-one, multi-purpose, multi-functional.

Inventive Principles that should always be considered for problems where we wish to improve this parameter:

15, 35

Averaged list of other Principles that should be considered where we wish to improve this parameter (decreasing order of frequency):

15, 29, 1, 35, 17, 40, 30, 3, 7, 6, 19

List of Principles relevant to each specific worsening parameter:

Worsening Parameter	Description	List of Relevant Inventive Principles (decreasing order of frequency)
1	R&D Spec/Capability/Means	30 25 29 1 35
2	R&D Cost	35 28 19 1 15 8
3	R&D Time	15 1 35 14 4
4	R&D Risk	2 40 31 28 35 29 7
5	R&D Interfaces	29 37 40 1 35 17 30
6	Production Spec/Capability/Means	1 15 17 2 28 38
7	Production Cost	1 30 10 38 29 35
8	Production Time	10 15 30 7 2 29 25 13
9	Production Risk	2 40 38 30 35 29
10	Production Interfaces	29 1 17 40 38
11	Supply Spec/Capability/Means	13 17 7 15 19
12	Supply Cost	1 17 40 3 29
13	Supply Time	15 1 10 27 7
14	Supply Risk	15 17 40 3 29 25
15	Supply Interfaces	29 28 30 3 15
16	Support Spec/Capability/Means	35 13 8 24 29
17	Support Cost	17 35 15 1 3 2

18	Support Time	3 30 40 29 17
19	Support Risk	1 30 40 17 14 15
20	Support Interfaces	29 30 17 14 18 1
21	Customer Revenue/Demand/Feedback	40 17 16 14 15 1
22	Amount Of Information	15 10 2 13 29 3 4
23	Communication Flow	25 6 37 40 15 19
24	Harmful Factors Affecting System	35 11 22 32 31
25	System Generated Harmful Factors	3 1 29 15 10 24
26	Convenience	15 34 1 16 29 36 19
27	Adaptability/Versatility	(see Physical Contradictions section)
28	System Complexity	15 29 28 5 37 6 35 25
29	Control Complexity	25 15 1 28 37 3
30	Tension/Stress	17 40 30 3 15 19 16
31	Stability	35 30 14 34 2 19 10

Notes:

28
Parameter We Want to Improve – System Complexity

Meaning: The number and diversity of elements, people, components, etc and their interrelationships within and across the boundaries of a system. The system may be internal or external to an organisation, or a combination of both. Includes issues like number of functions, number of interfaces and connections, excessive number of elements. Includes intangible as well as tangible parts and links between parts. This is the parameter to use when the 'big picture' perspective of a complex system is the issue under investigation.

Synonyms, Antonyms and Equivalent Meanings: network, web, chaos, edge-of-chaos, complex systems, size, extent, reach, interactions, holistic, small-world, whole-world, 'it's the whole thing, stupid, hierarchy, 'nobody understands', butterfly-effect, unexpected outcomes, ripple-effect, relationship network, population dynamics, perceptions, right-versus-wrong, right-versus-right, tipping point, cliff-edge, non-linear, cause-and-effect-net, viability (viable systems theory), culture.

Inventive Principles that should always be considered for problems where we wish to improve this parameter:

5, 25

Averaged list of other Principles that should be considered where we wish to improve this parameter (decreasing order of frequency):

35, 2, 25, 1, 28, 10, 17, 19, 37, 29

List of Principles relevant to each specific worsening parameter:

Worsening Parameter	Description	List of Relevant Inventive Principles (decreasing order of frequency)
1	R&D Spec/Capability/Means	17 25 1 19 35
2	R&D Cost	5 2 35 1 29
3	R&D Time	5 6 25 10 2 37
4	R&D Risk	28 30 35 1 17
5	R&D Interfaces	25 28 1 3 10
6	Production Spec/Capability/Means	12 17 27 26 1 28 24 13
7	Production Cost	35 5 1 2 29 25
8	Production Time	25 28 2 35 10 15
9	Production Risk	25 2 26 5 29 35
10	Production Interfaces	10 18 28 2 35
11	Supply Spec/Capability/Means	29 30 35 17 3

12	Supply Cost	35 19 1 25 2
13	Supply Time	38 24 16 15 3
14	Supply Risk	2 4 15 28 35 32
15	Supply Interfaces	28 5 3 25 37 40
16	Support Spec/Capability/Means	13 35 1 2 9
17	Support Cost	35 1 25 2 17
18	Support Time	28 15 17 32 37
19	Support Risk	13 35 4 2 37
20	Support Interfaces	28 17 29 37 10 4 13
21	Customer Revenue/Demand/Feedback	25 1 2 19 10 4
22	Amount Of Information	10 25 13 40 2
23	Communication Flow	1 25 4 37 6 18
24	Harmful Factors Affecting System	22 19 29 40 35 15 10
25	System Generated Harmful Factors	19 1 31 3 35 10
26	Convenience	26 27 32 9 12 24 17
27	Adaptability/Versatility	15 29 28 5 37 6 35 25
28	System Complexity	(see Physical Contradictions section)
29	Control Complexity	25 19 1 28 37 3 26
30	Tension/Stress	1 10 2 24 4 19
31	Stability	2 22 35 17 19 26 24

Notes:

29
Parameter We Want to Improve – Control Complexity

Meaning: Complexity of the means of control of a system – either the people, people-interfaces or physical components or the algorithms that it contains – used to enable a system to deliver useful functions. Like the preceding 'system complexity' parameter, this one assumes a high-level, whole system view of control. It is different from 'system complexity' in that it relates to the controllability aspects – a highly complex system can be very easy to control, and likewise, an apparently simple system can be very difficult to control and so the two things have to be treated independently.

Synonyms, Antonyms and Equivalent Meanings: negative feedback, positive feedback, feed-forward, missing-feedback, bottom-up, top-down, algorithm, self-re-enforcing, self-sustaining, automatic, input, output, integral, proportional, differential, response, inertia, lag.

Inventive Principles that should always be considered for problems where we wish to improve this parameter:

4, 10, 25, 37

Averaged list of other Principles that should be considered where we wish to improve this parameter (decreasing order of frequency):

25, 37, 28, 2, 15, 3, 1, 19, 7, 40

List of Principles relevant to each specific worsening parameter:

Worsening Parameter	Description	List of Relevant Inventive Principles (decreasing order of frequency)
1	R&D Spec/Capability/Means	25 15 19 35
2	R&D Cost	25 19 2 37 32
3	R&D Time	25 28 15 2 6 37
4	R&D Risk	25 1 3 37 40 12 24
5	R&D Interfaces	6 28 1 3 40 25 13 9
6	Production Spec/Capability/Means	28 1 13 16 25 37
7	Production Cost	6 3 25 10 32 37
8	Production Time	25 37 3 13 28
9	Production Risk	30 12 25 40 2 37
10	Production Interfaces	10 28 19 15 40 2 25
11	Supply Spec/Capability/Means	6 5 28 37 3 25
12	Supply Cost	22 2 37 4 32 25
13	Supply Time	28 32 25 2 37
14	Supply Risk	2 28 15 24 37

15	Supply Interfaces	25 8 22 28 32 37
16	Support Spec/Capability/Means	11 13 2 35 25
17	Support Cost	15 25 19 28 37
18	Support Time	28 25 37 15 3 1 4
19	Support Risk	10 15 1 34 37
20	Support Interfaces	25 15 10 30 29
21	Customer Revenue/Demand/Feedback	25 2 7 37 6 4 19
22	Amount Of Information	2 7 25 19 1 40 37
23	Communication Flow	25 1 19 37 10
24	Harmful Factors Affecting System	3 15 2 22 25 9 28 26
25	System Generated Harmful Factors	25 3 15 22 10 23 13
26	Convenience	25 5 10 12 24 28 3
27	Adaptability/Versatility	25 15 1 28 37 3
28	System Complexity	25 19 1 28 37 3 26
29	Control Complexity	(see Physical Contradictions section)
30	Tension/Stress	11 24 35 2 40 25
31	Stability	11 28 32 37 25 24

Notes:

Asymmetry (Principle 4) and Relative Change (Principle 37) are two commonly used conflict elimination strategies in the control context since the data they require is likely to already be available in the system, and therefore can be utilised very simply.

30
Parameter We Want to Improve – Tension/Stress

Meaning: Tensions and stresses at either an organisational or personal level – both of which use very similar strategies to achieve win-win outcomes. Tension is the outcome of an external influence that is in conflict with the perceptions, beliefs or behaviour of the recipient. Stress is interpreted here as a more severe version of tension that occurs when the conflict with the external influence passes beyond a threshold level. While not necessarily meaning stress in its medical sense, the interpretation here is that the conflict has forced the organisation or person out of its comfort zone. At the other end of the spectrum, the absence of tension or stress can also be the source of problems. This parameter covers all points on the spectrum.

Synonyms, Antonyms and Equivalent Meanings: pressure, morale, crisis, crisis-management, constructed crisis, lack-of-motivation, happiness, emotion, enjoyment, comfort-zone, dispute, illness, medical symptoms, sick-leave, absenteeism, bullying, harassment, discrimination, exploitation, 'them-and-us', threat, passive-aggressive behaviour, 'in-the-zone', high-performing teams, synergy effects, 'sum-greater-than-the-parts'.

Inventive Principles that should always be considered for problems where we wish to improve this parameter:

2, 12, 24, 36

Averaged list of other Principles that should be considered where we wish to improve this parameter (decreasing order of frequency):

2, 35, 24, 10, 25, 13, 19, 3, 1, 11

List of Principles relevant to each specific worsening parameter:

Worsening Parameter	Description	List of Relevant Inventive Principles (decreasing order of frequency)
1	R&D Spec/Capability/Means	3 2 25 35 9
2	R&D Cost	1 19 35 27 2 18
3	R&D Time	2 39 24 10 4 13
4	R&D Risk	1 23 2 25 13 39
5	R&D Interfaces	35 3 37 32 9 18
6	Production Spec/Capability/Means	35 1 3 10 16
7	Production Cost	1 35 2 25 13 17
8	Production Time	2 20 12 25 3 13 14
9	Production Risk	25 9 24 39 7 19
10	Production Interfaces	3 40 19 1 24

11	Supply Spec/Capability/Means	2 23 5 30 10 13 35
12	Supply Cost	10 3 25 7 40
13	Supply Time	1 10 15 25 24 2 19
14	Supply Risk	1 19 13 10 39
15	Supply Interfaces	5 3 17 29 13 35 2
16	Support Spec/Capability/Means	11 35 24 19 2 25
17	Support Cost	35 24 10 2 25 31 19
18	Support Time	2 24 10 40 25 8
19	Support Risk	10 11 39 1 24 35
20	Support Interfaces	10 8 2 24 6 21 13
21	Customer Revenue/Demand/Feedback	2 10 12 24 25
22	Amount Of Information	2 28 35 10 24 31
23	Communication Flow	3 4 6 7 13 26
24	Harmful Factors Affecting System	11 25 30 2 35 28
25	System Generated Harmful Factors	11 25 12 8 37 35
26	Convenience	10 5 14 12 13 35
27	Adaptability/Versatility	17 40 30 3 15 19 16
28	System Complexity	1 10 2 24 4 19
29	Control Complexity	11 24 35 2 40 25
30	Tension/Stress	(see Physical Contradictions section)
31	Stability	29 35 11 24 19 13

Notes:

Tension and stress problems often appear to occur during disruptive times and hence interpretation and use of Inventive Principles 36, Paradigm Shift, is always worth considering.

31
Parameter We Want to Improve – Stability

Meaning: The integrity of a system; the relationship of a system's constituent elements. The ability of a system to cope with de-stabilising influences, whether internal or external, real or imaginary. The parameter can be applied at the macro (whole-system) or micro (individual) level. In these chaotic times of ever more rapid change in the world, too much stability can be as big a problem as insufficient stability. The parameter includes both ends of this spectrum.

Synonyms, Antonyms and Equivalent Meanings: vulnerability, robustness, inertia, damping, chaos, edge-of-chaos, responsiveness, ability to recover, linear-range, non-linear change, disruption, consistency, predictability, tolerance, limits, extremes, boundaries, 'point-of-no-return'.

Inventive Principles that should always be considered for problems where we wish to improve this parameter:

4, 10, 12, 25, 36

Averaged list of other Principles that should be considered where we wish to improve this parameter (decreasing order of frequency):

35, 10, 1, 25, 19, 2, 3, 15, 29, 13, 24, 9

List of Principles relevant to each specific worsening parameter:

Worsening Parameter	Description	List of Relevant Inventive Principles (decreasing order of frequency)
1	R&D Spec/Capability/Means	25 2 15 36 29
2	R&D Cost	11 25 27 15 2
3	R&D Time	10 3 35 22 27
4	R&D Risk	9 14 1 12 4
5	R&D Interfaces	15 17 25 3 4 36
6	Production Spec/Capability/Means	35 1 23 3 19 13 5 39 40
7	Production Cost	10 1 35 27
8	Production Time	10 15 29 2 19
9	Production Risk	9 1 37 3 19
10	Production Interfaces	11 25 1 3 4
11	Supply Spec/Capability/Means	15 5 25 10 35
12	Supply Cost	19 3 35 10 4
13	Supply Time	35 3 5 27 20 18
14	Supply Risk	9 13 1 25 14
15	Supply Interfaces	33 15 23 17 7
16	Support Spec/Capability/Means	25 26 1 10 12

17	Support Cost	1 35 2 29 10
18	Support Time	10 15 2 30 29 12
19	Support Risk	10 35 7 9 19 1
20	Support Interfaces	11 1 40 13 22 23
21	Customer Revenue/Demand/Feedback	10 40 29 30 28 26
22	Amount Of Information	11 13 25 2 24
23	Communication Flow	37 1 39 40 9 31
24	Harmful Factors Affecting System	35 24 30 18 33
25	System Generated Harmful Factors	35 40 27 39 2
26	Convenience	32 35 30 25 13 19 3
27	Adaptability/Versatility	35 30 14 34 2 19 10
28	System Complexity	2 22 35 17 19 26 24
29	Control Complexity	11 28 32 37 25 24
30	Tension/Stress	29 35 11 24 19 13
31	Stability	(see Physical Contradictions section)

Notes:

Stability problems often appear to occur during disruptive times and hence interpretation of Inventive Principles 36, Paradigm Shift, is often particularly relevant.

40 Inventive (Business) Principles With Examples

Following systematic analysis of close to three million successful inventive solutions extracted from all areas of human endeavour – from the sciences, the arts, politics, engineering and business – researchers have discovered just 40 inventive strategies. These 40 inventive strategies or 'Inventive Principles' present a comprehensive series of solution triggers. They are in fact 'signposts' suggesting the directions in which successful – no compromise – solutions may be found.

The simplest way of using the Principles is in a brainstorming context. This is where we seek to make connections between a problem situation and the solution directions being suggested by each Principle. Whereas a traditional brainstorming session will begin to falter after a relatively short period, the Principles allow us to re-invigorate the idea generation process by simply moving on to look at a different Principle when we are no longer generating new ideas from the current one. It is frequently the case that brainstorming sessions managed using the Principles in this sequential manner can still be generating powerful new ideas after several hours. The traditional brainstorming process is largely random in the way that it works. One of the big underlying ideas behind the form and structure of the Inventive Principles is that they allow a complete solution space to be explored systematically and completely.

It is worth noting here that in order to ensure that the solution space coverage is as comprehensive as possible, there is some overlap between some of the Principles. To some users, this can be a little frustrating. To them, we say two things; 1) the overlap is intentional and, on the evidence of too many actual problem sessions to count anymore, ultimately beneficial, and 2) if you examine the next Principle in your sequence and think to yourself 'hey, I already saw this one', either try to force yourself to use the new one to generate more ideas, or simply move on to the next Principle.

Evidence from a growing user base clearly shows a benefit in becoming familiar with all of the Principles (you will begin to see them everywhere you look after a while). You might like to add your own examples to the database presented here.

Each Principle is presented with three levels of detail. At the most generic level is the basic title description of the Principle – 'segmentation' or 'the other way around'. At the next level of detail – presented as A, B, C, etc – are more descriptive definitions of how a given Principle has previously been interpreted by other problem solvers. And at the finest level of detail are a series of examples of each of the Principles and A, B, C sub-principles.

Principle 1. Segmentation

A. *Divide a system or object into independent parts.*
- Divide an organisation into different product centres.
- Autonomous profit centres.
- Use a work breakdown structure for a large project.
- Franchise outlets
- Red team/Blue team proposal preparation structures
- Kano Diagram – Excitement, Performance, and Threshold product attribute parameters.
- Marketing segmentation by demographics, sociographics, psychographics, lifestyles, etc (creation of 'micro-niches')
- Triage prioritization of problems
- Supermarkets have 'cash-only' or 'basket-only' tills to make it quicker for shoppers who are purchasing just a few items
- Strength/Weakness/Opportunity/Threat (SWOT) analysis
- Recognise difference between 'special' and 'common' cause failures

B. *Make a system or object easy to disassemble.*
- Flexible pensions
- Use of temporary workers on short-term projects
- Flexible Manufacturing Systems
- Modular accounts allowing customers to 'mix and match'
- Modular offices/'hot-desking'
- Container shipment

C. *Increase the degree of fragmentation or segmentation.*
- 'Segment of one' advertising – mass customization
- Virtual office/remote working
- Special Economic Zones
- 'Creative Segmentation' – 'high performance small car', 'easy to use SLR', 'cordless power tool'

Principle 2. Taking Out/Separation

A. *Separate an interfering part or property from a system or object, or single out the only necessary part (or property).*
- Breakdown barriers between departments (Point No.9 of Deming's Fourteen Points).
- Eliminate exhortations (Point No.10 of Deming's Fourteen Points)
- Eliminate targets (Point No.11 of Deming's Fourteen Points).
- Drive Out Fear (Point No.8 of Deming's Fourteen Points)
- 'Separate the PEOPLE from the PROBLEM' ('Getting To Yes').
- ATM banking
- USP advertising
- Just-In-Time inventory management
- Separate development and production activities – skunkworks, tiger-teams, etc.
- Smart software learns user preferences and filters out non-useful information.
- Semantic processors used to extract 'knowledge' from text
- Anonymous questionnaires of customers and employees
- Dis-intermediation

Principle 3. Local Quality

A. *Change the structure of an object or system from uniform to non-uniform, change an external environment (or external influence) from uniform to non-uniform.*
- Moves away from rigid salary structures/job grading.
- Skill/personality matching in project teams
- Flexible working hours.
- Franchise fast food outlets have local dishes in addition to normal product range.
- Casual ('dress-down') days.
- Regional advertising campaigns/coupon programmes
- Moves away from rigid salary structures/job grading.
- Red team/Blue team proposal preparation structures
- 'Quiet' work areas/meeting areas/etc.

B. *Make each part of an object or system function in conditions most suitable for its operation.*
- 'Empowerment' of individuals
- Have each employee's workplace customized to individual ergonomic and psychological needs.
- Working hours phased to accommodate people working on international, shifted time-zone projects
- Using coffee-breaks for informal (non-uniform) communication
- 'Early adopter' focused products and services
- Customizable software

C. *Make each part of an object or system fulfill a different and useful function.*
- Organisational division by function rather than product.
- Staff specialists in centres of excellence
- Hire local people to acquire cultural knowledge of local customers
- 'Kids areas' in restaurants, etc

Principle 4. Asymmetry

A. *Change the form of a system or object from symmetrical to asymmetrical.*
- 'Buy-now, pay-later'
- (Proportionately) more 'Plan' or more 'Study' in the Deming PDSA cycle
- Skewed normal distributions.
- Budget for different departments individually rather than using a constant percentage increase or reduction for all departments
- More 'customer' in the customer-supplier relationship
- Take account of seasonal variations in sales forecasting

B. *If a system or object is asymmetrical, change its degree of asymmetry.*
- 360º appraisals
- More equitable 2-way dialogue between management and workers
- Shift away from calendar-influenced sales bias (e.g. shift from annual to bi-annual car registration dates (to reduce August sales peak), greetings card companies, etc.)
- Honda's 4M – 'man maximum, machine minimum' product design philosophy.
- Bigger customer focus groups/Internet focus groups
- On-line, web-cam shopping – 'one store serves the world'
- Collaboration with 'complementor' organisations when competing for business with other directly competitive companies

Principle 5. Merging

A. *Bring closer together (or merge) identical or similar systems or objects, assemble identical or similar parts to perform parallel operations.*
- Cell-based Manufacture
- Toyota JIT/'Lean manufacture'
- Common-interest groups
- Multi-screen cinemas
- Shopping malls
- Banks, etc offer customers a full range of financial service packages – current, savings, mortgage, pension, etc.
- Debt-consolidation loan
- Collaboration with 'complementor' organisations when competing for business with other directly competitive companies
- Partner with non-competing companies in other countries
- 'Young engineers have ideas, old engineers have bad experiences' Japanese saying

B. *Make operations contiguous or parallel; bring them together in time.*
- Eli Goldratt's Theory of Constraints
- Enlisting customer and supplier help in designing the product (Boeing 777 'Working Together Teams')
- Multi-media presentations
- Groupware – mail/email/intranet/video-conference/etc
- Movie/book/soundtrack/Internet/merchandise tie-ins
- Package holidays
- Call centres

Principle 6. Universality

A. *Make an object or structure perform multiple functions; eliminate the need for other parts.*
- Multi-skilling of work-force
- 'One-stop shopping' – supermarkets sell insurance, phone, fuel, newspapers, etc.
- Rapid Reaction Forces in the military – cross-trained, equipment versatility, etc
- Semco – managerial staff set their own salaries, shopfloor workers set their own productivity targets, part of change agent's job is to eliminate need for his/her job
- Internet/Intranet allows improved communication across companies, project teams – everybody has access to all relevant information.
- Industry standards – e.g. communication protocols – HTML/Internet/TCP/IP
- ISO9000 and related universal standards
- Market-based cost standards
- Templates

Principle 7. "Nested Doll"

A. *Place one system or object inside another; place each, in turn, inside the other.*
- Store-in-store
- Profit centers inside an organisation
- Cash machines work for multiple banks

- Hierarchical organisation structures
- Four levels of knowledge – 1) Basic Skills, 2) Know How, 3) Process Management, 4) Strategic Vision – contained in effective company (e.g. Sony) training schemes

B. *Make one thing pass through another.*
- Expose traditionally inward facing job-holders to external events/customers (e.g. engineers shadow marketing people during customer visits)
- Door sensors count customers into and out of a store/office, etc (use data for market profiling, etc)
- Internet 'Navigator' companies

Principle 8. Counter-Balance

A. *To compensate for the tendency of a system or object to deviate from a desired path merge it with others that provide a re-stabilising effect.*
- In a merger of two companies, one 'lifts' the other with whatever its stronger features are (distribution system, marketing, methods, capital, etc)
- Companies increase flagging sales by making connections with other rising products (e.g. movie tie-ins)
- Attaching the word 'new' is the most powerful way of enhancing the sales of fast moving consumer goods
- Recruit 'champions' to assist during change initiatives

B. *To compensate for the deviation tendency of a system or object, make it interact with global/macro-scale phenomena.*
- A small company is 'lifted' by use of an external transportation network to the level of the larger companies
- Political parties boost poll ratings by attaching themselves to popular causes
- Attach product/service marketing to customer and business driving forces (Megatrends – aging population, desire for flexibility, simplicity, etc)

Principle 9. Prior Counter-Action

A. *If it will be necessary to perform an action with both harmful and useful effects, this action should be replaced with anti-actions to control harmful effects in advance.*
- When making a public announcement, include all the information, not just the harmful parts (e.g. Perrier's handling of their water quality problem)
- Use formal risk assessment methods to quantify risk and identify mitigation actions before and during a project – subversion analysis ('how could we destroy this system?)
- Customer trials/segmented launch of (high risk) new products (e.g. film companies film several endings to a movie and trial with different audiences before finalising selection)
- Asking to be 'paid to play' during a competitive bid when you are the new player and the customer is looking to get the incumbent to reduce price
- Use of voluntary redundancy/pay-cuts/short-time working/job-sharing as alternatives to down-sizing
- Telling someone that they can't have something is often a very effective way of making them want it
- Introduce deliberate mistakes then 'wow' the customer with the efficient way in which things are fixed

B. *Create beforehand stresses in a system or object that will oppose known undesirable working stresses later on.*
- Epson product development engineers spend time as sales and then service staff before they are allowed to work on product development activities
- Team-building tasks are done before the real project starts. (for example the team spends one week on a special seminar, so that they can learn to work together)
- Negotiate upfront stage payments in a long term contract

Principle 10. Prior Action

A. *Perform the required change of a system or object (either fully or partially) before it is needed.*
- Pre-pay/post-pay financing arrangements
- Project pre-planning
- Visit Gemba – go see how the customer actually uses products/services
- Perform non-critical path tasks early (where circumstances permit)
- Dialogue with employees before embarking on re-organization stucture
- 'Off-the-shelf'/'ready-made'/'pre-packaged' solutions
- Rent, lease or partial-purchase property instead of outright purchase
- Phone-in food order before arriving at restaurant
- Create buzz about a new product by 'leaking' news ahead of formal launch

B. *Pre-arrange elements such that they can come into action from the most convenient place and without losing time for their delivery.*
- Kanban arrangements in a Just-In-Time factory
- Cell-based manufacture
- Publish an agenda before meetings
- 'Hub-and-spoke' network delivery concept (e.g. FedEx)
- 'If I had 8 hours to chop down a tree, I'd spend 6 hours sharpening my axe' Abraham Lincoln.
- Benetton 'retarded differentiation' – clothing is knitted before it is dyed; colour only applied when the season's popular colours emerge.
- Car-servicing overnight (when most customers are not using their vehicles)
- Dealer-fit car accessories – CD player, alloy wheels, air-con, etc.
- Distributed systems – local depots, etc

Principle 11. Prior Cushioning

A. *Prepare emergency means beforehand to compensate for the possible problems that might occur later.*
- Contingency planning and definition of 'fall-back solutions'
- Establish a worst-case, fall-back position prior to negotiation - 'Best Alternative to a Negotiated Agreement'
- Back up computer data
- Anti-virus software
- Encourage short, effective meetings by removing the chairs
- Put clauses in contracts requiring arbitration/mediation to avoid litigation
- Begin with 'S' in the PDSA cycle
- Second-sourcing critical sub-systems
- '80% of a successful production is in the casting' Lindsay Anderson

Principle 12. Remove Tension

A. *Where harmful tensions may exist, create conditions to compensate, reduce or eliminate them*
  - Make 'horizontal' career changes to broaden skills
  - Team members distribute their own merit award money (rather than often divisive distribution methods employed by management)
  - Force-Field Analysis – group discussion of the phrase 'forces push in various directions' – teambuilding/problem-solving technique.
  - Empathy – manager tunes presentation to best suit audience of, for example, workers and directors
  - Beware of the Peter Principle – 'Every employee tends to rise to his/her level of incompetence
  - Single-union agreements
  - 'No-fault' termination clauses written into contracts
  - 'Communication is and should be hellfire and sparks, as well as sweetness and light' Aman Vivian Rakoff

Principle 13. 'The Other Way Around'

A. *Invert the action(s) used to solve a problem.*
  - Bring the mountain to Mohammed, instead of bringing Mohammed to the mountain.
  - Expansion instead of contraction during recession.
  - Benchmark against the worst instead of (or at least as well as) the best
  - Blame the process not the person
  - Transform the Maintenance department into the 'Robustness' department and get them to eliminate maintenance
  - 'I used to think that anyone doing anything weird was weird. I suddenly realised that anyone doing anything weird wasn't weird at all, and it was the people saying they were weird that were weird' Paul McCartney.
B. *Make movable parts (or the external environment) fixed, and fixed parts movable.*
  - Home-shopping
  - Home banking
  - Park-and-ride schemes in busy cities
  - Mobile car service – mechanic comes to you rather than you going to garage
  - Mobile library
  - Don't make changes just because they are fashionable management fads
C. *Turn the system, object or process 'upside down'.*
  - Cash-till assistant is the most important part of a retail organisation
  - Computer help lines were often originally set up with relatively no-technical staff at the front-end, directing calls to progressively more technically able staff the more complicated the problem is. Latest logic suggests reversing this trend – i.e. place the most qualified staff as first point of contact (e.g. IBM)
  - Pull rather than push-based organisation structures
  - 'Ready, Fire, Aim' – Tom Peters
  - Mercedes Benz vision changed from 'the best or nothing' to 'the best for our customers' – i.e. shift from internal to externally focused vision statement.
  - The Peter Pyramid

- Corporate 'unlearning' – acquiring the ability to forget about the past where appropriate
- 'Ours is the age that is proud of machines that think and suspicious of men who try to' H Mumford-Jones
- Russian government pays inventors for patent applications/West makes the inventor pay to apply.
- Chairman of company spends time in the complaints department answering customer complaints
- 'Nothing fails like success'
- 'We don't stop playing because we grow old, we grow old because we stop playing'
- 'When you reach the top, that's when the climb begins' Michael Caine

Principle 14. Curvature

A. *Turn flat or straight things into curved ones; .*
- Take the shortest path to the customer – around the organisation rather than point-to-point through the bureaucracy
- Levi Strauss' IS Department's organizational chart resembles a solar system, with the names of 20 managers appearing once on a large circle-and in many cases, also on one of four smaller circles intersecting the large one. The small circles represent action groups focusing on specific tasks, including customer service and business systems.
- Set up 'virtuous circles' – self re-enforcing activities
- 'Form the wagons into a circle' John Wayne

B. *Go from linear to rotary motion.*
- Rotate leadership of a team
- Revolving credit agreements
- Circular work cells
- Recognise that the Deming PDSA cycle is circular and that the 'Act' stage feeds into the next 'Plan' stage (e.g. project teams are often disbanded before any 'lessons learned' are recorded)

Principle 15. Dynamization

A. *Allow (or design) the characteristics of a system, object, external environment, or process to change to be optimal or to find an optimal operating condition.*
- Empowerment
- 'Customer Response Teams'/Rapid Reaction Force
- Continuous Process Improvement
- Seasonal pricing/advertising
- Regional pricing/advertising
- Flexible shift patterns
- 'Drum, Buffer, Rope' process operation scheduling
- Swatch design proliferation – design for specific market niches
- Adjust meeting frequency according to rate of change during a project
- 'In today's turbulent business environment, there are no hard fast conclusions – only transitions'
- 'Change is the only constant'

B. *Divide a system or object into parts capable of movement relative to each other.*
- Work teams oriented to achieve same goal, but work at different rates on different objectives
- Geographically or functionally independent business units
- Conglomerate structures

C. *If a system, object or process is rigid or inflexible, make it movable or adaptive.*
- On-line shopping webcam – customer is able to control and move cameras to point to different products in different parts of the store from home computer
- Changing the supervisor's role; avoid 'whack-a-mole' firefighting
- Usage-based warranties (instead of fixed time period)
- Virgin 'One' bank account – continuously optimizes funds to earn maximum interest without the customer having to do anything
- Flexible organisation structure (chaocracy)

Principle 16. Slightly Less/Slightly More

A. *If 100 percent of an objective is hard to achieve using a given solution method then, by using 'slightly less' or 'slightly more' of the same method, the problem may be considerably easier to solve.*
- 'If it ain't broke, improve it anyway' – Japanese process management philosophy.
- Use Pareto analysis to enable work to concentrate on the high return elements.
- Set stretch targets in the knowledge that achievement of less than the full amount is still well worth having
- Saturation advertising
- Aim to 'delight' rather than 'satisfy' customers
- Design deliberate overlap between the roles of managers in order to improve communications (commonly used Japanese strategy)
- 'The most important numbers are the ones you'll never know' – W.E. Deming (i.e. is it possible to ever know what '100%' means)

Principle 17. Another Dimension

A. *If a system or object uses only one or two dimensions; make use of the unused dimensions.*
- 360° appraisals.
- Continuous appraisals (i.e. use of the time dimension)
- Portfolio investment strategies – with deliberate selection of different but complementary stocks
- Buy in one location and sell in another
- Multi-dimensional organisation hierarchy charts – 3D (e.g. to show 'hard' and 'soft' relationships), or 4D – to include an element of time ('Buckyball Management')
- Distributed responsibility and authority – e.g. Quality department advises on technical details and conducts audits, but everyone is responsible for quality. Ditto Safety Office.

B. *Use a multi-storey arrangement instead of a single-storey arrangement.*
- Organisational hierarchy
- Multi-stack storage systems use the height of a building, and save floorspace
- 'Standing on the shoulders of giants…'

- 'When two people meet, there are really six people present. There is each man as he sees himself, each man as he wants to be seen, and each man as he really is.' Michael De Saintamo

C. *Tilt or re-orient the system or object, lay it on its side.*
- Horizontal (peer) communication
- Switch between Horizontally and vertically integrated operations
- Switch from vertical to horizontal (lateral) thinking – and vice-versa
- Shift from 'line' to 'project' management dominance in matrix organisation (and vice-versa – depending on prevailing market conditions)
- Shift from portrait to landscape report format

D. *Use 'another side' of a given system or object.*
- View your organisation from the outside – either directly or using consultants, 'mystery shoppers', etc.
- New ways of looking at the selling process - instead of selling carpets to its commercial and industrial customers, Interface offers what it calls the "Evergreen Lease." Its customers no longer buy carpets or pay an installation fee - they just pay a monthly service fee that guarantees they will always have clean, attractive carpets
- 'A good manager doesn't try to eliminate conflict; he tries to keep it from wasting the energies of his people. If you're the boss and your people fight you openly when they think that you are wrong -- that's healthy' Robert Townsend'
- The things we fear most in organizations - fluctuations, disturbances, imbalances - are the primary sources of creativity' Margaret J Wheatley.

Principle 18. Resonance

B. *Find and use the 'resonant frequency' of a system or object.*
- Use the process of hoshin planning to get the whole organisation 'vibrating'
- 'I don't think that you should ever manage anything that you don't care passionately about' D Coleman, VP & CFO Apple
- 'He inspired in us the belief that we were working in a medium that was powerful enough to influence the world' Lillian Gish on D.W.Griffiths
- Use strategic planning (policy deployment, hoshin Kanri) to select the right frequency and get the organisation resonating at that frequency to accomplish a breakthrough strategy
- 'In a start-up company, you basically throw out all assumptions every three weeks.' Scott McNealy
- 'Kansei' – Japanese term for resonance/one-ness between product and user

Principle 19. Periodic Action

A. *Instead of continuous action, use periodic or changing actions.*
- Batch manufacture.
- Tidal traffic flow schemes ease transport into and out of busy areas
- Change team leadership periodically (e.g. the EU leadership is rotated on an annual basis between different countries)
- Introduce 'time-out' periods in difficult negotiations
- Introduce 'breathing spaces' into contracts
- Introduce sabbaticals to refresh people's points of view

B. *If an action is already periodic, change the periodic magnitude or frequency.*
- Audit at irregular intervals
- Use monthly or weekly feedback instead of annual reviews
- Flexible savings schemes which pay higher interest rates the fewer the number of withdrawals made
- Ritz-Carlton hotels have 10 minutes staff training per day instead of less frequent longer sessions.

C. *Use pauses between actions to perform a different action.*
- Use travelling time to catch up on reading
- Perform maintenance work during vacations
- Introduce stimulating activities (external speakers, etc) during times of the week when work output is low – e.g. Friday afternoons.
- 24-hour car service operation – evening pick-up, return of serviced car by breakfast the following morning (customer perspective).
- 'Hot-till'ing in supermarkets – staff do other tasks during quiet periods and move to tills when they see queues developing

Principle 20. Continuity of Useful Action

A. *Make parts of a system or object work at optimal conditions continuously.*
- Run the bottleneck operations in a factory continuously, to reach the optimum overall pace. (from Theory of Constraints)
- Institute Constant Improvement (Point No.5 of Deming's Fourteen Points)
- Continuous on-line monitoring of elevators by Otis who take on total maintenance responsibility
- Continuous compounding of interest
- Perpetuities
- 24 hour car service operation – evening pick-up, return of serviced car by breakfast the following morning (garage perspective)
- 'Life-long learning'
- 'The power of a waterfall is nothing but a lot of drips working together'
- 'The more I practice, the luckier I get' Gary Player

B. *Eliminate all idle or intermittent actions or work.*
- Multi-skilling to enable working in bottleneck functions to improve workflow
- 24hour shift patterns
- Conduct training during pauses in work

Principle 21. Hurrying

A. *Conduct a process, or certain stages (e.g. destructible, harmful or hazardous operations) at high speed.*
- 'Incrementalism is innovation's worst enemy' Nicholas Negreponte, MIT Media Lab
- 'Don't be afraid to take a big step if one is indicated. You can't cross a chasm in two small jumps' David Lloyd George
- 'Fail Fast; Learn Fast'
- 'Fast Cycle – Full Participation' – method of involving the whole organisation simultaneously and rapidly in a major change, such as a re-organisation
- Get through painful processes quickly (e.g. firing someone)

- Rapid prototyping
- 'If you want to succeed, double your failure rate' JR Watson, IBM founder

Principle 22. "Blessing in Disguise" or "Turn Lemons into Lemonade"

A. *Use harmful factors (particularly, harmful effects of the environment or surroundings) to achieve a positive effect.*
- Recast an attack on you as an attack on the problem.
- Making a fuss over customers who have experienced a problem with your goods/services/etc, tends to re-enforce their overall positive feel about you – to a level greater than that where no problem had occurred.
- Turn contract negotiations into win-win situations – see a drive to reduce price as an opportunity to negotiate longer term or 'last-look' options
- 'Provocations' method of encouraging new ideas
- 'The Extra Mile will have no traffic jams.' Unknown

B. *Eliminate the primary harmful action by adding it to another harmful action to resolve the problem.*
- Eliminate fear of change by introducing fear of competition
- Put a 'problem' person on an assignment in another area where he/she can do well and not be a problem to the original group
- Loss-leader strategy for increasing sales
- Keep traffic out of cities by introducing low cost 'park and ride' and expensive downtown parking charges.
- Make potentially polluting industries place flow intakes downstream of flow outlets on a river

C. *Amplify a harmful factor to such a degree that it is no longer harmful.*
- Reduce resourcing levels to such an extent that new ways of doing the job have to be discovered
- Restrict supply of goods to create scarcity value (e.g. some sports car manufacturers seek to maintain a multiple year waiting list on vehicles giving them a certain cachet that they would not otherwise have)
- Borrow ten thousand dollars from the bank and they own you; borrow ten million and you own them!

Principle 23. Feedback

A. *Introduce feedback (referring back, cross-checking) to improve a process or action.*
- Statistical Process Control (SPC) -- Measurements are used to decide when to modify a process.
- Enlist customers in the design process.
- 'Extranets'/Electronic bulletin boards
- Customer surveys/customer seminars, etc
- 'Active Transition Management' as a way of controlling product development process between research, development and production phases.
- (Supermarket) loyalty cards – provide customer shopping profile information
- 'What you measure is what you get' Joe Juran
- Beta testing on-site with customer
- 'Active Transition Management' as a way of controlling product development process between research, development and production phases.

- 95% of customers who have a bad experience with your services will not complain, they will simply move to another provider. Introduce easy feedback mechanisms so customers can give (possibly anonymous) feedback

B. *If feedback is already used, change its magnitude or influence.*
- Change a management measure from budget variance to customer satisfaction.
- Expose designers as well as marketers to customers
- Allow customers to watch (e.g. via webcam) the manufacture or preparation of their order
- Multi-Criteria Decision Analysis (valid 'apples and oranges' comparisons).
- Toshiba medical systems division split into R&D, Engineering and Manufacture sectors. As a product is being developed, key personnel and leadership physically move from one sector to another to actively manage transitions between product development stages.
- 'Open the kimono' – everything out in the open – communication
- 'Supravision' rather than 'supervision'
- 'Co-evolutionary marketing' – e.g. Amazon.com invites readers to write on-line book reviews; other readers often prefer these views to professional reviewer evaluations, therefore people visit the site more often
- Motorola 'open dissent' policy – employees fill in a minority report to senior management when ideas they consider valuable are unsupported by colleagues and immediate superiors
- Use of 'half-life' as a measure of improvement (e.g. time taken to half product development time) to encourage large-scale thinking
- Feed-forward – anticipatory feedback

Principle 24. 'Intermediary'

A. *Use an intermediary carrier article or intermediary process.*
- Use of impartial body during difficult negotiation (e.g. ACAS)
- 'Po' (provocative operator) – a place between 'yes' and 'no', construct devised by Edward DeBono to help avoid premature discarding of ideas
- Sub-contract non-core business (e.g. cleaning services, transport)
- Franchisee acts as intermediary between corporate vision and customer
- Travel agent (NB can also mean removal of intermediary – e.g. direct selling).
- Collection Agent – debt
- Brokers, trustees, etc
- Product placement in TV shows or films
- UPS distribution system using core sorting centre.
- KLM 'feeder' airline concept – short flights from Germany, England pull passengers away from national airlines in order that they fly long distances using Holland as a hub
- 'Video Plus' – programme video using simple codes to represent channels, dates and times
- 'Cuckoo Investments'

B. *Merge one system or object temporarily with another (which can be easily removed).*
- Introduction of specialist trouble-shooting or fire-fighting teams
- Hire consultant.
- Use bridging loan arrangements to help cashflow
- Subcontract occasional services – grounds maintenance, etc.

Principle 25. Self-Service

A. *Make a system or object serve itself by performing auxiliary helpful functions*
- Quality Circles
- Self-help groups
- Viral marketing campaigns
- Brand image circularity – Harvard Business School produces bright people; these people enhance the School's reputation; hence lots of people apply; hence they only take on very bright people; bright people in equals bright people out; and so the circle re-enforces itself.
- 'Cookies' on the Internet gather data useful for future marketing activities, while performing a useful service for the 'surfer'
- Bar-codes in supermarkets provide instant pricing information, but the system also gathers information to assist future marketing decisions
- Edward DeBono's suggestion to Ford UK that they buy National Car Parks and then only let Ford cars into the parking lots – i.e. motorists buying a Ford are also buying a parking place in every city

B. *Use waste (or lost) resources, energy, or substances.*
- Re-hire retired workers for jobs where their experience is needed
- Loan out temporarily under-utilised workers to other organisations (load-capacity balancing across companies – e.g. footballers – win-win situation; the player stays match fit, the loaner saves wages, the loanee fills skill shortage)
- 'Industrial eco-systems'
- 'Brown-field' developments
- Body Shop re-cycles used containers brought back by customers – helps promote corporate green image
- Leveraged buy-out
- Re-cycle all packaging material

Principle 26. Copying

A. *Instead of an unavailable, expensive, or vulnerable object, use simpler and inexpensive copies.*
- Bench-marking.
- Rapid prototyping (e.g. stereo-lithography)
- On-line bookings/transactions/applications replace physical offices
- Problem-based learning/case-based reasoning
- Scan rare, historic books, documents, etc so they are accessible to all and the original remains protected
- Lascaux II – reproduction of Lascaux cave paintings which is open to visitors

B. *Replace a system, object, or process with optical or virtual copies.*
- Virtual product service manuals.
- Flight simulator reduces pilot training costs.
- Numerical simulation – operational analysis (virtual war-gaming, virtual business development, strategic planning modeling).
- Video-conferencing instead of physical travel
- Use a central electronic database instead of paper records in cases where multiple users would benefit from simultaneous access to data – e.g. medical records, customer data, engineering drawings, etc

- Keep your personal calendar on a web-site so you (and others?) can access it from any computer, and it can't get lost
- Novell 'iHome' system gives users an Internet accessible version of their computer hard-drive.

C. *If copies are already used, move to an out of the ordinary illumination and viewing perspective.*
- Evaluate employee morale using multiple methods such as interviews and questionnaires (2 different 'wavelengths')
- Evaluate customer satisfaction using multiple techniques
- Have your customers benchmark you/have your suppliers benchmark you

Principle 27. Cheap Disposable

A. *Replace an expensive system or object with a multiple of inexpensive alternatives, comprising certain less-important qualities (such as service life, for instance).*
- Use disposable paper objects to avoid the cost of cleaning and storing durable objects. Plastic cups in motels, disposable diapers, many kinds of medical supplies.
- Throw-away cameras/mobile-phones, etc
- 'Disposable organisation structures' in rapidly changing markets – i.e. little point in massively optimising structures in e-commerce businesses which are still in a state of rapid evolution.
- Swatch 'renewed impulse' buying ' - 'Change clothes? Change Swatch'.
- 'Cardboard police' – 2D policemen or police cars over freeway bridges used as a means of slowing down traffic

Principle 28 Another Sense

A. *Replace or supplement one sensory means with another (visible, touch, acoustic, taste or smell)*
- CEO of budget motel chain; 'our goal is that when you turn out the lights and climb into bed, you think you are at the Hilton'
- Multi-media presentations
- Learning by listening, seeing and doing
- Supermarkets pump bakery odours around the store to help advertise bread products
- 'The seeing of objects involves many sources of information beyond those meeting the eye when we look at an object. It generally involves knowledge of the object derived from previous experience, and this experience is not limited to vision but may include the other senses: touch, taste, smell, hearing, and perhaps also temperature or pain.' R.L.Gregory
- MBWA – Management By Walking Around

Principle 29. Fluidity

A. *Make solid things into 'fluid' things.*
- 'Water logic' versus 'rock logic' – fluid, flowing, gradually building up logic versus permanent, hard-edged, rock-like alternatives

- Flexible (fluid) organisation structure versus old fixed hierarchical structures
- Organisations traditionally viewed as 'competitors' may become collaborators on certain projects – this is happening increasingly in the aerospace industry; which now has a much more fluid approach to who works with whom
- Make use of the informal communication channels (grapevine) that exist inside the organization – e.g. spread important messages by utilising the natural connectors
- Liquidation of assets
- Floating deadlines in contracts

Principle 30. Thin and Flexible

A. *Use thin and flexible structures instead of large, three-dimensional ones*
- The thinnest film is a single molecule thick. Likewise, the thinnest organisation structure is one employee thick. Get faster customer service by having the single employee customer service agent have all the necessary data easily available, so the customer only deals with the single, flexible 'shell' of the organisation not the whole bulky volume.
- 'De-layering' within an organizational hierarchy
- 'We like to delegate and leave people as free as possible, so we try to push management decisions down the line. We run Rolls-Royce with a very thin corporate structure', Lord Tombs of Brailes, ex-Chairman of Rolls-Royce

B. *Isolate a system or object from a potentially harmful environment using thin and flexible structures.*
- Office workers in open areas can use flexible curtains to shut themselves off from the visual chaos of the open area when they need to concentrate rather than communicate
- Use 'trade secret' methods to separate company proprietary knowledge from general knowledge

Principle 31. Holes

A. *Add 'holes' to a system or object.*
- Think of the customer-facing layers of a company as a porous membrane which filters information flow both into and out of the organisation
- Introduce 'breathing spaces' into contracts
- Improve internal communications by creating Intranet accessible by all hierarchical layers; giving workers access to CEO and vice-versa.
- 'Nature abhors a vacuum' – deliberately eliminate certain roles in an organization as a way of exploring how the system will fill in the missing elements
- Government 'leaks' – used as a way of gauging public reaction to (usually) controversial issues

B. *If a system or object already has holes, use them to introduce a useful substance or function.*
- Empower the customer facing layer (information is the thing that fills the pores – see 30A).
- Use mind-maps, self-patterning capabilities, etc to improve the information/knowledge intake and filtering abilities of the brain
- Media relations department turns spin-doctor and/or marketing feedback gatherer

Principle 32. Colour Changes

A. *Change the colour of an object or its external environment.*
- Red/Blue proposal preparation teams
- Use of lighting effects to change mood in a room or office
- Six Thinking Hats
- Creation of 'corporate colours' – creating a strong brand image through use of bespoke colours – 'BP green', 'British Telecom red' phone boxes, 'Ford blue', etc
- Use colours to communicate state of alert (green, black, amber, red, etc)
- Security alert states – psychologically, people remember colours better than text
- Have software change the colour of presented data when it – for example – goes outside a prescribed range

B. *Change the transparency of a system, object or an external environment.*
- 'Transparent' organisations
- Transparent communications
- Importance of creating clear, concise mission statement
- Smoke-screen/mis-information to disguise confidential R&D etc activities

Principle 33. Homogeneity

A. *Make systems or objects interact with others of a similar form or with similar properties.*
- Co-located project teams
- Internal customers
- Product branding/product families
- Boeing 'Working Together Teams' – bring customers and suppliers into the design loop.
- 'Complementor' organizations – ones that are not competing with yours, but which enable the creation of a win-win benefit – e.g. toothpaste and chewing-gum companies
- 'Singing from the same hymn sheet'
- Common data transfer protocols between different organisations
- 'The best way to make a silk purse from a sow's ear is to begin with a silk sow. The same is true of money' (Augustine's Law #1)

Principle 34. Discarding and Recovering

A. *Make portions of a system or object that have fulfilled their functions go away or modify them directly during an operation.*
- Flexible, variable-sized project teams
- Load/capacity balance using contract labour
- Consultants
- Contract hire of specialised equipment/facilities, etc

B. *Conversely, restore consumable parts of a system or object directly in operation.*
- Need to periodically re-energise continuous improvement initiatives ('enthusiasm injections')
- Life-long learning (where individuals are given responsibility for managing their own personal continuing education, ensuring skills remain up to date)

Principle 35. Parameter Changes

A. *Change an object's physical state (e.g. from physical to virtual).*
- Virtual prototyping
- Numerical simulation
- Virtual shopping – e.g. Amazon.com
- e-Commerce/e-Business
- Telephone banking
- Electronic voting in elections

B. *Change the concentration or consistency.*
- Stock options
- 'Six Thinking Hats'/'Six Action Shoes'
- Change the team structure (e.g. football teams use substitutes)
- Stores introduce 'special offers' and other promotions

C. *Change the degree of flexibility.*
- Introduce intelligence into on-line catalogues (e.g. first generation catalogues were replicas of previous paper versions, latest generation incorporate search engines, expert systems, etc)
- Software with options for 'beginner' through to 'expert' usage
- Moves away from fixed clothing size partitions – e.g. 'Personal Pairs' - a customer at a participating store chooses which fabric he/she wants, then is measured. Those measurements are transmitted instantly to a Levi's plant in Tennessee where the data controls a laser cutter. The bar-coded pieces are stitched on the regular assembly line, and mailed directly to the customer.

D. Change emotional and other parameters.
- Get customers excited about the product by giving them ownership of the change
- Get employees excited about the future of the company by using full involvement strategic planning, or stock options, or... etc.
- 'A fired-up team wins games even if it's not the best team. A fired-up company can achieve the same result'

Principle 36. Paradigm Shift

A. *Use phenomena occurring during disruptive shifts in an economy. (Awareness of macro-scale business phenomena)*
- Awareness of the requirements of different stages – conception, birth, development, maturity, retirement – of a project (e.g. shifting manpower requirements, shifting budget requirements).
- Take account of transition from a 'bull' to a 'bear' market.
- Tendency to relax after receiving a Quality Award, Innovation Award, etc.
- Alvin Toffler's stated need for companies to 'learn, un-learn and re-learn' as economies shift from disruptive wave to the next
- Forming/storming/norming/performing phases of team development – e.g. take advantage of enthusiasm dip during storming-norming

Principle 37. Relative Change

A. *Use the relative differences that exist in an object or system to do something useful*
- Personality matching on work-teams

- Derivatives
- Creative tension – some organisations employ two independent teams to develop a new product or process, and then compete them. This is often done using one team constructed along 'traditional' lines, and the other using a smaller number of 'maverick' types; ones that don't fit well into traditional structures.
- 'It seems safe to say that significant discovery, really creative thinking, does not occur with regard to problems about which the thinker is lukewarm'. Mary Henle

B. *Make different parts of a system act differently in response to changes*
- Expand or contract marketing efforts depending on the product's rate of sales and profitability.
- Combination of high risk and high-stability investment strategies during market turbulence.
- Pincer movement during war-gaming
- 'Good-cop/bad-cop' negotiation/interrogation strategies
- Creation of off-shoot companies to better exploit new product developments

Principle 38. Enriched Atmosphere

A. *Replace a normal atmosphere with an enriched one.*
- Risk and Revenue Sharing Partnerships
- Guest speakers at a seminar
- Use internal subject matter experts
- Use simulations/games instead of lecture-style training
- Injection of new-blood/new challenge into a team'
- Lotteries and other gaming activities
- 'Free gift inside'
- Un-secured loan
- Underwrite insurance for others
- Set stretch targets that cannot be achieved without a significant re-think of the way things are currently done
- A fired-up, empowered, appreciated individual will do the work of three who aren't'
- South West Airlines POS – Positively Outrageous Service
- Consider personal chemistry issues when assembling a project team – find people who will spark-off interesting reactions with each other.
- Deming's 4th stage of learning – unconscious incompetence, conscious incompetence, conscious competence, *unconscious competence*
- 'Leadership is a potent combination of strategy and character. But if you must be without one, be without strategy.' General H. Norman, Schwartzkopff

B. *Expose a highly enriched atmosphere with one containing potentially 'unstable' elements.*
- Corporate Jester/'Trickster'/Fool – someone who is paid to provoke the system and ask the difficult questions that often don't get asked
- 'Devil's Advocate'
- Bring your 'worst customer' into design or planning meetings
- 'I like Bartok and Stravinsky. It's a discordant sound and there are discordant sounds inside a company. As president you must orchestrate the discordant sounds into a kind of harmony. But you never want too much harmony. One must cultivate a taste for finding harmony within discord or you will drift away from the forces that keep a company alive' Takeo Fujisawa, Honda co-founder.

Principle 39. Calm Atmosphere

A. *Replace a normal environment with an inert one.*
- Moves away from the (normal) disruptive performance appraisal, merit award, and reward environment to an (emotionally neutral) more fair system of working practice
- Tie finances to stable currencies
- Quarantine zones
- Hare Brain, Tortoise Mind
- Time-out during negotiation
- 'Away-day's/ team-building days
- Secured loans
- Corporate Retreats
- Operations Room – e.g. for planning organisational change, proposal submissions, contract tendering, etc.

B. *Add neutral parts or elements to a system or object.*
- Use of neutral third parties during difficult negotiations (e.g. Senator George Mitchell in Northern Ireland, ACAS, etc.)
- Introduction of 'quiet areas' into the workplace.
- Rest breaks/'pause for reflection' breaks in meetings.

Principle 40. Composite Structures

A. *Change from uniform to composite (multiple) structures, be aware of and utilise combinations of different skills and capabilities.)*
- Multi-disciplinary project teams.
- Do training with a combination of lecture, simulations, on-line learning, video, etc.
- Employ different personality types (e.g. Myers-Briggs) on a team
- Hard person/soft person negotiating team.
- 'Small is beautiful' – appreciation for diverse, interconnected systems
- Mix of thinking skills in a project team
- Positional players in a football team
- Combined high risk/low risk investment strategy

12.
Problem Solving Tools
Contradictions

"Nothing is more dangerous than an idea,
when it is the only idea we have."
Alain

As we mentioned at the beginning of the previous chapter, there are actually two kinds of conflict present in a business situation. In this chapter, we examine the second type of conflict; the contradiction. This is the situation where we have a single parameter with different, contradictory requirements. A typical example of a contradiction, therefore, would be a problem description like 'we want the interest rate to be high, AND we would like it to be low'. More generally, a contradiction will have the form

'I want A, AND I want –A'

where 'A' is the thing we want, and –A signifies the polar opposite of A, for example high and low, present and absent, big and small, etc.

Lest there be any confusion, there are very definite links between the trade-off or compromise situation described in the previous chapter and the contradictions under scrutiny here. We shall explore those links in just a second. The reason for examining both situations is that it seems that certain types of individual prefer one way of looking at conflict or contradiction elimination over the other. We suggest, therefore, that at some point you have a look at both strategies and find one that best suits your way of doing things. For those that will eventually learn the whole array of tools within the systematic innovation toolkit, it is worth the investment to know both conflict and contradiction parts of the toolkit as sometimes it is easier to find the conflicts, and sometimes it is easier to find the contradictions.

This chapter is divided into four main areas. In the first part, we explore the links between conflicts and contradictions and describe a method for connecting the two. In so doing we provide ourselves with a greater list of solution generation opportunities. In the second part, we describe the solution generation strategies available to us when we wish to 'eliminate contradictions'. This is an important part since, as with trade-off elimination, the elimination of contradictions offers extremely powerful means of evolving business situations in a direction of fundamentally increased ideality. In the third part of the chapter we look at a number of case study applications of the contradiction tool. Then, in the final part, we explore some issues concerning whether the contradictions we can find in a system are real or perceived. This can and very often does have some important implications since treating a problem in the wrong way can lead to some unfortunate and less than ideal solutions.

1) Link Between Conflict And Contradiction

To all intents and purposes, any problem that can be described as a trade-off or conflict between two different parameters can be re-framed into a contradiction problem involving just one parameter. If we take some of the conflict case studies presented in the previous chapter, for example, it is possible to convert all of them into contradiction problems. The process for doing this is similar to the strategies used in the Theory of Constraints (Reference 12.1) and that contained in the WOIS (technical) problem solving method (Reference 12.2). It offers, however, something more than either of those two individually or collectively might be able to offer.

The Maintenance Department problem from the previous chapter was initially formulated as a conflict between the desire to reduce downtime/defects and the desire to not lose jobs. Expressing the problem as a contradiction requires that we find a single parameter which both sides of the conflict-pair map to. In this case the linking parameter is 'Maintenance Department'. This is so because we may begin to see that 'we want a maintenance department AND we don't want a maintenance department'. We want the department because we don't want to lose jobs, and we don't want the department because if the conflict is solved, we won't have any downtime.

We can repeat exactly the same conversion for each of the other cases in the previous chapter. The link between richness and reach is 'personalisation' in this case since 'we want personalisation (to achieve richness) AND we don't want personalisation (to achieve reach)'. For the load/capacity problem, the contradiction equivalent problem description would be something along the lines of wanting a rigid system AND not wanting a rigid system.

Figure 11.1 provides a simple thinking framework that permits different problem definitions to be re-framed into other types. In the final part of the chapter, we will also see what else this framework can do for us.

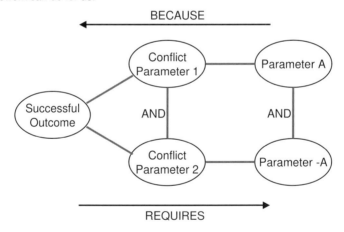

Figure 12.1: Method For Converting Conflicts To Contradictions (and vice versa)

In the meantime, however, we can see that the means of translating a conflict pair into a contradiction comes about by asking questions with the word '*requires*' in them (e.g. improved richness requires personalisation). Conversion from contradiction to conflict parameter on the other hand is performed by framing questions with '*because*' in them (we want personalisation because it gives richness). The figure also extends the conflict pair concept by adding a link to the desire to deliver a 'successful outcome'. Again the 'requires' and 'because' words are important in helping to connect the conflict pair to the desired outcome. The 'AND' word is also significant. Typical connections between the conflict pair and the 'successful outcome will be statements like 'a successful outcome requires richness and reach', or 'we want richness and reach because we desire a successful outcome'. The framework structure, plus the 'successful outcome' label is constant; our job if we are to use it is to fill in the missing conflict parameters and contradiction parameter in its positive and negative forms. The completed structure for the specific richness versus reach conflict will thus look something like the picture illustrated in Figure 12.2.

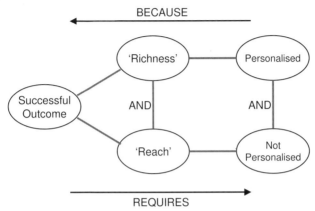

Figure 12.2: Conflict/Contradiction Conversion Framework For Richness versus Reach Problem

The purpose of the framework is to open up multiple opportunities for solving a problem. Tackling a problem by trying to achieve the 'AND' link between the conflict parameters in the middle of the framework will use the tools of Chapter 11. In the next section of this chapter, we concentrate on means of achieving the 'AND' connection between the contradictory parameter descriptions at the right-hand side of the picture.

2) Contradiction Elimination Strategies

Based on the same research that enabled the creation of the Business Conflict Matrix, a number of different strategies for successfully 'eliminating' contradictions have been uncovered. Essentially, there are four such strategies. We will examine all four here before moving on to look at a number of case study examples of the strategies in action on some real problems.

Four Separation Strategies

The four basic methods of 'eliminating' contradictions are:-

    1) Separation In Space
    2) Separation In Time
    3) Separation On Condition
    4) Separation By transition to an Alternative System

Generally speaking, this list should be viewed as a hierarchy of strategies, which we would use in a top-to-bottom sequence. The first three strategies are associated with a pair of questions with 'where', 'when' and 'if' perspectives respectively. The fourth is a category of solution routes we might explore if we have no success with the preceding strategies. So, a typical contradiction solution strategy would involve asking the questions:-

1) *Where* do I want condition A? and *Where* do I want condition −A?
2) *When* do I want condition A? and *When* do I want condition −A?
3) I want condition A *if*? and I want condition −A *if*?

Where, consistent with the earlier convention, −A represents the opposite of any parameter A.

Obtaining a difference between the answers of any of the question pairs, means that the contradiction is amenable to solution by the separation strategy in question.

So, to follow up the 'personalised and not personalised' contradiction from above, our three pairs of questions become:-
1) Where do I want personalisation? Answer – customer base
   Where do I want no personalisation? Answer – customer base
2) When do I want personalisation? Answer – when contacting customers
   When do I want no personalisation? Answer – when contacting customers
3) I want personalisation if? Answer – it is important to potential customers
   I want no personalisation if? Answer – it is not important to potential customers

Thus, we see from that this problem is not readily amenable to solution by separation by space or time – because neither of these question pairs that give us a difference in answer between the two sides of the separation. This leaves us with the option of solving by separating according to condition; since the questions have established that we require different attributes under different conditions.

Having established that the separate on condition solution route is a good one, we would now like to access the inventive solutions adopted by other problem solvers who have tackled the same generic 'separate on condition' problem we are facing. We do this using the data found in Table 12.1. This table is our equivalent of the Matrix developed to help solve conflicts and trade-offs. The first thing to note about this table is that the solution suggestions it contains are exactly the same Inventive Principles as are used to tackle conflicts and trade-offs. The second is that the table usually presents us with a rather larger list of Inventive Principle suggestions for each type of contradiction solution elimination strategies than are found in the Business Conflict Matrix. The advantage of this is that we have more solution options; the disadvantage is that our systematic application of each possible solution will take longer.

In the case of our personalisation problem and the separation on condition problem type, we have 11 possible solution routes. (Plus, it is worth noting, if we don't find a solution among these 11 options, we still have the opportunity to drop down the table into the fourth 'alternative ways' box and see if we can achieve any success with these Principles.)

While it is our intention to demonstrate the mechanics of the contradiction solving process rather than actually solving the personalisation problem, some readers may wish to take a moment to investigate how the 11 separate on condition solution triggers can be applied to help us design a system that does actually achieve the desired 'personalised and not personalised' characteristics. For those that are interested in comparing the outcome of the problem obtained through this contradiction route versus that obtained when it was solved as a 'richness versus reach' conflict problem, may note that Principles 35, 6 and 40 emerge from both methods.

Regarding the process, Table 12.1 represents an important systematic innovation tool; offering for contradiction problems the equivalent to what the Business Conflict Matrix does for conflicts and trade-offs. As such, you may wish to use keep this table to hand as you would if you like the Matrix.

Contradiction Solution Route	Inventive Principles Used To Tackle This Type of Contradiction
Separation in Space	1. Segmentation 2. Taking out 3. Local Quality 17. Another Dimension 13. Other Way Around 14. Curvature 7. Nested Doll 30. Thin and Flexible 4. Asymmetry 24. Intermediary 26. Copying
Separation in Time	15. Dynamics 10. Prior Action 19. Periodic Action 11. Beforehand Cushioning 16. Partial or Excessive Action 21. Skipping 26. Copying 18. Resonance 37. Relative Change 34. Discarding & Recovering 9. Prior Counter-Action 20. Continuity of Useful Action
Separation on Condition	35. Parameter Changes 26. Copying 1. Segmentation 32. Colour Changes 36. Paradigm Shift 2. Taking Out 31. Holes 38. Enriched Atmosphere 39. Inert Atmosphere 28. Another Sense 29. Fluid
Transition to Alternative System	
1. Transition to Sub-System	1. Segmentation 25. Self-Service 40. Composite Structures 33. Homogeneity 12. Reduce Tension
2. Transition to Super-System	5. Merging 6. Universality 23. Feedback 22. Blessing In Disguise
3. Transition to Alternative System	27. Cheap/Short Living
4. Transition to Inverse System	13. Other Way Around 8. Counter-Balance

Table 12.1: Contradiction Solution Strategies
(work from top-down when looking for solutions)

The list of Principles given for each separation category is in order of descending frequency of use by other problem solvers. Thus 'segmentation' has been used as a contradiction elimination strategy by the greatest number of investigated cases of 'separate in space' contradictions. As with the Business Conflict Matrix, the data contained in the Table is intended to be used as a 'good start' rather than as in any way an exclusive list; at the end of the day, any of the 40 Principles may possibly be capable of tackling any contradiction in an inventive way – the only limit being that of our imaginations.

The best way to understand the Table and the contradiction solving part of the systematic innovation toolkit is to see it in action. The rest of this chapter, therefore, describes a number of case study examples. As with case studies elsewhere in the book, despite the tendency of our brains to focus on the specific solutions obtained, the real aim is that we should focus on the process:

3) Contradiction Elimination Case Studies

a) The Maintenance Department

This case study is a repeat of the version presented in the previous chapter. The point of the repeat is to both save time in describing the problem, and also permits us to focus on the process without being unnecessarily distracted by the solutions we might generate. The start point for tackling the Maintenance case as a contradiction problem is the definition of what the contradictions are. As suggested earlier in this chapter, a good definition of a contradiction is that we 'want the maintenance department, AND we don't want the maintenance department.

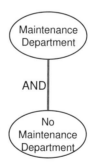

Figure 12.3: Maintenance Department Case Study As A Contradiction

The next step requires us to examine whether it is possible to separate the contradictory 'maintenance' and 'no-maintenance' requirements. Our list of start-point questions thus become:

    1) Where do we want the Maintenance Department?
       Where do we want no Maintenance Department?
    2) When do we want the Maintenance Department?
       When do we want no Maintenance Department?
    3) We want the Maintenance Department if?
       We want no Maintenance Department if?

In the case of the first pair of questions, the answer both times is 'in the company', and so this problem is not one amenable to solution by separation in space. When we ask the second pair of questions, we get two different answers:

> 2) When do I want the Maintenance Department? Answer – when there is maintenance to be done
> When do I want no Maintenance Department? Answer – when there is no maintenance to be done

And so, because we have two different answers, we know that the maintenance-and-no-maintenance contradiction is in this case amenable to elimination by a separation in time strategy. The types of solution we might generate when tackling the situation with these separation in time strategies are likely to include things like subcontracting or fool-proofing machines so that they don't need maintenance. These may be fine in some situations, but do not necessarily deliver solutions that the existing Maintenance Department might perceive as win-win. Thus, if we truly wish to reflect the position we are trying to achieve, we might review the answers we gave to the 'when' question as follows:-

> 2) When do I want the Maintenance Department? Answer – all the time
> When do I want no Maintenance Department? Answer – all the time

(Note: if this appears a little confusing, that explains why we originally worked this problem as a no-downtime-AND-no-job-loss conflict pair, rather than as a contradiction. Importantly, however, what this example does show is that we need to think carefully when asking the pairs of separation questions.)

Continuing down the list of questions, if we return to the contradiction solution route, should highlight that we cannot easily separate the maintenance-AND-no-maintenance contradiction on condition either. At least not if we apply the same logic as we just did to eliminate 'separation in time' as a possible strategy. This then only leaves us with the fourth group of contradiction elimination strategies; the ones associated with a transition to another way of doing things. Here in actual fact is where we start to see the same Inventive Principles as were actually used to generate a genuine win-win outcome emerging – and notably, Principle 13.

b) The Patriarch

The 'patriarch' case study involves a self-made and successful business-man, Mr Smith. The initial scenario for the investigation may be summarised as follows: Mr Smith has set up a semi-prepared food products company and nurtured its growth over a period of 20 years. The company now employs over 200 people. Mr Smith has been the source of nearly all of the sales made by the company to the extent that the company does not possess a sales team. The basis of Mr Smith's success has been the personal relationships he has built up with the client base over the life of the company. It is now time for him to retire, however, and he is in the process of handing over the running of the company to his son. He has stated that he still wants to help in the sales area during the transition. One of the first things the son does, however, is to appoint a sales manager. He does this because a) he is not interested in the sales side of the business, and b) he wants to help his father transition to a happy retirement as soon as possible. Within two months of the appointment of the sales manager, two major clients have been lost, and total sales are down by over 20%.

The first thing we need to do in order to try and solve the problem in this situation is to formulate a contradiction. Note how we do not suggest that we need to go away and conduct an investigation into why we have lost customers. This is an important point to notice at this stage. The case-study is based on an actual one, and our instinct upon being presented with this scenario was probably typical in that we wanted to know why the major clients had been lost. Upon trying to answer this question, however, by talking to both of them, it very quickly became clear that the answers we were being given were not the 'real' reason. We believe that this is a phenomenon that is very common and as such gives much more weight to the contradiction rather than root-cause analysis route; very simply, in many situations it is impossible to find the root cause. As soon as we snapped out of the 'more data' trap and started thinking about the problem as a contradiction, we were well on the road to generating some genuinely win-win solutions. The contradiction we formulated was:

'We want Mr Smith, AND we don't want Mr Smith.'

We want him because of his experience and good relationship with the customers, and we 'don't want him' because we wish him to go off and enjoy a happy retirement (note that the relationship between Mr Smith and his son was a very good one).

Having identified a contradiction, the next thing to do is ask the question-pairs that enable us to see which solution strategies will and won't work:

       1) Where do we want Mr Smith?
          Where do we want no Mr Smith?
       2) When do we want Mr Smith?
          When do we want no Mr Smith?
       3) We want Mr Smith if?
          We want no Mr Smith if?

What we find in this instance is that it is possible to generate different answers to each of the questions in a pair (we want Mr Smith where he has a relation with a customer; we don't want him where there is no relationship). This in turn effectively means that all four of the contradiction elimination strategies are available for use. As such, this case study is one we often use as an example in workshops since we can use a very wide range of different Principle suggestions to generate solution ideas.

Separation in both space and time using 'segmentation' (or 'periodic action' – which is the time equivalent of 'segmentation') offered an immediate resolution strategy to the contradiction – in that both the father's and the sales manager's maps were correct at different times and with different clients. Segmentation turned out to be simple and easy to apply, and it did indeed restore sales very quickly, but it didn't resolve the longer term issues associated with the fact that those clients who bought from the company because of their personal relationship with the father were eventually going to be disappointed when his retirement was full-time.

The eventual solution to the problem came from the – initially un-promising sounding – Principle 27, Cheap Disposable suggestion emerging from the transition to the sub-system solution direction. Here again we see the real trick to using the Inventive Principles to their best effect. Even though the initial suggestion sounds implausible, the process would like us to think of as many possible connections as possible. So, in this case, what could we transform into something cheap and disposable? The customers? The sales manager? Mr Smith?

The eventual answer; make a disposable version of Mr Smith by placing his image on the labelling of the company's products. The method; the clients who bought from the company because of the father could now see him on every product they bought from the company and thus felt that his memory was being respected.

c) Combinations of Separations and Principles

Instances like this 'Mr Smith AND no Mr Smith' situation where we find it possible to separate a given contradiction by more than one of the four strategies are quite common. Particularly common are cases where we find it possible to separate in terms of both time and space. We will explore this space **and** time separation possibility as the basis for examining strategies for tackling this kind of problem. Other combinations of contradiction separation possibilities will use exactly the same techniques as those described for this particular case. The two most important two-part questions associated with establishing whether a physical contradiction problem is amenable to solution by separation in space or time strategies are:-

1) WHERE do I want characteristic A and where do I want characteristic –A

2) WHEN do I want characteristic A, and when do I want characteristic –A

Anytime we obtain a difference between our answers between A and –A, we have then established that the problem is amenable to solutions separated by both time AND space.

Let's take another commonly experienced problem scenario; that of trying to establish the 'optimum' number of check-out tills in a bank or supermarket or store. Anytime we see that word 'optimum' and find ourselves performing the sorts of calculation that we shall see here in just a moment, the contradiction tool is trying to suggest that there is a better way of doing things.

As far as the calculation of the 'optimum' number of tills is concerned, we are likely to do a calculation of the sort illustrated in Figure 12.4 below:

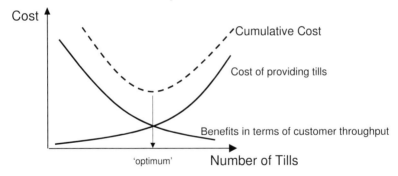

Figure 12.4: Typical Calculation Procedure For Calculating 'Optimum' Number Of Tills

Approaching the problem as a contradiction, on the other hand, will very quickly get us to the idea of 'wanting lots of tills, AND wanting very few tills'.

Asking the first two separation questions for this contradiction statement, we then get:-

Q. Where do I want lots of tills?	A. Where there are lots of customers
Q. Where do I want a few tills?	A. Where there are a few customers
Q. When do I want lots of tills?	A. When there are lots of queuing customers
Q. When do I want few tills?	A. When there are few queuing customers

I.e. different answers in each case.

The main point of this case study is to plant the suggestion that in these 'space and time' situations, it is a very good idea to look at Inventive Principles from *both* the space and time categories in Table 12.1, selecting at least one from each list, and then looking to use them in combination.

Thus, for example, supermarkets frequently use Principle 1, Segmentation strategies like having different types of till for people with a small number of items versus big trolley loads. They also increasingly use Principle 15, 'Dynamics' strategies by having staff who come and occupy tills only when they see that queues are beginning to build; otherwise they will be positioned elsewhere in the store performing other useful activities. By combining both the segmentation and dynamics solutions (and the masses of other ideas we ought to be able to generate using the other Inventive Principles), the idea is that we end up with an overall solution greater than the sum of the parts.

d) Graphical Representation of Contradictions

In the previous chapter we saw that a conflict or trade-off could be presented graphically as a hyperbolic curve (see Figure 11.2 for example). Figure 12.4 offers clues to the equivalent graph for a contradiction. A more general contradiction graph is drawn in Figure 12.5 below:

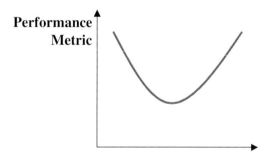

Figure 12.5: Graphical Representation Of A Contradiction.

This graphical approach is often a very good way of identifying a contradiction. The parabolic shape graph is extremely common. It is particularly prominent in optimisation processes – where the aim is to find the minimum 'optimum' point (or maximum if the parabola is drawn the other way up – also a representation of a contradiction).

Anywhere, in fact, where we find ourselves searching for an 'optimum' value of some parameter – like the search for an optimum number of tills – this contradiction part of the systematic innovation toolkit is encouraging us to think about re-defining the problem to derive a much stronger solution than the ones achievable through optimisation. Typical examples of this kind of scenario include:-

1) Attempts to find the 'optimum' number of employees in a firm
2) Attempts to find the 'optimum' selling price of a product or service, when clearly every customer is different from everyone, and will therefore have a different interpretation of what is an acceptable price they are willing to pay.
3) 'Optimum' interest rates.

4) In production processes, you will still find many organisations try and calculate an 'optimum' batch size during multiple operation manufacture. This optimum is typically actually the best compromise between conflicting requirements to have a high batch size (equals low set-up costs) and a low batch size (equals low inventory). A far better solution would achieve both low set-up cost and low inventory.

5) Attempts to find the optimum number of articles in a magazine; too few and people are unlikely to value the service; too many and they are likely to feel overwhelmed with complexity, and/or ignore valuable content that has cost money to create. Again far better to think about a magazine that had a large and small number of articles.

6) Attempts to find the 'right' number of products or services in a range. There can actually be no such thing as 'right', and someone, somewhere will thus be compromised by your decision.

And so on. Contradictions are everywhere around us. Sometimes optimisation strategies will offer adequate solutions; systematic innovation, on the other hand, is trying to encourage successive challenge of the contradictions as part of a desire to achieve ideality – Figure 12.6.

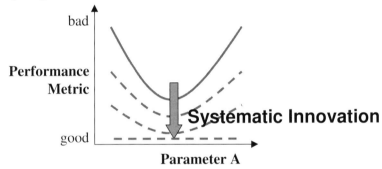

Figure 12.6: Graphical Representation Of Contradiction 'Elimination' Process .

The graph illustrates a parallel desire to not only move the optimum towards 'good', but to also remove relationship between changing values of the Parameter and the performance achieved – i.e. we wish to remove the parabolic correlation between parameter and performance.

Of course, the graphical approach is not the only way of recognising the presence of a contradiction. There are a host of situations where the contradiction is discrete rather than the continuous nature implied by a parabolic graph. Some of these are more obvious than others. A shareholder that 'votes AND doesn't vote' is an example of a non-obvious discrete contradiction. Identification of contradictions like this one are a very good way of innovating – in fact finding a good unresolved contradiction presents one of the best innovation opportunities of any of the systematic innovation tools – in that almost as soon as the contradiction is defined it becomes possible to identify new opportunities. For the shareholder that votes and doesn't vote, for example, the 'separate on condition' questions should quickly get us to the concept of a virtual voting system that permits the voice to be heard without the expense of having to send out ballot papers and count them, etc.

4) Real Or Perceived Contradictions?

A very significant factor in the contradiction elimination part of the toolkit is the determination of whether a contradiction is real or not. Experience to date would appear to suggest that in close to half of the cases we examine where the problem solver has determined that a contradiction exists, in actual fact it turns out not to be a real one. The primary issues at stake here those concerning the distinction between fact and perceived fact, and 'right-versus-wrong' or 'right-versus-right'.

A classic example comes from an early published example of the insensitive line-manager problem (Reference 12.4). This case study concerns line-manager, John. John runs a production line in a factory. He is very good at his job, but has the unfortunate trait of managing his line without any consideration of the negative impact he might have on other lines. Figure 12.7 provides a summary of the problem situation as described at the beginning of the investigation.

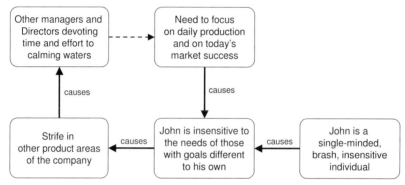

Figure 12.7: Classical 'John Must Be Present And Absent' 'Contradiction'.

The conclusion made in the Reference 12.4 article was that this problem was a 'John must be present and absent' contradiction. This is a classic case where if TRIZ is the only tool in your toolkit, every problem starts to look like a TRIZ problem. A simple test that can be applied in all contradiction cases to identify whether a contradiction is real or not comes from the world of NLP and specifically of Korzybski (Reference 12.5). The test involves the recognition of the difference between the map and territory.

The actual physical reality of a situation (the 'territory') is often not the same thing as the mental map we all draw of that territory. As suggested in Figure 12.8, John has one view of the reality – i.e. that he has been instructed to get the most out of his production line – while everyone else has a different view – i.e. John is sub-optimising the overall operation by optimising his own part.

John's view of reality is 'wrong' (actually, to give John the benefit of the doubt, we might say that his view is merely 'incomplete') and this should tell us that this is a 'right-versus-wrong' situation and hence not a contradiction.

The earlier patriarch problem on the other hand is a genuine 'right-versus-right' contradiction. Right-versus-right situations are those in which both sides of the contradiction are factually correct; in this case Mr Smith should be present because we are losing sales, and he should be absent because he has to retire.

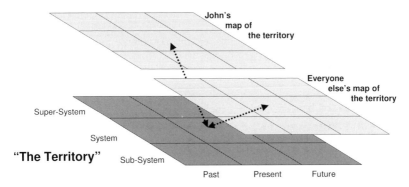

Figure 12.8: The Map Is Not The Territory.

When we find ourselves in the 'right-versus-right' situation, then the contradiction-elimination tool is precisely the right strategy to use to generate solutions.

In the right-versus-wrong situation, on the other hand is best solved using other strategies. In this scenario, we would be well advised to review the framework first illustrated in Figure 12.1. Rather like the 'Evaporating Cloud' model used in the Theory of Constraints, the idea behind the framework is that solving a problem requires us to break one of the links between the different elements. When we are solving a problem using the conflict or contradiction elimination tools, we are working in the two 'AND' links. When we are in the right-versus-wrong scenario, on the other hand, it is necessary to break one of the other links – Figure 12.9.

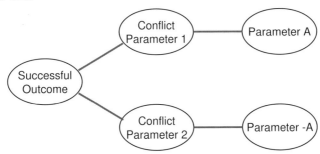

Figure 12.9: Required Link-Breaking Focus For 'Right-Versus-Wrong' Problem Situations

The figure highlights the presence of four different link-breaking opportunities:

  i)   Establishing *why* Conflict Parameter 1 requires Parameter A to be in place
  ii) Establishing *why* Conflict Parameter 2 requires Parameter -A to be in place
  iii) Establishing *why* a successful outcome requires Conflict Parameter 1 to be true
  iv) Establishing *why* a successful outcome requires Conflict Parameter 2 to be true

If we can successfully invalidate any one of the assumptions relating to any one of these four questions, then we have the ability to generate effective solutions. In the above 'John' problem for example, we might realize that the assumption that we don't want John because his presence disrupts the effectiveness of other production lines, can be invalidated if we explain to John that what we actually want him to do is think about the whole production system rather than just his own. Tackling right-versus-wrong problems like this John problem is much more effectively handled by examining and challenging perceptions and perceived realities than by trying to solve contradictions which, in reality, are not actually there. The John problem only becomes a genuine contradiction if John still fails to respond after being made aware of the bigger picture and he decides he doesn't want to change the way he does things.

What Do I Do?

The identification and elimination of contradictions represents an important part of the systematic innovation toolkit. In order to use the tool to best effect, the following general strategy is recommended (ultimately, of course, you should consider adapting these elements to best suit the way your individual brain likes to operate):

1) Identify a contradiction – this may happen via a number of routes, perhaps most commonly when you find yourself struggling to achieve adequate performance by optimising a given design parameter, or by seeing a parabolic profile graph, or by thinking about what the **ideal** attributes of a parameter might be.
2) Having identified a good contradiction, work through the three pairs of separation questions – where, when and if – in order to identify possible solution strategies.
3) Where a problem is amenable to solution by more than one of the separation strategies, think about using the Inventive Principle solutions triggers in combination.
4) If none of the separation strategies are possible, or if you wish to explore other solution routes, examine the strategies contained in the fourth 'alternative ways' box in Table 12.1.
5) Use the Inventive Principle suggestions to connect your problem to possible solutions – see the list of Principles with examples at the end of Chapter 11.

References

1) Scheinkopf, L., 'Thinking For A Change: Putting The TOC Thinking Processes To Use', St Lucie Press, Boca Raton, 1999.
2) HJ Linde, G.H. Herr, 'INNOWIS & WOIS', keynote paper presented at TRIZCON2002, St Louis, April 2002.
3) Mann, D.L., 'Systematic Win-Win Problem Solving In A Business Environment', paper presented at TRIZCON2002, St Louis, March 2002.
4) Kowalick, J., 'The TRIZ Approach: Case Study – Creative Solutions to a Human Relations Problem', TRIZ Journal, November 1997.
5) Korzybski, A., 'Science and Sanity', Institute of General Semantics, 1933.

13.
Problem Solving Tools -
Measurement Problems

*"It is safe to assume that the number of distributors, stockholders, products, pricing advantages
and customers are exponentially related, not tied in a linear way to the marketplace advantage. "*
Patricia Moody, Richard Morley

or

"It would have been cheaper to lower the Atlantic."
Lew Grade on the failure of his film Raise The Titanic

Problems of measurement form a special category in the systematic innovation framework.
In this chapter we explore the field of measurement in its business context, and detail the
tools available to help us to solve problems associated with measurement, or to help us
make measurements in a more effective way.

The chapter is divided into three main sections. In the first section we explore the 'what's'
and 'why's' of measurement; in the second we describe the 'how' aspects, and in the third
we present some brief case study examples of the tools in action, examining the remaining
questions of who, when and where.

1) What To Measure and Why To Measure It?

Managers love measurements. The world of measurement and data abounds with adages
and aphorisms. These cover an entire spectrum of opinion on the merits or perils of either
not having enough or of having too much. Most relevant of them – at least in the
systematic innovation context – are:
- 'you don't fatten a cow by weighing it'
- 'what gets measured gets done'
- 'the most important numbers are unknown and unknowable'

The first two are concerned with establishing just the 'right' form and quantity of
measurement. The third is more concerned with intangible factors. We shall examine both
aspects here.

A good place to begin the discussion is the ideality equation used throughout the
systematic innovation methodology. There are several subtly different forms of the
equation, but the one most relevant to the discussion here is:-

$$\text{Ideality} = \text{Perceived} [\text{ Benefits} / (\text{Cost} + \text{Harm})]$$

Whether we apply this equation at the level of individual elements within a system, or at
the macro 'whole-system' level, the four elements that make up the right hand side of the
equation are the only elements that should justify measurement for management
purposes. Of these, it appears clear that the 'cost' element is by far and away the one that
is easiest to measure. Consequently, in the large majority of management measurement

systems, this is the element that receives the most attention. Measurement of 'benefits' typically involves measurement of the value of the product or service being offered from the perspective of the person or persons receiving it. 'Benefit' in this context should be read as equivalent to the *functions* that the receivers wish to perform. Measurement of 'harm' is a relatively new phenomenon, one that has emerged primarily since the advent of 'lean' enterprise cultures (where 'harm' equates to 'waste') and, more recently, awareness of environmental and sustainability issues. Typically, all three of the benefit, cost and harm trio are connected using a fiscal scale of measurement.

The fourth important word in the equation is 'perceived'. This is a very simple label intended to hide the mass of complexity and uncertainty that emerges as we start to consider intangibles in our economic models. Historical evidence suggests that we are still pretty bad at measuring intangibles – whether they be positive ones like 'brand-value' or negative ones like 'lost-opportunity costs'. This 'perceived' element of the measurement story is the part of where the Deming statement 'the most important numbers are unknown and unknowable' comes from. Nevertheless, whether they are unknown or unknowable, too many businesses survive on intangibles today to ignore them.

However we eventually measure these four parameters, what is clear from the systematic innovation test of the viability of a system is that without a measure of the overall 'ideality' metric, the system is not viable. Figure 13.1 shows the essential elements of any system as defined by the viability test.

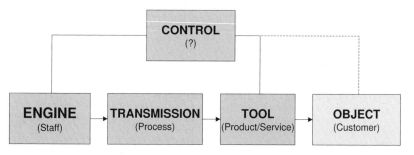

Figure 13.1: Need For Feedback And Control In A 'Viable' System

The lines linking each of the parts of the system to the box labelled 'control' represent the flow of control information. These lines are the parts of the system concerned with measurement and data.

Notice that the above description uses the term 'measure of the overall 'ideality'' and not the separate, individual measure of the four constituent elements of ideality. It is frequently assumed that benefits, costs, harms and 'perceptions' all need to be measured independently, but this need not be the case. This then leads us to another important element that the systematic innovation philosophy brings into play; complexity. Related to the test of the viability of a system is the evolution trend that says systems will pass through successive cycles of increasing and decreasing complexity. Complexity increases until such times as the system hits a maximum viable level of complexity; beyond this point, the only effective option is to evolve the system by maintaining functionality, but with reduced levels of complexity. A common phenomenon that occurs when systems reach this maximum complexity point is that cost and, particularly, reliability begins to decline. A sure sign that this point of maximum viable complexity has been reached is when you find that measurement systems to record the accuracy of other measurement systems are being introduced.

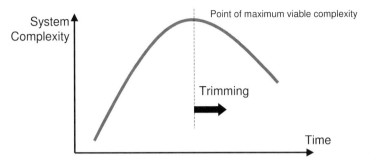

Figure 13.2: Complexity Increases/Decrease Trend And Measurement Implications

The 'need' to make measurements is one of the main drivers present in the increasing complexity portion of the trend cycle. The desire to understand the workings of a system necessitates the introduction of means of measuring what is happening – without data, in other words, it is very difficult to know which improvement aspects and directions need to be addressed. The reducing complexity portion of the cycle is the part where, having understood the workings of a system, those measurements that had to be introduced to aid understanding can become integrated or eliminated. The trend is there to suggest to us that there will be times when it is necessary to add measurements to a system, and there are times when we should be looking to integrate (i.e. measure ideality as a total rather than as four separate entities) and eliminate measurements. The measurement strategy recommendations described in the next section are consistent with this trend.

2) Strategies For Handling Measurement Problems

Following a programme of research to examine the most effective strategies for making measurements from across several hundreds of thousand examples of 'best practice' distilled from all areas of human endeavour (initially inspired by the measurement work in Reference 13.1), this section presents an ordered list of strategies that should be considered any time there is a desire to make any measurements in the business and management context.

The structure of the list is such that the generic strategies at the top of the list will give more ideal solutions than those found lower down the list (i.e. the ones at the top of the list are the ones most consistent with the 'reducing complexity' portion of the trend cycle). Consequently, it is recommended that the list should be used in a top-down sequence such that if you generate an effective solution from the suggestions in one generic strategy, then there should be no need to continue searching down the list. The only time we might chose to look at the whole list, therefore, is if we are wishing to generate a comprehensive list of possibilities.

The list of possible strategies follows. For each strategy, a series of additional information and examples is provided as a means of assisting the translation of the general strategy directions into specific solutions to a given measurement problem situation.

a) Modify the system so that there is no need to make the detection or measurement

- Self compensating/self-calibrating/self-monitoring systems all eliminate the need for measurement by allowing elements already contained within the system to perform measurements for themselves.
- 'You don't fatten a cow weighing it' – offers the suggestion that in many instances it is possible to eliminate the need to make a measurement by recognizing that the information it provides serves no useful function.
- Use existing resources in the system to perform the measurement (e.g. especially in computer systems there are massive amounts of known data that remains un-utilised from a measurement perspective – e.g. rate of mouse-clicks or key presses gives information on the capability and aptitude of the user, electronic filing of reports, minutes, etc gives automatic project management feedback data, use motion-sensitive lighting to identify when people are in an office).
- Increasing transparency within an organization reduces the need for explicit measurements to take place since very often the motivation for requesting a measurement is that something is hidden from view.
- Integration of different measures into one another is another possible strategy for eliminating the need for some measurements.
- (On the down-side the adage 'what gets measured gets done' means that we should apply care in deciding whether we literally eliminate a measurement.)

b) Make the detection or measurement on a copy, image or replica of the object or system

- Use of simulation or scenario planning software tools permit construction of a numerical model of a factory, organization, market, etc.
- Beta test networks act as a microcosm of the eventual full user base.
- Use of test audiences (e.g. film industry often tests several different endings to a film in order to identify which ones work better than others) or sampling techniques. Again, the idea is to make measurements on a representative sample of the full market.
- FMEA/Subversion Analysis (Chapter 21) risk analysis methods.
- Acquire customer feedback measurements using Internet-based forms and images.
- Virtual customers.

c) Transform the problem into one involving successive measurement of changes

- Measure the delta's between successive measurements in a sequence.
- In any system where there is recurrent, sequential acquisition of data, there is the potential to use the differences between successive previous measurements as a source of additional functional capability.
- Use rate of key-presses/mouse-clicks as a way of measuring competence of users.
- Use response rates on automobile controls to establish whether a driver has been drinking.
- Use changes in measurements as a way of establishing the frequency at which future measurements need to be made.
- Use change in rate of change of measurements as a way of identifying proximity to potential non-linearities and dangerous 'cliff-edge' changes.

d) Add a new element (communication or person or element) to provide an easily detectable parameter related to the parameter required to be measured or detected

- Mystery shopper provides potential to measure information (e.g. on customer service) that is otherwise difficult to obtain reliably.
- Suggestion schemes not only generate ideas, but give a good indication of the health and morale of an organization.
- Physical or virtual notice-boards offer the potential to allow people to contribute data or information.
- Cookies.
- Interactive TV.
- Bluetooth/Smart systems.
- GPS tracking systems.

e) If it is not possible to modify the system, then introduce an easily detected element to the surrounding environment

- Bring in a temporary consultant to make the measurement.
- 'Visit the Gemba' measurement gathering strategies.
- CCTV cameras.
- (Heisenberg Uncertainty Principles – any attempt to make a measurement inevitably affects the system.)

f) If it is not possible to introduce an easily detectable element into the environment surrounding a system, obtain the desired measurement by detecting changes in something already in the environment

- Use friends and family to obtain information on the morale of staff/team members.
- The press is particularly sensitive to changes in the world and so present an effective way of measuring shifts in markets/customer perceptions/etc – especially identification of disruptions and non-linearities.
- Key-presses on a computer keyboard.
- Use audience noise levels to measure enjoyment (in both senses – high background noise indicates low enjoyment, while excited clapping/cheering indicates high state of enjoyment).

g) Make use of psychological effects to help make the measurement

- Use of phenomena occurring at or close to the 'Tipping Point' of a system (Reference 13.2).
- Telling someone that they cannot have something is often a good way of making them want it. This phenomenon can often be used to improve response rate in questionnaires, surveys and similar customer feedback mechanisms.
- Most people have a built-in desire to be helpful and hence if they are approached in an appropriate manner, they will provide information even if it means they are inconvenienced.
- The human mind is often said to behave as a 'leaky integrator' (Reference 13.3). What this means is that a person is triggered into action only after an appropriate input signal has exceeded a certain total amount. Analogy: imagine a bucket that will tip over once it is full of water, and the signals to make it tip are the equivalent of water being poured

into the bucket. When sufficient water has been added, the bucket will tip. The 'leaky' part of the story is there to indicate the fact that the brain (the bucket) has a small leak, and so, over a period of time, water will leak and hence even more needs to be poured in to the bucket to compensate.

- It is better to be 'inclusive' when formulating questions – the psychological effect here is the same as in humour, where jokes that laugh at 'all of us', emphasizing how universal and common humans are, work much more effectively than ones that tend towards isolationist viewpoints.
- Bad news travels much faster than good news (see 'Seven and the Downward Spiral' in Chapter 6) – a customer is many times more likely to tell their friends about a bad experience they had than a good one.
- Customers often feel more positively about a product or service if something has gone wrong than if nothing bad has happened; provided that the supplier provides an appropriate rectification 'experience'.
- Make use of one of the great communication paradoxes; the more you tell people, the more they think you are hiding.

h) Use emotional effects to help to make the measurement

- Identification and use of 'exciters' (see Kano diagram).
- Identification and use of customer 'hot buttons'.
- Athletes and stage performers at the peak of their performance often talk of being 'in the zone' – the mental state where they are totally concentrated on the task at hand and are completely oblivious to external effects. Use this 'in the zone' phenomenon as a means of achieving customer or employee morale information.
- Empathic listening encourages people to reveal their 'real' thoughts (empathic listening that is perceived as in any way fake will cause the exact opposite reaction).

i) Use the inverse or opposite system to make the measurement

- Measure the empty spaces on a nearly-full aeroplane or in a cinema rather than the number of people (more generally; measure the thing that is missing rather than the thing that is present).
- Measure non-customers instead of (or in addition to) customers. This should include not just people who buy from competitors, but also people who are non-consumers of the product or service in any form.

3) Case Study Examples

In this final section we examine three short case studies, each intended to focus our attention on a different aspect of importance regarding measurement problems. In the first case we examine the issue of knowing *what* to measure; in the second we explore the close relationship between measurement and resources; and in the third we delve more deeply into methods of using the measurement problem solution strategies listed in the preceding section.

3a) Measuring Business Performance

All too often, organizations measure their business success based on what is measurable rather than what is important. Also, often, the measurable things turn out to be the things that will blindside the organization to what is *actually* important. This is particularly so in situations where disruptive or breakthrough innovations are emerging. What may be the 'right' things to be measuring today, may well turn out to be precisely the opposite of 'right' tomorrow.

Bearing in mind the 'what gets measured gets done' dictum from earlier, the theme of this first short case study is to examine strategies for ensuring that companies continue to be measuring the 'right' things even though the world around them is changing. The example we will use is based on one started by Clayton Christensen in his latest book 'The Innovator's Solution (Reference 13.4). Our intention here is to see if the systematic innovation methodology can help us to take the story a little further. The case centres around the photography industry and specifically the production of photographic paper.

The advent of digital cameras is having a profound effect on production of film for cameras. The impact on photographic paper is somewhat less, but still significant in terms of overall quantity demanded by the market. A large part of the reason for this is the fact that with a digital camera it is possible to delete or re-take images and so there is nothing like the amount of waste that occurred when whole reels of film were developed and printed. This aside, the manufacturer of photographic paper clearly needs to be able to measure what the market is doing in order to steer their business. The easiest things for the business to measure are streams of incoming and outgoing resources – either in terms of tangible product (tonnes of paper for example) or the usual financial parameters. Because they are easy to measure, these parameters tend to be the things that are used to guide the business. This data allows a company to, for example, respond to an unexpected fall in sales by instigating an advertising campaign or a discount, or respond to an unexpected rise in sales by exploring a rise in production or prices. Virtually all companies will do the same. There is nothing wrong with this approach of course – short-term survival depends upon it absolutely.

Clearly, though, just because something is easy to measure does not mean that it is the 'best' thing to measure. This is where the 'most important numbers are unknown and unknowable' dictum begins to play a role. Except, is it true that there are measures that are 'unknowable'?

The first clue towards helping us to identify better things for the photographic paper industry (or any other for that matter) to measure their performance against involves recognizing the function that the product or service delivers to the customer. (One of the key strands of Christensen's book in fact makes this leap – recognizing that customers buy functions rather than solutions – except Christensen uses the term 'jobs to be done' rather than function.)

In the film-dominated market, the main functions of the photographic paper were firstly to present a visible record of what pictures had been taken, and secondly to provide a permanent visible record of a memory. As digital photography has risen to the fore, the need for the first function has largely been transferred to the camera – the user now being able to filter out the rejects before they get printed. The second function, however, remains. So how does the photographic paper manufacturer measure the delivery of this 'visible record of a memory' function? Well, clearly it can continue to use the quantity of paper sold. But maybe there is more that could be done?

Something that the digital revolution doesn't appear to have helped resolve is the fact that the vast majority of collected 'photographs' are archived never to see the light of day again. In the pre-digital world, they sat in shoe-boxes; now they sit on hard-drives or CDs.

Either way, despite the intention of nearly everyone to put together memory 'albums', the effort of having to do it, means that it is a task that rarely gets done.

If we examine this issue through the lens of some of the business trends discussed in the next chapter, we can perhaps see a connection to the customer expectation trend. The shift from selling product to selling service, for example, might suggest the idea of selling a 'memory' service to customers rather than simply selling them paper. As soon as we make this kind of connection, we have the seeds of a discontinuous breakthrough innovation (which, after all, is what the trends are there to do for us). But the moment we have made it, the idea of using 'quantity of paper sold' as a measure of business success has become both useless and dangerous. Breakthrough shifts in the way things get done demand new ways of measuring success. In the 'memory' service business, much more appropriate measures of success will be things like number of subscribers, amount of time the subscriber spends looking at images, number of images recorded by a subscriber, number of images the subscriber requests to be turned into hard-copy prints (by which means we continue to remember that the selling of photographic paper – albeit now in an already printed form – is still a part of the business model).

As we extrapolate the customer expectation trend another step forward to 'experience', and we start thinking about an offering in which the supplier not only acts as a memory, but also connects to other family members or to friends (e.g. offering to send frequently opened images to other family members), or produces a hard-copy album of the images that have been viewed most during a year, or (to pick up breakthrough innovations emerging from other trends) archives not just pictures but a soundtrack to go with the pictures. Without getting too far off the radar screen, we might also imagine taking the whole idea of 'memory' a step further and think about cameras that record a soundtrack at the same time as they record a visual image, or (more difficult) record a characteristic smell to further help trigger the memory.

The point is that if we really do get what we measure, then we should be very careful that we chose the right things. The photographic paper company that only measures sales of paper is not going to be the one that is looking for the next generation offering. Just because something is difficult to measure ('how many memories were recorded today?' or perhaps even more importantly, 'how many memory capture opportunities were lost today because the right service was not made available to customers?'), doesn't mean that we should ignore it. Most important of all, we can use the idea of function and the discontinuous trends of evolution as ways of guiding us towards what the new 'right' things to measure are going to be.

3b) Project Management System Measurements

Global statistics on the performance of project managers make for depressing reading, with close to 85% of projects ending either late, over-budget, under-specification or a combination of all three. As a consequence, many organizations are devoting substantial resources to improving the way in which projects are managed. Several have introduced the concept of a project management 'dashboard'. This project manager as car-driver metaphor conveys the useful image of an instrument panel displaying all of the information required to successfully navigate from start-point A to end-point B – Figure 13.3.

Irrespective of how project management data is displayed and presented, it should possess three key attributes: it needs to be relevant, acquirable and accurate. The first of these three was the focus of the previous case-study example. In this one we start from the point where we have decided what is relevant and are now looking to the acquirable and accurate attributes.

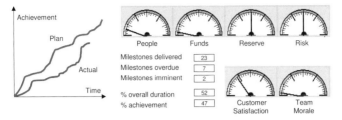

Figure 13.3: Hypothetical Project Management 'Dashboard'

Since so few organizations appear to have mastered the art of delivering projects to time, budget and specification, finding examples of 'best-practice' is not easy. Of the few things that can be stated with any degree of certainty, it would seem that successful project management has very little to do with managing Gantt charts. Yet another example of the most important numbers being unknown and unknowable. One of the most common failures occurs when organizations take the 'common-sense' view that poor project management results from not having enough project managers. The 'common sense' logic works something like this: successful project management needs data, acquiring data takes time, the project manager does not have enough time to acquire all the data, ergo, the project manager needs to recruit team members responsible for acquiring the data. In the very worst examples, we have seen this 'common sense' taken to an even higher level with project management systems where the project manager has felt the need to have people given the responsibility of verifying the accuracy of the data being acquired by the first fleet of data-acquirers.

At this point (or, hopefully earlier), we might chose to follow an alternative strategy and take a look at the recommendation at the top of the list of solution triggers for management problems:

Modify the system so that there is no need to make the detection or measurement

Or, stated another way, can we get the system to 'measure itself'. Our old friend 'self' again (Chapter 8) and the related concept of Ideal Final Result. The Ideal Final Result project manager involves the situation where we get the function (in this case 'management of the project') without the manager. Likewise, the ideal final result project management measurement dashboard is one that provides the relevant information, but requires no additional resource to acquire it.

As soon as we reach a problem definition like this one – where we want the measurement to make itself – we should begin to make a thorough search of the resources already available within and around the system we are trying to measure.

Typical of the sorts of things we might find in most modern organizations may then include:-

- electronic diary system that record when meetings happen
- electronic accounting systems that know when invoices have been approved
- expense claims that get submitted after trips have been made
- library systems onto which reports are automatically filed
- suggestion schemes (and related statistics that will also give an indication of the morale of a team)
- sick-days

- number of phone calls and/or visits from customers

A whole raft of things, in other words, that already contain – in electronic form – the information that managers will traditionally use to establish the status of their projects. The resources are already there, the only problem is that they just aren't connected to one another.

This whole concept of 'self' is vitally important in all areas, not just the acquisition of management data. Project managers get themselves into situations where they feel a need to recruit data verifiers because as soon as 'someone else' is made responsible for making something happen, it means that other people that could and would otherwise have cared about it, assume that someone else will now look after it. That person, in turn, assumes that those other people will continue to care about things and consequently doesn't feel a need to check everything. This is exactly the same situation as we can see happening in the Quality Department that quality go down rather than up phenomenon discussed in Chapter 19. The psychology of 'someone else' is a long and painful downward spiral that can absorb ever-increasing amounts of resource if left to follow its 'common sense' course. In the experience of the author, the only successful initiatives are those that were set up with an intention to not end up with an initiative department running them. This applies to knowledge-management, ERP, quality, suggestion schemes, and just about any other organizational function. Long-term success grows from initiatives set up with the aim of becoming self-sustaining – see Reference 13.5 for a seminal example of this type of philosophy in action.

By way of a final point regarding this example, it is worth noting another aspect of the ideality and ideal final result concepts contained within the systematic innovation method; that of the migration of functions to higher hierarchical levels. In this case study, most if not all of the information required to manage a project (including intangibles) is already there in the system. The problem is simply that no one at the higher level has for whatever reason sought to integrate it.

3c) Measuring Customer Satisfaction

In this last case study, we deliberately examine a very general problem setting. We do this as a means of demonstrating how the measurement strategies can be used as a way of adding focus to solution generation activities based on brainstorming techniques. Few measurement problems can be as vague and imprecise as those relating to the obtaining of information from customers. This is the dotted line feedback line required in order to achieve the required Control of what an organization does as indicated in Figure 13.1. Figure 13.4 below reproduces the part of that viable system model relevant to this case study.

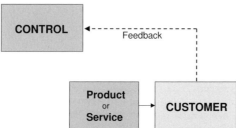

Figure 13.4: Customer Satisfaction Feedback Loop

In order to give the case study a degree of focus, we will focus on the acquisition of feedback from customers shopping in supermarkets. Hopefully, it will be possible to extrapolate the ideas and thoughts generated here and apply them in other situations. The following represents a list of ideas generated by simply brainstorming ideas using the measurement strategies described in the second section of the chapter (text in parentheses relates to the measurement strategy used to generate the ideas that immediately follow it):

(Modify the system so that there is no need to make the detection or measurement)

- *do a good enough job that an industry standard is set (e.g. become the organization that your competitors see as the benchmark)*
- *adopt a strategy of adding 'exciters' that appeal to ever-broader ranges and types of customer*
- *get customers to measure satisfaction 'themselves' – for example set up a customer administered web-site that facilitates and encourages dissent and sharing of experiences customer-to-customer.*
- *hand over control of the supermarket to customers (the concept of 'community shops' often works in rural areas, plus see Ricardo Semler for other examples of 'self-managing' systems – Reference 13.5)*

(Make the detection or measurement on a copy, image or replica of the object or system)

- *Internet shopping permits many electronic opportunities to acquire satisfaction data from customers – from the obvious (on-line surveys) to the less obvious (frequency of use, size of order, key-stroke rate, etc)*
- *use scenario planning techniques in order to empathise with different customer experiences*
- *use 'mystery shoppers' not to test supermarket staff, but rather to engage in conversations with other shoppers*
- *create special, permanent or temporary customer focus groups*
- *use thermal-imaging systems at key points around the supermarket (especially check-outs) to assess the stress level of customers*

(Transform the problem into one involving successive measurement of changes)

- *use credit card/loyalty card information to measure time between visits*
- *use the same information in order to identify seasonal patterns*
- *shift loyalty card swipe to store entry rather than check-out in order to establish patterns regarding how long customers remain in the store*

(Add a new element to provide an easily detectable parameter related to the parameter required to be measured or detected)

- *loyalty cards permit considerable monitoring of customer behaviour*
- *offer hand-held scanners to customers so that they can provide information as they progress around the supermarket (e.g. identify what things confuse them)*
- *add simple voting systems adjacent to new products on shelves so that next time people come into the store, they can pass judgement on some of the things they purchased on the previous occasion – thus other customers (and the supermarkets) obtain much more timely data on whether a product is going to be popular or not.*

(Introduce an easily detected element to the surrounding environment)

- *introduce GPS or equivalent position measurement system to trolleys and baskets in order to obtain patterns of use through the store – identifying where shoppers pause, where they avoid, how quickly they travel, etc*
- *in-store cafes and sit-down-and-relax spaces offer an opportunity for informal interactions, and can be particularly attractive to older customers – who very often visit the supermarket for the social interaction as much as for the shopping*

- introduce touch-screen (or equivalent) surveys at convenient post-check-out locations and display running average satisfaction (and other parameter) levels around the store so that customers receive immediate feedback that their input has been registered

(Detect changes in something already in the environment)

- Internet shopping permits considerable automatic data gathering opportunities
- have check-out staff engage in conversations with customers
- have car-park attendants engage in conversations with the customers (once outside the store, shoppers are more likely to make criticisms of things they have experienced inside the store)
- sponsor events at things like church-groups, young-mothers associations, old-people's homes, book-clubs, etc in order to acquire frank customer data in an environment where 'customers' are protected by the presence of like-minded others
- share data with other supermarkets in a pre-competitive manner – allowing each to use data in whatever way they feel is appropriate
- position survey forms in places like doctor's surgeries waiting rooms – places where people have nothing to do, and/or are in a negative mind-set – as a consequence of which, they are more likely to provide more useful information on how the supermarket might improve
- position survey forms in places of social interaction – like hairdressers – where communication is conducted in a neutral, frank and relaxed atmosphere (perhaps form some form of win-win relationship between supermarket and hairdresser)

(Make use of psychological effects to help make the measurement)

- most people dislike queuing at check-outs. This is often because they have nothing to occupy themselves rather than due to the lost time. Introduce simple survey methods – e.g. touch-screens – adjacent to queues in order to occupy customers (when they are in a probably negative mindset – and hence likely to give you the bad news that they may not otherwise do)
- use send-to-friend offers – meaning that people receiving them are not able to benefit personally. If people are not likely to win themselves, they are less inclined to act on the offer unless they are very happy with the service they receive from the supermarket
- identify 'influencer' customers and ensure they receive occasional 'experiences' that encourage them to tell their friends about what the supermarket 'did for them'
- when something goes wrong with a customer, use this time to find out what else the customer doesn't like about what you do – when they are in a negative mindset, they are much more capable and willing to divulge other negative aspects of their experience
- adding an element of discouragement or exclusivity to surveys is often a very effective way of making people want to participate

(Use emotional effects to help to make the measurement)

- introduce 'mySupermarket' personalization opportunities to on-line shopping methods – allowing customers to design for themselves how they interact with the site
- use schools and school projects to obtain information (e.g. several supermarkets run 'computers-for-schools' or equivalent schemes as a means of acquiring information on which locations and types of schools are involved most

(Use the inverse or opposite system to make the measurement)

- establish how many people come to do things other than shop – e.g. by introducing and monitoring quiet spaces, cafes
- obtain data from suppliers
- survey people at rival establishments (not just other supermarkets)

- *identify Omega Life View (Chapter 20) sectors of society to identify non-customers, and then find ways of establishing why they do not use your service, and how they may be influenced to do so*

And so on. Like the Inventive Principles and Trends in Chapters 11 and 14, the measurement strategies offer a way to systemize and structure brainstorming sessions.

The idea of this case study, of course, is merely to show how the Measurement Strategies can be used in this structured brainstorming mode. Clearly, some of the suggestions presented above are neither practical (today), nor necessarily effective. In a more real problem setting, all of the ideas generated would be evaluated in a downstream process to identify an implementable 'best' solution.

Final Thoughts

The Measurement tool and the measurement strategies play their biggest role in the creative problem solving arena in areas where the current 'system' either doesn't exist or it is still at a relatively immature stage in its evolutionary development and is suffering from inadequate feedback and control mechanisms. In a related fashion, it is also of great use when we decide to add a new function to a system – where some form of feedback will also be required. The missing key for many in these situations is failure to recognise the importance of feedback and control data requirements in systems – according to the viable system test, both are fundamental to the success of a system.

What Do I Do?

The most effective use of the measurement standards tool will emerge from the following basic deployment strategy:

1) Define in simple functional terms the measurement required from the system under consideration.
2) Determine whether the measurement is actually required by thinking about the useful function that the measurement is intended to deliver. Think specifically about the role of the measurement in providing the feedback and control functions required to ensure the viability of a system.
3) Work through the generic strategy suggestions in the Measurement Strategies section until you have identified a workable solution from one (or more) of them.

References

1) Altshuller, G. ,'Creativity As An Exact Science', Gordon & Breach, 1984.
2) Gladwell, M., 'The Tipping Point: How Little Things Can Make A Big Difference', Little, Brown & Company, London, 2000.
3) Grand, S., 'Creation: Life And How To Make It', Weidenfeld & Nicolson, London, 2000.
4) Christensen, C.M., Raynor, M.E., 'The Innovator's Solution', Harvard Business School Press, 2003.
5) Semler, R., 'The Seven Day Weekend', Century, The Random House Group, London, 2003.

14.
Problem Solving Tools -
Linear and Non-Linear Trends of Evolution

"First there is a mountain, then there is no mountain, then there is a mountain"
Buddhist Proverb

The trends part of the systematic innovation toolkit is, for many, emerging as one of the most powerful elements of the whole. It is one of those areas where the technical and business sides of the method are forced to have their closest link. If it may be true – as the technical trends suggest – that future technology trends are predictable, then this must have an impact on the way a business thinks about, plans and executes its activities. The technology trend story is covered in detail in the technical version of this book. Every manager and business leader is encouraged to explore – or have someone explore on their behalf – what systematic innovation has to say about the evolution of technical systems. All we have the time to say here is that in over a dozen years of researching and deploying those technical trends, we have not found an exception yet. The implications of this for managers are profound. That's 'are' as in 'right now'. It doesn't matter what business you are in, those technology trends are having an impact on where and when you or your competitors are going.

Our focus here is the business equivalent of those technology trends. Here as there, the real focus of the research has been somewhat different to what we might normally expect to find in a trend analysis. There is in fact a whole industry arranged around trying to do a better job of predicting the future. The general focus of that industry appears to be 'why are we so bad at predicting the future?' We believe that systematic innovation offers at least a partial answer to that question. In actual fact, the industry kind of knows it already. Why they don't do anything about it is wonderfully paradoxical. The story works something like this: a large part of the forecasting industry is made up of economists and mathematicians. Both are prone to try and build mathematical models of things. They are also both – especially the economists – prone to taking a top-down perspective of the world. Hence we get forecasting 'methods' like the Delphi approach in which groups of domain experts review past economic data and try to predict future economic data. This is an over-simplification which, of course, is harshly unfair, but nevertheless accurate in the sense that linear mathematical models get built. There are a number of techniques like Delphi used in various quarters. They all share a common lineage and ability to do a bad job. The only usual remaining issue is how quickly will they get things very badly wrong. All of these economists and mathematicians know that the real world is a non-linear place. There lies the heart of the paradox: attempts to build a linear mathematical model of a system that is fundamentally non-linear is doomed to failure from the moment the first equation is written down. It doesn't matter how sophisticated the mathematics gets, it will still fail to capture the fundamental dynamic governing the way the world operates. Linear models cannot model non-linear phenomena. All of those economists know this, and yet in a second twist to the paradox, their response is to say that the models are not sophisticated enough yet. Net result; reams of complicated mathematical formulae with a value as close to zero as you will ever wish to get. Take a quick glance at any copy of one of the (numerous) forecasting journals and you won't get past the first page without feeling like you are drowning in a mathematical swamp.

A non-linear world can only be modelled with non-linear models. This was the basic starting premise for the systematic innovation trends research. Fortunately the people doing this research also decided that mathematics was not going to be helpful in this endeavour. This chapter describes what has been uncovered. It is divided into a number of different sections:-

In the first section we examine 'conventional' linear trend directions. This might seem a little odd given the preceding discussion. Hopefully we will soon see that the inclusion of linear trends is useful on two counts; firstly as it will allow us to see why all of these linear trends – even though individually they may be absolutely correct – will eventually cause our predictions to go wrong. Then secondly, we will see how, even though they are wrong, they can still help us to better understand the *timing* of the non-linearities.

In the second section we examine the non-linear trends uncovered during the systematic innovation and explore how they can be used individually to help us generate solution ideas when we have a problem to solve. This section is complemented by a reference section at the end of the chapter, in which we detail all of the known non-linear business trends.

The third section then takes this story a step further by examining means of using the non-linear trends in combination with one another. Our real focus in this section is to introduce the concept of 'evolutionary potential' and the ability it gives us to establish – on a truly global benchmarking scale – how mature a given business model or organisation structure is.

In sections two and three we are primarily concerned with the where's, what's and why's of system evolution. In the fourth section, this story expanded to take into account the 'when's. Here we will see that, even though establishing when non-linear evolutions will happen, there are a number of guidelines that can help us to do a much better job than we would otherwise.

In the fifth and final section, we examine some of the special rules that apply to the non-linear trends. In particular here will be looking at situations where systems can apparently travel in the 'wrong direction', and identifying a series of rules that will determine why, where and how this can happen, and what we might do about it.

Before starting with these topics, however, it will probably be instructive to introduce one of the non-linear trends contained in the systematic innovation portfolio in order to obtain a grasp of what they look like, what information they contain, and how we might make best use of them.

Figure 14.1 illustrates an example of one of the trends. The trend is one known as 'customer expectation'. This is a trend that finds its roots in the work of Joe Pine, and the book 'The Experience Economy' (Reference 14.1). Like all of the other systematic innovation trends, this non-linear evolution pattern has been observed through analysis of how business systems across a wide variety of sectors have evolved. Like the other trends illustrated later, this trend works and is presented in a left-to-right fashion, such that systems at the right hand side are considered to be more advanced than ones to their left. Moreover, each box in the trend represents a discontinuous jump from one way of doing business to another. As such, even though we shall soon see it is an over-simplification, it is useful to think of each of the boxes as a new s-curve.

The relatively simple picture represents the distillation of a large amount of evolutionary data. It is worth examining some of the explicit and implicit data contained in what at first glance may appear to be an apparently simple image.

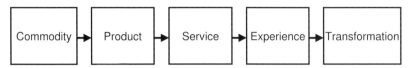

Figure 14.1: Example Evolution Trend: Customer Expectation

Firstly, we might ask why it is that systems evolve in this left-to-right direction (we will see later in the fifth section that there are predictable exceptions to this left-right rule, but generally we should assume evolution happens in a left-to-right direction). As the reference section at the end of the chapter will show, there are many examples of systems following this trend. By way of an illustration, we might think of a company like McDonald's. McDonald's business was never actually at the 'commodity' end of the trend, since the company was never in 'the beef business'. Neither was it a product-based business. When the company was started the main selling feature was that a McDonald's restaurant offered a service – i.e. the company actually began at the third stage of the trend. If a customer went to a McDonald's restaurant they weren't buying a hamburger (the 'product'), but rather a 'fast food' service. As the company grew, that service expanded to include the knowledge that a diner could go into any McDonald's restaurant anywhere safe in the knowledge that the food would taste the same, would be delivered in a consistently short time frame, would represent consistently good value for money, and would be served in an environment that was consistently clean, hygienic and friendly. Go into a McDonald's restaurant today and we can observe the company rapidly re-inventing itself as an offerer of an 'experience'. They are in the process, in other words, of making a jump from left to right along the trend. Very few of us now go to McDonald's because of the 'service' they offer, because very simply there are a large number of competitors now capable of offering a very similar level of service. What the company has realised is that in order to stay ahead of the game, they need to evolve their 'service' to another level. Hence, when we visit one of their restaurants (or rather when our kids visit), there are collectable toys, parties, hats, playgrounds and a host of other 'experiences'.

Actually, what the company has realised is that over time customer expectations increase, and that if your organisation is standing still then relatively speaking it is travelling backwards along the trend. McDonald's is thus offering 'experiences' as a means of fighting a commoditization battle, and as a means of continuing to be able to discriminate their offering from that of their competitors. According to the trend, when their competitors also start offering 'experiences', and when customer expectations have increased further, they may have to think about making another jump along the trend, to what Joe Pine describes as a 'transformation'. Given that a 'transformation' (what Pine describes as the 'fifth and final' stage of the trend) involves a transfer of responsibility from customer to provider, this possibility may be viewed by some as a rather frightening prospect in the McDonald's case. The 'transformation' stage exists because, while the fast-food restaurants haven't made this jump yet, other businesses have. If we go to a gym, for example, and employ a personal trainer saying that we wish to lose 20kg in the next month, and we *give that trainer the responsibility* to do all that is required to make it happen, then we have entered the 'transformation' stage of the trend.

Fortunately there are a cluster of other non-linear trends and so this transition from experience to transformation is not the only alternative available to McDonald's. As we shall see later, if we are going to use the trends to identify where a business is likely to evolve in the future, we need to examine all of the possible trend jumps rather than just look at one. We will see how the trends work in combination with one another in the third section.

Meanwhile, if we stay with the customer expectation trend for a few more moments, we might wish to look at the reasoning behind where the trend comes from and, more importantly *why*. An at least partial answer comes from the general message and single biggest key to using the trends effectively; '*somewhere there is a benefit from evolving from left to right along the trend*'. Every case where we have observed a business jumping from one trend stage to another, they have done it to achieve a benefit. As we see more businesses making the same sorts of jumps – which is where the trends have come from; observations of many systems making discontinuous jumps – we can also observe that the reasons why they made the jump can be quite different. The reference section at the end of the chapter reproduces the customer expectation trend along with a list of benefits that others have found for making the jumps. We need to have a little faith (at least initially) that these benefits exist, but the evidence from use elsewhere is that if we look we will find them.

The second point, then, related to this first one requires us to think again about the ideality equation, ideality = (perceived)(benefits/(costs + harm)). If we accept that increasing ideality is the over-riding evolution trend, and that moving from left-to-right along the customer expectation trend gives increased benefits, then it should be possible to also achieve an increase in ideality. This correlation may not appear immediately obvious. Indeed, for the evolution from selling a product to selling a service (a jump that many product-based industries are currently adopting or at least contemplating) there are a number of potentially painful lessons that need to be learned in switching from a model in which we would quite like customers to keep buying more of the same products from us, to one in which we potentially have to *give* them a product, or operate the product on their behalf. The ongoing switch from selling jet-engines to selling 'power-by-the-hour' in the gas-turbine industry, for example, has meant that engine companies have had to learn to live without the large capital injections that traditionally occur when a customer *buys* an engine, and instead rely on a continuous stream of income for each time a customer *uses* an engine that the engine company has now provided for free. The short-term cost has definitely gone up as far as the engine companies are concerned. But what they have also realised is that, provided they get their reliability calculations right and are able to make the engine last longer, the customer will be providing them with substantially more revenue over time. Like we see in this example, there is often a conflict between the top half of the ideality equation (benefits) and the bottom half (usually cost). The experience gathered from all of the systematic innovation research, however, firmly indicates that the evolutionary jumps described in the non-linear trends do give a net benefit. Even if cost or harm does go up initially (at least to certain customers), in the longer term, the benefit-versus-cost conflict is solved – very often as manufacturing technology advances – so that customers will always achieve the benefits they want with negligible cost or harm penalty. This phenomenon, of course, depends on the truth of the supposition that customers want benefits. We could fill another book arguing this point. As an alternative, we suggest that you observe how many systems around you have followed the trend patterns, and then have a go at using the trends to evolve a system you are interested in.

Incidentally, our research is constantly testing the validity and bounds of the trends. If we are ever able to find genuine exceptions to any of them (and we haven't done so as yet), we will be very happy – since an exception identified in one business may well open up a host of equivalent exceptions – and therefore disruption opportunities – in others.

The third general point about the trends before we look at their use in detail concerns goes back to the earlier comment about thinking of each of the trend stages as new s-curves. This is an important idea in the context of problem solving. The point is illustrated in Figure 14.2 below.

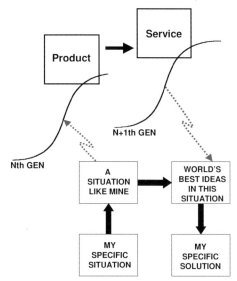

Figure 14.2: Each Stage Of A Trend Represents A New S-Curve

This point might be a little difficult to accept – but remember from Chapter 7 that every individual element within a system has its own family of s-curves – and it is, when analysed in detail later, an over-simplification. Even so, we recommend it as a very useful image to keep in mind.

The final general point is intended to act as a summary of the preceding discussions. The point is illustrated in Figure 14.3 – which repeats the customer expectation trend line again, but this time adds the labels describing the dynamics of what makes systems evolve in the way that they do. The absolute key to successful use of the trends in both strategic and problem solving contexts is the identification of the customer *benefits* that emerge as we speculate on *why* our system should jump to the right along the trend.

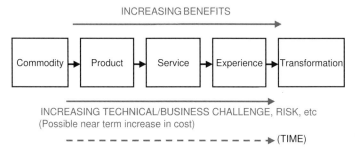

Figure 14.3: General Rules Concerning Non-Linear Trend Patterns

With two important exceptions, we will see that this picture applies to all of the non-linear trends described in the reference section at the end of the chapter.

The two exceptions – the trends for Mono-Bi-Poly and Trimming – we will discuss now, before we start to actually use the trends to do some problem solving or strategic planning work.

Mono-Bi-Poly

The Mono-Bi-Poly trend is essentially one that shows systems expanding from single entities, to double, triple and poly 'things'. As detailed in the reference section at the end of the chapter, the Mono-Bi-Poly trend has three main variants – firstly Mono-Bi-Poly(Similar) where the things that are increasing are all the same (e.g. different financial products offered by a bank), secondly Mono-Bi-Poly(Various) where the things that are increasing are different from one another (e.g. a bank that teams with a house-builder and a decorator to offer a complete home-purchase package), and the third Mono-Bi-Poly(Increasing Differences) in which we see systems inverting to deliver negative as well as positive functions (example – a bank that offers savings and loans services). The left-to-right evolution trend applies to all three of these examples, but needs to be qualified. The qualification basically works like this:

As we add more things to a system in order to transform it into a bi-system and then a poly-system, the normal rule says that benefits are increasing. The qualification with the Mono-Bi-Poly trend is that after we reach a certain number of things in the system, the benefits cease to appear any more and, if we persist in adding more, the overall ideality will actually drop. The phenomenon is illustrated in Figure 14.4 (and repeated in the reference section).

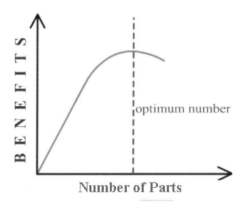

Figure 14.4: Qualification To The Mono-Bi-Poly Trend – Benefits Cease After A Certain Level

A simple example should serve to make the point: In order to offset the risks associated with market cycles in one sector, many companies take a decision to acquire or merge with companies offering products or services in markets operating on different cycles. If overall market fluctuations then begin to increase, the more risk and revenue sharing acquisitions a company tends to make in order to offset such fluctuations. The more volatile the markets, the more mergers and acquisitions required to achieve the desired financial stability. But, of course, every merger and every acquisition carries with it certain overheads and management challenges, and it usually doesn't take too long for these costs to outweigh the financial stability benefits; when this stage has been reached, there is no longer a net benefit in adding more companies and more sectors to the whole.

Another point related to this reducing-benefits characteristic, meanwhile, is that adding more things to a system almost invariably increases cost – the bottom half of the ideality equation. The usual consequence of this is that as the relative importance of benefits and cost varies, the 'optimum' number of things in the system will also tend to vary. A good example of this phenomenon in action can be seen in the shifting number of deposit account types and interest rates offered by retail financial institutions – the number going up during times when the market is strongly competitive and the banks have to adapt as much as they can to subtly different customer demands, and coming down when the economic conditions dictate the minimisation of overheads.

Trimming
The second qualification to the 'benefits increase from left-to-right' rule comes with the trend known as trimming. This trend, as described in detail in the reference section, is one in which systems are shown to evolve to contain progressively fewer elements as systems grow and mature. The basic mechanism of 'trimming' is that as managers get smarter in the ways they design and manage systems – progressively making better and better use of resources – they learn to make elements work harder. In other words, fewer elements are required to deliver the same (or even improved) functionality.

The qualification with this trend is that there are certain situations where it will not apply. One of the trend discoveries by the original TRIZ researchers was that as systems evolved along their s-curve they also followed through a characteristic path of, first increasing complexity, followed by decreasing complexity. This phenomenon is illustrated in Figure 14.5.

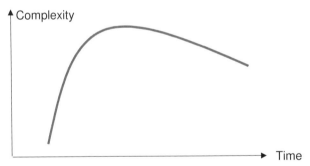

Figure 14.5: Evolution Of Systems Through Increasing Followed By Decreasing Complexity
(time span is equal to duration of corresponding system s-curve)

For all but the very simplest of systems, there is a strong correlation between complexity and the number of elements within the system. This in turn means that the increasing-decreasing complexity characteristic also correlates to the quantity of elements. The implications of this correlation, then, are that there are times during the evolution of a system when it is possible to reduce the number of elements, and there are other times when this is not a viable option. The boundary between the two scenarios is what might be seen as a point of maximum viable complexity. This is a point at which something (usually customer, or often a reliability problem – for complex systems at least – Reference 14.2) triggers a shift towards reduced complexity. This then is when the focus of managers and engineers is forced to shift in the direction of delivering benefits with reduced number of elements. Figure 14.6 thus shows when the 'trimming' trend can and cannot be used. We will talk about 'trimming' more in Chapter 18 – where we see how the trend can also help us to generate problem solving ideas.

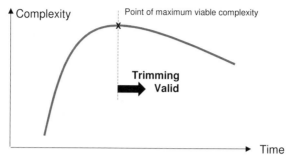

Figure 14.6: Where The Trimming Trend Applies

So there we have an outline of what the non-linear trends are and how we should interpret them. Before we go on to actually using them in either a problem solving or strategic sense, it is worth returning to what we conventionally think of when we think of 'trends':

1) Linear Trend Directions

The future forecasting industry has produced a raft of books and articles on the subject. The choice is overwhelming in many ways. Reference 14.3 provides a summary of over 700 sources of information on trends and trend directions. Figure 14.7 illustrates some of the main current customer and market trend directions that may be found at some of the sources identified in the reference. Without exception, all of this type of trend direction information has to be treated as transitory. One of the reasons that books like 'MegaTrends' are updated on a regular basis (and increasingly modified to suit different product niches or geographic regions) is that the trends often shift, and may in certain instances disappear altogether, and consequently 'keeping-up' with them can become a full-time career. Nevertheless, at a given point in time, we may observe the relevance and truth of any of these trends *if* we examine them individually.

```
* Increasing ELECTRONIC COMMUNICATION in private life
* Increasing GAP between have's and have-not's
* Increasing NEED FOR DIFFERENTIATION between business customers
* Increasing INFORMATION VOLUME
* Need for SIMPLICITY
* Decreasing HUMAN INVOLVEMENT
* Global AVAILABILITY OF SERVICES
* Wish for INDIVIDUAL SOLUTIONS (private customers)
* DEMOGRAPHIC TRENDS (aging population, DINKs)
* Wish for SELBSTVERWIRKLICHUNG ('making the most of one's life')
* TIME as a valuable resource
* Increasing RISK aversion/SECURITY consciousness
```

Figure 14.7: Example Linear Trend Directions

This 'individually' condition lies at the heart, then, of both the problem and the opportunity that customer trend direction information presents. The problem with the trends is that, while each of them may be seen to be logical and apparent when looked at in isolation, that is not how they operate in the real world. In the real world they all work together in a big complex and complicated mess of a structure. All 'keep it simple, stupid' attempts to simplify such complexity are almost inevitably doomed to fail. 'It's the whole thing, stupid' would, in this situation, make a far more appropriate aphorism. Scenario planning is often used as a middle ground between these two 'simple' and 'whole' extremes. In this trending method, we will typically take two or three trend directions that we think are appropriate to our situation, extrapolate them into the future time that we wish to analyse and see what happens. Usually what happens is we still end up with the wrong answer.

The reason that scenario planning and other trending methods 'go wrong' is that when the extrapolation into the future gets difficult the response is to make one or several simplifying assumptions to make the complexity manageable enough to proceed with the analysis.

The systematic innovation method uses this trend information in a somewhat different way. Rather than bailing out when things get difficult, it says that we should be actively looking for them. The 'difficulties' in this case are the things that happen when we take any pair of the trend directions. Any individual trend direction will be relevant only until something comes along and makes it irrelevant. That something is one of the other trends. Extrapolate along any two trends, in other words, and sooner or later a conflict is going to emerge. Figure 14.8 illustrates the phenomenon.

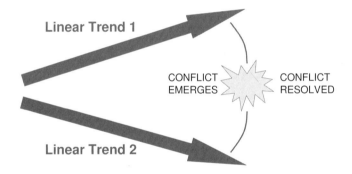

Figure 14.8: Pairs Of Linear Trends Result In Conflicts

When these conflicts emerge, scenario planning and other techniques bail-out. In systematic innovation – as we know from Chapter 11 and 12 – we see these conflicts as opportunities. According to systematic innovation, when we see two trends in conflict with one another, then we have also found an opportunity. Trends-in-conflict is a problem in scenario planning because we are forced into an either/or assumption. In systematic innovation, we have an opportunity to explore the conflict and identify means of resolving it in a win-win way. This again gets us back to the fundamentals of all system evolution; the dynamics of which we know are governed by the successive emergence and resolution of conflicts and contradictions. What is happening when we are using trend information to identify the conflicts is finding them before they actually emerge. By doing this, we have a crucial strategic opportunity to solve them before they become a physical reality.

One of the ways in which systematic innovation manages the bigger 'it's the whole thing, stupid' problem then is that in a full market trend analysis session we will be looking at many trends, but from the perspective that if we look at them in successive pairs and look for the conflicts and contradictions, that is where they are going to give us the most useful information. One of the things that we are presently building is a trend direction conflict matrix (Reference 14.4). We already use a version of this tool in many of the studies that we conduct either internally or on behalf of client organisations. We anticipate that ultimately there is at least a books-worth of valuable strategic information on trend-conflict analysis.

In the meantime, a simple example of how we use the trend-conflict idea will hopefully serve to illustrate why linear trend direction assumptions produce wrong answers, and why it is the conflict information where 95% of the value lies:

The first thing that needs to be done when using the trend directions, is to identify a focus. In this instance, let us say that we are interested in the future of grocery shopping. If we were then really interested in the likely future of grocery shopping, we would be likely to examine pairs of a whole series of trend directions. For the purpose of brevity, here we will simply look at two – decreasing human involvement and 'making the most of one's life'. The first trend is the one that will tell us that the majority of customers would prefer not to have to do their grocery shopping if they could avoid it. It is one of the trends behind the emergence and expansion of, first, Internet shopping, and then more recently, sophisticated online algorithms that remember what we bought on previous occasions so that the virtual supermarket can be re-designed to suit our requirements for future occasions. Hence, we can very quickly begin to see how a 'decreasing human involvement' trend may be applied to a grocery shopping scenario (if we were serious about the subject, however, we would also be examining the minority of customers who actually like grocery shopping). The same trend will also point us in the direction of us not even having to go to the store, and our purchases being delivered to us. It is a 'logical' direction. Why then has Internet grocery shopping grown and then – in many places – plateaued? If the trend is logical, why aren't we all doing our grocery shopping on the Internet?

One of the answers to that question lies in some of the other trend directions. The one we are looking at here is the 'making the most of one's life' trend. This is the one that will tell us that we are increasingly likely to:-
   a) want to eat foods from other parts of the world
   b) not have the time to 'learn' how to use a computer/the Internet
   c) not be home when the supermarket tries to deliver our on-line purchases.

What we have done here is identified several aspects of this second trend that could be in conflict with the first trend. The third aspect is probably the one that has had the greatest impact on the plateauing of Internet shopping growth. The conflict here is that we don't want to have to go to the supermarket to do our grocery shopping, but we aren't going to be home when the supermarket comes to deliver what we purchased virtually. As far as systematic innovation is concerned, this is the important part of the story. Until this conflict is resolved, future expansion of the market is likely to be hampered. The smart supermarkets, therefore, will be actively looking to resolve this contradiction. In actual fact, it may not be a supermarket that resolves it at all. Where the 'it's the whole thing stupid' issue raises its head again is that a good resolution to the conflict may come from the manufacturer of refrigerators: If the supermarket tries to deliver my food and I'm not home, they need somewhere to put it. If I have purchased refrigerated or frozen goods, then that somewhere needs to be appropriately chilled. It will also need to be accessible from outside. Or rather, accessible to the supermarket, but not to anyone else. Yet another contradiction that the forward thinking refrigerator manufacturers and the supermarkets might gain significant strategic advantage by resolving before their competitors do.

This example is obviously just a tiny fragment of a much bigger story. Big as that bigger story is, systematic innovation makes it a manageable one. Finding the conflicts between the trends is where the important strategic knowledge applies. Both in terms of *where* focus should lie, but probably more importantly, *when* markets are going to be ready for discontinuous innovation. Innovation timing is one of the most difficult aspects of the whole trend analysis story. It is an area that we return to later in the chapter. Meanwhile, the summary from this section is that trend direction information has a part to play in the overall story. Just not the one currently being thought about by futurists. Systematic innovation encourages us to use trend directions in a different way; it is not so much the individual trends that are important, but the connections and conflicts between them.

2) Non-Linear Trends As A Problem Solving Tool

Moving on from examination of linear trend directions, this section examines the discontinuous, non-linear trends in the first of their two roles; as a means of solving problems. As may be seen by the number of times the 'Select' part of the systematic innovation process (Chapter 10) references this chapter, the Trends tool has several diverse applications. Trends can be used to help us find new s-curves (one way of overcoming contradictions), for improving any actions we have determined to be insufficient or excessive, or simply as a way of improving any of the attributes of an element of a system or a process.

Many newcomers to systematic innovation find the Trends part the most attractive and easy to use from a problem solving perspective. The reason for this is that the trends encourage us to think in a slightly different way to the normal 'someone, somewhere already solved your problem' abstraction process. The difference is simple, but often profoundly important in its implications.

The Trends application process is similar to the general model of transforming a specific problem into a generic one, locating the general solution and then translating that general solution into a specific solution, albeit, as illustrated in Figure 14.9, the Trends process seems to by-pass parts of this process:-

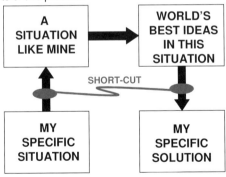

Figure 14.9: Trends in a Problem Solving Role

What the figure shows is that, although we still have to make the connections between the specific system under evaluation and the generic trends, once we have done that for an individual trend and have used that trend to identify the next evolutionary stage, we can use exactly the same connection we made to achieve the specific-to-generic jump in reverse to connect the generic solution back to a specific solution. In other words, the specific-generic transition only has to be done once. In many situations, the link from generic solution (i.e. the next stage in the trend to the right of the one the current system was connected to) back to the specific is so rapid that the user is often unaware that a transition has taken place at all.

A simple example should highlight the phenomenon, and demonstrate how we might use the trends in their problem-solving role. The system in question involves a typical customer-supplier relationship, and, for arguments sake, let's assume that the communications present in this relationship are not as effective as we would like them to be. The problem, as we have defined it, is that both sides of the relationship think that the other does not have their interests at heart; that the service is poor; that the customer is too demanding.

Using the Trends to help us to solve this problem demands first that we compare the customer, the supplier and their relationship with each of the non-linear trends in the reference section at the end of the chapter. In the case of each, the question we have to ask is 'where is this element positioned on this trend?' We are thus looking for connections between the customer or the supplier or the relationship between them and one of the trend stages for each trend. Figure 14.10 illustrates one such case – where we have successfully made a connection between the supplier and the first 'fixed' stage on the 'Connections' trend. (Note that we were able to make this connection despite the fact that there will clearly be elements of the supplier that are not 'fixed' – the point being that we are looking to make these connections in *any* sense – in this case, the fact that the supplier may have a number of 'fixed' elements in the way it does things. For example, there may be a single (fixed)-point contact with customers, or a fixed pricing structure, or a fixed order processing system – all of which indicate that the supplier is at the 'fixed connections' stage of the trend.)

As soon as we have made this connection, the trend pictures to the right of 'fixed' stage should begin to suggest generic solutions to us and, because we have already made the connection between specific and generic, we should already be picturing switchable pricing structures or order processing systems, or continuously switching interfaces.

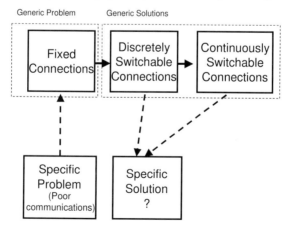

Figure 14.10: Trends In A Problem Solving Role – Customer-Supplier Communications

Several of these connections may in fact may turn out to offer excellent solutions to the stated problem. In many ways, this is where the trends have emerged from in the first place; someone somewhere has already solved their own problems by jumping from a fixed to a discretely or continuously switchable way of doing things. Quite possibly for different reasons to our own situation, but the jump is nevertheless (generically) common.

At least part of the reason for picking this example is to highlight the fact that the solution directions suggested by this particular trend run counter to the 'common-sense' view of many people. Prevailing 'common-sense' appears to tell many organisations that the right solution direction is to have precisely that kind of single-point contact between organisations; so that any one customer knows that there is someone dedicated to serving their needs at the supplier. The majority, if not all innovations run counter to prevailing common-sense of course. Single-point contacts sound like a good idea until it comes to vacation time, or there are differences of opinion. Likewise, single pricing structures sound like 'common-sense' until we realise that every customer is different from every other one, and that there are many value-adding propositions that one customer may want that others will not. The trends are there to tell us how other organisations and people have solved such problems in inventive ways.

Again, the consistent message when using the trends is 'somewhere there is an advantage in moving to the right along the trend'. In many instances, this means that our task when problem solving using the trends is not so much making the connections between trend and system, but working out *why* the answers emerging from the trends are answers. Again, the jumps are consistent across all the systems we analyse – this was the main criterion in fact for deciding whether a trend was a genuine one or not – but the reasons why the jumps can happen may vary considerably.

Relating to the important evolution cone shown again in Figure 14.11, what all of the non-linear trends are trying to do for us is act as signposts pointing towards more ideal systems.

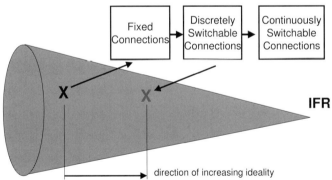

Figure 14.11: Non-Linear Trends Act As Signposts To More Ideal Systems

3) Non-Linear Trends in Combination

Deploying the non-linear trends individually is a frequently effective means of generating solutions to problems. At the very least they are a way of adding focus to brainstorming sessions – where we will use first use one trend to help generate ideas, then when we have run out of ideas from this trend, will move on to another, and then another, and so on until we have a set of answers that we like. This method of use is often effective, but inevitably carries the risk that we are generating solutions without having a true understanding of either the background to the situation we are in, or, more importantly, how other trend jumps might impact on the situation. It is this latter area that we turn our attention to in this section; how do we think about the non-linear trends acting in combination with one another?

One of the first and most effective ways of beginning to see the combinations involves a means of drawing the trends together. One such method of doing this is what we call 'evolution potential' mapping. The resulting picture is called an evolution potential radar plot:

Evolution Potential Radar Plots

The concept of evolution potential involves the idea that if we examine the position of our system along one of the non-linear trends and find that it is not yet at the final stage, then it has remaining untapped evolutionary potential. Alongside this idea is the related idea that we can also use the trends to identify the evolutionary limits of a given system. Both the evolution potential and evolutionary limits ideas are, we think, very important. Applied in a technical sense using the technical trends, the information contained within an analysis of the evolutionary potential of a given system may be expected to play a significant role in determining how best to spend R&D funds – there being little point investing in directions where the system is already at or approaching the fundamental limits of its potential, for example, and, conversely, there will be a lot of point investing in development of parts of the system right at the beginning of their evolutionary potential as likely benefit per unit of funds invested will be at its highest. Likewise, an evolution potential analysis using the business trends can be used to determine which parts of an organisation have more untapped potential than others, and which are beginning to hit some fundamental limits.

The 'evolution potential radar plot', then, is a means of plotting all of this potential and limits information in a single figure. As such, the plot is designed to help structure and present evolutionary potential thinking. An example evolutionary potential plot is illustrated in Figure 14.12. Each spoke in the plot represents one of the non-linear business trends relevant to a given element under investigation. For each relevant trend, the shaded area represents how far along each trend the current system has evolved. The outside perimeter of the plot represents the final known stage of each trend, and hence the evolutionary limit. Thus the area difference between shaded area and perimeter is a measure of evolutionary potential.

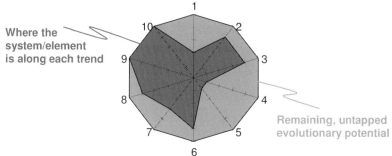

Figure 14.12: Evolution Potential Radar Plot

The construction of an actual evolution potential plot is probably best observed through consideration of a real example. The plots provide a means of analysing literally any type of business model, scenario, process or structure. Different trends will be relevant in each case – and therefore one of the first jobs will be to work out which trends are relevant and which are not. Ultimately, the greatest value of the method is that it offers us a means of comparing a system to a global standard. This 'global benchmarking' idea is, we think, another very important one – and is the underlying reason why we find ourselves constructing so many of these pictures when we are performing strategic studies. The example we will use to illustrate the process is the manner in which a typical motel chain presents itself to its customers.

We will usually begin by comparing our current system against each of the trends in turn. The sequence in which we look at the trends is not important, although if we wish to compare or overlay plots, it is useful to maintain a consistent sequence. The order of the trends in the reference section at the end of the chapter is designed to form such a consistent pattern. Although the details are not important here, the sequence of the trends has been chosen in accordance with a variety of psychological factors associated with the ability (or otherwise) of the human brain to make connections between their system and the trends.

The table below describes each trend in the context of our motel example:

Trend	Current Position Of Motel
Customer Expectation	Service (Stage 3 of 5)
Customer Purchase Focus	Price (4/4)
Self-Organisation Awareness	Unconscious (1/5) – most motels are managed in very top-down ways, with usually no awareness of complexity issues – 'keep it simple, stupid' is very much the order of the day
Knowledge	Information (2/4) – most motels have some form of customer tracking system, but few do anything useful with the information.
Competency	Consciously Competent (3/4) – thanks to high turnover of staff, relationships with customers tend to be on a scripted basis
Process Thinking	Single Process (2/4) – chains typically adopt one process for every motel in order to protect brand image
System Robustness	Transient Effects (3/6) – the motel is likely to operate on seasonal basis, but unlikely to think about longer term effects
Design Point	Single Point (1/4) – motels tend to be designed to attract a certain customer profile; they are unlikely to be designed to simultaneously appeal to multiple sectors – the direction being suggested by the trend
Mono-Bi-Poly (Similar) – Interface	Bi-System (2/4) – all customers likely to be treated in the same way, with the exception of a possible loyalty programme
Mono-Bi-Poly (Various) – Interface	Mono-System (1/4) – chain is not linked with any other kind of complementary business
Mono-Bi-Poly (Increasing Differences)	Similar Components (1/4) – all of the motels in the chain conform to a norm. (Marriott Courtyard, Residence, Suites etc represent a hotel chain that has evolved along this trend)
Segmentation – Interface	Homogenous (1/5) – similar to Mono-Bi-Poly in this case, but offering the additional thought that customers different from one another, and also different at different times during their visit
Nesting - Down	Difficult to see an immediate connection in this case
Sense Interaction	2 Senses (2/5) – motel is likely to harness visual and olfactory senses in customers, but not auditory, kinaesthetic or gustatory
Increasing Transparency	Opaque (1/3) – motel is unlikely to make its business processes and practices visible to customers

Connections	Fixed Connections (1/3)
Increasing Asymmetry	Difficult to see an immediate connection in this case
Boundary Breakdown	Many Boundaries (1/3) – traditional logic says that only reception staff are expected to interact with guests
Vertical/Horizontal Cycles	Vertical (1/2)* - motels today are a vertically dominated industry
Interaction With Others	Independent (2/3) – difficult to interpret in the customer context, but unlikely to be a feeling of 'we' between guest and hotel staff
Listening/Communicating	Selective (3/5) – another difficult one, experience in the large majority of motels would suggest that staff listen to guest comments only within a fairly narrow range of areas
Market Research	Findographics (2/4) – most motels will leave questionnaire forms in guest rooms, but are unlikely to actively seek to identify what customers want
Spiral Dynamics	Order (4/8) – a few motels might cater for materialistic needs but the majority do not
Generational Cycles	Difficult to interpret if customer-base spans a broad age range. In such cases it is more useful to plot this trend in terms of the four time stages. We are currently at the end of an unravelling (3/4) – implying imminent shift in focus of motel business
Action Co-ordination	Non-Coordinated (1/4) – guests are an inconvenience in many motels, and as such are expected to check-in and out, and eat at times specified by the motel, rather than the other way around
Rhythm Co-ordination	Continuous (1/3) – highly unlikely to be any time variation in the way in which the motel deals with customers
M-B-P (Similar) – Time	Difficult to see an immediate connection in this case
M-B-P (Various) – Time	Difficult to see an immediate connection in this case
Segmentation – Time	Difficult to see an immediate connection in this case
Nesting – Time	Difficult to see an immediate connection in this case
Damping	Difficult to see an immediate connection in this case
Feedback & Control	Two-Way Feedback (3/4) – most customers would expect to be listened to during their dealings with the motel, but very few have developed any kind of 'adaptive' capability.
Non-Linearities	Linear (1/3) – motel very unlikely to think about things that can go wrong outside a very tried and tested range of scenarios
M-B-P (Similar) – Space	Difficult to see an immediate connection in this case
M-B-P (Various) – Space	Difficult to see an immediate connection in this case
M-B-P (Inc.Diff) – Space	Difficult to see an immediate connection in this case
Segmentation – Space	Difficult to see an immediate connection in this case
Nesting – Space	Difficult to see an immediate connection in this case
Increasing Dimensionality	One-Dimensional (2/4) – linear, one-to-one staff-to-customer interactions are the norm
Degrees Of Freedom	Difficult to see additional relevance over that offered by MBP in this situation
Dynamization	Rigid (1/3) – relations with customers are unlikely to be adaptive in any way
Decreasing Human Involvement	Semi-Automated (3/6) – on-line booking systems reduce the effort a guest is required to make, but there are still a number of actions required – credit card, address details, keys, etc
Trimming	Partially Trimmed System (2/4) – most motel chains have been through at least one wave of business process re-engineering to eliminate waste in terms of what they offer to guests
Nesting - Up	Independent Structure (1/3) – not connected into higher level (non-motel) functional business model

* - this trend always tends to be drawn as 0.5 as the left-to-right sequence constantly switches

(Note: several of the trends are labelled 'difficult to see an immediate connection' – this will often be the case – the trends where this happens will be different in different applications. As experience with using the trends builds, users are likely to be able to make connections with progressively more of the trends.)

Figure 14.13 presents the radar plot resulting from the analyses presented in this table. As such, it offers us a much more compact and visibly significant image of the current evolutionary state of the motel in the example.

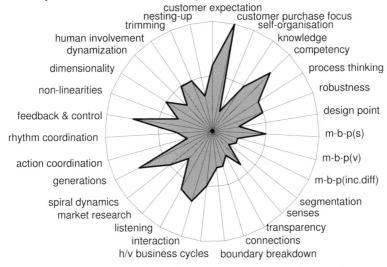

Figure 14.13: Exemplar Motel Chain Evolution Potential Example

As per the previously defined convention, the shaded area represents the current level of maturity of the motel. The white space between this shape and the outside edge of the plot represents the untapped potential of the current system. All of this untapped potential represents the opportunity to improve the way the motel operates and presents itself to its customers. We would typically use the prompts suggested by each of the trends to help us to generate ideas on which directions the motel should evolve.

It should be noted here that while this plot has been drawn for the motel chain as a whole, it is often the case that the analysis will be conducted at the level of individual elements contained within the chain in order to define a series of evolutionary plots. The process used during the construction of each of the individual plots is exactly the same as that used during the construction of the previous, overview plot. Such plot families offer significant potential in terms of identifying areas to focus improvement efforts – for example there will be little point in devoting resources to developing an element with little remaining evolutionary potential when there are other elements which are still at the un-evolved stages of several of the trends.

Figure 14.14 illustrates a typical evolutionary potential radar plot family showing the hierarchical structure of individual elements – in this case different areas within the motel chain – feeding into the higher-level radar plot from Figure 14.13 illustrating the evolutionary potential of the total. In this (hypothetical) example, we are able to see at a glance that the guest–services part of the business has more untapped potential than any other, and that the back office has used up most of its potential.

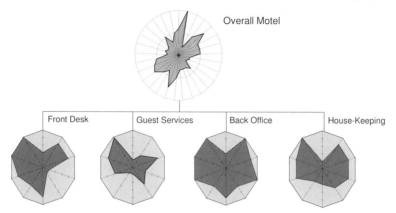

Figure 14.14: Motel Chain Evolution Potential Radar Plot Hierarchy
(NB: all plots have been show with the same number of spokes for convenience – in practice, each radar plot
will probably have a different number of relevant trends, and hence a different number of spokes)

This hierarchical structure is important as some of the trends that will not be relevant to a particular individual element – for example the 'action co-ordination' trend has little relevance to the design of the back office when we are thinking about external interfaces – but it does have relevance when we analyse the front desk or the overall system. Importantly, the plots drawn at the higher levels in the hierarchy are not simply an integration of the plots drawn at the lower levels – plots at each level need to be constructed independently of one another in order to make best use of the trends.

As a final point relating to the form and content of the radar plots, it is worth noting that the trends can be interpreted in both *internal* and *external* contexts. Figure 14.13, for example, compared the motel chain from the perspective of the external link to the customer. We could equally well have conducted an analysis by focusing on processes, relationships and structures internal to the motel. Figure 14.15 illustrates the fact that in any serious evolution potential analysis of a system, there are likely to be two families of plots – one internally and one externally focused. As suggested by the figure, the relevant trends in each instance is likely to shift as things that are relevant internally may not be when we look at relationships with the outside world, and vice versa.

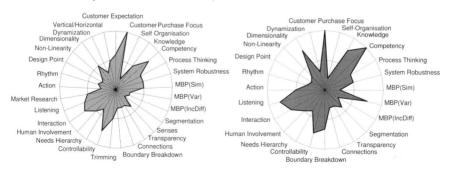

Figure 14.15: Internal And External Focus Of Evolution Potential Radar Plots

We should also note that the plots are intended to be flexible – allowing the user to include just those trends that are relevant to a given system (the recommendation is that all trends are examined as being *possibly* relevant however). Figure 14.28 at the start of the trends reference section illustrates the possible options, noting that certain trends have applications in more than one role – e.g. the Mono-Bi-Poly Similar and Various trends have space, time and interface contexts. In order to develop some order and commonality of approach when drawing evolutionary potential plots, we will find it useful to maintain the structure and sequence of trends presented in this example, especially with respect to the space, time and interface categorisations – in that way, any plot we see will always have, for example, 'interface' based trends at the top of the picture.

Combining Trends

As the Mono-Bi-Poly trend suggests, our deployment of the non-linear business trends can often be improved by considering interactions between multiple different trends as opposed to just singly.

This fact applies to all of the trends relevant to a system being evaluated, where they have some measure of untapped evolutionary potential. We will not discuss such cases any further than to merely mention that when examining unused potential, it is advisable to look for synergistic effects between different trend suggestions. In the above motel example, we can see this in action by combining the idea of a system with flexible connections with the listening/communication trend (and the jump towards attentive or even empathic listening) and the segmentation trend – which would prompt us to make the flexible connections adapt according to different customers, where we are actually wishing to empathise with the individual needs of a given customer.

The trend we need to mention in a little more detail in this combination role, however, is the Mono-Bi-Poly trend. This trend too can be used in the same manner as described in the previous paragraph. The reason for singling out the Mono-Bi-Poly trend for special attention in this 'trends in combination' section is that the bigger picture says that the number of options open to us when we use M-B-P to say 'add something else' – especially when it is something different that we wish to add – is potentially quite large and often 'non-obvious'. The addition of 'something else' to a motel's business model will sound obvious to some and not to others. In either case there has to be a question mark over what 'something else' might be.

Unfortunately, there does not appear to be any cast-iron rules regarding what sort of Mono-Bi-Poly action we might combine with other trends. On the other hand, someone, somewhere has already made a novel combination between the Mono-Bi-Poly and other improvements and we should take a note of these combinations. Figure 14.16 indicates some of the possibilities. The list is intended to be used as a solution trigger list. In the same way, problem solvers may care to examine some of the resources trigger sheets in Chapter 15 to identify other things they might combine into the way they use the trends.

Type of M-B-P Application	Example
Internal Additions	- adding things into gaps - addition of new functions - temporary additives – e.g. consultants, task-forces, tiger-teams - transfer of functions from other sub-systems
External Additions/ Additions Between Elements	- adding easily available elements to add new function - using resources available in the surrounding systems - addition of something capable of making measurements

	- addition of feedback mechanisms (ask the question 'what hasn't got any feedback?' in order to identify opportunities) - add something that will resonate when desired
Actions	- new actions - periodic action combined with multiple different actions - changing periodicity – addition of different functions at different times
Co-Branding	- add someone else's branded product to yours to benefit both

Figure 14.16: Examples Of M-B-P Combination Possibilities

Global Benchmarking

As soon as we have a globally generic means of comparing systems with one another, then a whole series of ways of using the capability emerge. One of the main uses to date has been the idea of global benchmarking. By analysing two or more equivalent systems against the trends of evolution, and then overlaying the two plots it becomes possible to benchmark not only one system versus another, but both can also be measured against a global scale of best practice. The basic global benchmarking concept is illustrated in Figure 14.17:

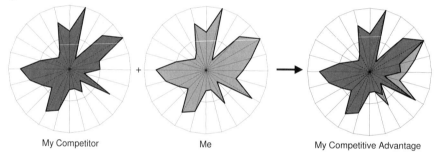

My Competitor   Me   My Competitive Advantage

Figure 14.17: Comparing Equivalent Systems versus Global Best Practice

The 'global' term comes into the name since all of the untapped potential (i.e. the white space between the shaded areas and the outside edge of the plot) is effectively comparing all of the systems included in the plot with best known practice taken from across all industries. Global benchmarking analyses can be performed at various hierarchical levels within a system, with an internal or external focus, for small niche sectors, for whole organisations, or, in some cases, for whole nations.

Mapping Changes In Evolution Potential With Time

Since each of the non-linear trends represents a discontinuous jump in the direction of a more ideal system, we may observe the evolution plots gradually filling up, or 'flowering' as a system evolves. Not only does the evolution potential concept then give us an indication of the maturity of a system, but if we examine how the plot changes as a function of time, we can also see how dynamic the market that that system operates within is. Hence another important use of the evolution potential radar plots involves producing plots at different times in the history of a system in order to establish the rate at which discontinuities are taking place. Figure 14.18 illustrates a typical sequence of plots for a system analysed over a period of time. At this point in time there is insufficient data to establish definitively how the rate of flowering corresponds to the perceived rate of change in an industry. What we can say with some degree of certainty, however, is that we have seen certain industries in which discontinuous shifts occur at a frequency of once-per-decade, while in others (particularly dot.coms) the shift rate may be as high as several discontinuous advances per year.

Figure 14.18: Plot 'Flowering' As A Function Of Time

The discontinuity dynamics phenomenon identifiable in these radar plots is but one of a number of things that needs to be done in order to better understand issues of innovation timing. In the next section we look at other aspects and see how we might be able to do a better job of knowing when the time is and isn't right to introduce which kinds of non-linear innovation into systems, products and services.

4) Non-Linear Trend Timing Effects

The non-linear business trends contained in systematic innovation offer a uniquely powerful means of identifying the where and how's of innovation. Innovation timing – the 'when's – on the other hand are somewhat less amenable to systematic prediction. Many books have been written on the subject (most notably Reference 14.5). We spend our time here examining the strategic implications of combining non-linear business and technology trends with customer and market evolution trends to provide organisations in the context of a systematic business concept innovation ('BCI' – Reference 14.6) methodology.

What we see acting as the primary innovation driver is the tension between the expectations of customers ('demand') versus the capability of organisations to meet those expectations ('supply'). The basic supply-demand concept is illustrated in Figure 14.19.

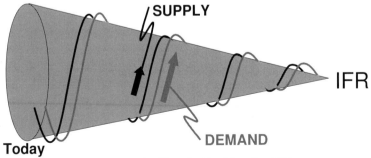

Figure 14.19: Plot 'Flowering' As A Function Of Time

The difference between supply and demand represents the primary driving tension force that will determine the need and therefore success of an innovation; the bigger the tension, the faster an innovation is likely to take-off. Conversely, without a driving tension, any innovation will fail. As indicated in Figure 14.20, the most difficult aspect of the demand side of the equation are those 'hidden failures' whereby a customer may be unaware that they have an unmet need.

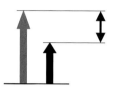 **Primary Innovation Driving Tension**

Note: sometimes the customer is not aware of the tension and it is up to the supplier to find it ('hidden failures')

Figure 14.20: Supply versus Demand Tension As Innovation Driver

Typical examples of hidden failures would be things like take-home pizzas (where the customer 'expects' the pizza to be cold and soggy), film cameras (where the customer expects to have to send their photos away to be processed) or retail banking (where the customer expects to have to take the time to shift finances from one sort of bank account to another). In each of these cases – and many more – as soon as the customer is shown a solution that eliminates the 'failure', the fact that it was a failure becomes immediately apparent. Paradoxically, prior to the emergence of the solution, customers are largely unaware that a failure exists at all.

Finding hidden failures is one of those areas where the systematic innovation method is at its most powerful. Very often we can use the non-linear trends as a means of identifying solutions to hidden failures. Although it may sound difficult to believe, the technical trends very definitely anticipated the emergence of the digital camera long before it was even a glimmer in the eyes of the photographic industry. Given this level of predictive capability, the systematic innovation trend tools are increasingly being used as a means of identifying solutions to hidden failures. Very often, in fact, finding the solution is substantially easier than finding the failures. A common question, then, when using the trends to predict what future solutions might look like is 'what hidden failures would this solution eliminate?'

Two other useful tools to help identify these 'hidden' failures are QFD and a variant of subversion analysis (Chapter 21) in which we might use simple but powerful provocations of the form 'how could a customer be unhappy with this product/service?' or 'who doesn't buy our product/service, and why?'.

Related to the issue of supply-demand driving tension, the next dominant influencing factor in business evolution timing is determined by whether the prevailing technology or business evolution precedes or lags behind customer expectations. Where technology or business model lags behind customer expectation (as in many service industries or the design of many household products), we see that the systematic innovation technology trends can be expected to play a major role in bridging the gap. Where technology or business evolution exceeds the expectations of a significant number of customers – as may be seen in a large number of case studies by Christensen (Reference 14.7) such as computer hard-drives, earth-moving equipment and accounting software – and the market becomes ripe for the emergence of 'disruptive' technology insertions, we show how modified definition and application of both the non-linear technical and business trends can also be used to develop potent BCI solutions. We will explore each scenario separately:

Technology Lagging Behind Customer Expectation

The picture reproduced in Figure 14.21 serves to illustrate the frequently observed scenario in which the fundamental limitations of a given solution become overtaken by customer expectations. This situation results in an 'administrative contradiction' – the customer knows what they want, but the system is unable to deliver it. This situation represents a classic example of demand-versus-supply tension. The inadequacy of a system relative to expectation is a vital innovation driver – and represents a significant element of the 'form follows failure' thesis found in Henry Petroski's excellent 'The Evolution of Useful Things' book (Reference 14.8).

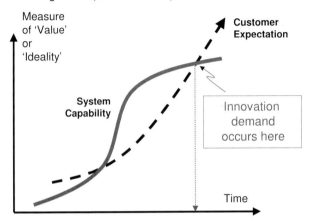

Figure 14.21: Common Innovation Driver I – Customer Need Exceeds Solution Capability

The characteristic of the customer expectation curve follows the trends suggested by the Kano diagram (Reference 14.9) and the inevitable shift of customer expectations as they become more familiar with products. The Kano model tells us that while we used to be excited by the idea of air-conditioning in a car, for example, we now almost take it for granted that the car will have this facility. In a similar manner, the idea of in-car GPS is still seen as an 'exciter' in many market segments – something that would actively delight us when we see it in the car. The rising characteristic of the customer expectation line in this scenario is in direct conflict with the inherent limitations created by the s-curve characteristics of a system.

The expectation curve and the system capability s-curve are of course plotted as averages. Particularly in the case of the customer expectation curve, this is a highly dangerous assumption. Certainly, one of the overriding messages from Chapter 7 on the dynamics of s-curves should leave readers in no doubt that not only does every element within a system possess its own family of s-curves, but that every individual customer may well also have a very different perception of the relative ideality of those different curves. Taking this into account will increasingly require us to plot these expectation pictures for every individual customer (leaving one or two important mass-customisation contradictions to be solved along the way!) if we are to truly understand the dynamics of when the innovation demand occurs.

The emergence of the administrative contradiction in this 'expectation exceeds capability' scenario meanwhile acts as the spur to innovation. The flattening of the top of the s-curve is symptomatic of the presence of a limiting contradiction in the system. The creation of a new or modified system that enables this s-curve to be lifted – i.e. presents the customer with sufficiently high new level of ideality or value – will only come about through resolution of a contradiction. This can be achieved through use of the Trade-Off Elimination/Contradictions part of the systematic innovation toolkit, or, using the non-linear trends described in this chapter – where, although already stated elsewhere as over-simplistic – it is possible to say that each new step along the trend patterns is a new s-curve opportunity.

In this 'expectation exceeds capability' scenario, then, it is evident that the innovation-timing question is answered by a definite 'now'.

Technology Exceeds Customer Expectation

Our thrust in this section now shifts to look at a different scenario connecting customer expectation to solution capability – that of the case where solution capability exceeds customer expectation (Figure 14.22). This scenario is the basis for much of the work reported by Clayton Christensen in the afore-mentioned Reference 14.7.

The central thrust and paradox of the Innovator's Dilemma is that traditional 'good' management practice can lead organisations into big trouble when the solutions they offer **exceed** the needs of their customers. In Christensen's words, these situations lead to opportunities for the entry into the market of 'disruptive' technologies. A disruptive technology is essentially one that changes the prevailing business model in a downward direction. True disruption will see the emergence of a product or service which in the eyes of the current customer base is inferior to the prevailing solutions, but which finds a new set of customers who can live with the inferior performance of some attributes provided that the solution gives superior capability in other attributes. Historically speaking, companies almost inherently fail to thrive (or often even survive) in situations where the market is expecting less of a product than it is capable of delivering.

One of the aims of this section is to encourage readers to think about possible disruptive technology opportunities or threats in their business, and, more importantly, to show how the non-linear trends are uniquely placed to help determine what the 'right' disruptive jumps might be.

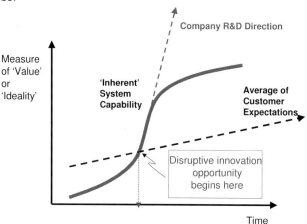

Figure 14.22: Common Innovation Driver II – Solution Capability Exceeds Customer Need

Case Study – Earth-Moving Equipment

In realising that probably not all of the readers of this book are interested in heavy earth-moving equipment, we hope that everyone can nevertheless extract some useful learning points from this discussion. Those that feel happier thinking about computer disc-drives or accounting software or retail shopping or electric cars might like to explore the details given for those cases given in Christensen's book and see the uncanny parallels to the earth-moving equipment case illustrated here.

Christensen details the evolution of earth-moving equipment from the original steam-driven mechanical devices of the type illustrated in Figure 14.23 to the hydraulic machines prevalent in today's earth moving environment. The introduction of hydraulic machines was indisputably 'disruptive' to the mechanical excavator business model.

To over-simplify grossly (and yet hopefully justifiably), the evolution of mechanical excavators was largely driven by the manufacturers (initially correct) belief that their markets were interested in moving ever greater amounts of earth per shovel load, and that this was particularly so for their most profitable customers. Consequently 'sound' management practice meant that the evolution of mechanical excavators was targeted at the earth-moving needs of the most profitable customers. As time went on, the industry found that it was possible to make bigger and bigger machines capable of moving more and more earth.

Figure 14.23: Disruptive Shift From Mechanical To Hydraulic Earth-moving Equipment

Further evolution of the earth movers to increase shovel load size, however, although serving customers at the high end of the market began to exceed the requirements of other customers to whom shovel size increase was not worth the increase in cost and other down-sides that came attached to such big machines. These customers were becoming ripe for a disruptive technology insertion.

They got one when JCB introduced the first hydraulically powered earthmovers in 1947. The first hydraulic 'backhoes' were inferior to the cable-actuated mechanical machines in just about every traditional performance measure used by the existing customer base: to these (high profit generating) customers the new machine was not particularly attractive. On the other hand, the new machines did offer a considerable number of new advantages, not least of which was a whole new level of compactness, portability and flexibility of operation, and a marked improvement in safety if something went wrong (insert image of snapped cable moving at uncontrollably high speed here).

The new hydraulic machines thus carved themselves a whole new market of customers to whom the new advantages outweighed the deficiencies of a smaller load carrying capability. The new machines began to sell in large quantities, but principally to a newly created customer base.

As is so often then the case, the revenues from this new customer base (albeit they were still not sufficient to be of great interest to the established cable-activated machine manufacturers – hence 'good management practice' said to ignore them) funded the development of increasingly capable hydraulic systems. The hydraulic machine evolution entered a phase where it was able to rapidly catch-up with the performance capabilities of the mechanical machines. It did this whilst simultaneously preserving the advantages of compactness, portability, flexibility and safety. In another highly reproducible evolution pattern, the increasing capability of the hydraulic machines was happening at a rate greater than the changing requirements of the customers with the highest earth-moving requirements. Before too long the net value of the evolving hydraulic machines thus met and exceeded both the customer expectation and the fundamental ideality limits of the mechanical machines – Figure 14.24. As is so often the case, the disruptive technology eventually won the day – and today the mechanical, cable actuated earthmovers are restricted to confined very-high load niche applications.

The connection with the systematic innovation trends here is that the technical versions would very definitely have predicted the evolution from mechanical to fluid-based systems.

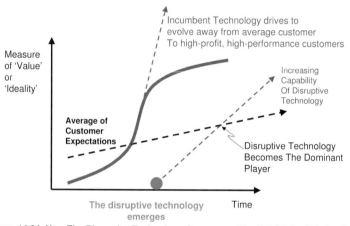

Figure 14.24: How The Disruptive Technology Overcomes The Established Technology

The relevant technology evolution trend in other words, could have been used to predict the eventual dominance of the hydraulic systems over the mechanical. The trend, however, doesn't end with the hydraulic system; it suggests that these will eventually be overtaken by another discontinuous shift from a hydraulic to a 'field'-based system.

Seeing as the hydraulic backhoe is the currently dominant earth-mover, we might now switch from historical analysis to future prediction mode by using the non-linear trends alongside Christensen's disruptive technology model to have a go at showing what both together would tell us about the future of earth-moving:

Field-Based Earth Movers
The reasons systems jump from hydraulic to field based solutions are various – increased reliability, increased design flexibility (positioning of components), increased efficiency, increased controllability, increased safety, reduced harm from fluid leaks, etc.

As far as load-carrying capability is concerned, however, an electrically actuated backhoe using the best of today's electrical actuation capability will not match the earth-moving performance of the hydraulic systems. The current customer base is thus unlikely to be attracted to an electrical machine.

According to the disruptive technology model, the new electrically based earth mover needs to find a new customer base – for whom shovel load size performance is not as important as some of the inherent benefits of shifting away from hydraulics – if it is to define a foundation from which to grow. Almost inherently, these customers don't exist today, or, if they do, they are highly unpredictable in terms of what they actually want. Hypothetically, for an electrical earth-mover, they might include a growing market of domestic users (see how the market for sit-on lawn-mowers evolved for example), or anyone requiring to dig lots of small holes with as little human labour as possible – e.g. cable companies – where the increased controllability and flexibility (i.e. the tool needs connecting to the power source by a simple wire only) of an electrically operated system would outweigh the reduced shovel-load performance. According to the model, these applications will in the short term be less profitable than the high performance hydraulic systems (which explains why the incumbent hydraulic companies are unlikely to be interested – at least based on historical evidence).

The next part of the prediction then goes something along the lines that because the electrical system is at the start of its evolutionary potential path, it doesn't need nearly so much investment to begin increasing the performance of the machines. Revenues from the new customer base fund development of higher shovel load systems; the electrical systems will then eventually become able to match the performance of the hydraulic systems, while retaining the other flexibility, controllability, reliability, etc advantages the hydraulic systems will never match – Figure 14.25.

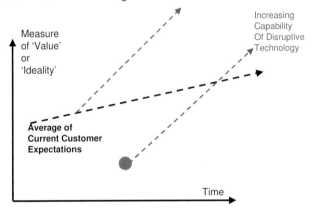

Figure 14.25: Disruptive Technology Wins Because Technology Evolution Eventually Exceeds Customer Expectation

Eventually, the electrical systems will achieve the performance capabilities of the hydraulic systems, after which point, the days of hydraulics will be numbered.

So what does this all mean? Disruptive technologies usually 'win' because technology performance capability often rises more quickly than customer expectations.

The disruptive technology is highly likely to be initially inferior in terms of the traditional performance measures of the incumbent technology. The disruptive technology thus usually has to find a new customer base to sustain it in the initial development stages.

The new customer base is unlikely to match the profitability of the existing market in the short term. 'Good management practice' thus means the existing companies will not exploit the new technology (NB Christensen's latest book 'The Innovator's Solution (Reference 14.10) offers strategies to remedy this problem – albeit they are almost inherently painful and come attached to a short term drop in profit.)

The cycle repeats every time an established technology 'grows' away from the evolving customer requirement.

When a customer's appetite for 'performance' is sated, they will increasingly make purchase decisions based on reliability, convenience and price – in this regard, take particular note of the 'customer focus' trend in the trend reference section.

In the meantime, the major point of this section is to implant the vital connection between the disruptive technology business model and the non-linear evolution trends. It is highly likely that the form of the disruptive technologies can and will be predicted by systematic innovation. Almost the absolute key to successful business concept innovation in this 'technology exceeds expectation' scenario is the identification of the new markets (and new players) that will suit the apparently 'inferior' disruptive product. Thinking back to the supply-demand tension driver in Figure 14.20, the key issue when we are in this 'solution exceeds expectation' scenario is the identification of new customers where the tension between requirement and capability is acting in the right direction.

The Christensen example of electric cars being more likely to emerge from the industries making golf-carts and milk-vans rather than any of the big car manufacturers is particularly apposite in this BCI scenario. The more organisations look outside their current self-imposed boundaries, the more likely it is that they will identify the threats, and (in the case of the golf cart manufacturers) opportunities awaiting those who can spot the discontinuities. Reference 14.7 discusses this side of the equation in more detail.

5) Special Non-Linear And Linear Trend Rules

In this section we examine some of the more sophisticated interpretations and uses of the non-linear trends. Specifically, we will look at situations in which systems apparently go the 'wrong way' along the trends:

Trends In Reverse?
All of the trends plotted in this chapter show systems evolving in a left-to-right direction across the trend stages. This is done because this direction is the most common evolution direction. There are, however, a number of exceptions to this left-to-right rule, such that there are occasions when systems can be seen to evolve in the opposite direction. Fortunately these instances are predictable in nature. For the purposes of obtaining a complete understanding of the trends and the way we can deploy them most effectively, we need to examine these exceptions. They fall into two general categories; the first associated with the so-called Law of Non-Uniform Evolution – and the second a more loosely connected series of rules we shall label 'market anomalies'. We will examine both in turn, starting with the Law of Non-uniform Evolution and its implications for trend deployment.

The Law of Non-Uniform Evolution
Previous statements describing increasing ideality as the over-riding trend of system evolution are true, but over-simplified (they are nevertheless useful concepts to keep in

mind – which is why the statements have been used repeatedly in the book). The over-simplification comes because, although the statement is true at the system level, it is not necessarily true as we zoom-in to look at the evolution of elements and components within a system. Indeed, at the sub-system level, it is clear that sometimes a sub-system will travel in a direction of decreasing ideality in order to enable the overall system to achieve net increasing ideality. This sub-system exception to the increasing ideality rule emerges from the Law of Non-Uniform Evolution. The Law states:

> The rate of evolution of different parts of a system
> and its associated sub-systems is not uniform

Evolution at the system level often causes a wave of consecutive changes in adjacent systems and sub-systems. The Law implies that sometimes some elements of a system need to get worse in order to serve the greater good of the overall system. The more complex the system, the more non-uniform the evolution of the sub-system parts, and therefore the greater the likelihood that some elements will *have to* markedly decrease in ideality in order to facilitate the advancement of the overall system. It will be instructive to look at an example of the Law in action before discussing its implications on the trends and our application of them:

The bottom half of Figure 14.26 illustrates key stages in the evolution of laundry detergents. Detergent evolution from solid blocks to powders to liquids are entirely consistent with the non-linear technical trends. But then recently the industry introduced detergent blocks again – an apparently backward step along a trend which would eventually have pointed the industry to field-based solutions (and the ultrasound-based machines that have recently emerged). So what happened? Why did the trend go backwards? The answer to that question is hinted at in the top part of the figure.

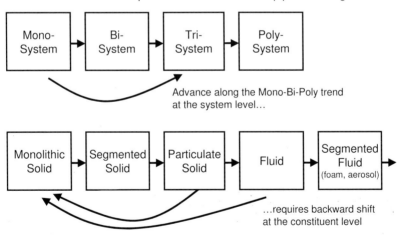

Figure 14.26: Evolution History Of Laundry Detergents

The reason for the reversion back to detergent blocks was that, at a higher-level, the desire to add new functions to the laundry (e.g. separate pre-wash, soak and main-wash functions) has so far meant that the only way to prevent the detergent for the later stages being used up during the early stages is to encapsulate it inside the product delivering those early stages. The technical details here are unimportant. What is important is the idea that sometimes systems at one level have to travel backwards along the trends to facilitate an advance at a higher level – Figure 14.27.

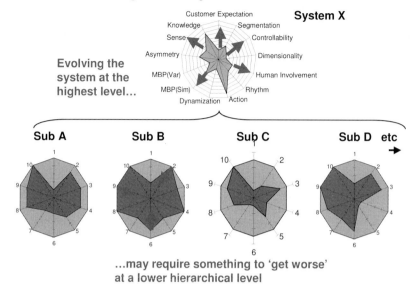

Figure 14.27: Advance At One Hierarchical Level May Require A Retrograde Step At A Lower Level

The main point emerging from the Law of Non-Uniform Evolution is that we need to be very careful when conducting a trend analysis of a system – particularly so when we are examining several hierarchical levels – that we take into account that the overall direction of evolution is driven by the increasing ideality of the highest level system being considered. Some of the sub-systems and components supporting the overall system – even if they are seemingly independent – may have to become 'worse' in order to support the greater good.

Market Anomalies
The effects of the market on the application and relevance of the non-linear trends can be somewhat difficult to predict. Fortunately, their duration is often short-lived and so, although a market shift can cause a system to reverse direction along a trend for a while, the effect is usually transitory – being reversed again either by a return to 'normality' in the market dynamic, or the resolution of a contradiction.

By far the most difficult of the market anomalies to predict is one usually described as 'form follows fashion'. Examples of 'form follows fashion' include things like portable radios (for which increasing size was a distinct trend direction for a period), clothing (where we are to a large extent subject to the whims of a supposedly learned few designers from one season to the next), and assorted shifts towards 'retro' styling in things like motorcycles and a variety of consumer goods. Evolutionary shifts driven by such fashion considerations are very difficult to predict, despite the fact that there are often predictable cycles contained within the bigger picture (think of the cyclic nature of skirt lengths for example). Fortunately, the evidence from all examples of 'form follows fashion' is that eventually the allure of increased ideality eventually triumphs. The least predictable part of the whole story, is knowing *when* the shift will take place.

The most common market anomaly is a sudden increase in the dominance of the cost element of the ideality equation. This anomaly is often consistent with the overall drive to increasing ideality, but results in a shift in focus from the benefits or harms elements. If the increased emphasis on cost can only be achieved by a reduction in benefits, that is the time when we can see systems switching their trajectory across the trends from left-to-right to right-to-left.

By way of example is the earlier discussion concerning the economics of retail banking and the oscillation in the number of different types of accounts offered by the banks as economic factors shift from buyer- to seller-dominated market conditions. The often precarious economic balance between overhead cost and revenue for the different combinations of number and types of accounts is usually manifest in quite wide swings between diversification and consolidation.

This cost-focus shift in a market is often transitory. As such, it means that systems will be forced to evolve in the reverse (right-to-left) direction only until the prevailing economic situation reverts to emphasis on the benefits side of the equation. What happens in the longer term, of course (especially when we think of systems at the mature end of their s-curve and cost is the only thing left to focus on) is that the fight between top half and bottom half of the ideality equation is resolved by the elimination of a contradiction.

So, while the traditional economics of 'optimizing' the account diversity versus overhead trade-off will prevail for a period, ultimately, this type of benefits-versus-costs, top half/bottom half contradiction will be resolved. Increasingly in this type of scenario, such a resolution is being offered by a shift to on-line systems, where the overhead of having many different types of accounts can become negligible very quickly.

In summary then for this discussion on 'trends in reverse', although market conditions can temporarily drive evolution the 'wrong way' along the trends, these aberrations are either halted by a reversal in the market or, if the drive towards lower cost remains, by the resolution of a contradiction between the top and bottom halves of the ideality equation.

6) Trends Reference

This final section presents a collection of 35 disruptive-trend lines uncovered by systematic innovation researchers during the extensive additional research that has informed this book. The general format of presentation in each case involves the basic trend being presented across the top of the page. This trend image is then followed by, first a list of examples of the particular trend (note how some systems have not evolved all the way along a particular trend, or didn't start at the first stage, or have sometimes missed a stage out – all of these characteristics being relatively common), and then second, a list of reasons distilled from other solutions to suggest why the jumps might offer a benefit to us in our situation. These lists are not intended to be inclusive, and as such, if you find other reasons for the jumps, you might like to add them to the table for your future reference.

The sequencing of the trends is quite important. Whether you intend to use the trends as strategic tools or problem solving aids, it is important to try and connect each trend to your situation in the sequence presented. Some may not be relevant, but the point is that the question should at least be asked. We have tried to sequence the trends in accordance with a logical progression that makes the connective jumps our minds have to make a manageable size.

Some, of course, will prefer to use a more random approach. This is perfectly acceptable, although we recommend that you keep in mind the following important image: Figure 14.28 shows how the trends cluster into three broad (sometimes slightly blurred) categories covering space, time and interface situations. We have found this grouping useful in determining which of the trends are going to be relevant to a given situation; if, for example, the system being evaluated involves the definition of a particular advertising campaign, then the most likely matches to the trends will come through examination of the 'interface' (i.e. relationship between vendor and potential customer) trends rather than the 'time' or 'space' based ones.

This space, time, interface clustering represents a recurring theme in the systematic innovation method – see also the Chapters on 9-Windows (4) and Conflicts (11) – particularly Figures 4.8 and 11.14. The space-time-interface theme is also consistent with the evolution of systems towards free-perfect-now end-points (Reference 14.17) – space-free; time-now; interface-perfect.

SPACE RELATED BUSINESS TRENDS
Mono-Bi-Poly (Similar) – Space
Mono-Bi-Poly (Various) – Space
Mono –Bi-Poly (Inc.Diff.) – Space
Segmentation – Space
Nesting - Space
Increasing Dimensionality
Degrees of Freedom
Dynamization
Human Involvement
Trimming
Nesting - Up

TIME RELATED BUSINESS TRENDS
Action Co-ordination
Rhythm Co-ordination
Mono-Bi-Poly (Similar) – Time
Mono-Bi-Poly (Various) – time
Segmentation – Time
Nesting - Time
Damping
Feedback & Control
Non-Linearity

INTERFACE RELATED BUSINESS TRENDS
Customer Expectation
Customer Purchase Focus
Self-Organisation Awareness
Knowledge
Competency
Process Thinking
System Robustness
Design-Point
Mono-Bi-Poly (Similar) – Interface
Mono-Bi-Poly (Various) – Interface
Mono –Bi-Poly (Inc.Diff.) – Interface
Segmentation – Interface
Nesting - Down
Sense Interaction
Transparency
Connections
Asymmetry
Boundary Breakdown
Horizontal/Vertical Business Cycles
Interaction With Others
Listening/Communication
Market Research
Spiral Dynamics
Generations

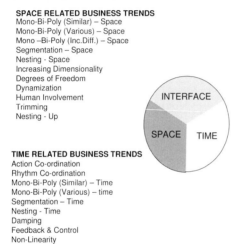

Figure 14.28: Clustering of Disruptive Business Evolution Trends

(Note that some of the trends in this list have connections to more than one of the space, time and interface categories – there are 35 different trends, interpretable in a total of 44 ways. The Reference section contains one entry for each of the 35 individual trends.)

What Do I Do?

The Trends tool is one of the single largest parts of the systematic innovation total. It is also the tool that a high proportion of newcomers seem to obtain early success using. In this sense it appears to operate in a manner consistent with the way many people naturally think. Experience shows that an awful lot of problem situations can be tackled just by using the trends. There are two main application roles for the trend; one in a strategic context, the other in a problem solving context. Both require that users are familiar with the trends illustrated in the following reference section, and are capable of connecting their situation to those trends. In the first instance, we recommend that you become familiar with this process.

Specific, then, to their role in a problem solving context is the need to be able to work out *why* the solutions being suggested by trend patterns are in fact solutions to the problem under consideration.

In their strategic role, concepts like evolutionary potential (and the idea of the evolutionary potential radar plot) make a useful start point. This start then needs to be matched with a good understanding of market dynamics – for which, you should refer to the fourth section of the chapter. This then needs to be backed up by some of the more detailed knowledge contained in the later sections of the chapter – in which we see some of the exceptions to the general trend directions and complications caused by combination effects coming in to play.

Finally, as with so many other parts of systematic innovation, you may like to observe the Trends in action in the world around you and to keep a note of them in the spaces left in the reference section. This will serve to both extend your familiarity, and provide additional solution triggers for future reference.

References

1) Pine, J., 'The Experience Economy', Harvard Business School Press, 1999.
2) Mann, D.L., 'Trimming Evolution Patterns for Complex Systems', TRIZ Journal, June 1999.
3) http://trends.creax.net
4) Mann, D.L., 'Trends', CREAX Press, to be published 2004.
5) Utterback, J.M., 'Mastering The Dynamics Of Innovation', Harvard Business School Press, 1996.
6) Hamel, G., 'Leading The Revolution', Harvard Business School Press, 1999.
7) Christensen, C.M., 'The Innovator's Dilemma: When New Technologies Cause Great Firms To Fail', Harvard Business School Press, 1997.
8) Petroski, H., 'The Evolution of Useful Things', Vintage Books, 1994.
9) Walden, D., 'Special Issue on Kano's Methods for Understanding Customer-Defined Quality', Center for Quality of Management Journal, Reprint RP02700, Fall 1993.
10) Christensen, C.M., Raynor, M.E., 'The Innovator's Solution', Harvard Business School Press, 2003.
11) Kelly, S., Allison, M.A., 'The Complexity Advantage: How The Science of Complexity Can Help Your Business Achieve Peak Performance', McGrawHill BusinessWeek, 1999.
12) Handy, C., 'Understanding Organisations', Penguin, 1976.
13) Wilson, R.A., 'Prometheus Rising', New Falcon Publications, 1988.
14) Covey, S., 'The Seven Habits of Highly Effective People: Restoring The Character Ethic', Simon & Schuster, 1992.
15) Shapiro, E.C., 'Fad Surfing In The Boardroom – Reclaiming The Courage To Manage In The Age Of Instant Answers', Addison-Wesley Publishing Company, 1995.
16) Fine, C.H., 'Clockspeed', Little, Brown, London, 2000.
17) Systematic Innovation E-Zine, 'Space/Time/InterFace and Free/Perfect/Now', Issue 50, May 2006.
18) Beck, D.E., Cowan, C.C., 'Spiral Dynamics: Mastering Values, Leadership And Change', Blackwell Publishers, 1996.
19) Mann, D.L., 'If TRIZ IS So Good, Why Isn't Everyone Using It, Part 7: Plausible Deniability & Spiral Dynamics', paper presented at TRIZ Kongress, Mainz, 2005.
20) Strauss, W., Howe, N., 'The Fourth Turning: An American Prophecy', Broadway Books, New York, 1997.

CUSTOMER EXPECTATION

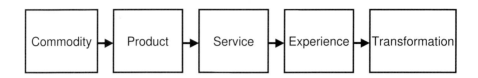

Examples

Commodities – steel, aluminium, timber, chemicals, generic drugs, filters, CDs, videos,etc.
Products – cars, phones, televisions, DVD players, washing machines, etc
Services - Clean clothes, power-by-the-hour, fast food, package holidays, home delivery,
        car rental, library, hotel shuttle, contract cleaning
Experiences – Disney, adventure sports, McDonalds,
Transformation – personal trainers (where – importantly – responsibility for a desired
        transformation switches from the individual to the trainer)

Reasons For Jumps

Evolution Stage	Reasons for Jumps
Commodity to Product	-increasing customer involvement -increasing company involvement and therefore possibility for profit -greater leverage in supply chain -less work for customer -greater branding opportunities -greater customization -increase in 'added value' -improved control over product and customers -direct sales/direct marketing to consumer
Product to Service	-increasing customer involvement -increasing company involvement and therefore possibility for profit -greater leverage in supply chain -increased customization possibilities -ability to build long-term relationship with customer -increased possibilities for customer feedback -forces emphasis on quality

Service to Experience	-increasing customer involvement
	-increasing company involvement and
	  therefore possibility for profit
	-greater leverage in supply chain
	-'wow' creation opportunities
	-customer relationship building based on emotion
	-relate your company to the customers'
	  psychological needs

Experience to Transformation	-increasing customer involvement -increasing company involvement and

	therefore possibility for profit -greater leverage in supply chain -building intimate relationship with customers -ability to increase revenue/margin due to transfer of responsibility from customer

Notes:

This trend is focused on the recipients of the products and processes we design. The trend emerges from the work of B.J.Pine in his book 'The Experience Economy' (Harvard Business School Press, 1999)

The general concept behind the trend is that customer expectations increase with time. Therefore, if you stand still, you are actually going backwards. So, in order to remain competitive, we should be looking to the right along the trend.

The idea that we are actually going backwards if we are standing still on this trend comes from the quality work of Kano – and the idea that things over time our expectations as customers increase such that the things that used to 'excite' us – air-conditioning in cars for example – rapidly become the norm and we become dis-satisfied if they are suddenly not there.

Appropriate use of the trend requires adequate customer data.

CUSTOMER PURCHASE FOCUS

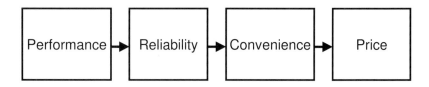

Performance → Reliability → Convenience → Price

Examples

Automobiles, hydraulic components, filters, light-bulbs, CDs, computer hard-drives, televisions, video/DVD players, mobile phones, insurance products, banking services, just about anything that has become 'commoditised'.

Reasons For Jumps

Evolution Stage	Reasons for Jumps
Any stage to the next	-customers desire for more of the parameter has been fulfilled -competitive advantage -overcomes common problem of technology capability overtaking customer requirement

Notes:

This trend operates a little differently to most of the others. The jumps from stage to stage here are made when a given customer has received 'enough' of the current purchase focus. Most car-buyers for example care little about better car performance, and most have shifted to purchasing 'reliability'. Anyone still interested in high performance is unlikely to be unduly concerned by reliability, convenience or prices. When a majority of customers are at the 'price' stage, providers need to find new functions that will encourage a focus on new measures of performance.

The trend is related to positions on the s-curve for a system:

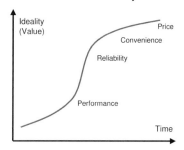

Different customers will be at different positions along the trend.
Trend is based on Windermere Associates model described in 'The Innovator's Dilemma by Clayton Christensen (Reference 14.7).

SELF-ORGANISATION AWARENESS

Unconscious Self-Organization → Conscious Self-Organization → Guided Self-Organization → Qualitatively Guided Self-Organization → Consciously Competent Autopoiesis

Examples

A trend which as yet has very few examples, due to the fact that the connection between complexity theory and organisation systems has only just begun. Citibank/Citigroup is a leading proponent of this trend. Other examples: the concept of 'commander's intent' in a military leadership context, so-called 'chaocracy' organisation structures, 3M employees ability to spend 15% of their time working on whatever they want.

Reasons For Jumps

Evolution Stage	Reasons for Jumps
Unconscious to Conscious	-survival -improved change management -ability to design robust systems -threat management -risk/crisis identification -risk/crisis management -risk mitigation strategy management -reduce internal tensions -stronger strategic planning
Conscious to Guided	-improve morale -improve risk management -improve change management -robust systems capability -instil complex systems thinking
Guided to Qualitatively Guided	-empowerment -improve morale -re-enforce complex systems thinking -improve receptiveness to change -autonomy -process 'ownership'
Qualitatively Guided to Autopoeisis	-sustainable business growth -complexity management -improved crisis management -improved operational flexibility -autonomy

Notes:

A very new trend emerging from work on complex systems theory applied to organisation structures. The trend was first identified and discussed in 'The Complexity Advantage' (Reference 14.11). Interpretations of the various stages of the trends are as follows:-

Unconscious – organisation is unaware that all human systems are complex, chaotic and cannot be successfully managed in the longer term without taking these factors into account

Conscious   -   organisation becomes aware of complex, chaotic nature of human systems but doesn't yet know what to do to manage such systems effectively

Guided   -   organisation begins the process of managing self-organisation initiatives. Signs – Quality circles, 'empowerment', ''bottom-up'. Possible use of external facilitators and someone in organization with specific responsibility for managing the transition to self-organization

Qualitatively -   amount of facilitation decreases, success stories emerge, initiatives begin to become self-expanding

Autopoietic   -   organisation has self-sustaining, self-organizing structure

KNOWLEDGE

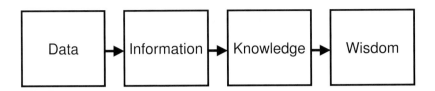

Examples

The evolution of business information from collection and display of raw-data, to presentation in spreadsheets, to incorporation of sophisticated interpretation algorithms, to the wisdom to know that 'the most important numbers are unknown and unknowable' (W.E. Deming). Written text converts data into usable information; 'semantic processor' technology extracts useful knowledge from this textual information; addition of context then permits transition to wisdom.

Reasons For Jumps

Evolution Stage	Reasons for Jumps
Data to Information	-provision of structure -addition of meaning -permit interpretation
Information to Knowledge	-ability to filter out the 'irrelevant' -time management -provision of transferable structure
Knowledge to Wisdom	-measuring the 'right' things -making the 'right' responses -inclusion of context and relevance -recognition that sometimes the right data gives the wrong answer ('anti-logic')

Notes:

The emergence and increasing dominance of computer technologies that generate massive amounts of 'data' is the prompt for inclusion of this trend. Many managers find themselves drowning in data. The trend is essentially about the distillation of appropriate management and leadership wisdom from the mass of available content.

'Knowledge is knowing that a tomato is a fruit; wisdom is knowing not to put tomatoes in a fruit salad'. Wisdom, in other words, is about the contextualization of knowledge.

COMPETENCY

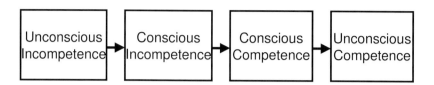

| Unconscious Incompetence | → | Conscious Incompetence | → | Conscious Competence | → | Unconscious Competence |

Examples

All aspects of the learning process – acquiring new skills, new work-roles, new customers, new employees, etc.

Reasons For Jumps

Evolution Stage	Reasons for Jumps
Unconscious Incompetence to Conscious Incompetence	-survival -improved change management -ability to design robust systems -threat management -risk/crisis identification -risk/crisis management -risk mitigation strategy management
Conscious Incompetence to Conscious Competence	-improve morale -improve risk management -improve change management -robust systems capability -instill process thinking
Conscious Competence to Unconscious Competence	-save time -openness to accept other capabilities -automated processes -system optimisation -self-organising systems -(negative) psychological inertia

Notes:

Unconscious incompetence: Blissful ignorance, confidence exceeds ability, we are not knowledgeable/skilful. *We don't know we don't know.*
Conscious incompetence: Discovery that there is something we need or want to know, but that we don't know how to do it. *We know what we don't know.*
Conscious competence: We acquire the skill. We have to concentrate on what we are doing. *We know that we know.*
Unconscious competence: Lastly, we blend the skills together and they become habits. Our confidence and ability have peaked so that we no longer have to concentrate on what we know/do. This can then often lead to psychological inertia issues, which in turn eventually prompts the start of the next learning curve. *We don't (necessarily) know we know.*

PROCESS THINKING

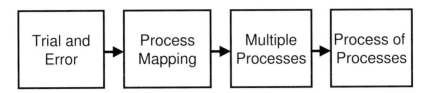

Trial and Error	→	Process Mapping	→	Multiple Processes	→	Process of Processes

Examples

The 1950s and 60s saw organisations recognise that processes were important. This prompted a phase of trial and error evolution of 'successful' process models. The emergence of successful models allowed definition and transfer of the 'right' process; which in turn became to be seen as a range of different processes, each relevant in different contextual situations. More recently, the emergence of guidelines that allow processes to be designed in situ for specific individual situations: emergence of 'plan-do-study-act' continuous improvement initiatives, followed by 'design the process' guidelines in Design for Six Sigma philosophy.

Reasons For Jumps

Evolution Stage	Reasons for Jumps
'Trial and Error' to Process Mapping	-reduced time/cost/risk -higher quality end result -improved communications -improved progress monitoring -certification/accreditation issues
Process Mapping to Multiple Processes	-improve flexibility to change -improve communications -improve quality -improve customer response -improved portfolio management
Multiple Processes to Process-of-Processes	-improve flexibility -improve change management -improve ability to handle crisis -improve customer response -improved portfolio management -improve quality -empowers employees -improved 'ownership' of systems

Notes:

Process Mapping – (where most organizations are) There is a set of procedures that dictate how a certain job should be performed. Everyone is expected to understand and conform to this map

Multiple processes – the process for a certain function or operation is designed for each specific situation.

Process of processes – there is a process by which the process can be designed for each individual job processes are effectively adaptive to suit changing situations. Further, the processes know how to change should the operating situation changes. The process is capable of optimizing and re-optimizing itself.

SYSTEM ROBUSTNESS

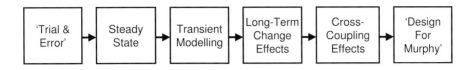

Examples

A general trend observable across many industries – automotive, fast-moving consumer goods, aerospace. Nuclear and space represent the state of the art in terms of 'if anything can go wrong, it will go wrong' design philosophy in a technical sense. The trend is still relatively new in terms of the design of 'robust' business models. Organisations embracing ideas of 'constant change' and 'operating at the edge of chaos' are beginning to think about the third and subsequent stages of the trend

Reasons For Jumps

Evolution Stage	Reasons for Jumps
'Cut & Try' to Steady-State	-improved use of system resources -reduced waste in development time/cost -reduced waste of materials -reduced product development time
Steady-State to Transient to Long-Term Change to Cross-Coupling	-improve system reliability and robustness -long-term survival/sustainability -competitive advantage -increased market awareness -improved understanding of customers
Any of the above to 'Design for Murphy'	-improve reliability -enable easy shift to 'functional sales model' -ability to adapt to unexpected change -reduce vulnerability to disruptive shifts

Notes:

This trend is closely linked to drives for improved robustness in systems. See Chapter 20 for more details of this trend in operation.

Generally speaking, if the manner in which your organisation is managing the way it operates both internally and externally using is not at the right hand end of the trend, someone out there has already identified ways to allow you to do a better job.

Examples of the different stages of the trend:-
Transient – taking account of temporary effects – starts and stops, seasonal variations, holidays, disputes, etc
Long-Term Change – taking account of things like economic cycles, recession, initiative fatigue, etc
Cross-coupling – recognising that things in a system that should in theory have no effect on one another can sometimes actually have a cross-linking effect. The way check-out tills in supermarkets are configured ought not to be influenced by (say) the design of the

car-parks (to take an extreme example) – prevailing logic says the performance of one will not impact on the performance of the other. The cross-coupling effect says that one is actually quite likely to affect the long term behaviour of the other.

Design for Murphy – under normal circumstances, if a customer does something stupid with a product, they pay the consequences; under emerging 'service' markets, the supplier is increasingly liable for these consequences. It is thus becoming important to include consideration of 'if the customer can do something stupid with this, they will' into the design process.

DESIGN POINT

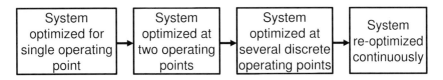

Examples

Many business systems are designed for an 'optimum' operating condition – e.g. factories operated at 'full capacity' all the time for the purpose of 'maximum efficiency. Long and short shift patterns allow the creation of a dual optimum; floating shifts allow a system to be continually re-optimised.

Reasons For Jumps

Evolution Stage	Reasons for Jumps
Any stage to the next	-improved performance at all operating conditions -reduced wastage -increased user operational flexibility -broader operating range -increased operating safety margin -solving a physical contradiction

Notes:

This is another emergent trend. Many business systems have their performance optimised at a single condition since there is a parallel desire to be 'optimum and recognition that highly complex systems are difficult to measure. This trend is emerging to help reduce inefficiencies as the system in question operates at points distant from the optimum design point.

The trend is related in several senses to the Mono-Bi-Poly trend. It is included as a specific reminder of the importance of thinking about design point, and because the idea of 'continuously re-optimised' designs does not emerge from M-B-P thinking adequately.

MONO-BI-POLY (Similar)

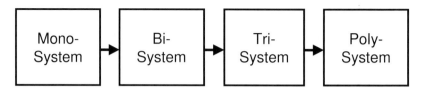

| Mono-
System | → | Bi-
System | → | Tri-
System | → | Poly-
System |

Examples

Financial services – current, deposit, mortgage, etc accounts. Portfolio of stocks and shares. Franchise operations. Double-entry accounting. Customer relationship management ('every customer is different').

Reasons For Jumps

Evolution Stage	Reasons for Jumps
Any stage to the next	-improve amount of useful function deliverable -improve user convenience -synergy effects -reduced cost per system component -greater customer benefits -greater customer tie-in -distribution of risk by diversification -wider customer range

Notes:
The principal issue with the M-B-P trend is that a point is reached, beyond which it is no longer possible to continue obtaining benefit by adding any more of the similar objects:

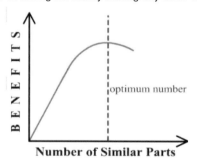

optimum number

Number of Similar Parts

The equation determining what exactly this optimum number is may be relatively fixed, but it may also be highly dynamic. This is especially so when considering that the top and bottom halves of the ideality equation both change as more things are added to a system. The conflict between increased benefits of adding more versus the almost inevitably increased cost with adding more can be a turbulent one – see the frequent shifts in the number of different financial products offered by banks and loan companies.

Applies to each of time, space and interface issues.

MONO-BI-POLY (Various)

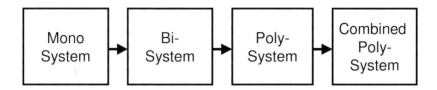

Examples

'Complementor' strategies – Virgin Brides brings together all of the services required to get married into one place. Movie tie-ins (book, t-shirt, website, toys, etc). Co-branding – chewing-gum with toothpaste, house-builder with mortgage provider, mobile phone with iconic apparel. The key difference between this trend and M-B-P(Similar) is that in that trend the emphasis is on more of the same, whereas here the 'various' element is about adding new functions.

Reasons For Jumps

Evolution Stage	Reasons for Jumps
Any stage to the next	-increased system functionality -increased operability -increased user convenience/benefit/lock-in -reduced packaging -(synergy effects) -reduced number of systems/expenses -reduced net system size -distribution of risk by diversification

Notes:

The principal issue with the M-B-P(Various) trend, like M-B-P(Similar) is that a point is reached, beyond which it is no longer possible to continue obtaining benefit by adding any more of the different objects:

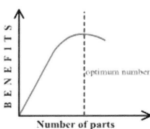

Applies to each of time, space and interface aspects.

A highly significant trend at this point in time, as many organisations look to find their 'complementors' – other, non-competing organisations with complementary products or services that together produce *combined functions* with win-win outcomes

MONO-BI-POLY (Increasing Differences)

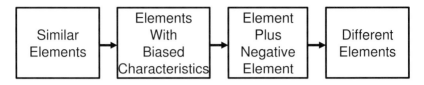

Examples

Savings and loans. Production and recycling. Use of ex-thief to help design security systems. Internally competing red-team/blue-team development strategies – where one team tries to put the other out of business, in the spirit of creating a more robust business.

Reasons For Jumps

Evolution Stage	Reasons for Jumps
Similar to Biased	-increased system functionality -increased operability -increased ability to adapt to different customer circumstances -increased user convenience -(synergy effects)
Biased to Negative	-add ability to achieve the opposite function -increased adaptability -increase operational flexibility -robust systems -(synergy effects) -ability to target niche customers
Negative to Different Components	-increased system functionality -increased operability -better use of individual skills -increased user convenience -(synergy effects) -reduced number of systems -reduced net system size

Notes:

The jump to the 'negative' element (i.e. that element, component or constituent part that delivers the opposite function to the exiting function) is a very important one – someone, somewhere can make positive use of a system that delivers the opposite function to that conventionally expected. Although not always instinctively obvious today, someone, somewhere wants the 'negative element'.

The timing of these jumps to negative is difficult to predict as the size of market for the negative thing, if it doesn't already exist is unknown, and hence risk is high.

Applies to both space and interface aspects of a system.

SEGMENTATION

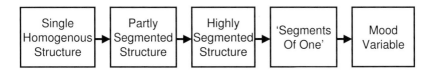

Examples

Internal to an organisation – corporation/division/cost-centre/department/individual.
External (thinking about customers) – 'the customer'/customer segments/segments of one
(mass customisation)/each customer is different at different times of the day.

Reasons For Jumps

Evolution Stage	Reasons for Jumps
Any stage to the next	-increased understanding of system structure -more effective use of resources -improve deployment of individual skills -improve individual motivation -reduced overall size of system -improve system performance efficiency -better customer awareness -improved customer responsiveness -clearer understanding of responsibilities -ability to respond to individual/local conditions -ability to identify and resolve conflicts

Notes:

The segmentation trend is essentially the first half of the complexity increases and then
decreases trend. When a segmentation strategy is adopted, benefits generally increase,
but usually at the expense of added system complexity.

The 'mood variable' stage is intended to indicate that it is possible to segment even further
than simply individual people. Classic example; a hotel room in which the occupant is able
to change the colour (through lighting effects) according to their mood.

Segmentation has meaning in all three of the space, time and interface trend clusters in
that we can segment something physically, we can segment time and we can segment the
interfaces and interactions between different entities. It is advisable to specifically think
about all three aspects when deploying the trend

NESTING (DOWN)

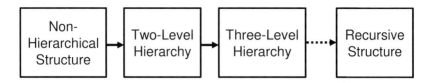

Examples

'Store-in-store', hierarchical organisation structures, multi-tier supply chains.

Reasons For Jumps

Evolution Stage	Reasons for Jumps
Any stage to the next	-increased stability -increased efficiency carrying out specialized tasks -improved co-ordination -improved knowledge management -solve a physical contradiction('transition to sub-system')

Notes:

Trend applies to both physical (e.g. organisation structures)) and temporal (e.g. action-within-action) perspectives. In the temporal sense, the final stage of the Action Co-ordination exists as a further reminder to think about Nesting of activities and processes within a system.

The trend is applicable and should be explored at both macro and micro scales.

It applies to time, space and interface aspects of a system.

SENSE INTERACTION

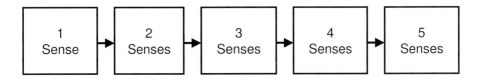

Examples

Silent movies – talking pictures – 'Sensurround' – addition of smell, taste, multi-media computers, virtual reality, theatre, communications in general (e.g. emergence of video-phones), food products.

Reasons For Jumps

Evolution Stage	Reasons for Jumps
Any stage to the next	-improved interaction control -increased human involvement -'sensual immersion' -improved realism of simulation -more efficient communication -richer customer experience -greater customer involvement

Notes:

The trend is about increasing interaction of systems with human faculties. The trend relates only to the number of trends incorporated into a system not the sequence.

In all there are five key senses involved in the trend – visual, auditory, kinaesthetic (touch), olfactory and gustatory (taste). The acronym VAKOG is widely used to assist in the remembering of these senses. While primarily a trend associated with the technical attributes of a product or service, it has very distinct meaning and relevance in the business context and use of different senses is an often very effective way of solving business and (particularly) communication problems – since different individuals respond to different sensual stimuli in different ways.

INCREASING TRANSPARENCY

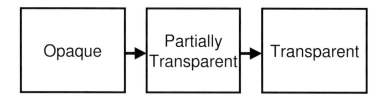

Examples

Company accounts, double-entry accounting, 360degree appraisal systems, open-source software, public posting of salary levels/ratios, Ben & Jerry's company vision and mission shared with and influenced by employees.

Reasons For Jumps

Evolution Stage	Reasons for Jumps
Any stage to the next	-improved employee morale/commitment -improved shareholder trust -improved relationship with customers -improved 'buy-in' to mission/vision -facilitates open and frank dialogue -eliminates destructive covert agendas -improved time-management -improved quality – more likelihood of 'right-first-time' -improved ability to respond to change

Notes:

Increasing pace of change in and around organizations, increasing lack of trust by shareholders and employees in company trustees, and massively increased quantities of data means that the infra-structure required to maintain and protect 'confidential' information becomes prohibitive is the primary spur towards the increase in transparency.

The intermediary 'partially transparent' stage of the trend is indicative of smaller scale disruptive shifts that take place as certain families of data switch from being 'hidden' to being accessible to all interested parties. This is usually classed as 'non-critical' data. The final 'transparent' stage should thus be interpreted as that stage in the evolution of an organization in which any and all business information is available to all (e.g. salary information, operating costs, etc). The Internet is the first communication media that makes this practically possible – at least from a technological perspective.

CONNECTIONS

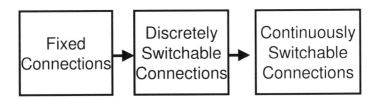

| Fixed Connections | → | Discretely Switchable Connections | → | Continuously Switchable Connections |

Examples

Fixed organisation structure to seasonally variable (e.g. pre-Christmas mail delivery organisations), to fully flexible systems (e.g. floating shift patterns). Project-team methods of operating shift from a fixed organisational hierarchy to temporary working units.

Reasons For Jumps

Evolution Stage	Reasons for Jumps
Fixed Connections to Discretely Switchable	-ability to adapt to changing customer needs -increased operating flexibility -reduced duplication of effort and waste
Discretely Switchable to Continuously Switchable	-robust organization design -ability to handle disruptive change -ability to offer customer 'experience' -multi-skilling of workforce -reduced tedium of unpopular (but necessary) tasks -improved employee commitment (if done well!) -reduced duplication of effort and waste

Notes:

Another trend that has emerged only relatively recently. Definite (and deliberate) overlap with the degrees-of-freedom and process thinking trends. Flexible connections are the primary enablers of adaptive business process capabilities. This trend is included separately in order to ensure due focus on the connections within a system as well as the people and entities that it contains.

INCREASING ASYMMETRY
(To match External Asymmetries)

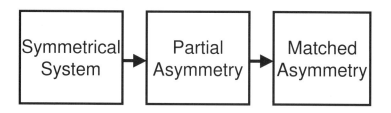

Examples

One-to-many or many-to-one communications, B2C, B2B, boss-to-staff, everyone is different in some respect to everyone else and so asymmetries may be seen in abundance.

Reasons For Jumps

Evolution Stage	Reasons for Jumps
Any stage to the next	-improved communications/relationships
	-reduced waste
	-recognition of niche markets
	-improved product/service discrimination
	-customer 'experience' potential
	-improved buy-in/morale

Notes:

In many ways, a trend to be interpreted in a very general sense. The important issues when looking for relevance of this trend are the presence of 'external asymmetries' and assessment of whether the current system matches those asymmetries; if it doesn't, the trend should be used.

A more specific interpretation of the trend is the 'winner-takes-all' asymmetry – in which systems tend towards a marked polarisation between, say, the 'haves' and 'have-nots'.

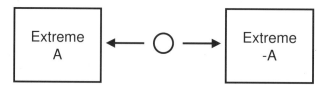

'Partial asymmetry' is intended to recognise that there are often non-linear, intermediate steps between a fully symmetrical system and one which is fully able to match the asymmetries of an external influence.

BOUNDARY BREAKDOWN

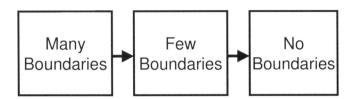

Examples

Flattened organisational hierarchies, 'empowerment' of individuals to deal appropriately with their customers, 'working-together' teams, physical placement of subcontractors into contractor facilities.

Reasons For Jumps

Evolution Stage	Reasons for Jumps

Any stage to the next	-improved system robustness
	-reduction of activities inconsistent with
	  company mission
	-improved communications
	-improved ability to achieve unity of purpose
	-reduced 'mis-communication'
	-improve morale
	-ability to involve customer in design process
	-(downside that requires to be managed –
	  people expectant of promotional
	  opportunities can become highly frustrated
	  in the boundary-les organization)

Notes:

The main thought intended to be provoked through comparing this trend to a given innovation situation is one of interfaces; interfaces generally mean weak-points and inefficiencies, and evolution suggests we gradually get better at eliminating them. Again some deliberate overlap with the preceding 'connections' trend – the emphasis there was in adaptation capability, the emphasis here is on the number of interfaces.

The trend can contain both continuous and discrete stages. The link to disruption is that the removal (say) of a layer of management fundamentally creates a non-linear shift in the way of doing things. Or at least it should do – hence the adage concerning the impossibility of crossing a chasm in small steps.

VERTICAL/HORIZONTAL BUSINESS CYCLES

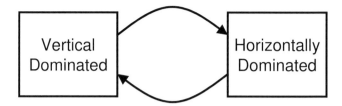

Examples

The computer industry has shifted from being dominated by the vertically dominated integrators like IBM in the 70s to horizontal stratification and the dominance of Intel ('Intel Inside') and Microsoft in more recent times. According to the trend, the future will see a further shift towards dominance by a vertical integrator (e.g. Apple's latest range of I-products or Samsung?). A similar example of a shift from vertical to horizontal dominance may be seen in the bicycle industry, where gear/brake manufacturer Shimano has become the most well known name. Likewise, in the automotive sector, the vertically organised integrator companies like Ford, GM, Toyota are increasingly being challenged by horizontally organised component suppliers (Delphi for example).

Reasons For Jumps

Evolution Stage	Reasons for Jumps
Any stage to the next	-the desire for the currently dominant organization to preserve its dominance coupled with the desire of the smaller player to exploit niches and achieve growth leads to oscillatory behaviour -technology shortfall relative to customer demand leads to integration -technology surplus relative to customer demand leads to modularization and horizontal stratification

Note:

The perpetual oscillation from vertical to horizontally dominated supply structures was first reported by Charles S Fine in his book Clockspeed (Reference 14.16). The book connects this oscillatory behaviour to complex systems theory and the idea that 'good management' strategies in both vertical and horizontal companies inevitably lead to dominance switching between the two – see accompanying figure.

(Note: this trend has only been observed relatively recently. There is insufficient evidence to indicate whether the dominant player is capable of altering their guiding principles ('business DNA') sufficiently to avoid the opposite model from eventually taking over the dominant position. Quite possibly Intel will be the first time the trend has an opportunity to be over-turned. All past evidence suggests that they will be unable to succeed. Time will tell.

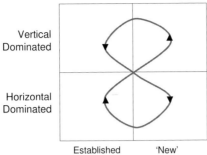

Vertical
Dominated

Horizontal
Dominated

Established 'DNA'	'New' 'DNA'
-protect strength	-growth
-stability	-focus on niches
-profit	-exploit weaknesses in big players
-growth	-dynamicism
-focus on 'high-value' products	-adaptability
-focus on 'core-competences'	-try to increase stability

INTERACTIONS WITH OTHERS

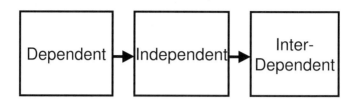

Examples

Organisation structures switching from a 'them and us' culture to one of co-operation and ultimately, integration into a way-of-life. Marriage. Long-term friends.

Reasons For Jumps

Evolution Stage	Reasons for Jumps
Dependent to Independent	-morale -autonomy -improve survival skills -change management capability -risk management -complexity reduction -improve cost control -improve time control -improve crisis management capability
Independent to Interdependent	-realise win-win benefits -'symbiosis' -reduce overhead -risk management -increased operational stability -empowerment -self-organisation opportunities -growth -increased innovation opportunities

Notes:

This trend has been distilled from the extensive coverage received in the Steven Covey classic, 'Seven Habits of Highly Effective People' (Reference 14.14). The stages are interpreted as follows:-

Dependent – interactions where we are dependent on the other party
('them', 'the boss says…', 'I feel lost without you', etc)

Independent – interactions where we are or feel independent of the other person; we feel free to make our own decisions irrespective of what another person might feel ('me', individual, everyone for themselves, etc)

Inter-Dependent – a higher state of interaction. Interdependence demands that we have already been through the independent state. Interdependence does not mean giving up our independence, but rather choosing to integrate the wishes of the other party into what we do. Strongly linked to the desire and ability to seek out genuine win/win outcomes

('we', 'the team', marriage, etc)

LISTENING/COMMUNICATION

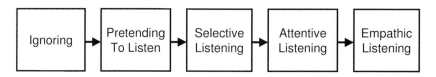

Examples

All forms of inter-personal communication. Many organisation communication systems – either internal or to customers – still appear to be at the left hand side of the trend.

Reasons For Jumps

Evolution Stage	Reasons for Jumps
Ignoring to Pretending	-awareness of others -awareness of outside world
Pretending to Selective	-awareness of others -awareness of outside world -re-enforcement of perceptions -highlight lack of perception re-enforcement by others (particularly customers)
Selective to Attentive	-'voice of the customer' -gain perspective -open collaboration opportunities -improve morale -improve popularity -improve level of feedback -reduce tensions/conflict potential
Attentive to Empathic	-open possibility for win-win -effective collaboration -understand the customer before they understand themselves -anticipatory awareness -long term relationship building -reduce conflict potential

Notes:

Another trend inspired by the work of Steven Covey (Reference 14.14). Interpretations of the different stages:-

Ignoring – making no attempt to listen to what the other person/customer/company is saying

Pretending to listen – making signs that you are listening, when in fact you are not

Selective listening – listening to only those parts that we wish to hear
("Hi, ****** ** **** profit **** *** up ** 20% *** ***")

Attentive listening – paying attention and focusing energy on the words that are being spoken ("Hi, according to the press, profit targets are up to 20% too high")

Empathic listening – listening with a genuine attempt to understand what the speaker is trying to communicate (trying to get inside the mind of the speaker)

MARKET RESEARCH

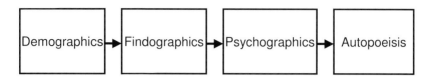

Demographics → Findographics → Psychographics → Autopoeisis

Examples

Activities of the leading advertising agencies frequently adopt the 'psychographics' stage of the trend – developing accurate techniques for mapping the intangible desires that customers are unable or unwilling to divulge. Essentially, the evolution of the whole advertising industry has followed this trend, at least to the third stage.

Reasons For Jumps

Evolution Stage	Reasons for Jumps
Demographics to Findographics	-increased understanding of customer -reduced risk of product failure -ability to build strong tie to customer -competitive advantage
Findographics to Psychographics	as above plus -awareness of importance of intangibles -(downside – customer can feel manipulated unless care is taken)
Psychographics to Autopoeisis	-reduced labour requirement -increased operational flexibility -faster awareness of emerging changes

Notes:

Trend based on the writings of Eileen Shapiro (Reference 14.15) and relate to the evolution of methods used to understand and extract knowledge from customers. The first three stages should be interpreted as follows, based on Shapiro's discussion:-

Demographics - research is based on public record demographic information

Findographics - research is based on information that can be illicited from customers based on surveys – favourite colour, favourite X, etc.

Psychographics - research is based on intangibles – information very difficult to extract from surveys (interaction, subconscious, etc effects)

The fourth 'autopoeisis' stage – which is not in Shapiro's text – relates to the evolution of the market knowledge gathering activity evolving towards an autonomous, self-updating capability (e.g. the current product or service automatically sends feedback on what the requirements of the next one should be).

SPIRAL DYNAMICS

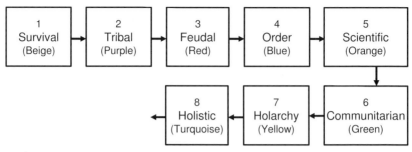

Examples

All humans are born at the first stage of the trend. Then at various life stages, prompted by emergence and resolution of contradictions, we may shift from one stage to the next. Classic archetypes – Tribal – gangs; Feudal – power-gods, heroes; Order – 'moral majority', codes of conduct, rules; Scientific – nature-tamed, materialism, management-by-objective; Communitarian – politically correct, consensus, equality; Holarchy – inter-dependence, co-opetition, natural-order; Holistic – theory-of-everything, spiritual harmony

Reasons For Jumps

Evolution Stage	Reasons for Jumps
Survival to Tribal	- fundamental limits to individual survival ability (need for sleep, parenthood, catching prey, etc) means there is a benefit to becoming part of a social group
Tribal to Feudal	- when times become tough in the social group, the fittest will survive, and so there is evolutionary pressure to fight through the group hierarchy
Feudal to Order	- there are limits to how much a single dominant person can achieve without 'buy-in' from others. This can only be achieved (in the long term) by introducing 'fair' rules
Order to Scientific	- the ordered rule-bound system does not respond well in times when there is a need for adaptation and change. Need for innovation emerges; which prompts need for knowledge
Scientific to Communitarian	- individual materialism eventually impacts on external factors that prevent further growth, prompting a need to think about 'system' and the concept of 'enough'
Communitarian to Holarchy	- the drive for equality and 'fairness' eventually hits a limit of indecision, procrastination and in-action, which then provokes recognition of the existence of 'natural hierarchies'
Holarchy to Holistic	- recognition that all systems hit limits applies to all systems, and that sometimes it is necessary to completely shift to a new (higher level) integrated alternative

Notes:

This trend represents an evolution of the pioneering work of Maslow. Maslow introduced the five level 'hierarchy of needs'; 'Spiral Dynamics' by Beck and Cowan (Reference 14.18) expands the model to include a number of more explicit stages. The trend shows discontinuous shifts that occur from one type of thinking/consciousness to another. The trend operates somewhat differently from other trends in that it is very dynamic. Thus, although every individual will have a 'normal' level of thinking, their prevailing emotional state may cause them to shift to any of their earlier levels.

Beck and Cowan suggest that until an individual experiences the contradiction that emerges at one level, they will not shift to the next. As such, it is not possible to 'leap-frog' and miss stages out.

An important finding from the research is that human communications are only likely to result in meaningful outcomes with a relatively small number of combinations of thinking level of the person providing the message and the person receiving it (Reference 14.19):

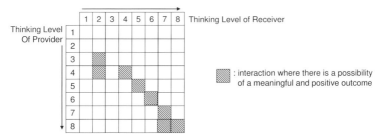

Of particular significance is a trend within the trend: odd number trend stages are closely associated with the individual. Even number stages, on the other hand, are strongly biased towards social groups.

The trend is most significant when we are thinking about using the trends in their problem-solving role. Recognising that the reason (say) quality levels are not improving is because one work group is thinking in 'blue' mode, while their manager is thinking in polar-opposite 'orange' is an important (albeit difficult) step towards developing real, sustainable solutions. To help in these situations it is important to recognise what motivates and de-motivates people at the various different levels:

Thinking Level	Pleasure Seeking…	Pain Avoidance…
1. Survival	-	food, water, warmth, safety
2. Tribal	good fortune, 'one of the gang', revenge	curses/spells/rejection/isolation
3. Feudal	ego-gratification, 'my way', mass adulation, rebellion	defeat, loss of power, rivals/threats
4. Order	stability, obedience, medals, status, promotion	change, rebellion from others, loss of status, outcast
5. Scientific	peer recognition, 'best in show', biggest/best/fastest, merit pay	losing, 'keeping up with the Jones'
6. Communitarian	'making a difference', harmony 'maximize my potential'	orange or blue attitudes, aggression/conflict/hierarchy
7. Holarchy	knowledgeable/'wise', 'life-long learning', discovery/challenge	sub-optimization, rigidity, 'stupid rules'
8. Holistic	'defining the jigsaw', 'wrong-jungle', empathy/trust	non-holistic, non-spiritual

GENERATIONAL CYCLES

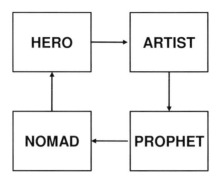

Examples

The trend emerges from the work of Strauss and Howe (Reference 14.20), and relates to a repeating pattern of generational archetypes. Typical examples: the GI Generation was classic 'Hero' (John Wayne). Just before and during WW2, the GI Generation gave birth to 'Artist's, now generally known as the 'Silent Generation' (Bob Dylan, Paul Simon). The Silent Generation in turn gave birth to a generation of 'Prophets' – the Baby-Boomer generation. Baby-Boomers in turn gave birth to Generation X – a typical 'Nomad' generation. The most recent 'Generation-Y' – the offspring of mainly Generation-X parents, are another 'Hero' generation.

Reasons For Jumps

Although this trend is consistent with the others in terms of its focus on discontinuous shifts, because it works over much longer periods (a typical generational cycle being 20-25 years) the underlying mechanics are a little different. The reasons that one generational archetype gives birth to another different archetype emerges from the different manner in which each generation was raised. 'Hero' generations are very protected in childhood (think of 'Baby On Board' signs in cars in recent times) and as such make very different parents to 'Nomads' – who were abandoned ('latch-key kids') while being raised by their Baby-Boomer parents. The main Strauss and Howe point is that these generational archetypes produce patterns that have repeated for at least the last 400 years. The following table summarises the main characteristics of each archetype at different ages during their life:

	0-20	21-41	42-62	63-83
HERO	protected	heroic	hubristic	powerful
ARTIST	suffocated	sensitive	indecisive	empathic
PROPHET	indulged	narcissistic	moralistic	wise
NOMAD	abandoned	alienated	pragmatic	tough

This trend is included here since it is thought to be a strong driver on the shifting pattern of consumer and market trends. According to Strauss and Howe, around the middle of this decade, the new generation of 'Hero's' were entering adulthood, thus marking the start of a major shift in societal behaviour.

What Strauss and Howe have also noted (although it is mapped to the idea of discontinuous shifts for the first time here) is that the various different combinations of archetypes at different ages in society correspond to a series of again repeating societal characteristics. The pattern can be mapped to four main phases of a societal s-curve:

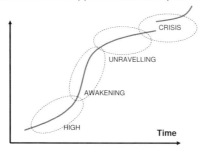

This high-awakening-unravelling-crisis pattern exists and repeats every four generations because of the characteristics of each generation living during that period:

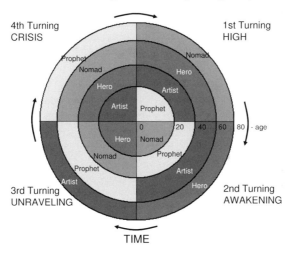

According to Strauss and Howe, the world is currently at or around the transition from an 'unravelling' to a 'crisis' period. The 'unravelling' occurs because of the combination of moralistic Prophets in political power and alienated Nomads in young adulthood. The 'crisis' period then sees the Prophets (Baby-Boomers today) becoming wise, Nomads becoming pragmatic, and newly-adult Hero generation entering their heroic period. Again according to Strauss and Howe, this combination of characteristics will respond very differently to random and unplanned world events (such as 9/11, tsunamis, etc) than other combinations. Alas the likely reactions during a 'crisis' period will tend to amplify rather than attenuate these world events, and hence the emergence of crises like those that occurred during the previous historical crisis period between 1926 and 1946.

This trend presents a good example of complexity theory – and specifically the idea of how apparently subtle micro-scale shifts can create enormous macro-scale societal impacts.

ACTION CO-ORDINATION

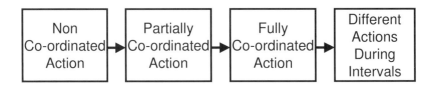

Examples

Manufacture processes, manufacture scheduling (run factory at full capacity irrespective of demand; manufacture to forecast; pull-based manufacture-to-order systems), supermarket check-out staff scheduling, time-outs for staff training, maintenance, etc.

Reasons For Jumps

Evolution Stage	Reasons for Jumps
Non-Co-ordinated to Partially Co-ordinated	-reduce time wastage -increase system efficiency -improve response to external changes -improve safety -reduce likelihood of system damage -reduce system wear -increase user convenience
Partially Co-ordinated to Fully Co-ordinated	as above
Fully Co-ordinated to Action During Interval	-insert a new useful function -improve overall efficiency -increase user convenience -improve safety

Notes:

The key connecting word in this trend is 'action' – what actions are being performed in the system being investigated?

The 'Action during interval' evolution step could actually be seen as an example of the Mono-Bi-Poly trend. It is included here as a stage in this trend because the explicit evolution trigger 'can you find any intervals in your current system?' is not covered explicitly enough in the Mono-Bi-Poly trend.

This trend relates to both time and interface aspects of the trend clusters – i.e. thinking explicitly about the time element of actions, and also the manner in which communication actions will evolve.

RHYTHM CO-ORDINATION

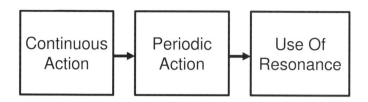

Examples

Shift-switching patterns that rotate tedious jobs. Revision for exams is most effective in short, sharp bursts rather than prolonged sessions. Short, punchy workshops and seminars recognise that the human attention span is typically less than 30 minutes (and falling!) and so schedule different activities between the formal lecture parts.

Reasons For Jumps

Evolution Stage	Reasons for Jumps
Continuous to Periodic	-reduction in energy usage -overcome a physical contradiction (separated in time) -increase efficiency of useful effect -introduce time measurement capability -reduce waste
Periodic to Use of Resonance	-increase magnitude of useful effect -increase efficiency of useful effect -reduce energy usage -reduce waste -reduce system complexity -reduce cost (resonance is a free resource)

Notes:

Many systems will be found at the left hand end of this trend. This is at least partially because resonance is usually viewed as a 'bad' thing. The trend shows that (like the Inventive Principle 'Blessing in Disguise' – Chapter 10) somewhere resonance can be put to useful effect. There is considerable evolutionary potential in this trend for many systems.

The trend is designed to be complementary to the preceding 'Action Co-ordination' trend. That trend is designed for relatively long time periods, while the rhythm co-ordination trend is generally focused on time periods of seconds or minutes.

'Resonance' in the business context means recognizing that 'in-the-zone' state that athletes and performers achieve when they are wholly concentrated on the task at hand and become oblivious to distractions.

REDUCED DAMPING

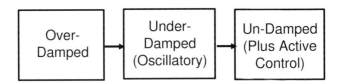

Examples

'Damping' is the engineering term for the inertia within systems. A heavily damped system is one that is very stable and resistant to change – e.g. the legal system. An un-damped system is inherently unstable and thus may fluctuate wildly in turbulent conditions – e.g. forward thinking venture-capital companies, rapid reaction force, e-commerce (any kind of virtual enterprise, in fact, as virtual systems are much easier to change than physical ones). These latter systems become stable only when active control management methods are deployed.

Reasons For Jumps

Evolution Stage	Reasons for Jumps
Any stage to the next	-reduced waste and inefficiency in system -improved dynamic performance -improved response time -improve ability to respond to disruption and non-linear change -'change is the only constant'

Notes:

A perhaps non-instinctive trend, this trend mirrors a technical equivalent. Increases in the dynamic nature of the business environment mean that the ability to respond to change is emerging as *the* dominant business survival skill.

Damping (or 'inertia' or 'resistance to change') is an inherent property of all systems. Over-damping relates to a system where change happens only slowly. When a target is set, for example, the system will edge slowly to that target.

As damping is removed from a system, oscillatory behaviour is able to occur – in order to meet a target, the system may over-shoot then correct and under-shoot, with the over-shooting and under-shooting progressively reducing until the desired target level is achieved.

Elimination of inertia ('un-damped') allows a system to potentially converge very rapidly on target values, but at the expense of potential instability. As such, an un-damped system demands the incorporation of effective ('active control') turbulence-management strategies.

This trend is still at a relatively immature stage – being largely dependent on the emergence of sophisticated control algorithms and deep understanding of complexity and chaos theories.

FEEDBACK AND CONTROL

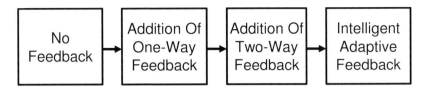

Examples

Staff appraisals and evolution to 360degree appraisal systems. Boss-worker relations. Quality circles. Customer relationship management and evolution to a stage where customers actively participate in the design of the products and services they receive. Amazon (and a host of e-businesses) that 'learn' what their customers like and don't like and respond accordingly.

Reasons For Jumps

Evolution Stage	Reasons for Jumps
No Feedback to One-Way Feedback	-improved morale -reduced misinterpretation of communication -reduced passive-aggressive behaviour
One-Way to Two-Way Feedback	-system self-correction -reduced likelihood of non-linear failure -ability to control function delivery to specified requirements -improved user-proofing -improved involvement and morale
Two-Way to Adaptive, Intelligent Feedback	-adaptive systems -self-learning systems -self-repairing systems -reduced likelihood of system failure

Notes:

One of the most effective uses of this trend is to examine any and all relationships present in a system and establish whether there is feedback in that system. A frighteningly large proportion of business systems still have no adequate feedback loops in them – see the large number of innovations that failed because the 'voice of the customer' was missing, or the number of in-company change initiatives that fail because the voice of the staff is not taken into consideration.

In addition to the central concept of adaptiveness, 'intelligent feedback' also specifically includes the concept of 'feed-forward'. This is most usually seen in a business context as pro-active 'anticipate and pre-empt' strategies.

The Controllability trend is the most common example of the phenomenon 'the need for the system disappears' when the end of this trend has been reached. I.e. something else already in the system performs the function of the control system – the system achieves autopoeisis and becomes 'self-controlling'.

NON-LINEARITIES

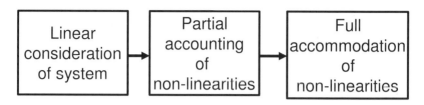

Examples

Very few. The large majority of organisations fail to recognise that non-linearities (brought about by disruptive innovations, or environmental changes or political events, etc) exist, never mind the thought that they might be able to plan for them.

Reasons For Jumps

Evolution Stage	Reasons for Jumps
Any stage to the next	-improved organizational robustness -improved ability to change -improved user safety -reduced likelihood of (cliff-edge) catastrophic failure

Notes:

Another emerging trends – the large majority of both business and technical systems are designed to avoid exposure to non-linear areas of operation by being forced to stay within established envelopes of known safe operation ('operating procedures'). Unfortunately, we sometimes get these boundaries wrong, or accommodation of their existence unduly compromises the performance of the system as a whole.

Recognising the existence of an existing or emerging non-linearity is one thing, knowing what to do about them when we see them is another. There are as yet still precious few examples of organizations developing successful strategies for dealing with on-linearities. We do know that the use of the win-win conflict resolution strategies within systematic innovation is a very clear step in the right direction.

INCREASING DIMENSIONALITY

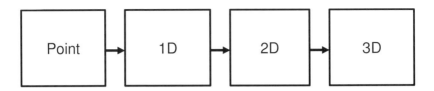

Examples

Organisation structures – no-organisation to unitary hierarchy to matrix structure to 'bucky-ball structure (after the Buckminster-Fuller C60 carbon atom arrangement in which every atom (person) is both externally facing and connected to every other atom).

Reasons For Jumps

Evolution Stage	Reasons for Jumps
Any stage to the next	-improved employee relations/involvement -improved communications -improved system adaptability -closer proximity -improved information flow -greater exposure to and awareness by market -greater accessibility -improved backup procedures

Notes:

Close relative of the 'Another Dimension' inventive strategy from Chapter 10. The trend is deliberately designed to be generic in nature in order to encourage consideration of all possible interpretations of things that are points or straight-lines or 2-Dimensional within and around a business.

Systems can, of course, evolve beyond the three dimensions suggested in the trend graphic (e.g. a time variant buckyball organisation structure, may be seen to have added the dimension of time).

DEGREES OF FREEDOM

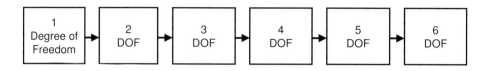

| 1 Degree of Freedom | 2 DOF | 3 DOF | 4 DOF | 5 DOF | 6 DOF |

Examples

Reporting structures, inter-personal relations, communication links, functional/intangible relationships in organisation structure, relationships with customers and complementors.

Reasons For Jumps

Evolution Stage	Reasons for Jumps
Any stage to the next	-increase operability -increase organisational flexibility -improved co-ordination -improved ability to respond to change -improved morale -reduced waste (time, risk)

Notes:

A trend that may be seen to have parallels with the earlier Mono-Bi-Poly trends, but included here as a separate entity in order to give more specific focus to the importance of the links and connections that join one person to another, one department to another, one company to another, etc.

DYNAMIZATION

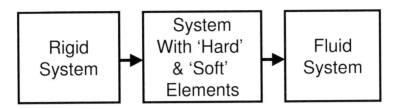

Examples

Organisation structures evolving from single fixed structure to one with some fixed and some flexible relations (e.g. matrix organisation uses combination of line and project managers to look after staff), to one capable of continuously adapting to changing situational requirements. Supermarket 'one-in-front' check-out systems – where the number of staff at the tills varies according to number of customers in the store and the number queuing to get out.

Reasons For Jumps

Evolution Stage	Reasons for Jumps
Any stage to the next	-improved system responsiveness
	-improved operating flexibility
	-solving physical contradiction
	(e.g. wide and narrow)
	-compound properties
	-greater responsiveness
	-ability to create self-propagating systems
	-reduced risk
	-increased efficiency
	-greater chance of synergy effects

Note:

A trend primarily about adding the capability within systems to adapt to change. 'Fluid' in the sense intended by the trend should be interpreted as the ability to change seamlessly from one thing to another. We might interpret the increasing use of e-communication channels and virtual businesses in general as an important (some might say, 'dominant') example of the fluid business system.

REDUCING HUMAN INVOLVEMENT

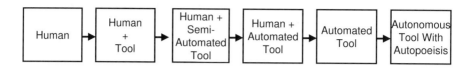

| Human | → | Human + Tool | → | Human + Semi-Automated Tool | → | Human + Automated Tool | → | Automated Tool | → | Autonomous Tool With Autopoeisis |

Examples

Use of computer aided systems, touch-tone phone services, e-commerce, supermarket ordering systems that record what we like and what we have run out of, automatic re-ordering inventory control systems, e-booking of airline tickets.

Reasons For Jumps

Evolution Stage	Reasons for Jumps
Any stage to the next	-reduced human drudgery -reduced likelihood of 'human error' effects -increased accuracy -ability to deliver extremes of a function outside the human range – e.g. memory, processing mathematical information, etc -reduction of fatigue effects -reduced cost

Note:

'Tool' should be interpreted in the trend in its most general possible sense – i.e. as the thing that delivers an action onto an object.

TRIMMING

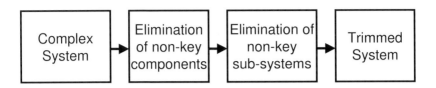

| Complex System | → | Elimination of non-key components | → | Elimination of non-key sub-systems | → | Trimmed System |

Examples

'Business Process Re-engineering'. 'Right-sizing', lean-enterprises, 'beyond-lean'.

Reasons For Jumps

Evolution Stage	Reasons for Jumps
Complex to Elimination of Components	-reduced complexity -reduced cost base -improved reliability -improved communications -(downside – tendency to eliminate the muscle as well as the fat)

Notes:

All trimming operations are aimed at reducing part-count/overall complexity of a system without negative impact on functionality.

The main thing to remember about the trend is that there are times in the evolution of a system when trimming is an appropriate action, and times when it is not:

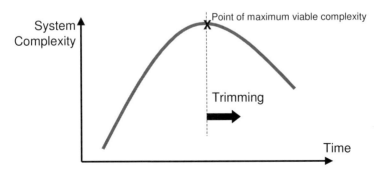

Typical signs that the 'point of viable complexity' has been reached: plateauing of key business measures, customer complaints that they don't understand you, high staff turnover, operating procedures that fill several filing cabinets and hence never get opened, Dilbert cartoons posted on the walls.

NESTING (UP)

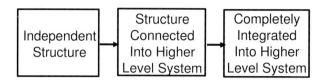

Examples

A large proportion of Merger & Acquisition activities, and just about all of the ones where a smaller entity is brought into a larger one – Lloyds Bank and TSB, British Steel/Corus, Vauxhall/General Motors, etc.

Reasons For Jumps

Evolution Stage	Reasons for Jumps
Any stage to the next	-improved system co-ordination -reduced system complexity -improved co-ordination -solve a physical contradiction ('transition to super-system')

Notes:

As systems evolve towards more ideal states, functions tend to migrate from sub-system elements to higher levels. There is a strong relationship between this trend and the increasing-decreasing complexity trend cycle:

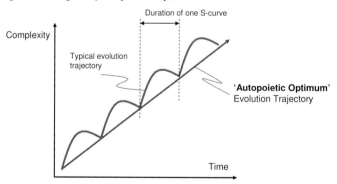

Over the course of several increasing-decreasing complexity cycles, the overall pattern is in an increasing complexity direction.

15.
Problem Solving Tools
Resources

"A wise man will make more opportunities than he will find"
Francis Bacon

and

*"The test of a first rate intelligence is the ability to hold two opposed ideas in the mind
at the same time, and still retain the ability to function."*
F. Scott Fitzgerald

and

"The world is an oyster but you don't crack it open on a mattress"
Arthur Miller

Anything in or around the system that is not being used to its maximum potential is a resource. Resources play a big part throughout the systematic innovation methodology. Identification of an untapped resource in or around a system is often a sign that a solution to a problem is nearby. In systematic innovation terms, even the things that we currently think of as harmful may also be transformed into useful resources if we are able to change our perspective. The world of business – particularly in the West – is prone to inefficient use of resources. Few if any business models in existence today will meet our definition of using resources to their maximum effect. All managers like to think that they are able to get the maximum out of the resources available to them. Discovering that there is still considerable untapped resource in the systems we may have been improving and optimising for possibly years can be a difficult message to absorb and accept. The prevailing logic in many organisations is that problems are solved by adding things; quality is improved by adding a Quality Department; human relations are improved by adding an HR department, etc.

This chapter is all about helping to identify the resources that will allow us to solve problems using what is already there. Or possibly even by taking things away. Our 'Ideal Final Result' thinking should tell us that the ideal quality department is the one that delivers quality but doesn't exist. This chapter is the one that will help us to identify the resources that will help to make that ideal possible. The chapter is divided into four main parts. The first one follows on from the preceding trends of evolution and evolutionary potential chapter and details its relationship to resource identification. The second part then provides a check-list of resources. The basic idea behind this part is to offer a comprehensive array of places and times to go look for available resources. The third part takes this idea a stage further by examining the 'turn lemons into lemonade' resource creation strategy. The final part of the chapter then puts all of the first three parts together by describing a case study example.

Resource Identification Triggers I – Evolutionary Potential

The first of the three main ways of identifying resources involves the identification of untapped evolutionary potential within and around systems. Evolutionary potential links in with the Trends of Evolution in the previous chapter. There we saw the concept of 'evolutionary potential' and the idea of a radar-plot as a means of describing how much further a given system is able to evolve. When examining the evolutionary potential in and around business systems it is usual to take both inward looking and outwardly focused perspectives. In terms of these plots (Figure 15.1), every bit of unused evolutionary potential, whether internal or external, represents a resource.

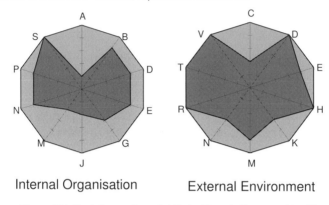

Internal Organisation   External Environment

Figure 15.1: Evolutionary Potential Radar Plots As Resource Identifier

Resource Identification Triggers II – Check-Lists

The second means of identifying things that can be utilised as resources is to provide a series of lists of things that other problem solvers in other fields have at some time successfully harnessed as resources. We present these lists here (based on work first reported in References 15.1 through to 15.4) with the expectation that you will peruse through them when in a position where you are looking to explore the complete resource space in and around the system you are evaluating.

For ease of use, the resource trigger lists have been segmented into the following major categories:-

- Internal Resources
- External Resources
- Human Resources/Resources Associated With Humans
- Low-Cost Resources
- 'Unexpected' Resources and Turning Harm Into Good

For all of the trigger lists, data has been arranged in terms of relevance to tangible and intangible categories. There is an inevitable overlap between the different categories used (e.g. 'humans' are likely to be involved in both internal and external situations). The intention has been to end up with something that can be considered to be comprehensive in a generic sense (there is empty space in each table for readers to add their context specific resources, however). The basic recommended means of using the lists is simply as a series of memory joggers. The problem solver is effectively being prompted to ask the question *'is resource X present in my system, and if it is, could I harness it as a resource?'*

Internal Resources

Internal resources are the things that exist inside an organisation. Resources identified in this category are generally within our control, and hence are (theoretically at least) easier to harness than things that lie outside the organisation. Within this category of resources are a number of sub-categories – elementary, organisational, functional, informational, financial and social. The following table details resources that may be available in each of these categories in both tangible and intangible contexts:-

Category	Tangible	Intangible
Elementary	geographical location size (turnover, profit, market share, etc) divisions/other facilities products services unoccupied space space between elements space inside elements unoccupied surfaces of elements space occupied by unnecessary elements time before a process starts (preliminary work) time during a process duration of a process parallel work/processes breaks, interruptions post-process time (feedback) speed/ability to react/dynamicism	market perception market value brand image
Organisational	labour structure – hierarchy/formal links reporting structure overlap between roles co-ordination/monitoring systems concessions succession plans	philosophy vision strategy informal networks 'team spirit'
Functional	gaps in a function function databases insufficient/excessive functions periodic/occasional functions back-up/contingency activities temporary actions duration of actions safety	casual functions non-mandated functions
Informational	intellectual property/patents copyright technical data/knowledge databases formulas customer lists/contacts processes (written) 'core competencies'/methods software/Intranet redundant knowledge (ability to forget)	know-how/'wisdom' rights-of-use forecasts/estimates processes experience past failures/successes 'lessons learned'

Financial	fixed assets licenses contracts equipment (e.g. machinery, software) inventory raw material work-in-progress/semi-finished goods facilities, plants land investments cash reserves incentives – company car, gifts, etc	incentives: social/prestige
Social	personnel records training	corporate culture peer-group culture working atmosphere 'unspoken rules' 'Old Pals Act' 'Not Invented Here' esteem 'family'/team political/religious stance

Figure 15.2: Internal To Organisation Resources

External Resources

External resources are the things that exist outside an organisation. Resources identified in this category are generally outside our direct control, and hence to harness them may require careful negotiation with external authorities. In addition to repeating the table structure used to examine internal resources, this section also includes an additional section aimed at helping to identify so-called 'complementor' resources.

Category	Tangible	Intangible
Elementary	products/services share price	market valuation customer 'experiences'
Organisational	franchises suppliers/supplier networks collaborative partners risk/revenue sharing partners joint ventures retired staff	ex-employee links
Functional	main delivered customer functions auxiliary functions	perceived functions (fashion/status/etc)
Informational	media universities/colleges published articles/papers 'Rembrandt's In The Attic' (Reference 15.5)	trade-marks trade-names
Financial	laws/taxes national/international policy loans investments	awards/medals (indirect financial benefit)
Social	charity/sponsorship	brand image

	community links customer loyalty business environment trade bodies/common-interest groups political connections – local/region/national/international	reputation goodwill

Figure 15.3: External To Organisation Resources

Complementor Resources

Complementors deserve a special mention in the context of resources. This is because they represent a whole range of possible opportunities that lie off the radar screen of many organisations. The idea of complementors was first discussed in the classic management text 'Co-opetition' (Reference 15.6). As indicated in Figure 15.4, complementors are a class of potentially value-adding entities that sit beyond your current customers, suppliers and competitors. They are the organisations and entities that currently have no connection to you or your products/services, but may offer the potential of a mutually beneficial win-win opportunity. Such opportunities may be one-offs or may turn into full blown collaborations and even mergers. The emergence of the complementor collaborations are still relatively infrequent. It is only, in fact, the difficulty of maintaining a competitive edge in the fast-moving modern world that has caused organisations to start thinking about them. In a market climate where competitive pressures are low, there is little incentive to attempt to break down the barriers that exist between any kind of organisations. Now that climate is changing, and organisations are finding it increasingly difficult to discriminate their offerings relative to those of their competitors, complementors are beginning to be seen as relatively easy opportunities to re-vitalise a business or a product/service range.

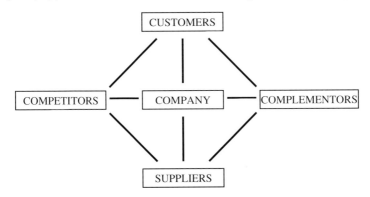

Figure 15.4: Complementors Form An Important Element In Determining Value Networks

Typical examples of complementor relationships between organisations might include the co-branding of toothpastes inside chewing-gum, packaging of products and services associated with the process of getting married (Virgin Brides – a name that could probably not fail in any case – offers a single-stop shop for ceremony, reception, flowers, photography, outfits, etc), integration of car-purchase and financing packages, or house-builder and mortgage companies. In each case the 'complementary' element is the crucial element. Co-branding of toothpaste and wedding dresses would be unlikely to succeed as the two things are completely independent from one another. But, make the connection between toothpaste and chewing gum – both things that sit inside the mouth – and you have the seeds of a potential win-win success. Let's have a look at a fairly simple one to see why the idea of complementors is such an important one:

Yoghurt products are typically sold in the UK as an after-dinner dessert product. The market is dominated by a small number of large players and a host of small niche operators. The market is considered to be a mature one, with no single company capable of any significant growth except at the expense of other players – which would probably lead in any event to a mutually destructive price-cutting war. So what does a company do in order to continue to feed their growth ambitions? Well, one company decided to go out and look for potentially complementary products – went outside their traditional 'yoghurt industry' box and tried to identify other products that might make a good combination with their own. Net result; they team with a well-known breakfast cereal manufacturer and begin selling yoghurt products with a side portion of breakfast cereal. Why are these two 'complementary' in the complementor sense of the word? To see the answer to that question, we need to look at the wins that both yoghurt company and cereal manufacture achieve:-

Yoghurt Company Wins	Cereal Manufacturer Wins
* Sell more yoghurt * Co-branding with a bigger name * Get customers familiar with the idea of eating breakfast cereal and yoghurt together	* Sell more cereal * Sell at a premium per-portion price * Get customers familiar with the idea of eating breakfast cereals at other times of the day besides breakfast

As is common in the fast-moving consumer goods sector, the benefits of the co-branding exercise are likely to be fairly short-term (Although the products are still selling well two years after introduction). Because this is a genuine complementor relationship, however, there are also long term wins for both companies that emerge from the relationship – so that, even when customers work out that they can buy an ordinary yoghurt and an ordinary packet of cereal and mix them themselves much more cheaply than the per-portion cost of the integrated product, both companies still have the opportunity to have their market expanded since they have made visible the connection between yoghurt and cereal and the attractions of eating at different times of the day besides post-dinner dessert and breakfast time respectively.

So, from this rather specific example, let us explore some of the more general guidelines that might help to steer us towards finding the complementors to our organisation. Figure 15.5 illustrates the main questions we might ask in order to establish the presence of products and services that might complement our own:

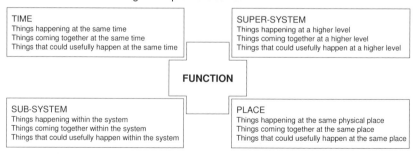

Figure 15.5: Complementor Resource Identification Questions

First thing to note about the picture is that 'function' acts as a common thread throughout. In all of our efforts to find complementors, we should be thinking about the functions that our systems perform and the other functions that a customer may also wish to perform. Beyond that, the basic idea is to examine our current system from the perspectives of space, time and interface with other things – either at the sub-system or super-system level.

When looking at time issues, we are interested in things that are happening or coming together at the same time. Virgin Brides is a classic example of this kind of temporal complementarity – since all of the activities performed by the company are delivered in this case at a single event called a wedding.

Spacial complementarities are things like the toothpaste/chewing-gum example – since these two products both operate within the same physical space (albeit, traditionally at different times).

The next two complementor finding options involve either zooming in to sub-systems (the classic complementor example here would be the 'Intel Inside' example – in which it becomes beneficial for computer manufacturers to advertise the presences of Intel products inside their box) or out to super-systems. Examples of finding complementors at the super-system level are less frequently observed, but nevertheless an example like football clubs seeking shirt sponsorship from organisations with a football-friendly/'cool' name (e.g. Newcastle United and Northern Rock insurance company) gives an indication of what it means to find complementors at this level.

The most difficult aspect of the complementor-finding story (and therefore the one that offers the potential for the biggest wins if we can make the non-obvious connections before others do) involve the questions involving the word 'could'; 'things that *could* usefully happen at the same time', 'things that *could* usefully happen at the same location', etc. By definition, things that 'could' happen together, currently do not. And so the key to find a complementor is to identify the functions that a customer might benefit from being able to do together. The strongest advice here is to examine the human drivers listed in Figure 15.8 later in the chapter and us them as a way of identifying such functions.

A simple example may serve to illustrate the process: apart from different strengths and brands, all sun-tan crèmes and sprays are the same. They all serve the function 'protect against the sun'. If we are to find a good complementary product to this product, we need to identify things that a consumer *might* usefully want to do where or when the sun crème is being used. Human attractors listed in Figure 15.8 include 'sweet smells'. Connecting this driver to the idea of a sun-crème might immediately suggest to us that when a consumer puts on a sun-crème they smell of sun-crème. This is not such a bad thing, but on the other hand, when someone is going out for the evening and want to smell attractive, they are unlikely to put on a sun-crème to achieve the desired effect. They are much more likely to put on after-shave or perfume. Take one more step from here, and we get ourselves to the idea of a sun-crème co-branded with a perfume and the pleasant prospect of Chanel No.5 on the beach.

Human Resources

In this section, we have segmented resource lists according to internal and external categories again. This time, however, the 'internal' category needs to be further divided into a section listing human resources internal to an organisation that can be harnessed as resources, and then a category examining psychological and physiological aspects of humans in general. Having described such physiological/psychological resources, we then go on to include a further short section exploring issues of culture, and whether there are more resources to be obtained by harnessing the differences between different global perspectives in a positive manner. All will hopefully become clear as we see each of the check-lists. We begin with the first two categories:

Category	Tangible	Intangible
Within The Organisation	employees employees with specific skills communication skills subject-matter experts leaders ethical standards health	seers influencers/motivators creators goals/aims expectations moral standards intelligence creativity charisma trust/loyalty consistency life experience flexibility social acceptance intuition
External To The Organisation	customers suppliers channels competitors shareholders sponsors/stakeholders mediators/brokers politicians media potential employees retired/semi-retired people	customer loyalty 'Tipping Point' (Reference 15.7) family ties extended family

Figure 15.6: Human Resources

Physiological and Psychological Resources In Humans

One of the elegant ideas contained in Steve Grand's work on artificial life (Reference 15.8) is that humans and the human brain in particular are 'wired' to minimise the difference between actual state and desired state. Thus, for example, if our actual state is that we are cold, and our 'desired state' is to be warm, we are driven to try and reduce the tension between the two states. We will 'feel cold' until such times as we have equalised the tension between actual and desired state and are 'warm enough'. From a resources perspective, whenever such a tension between actual and desired state exists – Figure 15.7 – then we may think of that tension as an untapped resource.

Being warm or cold is but one of a whole range of different attributes that can act as the source of a tension between actual and desired state. Figure 15.8 lists a range of things that act as either attractors (desired states that we wish to achieve) or repulsors (states that we desire to get away from) to humans. Mainly they operate at a visceral or instinctual level. The list is an expanded and re-structured form of a similar list in Reference 15.9. In some of the cases, the desired state may be seen as some kind of 'optimum' point. With temperature, for example, we each of us have a temperature at which we are most comfortable.

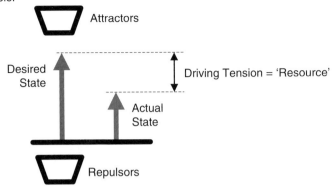

Figure 15.7: Tension Between Actual And Desired States As A Resource

Actually, we all of us have a range of different temperatures that we might view as optimum under different conditions – so that I might prefer to sleep in a cooler environment than that in which I read a book. These 'optimum' values, in other words, may well be dynamically changing, but at any point in time there will be an optimum desired state. Other of the attractors or repulsors do not feature such an 'optimum' point – there is no such thing as an 'optimum' grating noise, for example – and our desired state will always to be as far away from them as possible. We might think of the desired state of such attractors or repulsors as infinite in nature – in that we will never be able to have enough of an infinite attractor, and never too little of an infinite repulsor.

Whether a desired state is either towards a (dynamically changing) 'optimum' or one positioned at infinity, if there is a difference between our desired state and our current state then we have an untapped resource. Consequently, when we come to think about resources associated with humans that might help us to solve problems, we should be thinking about these attractors and repulsors and for each of them, ask the question 'is there a difference between where we are and where we would like to be?

	Things That Attract Humans	**Things That Repel Humans**
Visual	natural/comfortable lighting sunlight bright, highly saturated hues smiling faces dilated pupils (eye) 'attractive' people symmetry rounded/gently curved objects 'sensuous' shapes	darkness extremely bright/artificial lights empty, flat terrain crowded scenes straight lines perpendicular lines away-from-norm human forms
Auditory	'soothing' sounds 'sensuous' sounds simple melodies simple rhythms & rhythmic beats harmonious sounds loud musical noises (between 110 & 140 dB)	sudden, unexpected noises loud noises (70 to 110dB, & above 140dB) grating noises discordant noises noises at resonant frequency of ear

Kinaesthetic	warmth	extreme heat
	caresses	extreme cold
	smooth textures and objects	
Olfactory	sweet smells	rotting/decaying smells
	food smells	stale sweat
	fresh sweat	faeces
	pheromones	vomit
Gustatory	sweet tastes	bitter tastes
Other	'sensuous' feelings	heights
	controlled fear	crowds of people
	sexual features	other people's body fluids
	exaggerated body features of the	uncontrolled fear
	young	sharp objects
	water	snakes
		spiders

Figure 15.8: Human Attractor/Repulsor Resource Check List

Cultural Resources

Different parts of the world are culturally very different from one another. In many instances such differences cause tensions which in turn have often turned into conflict and, in extreme cases, bloodshed. The work of Charles Hampden-Turner and Fons Trompenaars on cross-cultural competence represents an important study into the differences between different cultures, and how we might begin to think about those differences as resources (Reference 15.10).

Of particular importance when trying to identify cultural resources are the six dimensions of cultural diversity uncovered by the authors. These dimensions represent contradictions or dilemmas between apparently opposing views. We say 'opposing' because traditionally we think of things like universalism and individualism as two polar opposites. According to Hampden-Turner and Trompenaars, however, rather than being at two opposite ends of a spectrum, these parameters are actually mirror images at opposite sides of a circle, and that if we are smart we will not let the fact that we believe one thing and someone else believes another to lead to an either/or conflict but instead to a recognition that elements of both are needed. There is much in common here with the systematic innovation perspective on contradiction that in any either/or kind of argument, there is a very high probability that the correct answer will turn out to be neither. So, rather than getting into cultural disagreements over universalism versus particularism, it is far more productive to see what good things happen when the best bits of both are taken and used in combination; universalism is useful up to a point, beyond which it becomes problematic; and the same applies to too much or too little particularism. As illustrated in Figure 15.9, if we are able to see such 'polar opposite' parameters in a both/and light then we have created 'resources' and hence an opportunity to generate new solution possibilities.

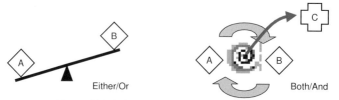

Figure 15.9: Cultural Diversity As Both/And Resource

Closer examination of the six cultural diversity dilemmas uncovered by Hampden-Turner reveals a number of potential resource opportunities. As was the case in the previous section, we might think of any of these dilemmas as a resource when there exists a tension between an actual and a desired state. Alternatively, the 'resource' element may simply come about as a result of recognising the presence of a cultural diversity and seeking to make a positive use of that diversity.

Figure 15.10 illustrates the six main dilemmas. The best way to think about and use them is to examine them in the context of any culture that you are contemplating working with. Any differences that you can identify between the culture of your organisation and that of the other company or country involved are potentially threatening to the success of the possible collaboration. By recognising the differences and thinking about them from the perspective of resources, we open up the possibility of turning potential negatives into win-win positives. To try and reduce the massive issues involved in understanding and make a positive out of cultural differences in the space of half a page is probably somewhat over-ambitious. Interested readers are encouraged to acquire a copy of the Hamden-Turner book.

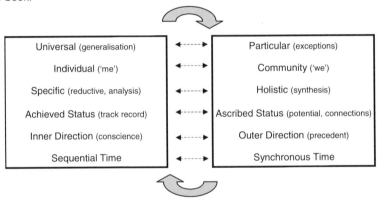

Figure 15.10: Six Dimensions Of Cultural Diversity (adapted from Reference 15.10)

Perhaps a simple example may serve to illustrate the threats – and hence opportunities – that the cultural differences described in the figure present. The differences between cultures that see time as essentially sequential in nature (e.g. although it is very difficult to justify generalisations on a national scale, the US with its ideas of 'time is money' and trying to get the most out of systems in the available time) and those that see it as a much more soft and elastic entity (overlapping time, JIT – and hence strongly connected to the Japanese way of doing things) can lead to all sorts of collaborative problems. Force someone used to working in a synchronous culture to give you a specific start date for an activity and you are likely to insult them. But recognise that they are attuned to synchronous ways of doing things and allow them the freedom to work in that way and you have tapped in to a resource that will allow both parties to win – one gets autonomy and the other gets an earlier delivery date because the synchronous party has had the opportunity to take advantage of doing things in parallel where necessary.

Low Cost Resources

Low cost resources can be useful if we determine that we are unable to solve a problem with a system using the resources it presently contains, and are fundamentally required to add something. Appropriate addition of a – genuinely – low cost resource should be examined before looking to more expensive alternatives. The following are all readily available things:

Resources Available in the Environment

Physical	Non-Physical
sunlight intensity, UV, IR	colour
water/humidity	music
magnetic fields	smell
barometric pressure/variation with altitude	sound (e.g. quietness)
ambient temperature/variation with altitude	imitation
altitude, density	
rock, stone, sand (silicates), earth, clay, chalk, dust	
(sustainable) timber, biomass, natural fibres – hemp, hair	
water, steam, ice, salt, foam, bubbles	
wind, rain, snow, hail, fog, mist, lightning	
aerosols, smoke	
air, voids	

Figure 15.11: 'Low-Cost' Resources In The Environment

Miscellaneous other low-cost resources available within and around organisations (all of these are only genuinely 'low-cost' if they are treated in an appropriate win-win manner – any attempt to exploit these resources unfairly will inevitably turn out to be 'high-cost'):

	Tangible	Intangible
Internal	interns/placement students suppliers	goodwill trust
External	charities community associations trade associations universities/colleges (projects) local schools councillors/politicians competitive tender bidders (tread carefully with this one!)	(unlikely to be anything meeting the 'low-cost' criteria)

Figure 15.12: 'Low-Cost' Resources In And Around Organisations

'Unexpected' Resources and Turning Harm Into Good

Tales of the Unexpected – the search for resources in and around systems is supposed to be a creative activity. The use of check-lists can often detract from the creative imperatives of resource identification. A very effective way of making the job feel more creative is to conduct an exercise in which we look for the things in a system that are the least likely to be useable as resources and to then see how they can be transformed into something useful. A simple but often effective question, having found a suitably unlikely resource candidate is 'how can this thing be turned into a useful resource?' This kind of provocation can often generate some surprising new thoughts.

Most retail financial institutions 'suffer' from what they know as over-indulgent customers. An over-indulgent customer, in case you have never heard the expression before, is the sort of customer who devotes a significant proportion of their time asking the institution what the institution sees as time-wasting questions – 'how did you calculate my interest-rate?', 'why didn't you send me a new folder for my statements?', 'why was the debit made a day late?', 'why doesn't the bank open on a Saturday?', 'how come there are never enough staff at lunchtimes?' The list can appear to be a seemingly endless one, particularly when it involves a customer who has perhaps retired from full-time work and has plenty of time on their hands, and plenty of opinions on what represents 'good service'. For most banks, these over-indulgent customers can absorb an inordinate amount of staff time and resource. Consequently, several banks harbour desires to encourage these customers to move their business elsewhere.

However, by asking the question 'how can these over-indulgent customers be turned into a useful resource?' we can begin to see how perhaps all of the down-sides they are perceived to bring to the institution might be re-framed as positive things. Like for example:-

- using them in focus-groups aimed at improving the banks service (in many ways these over-indulgent customers are merely trying find an outlet for their frustrations and so giving them a formal opportunity to vent them is helpful on both sides)
- using them as a way of testing the robustness of systems (ask an old person with no computer experience to try out your brand new ATM system as a way of *really* proving its friendliness)
- recognizing that these over-indulgent customers are just as happy to spend their time doing sociable things as they are complaining to you; hence why not think of them as word-of-mouth advocates of how good your service is – no-one comes into a shop or bank to be deliberately disruptive (or not for long; unless you treated them really badly in the past), so why not give them the benefit of the doubt and the opportunity to phone their friends to tell them what the nice bank did for them this week.

Moral of the story; even the most unexpected things in a system can turn out to be useful resources if we force ourselves to think about it hard enough. The same goes for things in the system we currently view as harmful:

Turning Harm Into Good – the same basic provocation 'how can this thing be turned into a useful resource?' as described above can be taken a step further and applied to things in the system we are currently seeing as bad things. 'How can this bad thing be turned into a useful resource?' is thus a good start point for some serious thinking about turning harm into good.

Related to this basic start point are the follow up questions:-

- under what circumstances would the bad thing become a good thing? (and how could we make these circumstances happen?)
- who might view the bad thing as a good thing? Why?
- where might the bad thing be seen as a good thing?

Other examples of things traditionally viewed as 'bad' being turned into useful resources are the various aspects of 'waste' to be found in organisations. Waste takes on a host of forms, and is a central theme in 'lean' thinking. Figure 15.13 highlights a series of different types of waste that we might consider re-thinking from a resources perspective as may be found in the lean context:-

- *waste – process, business (employees, managers suppliers, etc), pure*
- *waste of over-production*
- *waste of waiting (internal and external)*

- *waste of transporting (internal and external)*
- *waste of inappropriate processing (using a hammer to crack a nut)*
- *waste of unnecessary inventory*
- *waste of unnecessary motions*
- *waste of defects*
- *waste of untapped human potential (empowerment)*
- *waste of inappropriate systems (over-specified computers, machines, etc)*
- *waste of energy and water*
- *wasted materials*
- *service and office wastes (excess meetings, food, photocopying, etc)*
- *waste of customer time*
- *waste of defecting customers*

Figure 15.13: 'Waste' Resources

See also Inventive Principle 22 'Blessing in Disguise' in the reference section of Chapter 11 for other examples of things traditionally thought of as 'bad' being turned into something useful.

By way of practice at turning bad things into good things, as a more extreme than the 'least likely' resource identification question from the previous section, try thinking about the absolute worst, most harmful, destructive thing about a system you can, and then force yourself to see how it could be viewed as a resource.

'Devil's Advocate As A Resource

Many of us have also suffered at the hands of those people in meetings with the perpetual propensity to take on the role of devil's advocate. Taken in a positive spirit, the devil's advocate role is a very important one – one, indeed that we will return to in the red-team/blue-team subversion analysis discussion in Chapter 21, and the design of business systems that are as robust as possible. However, there are some devil's advocates that decide to take on the role as a full time occupation, and as a consequence what could have been a positive contribution becomes disruptive and destructive. It can be difficult, but if you imagine that these characters are the most important people present in your meeting (for one thing, if you answer all of their 'yes, but's...' you can guarantee that you have also answered everyone else's), then they can be transformed into the most useful resource you ever had.

Here are a few typical 'devil's advocate questions that can be helpful when we are trying to identify untapped resources in and around systems:-

- *what resources do we need to maintain the unity of the team?*
- *what resources do we need to prevent initiative fatigue?*
- *is there someone outside the team that can act as a guide/teacher/inspirer?*
- *what resources do we need to make the project fun?*
- *what might cause us stress?*
- *where are the overlaps and how can we use them positively?*
- *what might we do when project begins to lose momentum?*
- *who could offer us team coaching?*
- *what will customers get confused about?*
- *what space has been created for doing things differently?*
- *who should keep a day-to-day diary of the project?*

- *who will tell us when we are becoming too insular?*
- *who will tell us the truth when things are not going well?*

Figure 15.14: Good 'Devil's Advocate Questions To Help Find Resources

'False Givens' As A Resource

A final useful thing to think about when searching for resources is 'what are the things we have assumed to be true, that in actual fact are not true'. It is worth exploring this direction because the psychological inertia phenomenon discussed in Chapter 3 very often leads us to make premature judgements about things. We also have a strong tendency to simplify and average things. A classic example of a 'false given' occurs when someone asks a question like 'how tall are you?' Almost invariably, we each of us have remembered a single number. A single number that turns out to be incorrect. Or rather only right at one moment during the day since between getting out of bed in the morning and returning to bed the next night we are likely to have shrunk by between 12 and 20mm due to the effects of gravity. This kind of 'false given' is everywhere and every time we fall into the trap we miss a potentially important resource.

Optical illusions represent another common kind of 'false given'. Because the human brain is effectively a prediction engine, it tends to be very easy to fool it with things that are not as they appear. Take Figure 15.15 for example. The question here is about which of A or B is shaded darker. Most people will tend to answer A. The actual answer is that both squares have exactly the same shade.

Figure 15.15: Which Square Is Darker A Or B?' Illusion (Edward H Adelson)

The simplest and most effective way to explore and find 'false givens' is to periodically look at the things that have been written down in the Problem Explorer templates or in FAA diagrams or Perception Maps through an '*is this really true?*' lens. Use this lens to challenge everything; and be aware that the less likely the exercise appears to be useful, the bigger the false-given resource finding opportunity.

Resources Case Study – Retention Of High Potential Personnel

Let us now try and put some of these pieces together via a simple case study example. The case involves a problem common in many large organisations – that of how to retain high potential individuals. Scarce skills will always operate in a seller's market, and consequently, people possessing such skills are able to command high salaries and terms and conditions of employment. Increasingly, too, such individuals are decreasingly likely to want to be bound by the seemingly inevitable restrictions of the large organisation.

So, what might we do to help resolve such retention problems? Well, the identification of 'resources' is likely to play an important part, and so let's put ourselves in the position of the HR department in a large organisation and see what we might be able to find that is 'not being used to its maximum potential'. In an attempt to keep the example relevant to as many applications as possible, we will focus on those parts of the resource search that can be applied generically. We will begin by constructing an evolution potential radar plot based on the trends and methods discussed in Chapter 14. Figure 15.16 illustrates the results of this analysis. The plot has been drawn from the perspective of a high-potential individual residing inside a typical leading-edge large employer organisation.

Figure 15.16: Evolution Potential Plot For High Potential Personnel Resource Search

As is typical in many advanced organisations, a significant amount of the evolution potential has been used already. There are, however, a number of trend jumps that have not yet been made that may help us to solve our retention problem. A number of potential ideas emerge:-

- the Maslow Hierarchy of needs trend is an important one in all internally facing evolution potential exercises. In this case, we have recorded an organisation the opportunity to afford the high potential employee 'esteem' in the form of bonus payments, awards, prizes, etc (as per conventional logic). This organisation – like most others – does not however consciously think about the final 'self-actualisation' stage of the trend, and the implied need to help take an individual to a point where they feel genuinely involved in the business, and motivated to 'make a difference'; that their purpose is to translate their talent into a tangible effect on the performance of the business.
- 'Customer Expectation' – while normally applied in an externally facing context, this trend can also be applied looking within an organisation. In this case, the organisation offers the high potential employee a 'service' (employment), but does not deliver an 'experience'. Very few organisations presently think about delivering a (positive!) experience to their employees. Hopefully injecting the word 'experience' into the thinking process offers the potential to generate useful ideas.
- 'Self-Organisation' – few organisations are actively recognising and taking advantage of the possibilities that complex systems theory involves. Pointing the high potential individual in this direction does much for their learning skills, involves them in the very DNA of the business (thence hopefully increasing commitment to the organisation), and most importantly, puts the right person in a highly influential position in a company.

- 'Transparency' – giving high potential individuals (everyone in fact) access to company information is another effective way of increasing involvement. See Ricardo Semler again (Reference 15.11) – SemCo has some of the lowest employee turnover figures anywhere in the world.
- 'Connections' and 'Dynamization' – tying a high potential individual to a rigid organisational structure is a sure-fire way of de-motivating them. A jump along this trend to give the individual a more flexible role will often pay dividend in terms of involvement and interest.
- 'Rhythm Co-ordination' – it is difficult for any large organisation to find the 'resonant frequency' of individual employees, but on the other had, very few of them ask the question, or indeed permit individuals to find their own resonant niche.

Switching now to the more general resource check-lists in this chapter, there is probably little value in applying many of the triggers to such a general application – far better to think about them through the context of a specific example. There are, however, one or two aspects from the lists that can offer some useful insight into this case study:
- 'Low-cost' – statistics will show that very few high potential individuals cite 'low pay' as a reason why they will move from one job to another. Most commonly cited reasons are that they felt that their potential was not being used to the full. It is true that in many cases, the role that individual find themselves in is not 'big enough' for that person, but at the same time, the organisation has no other role to offer. The 'low-cost' resources suggest a number of possible win-win additional tasks that can be offered to individuals in this 'untapped capacity' situation – setting up college/community/charity projects, working with trade associations, politicians and other influencers can also be beneficial to all concerned if the right matches are made.
- 'Complementors' – are normally thought about at the organisational level rather than for individuals, but perhaps here it leads to the thought that high-potential individuals can be 'partnered' with equivalents in other complementary companies. Not only do the individuals benefit from exposure to other corporate cultures (and see that the 'grass is *not* greener on the other side'), but they also bring back the things they have learned to tangibly and intangibly benefit their employer.
- 'Cultural Diversity' – suggests the possibility of secondment to other parts of the world. Several possible win-wins here – broadening of skills, satisfying the 'wanderlust' present in many highly-educated people, and (combining this idea with the 'complementor' idea from above) the opportunity to import skills from equivalent companies in other parts of the globe.
- 'Tipping Point' – given the drive to 'make a difference' in many high potential individuals, there is much to be said in giving 'killer application' new project development tasks to such people; giving them responsibility for not only developing the idea, but also constructing business plan, marketing plan and exploitation plan. In many organisations this kind of responsibility is matched with the offer to take a sometimes significant ownership stake in the emerging business.

(Acknowledgement: many thanks to Sandra Müller at the University of Bremen in Germany for her thoughts and inputs on this case study.)

What Do I Do?

Resources and the concept that everything in and around a system that is not being used to its maximum potential is one of the cornerstones of the systematic innovation philosophy. In systematic innovation terms, even the bad things in a system are good things, if only we can think about them hard enough.

The aim of this chapter is essentially to collate lists of things that we don't always think of as resources, but that someone, somewhere has somehow been able to successfully harness. The best way to use these lists is as simple solution triggers. In this regard it is recommended that you peruse the lists when you are unable to develop an elegant enough solution to the problem you are working on.

In the case of turning bad things into good things, the key provocation to be used is 'how can this bad thing be turned into a good thing?'

References

1) Collis, D.J., Montgomery, C.A., 'Competing on Resources Strategy in the 1990s. How do you create and sustain a profitable strategy?' *Harvard Business Review*, 73, 4, pp118-128, 1995.
2) Montgomery, C.A., 'Of Diamonds and Rust. A New Look at Resources.' In Montgomery, C.A. (ed.), <u>Resourced-Based and Evolutionary Theories of the Firm: Towards a Synthesis</u>. Kluwer Academic Publishers, Boston et al., pp251-268.
3) Wernerfelt, B., 'From Critical Resources To Corporate Strategy', *Journal of General Management,* 14, 3, 4-12, 1989.
4) Wernerfelt, B., 'A Resources-based View of the Firm', *Strategic Management Journal*, 5, 171-180, 1984.
5) Rivette, K., Kline, D., '<u>Rembrandts in the Attic: Unlocking the Hidden Value of Patents</u>', Harvard Business School Press, 1998.
6) Nalebuff, B.J., Brandenburger, A.M., '<u>Co-opetition</u>', Harper Collins Business, London, 1996.
7) Gladwell, M., '<u>The Tipping Point: How Little Things Can Make A Big Difference</u>', Little, Brown & Company, London, 2000.
8) Grand, S., '<u>Growing Up With Lucy: How To Build an Android In Twenty Easy Steps</u>', Weidenfeld & Nicolson, London, 2003.
9) Norman, D.A., '<u>Emotional Design: Why We Love (Or Hate) Everyday Things</u>', Basic Books, Perseus, New York, 2004.
10) Hampden-Turner, C., Trompenaars, F., '<u>Building Cross-Cultural Competence</u>', John Wiley & Sons Ltd, New York, 2000.
11) Semler, R., '<u>The Seven Day Weekend</u>', Century, The Random House Group, London, 2003.

16.
Problem Solving Tools
Knowledge

"If railroads had understood they were in the transportation business instead of the steel rail business,
we'd all be flying on Union Pacific Airlines."
Anonymous

and

"Information networks straddle the world. Nothing remains concealed. But the sheer volume
of information dissolves the information. We are unable to take it all in."
Günter Grass

When the 'select' part of the systematic innovation process is directing us to this 'knowledge' part of the toolkit, we are basically being prompted to look beyond our current horizons to see if anyone has already solved the type of problem we are facing. Other solution generation parts of the toolkit enable us to tap into the good solutions of others in an abstracted form. The interest here, though, are strategies that may be used under circumstances in which the abstractions we are required to make become too general to be able to make useful connections to our specific situation. Here, then, we are interested in means of accessing solutions that require little or no abstraction, but rather access directly existing solution databases:

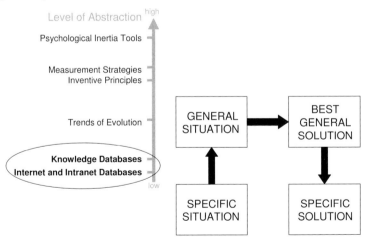

Figure 16.1: Levels of Abstraction In The Systematic Innovation Process

The chapter is divided into four main sections. In the first section we explore sources of useful business knowledge and strategies for searching them effectively. In the second

413

section, we explore new and emerging tools designed at assisting in the knowledge search task. In the third section, we explore the bigger questions of context and translation of knowledge into wisdom. Business problems are as different as fingerprints, and one of the great fallacies of management is the idea that it is possible to transplant solutions known to be effective in one situation into other situations. It is impossible to quantify the damage that has been caused to businesses by managers and consultants when they introduce so-called ready-made solutions (think of TQM, 'zero-defects', 'right-first-time' and just about every other management flavour of the month) that turn out not to match the specific context of the problem at hand. Any reader that does not believe this possibility, or simply wants some verifiable evidence is recommended to have a look at Reference 16.1. In this third part of the chapter, we explore what can be done about such knowledge transplant issues. Finally, in the last section of the chapter we draw a few conclusions on knowledge issues and reflect on some of the implications and opportunities for knowledge management.

1) Accessing Knowledge

One of the main underlying ideas of the technical version of the systematic innovation toolkit is that knowledge sharing between different scientific and engineering disciplines becomes much more readily achieved when solutions are arranged in terms of *function*. As discussed in earlier chapters, function is important because this is what a customer is first and foremost looking for when they are selecting one product or process over another one. The evolution from selling product to selling function may be seen in examples as diverse as jet-engines to carpets, dietary supplements to laundry. Given the choice of paying several million dollars to buy a jet engine or receiving a 'free' engine and paying on a 'power-by-the-hour' basis, customers are far more likely to choose the latter option. Likewise given the choice of buying a generic vitamin tablet or a personalised health maintenance plan, the customer is always opt for the solution that maximises their personal benefit and minimises all of the downsides.

The shift from selling washing powder to selling 'cleaned clothes' represents a subtle but profoundly important change in the way companies present themselves to the market. When combined with knowledge repositories arranged in terms of function this shift becomes even more important. Historically good ideas have travelled very slowly between different industries and disciplines. It took nearly 40 years for brush seal technology to travel from doors to jet-engines; conversely jet-engine originated squeeze-film damper bearing technology has been around for over 20 years and, despite its simplicity and amazing performance benefits, still hasn't transferred to the automotive and other sectors. The advent of knowledge databases arranged in such a way that allows us to immediately see all of the known ways of moving a liquid or joining things or separating things or heating things or cooling things or, to get back to the laundry theme, cleaning things means that those companies using them have a distinct advantage over those that don't. The emergence of ultrasound-based washing machines from Sanyo (not from Electrolux or Whirlpool or any of the other traditional manufacturers, note) that don't require the use of any detergents are the sort of consequence we will see increasingly frequently in the coming years. Ultrasound is an extremely commonly used means of cleaning things in an industrial process context; putting a description of it into a database marked 'all the ways of cleaning things' means that everyone else can also recognise its existence.

This is a 'business' book and not a 'technical' one, but the implications for business of not recognising the importance of function and the availability of technical knowledge databases arranged in terms of function are too important to ignore. Business readers may care to check out Reference 16.2 to see just how easy it is to access the technical knowledge of different industries. Business readers with an acute aversion to anything with the word 'technical' in it, may wish to delegate the job to someone else. Either way, someone in the organisation needs to be aware of the threats (and opportunities – since someone, somewhere may well be desperately looking for the solution your organisation has already found – References 16.3 and 16.4) posed by these databases.

From the perspective, then, of searching for knowledge in a business context, one of the main things that the research on the technical side should tell us is that it is the function words that are the ones where we should concentrate our attention. This is maybe another of those subtle but profound shifts in thinking that the systematic innovation method causes us to think about. We are all of us conditioned to think about 'things' – people, objects, companies, etc – rather than the connections between the things. We focus on nouns rather than verbs. If we think about the general idea of 'something does something to something' (e.g. 'John directs Peter') it is the 'does something' part that allows us to map ideas from one place to another. Of course the 'John' and 'Peter' parts of the system are important, but unfortunately neither of them allows us to shift our thinking from its current box to one that might allow us to identify a better way of doing things.

In the next section we list some of the key verbs relevant to knowledge searching in the business and management contexts. Unlike the technical version of the knowledge databases, we have opted to not list all of the ways we can find to achieve the 'reward' or 'motivate' or 'discipline' functions. This was a decision we have argued about long and hard. What manager, for example, wouldn't be interested in seeing all of the known ways of motivating his or her staff? Managers are busy people and therefore they need answers fast. The big danger with these perfectly logical statements, as hinted at the beginning of the chapter, is that all the evidence we see says that transplanting of ideas from one place to another without a genuine understanding of context leads inexorably to failure. According to the quotation in one of the warnings at the beginning of the book, people will do almost anything to avoid having to think. We ultimately decided that a knowledge database including known ways of motivating people carried far more dangers than benefits. Many would argue that there are no ways to motivate people, and that managers can only de-motivate. Whether this is true or not, it is definitely one of those complex issues that cannot be solved by a look-up table of other peoples solutions that might not even have actually worked in their own context never mind yours. There are simple, top-down solutions to all simple problems. Complex problems have no simple, top-down solutions.

So, the following table is intended to act merely as a start to the knowledge search process. At the end of the table and in the next section, we explore additional knowledge search strategies that offer at least the potential to match solutions and context. Firstly, in order to give the list some form of structure, Figure 16.2 illustrates the basic categories of function words most useful to the business and management context.

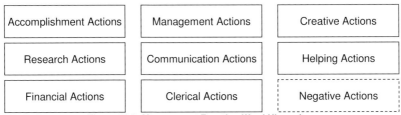

Figure 16.2: Management Function Word Hierarchy

Accomplishment Verbs

achieve
become
elect to
establish
expand

improve
increase
move
pioneer
reduce (loss)

resolve (problems)
restore
spearhead
transform

Creative Verbs

act
anticipate
conceptualize
create
customize
decorate
design
develop
direct

display
draw
edit
entertain
establish
fashion
film
found
illustrate

initiate
innovate
institute
integrate
introduce
invent
originate
perform

Clerical or Detail Verbs

approve
arrange
catalogue
chart
classify
collect
compile
deliver
dispatch
distribute
draft
edit
execute
file
generate

host
implement
inspect
keep
memorize
monitor
operate
organize
outline
prepare
process
purchase
record
register
relay

reorganize
reproduce
retrieve
scan
schedule
screen
separate
simplify
specify
systematize
tabulate
transfer
type
update

Communication Verbs

address
advertise
arbitrate
arrange
articulate
attend
author
collaborate
commit
convince
correspond
demonstrate
describe
develop
direct

discuss
divert
draft
edit
elicit
empathize
emphasize
enlist
entertain
express
facilitate
formulate
harmonize
influence
inform

inquire
interact
interpret
interview
invite
justify
lecture
listen
manipulate
market
mediate
moderate
motivate
negotiate
network

perceive
persuade
present
promote
propose
publicize
recommend
reconcile
recruit

reflect
relate
report
represent
respond
settle
show
signal
solicit

specify
speak
talk
testify
translate
visit
write

Financial Verbs

administrate
allocate
analyze
appraise
audit
balance
bargain
buy

budget
calculate
compute
develop
exchange
forecast
insure
manage

market
plan
project
purchase
research
sell
spend

Helping Verbs

accompany
adopt
advocate
aid
assess
assume
clarify
coach
collaborate
combine
counsel
demonstrate
devote
disclose
educate
effect
enlarge

ensure
execute
expand
expedite
facilitate
familiarize
fortify
guide
help
increase
involve
maintain
modify
motivate
offer
participate
protect

provide
reduce
refer
rehabilitate
reinforce
represent
retain
review
revise
sample
serve
set up
share
suggest
supply

Management Verbs

administer
allot
assign
attain
broaden
call for
chair
change
consolidate
contract
coordinate

decide
define
delegate
develop
devise
direct
eliminate
enforce
evaluate
execute
expand

focus
handle
hire
implement
improve
incorporate
increase
inspire
institute
integrate
judge

lead	produce	shape
manage	recommend	solve
mobilize	regulate	seek
motivate	resolve	specialize
narrow	restore	strengthen
organize	review	structure
overhaul	schedule	supervise
oversee	screen	terminate
plan	scrutinize	verify
prioritize	select	

Research Verbs

apply	evaluate	interview
check	examine	isolate
cite	explore	locate
clarify	extract	observe
collect	forecast	organize
compare	formulate	predict
deduce	find	read
determine	gather	research
diagnose	graph	study
discover	identify	summarize
dissect	inspect	survey
estimate	interpret	systematize

Technical Verbs

adjust	excavate	plot
advance	extinguish	produce
alter	fabricate	programme
amplify	install	remodel
assemble	make	renovate
attentuate	maintain	repair
build	map	restore
calculate	measure	rotate
compute	navigate	solve
design	obtain	synthesize
devise	operate	upgrade
engineer	overhaul	

Finally, there is a class of business words associated with negative aspects of the management process. While – hopefully – there will be few instances where we are looking to achieve a negative effect, it is worth noting some of the main negative words since often some very positive ideas can emerge from studying the negative.

Negative Verbs

Corrupt	Eliminate	Mis-interpret
Damage	Exaggerate	Obscure
Delay	Harm	Prevent
Destroy	Hide	Spin
Divert	Mis-inform	Subvert

Knowledge Search Strategies

The recent availability of on-line knowledge database resources opens up the prospect of easy access to potentially vast amounts of business and management data. To some, the amount of data available can be overwhelming. Searches built primarily on functions rather than objects allow us to take a powerful first step towards extracting the material that will be useful from that which will not.

Systematic innovation methods are built around a 'something does something to something', subject-action-object (or noun-verb-noun) template (see also Chapter 6) because it allows us to find the useful stuff. It is comparatively easy for people to hide what they are doing by using nouns that are different from the norm (as we see happening increasingly in invention disclosures – where we might find ourselves filing a claim for a wheel that doesn't use the word 'wheel'). It is very difficult, on the other hand, to disguise the function words.

The simplest, most effective search strategies, therefore, are built around the function words. If – as is frequently the case – searching on just function words provides too many hits, then the search can be qualified using the subject or action parts of what you are trying to find. Hence, if you are looking for ways to allocate funds in the most effective way, search using 'allocate funds' (and synonyms if necessary – see next section). Alternatively, if you are looking to find out who else might want the solution you already have you might search using the subject and action part of the subject-action-object template – e.g. an 'agent-based software allocates' search would locate things that agent-based software has been used to do.

2) Emerging Knowledge Search Tools

One of the big ideas from the contradiction related elements of the systematic innovation method is that the whole dynamic of evolution of systems takes place through the successive emergence and resolution of contradictions. Not so long ago, in the dark days before the Internet, the limitations on finding knowledge centred around the creation and appropriate filing of printed media. The library was the limiting contradiction. The Internet has now almost completely eliminated the limitations of the library and cost of creating and making information accessible to all. But, of course, the dynamic of evolution says that when one contradiction is resolved, another one is eventually bound to emerge. For most users of the Internet, that new contradiction has already emerged and is indeed getting more serious every day – it is the fact that although the amount of information is increasing at incredible rates, the amount of time we all have available to us to sort through all of that information is the same or reducing – Figure 16.3.

The smart companies are those ones that try and stay at least one resolved contradiction ahead of their competitors. Undoubtedly, in the world of knowledge management and surfing the stormy waves of the Internet, the smart companies are the ones that are developing solutions to this time-versus-content conflict. For some that means finding themselves a role as 'navigators' – people that will find what you want for you. For the more far-sighted others who recognize the likely temporary role of the navigator, it means finding more effective search methods. These are the things we focus our attention on in the rest of this section.

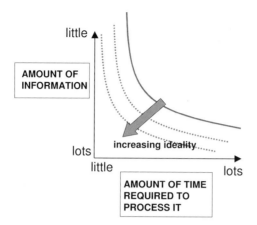

little

AMOUNT OF
INFORMATION

lots

little

increasing ideality

lots

AMOUNT OF TIME
REQUIRED TO
PROCESS IT

Figure 16.3: The Information Versus Time Conflict

There are currently four significant classes of knowledge search tools available to help managers challenge this time-versus-content conundrum:-
a) Search Engine
b) Semantic Search Tools
c) User-Defined-Context Search Tools
d) Intelligent Agent-Based Search Tools

We will explore all four in sufficient detail to permit managers to determine which level of capability is appropriate to their needs.

a) **Search Engines** – from the sea of different search engines that emerged once the Internet became established, a few giants have emerged. Among the most popular has been Google (www.google.com), an engine that very quickly built a reputation of uncannily finding what users were looking for. There is a very high likelihood that, even though engines like Google will present a user with several thousand hits, what you will need will be in the top ten or twenty. With a little practice, this already high success probability can be made even higher. Key to more effective searching on Google type engines is to understand a little about the method by which they sift through information. The first generation engines used simple searches based on strings of text. The Google generation still uses key-words, but has added the conceptually simple idea that in addition to simply finding words in text, the distance between those words is a very effective indicator or relevance. Say you are searching for motivational techniques in a service industry context, then you are likely to input a search string something like 'motivation service industry'. A first generation engine will identify documents containing these three words. A Google generation engine will do the same, but then place the documents in which the three words appear closest together – e.g. all in the same sentence – at the top of the prioritized list of hits that it creates.

b) **Semantic Search Tools** – more closely related to the systematic innovation subject-action-object knowledge structuring idea are the new generation of semantic search tools. The Goldfire/Knowledgist products from Invention Machine (Reference 16.5) are among the most widely used. These tools are built specifically on the subject-action-object concept; they will 'read' sentences and then extract all of the subject, action and object aspects of those sentences. Type in a search like 'reward staff' and point the processor at whatever knowledge source you like (usually either the Internet or a within-company electronic library) and it will not only find all the sentences in which 'rewards' (and synonyms) is the action and 'staff' (and synonyms) is the object, but will also extract the subject of those sentences. These 'subject's represent the known ways of achieving the 'reward staff' function. Current limitations of these semantic tools are that they work only on text written in English. The next generation of semantic tools (e.g CREAX 'Word-Wise' tool) is expected to operate in multiple languages.

c) **User-Defined-Context Search Tools** – as will be discussed in the next section of the chapter, the big problem with the first two search techniques is that they know nothing about the context of your search – why are you searching, what application are you looking to apply the knowledge to, what constraints you have to work within, etc. The first generation of search tools aimed at tackling the challenge of context are those constructed around pre-defined or user-defined knowledge classifications/taxonomies or ontologies. In this type of context ontology tool, the user (or someone) has to pigeonhole information into a pre-defined knowledge structure. The problem with this approach is that a piece of information rarely fits into a single category. As a result, classifications can quickly become hugely complicated and then slowly drown in their own complexity. Latest generation context tools have added a degree of adaptivity (see Reference 16.6 for example) that permits information to migrate from one pigeon-hole to another as the user changes the context in which they wish to use it. The major hurdle that needs to be overcome before this technology is likely to become an everyday as opposed to specialist tool is the need for someone to define some form of knowledge structure before the tool can begin to 'understand' what the user context might be.

d) **Intelligent Agent-Based Search Tools** – agent-based software architectures adopt a fundamentally different approach to knowledge and the matching of knowledge to context, in that they operate from bottom-up rather than top-down rules. In the most advanced systems, the search tool 'learns' about the context of a user by watching what the user does. Have an agent-based search tool watch you visit the Bradford City football club website once a day for a week and it will begin to recognize that your context involves a liking of depressingly meager forms of the game. From there, it will then begin to give particularly high priority to the findings of a different search on, say, currency exchange rates that connect to Bradford City or football. The more you visit the Bradford City page, the more the agent re-enforces the strength of the Bradford City context in which you are living. Amazon.com offers a crude version of this agent-based idea when it offers you recommendations for other books for you to buy based on what you already bought. Rather more sophisticated (and hence expensive) variants utilize Bayesian algebra to find patterns in the electronic 0s and 1s of all of the electronic information you are interested in and use this information to create context. The key advantages of agent-based tools are that they require little or no specialist knowledge (only the patience to stick with the software long enough for it to 'learn' what you like and what you don't) and that, if they use Bayesian techniques, they are also able to recognize pictures as well as text (see Reference 16.7 for example).

3) Context And Wisdom

As discussed in Chapter 14, there is a trend of discontinuous jumps relating to the use of data and knowledge – Figure 16.4. The final jump in that trend involves the shift from knowledge to wisdom. The difference between the two is not always apparent. A simple but vivid illustration of the difference under discussion here comes from the well-known expression; 'knowledge is when you know that a tomato is a fruit; wisdom is when you know not to put tomatoes in a fruit salad'.

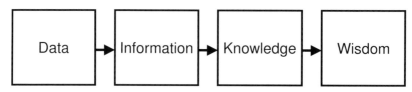

Figure 16.4: The 'Wisdom' Evolution Trend

To some extent the emerging context-based search tools described in the previous section will help to ease the transition of knowledge to deployable wisdom. Given the vagaries and complexities of humans, they are, of course, unlikely to offer a complete answer in the foreseeable future.

Which then leaves us with a problem. A discussion about 'wisdom' can take one of two extremes – it can be the subject of a few seconds discussion or a whole lifetime's research. It is not exactly clear what can be said of any value in the 'few second' route, but perhaps it is merely sufficient to re-enforce the connection between wisdom and context. Wisdom may be thought of as the successful application of knowledge; the successful application of knowledge means setting that knowledge into the specific and unique context of the situation. There are not short-cuts. Our brain will often try and convince us that there are, but it will undoubtedly be trying to fool us into ignoring an assumption or a difficult connection or something that doesn't fit with our current perception of reality. The overall systematic innovation process is in many ways designed to prevent us from allowing those short-cuts from diverting us to solutions that will ultimately be in-effective. It tries to keep the brain in an analytical 'defining' mode, for example, long after our brain has tried to tell us that it is time to get on with the 'solving' part of the process.

There is probably no good way to conclude any discussion on wisdom, never mind one this short, but a reference to one of the wisest business books ever written – The Mind Of The Strategist (Reference 16.8), now coming up to its 30th anniversary and still as conceptually relevant today as it was in 1975 when the first (Japanese) edition was printed – may serve as some kind of end:-

"Strategic success cannot be reduced to a formula, not can anyone become a strategic thinker merely be reading a book. Nevertheless, there are habits of mind and modes of thinking that can be acquired through practice to help you free the creative power of your subconscious and improve your odds of coming up with winning strategic concepts."

4) Knowledge Management

Knowledge management is big business. Almost every large organization has suffered from problems along the clichéd lines of 'if only the organization knew what the organization knows then we would be unbeatable'. The problem is undoubtedly a very serious one, with countless stories of companies spending millions re-inventing what someone in a different part of the company already invented two decades ago. There are of course no easy answers to the knowledge management problem. For a start, there are massive organizational culture issues relating to 'knowledge is power' mentalities within individuals. A single instance of a person passing on their knowledge to another person (or increasingly to a computer) and then subsequently losing their job is enough to prevent anyone else from making the same mistake for the next n years. Unless the knowledge-share-equals-job-loss correlation – whether real or imagined – is convincingly destroyed, no knowledge management structure will ever work.

Looking beyond such cultural issues, what then becomes clear is that the function-based knowledge ideas present in the systematic innovation method offer the ability to create a universally applicable knowledge framework. How universal the word 'universal' turns out to be is an issue of some doubt at this point in time, but since the whole systematic innovation philosophy is formed around the idea of making the good ideas from one person accessible to others in widely different areas, many organisations are beginning to recognize the relevance of using its trans-disciplinary structure as the foundation of their own specific internal structure. In true 'someone, somewhere already solved your problem' fashion, systematic innovation has created a structure that has so far found a logical place for every single piece of knowledge that has been studied. Systematic innovation researchers continue to test the bounds of the framework every day when they look at new patents, business innovations, laws and any other piece of 'new' thinking.

Given the framework that functionally classified databases give, the next challenge is usually one of integrating all of the know-how that exists within a company. Protection of knowledge (and wisdom) that exists within a company, but which has never been exposed outside can highlight serious issues of trust, which in turn very quickly get into the territory of company culture and recognizing the true value of every employee in an organization. There are no easy answers to these issues. Common factors of the few successful models (see the SemCo group of companies again – Reference 16.9 – to name one) include:-

i)   trust
ii)   faith in the power of self-organisation in systems once pre-requisite i) has been achieved
iii)   implicit in ii), the idea that there should be no 'knowledge management department' at the end of a knowledge management implementation. Knowledge management departments exist first and foremost to protect the interests of the knowledge management department rather than the business. They also send the clear message to everyone else that knowledge management is someone else's responsibility
iv)   the ability to forget knowledge that is no longer relevant. Corporate memory is both a good and a bad thing. The transition from good to bad occurs when managers fail to note when the context has changed and the application of a piece of knowledge no longer fits the context. Which brings us full circle back to wisdom again.

What Do I Do?

Using the knowledge part of the systematic innovation toolkit in a problem solving context involves one or more of three possibilities:

1) The 'someone, somewhere already solved your problem' idea is applicable up to a certain point. The method offers a number of strategies to assist in the search for other solutions. First among these is the recognition that function is the most important way of connecting a problem to the solutions of others.

2) More sophisticated knowledge search capabilities – some now incorporating a context-matching capability – are becoming ever more affordable. Use the second section to determine which of the four main tools are most appropriate to your needs (and budget).

3) The most difficult one; recognising and accepting that there are no short-cuts in matters of business and management problem solving, and that there is no substitute context-driven application of knowledge.

If you are looking to create a knowledge management capability within your organisation, beyond the inevitable people issues that will always tend to dominate, you could do much worse than to consider using the function-based structure offered by the systematic innovation knowledge framework.

References

1) Shapiro, E.C., 'Fad-Surfing In The Boardroom – Reclaiming The Courage To Manage In The Age Of Instant Answers', Capstone Publishing Ltd, Oxford, UK, 1998.
2) www.creax.com, Free Resources – Function Database.
3) Rivette, K., Kline, D., 'Rembrandts in the Attic: Unlocking the Hidden Value of Patents', Harvard Business School Press, 1998.
4) Systematic Innovation E-Zine, 'More Opportunities', Issue 6, July 2002.
5) www.invention-machine.com
6) www.adiuri.com
7) www.autonomy.com
8) Ohmae, K., 'The Mind Of The Strategist – The Art of Japanese Business', McGraw-Hill, 1982 (originally published in Japanese in 1975).
9) Semler, R., 'Maverick! The Success Story Behind The World's Most Unusual Workplace', Random House, 1993.

17.
Problem Solving Tools
Re-Focus/Re-Frame

"Chaos often breeds life, when order breeds habit."
Henry Brook Adams

or

"You can eat an elephant one bit at a time."
Mary Kay Ash

Sometimes there will be situations where the basic systematic innovation process fails to do what you would like it to do. Hopefully these situations will be rare. To set the level of rarity into some kind of context, this author has had occasion to need a different way of looking at things two times in the last twelve years. This chapter describes the 'different way' that has been designed to help handle those situations.

The roots of this 'different way' connect to the Soviet-originated 'Algorithm for Inventive Problem Solving', ARIZ (References 17.1-17.4). Without wishing to dwell on the history of this method, it is nevertheless worth noting that it was originally conceived as a complete start-to-finish problem definition and solution method for 'complex problems'. Attempts to use ARIZ in business situations, however, has shown that it fails to offer the necessary flexibility and ability to handle the complexities and 'fuzziness' inherent to many problem scenarios. Consequently, it is featured only indirectly in the overall systematic innovation picture. Firstly, it finds a place only here as an 'emergency back-up' alternative to the main systematic innovation process. Secondly, in the 're-focus/re-frame' mode described in this chapter, much of the original ARIZ structure has been modified.

If you use this chapter in the way that it has been configured, you will visit the re-focus/re-frame tool only on very rare occasions. It is also possible, however, that the method – like some of the various versions of ARIZ – meshes with your natural way of thinking, and as a consequence you may decide to use its structure as an alternative to the systematic innovation process. The choice, of course, is yours; as ever, the only real point of having any of the tools within the systematic innovation toolkit is to enable you to create some real solutions to real problem situations.

The chapter is divided into two main sections. The first section describes a step-by-step description of the re-focus/re-frame tool in its preferred 'emergency back-up' role within the overall systematic innovation structure. The second section then features a case study example of the process in action.

Re-Focus/Re-Frame Method Description

The re-focus/re-frame (RF^2) method starts at the point where problem solvers have already made an attempt to work through the various situation definition steps of the systematic innovation process. That is, they have filled in the problem explorer (Chapter 5), constructed a function and attribute analysis (Chapter 6), performed some kind of assessment of the maturity of the situation under consideration (Chapter 7), and, where appropriate, had a look at the Ideal Final Result (Chapter 8) and Perception Mapping (Chapter 9) tools. If the problem solver, having done those things, finds that they are in the position where they don't know what to do next, then this RF^2 chapter is the place they will find themselves.

The following series of steps start from that point. The steps have been designed to follow a logical sequence that effectively causes the user to re-trace their steps through the already completed situation definition part of the process, but this time with a somewhat shifted perspective. The following text describes that sequence:

a) Define the 'mini-problem'.

From the already drawn functional and attribute analysis model of the system under consideration, identify a single *key* harmful, insufficient or excessive functional relationship – i.e. the one that caused us to have drawn the FAA in the first place; the one that, if it wasn't there any more, you would consider the problem to have been solved? This can be a difficult process, and to be honest, requires more than a little faith that solving the problem concerning this relationship will also solve some of the other adverse relationships present in the system. A good principle to keep in mind is that it should be something that is close to the Main Useful Function (MUF) of the overall system under evaluation – the section on functional hierarchies in Chapter 6 should suggest to us that the MUF delivering parts of the system would still be around when everything else has eventually evolved away.

b) Define the Problem Space, Time and Interface Scope

For the selected key problem functional relationship selected in the previous step, identify the operational space, operational interval and operational interfaces. These are, respectively, the relevant physical space around the problem, the relevant time space around the problem, and the relevant interfaces around the problem. In the case of the operational space, it is often useful to make drawings of the problem, and then to draw an enclosing dotted line to denote what is in and what is outside of the conflict zone. It is helpful to focus this space as closely to the problem relationship as possible, so trying to make it as small as possible is a good objective – it could, for example, be an individual element or a single relationship between two persons within an organisation. For the operational interval, the task is similar in that the aim is to draw a time envelope defining the boundaries of when we do and don't have the problem. Of particular interest are the time when the problem is occurring (to define one boundary of our time-window) and the time immediately *before* the problem occurs, or (less likely, but by no means impossible) immediately after it has disappeared. As with the operational space, the objective is to define these boundaries as close together as possible in order to try and define the tightest possible focus for the problem. The same applies when we define the operational interfaces. Operational interfaces are all of those connections that exist across the boundaries defined by the operational space and time. Interfaces, as elsewhere in the systematic innovation methodology, are all of the connections and relationships that exist 'between the things' inside a system. Taken together, the operational space, time and interfaces define the boundaries within which the problem is observed to exist.

c) Define a Conflict Pair

Keeping our thinking within the operational space, time and interface from the previous step, think about the negative functional relationship under evaluation and, looking at the system element *from* which the relationship arrow leaves, identify the useful thing(s) that this element delivers. If there are multiple other things (positive or negative) that this element delivers, pick the one closest to the MUF of the system. The selected useful function plus the previously selected negative functional relationship together define a conflict pair – in that you want the useful thing, but in the process of obtaining that, you also get the negative thing. Record what this conflict pair is. If there are insufficient functional arrows leaving the component in question to formulate a conflict, check the attributes of the element under consideration in order to establish which of them is involved in producing a conflict. In order to check that whatever conflict derived is a true conflict, think about what happens to the useful function at the time (from step b) above) immediately before or after the time the conflict occurs – i.e. immediately outside the defined operational interval; if the useful function has either become insufficient, excessive or has disappeared altogether, then it is safe to assume that your chosen positive and negative pair (or an attribute) are in conflict with one another.

d) Define the Contradiction

Select one of the pair of positive and negative functional relationships from the previous step and use this as the basis for defining a contradiction. Although there is no general rule dictating which of the two relationships to use during this process, it is more usual to configure the contradiction around the negative relationship – if only because the idea of 'wanting the MUF and not wanting the MUF' or rather the 'not wanting' part of the contradiction, is often meaningless. Use the already defined operational space, time and interface to explore the boundaries of when or where you do and don't want the different requirements of the chosen contradiction parameter. Record the formulated contradiction in the form '*I want condition A at* (define space, time or interface where you want condition A), *and I want condition –A at* (define space, time or interface where you want condition – A)'. –A is taken to represent the opposite function to A – for example if A='high interest rate', then –A='low interest rate'. (See Chapter 12 if you need more help in formulating and converting between conflicts and contradictions.)

e) Define the Ideal Final Result Outcome

Thinking about the contradiction defined in the previous step, define the Ideal Final Result (IFR) outcome to this contradiction. This should take the form of a statement like '*I achieve condition A and condition –A without complicating the system*'.

f) Define The X-Element

The x-element may at first sight appear to be a somewhat strange concept. Its basic function is to help us to break out of psychological inertia. The x-element should be viewed as 'something' that is magically able to come along and solve our problem. At this point in the process, we are asked to put all preconceptions about what is and isn't physically possible on one side when thinking about the x-element. In effect, what we are doing is using the concept as a way of defining the specification for what it is we would like this magic element to achieve. The definition of the x-element should be closely tied to the negative functional relationship defined in a) and contradiction defined in step d). Record the resulting specification for the x-element in a form something like; '*the x-element is able to eliminate the harmful function B and/or to solve the contradiction, C*'.

g) Analysis of Resources

Having defined conceptually what the x-element is required to do, the next step in the process involves a search to establish whether there is something already in or around the system capable of fulfilling the specification defined in the previous step. The system resources should previously have been recorded during the problem explorer part of the overall systematic innovation process detailed in Chapter 5. The slight difference in the way we now use those resources we have identified, is that we are now looking to compare them to the specification outlined in step f). There are various ways in which to conduct this comparative x-element/resource search. The way recommended here is to begin the search within the operational space, time and interface boundaries, and to move gradually beyond these boundaries to look at, next, things already in the system, and then things we might easily add to the system – see the list of 'easily available' resources checklist from Chapter 15. The generally recommended search strategy is illustrated in Figure 17.1. If we *can* find a resource matching the x-element specification, chances are we have solved the problem.

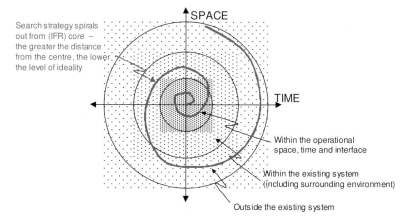

Figure 17.1 X-Element/Resource Match Search Strategy
(Note: the IFR defined in step e) defines the minimum disruption point at the centre of the circle)

h) Modification of Resources

This step is similar to the preceding one, but takes things a step further by prompting the problem solver to think harder about the resources issue. This step assumes that a suitable resource has not been identified in the previous step. The new questions provoked in this 'modification' step are:-

i) would it be possible to reproduce the specification of the x-element by *modifying* one of the things already in the system?

ii) would it be possible to reproduce the specification of the x-element by *combining* two or more of the things already in the system?

As with the preceding step, the most logical sequence of events here involves starting within the operational space, time and interface and gradually working outwards to other system elements and then things we could add to the system. Likewise, any of the evolutionary steps illustrated in the trends of evolution when coupled with the idea of untapped evolutionary potential (Chapter 14) also suggest the presence of resources. As in the previous step, if we can find a modified resource matching the x-element specification, chances are we have solved the problem

i) Use Principles for Eliminating Contradictions

Apply the strategies described in Chapter 12 for the elimination of contradictions on the contradiction defined during step d).

j) Use Principles for Eliminating Conflicts
Apply the strategies described in Chapter 11 for the elimination of conflicts on the conflict pair defined during step c).

k) Use Knowledge
Examine the useful function in contradiction with the negative functional relationship defined in step a) and examine the possibility of using existing knowledge from other places (Chapter 16) in order to establish whether there are other ways of delivering that useful function that may avoid the generation of the negative effect.

l) No Solution?
If no solution has been obtained by this stage, the most pragmatic strategy to adopt is to return to either one of the options emerging from the preceding steps (e.g. picking the second of the two contradictions defined in step d)) or to go back to the original FAA model and identifying an alternative negative functional relationship on which to base the RF^2 analysis. Repeat the steps a) to k) for the new mini-problem arising from the newly selected alternative negative function.

Summary

In several senses, the RF^2 tool presented here represents 'just' another way of linking together some of the steps already contained within the bigger systematic innovation process. It differs in several minor (introduction of x-element, combination of resources) and one key respect, however. The key difference builds from the underlying assumption within RF^2 that we wish to solve the problem with the *minimum level of disruption* to the system (as opposed to the systematic innovation process where we use the constraints defined in the initial problem explorer to drive the direction and strategy). A useful image to keep in mind as you progress through the various RF^2 steps is the convergent-divergent picture illustrated in Figure 17.2.

The basic idea is that we use the process to gradually define a progressively more exacting problem – the extreme limits of which being our definition of the Ideal Final Result – and then, as we shift into the solution part of the process we migrate away from this ideal only when we are unable to obtain solutions at or close to that ideal definition.

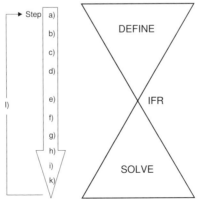

Figure 17.2 Overall Convergent-Divergent Structure of RF^2 Process

One final point regarding the mechanics of the Re-Focus-Re-Frame tool; our brains tend to want us to stop going through the process once we hit upon a solution that looks promising. It is always useful to avoid this tendency and carry on with subsequent steps, in the same way that it is useful to cycle more than one time around the systematic innovation process.

RF^2 – Case Study Example

If systematic innovation is in large part about eliminating contradictions, one the whole community of experts has thus far failed to solve involves 'good' case study examples of ARIZ in action. The roots of the contradiction lie in its role as a tool to help tackle complex problems; complex problems tend to require masses of detail that cause the reader to focus on the problem rather than the process, while simple problems focusing on the process tend to be frustrating because it very quickly becomes apparent that you don't need ARIZ to tackle it. In other words, we would like a case study that is both complex and not complex. We will examine a problem involving an ethical dilemma. Which probably veers towards the complex end of the spectrum.

The initial problem scenario involves a company involved in a large sale to a customer in a country they have not dealt with before. The sale is an important one because the company's business is in the middle of a down-wave and without it, there is a strong likelihood that redundancies will have to be made. The sale has been the result of a lengthy competition with several other potential vendors. During the latter part of the sales process, it becomes apparent that the third party agent responsible for completing the sale with the customer is beginning to hinder the process. When things eventually come to a head, it becomes clear that even though the agent is being paid for his services by the customer, he wishes to receive an additional sum from the company. This sum represents 10% of the total value of the sale. Financially, the company has established that, although this figure is high, it alone should not be a cause to halt the sale. Upon investigation, the company learns that although the commission demand is not legal in the country of the sale, it is something that happens on a regular basis; in fact it seems that not only is the practice rife, but the government turns a blind eye to it. Covert questioning reveals that there are no known cases of the government intervening or taking action when the law is broken. As the delay drags on, the agent begins to suggest that he may have to encourage the customer to re-open the competition. This threat coupled with the increasingly precarious financial situation of the company forces the board to make a decision about whether to pay the 'commission' or risk losing the business. The company has a clear ethical policy relating to the types of situation it now faces. That policy states that no illegal payments of any kind are acceptable. The plight of the company coupled with the knowledge that it is unlikely that the payment will ever become public knowledge makes it tempting to simply make the payment and close the deal. At the decision-making board meeting, the personnel director displays his outrage that anyone could even make the suggestion that the company should ignore a clear legal and ethical policy. The personnel director stands up and states openly to the other directors that he will consider it his duty to 'go public' with the information if the payment is allowed to happen. The managing director calls for a time-out, suggesting that everyone re-convenes the following morning to discuss the matter again and make a decision in a less charged atmosphere.

Here then is the point at which we begin the RF^2 analysis in an attempt to help the managing director make the most appropriate decision.

Referring to the steps detailed in the previous section, we should then proceed through this problem as follows:-

a) **Define the mini-problem** – the first step demands that we have already constructed some form of function analysis of the initial situation. The analysis for this problem looks like the model illustrated in Figure 17.3 below:

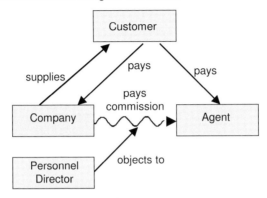

Figure 17.3: Initial Situation In Buyer's Commission Ethics Problem

The most appropriate 'mini-problem' in this situation is the 'pays commission' link between the company and the agent since this is the issue that provoked the concern at the board meeting and the objections of the personnel director.

b) **Define the Problem Scope** – here the requirement is to define the operational space, time and interfaces. We will define the operational space as that space containing each of the elements drawn within Figure 17.3. The 'company' specifically involves all of the directors involved in the board meeting. The operational space also needs to include the home country of the customer and agent since this is the location where the commission payments are deemed illegal.

With regard to the operational interval we should be looking for a time when a conflict occurs and the time immediately before it occurs. The time when a conflict occurs would be precisely the moment that a decision to pay the agent a commission is made. The managing director has stated his intention to make the decision the following morning. He need not do this of course; in which case the operational interval will expand up to the point at which the company financial situation reaches the critical state. The company expects that, without the sale, they will have to begin making redundancies within the next two months. This then defines the true operational interval.

The operational interfaces are again represented in Figure 17.3. The main interactions of concern involve the relationship with the agent and the personnel director's threat to reveal any illegal transaction.

c) **Define a Conflict Pair** – in order to identify a conflict pair we need to examine the functional space around the problem commission payment. The essence of the problem as observed from Figure 17.3 is that the company needs to make the sale to the customer, but does not want to make a commission payment that contravenes its legal and ethical policies. This combination defines our conflict pair.

d) Define the Contradiction – the most appropriate half of the conflict pair from above to use as the foundation for formulating a contradiction relates to the commission payment. This is so because there is little value in formulating a contradiction focused on 'making the sale and not making the sale' – since not making the sale is not an option that we would realistically wish to contemplate. The contradiction 'we don't want to pay the commission and we might have to pay the commission' is thus the one that we will formulate here. We don't want to pay the commission in this case because it is illegal and against our policies, and we might have to pay it in order to ensure the sale. Figure 17.4 illustrates the relationship between conflict pair and this contradiction according to the convention described in Chapter 12.

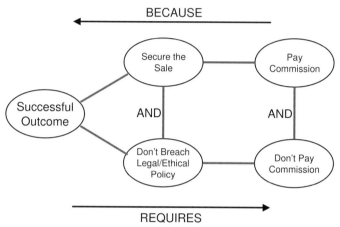

Figure 17.4: Conflict Pair And Contradiction Relationship

e) Define the Ideal Final Result Outcome - '*The company 'pays the commission and doesn't pay the commission' without complicating the system'*.

f) Define The X-Element – '*the x-element is able to eliminate the harmful illegal commission payment and/or to solve the contradiction, 'pay the commission and don't pay the commission'*.

g) Analysis of Resources – here we should refer to the 9-Windows based list of resources that we should have compiled during the problem explorer part of the systematic innovation process that preceded our entry into the RF^2 tool. We will not seek to duplicate such a list, merely reproduce some of the resources identified that might be relevant to the problem at hand (a complete analysis would examine all of them – here we are simply picking out a few that appear to have some similarities to the specification of the x-element from the previous step). More important than completeness for the purposes of this case, is the process adopted; in keeping with the search direction progressing outward from the operational space, time and interface as illustrated in Figure 17.1, we have compiled a table comprising the three different search spaces. The table has also been divided into two data columns – the first for listing resources as identified in the problem explorer, and the second emerging from a trends of evolution based 'evolutionary potential' analysis.

Search Space/Time	Resources (from Problem Explorer)	Evolutionary Potential Resources (from Trends of Evolution)
Inside the operational space, interval and interface	• interim payments • delayed payment to agent • shareholders • employees • relationships between directors • relationship between agent and customer • ethical policy • 'time-out' • warranty periods	• better two-way dialogue with agent (find out what purposes he wants his commission for) • better dialogue with customer (are they happy with what the agent is doing?) • periodic payments/installments to agent • personal esteem of agent • need for transparency • local knowledge
Within the overall system	• in-country authorities • authorities in the company's own country • other companies in the competition • other customers • intangibles – trade-name, brand • non-financial rewards	• switch to service business model • other 'experience' possibilities • shift in level of 'convenience' to customer and/or agent • additional skills/knowledge of agent • phased contract payments • in-kind offerings to customer (IP, design assistance, etc)
Outside the system	• leads in other countries that the agent could be given • press/media • third-party conflict resolution negotiators • other agents • neighbouring countries • social contributions and sponsorships • inter-cultural training • possible future changes in the law • possible future changes in currency exchange rate	• possible 'complementor' organizations • set up a new company in the customer country

Again, the point of the case-study is to focus on process, but nevertheless, hopefully it should be possible to see that the table describes several things that are not currently being utilized by the directors involved in the problem.

h) Modification of Resources – the next step involves the re-examination of the resources identified in the previous step in the context of their possible beneficial effect on the insufficient lift problem when either modified or used in combination. Again we are more interested in process than actual solutions, but below are some examples of how combining resources may result in synergistic benefits for the problem at hand:-

  o reduce the amount to be paid by the customer by the amount of the customer (possibly justifying the decrease by offering a shift in terms and conditions) and allowing the customer to increase their payment to the agent
  o re-phase rather than reduce the amount to be paid by the customer
  o pay the agent for alternative services (e.g. educating the company on cultural issues)

433

- o recruit the agent
- o pay the commission amount to a different party nominated by the agent (e.g. a charity, education institute, etc)
- o pay the commission to the agent in a country where the arrangement is not illegal
- o switch to service sales model and use the agent to somehow facilitate the delivery of that service – hence allowing him to be paid for services that are legal
- o switch to a service model that effectively means the customer is made no purchase – and hence offers the potential that neither company nor customer has to pay the agent anything
- o inform the customer about the company's ethical policy (which may well enhance the reputation of the company in the customer's eyes) and ask for their thoughts on how a legal transaction might be paid
- o offer agent non-financial reward – making connections to other companies that might wish to do business in his country for example
- o make a commitment but delay payment to agent until legal position becomes clear
- o make use of the press/media to highlight the actions of the agent (this needs to be done without the potential to cause any embarrassment to the customer)

i) Use Principles for Eliminating Contradictions – taking the 'pay the commission and don't pay the commission' contradiction as a start point, the contradiction solution strategies described in Chapter 12 can be used to identify solution possibilities. Using the separation in space, time and condition questions, it should be possible to find conceptual solutions in all three directions:

Separation in space – pay the commission in a different country; 'nest' the commission inside the payments expected from the customer; segment the sale so that the agent only gets paid (by both company and customer) for a much smaller chunk of the overall sale; make a legal payment to a third party intermediary (e.g. in-country education establishment) who may then pay the agent in either cash or kind.

Separation in time – since there is an urgent need to secure the sale and to begin receiving revenues, offer the customer some time-phased benefit to go ahead with the sale now; pay the agent 'under duress' and seek to have the money returned (possibly by legal action) in the future; make a legal payment of some description to the agent now, and tie subsequent payments to changes in the law or other conditions.

Separation on condition – pay the agent in shares or other non-cash means; pay the agent for services other than the commission; pay the commission to the customer and allow them to decide what to do with the amount; use the inappropriate agent demands as a means to demonstrate to the customer that they may have a legitimate excuse to not pay him the fees that they owe him – i.e. the customer benefits financially.

All three definitions should, in combination with the appropriate Inventive Principles (see Table 12.1), enable us to generate several useful solution directions. The fourth contradiction elimination strategy – transitioning to an alternative system – should likewise generate several solution opportunities:

- o go to the press with the story and offer to pay the commission to any in-country charitable cause that the customer nominates – possibly presenting the matter in such a way that the customer emerges from the story with a better public profile and the illegal commission system becomes exposed. At the very least, this strategy would make it very difficult for competitors to step in to the picture
- o ask the customer to pay the agent's additional demands and see how they react
- o find potential 'complementor' companies who may also have something to contribute to the requirements of the customer and connect these to the agent so that he gets paid (legally) by arranging purchases from such new sources
- o thinking about the 'other way around' Principle, it appears clear that the agent is in the wrong in this situation. Now that he has made the commission demand, it has inevitably become very difficult for him to retract it without causing an adverse effect on his pride

and esteem. Hence find a way of making the agent feel good about *not* accepting the commission – e.g. donation to charitable cause credited to the agent; obtain public awareness of the moral actions of an agent unwilling to abuse the law; recommendations to other potential sellers of an agent of 'high ethical standing'; name some kind of (publicly known) ethics award to the agent – this in turn will ensure that he will get more business in the future, etc.

j) Use Principles for Eliminating Conflicts – in order to identify how others in the same position as the company have solved similar problems, the conflict pair defined in step c) needs to be translated into a pair of parameters featured in the Business Conflict Matrix featured in Chapter 11. A good match to the 'make the sale' and 'don't breach legal/ethical policy' pair is illustrated in Figure 17.5.

Parameter We Want to Improve – Customer Revenue/Demand/ Feedback
:

List of Principles relevant to each specific worsening parameter:
:

24	Harmful Factors Affecting System	39 3 5 17 26 35

Figure 17.5: Conflict Pair Mapped Onto Business Conflict Matrix

As soon as this pair has been identified, the Matrix suggests the Inventive Principles most likely to help generate win-win solutions. The recommended Principles for this case are illustrated in the figure. From these, the following ideas might appear:

- o   add neutral third party to the negotiation (e.g. government arbitration service)
- o   establish more detailed knowledge of in-country law in order to identify legal ways to pay the agent – e.g. local rather than national-level regulations
- o   somehow customize the offering to the customer in order to make the sale uniquely valuable to them and seal advantages that competitors will not be able to match
- o   personalize the sale by offering to position someone from the company inside the customer for a while to ensure smoothest possible delivery/integration process
- o   employ local banks to manage the transactions – in which case the decision to make the illegal payment to the agent shifts to entities inside the customer country
- o   employ the services of a well-known public figure within the country to progress the sale and emphasise local benefits
- o   personalize the offering to the customer and bridge the geographic gap through virtual communication means – e.g. dual language project management intranet (again with the idea of making the offering to the customer good enough that they will not want to go elsewhere); possibly employ the legal services of the agent to create the virtual capability (and license him to expand the idea to other of his clients – hence giving him additional revenue earning potential)

k) Use Knowledge – here our search needs to clearly focus on the local knowledge that is lacking within the company; what are the precedents and implications of the agents actions; press stories on corruption; local or national action groups fighting against corruption; politicians standing on anti-corruption platforms; sympathetic media; local celebrities; charitable causes that the customer has sponsored in the past; shareholders of the customer company (to solicit their views on corrupt practices); local causes of interest to the customer; hobbies and passions of the key customer personnel and their families; ethical policies of the customer; other clients of the agent (any common-interest groups?); hobbies and interests of the agent.; etc. (The principle aim here is to identify those unique-to-situation resources that may be able to offer additional insight into solving the problem in a win-win way.)

l) No Solution? – even though we have been focusing on process rather than generating actual solutions to the illegal commission payment problem, it appears evident that a number of conceptual solution opportunities have been generated using the RF^2 tool. If, on the other hand, we had failed to generate any such solutions, step l) of the process would return us to previous steps in order to force exploration of other problem definition opportunities (for example in step b) we identified a number of possible operational interfaces and chose to pick one; step l) would send us back to try the discarded opportunities – for example focusing more on the personnel director aspect of the situation).

Final Point – 'The Third Way'

A general point that arises out of this very specific RF^2 example is the manner in which it forces people to leave the (traditional) binary 'either/or' mentality approach to problems. If your brain was operating in the same way as the large majority of others after you read the introduction to this case study, it is highly likely that you saw the problem exactly as the managing director did – a simple black and white choice of pay the commission to secure the sale or don't pay the commission and lose the sale. What the systematic innovation method in general and the RF^2, conflict elimination and contradiction elimination tools suggest more specifically is that there is always a 'third way' alternative. This way is the one that delivers something other than the either/or choice. Specifically it is aimed at delivering a solution in which both sides of the either/or choice are achieved. The 'third way' idea has been dismissed in many management circles as 'pie-in-the-sky' or a value-less abstraction. Systematic innovation makes the 'third way' into a practical and systematically achievable reality.

What Do I Do?

If you are looking to use the Re-Focus/Re-Frame process described here, follow the steps a) to l) and repeat as necessary until you have achieved a clearer view of what your problem actually is and have (hopefully) generated some good solutions.

It often happens that going through some of the definition steps within RF^2 clarifies the problem situation to an extent that it becomes possible to re-visit the systematic innovation 'Select' step (Chapter 10) and be guided by that in terms of which solve tools to be used. The key to recognising that this has happened is the (usually sudden) dawning of the 'its obvious, why didn't I think of that before?' moment.

References

1) Altshuller, G., 'To Find An Idea', Nauka, Moscow, 1985 (in Russian)
2) Salamatov, Y., 'TRIZ: The Right Solution at the Right Time', Insytec, The Netherlands, 1999.
3) Ikovenko, S., 'Algorithm for Inventive Problem Solving', tutorial session at TRIZCON2000, Nashua, NH, April 2000.
4) Zlotin, B., Zusman, A., 'ARIZ on the Move', TRIZ Journal, March 1999.

18.
Problem Solving Tools
Trimming

"One company, one strategy, one message."
Ken Olsen

or

*"Our dream... is a boundaryless company... where we knock down the walls that
separate us from each other on the inside and from our key constituencies
on the outside."*
Jack Welch

Trimming is one of the conceptually more simple of the systematic innovation tools. It has links to the 'Trimming' trend described in Chapter 14. The trend describes how systems eventually evolve to contain progressively fewer and fewer elements, whilst simultaneously managing to maintain (or in some instances increase) functionality. The trend also contains a note of caution that sometimes in the evolution of a system it is correct to 'trim' elements, while at other times it is not possible. Figure 18.1 describes the correlation between complexity and position on the s-curve of the system. This examination of the 'trimming' tool here, then, considers itself only in those times in the evolution of a system where a reduction in the number of elements in a system is a viable option.

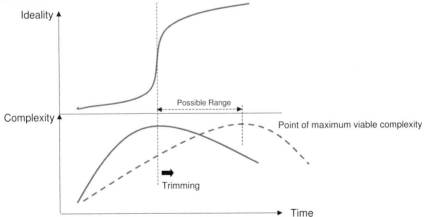

Figure 18.1: Trimming Possibilities versus System Maturity

The chapter is divided into three main sections. In the first section, we will describe the basic rules of the Trimming tool and the system improvement solution generation suggestions that it offers. The second section of the chapter then goes on to examine some of the dynamics of system evolution and the impact they should have on the way in which we interpret and deploy those basic rules. The third and final section then provides two simple case study examples of 'trimming' in action.

1) Trimming Tool

The Trimming tool should ideally have a completed function and attribute analysis model (Chapter 6) as its start point. Some might argue that the simple trimming provocation 'how could the system work if element X was trimmed?' is a far simpler start point – and undoubtedly it is, but unfortunately it is a simplification than filters-out rather than distills useful data, and consequently often leads to a variety of downstream problems. As far as this book is concerned, the only way you will be directed by the systematic innovation process into this Trimming chapter is after a function model has been constructed.

Once the FAA model exists, the underlying principles of the Trimming tool are then very simple. The main objective is to eliminate excess elements from a system. We need to decide which elements are potential candidates for trimming, and in what order we should examine them, but first it is useful to examine the provocations contained in the tool to start the process. The crucial first Trimming provocation is

Why don't we eliminate this element?

Essentially, then, we have a series of Trimming questions that we can use to determine whether or not an element we have selected as a possible candidate for trimming can *actually* be removed. The questions will vary slightly depending on whether the 'element' we are considering is physical (a department, say, or a product, a role, a job) or a time-based process step. We will examine the questions for trimming process steps shortly. In the meantime, the questions we can use to consider trimming physical entities are illustrated in Figure 18.2 below.

> Do we need the useful function(s) performed by this element?
> Can one of the other elements in the system perform the useful function(s) instead?
> Could we modify one of the other elements to perform the useful function(s)?
> Is there an element or resource around the system that can perform the function(s)?
> Is there an element or resource around the system that could be modified to perform the function?
> Can we perform the function(s) by combining other elements and resources?

Figure 18.2: Trimming Questions For Physical Entities

The list in the figure is designed as a top-down sequence. Hence any element that we are contemplating trimming from a system should be compared against each question in turn, starting with the question at the top of the list. At any point on the list when we achieve a positive answer then we know we have established the potential to trim the element under consideration. The sequence of the list is important. If we can trim an element on the basis of the first question this will tend to give a more ideal solution than one obtained from the second question, which in turn will be more ideal than a solution generated from the third question, and so on. Let us have a look at each of them in turn, starting at the top of the list:

Do We Need The Function(s)? An important first question. If we are looking to eliminate a particular element, **all** of the useful functional connections between that element or its attributes and other elements or their attributes (i.e. all of the 'useful' arrows pointing out of the component – see Figure 18.3) will disappear. The question is about establishing whether those useful functions are actually required.

Note how it is only outgoing arrows on useful functions that we are required to question. We don't mind if outgoing arrows representing harmful functions disappear (these are probably among the things that are prompting us to consider trimming the component in the first place!), and likewise, we don't mind if the incoming arrows disappear as these are functions that exist only because the element we are looking to trim does – in many instances in fact, they are only present because the element functions inadequately without them.

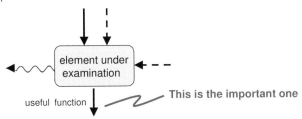

Figure 18.3: Useful Outgoing Functions Will Determine Whether We Can Trim An Element

An important side issue here is ensuring that there are no other useful things that an element is performing in a system. In part the answer to this question depends on how rigorously we have defined the FAA model. There are however reasons other than the purely functional that will determine whether an element can be trimmed without causing negative side effects. The most common of these reasons is that we trim an element only to find afterwards that it compromises our ability to adapt to changes in circumstances that might occur in the future. The only sure way to establish whether this will be an issue is to consider the trimmed system in the context of a future scenario containing considerably more uncertainty, and ask 'does the trimmed element help me to manage this uncertainty any better?'

Can One Of The Other Elements Perform The Function Instead? Here we are explicitly looking at the other elements already included in the FAA model to see if they are able to perform the useful function(s) that we would lose if the element under consideration were to be trimmed. The implicit assumption here is that we have determined from the first question that we *do* want the function. If the FAA model has been drawn in a hierarchical manner (see Chapter 6, section 6a), the search for something else in the system to deliver the function should start from the elements most closely connected to the trimmed part, and work gradually away to the extremes of the model. Experience suggests that, if an answer exists, it will tend to be found at a position higher up the hierarchy, but this should not be considered as an absolute rule.

Could We Modify One Of The Other Elements To Perform The Useful Function(s)? – if it not possible to use one of the other elements in its current state, this third question asks us to consider the possibility that we might be able to modify one so that it will become able to perform the functions we are interested in.

As suggested by Figure 18.4, there is a strong connection with the evolution potential part (Chapter 14) of the systematic innovation toolkit. In the figure, element 'D' is a candidate for trimming. If it transpires that none of the other elements are capable of performing the useful functions of D in their current form, then we may examine their evolutionary state in order to see what sorts of modification potential they may possess. The radar plots give a good indication as to which of the surrounding elements have the most potential to evolve to fulfil the desired functions. While we are thinking about modifying existing elements, it is also useful to explore whether there is something in the attributes of one of the other elements that might make it able to perform the required function(s).

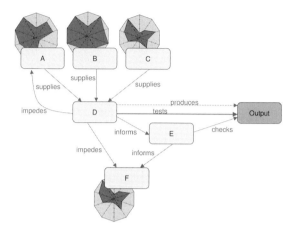

Figure 18.4: Evolution Potential Radar Plots For Elements In FAA Model

Is There An Element Or Resource Around The System That Can Perform The Function(s)? In several senses, this is similar to the second question, but, importantly, it extends that question to look beyond just the other elements drawn on the FAA model. In the terms of our definitions of what resources are (see Chapter 15 and the resources section in the Problem/Opportunity Explorer in Chapter 5), this question provides two new opportunities to identify something already in the system that may be able to help deliver the function(s) we require to have performed:

a) Thinking about the resources identified during the Problem/Opportunity Explorer analysis, is there an element or resource in that list that can be used?

b) Thinking more generally about resources, do the resource check-lists detailed in Chapter 15 suggest the presence of anything that may be able to deliver the required useful functions? Pay particular attention to the category of 'low-cost resources'. This question is more one of 'substitution' than 'trimming', but if the element we are looking to eliminate can be replaced by a cheaper alternative, then at the very least we will have acquired the opportunity to trim cost.

Is There An Element Or Resource Around The System That Could Be Modified To Perform The Function(s)? This question takes the previous one a step further towards looking at the untapped evolutionary potential in elements or resources outside to see if using any of it can help deliver the function. In other words, if we evolve something along one or more of their unused trend jumps, could it then perform the function we require?

Can I Perform The Function(s) By Combining Other Elements And Resources? deliberately at the bottom of the priority list, this question requires us to look at the possibilities generated in the previous four questions to see if anything there can be combined in order to deliver the functionality that we require. 'Combination' in this context may be between two or more existing elements, or an existing element plus outside resource, or two or more outside resources. By the time we have reached this far down the list of questions, the possibilities for successful trimming have reduced substantially, and we will have to conduct some significant creative thinking if we are to achieve a valid combination that both delivers the required function *and* avoids compromising the system in other ways.

Time-Based Process Steps

The above questions need to be modified slightly in situations where the system under evaluation is process based. In these situations, while we might well have drawn FAA models for each of the different stages of the process, it is useful when thinking about Trimming to establish whether whole process steps can be trimmed. Conceptually, the basic questions are the same as before. The only difference is that the context needs to be shifted slightly away from physical entities towards the process steps we are looking to trim. Figure 18.5 lists the questions we should work through when we are considering whether a process step can be trimmed from a system.

> Do we need the useful function(s) performed by this process step?
>
> Can one of the other steps in the process perform the useful function(s) instead?
>
> Could we modify one of the other existing process steps to perform the useful function(s)?
>
> Can we introduce a new, simpler, process step that can perform the function(s)?
>
> Can we modify a process step from a different existing system to perform the function?
>
> Can we perform the function(s) by combining other process steps?

Figure 18.5: Trimming Questions For Process Systems

The details of how we interpret and deploy these questions are exactly the same as was described for the earlier physical entity trimming section. We will see the questions in action in the case study in the final section of the chapter.

Before that, we need to explore the guidelines that will help us to decide which elements – whether physical or process based – we should seek to trim from a system and in which sequence:

Trimming Sequence

The Select part of the systematic innovation process (Chapter 10) provides guidelines on when trimming will be used, but unfortunately it is not able to help us determine *which* specific elements should be trimmed or in which specific order. Unfortunately, the rules that could help us to answer this question – if indeed they exist – are not fully understood and mapped at this point in time. At least not in any generic sense. What can be determined, however, is that there are useful guidelines that do appear to be generically applicable. We examine four in particular here:

1) Those elements with the highest number of harmful, excessive and inadequate functions connected to them are a prime candidate for trimming. This is especially so where the negative function arrow directions are pointing towards the element (i.e. where the element is the *object* of a functional relationship).

2) Those elements with the highest relative value (usually financial) offer the biggest trimming benefit opportunities and should be given a higher priority over lower value entities or process steps. This guideline is about Pareto analysis and focusing our creative efforts on those places where we are going to achieve the biggest benefit per unit of effort expended.

3) Those elements that sit highest up the functional hierarchy in a system likewise offer the highest potential prize if they can be successfully trimmed.

4) Related to this third question, elements that deliver the smallest number of useful functions – especially when they are functions low down the hierarchy – should also be a prime candidate for trimming.

The relative priority of these four guidelines will be dependent on the specific circumstances surrounding a given problem. The case study examples at the end of the chapter illustrate typical strategies. Before those case studies, however, it is prudent to explore some of the generic dynamics of system evolution and examine the impact they should have on the way in which we interpret and deploy the basic Trimming rules:

2) Trimming – The Bigger Picture

In this section we explore three aspects of the Trimming story relating to higher level phenomena that will influence when we can and cannot contemplate using the tool:-
   a) function capture
   b) viable system tests
   c) managing situations where elements are functionally coupled

a) Function Capturing

The biggest single factor affecting the success or otherwise of a trimming action is functionality. Specifically it is about knowing that **all** of the functions present in a system are present and recorded. Unfortunately there are no hard and fast guidelines to help in this task; there are simply too many possibilities. The only real 'secret', therefore, is that the function and attribute analysis has been comprehensive. It should also, preferably, have been validated by more than one person.

The simplest and most effective strategy to help ensure that we have successfully captured all of the functions delivered by an element is to use the 9-Windows tool. The tool is intended to be kept in mind throughout our application of systematic innovation methods, but here is a useful place to remind ourselves to use it to perform a specific checking task. As suggested in Figure 18.6, the tool can give us a number of test questions designed to help identify any functional connections that may be missing from our FAA analysis.

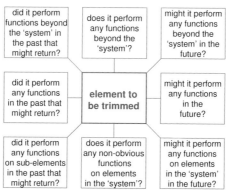

Figure 18.6: 9-Windows Tool Function Capture Completeness Questions

442

The general point from this first trimming rule, then, is make absolutely sure you have recorded all of the useful function arrows pointing away from the element you are aiming to trim. The 9-Windows concept is designed to help you to make sure that 'all' really does mean 'all'.

b) Viable System Model

There has been considerable work done over the years to better understand the workings of organizations. Much over-looked in recent times has been the work done on cybernetics by Stafford Beer and colleagues starting during the 1960s and 1970s (Reference 18.1). Beer was particularly concerned with establishing the fundamentally necessary elements that would determine whether an organisation was 'viable' or not.

The resulting 'Viable System Model' (VSM) (Reference 18.2) describes the necessary conditions for system viability, concluding that there are five; policy, intelligence, implementation, control and co-ordination. We examine each of them briefly here in order to identify possible connections with the Trimming tool and our desire to establish whether an element can be successfully trimmed from a system or not.

Implementation – defined as the parts of the system responsible for the conducting of primary activities. Those responsible, in other words, for producing the products or services implied by the organization's identity. A second of Beer's key ideas is that the Viable System Model operates recursively, and that a company offers products and services through the combined actions of different levels of 'viable systems'. Generally speaking, although the level of recursion in any given organisation can be taken to the level of an individual, it is more likely to stop unfolding a structure at the complete work task level (e.g. a manufacturing cell). We would expect to see most viable systems, at whatever structural level they occur, containing further sub-systems as a way to help them handle the complexity of their environments. These sub-systems are responsible for carrying out the value-adding tasks of the system-in-focus.

Co-ordination – a viable system also requires systems in place to co-ordinate the interfaces of its value-adding functions and the operations of its primary sub-units. In other words, co-ordination is necessary between the value-adding functions as well as between the embedded primary activities. 'Co-ordination' in the VSM context also suggests that the more teams "share common standards, approaches and values, the greater the chances that spontaneous lateral communication will occur, resulting in less 're-invention of the wheel' and more chance of synergy. The stronger these lateral links, which are of both a technological and human nature, the less the requirement for management to attempt to impose control from above and the greater the sense of autonomy and empowerment experienced by the subsumed primary activities" (Reference 18.2 again). The 'co-ordination' definition is highly suggestive of the need for effective two-way communication links within and between elements within a system.

Intelligence - is defined as 'the two-way link between the primary activity and its external environment'. Intelligence is described as fundamental to adaptivity; firstly, it provides the primary activity with continuous feedback on marketplace conditions, technology changes and all external factors that are likely to be relevant to it in the future; secondly, it projects the identity and message of the organisation into its environment. The intelligence function is, in Beer's definition, strongly future focused. It is concerned with planning the way ahead in the light of external environmental changes and internal organisational capabilities so that the organisation can invent its own future.

443

Control - is defined in the VSM as the (two-way) communication between sub-unit and meta-level unit.

Policy - is the last function in VSM, and as such the policy making function gives closure to the system as a whole. The main roles of Policy are to provide clarity about the overall direction, values and purpose of the organisational unit; and to design, at the highest level, the conditions for organisational effectiveness.

Incidentally, both Game Theory (Reference 18.3) and TRIZ (Reference 18.4) have both also described the need for five elements to define a complete and viable system. Reference 18.4 discusses the three different perspectives in more detail for those interested in gaining a broader insight into the importance of the three. Figure 18.7, taken from that reference summarises the three perspectives. It's main value here is to suggest the intimate connection between the three, and, more importantly, to display the different terminologies used – the hope here being that it will be easier to connect the language they are most familiar with to the concept of system viability

Stafford Beer Viable System Model	'Co-opetition' Game Theory	TRIZ Law Of System Completeness
Policy	Added Values	Engine
Co-ordination	Rules	Transmission
Control	Tactics	Control Unit
Implementation	Players	Working Unit
Intelligence	Scope	Interface

Figure 18.7: Comparison Between Different System Viability Tests

The Viable System Model is, unfortunately, not a tool that is used widely. Part of the reason for this may lay with its apparent complexity to the newcomer. Certainly the commonly used pictorial representation of the Model viewable at Reference 18.5 does not help in this regard. Whether more people will adopt more of the ideas contained in Beer's work remain to be seen. In the meantime, from our specific Trimming validity perspective, the thing that it and the Game Theory/TRIZ elements offer is a test of whether an element can be trimmed from our system or not.

The main message, meanwhile, is that if we are seeking to trim any of these essential elements from our system, we fundamentally have to find replacements for them since, without them, the system cannot be viable.

c) Coupled Functional Requirements

For those organisations fortunate to survive and thrive through multiple discontinuous evolutions (s-curves), the Trimming possibilities may be influenced by coupling effects.

Figure 18.8 illustrates a modified version of the picture shown at the beginning of the chapter. This new figure illustrates the 'complexity-increases-complexity-decreases' trend plotted over several s-curves. What it shows is that the overall level of complexity of organisations tend to increase over time. This phenomenon is one that carries across from research on the manner in which biological systems evolve (Reference 18.6).

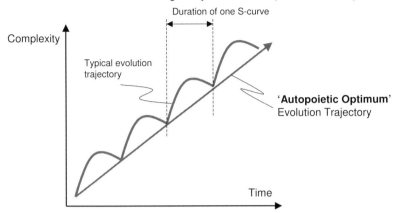

Figure 18.8: Combined Natural plus Technical System Complexity Evolution Trend
(Note: 'Complexity' is not the same as 'number of elements' – the number of elements in a system at the end of the evolution of one system may well be less than the number at the beginning; the complexity, on the other hand is almost always going to be higher at the end than it was in the beginning, albeit often in an embedded rather than explicit form)

The figure hypothesises that there is an 'optimum' level of complexity at any stage during the evolution of a system. That 'optimum' is defined by the minimum level of complexity necessary to give the system autopoetic properties – i.e. properties that allow a system to survive and reproduce in a sustainable manner. The increasing-decreasing complexity pattern followed by non-biological systems is symptomatic of the fact that we don't have the same short term survival drives as a natural system. An unfit biological system will almost invariably not survive for very long, whereas a non-optimal business system can survive for sometimes considerable amounts of time before the drives to become optimal become acute enough for anyone to want to do anything about it. Also, in the vast majority of cases, we simply aren't smart enough to know what the 'optimal' system should look like (never mind be able to achieve it) during the early stages of evolution.

So what does this have to do with Trimming? The answer is easiest to see when we look at an example. Of the five elements that define the 'viable' system, the one that is the most likely one to be trimmed is usually the 'control'. We see this happening to managers in any 'de-layering' or 'right-sizing' or 'business process re-engineering' activity. The aim in all of these programmes is to instill a self-organizing capability into the people and elements that remain when the 'surplus' has been trimmed. Too often, however when these things happen, the system that is left behind drops below its autopoetic capable level – Figure 18.9. When this happens, the system is in trouble. Too many organisations fall into this trap of 'cutting away at the flesh and bone as well as the fat'. They do it inadvertently of course, but nevertheless, when the damage is done, it is very difficult to recover. The issue here is one of coupling. Coupling and the fact that when we are looking at the 'control' mechanisms in place in an organisation there are relationships and connections that can be written down, but there are also higher level things going on that our modelling capabilities find it difficult to map adequately. Figure 13 from Chapter 6 suggests one means of formalising the coupling that can exist between different functions. This is a start, but there still remain issues concerning the higher-level appreciation of how systems operate. This is the essence of the VSM emphasis on recursion. We may think we are trimming out excess Control in the system, but in actual fact we have failed to recognise that the elements we are trimming also need to have an appreciation of their links to the higher-level system.

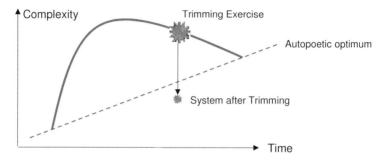

Figure 18.9: Trimming Below Autopoetic Level Will Cause Problems

It would be possible to enter into a long discussion about the mechanics of recursion at this point, but it will probably be mostly unhelpful in helping us to use the Trimming tool in a practical sense. We will therefore end this section by making the suggestion that there are important questions to ask when we look to confirm that it is possible to trim an element from a system:

- 'are there any coupled functions present here?'
- 'are there any aspects of the element to be trimmed that link our system to the system operating at the next higher hierarchical level?'

If the answer to either question is 'yes' then we should think twice before we proceed with trimming the element. It may still be possible, but – according to the Figure 18.8 characteristic – it means that whatever is left in the system needs to embrace the coupling effects and particularly the links to the higher system.

3) Trimming Case Study Examples

We will now examine two case study examples of the Trimming tool in action. The first case focuses on trimming of a typical business value network system, while the second examines a process-based system where the time dimension plays a much more important role. Both cases have been chosen to also bring out a number of additional, hopefully useful, thoughts regarding Trimming and our effective deployment of the technique. For the sake of brevity, in both cases, we do not present the whole of the preceding problem definition activity that lead to a decision to use trimming – our purpose being to focus on process rather than specific outcome.

The first thing we have to do before it is possible to begin a trimming analysis is to construct a functional model of the system. We do this using the procedure defined in Chapter 6. In the first case study we use as a foundation a case first described in Reference 18.7. The case involves a hypothetical value network involved in the creation and sale of pharmaceutical products. The resulting model drawn for the value network system under consideration is reproduced in Figure 18.10.

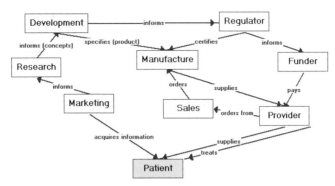

Figure 18.10: Function Analysis For Pharmaceutical Product Value Network

The model actually describes only the main tangible functions of each of the elements of the system. Reference 18.7 uses the case as a means of detailing the extensive network present in systems like this. Three different shading schemes are used for the different boxes in the model – one to represent the internal divisions of the pharmaceutical organisation, and two to represent external elements. We have chosen to discriminate between the patient and the other external agencies since without the patient, the need for the system completely disappears. As such, we might think of the patient as the one element of the system that cannot be changed. Taking the Figure 18.10 story a little further, Figure 18.11 presents a relationship table that includes a more comprehensive list of the functional relationships present in the system. Unlike the Reference, we have also added the negative relationships that we might expect to be present in such a system.

	patient	provider	funder	regulator	sales	marketing	research	dev	manf
patient		informs pays(E)				informs (I)			
provider	treats (Main) supplies		claims confirms		orders confirms pays(E)	knowledge (I)	knowledge (M)	informs	
funder		pays		informs (M)					
regulator		knowledge	informs						inspects(E) certifies
sales	informs	informs knowledge	informs						orders
mrkting		knowledge biases(H)					informs		
research								informs supplies	
dev				informs (I)					specifies (I)
manf		supplies		informs	informs (I)				

Figure 18.11: Comprehensive Functional Relationships For The Value Network
(descriptions in italics represent intangible relationships,
M – missing, E – excessive, I – insufficient, H – harmful)

For function analysis models like this, where there is little influence of time on the problem, we are basically presented with two main directions when we begin to contemplate

447

Trimming. The first is to focus on the elimination of the negative things happening in the system, while the second is to focus on reducing the number of elements in a way that has greatest impact on the cost (or whatever other attributes we choose to focus on) of the system. In the case of this pharmaceutical value network, those two approaches lead to quite different foci:

If we choose to focus on the 'eliminate negative effects' part of the current system, the function analysis shows us immediately that there are several insufficient relationships centred around the transfer of knowledge in what we might think of as the market research activities. Then there are several parts of the value chain who perceive that they are paying too much, a harmful relationship relating to biased (in the eyes of the provider) marketing and an excessive inspection (in the eyes of the manufacturer) by the regulator.

Should we chose to use this information to guide us towards which elements of the system we might trim, then we will immediately find our options are quite limited. In the first instance, the 'insufficient' relationships often suggest that we need *more* of a system rather than trimming to produce less. This is not always the case, however, and often the answer to an insufficient action – especially one that feels like it will always be limited – is to trim and find a better way of doing things. In this particular case, for example, the identification of a missing knowledge transfer between the provider and the research department in the pharmaceutical company (the people that will actually use the information) might well suggest to us that the marketing department might make a suitable trimming candidate. Then, in terms of the trimming question 'do we want this function?' and the likely positive answer, we will eventually get to the question 'is there something else in or around the system that can perform the function?' At this stage we might identify several means by which the Provider can provide the information that Research needs that don't involve going through the Marketing department – e.g. Internet system.

With regard to the other trimming possibilities that arise from looking at the negative relationships, excessive payments suggest trimming of either the Provider or the Sales. Both sound quite difficult, at least in the short term. Several organizations are, of course, working on patient diagnosis expert systems that require either no provider, or a less qualified provider. Similarly, increasing use of Internet systems is paving the way for more direct, automated sales requiring less sales people.

The final trimming possibility relates to the apparently excessive inspection of Manufacture by the Regulator. Trimming of either of these options appears to offer little practical prospect – Manufacture because there is a product that has to be made, and the Regulator because this is an external agency and therefore not under the control of the pharmaceutical company. The general point that emerges here is that those elements of a system that are outside of our direct control are usually not good trimming candidates. The best prospect for the pharmaceutical company in this situation is to lobby for (say) the regulator function to be integrated with that of the funder.

The second overall Trimming option involves focus on reducing the number of elements in a way that has greatest impact on the cost. In order to achieve success in this direction, we need to supply some more data into the function analysis model. Specifically, we need to supply some relevant attributes for each of the elements. In simple terms, each element identified in the function analysis model has a whole series of attributes – size, running cost, skills, etc – some of which will be relevant to the problem and some not. The cost attributes are particularly useful metrics from a trimming perspective.

The task, once the relevant attributes have been identified, involves selecting the most appropriate of the current elements for Trimming. The simplest rules here are to opt either for the most expensive elements or the elements generating the fewest useful functions first. In the absence of specific cost information for this system (which we would obviously have in our possession if this were a real case), we might instead chose to examine elements that deliver the fewest useful functions. A simple way to do this is to look along the rows in the table of functional relationships. According to Figure 18.11, it looks like the Funder is the most likely external element, while Marketing, Research and Development are the three most likely internal candidates. Again, we will have the debate about whether it is within our power to trim external elements. If we chose to focus on the internal elements under our control, we are left with the three areas. The sequence of Trimming questions might then take us through a sequence something like:-

1) do we want the function? Answer – yes in all three cases.
2) Can another element perform the function? – no in the case of Research and Development, possibly yes in the case of Marketing (e.g. Sales)
3) Can we modify one of the elements? – possibly integrate Research into Development, but probably unlikely.
4) Can we use an external resource? – possibly again – there are several agencies that can do Marketing and Research, for example.

In most cases like these we are faced with a trade-off between ease of achieving the trimming result and the resulting benefit we achieve – difficult trimming equals big benefit, and vice-versa. The only exceptions to this general rule appear to be systems that have not been the subject of any kind of function analysis before. In these situations, it would seem that almost any kind of Trimming analysis can result in big benefits.

A good way to focus the search of other elements that may be able to take on the function of one that is looking to be trimmed is to start with the ones that are physically closest and to work away to the most distant ones. The closest elements are in the majority of cases the ones already functionally related to the Trimming candidate and are the ones most likely to be capable of taking on the function.

As a final thought on the subject of Trimming this kind of FAA model, it is absolutely essential to double-check the completeness of any FAA model before concluding that an element can be trimmed. 'What's stopping me?' is a very good double-check question. A relationship between the element and something from the super-system that we haven't thus far included is a very usual reason why something is stopping us.

Case Study 2 – Time-Based Process Situation

Figure 18.12 illustrates a typical international air travel process that we have selected as a possible candidate for trimming. Paradoxically, many process-based situations often appear to be full of Trimming opportunities, but trimming is often experienced as 'difficult to achieve' in reality. They are 'full of opportunities' because it is often the case when analyzing processes that the function of many of the steps only exists because some other step is performed inadequately.

We could apply Trimming at two main levels in this kind of process situation. The first would be the level where we look to eliminate process steps. Our aim in doing this may be either reduction of process time (something the passenger is most likely to be interested in), or it may simply be to achieve increases in efficiency or reductions in cost (something the airport is most likely to be interested in). In terms of reducing process time, our Trimming emphasis needs to focus on bottleneck activities. Since this process is essentially built on a linear sequence of events, we know that elimination of any one will have a beneficial effect on the throughput. In other processes, where there may be a host of parallel processes, the trimming emphasis needs to focus on those elements that determine the overall process time. If our focus is more concerned with improving efficiency or removing waste, we may deploy the Trimming tool more broadly to look at any process step, even though it may not exist on a critical path.

Check-in
- Check ticket
- Check passport
- Weigh luggage
- Label luggage
- Issue luggage receipt
- Check hand-luggage
- Ask security questions
- Issue boarding pass
- Issue immigration forms
- Inform gate number

Security
- Check boarding pass
- Remove coat/metal objects
- Security check belongings
- Screen passenger
- Locate gate

Gate
- Enter boarding pass
- Check passport
- Hand over boarding pass stub

Plane
- Check boarding pass stub
- Identify seat
- Stow hand-luggage
- Issue customs form
- Complete forms

Destination
- De-plane
- Immigration check
- Baggage claim
- Customs
- Ground transportation

Figure 18.12: Operation Sequence For Typical Air Travel Process

As may be seen from the large number of steps that occur, process improvement in air travel holds the potential for some significant improvement, despite the security checks that have become an inevitable part of the ordeal. We would typically use the questions detailed in Figure 18.5 in order to identify and confirm potential trimming opportunities in the system. Rather than do that here, however, we will instead focus our attention on a second aspect of Trimming that can be useful in these types of system.

The second kind of Trimming is the one operating at a higher hierarchical level. This is the level where our interest is usually focused on the main function of the overall process – which, after all, is the reason the whole system exists – and trying to find ways of improving it. We will often resort to using this higher-level type of strategy when we are looking at processes – like this one – where there are many different variations that can occur. The biggest source of variety in the air-travel process is that every passenger is different from every other one, and thus has requirements that are distinct and in many instances unique. One of the reasons the process outlined in Figure 18.12 is so complex is that it has to cope with so many different kinds of passenger requirements. In this kind of situation, we can find ourselves having to construct very large quantities of process maps for different types of passenger. When we are facing this type of situation, only the most systematic users will have the energy to construct such models. For the rest of us, there is an alternative. In actual fact there are two, but since one involves recognizing that different customers with different requirements are in fact contradictions, it is more relevant to Chapters 11 and 12 than here.

The alternative relevant to the process of Trimming involves focusing on elements that form a common thread through most if not all of the process. The element that is involved at every step of our process here is the long-suffering passenger. So, if we focus on the passenger, a very useful way of thinking about the Trimming possibilities is to examine all of the things that the passenger needs to get them through the process. Figure 18.13 illustrates the things that passengers are likely to have with them, and are likely to need on an international flight.

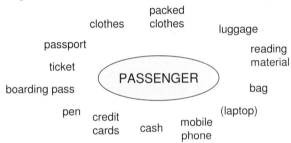

Figure 18.13: Alternative Trimming Perspective: What Resources Does An Element Require To Proceed Through The Complete Process

Any attempt to Trim the air-travel process is likely to have an impact on what the passenger is required to do at different stages, and consequently on what they need to have with them at each stage. If we then think about Trimming as a route intended to take us in the direction of the 'more ideal' system, then we might begin to imagine that as time advances, the process will move in the direction of requiring the passenger to carry fewer and fewer items. A useful way of thinking about Trimming in this context, then, is to look at all of the things that the passenger has to have with them, and to consider how the system would work if items were eliminated. Some airlines have already, for example, Trimmed out the need for the ticket and transferred the function to the passport or a credit card. The ticket is the easiest of the passenger listed passenger items to trim, but it is by no means the only one. In this regard, we might imagine that over time, the number of things the passenger will be carrying around with them will progressively reduce down to the clothes they are wearing. Next easiest items to trim from the system might be:-
- boarding pass – useful functions 1) inform staff that a passenger is on the right plane, 2) inform the passenger what their seat number is. The former function could easily be transferred to the passport, the second could perhaps be SMS'd to a mobile phone.
- cash – not specifically related to the air-travel process per se (but no reason why the airport can't add some value), but as e-cash and m-cash (where your mobile phone becomes your local currency) expand in use, then the hassle of having to carry around multiple currencies may disappear
- credit card – functions transferred to either passport or mobile phone
- laptop – functions transferred to mobile phone (?)

This kind of high-level focus is important in system evolution terms as well as from a Trimming standpoint. The dynamics of evolution (Reference 18.8) are such that, whether we like it or not, different parts of the value chain are increasingly going to try and take our business away from us. The credit-card industry is busy trying to maintain and grow their business; the same with mobile phone companies, laptop manufacturers, textile manufacturers (smart clothing?). If we're not thinking about Trimming, almost guaranteed that someone else from a different part of the value network is.

In summary, when thinking about trimming in the context of processes, the idea of hierarchy is fundamental to our thinking. Trimming at the higher levels, perhaps unsurprisingly, are the most difficult to realize, but on the other hand, they are usually the only ones to make a significant effect on overall process throughput.

What Do I Do?

Conceptually, Trimming is one of the simplest of the systematic innovation solution generation tools. The whole thing basically operates from the provocation 'why don't we eliminate X?' where X could be any kind of physical entity or process step.

All of the necessary ground-work for Trimming should have been done in the construction of Function and Attribute Analysis models during the problem definition part of the systematic innovation process.

The strategies open to us once we have decided to attempt trimming of an element from a system involve working through the questions detailed in Figure 18.2 for physical entities, and Figure 18.5 for process steps.

These questions may then lead us on to other parts of the toolkit (for example the question 'can something else in the system perform the function?' often leads to the idea of 'self-x' functions and Chapter 19 in order to find out if anyone else has already achieved a solution to your trimming problem.

References

1) Beer, S., 'Brain Of The Firm: The Managerial Cybernetics of Organization', The Professional library, Allen Lane, The Penguin Press, London, 1972.
2) Espejo, R., Harnden, R., 'The Viable System Model', John Wiley & Sons, New York, 1989.
3) Nalebuff, B.J., Brandenburger, A.M., 'Co-opetition', Harper Collins Business, 1996.
4) Mann, D.L., 'Laws of System Completeness', TRIZ Journal, May 2001.
5) Espejo, R., Gill, A., 'The Viable System Model as a Framework for Understanding Organizations', www.phrontis.com/vsm.htm
6) Mann, D.L., 'Complexity Increases And Then... (Thoughts From Natural System Evolution', TRIZ Journal, January 2003.
7) Allee, V., 'The Future Of Knowledge: Increasing Prosperity Through Value Networks', Butterworth-Heinnemann, 2003.
8) Utterback; J., 'Mastering The Dynamics of Innovation', Harvard Business School Press, 1993.

19.
Problem Solving Tools
Ideality/Ideal Final Result

"The indefatigable pursuit of an unattainable perfection... is what alone gives
a meaning to our life on this unavailing star"
Logan Pearsall Smith

Chapter 8 examined the use of the Ideality and Ideal Final Result (IFR) concepts in the context of their application in a problem or opportunity definition context. In this chapter we examine aspects of both that are relevant to their use in a problem solving context – that is their application in the role of helping to generate solutions.

In all, there are two main aspects of Ideality and IFR that offer problem solving tools. These are:-
1) 'self' solution trigger tool
2) connection to resources and system hierarchy tool

Each of the two will be described individually in the following sections:

1) 'Self' Solution Trigger Tool

This section discusses the importance of systems that incorporate solutions incorporating the word 'self' – self-organizing, self-correcting, self-managing, etc – in the context of their relationship – in the true systematic innovation sense – to the concept of ideality. We discuss the state of the art regarding business system design solutions achieving self-x delivery of useful functions through discussion of a series of examples where managers and strategists have sought to build 'self-x' into the fundamental design of the systems they wished to create.

Anyone that has used the Ideal Final Result part of the systematic innovation suite of tools will have come across the word 'self'. If we accept that the Ideal Final Result occurs when we achieve the desired function without cost or harm, then we often derive statements like 'the system achieves the function itself', or 'the problem resolves itself' when conceptualising ideal solution directions. Although in practice we may have to back away from such an ideal end point, there is a growing database of solutions where others have not. Systems that have solved problems 'by themselves' thus represent an important part of the global knowledge database.

It is these solutions that we discuss here in the context of the way they can help to generate good solution directions and ideas. The basis for establishing the validity of the tool has been an analysis of the published management literature. That analysis has taken as its start point, the range of solutions featuring 'self-X' properties, where X may be just about any useful **function** other business leaders, strategists and entrepreneurs have required a system to perform.

Before examining these examples in detail, it is first necessary to clarify the relationship between 'things that do things for themselves' and the systematic innovation concept of ideality. We must do this, because examination of the many business solutions quickly reveals a large number of 'self-x' solutions that have little in common with the concept of an Ideal Final Result solution.

Figure 19.1 illustrates the difference between conventional and ideality-driven strategies. In this characteristic, we see the 'conventional' evolution of systems following a trend of increasing complexity followed by decreasing complexity. This trend can be observed in all organization systems as they evolve from birth through growth and on to maturity. In the early stages of a business, if their offerings to the market are in sufficient demand to create opportunities for growth to happen, it is usually the case that the focus of the business is very much on increasing output rather than optimization of processes. This optimization in fact frequently only becomes a consideration *after* several competitors have emerged and the organization needs to find better ways of conducting its business in order to maintain an edge. Examples of this phenomenon can be seen in industries from the old bricks and mortar manufacture sector through to the more recent e-businesses – which have only relatively recently been forced to transform themselves from burn-rate supernovas into professionally managed operations.

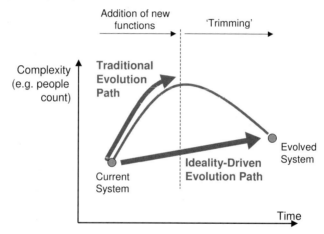

Figure 19.1: Conventional versus Ideality-Driven Evolution In Business

In the evolution of technical systems, the trend towards increasing and then decreasing complexity is often driven by a fundamental lack of knowledge regarding the technology during the early stages of evolution. In business, a similar lack of knowledge can also be a factor, but more often it may be speculated that the characteristic actually occurs because the emphasis of the business is heavily driven by a need to grow the customer base as fast as possible, and the need for things like operating procedures, quality manuals, human resources functions, etc – all of which are frequently added without due consideration of their impact on the existing systems – are often given a lowly second place in the full scheme of things. It may well be, therefore, that there are rather fewer justifiable reasons why the increasing-decreasing complexity characteristic needs to be present in a business system, provided the right foundations can be put in place early in the life of the business. See also Reference 19.1 for additional interpretations of this trend – which, although discussed in the context of technical systems, are also highly applicable in business settings.

What the systematic innovation interpreted use of the word 'self' (and its synonyms of course – 'automatic', 'remote', 'autonomous', etc.) is trying to imply is that by thinking about getting systems to deliver useful functions 'by themselves', it is highly possible that systems will be able to avoid some of the waste that inevitably accompanies the excessive increase in complexity suggested by the trend.

The rest of this section now looks at a number of examples where such ideality-driven 'self-x' cases have been shown to produce important success in the business context. Rather than focusing on simply those instances where businesses are at the start of their s-curve, we will also examine examples in which relatively mature organizations have successfully adopted self-x strategies later on in their evolution.

Case Study 1 – Self Regulation of Quality at Toyota

The first such case involves Toyota specifically, but also, thanks to the extensive studies published on the Toyota 'lean' model, to an increasing number of other organisations. Albeit, few of these new examples have successfully managed to introduce the full philosophy behind the Toyota model. Particularly when it comes to thinking about the human elements of the design of that model. The case study itself is very simple. It relates primarily to the role of inspection and Quality functions within an organisation.

In many organisations, the creation of a 'Quality Department' or recruiting of inspectors, etc occurs in response to failures of the system to deliver the desired levels of quality during the production of whatever the product or service that is being delivered to the customer. The 'common sense' logic underlying the increase in complexity of the system resulting from adding people with specific responsibilities for quality is that these people will be able to check the output of the producing elements of the business in order to identify defects before they hit the customer.

Common sense has the unfortunate habit of turning out to be flawed as we think harder about situations (see Reference 19.2 which suggests that in fact just about all successful new ideas and models run counter to the prevailing common sense logic). With regard to quality systems, the logic has proved itself to be severely flawed on just about every possible occasion. The net result of that flawed thinking is that most 'quality systems' actually serve to decrease overall quality (albeit the customer fortunately doesn't get to see any of it – at least not directly), and increase costs (the bit the customers do see).

Why is this so? From the perspective of the people doing the productive work, the appearance of a downstream Quality checking function sends out a strong yet unspoken implication that 'someone else' will worry about quality. The consequence of this is that there is less need to worry about doing things right. From the perspective of those people put in place to worry about the quality, there is an opposite perception that the upstream producers will produce quality goods and that only a small amount of poor quality will reach them. The net result of the two perceptions is that more mistakes get made during production, and the inspectors pick less of them up.

At Toyota, they have achieved the ideal 'Quality Department'. The ideal final result quality department is one in which we get quality without the quality department. At Toyota, the system 'itself' delivers the required levels of quality.

Toyota, of course, didn't use any systematic innovation technique to get to this outcome. By applying the 'get the system to deliver the function by itself' question, on the other hand, it becomes possible for us to at least be thinking about the same end point that Toyota have reached. Furthermore, the self-regulating capability achieved at Toyota represents part of a database of 'someone, somewhere has already solved our self-x problem' that we can apply in our own context.

Case Study 2– Self Regulating Systems at Semco

Ricardo Semler is the CEO of Semco, a Brazilian company made famous (in the US and Europe at least) following the publication of the book Maverick (Reference 19.3). Semler is the son of a wealthy Brazilian industrialist. He was not accepted at Harvard University and so at 21 was instead placed in charge of Semco. Maverick tells the story of the revolutionary changes Ricardo Semler made in the company. When he started, Semco was a traditionally structured and struggling industrial pump manufacturer. Young Semler proceeded to fire most of the top managers in an effort to perform emergency surgery on the foundering company. Initially, Semler concentrated on keeping the company afloat. But once the company's financial position stabilized, he proceeded to buy other companies and diversify. As Semco grew, Semler gradually made innovations, such as doing away with dress codes, introducing flex time, and encouraging employees to take more ownership of their work. These are all areas that many companies have experimented with over the last fifteen years. However, Semler went much further. He questioned many standard office practices and reinvented many of them – often with a very IFR-like 'get the system to fix the system by itself' strategy in mind. After seeing a company order for $50,000 worth of file cabinets, for example, he decreed that every person would clean out their own file cabinets and keep only what was absolutely necessary. The system, in other words, became transformed into a self regulating system in which only the stuff important to the future of the business (as opposed to future of an individual bent on covering his/her tracks) was retained. Everyone takes on a responsibility for determining what gets stored and what gets thrown away.

Another explicitly self-x solution from the Maverick book is the example of self-regulating pay and reward systems. The basic concept may appear to be quite radical in the context of many business systems, but appears to be one of the major success factors underlying the Semco strategy. From the book:-

"Paying people whatever they want seems a sure route to bankrupcy, but we've been doing this for years and we've never done better. A 10% rise turns out to be an exception. Nearly 25% of our employees now set their own salaries, including most of our co-ordinators, and I don't see why factory workers shouldn't one day determine their own pay."

Yet another piece of prevailing common sense (i.e. if you let people set their own salaries they will take a lot and in the process suck all of the resource out of the business) that proves to be a fallacy in the cold light of day.

One reason for the continuing existence of Semco has been the willingness of Semler and the Semco's manager to adapt themeselves to changing external circumstances. Brazil's economy has forced thousands of companies to shut down, laying off hundreds of thousands of workers. While Semco has had some layoffs and has closed some plants (in several instances, a manager's job is often to try and remove the need for his job and have the system be self-regulating instead), it also spun off nearly two dozen satellite companies. In an effort to decentralize, these satellite companies contract back some services to Semco in addition to soliciting independent business.

This whole concept of self-regulation and self-organisation within business systems lies also at the heart of the book 'Complexity Advantage' (Reference 19.4) – which contains many fine examples of how this Semco kind of self-x direction setting in the DNA of the business results in a successful system that emerges ('by itself') from the complex soup of employees, structures, interactions and customers.

Case Study 3– Self Limiting Systems

Many organisations talk about the need for some kind of tension within the business in order to get things done. Tension, as we probably all know can be both a useful and a harmful thing. The tension of an upcoming deadline is often the essential incentive to spur us into action (think of how many college assignments you used to begin writing only on the day before they were due to be handed in). On the other hand, too much tension can be highly destructive – resulting in, amongst other things, depression, illness and time off work. Taken together, it seems clear that we have contradictory requirements for both tension and no-tension. The phenomenon is illustrated in Figure 19.2. The figure describes the effect of changing tension (x-axis) on the outcomes from a system. System in this sense meaning anything from an individual to a whole organisation. What the characteristic of the graph shows is that as tension increases up to a certain 'optimum' level, its effect is beneficial. Beyond this level, however, and the positive effect rapidly turns into a negative one. In this situation, no matter what happens, the tension level will not go beyond a certain level (since either people will become ill or leave for a more amenable environment). Tension, in other words, self-limits inside a system.

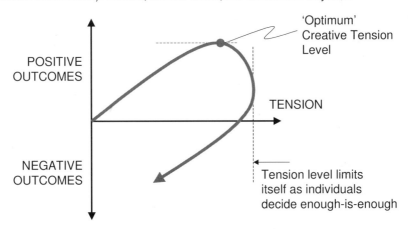

Figure 19.2: Self-Limiting Tension And Impact An The Overall Business

The characteristic further describes a high level of hysteresis in the system – since trying to force the tension level above the self-limiting maximum serves only to force more and more negative outcomes. In many senses, we might think of this lower part of the hysteresis curve as the Dilbert zone – the place where things are so bad that the only possible human response is to laugh.

The self-limiting tension phenomenon is in itself hardly an IFR-like definition of the self-x and ideality concepts. What is, however, are systems that are able to manage themselves into the 'optimum' tension position (recognising that this value is dynamic and variable depending on a wide variety of different external situations). Several organisations are beginning to talk about 'creative tension management' and, in keeping with the emergent systems ideas of Reference 19.4, attempts to define the DNA rules that allow systems to find this 'in the zone' tension level by themselves.

Case Study 4 – Self Financing

How does a rock band finance their next record when the record label has dropped them? That is the problem faced by famous progressive rock band Marillion when it came to writing, recording and releasing new material at the beginning of this century. Although the band was not expecting to sell the millions of records it was able to ship during the 80s and early 90s, the band nevertheless knew that there was a substantial audience still wanting to hear from them. The strategy used by the band to resolve the problem of self-financing the new record involved tapping into the existing resource provided by that loyal fan base. The band asked fans to buy the album before they had even written it. This advance money (which would normally have come from the record company) was then used to buy the studio time needed to write, record and release the record. In all over 13,000 fans had sufficient faith in the quality and integrity of the band to pay for the new record in this way (Reference 19.5). The record – Figure 19.3 – has since become a high selling record (not chart-wise, but nevertheless very respectable) and the basic idea of pre-financing the record is undoubtedly still being talked about in music industry circles and in the press over two years later. In many senses, the self-financing idea of using existing resources, looks set to play a strong influence in the future of an industry that has been subject to increasing levels of fragmentation and Scarcity Theory effect (Reference 19.6) in recent times.

Figure 19.3: Marillion Album Anoraknophobia – Financed By Fans Before It Was Recorded
(the names of all 13,000 fans that pre-ordered were included in the album cover art)

Case Study 5 – Self Organisation

The traditional role of management within businesses is to 'manage' the activities that take place within the organisation. The evidence emerging from books like the Complexity Advantage (Reference 19.4) is that this kind of top-down approach to management is in many instances fundamentally flawed. Bad top-down management results in unhappy workers who devote increasing proportions of their creative efforts designing ways around the systems imposed on them. The way that SAP, for example, is deployed (or rather mis-deployed) in several organisations offers powerful evidence of the conflicts that can arise when a management team think that SAP has given them more control over their business, while the day-to-day working level reality is that the 'real' work goes on despite the system – with workers devoting ever more time to servicing a system that delivers the required rather than actual truth. Management phrases like 'don't ever let me catch you doing that again' often give the manager what he or she wants. Whatever it was that was going on will probably still be going on, but now the perpetrator's will use their creative energies to make sure the manager doesn't indeed ever catch them.

There are an increasing number of examples of organisations taking heed of the problems created by top-down management styles (another example of common sense pointing managers in the wrong direction) and are instead shifting to higher and higher degrees of self-organisation. SouthWest Airlines (Reference 19.7), for example, is famously free of bureaucracy and top-down rules, insisting instead that everyone takes responsibility for not just their own jobs, but also for the welfare of the organisation as a whole as they perform their work.

Perhaps even more striking is the shift in management that has taken place in military circles in recent times. Traditionally, the military has represented the epitome of top-down management – the prevailing logic being that people following order without question is the best way to achieve a desired end. The evidence provided by campaign after campaign, and exercise after exercise is that this kind of approach often produces highly non-ideal results. If soldiers are encouraged not to think; they won't think. This can be okay if the situation in which those soldiers find themselves is as per the plan, but if the plan changes, what used to be an appropriate command, can turn into something that is quite the opposite. NATO commanders, having recognised this phenomenon, and the high likelihood that plan's will change on a very regular basis, have shifted to a structure known as 'Commanders Intent' (Reference 19.8). Commanders Intent works by passing on instructions in the form of desired outcomes (e.g. 'capture that bridge and hold it, because it is a unique supply route that will both cut off the enemy and help us'), and then allowing soldiers to organise themselves to deliver the desired intent. This level of flexibility permits the soldiers to adapt (themselves) to suit emerging conditions in the field, without the need to wait for further instructions from the commander when a situation changes from a fixed plan.

Case Study 6 – Self Replicating

All life forms have a pre-determined maximum potential life-span. The same applies to businesses, although few managers have recognised that a connection exists as yet. Nature solves the problem of death by having systems that are capable of reproducing themselves. The self-reproducing idea is rather less well established in industry, but is beginning to be seen as a natural (albeit often also uncomfortable) way of enabling businesses to achieve long term survival. As one product or market dies out, another one emerges to take its place. We can see this shift taking place in the photographic industries at the moment – where all the smart organisations are busy trying to shift from film to digital products and services.

One of the best self-replicating examples comes from Richard Branson's Virgin group of companies. Virgin has spawned a broad range (airlines to banks to cola drinks to name but three) of outlets for its capabilities, and frequently uses the 150 people rule (which says that when an organisation structure gets above 150 people, the evolution of a social network makes it increasingly unlikely that everyone can know everyone else, and that bonding and interaction suffers exponentially – Reference 19.9) as a means of deciding when an organisation is ripe for (self-)dividing into new entities. The culture within the company actively supports this kind of self-replication function – the most well known case perhaps being Virgin Brides (a no-fail name if ever there was one!) – which was the brainchild of a cabin attendant flying Virgin Atlantic who was having logistical difficulties organising the multitude of different elements of her wedding, and had the idea of a one-stop shop for bringing into one place the co-ordination of church, flowers, photographer, reception, cake, dress, etc, etc. The organisation gave her the freedom to develop the idea into a business plan that subsequently turned into a successful part of the Virgin empire. Similar self-replicating strategies can also be seen to be emerging in companies like GE, AOL and IDEO.

'Self' and Your Problem

Solutions that achieve functions 'by themselves' are very important in the sense of a world in which the overall business evolution driver is increasing ideality.

In this sense, the concept of Ideal Final Result, and the idea of looking for solutions which incorporate the word 'self' – i.e. the problem solves itself – is a very powerful tool in the systematic innovation armoury. There is some overlap here with the contradictions part of the systematic innovation toolkit and Inventive Principle 25, 'Self-Service'. Tying 'self' and the IFR concept more specifically together, however, tends to allow the creation of more holistically valid solutions.

Some problems contain constraints which make it difficult if not impractical for the problem owner to consider using the IFR method, but that being said, the 'define the IFR and then work back' schema illustrated in Chapter 8 is a useful start point for a good number of problems. Ideal Final Result thinking encourages problem owners to first register the function that they are wishing to deliver, and then gets them to think about how the system could deliver that function by itself – i.e. without the addition of the increased complexity inherent to traditional problem solving methods.

The growing catalogue of ideality-driven 'self-X' solutions are testament enough to the fact then that someone may already have successfully achieved the 'self' delivery of a function we wish to achieve ourselves.

'Self' is a very important word in the context of looking for good solutions to problems; if a system can solve a problem 'by itself', it will be a more ideal solution than one that requires the inclusion of external factors which serve to complicate the system.

There is a difference between traditional and ideality-driven definitions of 'self'. Traditionally, if we add new functions, the system has to become more complex. The ideality-driven definition gets us to think harder about whether we can achieve the additional functionality using resources that already exist in or around the system, and without increased complexity.

Someone, somewhere is increasingly likely to have thought about and solved your 'self-x' problem. As such, adding the word 'self' to the front of any function you are looking to deliver within a system is a simple yet extremely powerful solution trigger.

Resources and System Hierarchy Tool

As described in Chapter 8, the ideality part of the systematic innovation toolkit is closely linked to the identification and maximal utilisation of resources within a system. The underlying concept of increasing ideality involves the desire to achieve functionality with ever fewer resources. As discussed in Chapter 1, the identification of resources is one of the pillars of the overall systematic innovation philosophy. There are three main routes to the identification of resources. Two of these three ways are discussed in other chapters; Chapter 15 specifically discusses the identification of resources through use of a series of resource trigger databases – things that other successful problem solvers have successively found to be resources; Chapter 14 discusses the discontinuous-jump business trends and the concept of evolutionary potential – the unused evolutionary steps in a given system.

The third route to the identification of resources is more closely linked to ideality and is thus described here.

The basis of this ideality/resources link is the hierarchical nature of systems. Figure 19.4 illustrates a typical system hierarchy diagram for a system called 'moving money'. The hierarchy plots a simplified structure from the high level functional requirement to the individual people employed to in place to achieve the desired function.

The construction of this type of hierarchy is a very useful first step to the identification of resources that will hopefully enable us to evolve systems and system components towards their Ideal Final Result destination.

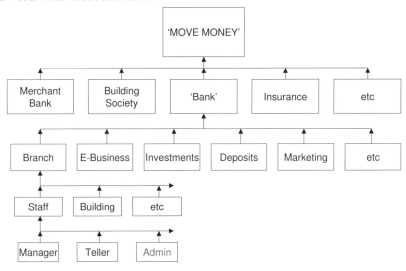

Figure 19.4: Simplified 'Move Money' System Hierarchy

In certain circumstances (e.g. if we do not work in the financial services sector) we might chose to explore the IFR concept at the hierarchical level of 'bank'; in which case the IFR car is that we achieve the function ' move money' (or more specifically 'move my money') without the presence of a system called bank. For most practical purposes, defining the IFR at this level is not particularly useful. Defining it at lower levels of the hierarchy, on the other hand, can prove to be extremely useful.

As an example, we will examine an Ideal Final Result administration post within the bank. Our definition here would involve achieving the function(s) of the department ('process transaction forms' primarily) without the need for the department. This definition can turn out to be much more practically realizable.

The main point, and the principal connection between this kind of IFR definition and a solving tool is that the hierarchy offers us the opportunity to identify other things that already exist in the system that may be able to fulfill the function of the component or assembly we wish to evolve to its IFR.

Thus, in the case of the components drawn in the figure, we might hypothesise that something else in the system – for example the other staff *themselves* – might be able to achieve the administration function– Figure 19.5. Indeed, in many banks this is beginning to happen. The previously untapped resource that is enabling the shift involves the amount of time that a customer expects to a transaction to take; above a certain amount of time and the customer is unhappy because the time spent could be better spent elsewhere. But conversely, make a transaction happen in a very small amount of time and customers will also become unhappy; this time because they perceive that their presence is not being acknowledged by the teller. Hence, use the few seconds of 'unused' time during the transaction to process the transaction directly (with the appropriate computer support systems obviously) – net result, the customer feels they are being attended to, they can directly see that their transaction has 'entered the system' and the admin is done.

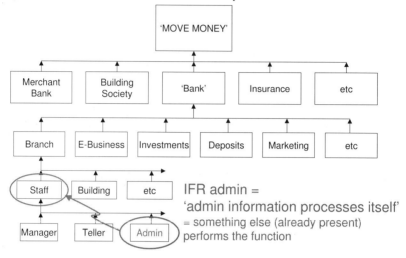

Figure 19.5: The Hierarchy Mechanics Of Evolution Towards Ideality

There are obvious links to the idea of Trimming (Chapter 18) here of course. The difference – and thus the additional problem solving idea offered by this combined ideality/resources thinking – comes with the crucial image of first the construction of this kind of system hierarchy, followed by an evolution process in which the things at the bottom of the hierarchy are progressively evolved to their IFR and disappear. Thus we have an image of a hierarchical structure progressively being eaten away from the bottom up.

In terms of the search for resources to help evolve a given component to its IFR then, the key part of this hierarchy tool is that we should be looking at other parts of the hierarchy (particularly those things at a higher hierarchical level) to see if they can take on the useful functions of the component we wish to eliminate.

What Do I Do?

Using the ideality and ideal final result concepts in a problem solving context involves one or more of two main possibilities:

1) Add the word 'self' onto the front of a function you require to have performed and use this 'self-x' function description as a trigger to first see if anyone else has already solved a similar problem (e.g. by searching patent and other knowledge databases), and second, as a prompt to generate ideas (akin to the 'Self-Service' Inventive Principle in Chapter 11).

2) IFR and resources are intimately linked to one another. Construct a system hierarchy as a means of seeing if there is a resource somewhere else in the system that may help you to achieve an IFR outcome for the component or assembly you are investigating – in other words, can something else already in the system perform the useful function(s) of the part that you wish to extrapolate to its IFR conclusion.

References

1) Mann, D.L., 'Complexity Increases And Then...(Thoughts From Natural System Evolution)', TRIZ Journal, January 2003.
2) Wolpert, L., 'The Unnatural Nature of Science' Faber and Faber, 1992.
3) Semler, R., 'Maverick: The Success Story Behind The World's Most Unusual Workplace', Random House, 1993.
4) Kelly, S., Allison, M.A., 'The Complexity Advantage – How The Science of Complexity can Help Your Business Achieve Peak Performance', McGraw-Hill BusinessWeek Books, New York, 1999.
5) www.marillion.com
6) 'Abundance Theory versus Scarcity theory', CREAX Newsletter, April 2003.
7) Freiberg, K., Freiberg, J., 'Nuts! Southwest Airlines' Crazy Recipe for Business and Personal Success', Bard Press, Austin, Texas, 1996.
8) Pascale, R., Milleman,M., Gioja, L., 'Surfing the Edge of Chaos', Crown Business Press, New York, 2000.
9) Branson, R., 'Losing My Virginity', Virgin Books (naturally!), 2002.

20.
Problem Solving:
Psychological Inertia Tools

"Every creative act is a sudden cessation of stupidity."
Edwin Land

or

"If it ain't broke, break it."
Richard Pascale

Introduction

The psychological inertia (PI) breaking tools contained in systematic innovation are used in two main scenarios. The first involve situations where we are having difficulty solving a problem; perhaps a situation in which we have passed through the 'generate solutions' part of the process and have not generated anything that looks like an answer. The second involves use of one or more of the PI tools specifically as a problem solving tool simply because they fit into our particular way of doing things. Generally speaking, the first scenario is the only one in which the overall systematic innovation process will direct you to this chapter.

In either scenario, the basic underlying idea behind the tools is that our brains are somehow 'blocked', and that we need something to give us a jolt. In the problem solving as 'digging for treasure in a field' analogy, the psychological inertia tools are there to help us make a systematic shift to another part of the field. More than this, the tools are hopefully going to send us to a part of the field in which the probability of finding new or better treasure is high.

There are many forms and types of psychological inertia breaking tools in existence. The work of DeBono, Buzan, Osborn and, to a lesser extent, Dilts (see the bibliography at the end of the chapter for more information) are worthy of specific mention. In the majority of circumstances the strategies recommended by these other authors can be included in this part of the systematic innovation process, either as a replacement or, preferably, a supplement to the tools originating from the original TRIZ framework.

The discussion here will examine only those tools that have had demonstrably beneficial impact in a management problem-solving context. We will examine five different tools. One – the 9-Windows or system operator tool – has been the subject of a whole chapter earlier in the book and, in keeping with its importance, a 9-windows image features on every page. We will confine our discussion of the tool in this chapter to just its specific application as a psychological inertia breaking strategy. The other four tools within the armoury are:-
- Least-Ideal Final Result
- Size-Time-Interface-Cost (STIC) Tool
- Why-What's Stopping Analysis
- Omega Life View (OLV) Tool

We will start by looking at the 9-Windows tool in its purely psychological inertia breaking context.

9-Windows/System Operator

As initially discussed in Chapter 3, our brains sometimes play some cruel tricks on us. Take a look at Figure 20.1, for example, and write down what you can see.

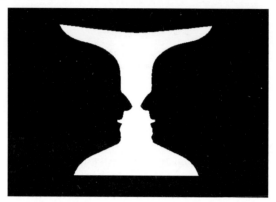

Figure 20.1: What Can You See?

Because everyone has seen something like this picture before, the usual response is something along the lines 'aha, yes, I can see both things – two faces and a vase'. There are two types of psychological inertia happening here; the first comes from exactly that familiarity – we are simply too used to seeing this kind of annoying puzzle. The second, however, is somewhat more serious. It comes from a rule that in all probability your brain has just imposed on itself, even though it is a rule that was never stated, nor was it actually there. That unstated, self-imposed rule was 'I must form images from the *whole* picture'. Admit it, its one you applied.

But the rule was never there. Just as similar 'rules' are never there in many of the 'problems' we look at. The simple truth about the Figure 20.1 image is that there are lots of images there that can be formed from just a part of the picture. Maybe now we have dispensed with the false rule, you can see things like

- a man in a pork-pie hat or a light fitting? (bottom half of picture)
- a whale's tail? (top half of picture)
- profile of an overweight person? (bottom right quarter of picture)

Or maybe you can zoom out and see the picture as that of a small key-hole? Or how about a close up of the back of two cars parked back-to-back?

Or maybe you turned the picture upside-down (one of the first resolution strategies our brain will apply if we get stuck with a problem), in which case you may have seen a coat-hanger in what has become the bottom half of the picture.

The point? We often need a little help to break us out of the ways we 'normally' look at things. In terms of the 9-Windows/System Operator tool, that 'normal' way involves someone giving us a problem and us heading straight for the system-present window at the center of the 9 boxes – Figure 20.2.

In other words, we immediately begin to assume a definition of what the 'system' is – where system is very often the first image your mind conjures up when the problem is described to you; 'the car won't start' leads to an immediate mental image of a system called 'car'. Similarly with respect to time; 'the car won't start' leads to an immediate mental image of someone sat in the drivers seat, turning the key, and nothing happening (except, maybe you can hear the engine turning over and not firing).

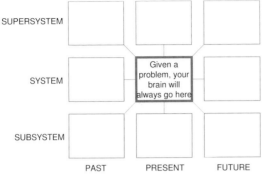

Figure 20.2: Where Our Brains Go When We Give Them A Problem To Solve

The Figure should give you a clue on how the 9-Windows tool can help us to overcome the system-present trick our brain plays on us. Very simply, what the 9-Windows asks us to do is think about the problem from the perspective of the other 8 boxes, asking the question in each 'is the *real* problem here?'

In other words, while the *manifestation* of the problem we are experiencing ('my car won't start') may well appear in the middle box, the actual problem requiring to be solved may well be in another box.

Chapter 3 talks about the practiced ability of systematic innovation experts to be able to continuously changing their frame of reference and viewing perspective on a problem, and Chapter 2 talks about how some of the solution triggers provided by the method help push us to different Windows. The 9-Windows tool is mentioned again specifically in this Chapter, because chances are, if the overall systematic innovation process and Chapter 10 has directed you to this Chapter that a little reminder about using the 9-Windows wouldn't go amiss.

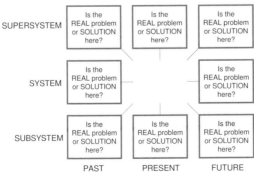

Figure 20.3: 9-Windows From A Problem Solving Context

Least-Ideal Final Result

Anyone familiar with the pillars of systematic innovation will know about the concept of the Ideal Final Result as a destination point towards which successful innovations are attracted. More experienced users will also be aware of the trend known as 'Mono-Bi-Poly (Increasing Differences)'. In this trend we see the emergence of an opposite function. The classic example is the pencil with the eraser fitted at the end. Or savings and loans. Mergers and divestments. According to the trend, ultimately, someone, somewhere will find a need for the opposite function.

By combining the Ideal Final Result (IFR) concept with this Mono-Bi-Poly (Increasing Differences) trend, we might come to the idea of a negative Ideal Final Result (-IFR), or least Ideal Final Result. The –IFR may thus be seen as the polar opposite of the IFR as shown in Figure 20.4.

Figure 20.4: Ideal Final Result And Least Ideal Final Result

The characteristics of this negative IFR may be seen as all those attributes that we really don't want to find in a system – infinite cost, zero reliability, etc. Not much use at first sight, but actually very similar to an often extremely effective idea generating technique found outside of the traditional systematic innovation territory.

'What would be the worst possible way to solve this problem?' is often used by creativity educators as a means of getting people to think out of the box. The technique also resognises that many people find it easier to engage the negative thinking aspects of their brain than the positive and generative parts. If you've not tried it before, an experiment you might like to make with a group sometime is to divide into two smaller groups and then get one to think about 'best' and the other 'worst' ways of solving a problem. At the very least, the number of ideas generated by the negative group will be significantly longer than that produced by the positive group. Very often, also, you will observe that the ultimate solution to the problem also emerges from the negative group. Not that anyone really wants to solve a problem in the 'worst possible way' – ultimately what we should be seeking to do is invert the 'worst' solution ideas into what might hopefully become 'best' ideas. The big point about going to the worst case first is that it forces you to get away from all of the psychological inertia associated with always being expected to think in the purely positive direction.

During a recent workshop, someone asked the question 'why do we always try to jump straight into solution mode when we are given a problem?' If you think about it, it nearly always happens; as soon as someone describes a problem to us, our immediate instinct is to start generating possible solutions. We think the answer to this is closely related to the above psychological inertia effect of always wanting to be heading in the positive direction. We are very often reluctant to challenge problem definitions because by doing so we might end up further away from a solution than when we started. Even if this ultimately turns out to be a good thing, at the time we are doing it, it can feel extremely uncomfortable. In many ways this effect is the same as the one that causes us to spend so little time (comparatively) planning an activity before we get stuck into the 'doing' part. When we are 'doing' we look busy, and we very easily trick ourselves into believing we are making progress. When we are 'planning' we often don't look like we're busy, and, more importantly, we feel that we are not making progress. Even worse, very often 'planning' opens up the possibility that we may be heading in the wrong direction and that therefore we will have to make some very definite backward steps.

So, the 'what would be the worst way...?' prompt is a way of getting us out of this kind of psychological inertia rut.

In many senses, the Subversion Analysis part of the systematic innovation toolkit (Chapter 21) works using a very similar reverse-psychology basis – prompting users to actively invent failures ('what would you do to make this system fail'). Again, experience using the method demonstrates that many people are much more capable of dreaming up ways of making bad things happen than they are of producing generative ideas. The Size-Time-Interface-Cost psychological inertia tool described in the next section is also very similar ('how would you solve the problem if you had zero money?' for example).

The 'what would be the worst way...?' technique is most commonly used as a light-hearted icebreaker type exercise (almost guaranteed in fact that if you are in a workshop and things are not going well, the facilitator will suggest doing this kind of exercise). Its purpose in this role is very much to get people thinking out of the box. By taking the output from this kind of activity and re-inverting it back to a positive direction, however, we can very often generate some very interesting new and useful ideas.

Example:-
    Q. 'What would be the worst way to motivate students to learn?'
    A. Tell them it won't be on the exam

Okay, an obvious one when we come to invert it, but what about:-
    Q. 'What would be the worst way to motivate students to learn?'
    A. Lecture at 9am.

Here's a negative solution direction that might enable us to generate some very interesting positive direction solution options – taking a direct opposite, we might think about lecturing at 9pm (when many students are just beginning to get their brain into gear for the day). A more general 'opposite' might cause us to think about other times of the day or moving from thinking about a fixed time to one that is completely flexible – e.g. putting lectures on a website or on CD-Roms so that students can look at them at times of their own choosing.

During a serious application of this tool, we might well list out a whole series of 'worst possible' ways of doing something and inverting all of them, rather than the single example cited here.

The negative Ideal Final Result is very simply a way of adding a more specific focus to the whole concept of problem solving by first looking to the worst possible ways of doing things.

Size-Time-Interface-Cost (STIC) Tool

The Size-Time-Interface-Cost (STIC) tool is an extension of the size-time-cost tool described in some of the original Soviet TRIZ texts (see Salamatov for example –

Reference 20.1). We make the extension to include 'interface' as a new category based on its philosophical importance in the overall context of the systematic innovation whole we are describing in this book.

The basic idea contained within the tool is that we tend to think of whatever problem it is that we are looking at in the context of its current size, the timeframe in which it currently operates, the number and form of interfaces that it currently has, and its current cost. We might see all these as the center point in a field with four dimensions (a little bit difficult to visualize perhaps – which might explain why the original tool had three dimensions to it). The tool is trying to get us to shift to the extreme edges of the field in order to see if we can find a better solution in one or more of those new viewing positions.

The tool gets us to take each of the four STIC parameters and systematically place ourselves at the extreme edges of each in turn. In each of the new positions, we then ask ourselves the question; 'how would I solve the problem if....?' Each extreme point provides us with a new if question. Taken all together, the questions the tool is prompting us to ask are; How would I solve the problem if.....

Physical Size (S) was	Zero	Infinite
Time (T) to deliver function was	Zero	Infinite
Number of Interfaces (I) was	Zero	Infinite
Allowable Cost (C) was	Zero	Infinite

Each of the eight questions is then used as the basis for a systematic brainstorming session. Figure 20.5 illustrates the STIC tool idea graphically, showing the idea of movement away from the current perspective to another at the extreme end of a spectrum of possibilities.

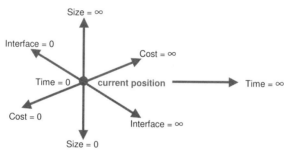

Figure 20.5: Size-Time-Interface-Cost PI Tool As A Means Of Shifting To A Different Problem Perspective

An example will probably help to illustrate how to use the tool in the most effective manner:

Anyone that has to undergo the rigours of air travel more than twice a year will know that the novelties of queuing to check-in, to pass through security, to board, to un-board, to pass through immigration, to collect baggage, to clear customs very quickly wears thin. Frequent air travelers might well chose to call themselves the 'bitter-class'. So, what might the STIC tool have to say about making the process of air-travel less cattle-like and less time-consuming?

These are the sorts of questions the tool is prompting us to think about:-

(S→∞) - What would air travel and the process of checking and unchecking luggage, etc be like if the airport was infinitely big?

(S→0) - What would air travel be like if the airport was so big enough for only one plane? Or one passenger? Or if the airport did not exist at all?

(T→∞) - What happens if check-in time was even longer? What if it took a whole day? Or a week?

(T→0) - What would air travel be like if check-in time was zero? Or flight time was zero? Or there was no waiting time anywhere?

(I→∞) - What would air travel be like if there was a staff member for every passenger? At every stage of the entering and exiting procedures?

(I→0) - What would air travel be like if there were no staff? No cabin crew?

(C→∞) - What would air travel be like if the cost was infinitely high? High enough that only a few passengers could afford it? What if passengers had to pay for the true environmental cost of their journey?

(C→0) - What would air travel be like if the cost were reduced to zero?

Undoubtedly some of the solution directions will generate ideas that make no sense no matter how long you spend looking at them. Undoubtedly also, it is very rare that none of the eight direction shifts prompted by the questions produce an idea that turns out to be a very useful one.

By way of example of some of the things the tool may prompt us to think about in relationship to the above air travel unpleasantness problem are:-

(S→∞) - personal transportation systems for every passenger, GPS tracking systems, personal announcements on local communication system (mobile phone?)

(S→0) - home pick-up service, all transactions done in transit to airport, car takes passenger directly to the plane, and their luggage to the hold, network of highly localised airports – 'super-hubs'.

(T→∞) - telephone check-in, Internet check-in, check-in by travel agent or holiday rep, hotels, meeting rooms, cinemas, entertainment facilities (i.e. make people want to get to the airport early rather than have them try to leave everything as close as possible to the due departure time),

(T→0) - terminal-wide security systems (e.g. radar, GPS tracking), one-time safety briefing that actually adds some value (e.g. making people actually put a life-jacket on rather than just telling them about it), combined check-in/security, perform immigration processing at check-in or on the plane not after the flight

(I→∞) - a staff-member for every passenger; personalised service, a system that remembers passenger preferences in an intelligent fashion, adaptive learning systems, software agent tracking-simulation tools, a system where passengers are regularly asked for their opinions and their suggestions are acted upon.

(I→0) - automated security systems, e-ticketing, e-passport, carry-on only services, transfer responsibility to get to appropriate gate on time to passenger (as happens at several so-called 'silent' airports already), GPS navigation aids for passengers requiring assistance, make use of the mobile phone that nearly everyone carries around with them – SIM-ticketing, SMS-flight information

(C→∞) - no useful ideas generated

(C→0) - have free flights at unpopular times in order to reduce congestion during peak times, no in-flight refreshments - passengers bring their own provisions, virtual travel, simulators

Depending on the individual or group using the tool, the likelihood of maintaining the energy to keep generating new ideas for all eight questions is relatively low. If you are trying to use the tool and find yourself saying things like 'oh, well, it obviously can't be possible to solve the problem if there's no money to do it', chances are you have reached the low-energy point. The temptation is to call it a day at this point. You can of course do this. A better strategy in such situations would be to go and do something different for a while and come back to the session later. Or it might mean splitting a group into smaller group and dividing the trigger questions between the different parts.

Why-What's Stopping Analysis Tool

The Why-What's Stopping? Tool is one that has been imported in a modified form into the systematic innovation toolkit. A version of the basic idea behind the tool may be found in several places. We include it here because it is the best thing we've found to help establish a hierarchy of problem statements in order that we might identify from that hierarchy 'the' problem we should be tackling. As we will see, this is important because very often we will discover that the problem we start with turns out not to be the one we should be solving. You will also find the Why-What's Stopping tool inside the Problem Explorer part of the Problem Definition sector of the book (Chapter 5). In that context, the tool is trying to provide some guidance at the beginning of a project. Here it is being used in the context of the situation where we have been through all the problem definition, tool selection and solution generation stages and still not generated a workable solution.

The 'Why-What's Stopping' tool represents a modified version of the analysis tool first developed by Basadur (Reference 20.2). The tool provides users with a structure through which to visualise an initial problem statement in the context of its broader and narrower contexts. The tool is aimed at overcoming the highly common situation which starts with statements like 'the problem is…' and continues a few seconds later with a headlong plunge into problem solving mode. This phenomenon is one of the most important manifestations of psychological inertia. Countless situations point to the fact that the initial problem definition turns out to be anything but the 'right' one. So, the tool takes the initial 'the problem is…' statement and forces the user to think about the broader and narrower problem. The typical schema is reproduced in Figure 20.6 below.

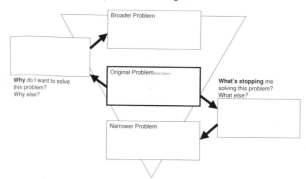

Figure 20.6: Why-What's Stopping? PI Tool Framework

Basically, the user uses the 'Why?' question to broaden the problem and uses the question 'What's Stopping?' to narrow the question. In keeping with the Deming (Reference 20.3) 'ask why 5 times' philosophy, the schema can be broadened or narrowed multiple times. (In line with Deming's statement, it would be very unlikely that we would have to repeat the why cycle more than five times to get to the root cause – in practice it will usually take less.) At the end of the process, the user has obtained a vertical stack of hierarchical problem definitions, from which a much clearer picture of what the 'right' problem is should emerge.

It is often useful to combine this mode of questioning with not just the '5-why's', but also the '5W's plus an H' approach: Who, What, When, Where, Why, and How. For more details on the combination of these approaches into the systematic innovation process in general, the reader may care to check out Reference 20.4.

For the purposes of breaking psychological inertia, we will retain our focus on the 'Why-What's Stopping?' approach. An example problem should hopefully help illustrate how the tool can encourage us to view a problem from different perspectives. We will look at the general problem of late payment of invoices by customers in a business-to-business context. This is a problem many organizations face and one that most will try to tackle as such a problem. Hence we will define that as our original problem.

The tool then encourages me to head upwards in the direction of broadening the problem by asking 'why' questions, and also downwards in the direction of narrowing the problem by asking the 'what's stopping' questions. It is important to notice the 'why else' and 'what else' questions – the intended implication being that we should be looking for as many possible answers as possible.

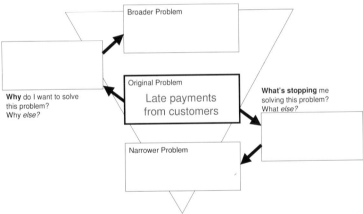

Figure 20.7: Why-What's Stopping? Tool At The Beginning Of The Late Payment Problem

Figure 20.8 illustrates a possible combination of questions and answers for the initially stated late payment problem. Some of the solution directions suggested by the tool are consistent with some of the things many companies already do (incentives/discounts to make customers happier to pay earlier, better communication, etc), but interestingly, some of them are not. The idea of making accounting systems transparent for example is actually quite interesting if customers can be convinced that two-way transparency makes for several win-win possibilities in terms of, say, spreading risk and building a stronger, longer term collaborative relationship. Similarly, the definition of a need for transparency that doesn't compromise either the confidentiality or the security of the company may lead to several interesting possibilities. (Note that in this latter regard, we have also identified a conflict between transparency and security. We may choose this opportunity to explore the conflict elimination part of the systematic innovation toolkit (Chapter 11) to see how others may have already found a win-win to such a conflict. This identification of a conflict is a phenomenon that often occurs when using the Why-What's Stopping tool.)

The basic point of the tool then is that it encourages exploration of the space around the initially perceived problem. As in this case, a better problem than the one initially identified often emerges.

Note that it is also possible to take one of the broader problem definitions and ask the 'what's stopping?' question on this in order to expand the scope of the problem exploration exercise. Similarly, it is possible to expand the scope of the narrower problem definitions by asking the 'why do I want to solve?' question.

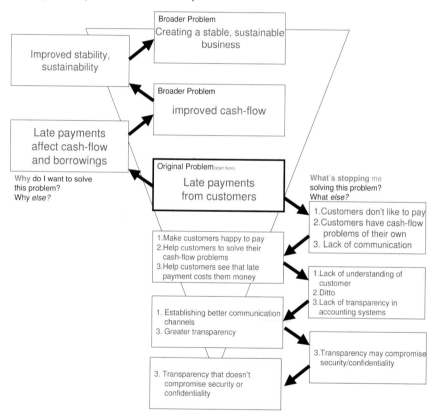

Figure 20.8: Why-What's Stopping? Analysis for the Late Payment Problem

See Chapter 5 for another example of the Why-What's-Stopping tool in action in its purely problem definition assistance role.

474

Omega Life View (OLV) Tool

In this final section we explore a new strategy we can use to overcome psychological inertia; The 'Omega Life View' (OLV) tool. It has been designed specifically for situations in which we are examining customer needs when we have a parallel desire to identify disruptive innovation opportunities.

The tool is based on two important pieces of psychology research; in the first instance, it builds on the 'Other People's Views' (OPV) development work of Edward DeBono (Reference 20.5). The OPV 'tool' very simply encourages problem solvers to shift their perspective to that of someone else. Typical OPV questions would be things like 'what would my manager think in this situation?' By putting ourselves in the position of others – empathizing with them – according to DeBono, we are able to think out of the box defined by our own psychological inertia. Secondly we build on the work of Liam Hudson (Reference 20.6) and his research finding that if we force people to try and solve problems while taking on the role of someone else, they very often do it better than if they had remained in their own mindset. The basis of this 'frames of mind' research is that if we can get outside the confines of the box defined by our own psychological inertia, or 'get outside our zone of comfort', we are often much better able to generate new ideas. One of the most amazing findings made by Hudson and his team was that by asking people who were normally not felt to be very creative to work on a task by taking on the perspective of a creative person ('how would a creative problem tackle this situation?) they were able to markedly improve their performance.

So, in its very simplest terms, the Omega Life View uses exactly the same strategy as both the DeBono and Hudson techniques; shift your perspective to match that of someone else. In both of those techniques, however, users are encouraged to shift to some fairly conventional 'other people' perspectives. This is great if, say, we are involved in an argument with another individual and wish to see the world from his or her perspective, and very often this kind of shift to seeing things from the 'other side' can be very effective. It becomes less effective, however, as we broaden the scope of which other people we chose to become. Microsoft, for example used to have a series of pre-defined customer characters that they used during product development. Thus, there may be a character called 'Bert'. 'Bert' is defined by a series of characteristics – say not very used to using computers, manual worker, etc – and then the developers would put themselves in Bert's position ('what would Bert do now?') in order to hopefully create a product that Bert and all of the other pre-defined characters would be happy to buy and use. Again this 'other people' technique can be very useful in helping us to design products that are robust and popular with a wide range of customers. Clearly, the more sorts of 'other people' we build into this thinking framework, the more popular our output ought to be. Except. Except there are two big problems here. The first is that pretty soon we can have so many different 'other people' types that it becomes impractical to manage them all (in most design teams using this kind of technique, the number is usually limited to 7 or 8); the second is that our common sense tells us to pick the most useful types of customer profile to become. Here comes our old friend the normal curve again. Common sense and the normal curve – a potentially fatal combination. Fatal? How come?

Let's have a look at what might typically happen when we go through the process of selecting which 'other people' to empathise with and design our products or services to please. The supermarket business is trying to make sure it attracts and retains the maximum number of customers. This is the common sense part. As a consequence of this common sense, the supermarket commissions all sorts of research to identify and understand the profiles of its different customers. This research will produce lots of useful data on things like average age of customer, average shopping bill, queue time, proportion of males to females, percentage of customers with small children, etc. All very useful. Then someone comes along and fits all of the data into an array of normal curves. Then as shown in Figure 20.9, they are able to find the 'optimum' average value of all of those measured parameters. It is only one small additional step then to design the supermarket to best match those 'average' values. If we do this well enough then our supermarket will become successful. What could possibly be wrong with this strategy?

The answer is our standard one whenever we see the normal curve or its cousins. What about the things at the extremes? What, in other words, about the Omegas?

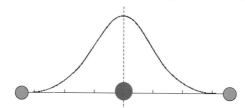

Extreme B   OR   'Average optimum'   OR   Extreme B

Figure 20.9: The Normal Curve And 'Omega Life Views'

The whole point of the normal curve, of course, is to allow us to make sure that we cover as much of the solution space as possible. Thus we can be pretty certain that supermarkets have designed their stores, check-outs, car-parks, etc to cover a pretty wide range of ages and customer types. Again, what's the problem?

Well, one problem is that every other supermarket has probably done exactly the same research, and drawn more or less exactly the same sorts of normal curve, and made all the same design decisions that we have. That's what makes it 'normal'. That's what makes just about every supermarket the same as every other one. Inevitably, there are some minor differences, but you only have to see how quickly one supermarket copies the shifts of another to see how this normal curve world-view spreads itself. One supermarket gets some new data to suggest that customer incomes are increasing and decides to launch a range of 'luxury' products. Guaranteed that within a couple of months, the second, third and fourth supermarket chains have launched their own 'finest' or 'gold-standard' or whatever equivalents. See also 'mother-and-baby' car-parking spaces, 'one-in-front' check-out queue strategies, loyalty cards, on-line store, in-city 'boutique'/Express stores, or just about every other 'innovation' you've ever noticed, and see how quickly the second supermarket follows the first.

The other problem – the apparently less serious one – is that those people that sit outside the bounds defined by our normal curve are not going to be our customers. This one looks less serious because if we've designed a model to cater for 99% of the population, why should we worry about the last 1%?

This sounds logical. Potentially losing 1% of a market sounds like a fairly acceptable situation to most businesses. 99% is a big customer base after all.

Here, however, lies the big paradox. *Our common sense focus on the 99% means that we miss the disruptive and discontinuous innovation opportunities*. What? It's true; the overwhelming evidence from just about every type of innovation is that the spark for that innovation has come from the Omegas; the people outside the normal curve. Think about it. Those Omega extremes are not being catered for by the 'normal' system. Consequently, they have to find other ways of getting what they want. Ironically, the Omegas also tend to be the sort of characters that are the entrepreneurial rebels that are likely to do something to get what they want. Net result? The Omegas find alternative ways of doing things, and – crucially – some of these ways will turn out to be the things that will eventually displace the 'normal' way of doing things.

Now we have a new problem because the large majority of the solutions derived by the small population of Omegas will turn out to be effective niche solutions but completely useless in the wider context. As a consequence of this usually extremely poor success/failure ratio, most organizations tend to ignore the Omegas altogether. This happens until either it's too late, or they have to spend large sums of money to buy the Omega out. See the Ben & Jerry's ice-cream story for an archetypal example (Reference 20.7).

The 'Omega Life View' tool has been designed to improve the success rate of this kind of disruptive innovation finding problem. There are two important elements to the methodology. The first involves the selection of which Omegas to select. If it were just this part then we will not really have helped the situation very much as finding the 'right' Omega can be as difficult as finding the 'right' disruptive innovation. The second part of the method is thus aimed at resolving this 'right'ness problem. The second part takes advantage of the systematic innovation research discovery about the importance of contradiction elimination in the creation of disruptive innovations. Identifying a 'good' conflict opens the way to use of the Inventive Principles to remove them. The OLV tool is aimed at helping to find such 'good' conflicts and contradictions.

The method is very simple, comprising the following steps:-
   a) identify the thing to be improved
   b) identify a range of Omegas – potential customers who currently lie outside the normal curve(s), preferably at both extremes
   c) put yourself into the life of those customers and write down the 'ideal' wish-list sorts of things they would like to have
   d) compare the wish-lists of each of the Omegas in order to identify and define common themes and conflicts
   e) ask whether any of the common themes suggest possible disruptive opportunities
   f) for the common themes, also ask 'what stops us from delivering these requirements?' in order to identify other conflicts
   g) explore means of 'eliminating' some or all of the conflicts

The power of the method lies in the fact that very often when we 'eliminate' a conflict – as opposed to making the usual trade-offs and compromises – that all sorts of nice things happen that we weren't expecting.

Let's take a look at an example of the process in action in order to explore the basic mechanics and to explore a situation that is currently ripe for disruptive innovation:

Cell Phone Services

Thing to be improved: cell-phone services
Omegas: a) CEO of Fortune 50 company
           b) Epileptic traveller
           c) Single mother with kindergarten-age triplets

(The general idea here is to identify a spectrum of people at different extremes laying outside the realms of the 'normal' curve. It is worth noting here that we have tended to identify specialized niches containing very few people at the edges of the societal structure. According to 'The Deviant's Advantage' (Reference 20.8) we ought to push the spectrum even further to those living at the very fringes of society. We will stick with 'edge' rather than 'far-fringe' for two reasons – 1) it is (hopefully) easier to empathise with a single mother or a company CEO than it is to empathise with a member of the Jim Rose Circus (www.ambient.on.ca/jimrose/jimrose.html - please take care!), and more importantly, 2) identifying and solving a 'good' conflict will likely as not also deliver a solution that a wrestling Mexican body-piercer might well also want.)

The next stage:-

Omega	'Ideal Product' Wish-List
CEO	- a handset that symbolises status - small as possible handset/integration with other tools - handset 'auto-charges' battery - instant access to share prices - instant access to PA and direct-reports - one-to-many conference calls - no loss of signal when on trains/planes - zero learning curve - direct voice-to-e-mail - boundary-less international calling - ability to store all desired information - theft-proof - 'scramble' facility for confidential communications - always the 'latest version'/'no-phone' - stress monitor
Epileptic traveller	- single-press emergency call to nearest emergency service irrespective of location - handset invulnerable to damage if dropped - power always available (battery always charged) - phone able to transmit vital-signs to emergency services - theft-proof - language translation facility - combine with airline e-ticket - combine with local currency e-cash/m-cash system
Single mother	- low-cost - rugged handset – invulnerable to damage from a wide range of (infant generated) situations - impossible (for baby) to accidentally press keys and make calls - story-telling facility/entertain infants simultaneously - loss-proof – handset able to inform mother where it is - hands-free, attachment feature - baby monitor facility connected to kindergarten CCTV - panic button - support-group communications (multiple users)

Each of these lists would typically be much longer if we were conducting the exercise for real. We have stopped at this stage in order to concentrate on the process rather than any specific solutions that might emerge.

Conflicts: - open-access AND confidential
- low-cost AND high status
- long calls AND low cost
- long calls and battery capacity
- small AND loss-proof/theft-proof
- latest version AND zero learning curve
- 'One-touch' calling AND no accidental calling
- communication AND 'no-phone'

Common themes: - damage tolerance
- auto-location of important numbers
- auto-link to external information sources
- one-to-many/many-to-one
- integration of different capabilities
- input of sensing information
- auto-charging/'self'-powered
- hands-free

Conflicts caused by these themes: - rugged AND low-cost
- integration AND security
- sensing AND reliable
- battery AND no-battery
- hands-free AND theft-proof

Taken together, we may begin to see a number of interesting new possibilities and facilities emerging once some of these conflicts become resolved.

What this example shows is that even though it is not immediately obvious that any of the Omegas considered have anything at all in common with one another, nevertheless a cluster of common themes emerge (e.g. each one wants single-press access to key numbers; but for very different reasons). Similarly, a number of conflicts emerge that we can quickly see that if they are resolved, the resulting capability satisfy the often wildly different specific requirements of each Omega.

Above all, the example demonstrates that the OLV tool is very simple to use and an effective way to 'get out of the box' and to places that will generate valuable new solutions.

What Do I Do?

As discussed in Chapter 3, psychological inertia appears to be a fundamental phenomenon of the human brain. Awareness of the problem is a start, but many people find they need active strategies to help them to overcome psychological inertia.

Four main tools are recommended in the overall process we have labelled 'systematic innovation'. The 9-Windows 'system operator' concept is required throughout, and thus received its own chapter earlier in the book. In this chapter we have examined four other tools – Least Ideal Final Result, Size-Time-Interface-Cost, 'Why-What's Stopping' Analysis and Omega Life View. These are collectively the five we have found to be most useful in countering psychological inertia, for the greatest number of users. Everybody's psychological inertia appears to have its own uniquely individual quirks, however, and so the most effective way of using the techniques in this chapter is to try each of them out and see which fits best into your way of doing things.

The PI tools are most useful in helping us to re-frame a problem if we have not been able to generate solutions using any of the other tools in the systematic creativity armoury, but some people will find they have a particular affinity to a certain tool and will naturally incorporate it into their everyday use. This is to be commended – the greater the number of working tools in the toolkit, the greater our chances of deriving better solutions.

For readers who find that none of the tools recommended here fit into their scheme of things, check out the bibliography at the end of the chapter for a more comprehensive list of what the wider world knows about overcoming psychological inertia.

Whatever PI tools you are attracted to, the real requirement is to use them as often as possible.

References

1) Salamatov, Y., 'TRIZ: The Right Solution at the Right Time', Insytec nv, The Netherlands, 1999.
2) Basadur, M., 'The Power Of Innovation', Financial Times Prentice Hall, 1995.
3) Deming, W.E., 'Out of the Crisis', Cambridge University Press, 1986.
4) Apte, P., Shah, M., Mann, D.L., '5W's and an H of TRIZ', TRIZ Journal, June 2001.
5) DeBono, E., 'Serious Creativity', Penguin Books, 1992.
6) Hudson, L., 'Frames Of Mind', Methuen, 1968.
7) Cohen, B., Greenfield, J., 'Ben & Jerry's Double Dip', Simon & Schuster, 1997.
8) Mathews, R., Wacker, W., 'The Deviant's Advantage: How Fringe Ideas Create Mass Markets', Random House Business Books, 2003.

Bibliography (in descending order of importance)

1) DeBono, E., 'Serious Creativity', Penguin Books, 1992.
2) DeBono, E., 'Po: Beyond Yes or No', Penguin Books, 1972.
3) DeBono, E., 'The Mechanism of Mind', Penguin Books, 1969.
4) Dilts, R., 'Tools For Dreamers', Meta Publications, 1982.
5) Dilts, R., 'Strategies of Genius', Volumes 1-3, Meta Publications, 1996.
6) Koestler, A., 'The Act of Creation', Penguin Arkana, 1964.
7) Hall, L.M., Bodenhamer, B.G., 'Figuring Out People: Design Engineering with Meta-Programs', Crown House Publishing, 1997.
8) Lawley, J., Tompkins, 'Metaphors in Mind: Transformation Through Symbolic Modelling', The Developing Company Press, 2000.
9) MacKenzie, G., 'Orbiting the Giant Hairball', Viking, 1998.
10) Root-Bernstein, R. and M., 'Sparks of Genius – the 13 Thinking Tools of the World's Most Creative People', Houghton Mifflin, Boston, 1999.
11) Gelb, Michael, 'How to Think Like Leonardo da Vinci – Seven Steps to Genius Everyday', Thorsons, 1998.
12) Allan, D., Kingdon, M., Murrin, K., Rudkin, D., 'What If? How to Start a Creative Revolution at Work', Capstone Publishing, 1999.
13) Charlotte, S., 'Creativity – Conversations with 28 Who Excel', Momentum Books Ltd, 1993.
14) Foster, R., Kaplan, S., 'Creative Destruction: Turning Built-to-Last into Built-to-Perform', Financial Times Prentice Hall, 2001.
15) Horn, R.E., 'Visual Language – Global Communication for the 21st Century', MacroVU Inc, Washington, 1998.
16) Oech, R., von, 'A Kick in the Seat of the Pants', Harper Perennial, 1986.
17) Buzan, T., 'Use Your Head', BBC Books, 1997 updated edition.
18) Claxton, G., 'Hare Brain, Tortoise Mind', 4th Estate, London, 1997.
19) Wallace, D.B., Gruber, H.E., 'Creative People at Work', Oxford University Press, Oxford, 1989.
20) Grand, S., 'Creation: Life and How to Make It', Weidenfeld, 2000.
21) Nalebuff, B., Ayres, I., 'Why Not? How To Use Everyday Ingenuity To Solve Problems Big And Small', Harvard Business School Press, 2003.
22) Osho, 'Intuition, Knowing Beyond Logic', St Martin's Griffin, New York, 2001.

21.
Problem Solving Tools
Subversion Analysis

*"A common mistake that people make when trying to design something completely
foolproof is to underestimate the ingenuity of complete fools"*
Douglas Adams, Mostly Harmless.

or

"But the Earth turns for its own reasons, ignoring mine, and these human mis-calculations"
Margaret Atwood, The Circle Game.

This chapter is all about techniques and strategies for creating more robust business solutions. It doesn't matter whether we examine the world of business at a macro-level or zoom-in to look at departments and sections inside organisations, there are very few examples of businesses that have stood the test of time. We only have to examine how the list of Fortune 100 companies has evolved and shifted in the last 40 years to see just how bad business leaders are at building long-term sustainable success into the way that they go about their activities. Of course there are exceptions – organisations that have thrived and survived for hundreds of years – but the average life expectancy of an organisation here in the first part of the 21st Century is more usually measured in years rather than in decades or centuries. In some sectors, like the restaurant trade for example, the failure statistics will show that 95% of businesses will go out of business within five years of their launch. In nearly every sector, the average life-expectancy figure has been and on a consistently downward trajectory for some considerable time. The words 'business' and 'robust' are not often used in the same context as one another.

So, what can systematic innovation offer to help us in those situations where we are looking to build more robustness into the way we go about managing the sections, departments, divisions, companies and corporations we are responsible for? Well, in true 'someone, somewhere already solved your problem' fashion, there are many people who have had to think about designing systems that are considerably more robust than not only the average, but also the most robust business models. In this case those people are the engineers of the world. At the cutting edge of engineering robustness design are probably the nuclear, aerospace and space industries. If you have invested several hundred million dollars to produce a satellite that you are going to launch into the most hostile environments possible, and never be able to get your hands on ever again, there are no such things as 'having a second go at it'; it has to work, and work reliably from the first moment of launch.

One of the main parts of the chapter, therefore, is to present a version of the tools being used by these engineers re-framed into a business and management context. That will be the second and single biggest part of the chapter. The first part of the chapter describes some of the definitions and metrics used to define what we mean by robustness in the business context. Beyond those two sections, the remainder of the chapter then goes on to offer a series of 'check-lists'. These lists are designed to help us to think about and ask the right questions when we wish to design as much robustness as possible into a business situation.

1) Defining 'Robustness'

Robustness (or 'reliability' as it is more often referred to in an engineering context) appears to becoming one of the dominant aspects of system design in many industry sectors. This is in part due to the fact that managers are increasingly expected to manage their parts of the business to survive and thrive into the future. Unfortunately and ironically, the great weight of history suggests that we only become truly concerned by issues of robustness after it is too late. Figure 21.1 illustrates a typical correlation between the evolutionary state of a business and the focus of the managers and people within the business during its different stages. The figure shows that robustness only becomes a serious concern and focus during the latter maturity and retirement phases of the lifecycle of the system. This phenomenon occurs because often in the early stages we are simply trying to get the product or service offering to a sufficient quality level that any customer will want it, then, during the phase of rapid growth we are too busy shipping product and collecting the money. Only when improving the offering becomes more difficult – and consequently it becomes more and more difficult to discriminate ourselves from our competitors – does the focus shift to building longevity into the business. Unfortunately again, this turns out to be 'too late' (see Reference 21.1 for a catalogue of examples) because it is extremely difficult to bolt robustness on to a model that has never considered or had to think about it before.

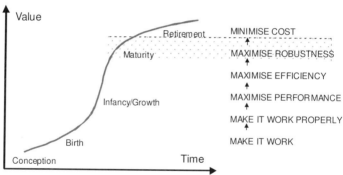

Figure 21.1: Reliability Consideration On System Evolution Curve.

A very big consequent problem in terms of designing to improve robustness is that it almost demands consideration of the relevant issues from day one. The second big problem is that there is comparatively little design database upon which to build an effective business design methodology.

Before getting in to the details of what we might do to help improve this situation, it is first useful to define a few important robustness metrics: Robustness is defined as the probability that a system will perform to a specified standard without failure, for a given time, when operated correctly, in a specified environment. Since robustness is in this definition a probability, it is defined as a number between 0 and 1.

A robustness of 0 indicates that a system will definitely fail; whereas a robustness value of 1 means that the system will never fail. Sometimes it is also helpful to talk in terms of a probability of failure. Robustness and probability of failure are connected by the simple formula:

$$\text{Robustness} = 1 - \text{Probability of Failure}$$

Many robustness metrics are described in terms of failure rates per number of operating hours. Six Sigma, for example uses the idea of 'number of defects per million opportunities' as a way of defining the robustness of a system. Thus, within Six Sigma terminology, achieving a six-sigma level of quality would mean (depending on how you do the maths – Reference 21.2) 3.4 failures per million opportunities. Different industries tend to use different methods of presenting data. We will use the conventions of the space and aerospace industries – describing failure rates in terms of a probability of failure per hour of operation. Thus 10^{-6} is used to record a failure rate of 1 failure per million operating hours. Obviously, the lower this number, the more robust a system is. Leading edge engineering systems are typically capable of failure rates of 10^{-8} or better – i.e. one failure per hundred million hours. Few if any business systems can justifiably claim such low failure rates.

To some, it may appear strange that we need to be talking about robustness at all since, conceptually at least, it ought to be highly possible to configure systems that will never fail. In simple terms, the robustness of a system depends upon the relationship between the tasks that we expect it to do and the corresponding capacity and capability of the elements that we put together to deliver the required output. Figure 21.2 shows possible task and capability distributions plotted on a common axis. We include statistical variation on the two distributions since we know that both the task and the capability will be subject to some degree of variation. Irrespective of the amount of the variation in either task or capability (both of which could be considerable), if we can design the business so that there is no interference between the two distributions – i.e. ensure that the worst case capability is always better than the most testing task – then there will be no possibility of failure. This may be seen as the ideal situation; if a system is designed with these curves and this separation in mind, they will have a robustness value of 1. This being the case, despite the inevitable conceptual over-simplifications in the analogy, we must ask why it is that robustness, or rather the failure of so many systems continues to be such a big issue.

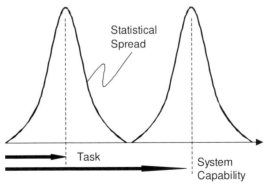

Figure 21.2: Task-Capability Diagram With No Interference.

What actually happens, however, is shown in Figure 21.3. In this scenario there is an interference region. This region indicates that some aspects of the system may have capabilities less than that demanded by the task. Consequently there is a risk that some system failures will occur. This intersection between the two curves occurs due to two primary drivers – firstly, thinking about the ideality equation, the desire for increased 'benefits' (e.g. task conducting capability) tends to push the design curve to the right, and secondly, the demands of competition and cost reduction tend to cause organizations to pull the capability curve to the left.

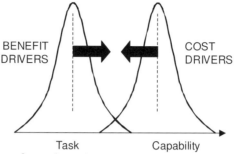

Figure 21.3: Task-Capability Diagram With Interference.

In practice, of course, it is common to try and cut off the tail of the capability curve by inspection and testing. Likewise, we limit the task by specifying what customers can and cannot ask for, and designing systems that prevent customers from straying into unwanted excessive-demand territory. The paradox in both cases, is that these actions tend to create their own robustness problems – in that very often it is the systems we put in place to measure and limit that turn out to be the things that fail. In other words, we look to solve one set of problems and in so doing introduce another set.

An issue related to this paradox is also worth discussing briefly in setting the scene for understanding what we mean by the term 'system robustness' and then in doing a better job of designing for robustness. Historically, the way we design systems is that we spend some time assessing what customers want and then designing and constructing a business model to deliver it to them. Because there is an inevitable amount of uncertainty in both of these activities, we multiply in a range of 'fudge factors' that basically says 'we don't really understand what's going on, so let's add in some margin'. And so usually we end up with a system that we later come to describe as 'over-engineered'. This offers an at least partial explanation for the increasing-followed-by-decreasing-complexity trend that all systems follow over the course of their evolution (Chapter 14). If a system finds itself in this state, then very quickly competitive pressures (in the form of 'business process re-engineering' initiatives often) cause us to say 'hey, we over-engineered the system; perhaps those fudge factors were too big. Next time, let's make them a bit smaller (and hence use less resources)'. This process then tends to repeat until, surprise, surprise, failures begin to occur. In effect this kind of optimization is one of the basic tasks of management – trying to get the maximum output for the minimum input, and in so doing, inevitably pushing systems to the limits of their capability. As has already been discussed in Chapter 10 when we were talking about short-cuts, in our experience over 80% of business situations are in a state where systems have been pushed to such a fundamental limit.

2) Tools And Strategies To Help Improve Robustness

There are a number of tools and techniques that can be deployed to help us to design business systems that are more robust. We shall explore five in particular here:-

a) Top-down analysis
b) Bottom-up analysis
c) Red-Team/Blue-Team subversion analysis
d) Robustness Trend Patterns
e) Robustness Contradiction Elimination

a) Top-Down System Analysis

Business systems of any description are complex. That is 'complex' meaning 'on the edge of chaos'. Top-down methods of analyzing the robustness (or lack thereof) associated with such complexity generally involve the construction of fault trees. Fault tree analysis (FTA) is particularly useful at the design stage of a business operation, since it should identify likely causes of system failure. It corresponds to a question of the type *"How could this failure event occur?"* The general pattern of analysis usually follows a number of steps:

i) System definition – process flow charts and FAA models of the system under evaluation are required. These identify the elements and steps that define the system and the interconnections that it contains.

ii) Selection of top events - A 'top event' is an operational failure (or partial failure) of the system. It may represent either a complete breakdown or a failure to meet the desired performance specification: e.g. a customer order fails to ship, or arrives late. A new fault tree is associated with each new top event. Hence it is important to select those top events that will have the most serious consequences, particularly those that are more likely to happen.

iii) Fault tree construction - By following the FAA models from the element associated with the top event along the function relationship lines that connect it to other elements of the system, the top event may be linked to more basic fault events. The event statements are linked through logic gates. OR gates require only one input to be available before the output event occurs. AND gates on the other hand require both input events to have occurred before the output event can happen. In the simplest models, only OR gates are required, linking alterative fault events, e.g. there will be no dispatch of an order to a customer if the warehouse doesn't receive the appropriate instructions, OR the sales-person doesn't enter the relevant details into the system, OR production doesn't deliver the goods to the warehouse. And so on. In systems with in-built redundancy, AND gates are also required. Here we might have failure situations like; there will be no dispatch of an order to a customer if the accounts department processes the order information late AND the order processing system fails to flag to the rest of the system that it is late. A fault tree may thus be built up by piecing together many such small segments.

iv) Primary events - Each branch of the fault tree must terminate in a primary event representing a basic element failure which requires no further analysis (like 'sales-person doesn't enter details into the system'). All primary events should be fully independent. An analysis of these events should indicate the most likely cause of the top event. If the top event represents catastrophic failure of an important system, it may be desirable that no single primary event should be sufficient to cause the failure. Multiple redundancy may be fitted in order that failure will occur only if there are simultaneous primary events in several independent elements.

v) Probability analysis - The probability of occurrence of a primary event is defined as the probability that the event occurs at least once during the intended life of the system. Such probabilities may be estimated from data obtained through records of the failure rates of similar elements in service in the past, or – much more likely since very few organizations collect this kind of information – from estimates. This final stage of the analysis is usually only carried out if it is required to produce some kind of quantified assessment of the robustness of a system. It is not entirely clear what the tangible benefits of such approaches are in absolute terms. As a relative-improvement measurement tool on the other hand, there is something to be said for the technique. It certainly matches the trend in many organizations towards measurement of previously intractable things like 'how much risk am I carrying'. This trend is in large part driven by Six Sigma type quality improvement initiatives.

b) Bottom-Up System Analysis

This is a complementary form of analysis to the fault tree analysis just considered, except now a *bottom up* approach rather than a *top down* approach is adopted. That is, it corresponds to a question of the type *"What happens if this element fails?"* It is most usefully applied to non-redundant systems, concentrating on those elements that are associated with probable causes of system failure.

This type of bottom-up 'what happens if' approach has its roots in Failure Modes and Effects Analysis (FMEA). Unfortunately, FMEA is often tedious and time consuming work. It usually comprises the following stages:

i) System definition - This is similar to the first step in fault tree analysis, beginning again from FAA models.

ii) Failure mode analysis (FMA) - For each system element and for each operating sequence and corresponding component state, all potential failure modes should be identified – e.g. 'accounts department processes the order information late'. Where possible their relative frequency of occurrence may be compared.

iii) Failure effects analysis (FEA) - For every defined failure mode of each element within a system, the local effects on the function of that element, the effects on the system and on the operation should be identified and recorded. A limitation of most analyses is the practice of considering only single failures. Each failure mode should be evaluated to determine the worst possible consequences and a severity classification may be assigned. These range from catastrophic (loss of equipment or injury to staff) and critical (failure of operation) to marginal (reduced performance or availability) and minor (unscheduled repair required).

iv) Criticality analysis (CA) - Each potential failure mode may be ranked according to the combined influence of its severity classification and the probability of its occurrence. Often there is a lack of appropriate data, and this work can only be carried out qualitatively. A criticality matrix may be drawn, points representing different failure modes being plotted on axes representing severity and frequency of occurrence. Alternatively, an arbitrary scale of numerical values may be assigned to the severity classification and to the estimated frequency of occurrence, and the criticality may be defined as the product of the two numbers for any particular failure mode. Other factors might also be introduced into the criticality rating. Where system monitoring techniques are used, it might be appropriate to include a factor representing the difficulty of detecting an incipient failure mode. In industrial applications one might include a factor representing the maintenance cost associated with a failure. For the most critical items, particularly those with high severity ratings, robustness may be improved by changes in design, changes in system design, duplication and redundancy. Condition monitoring systems may be used to give warning of deteriorating performance and impending failure. Planned inspection and maintenance may be directed to the more critical components.

v) Documentation - The results of FMECA are normally presented in tabular form; separate forms being used for FMEA and for CA due to the large number of columns required. Following a definition of an element and its function, the first form should list the possible failure modes, the system operating modes, the failure effects (both local and general), the severity of the effects of each failure mode, failure detection methods and general remarks. The second form would also identify the element, its failure modes and severity classification. Columns would then be provided to list the probability of each failure mode, the probability of each failure effect, failure rates and operating times, the criticality of each failure mode and each component and general remarks.

For examples of the process in action, interested users may care to check out Reference 21.3. One of the pleas made in the reference, and the essential idea behind FMEA (and FTA for that matter) is that it is supposed to *influence the design* of systems. Unfortunately, this feedback loop is very often missing, and an analysis is very often performed because of a requirement to have an appropriate 'tick in the box', rather than to improve the system. This is a pity.

Limitations of FMEA and FTA

i) They are both tedious time consuming processes in large systems. It is usual to apply the *Pareto Principle* - concentrate on the vital few, i.e. those elements whose failures have catastrophic or serious effects, or occur most frequently, and those failure events (top level events) which are perceived as being of most importance, and ignore the *trivial many*.
ii) The processes do not positively identify failure modes or effects or top level events, and some may be missed. FMEA tends to focus on the physical system structure and can miss the effects of external hazards such as operator error or errors inadvertently introduced by customers. Hazards caused by intangible factors ('we didn't check it because of your reputation for quality') can also be difficult to identify and mitigate against. FTA may entirely overlook the existence of significant classes of system failures by failing to consider their possibility.
iii) It is difficult to combine the robustness data of system elements in series and parallel particularly when the relationships between them are temporary or periodic.
iv) It is difficult to allow for gradual degradation processes – particularly those involving intangible factors. Modeling a gradual decline in morale, for example, can be extremely difficult to analyse in any kind of meaningful way.
v) There is a lack of published data describing what happened in the past. Since business systems are also fundamentally complex, it is also very difficult to use any data that does exist from the past to assess what might happen in the future; there will *always* be something that is different.

c) Red-Team/Blue-Team Subversion Analysis

For some the most striking aspect of the descriptions of FMEA and FTA above are that they both sound like a lot of hard work that may result in little benefit. There are also a number of psychological inertia issues associated with the fact that the process can become very dull very quickly. Many organizations have sought to overcome at least the boredom/motivation problem aspect by taking a more pro-active approach to finding where and how business systems can go wrong. In some of those organizations, the approach is known as Red-Team/Blue-Team. In this approach, the job of the Red Team is to actively try and put the Blue Team out of business. GE has used such an approach very successfully to make their various operating units more robust. The Red Team may be just one or two people versus several thousand that exist in the Blue Team, and clearly their job is not to *really* put the company out of business, but to identify the things that competitors might do before the competitors themselves find ways to achieve the objective. The Red-Team approach works because the members of the team are expected to engage their creative capabilities rather than the analytical skills that FMEA and FTA would expect.

Subversion Analysis (SA) operates along very similar psychological lines – requiring users to be thinking in a divergent, creative mode rather than a convergent analytical way. The key subversion analysis question is *'how could we destroy this system?'*

As soon as we have expressed a robustness problem in this way, we have turned it into an inventive one. As such, we can use all of the systematic innovation toolkit to help us generate 'solutions'. The basic idea then, of course, is that if we are able to invent ways of destroying a system, we can then put into place strategies that will prevent such ways from happening. Subversion analysis is in many ways about using systematic innovation tools in reverse.

Let us now use some of those systematic innovation tools in this 'reverse' mode to see what they may have to say about the design of more robust systems:

A first simple connection comes from thinking about the dynamics of system evolution and the cone image reproduced in Figure 21.4. What this figure suggests is that one of the main threats to the robustness of any business system is that someone introduces a more ideal solution than yours.

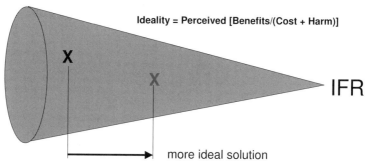

Figure 21.4: A 'More Ideal' Solution Will Threaten An Existing System.

What this picture and the ideality equation definition tells us is that there are four main focus areas to look at when we are trying to identify potential threats to our system; systems that deliver more benefits; systems that cost less; systems that produce less harm; and systems where customers *perceive* that the overall ideality is better (even though in actuality it may not be).

Beyond this, the law of system completeness (Chapter 18) will tell us that not only must a threatening solution be more ideal than our own, but it must also possess a further three attributes. Firstly, the solution must be 'producible' – it can be the best solution in the world, but if it cannot be produced in sufficient quantities then it is not a threat to our solution. Secondly, and related to the producibility, the solution must also have a route to market. This may literally mean the logistics of delivering the product or service, but it can also include anything else relating to the ability to get the product or service from the supplier to the customer. Thus it may include things like a relationship with appropriate channels, order processing systems, after-sales support, and – occasionally very important – compliance with legal requirements (changes in legislation can often become a significant threat to robustness and hence need to be included in any subversion analysis). Finally, and most importantly, there must be a demand from the market for the more ideal solution. As discussed in Chapter 14, this demand may be explicit or it may be hidden. Without it, however, a solution can be the most effective one in the world, and it will not succeed. Taken together then, before an alternative to our system can be classed as a real threat, we can see that it must be at least perceived to be more ideal, producible, have a route to market, and there must be a demand for it. These four (necessary and sufficient) attributes are illustrated in Figure 21.5.

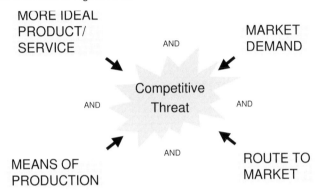

Figure 21.5: Essential Attributes Of A Competitive Threat.

What we must take into account when we look at these attributes is that different customers have different definitions of what 'ideal' means. Of specific concern when we are thinking about robust businesses is the concept of a disruptive innovation. As far as our current customers are concerned, a disruptive innovation fails the 'more ideal' test of a competitive threat. However – and it is a very big however – to people who are not your current customers, the disruptive innovation may be perceived to be more ideal because they are measuring ideality against a different set of metrics to the ones that you and your current customers are using. Chapter 14 talks about this subject in more detail. From the perspective of building more robust systems, suffice to say that in a very large proportion of cases, the thing that comes along and destroys your system will be precisely one of these disruptive innovations. The non-linear trend (Chapter 14) and Omega Life View (OLV – Chapter 20) tools are the ones with most to offer in helping us to identify where these threats to our business are going to come from.

Finally in terms of scoping where and when threats might emerge, we return to the 9-Windows tool from Chapter 4. As suggested by Figure 21.6, what the 9-Windows will do is fully define where and when a threat may emerge from. While this might not sound like a great deal of help in terms of inventing ways to destroy systems, at the very least it offers a systematic way of segmenting the search space.

One of the things that the 9-Windows implies to us is that threats to robustness may just as easily come from within our own system as from an outside threat. In this sense, we should again focus on the four necessary and sufficient threat elements defined in Figure 21.5. If we lose any one of these four elements then again our robustness will be under serious threat.

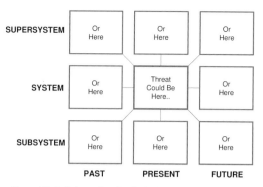

Figure 21.6: Subversion Analysis And The 9-Windows.

The final section of this chapter contains three check-lists of important subversion analysis questions. These are designed to help us to take the general rules and guidelines described here and turn them into a series of practical things to think about. In the meantime, we need to examine two more general aspects of the design-for-business-robustness story:

d) Robustness Trend Patterns

According to the systematic innovation 'someone, somewhere already solved your problem' statement, the robustness problems we are facing have already been faced and solved by someone. Quite likely they were working in a very different field to our own, but nevertheless, according to the underlying systematic innovation thinking, it ought to be possible to distil some generically applicable solution directions from the good practices of others. One thing that may be observed if we examine large numbers of such successful robustness-building solutions is that there are some definite patterns that recur across wide ranges of different sectors.

In this section we examine a robustness trend pattern that emerges from the analysis of the successes of others. This pattern may be thought of as a series of discontinuous jumps that emerge as progressively more sophisticated robustness capabilities are developed and proven. The basic pattern is illustrated in Figure 21.7.

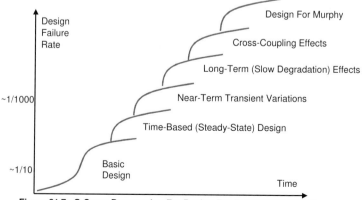

Figure 21.7: S-Curve Progression For Design For Robustness Paradigms.

Again we observe the idea of the evolutionary s-curve in action. Each of the new curves in the figure represents one of the discontinuous jumps in system design capability (we have only drawn the top portion of them, since the shift from one method of improving system robustness will only fully occur when the new capability is better than the existing one, and thus the bottom portion of the curve may not be relevant).

A good way to think about and use this s-curve progression is like that recommended for the trend of evolution detailed in Chapter 14. I.e. if you observe that the design strategy you are applying is not at the end of the progression, there is untapped evolutionary potential that once exploited will enable you to improve robustness. Like the trends, the progression is there to illustrate and suggest good solution directions. A simplified version of the trend progression may also be found in the reference section at the end of Chapter 14.

From the perspective of using the progression as a means of designing more robustness into a business model or organization structure, or for that matter any kind of business situation, the jumps may be seen to form a progression. That is, there is little point in trying to improve the robustness of a system by looking at long-term degradation effects if we have not first tackled short-term, transient ones. The basic jumps, then, comprise the following:-

Basic Design – a first stage design capability in which we construct a system to deliver certain functions. This may be done on a trial-and-error basis, or there may be an element of design that says, for example, that if we wish to set up and run a shop that there are certain fundamental things like ordering stock, transacting business, receiving money, etc that will need to be done.

Steady-State – an advance on basic design in that we now realize that not only do we require certain actions to take place in order to run our shop, but that they need to happen in a certain sequence. Thus, for example, a system in which we don't actively manage the flow of income and outgoings is not going to last for too long. To be honest, any business that has not reached this second level of robustness is unlikely to survive for very long in today's competitive environment. Time issues may not be as important during the birth phase of a business, but they will very quickly become so in even the most immature market sectors.

Near-Term Transients – where we take into account the likelihood that the way we operate needs to change as a function of time. Things like seasonal variation, end-of-year fiscal events, different times during a project cycle, shifting load/capacity balance, over-time working, disputes, etc are all examples of transient effects that can have a significant effect on the robustness of a business system.

Slow Degradation – when we are thinking about slow degradation effects, we are generally switching from the above short-term (daily/weekly/monthly/annually) perspective to a longer term perspective of a business. In this longer-term view, we are interested in things like shifts in interest rates, legislation changes, inflationary pressures, increasing competitive pressures, etc and the impacts they might have on the robustness of our business.

Cross-Coupling – by the time we are beginning to incorporate cross-coupling effects into the way that we design our business, we will typically already be approaching failure rates of one-per-hundred-thousand or better. Cross-coupling effects here means that we examine individual failure modes identified in the above robust design models and begin to examine what happens to our business if those failures begin to occur in combination with one another. Thus, for example, we might find ourselves considering things like what

491

happens when we get a series of late payments, at the end of the financial year, during a labour dispute. Even if we think that some of the events we have identified in the earlier methods can never ever happen together, there is a deal of evidence from failed companies to suggest that the worst-case scenario has an uncanny habit of becoming the actual scenario.

Murphy – leading-edge robust design capabilities work on the premise that if something can possibly go wrong with a system, it will. In essence, the 'design for Murphy' paradigm emerges from engineering sectors where the responsibility for the reliability of a product shifts from the customer to the supplier; sell someone a jet-engine and they do something stupid with it, then traditionally they pay for the mistake. Increasingly, however, customers are expecting that the liability for a product or service resides with the supplier no matter how stupidly they the customer uses or abuses it. 'If something can go wrong, it will go wrong' is the basic premise behind the Murphy-based robust design method. Not so long ago, none of us would have dreamed that a person would tamper with baby-food products sitting on a supermarket shelf, but nowadays we know that it has happened. The world is a more frustrating place as a result of some of the safety counter-measures that are put in place to counter this kind of once-in-a-billion possibility (a whole series of new contradictions that need to be solved!), but if we are interested in designing the most robust business possible, at the very least we may find ourselves having to contemplate such failure modes.

e) Robustness Contradictions

There is an emerging school of thought that says you can analyse and analyse a system from now until eternity and still not understand what is *causing* a robustness problem. This is the theme expressed by the WE Deming quote that the most important numbers are 'unknown and unknowable'. In the context here, the most important robustness numbers – cost of customer dissatisfaction, failure rate of a system when used in 'real' operating conditions, etc – are indeed both unknown and to all practical (affordable) intents and purposes unknowable.

The idea suggested here, however, is that if it turns out to be impossible to really get to the root cause of a given robustness problem (or if we identify a root cause that there is absolutely nothing we can do to influence), so long as we can identify a contradiction associated with the problem, we might still be able to improve the situation. The idea is based on the belief that if the strongest reliability improvement solutions are those that move away from the traditional compromise based optimization solution approaches (optimization can fundamentally never work if we don't have the data to drive it) and think instead about changing the paradigm. Figure 21.8 re-presents the idea first described in Chapter that eventually all systems will hit fundamental limits beyond which they are incapable of performing, but now from the specific robustness and failure rate perspective. It also turns out that finding a root contradiction is considerably easier than finding a root cause. The next section will detail some of the signs that will help to identify these contradictions. The reader should also, however, keep in mind the strategies for utilizing the contradiction tools described in chapters 11 and 12.

As far as the Matrix is concerned, 'robustness' is considered to be too general a term. Therefore, if we are to translate a specific robustness problem onto the Matrix, we need to map our situation onto one or more of the parameters that make up the sides. The parameter 'Stability' is the closest match in many cases, but other likely connections will include any of the 'quality' or 'risk' parameters, or 'system complexity', or 'tension/stress' (particularly if the robustness problem centres on people issues).

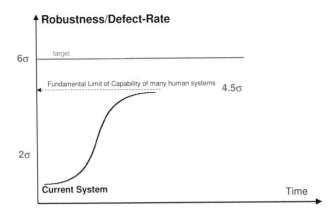

Figure 21.8: Fundamental Limits And System Robustness.

Alternatively, if we do not wish to use the Matrix, we might say that if we are in a situation where we wish to improve robustness, but that something is stopping us, then use all 40 of the Inventive Principles to help generate solutions. In order to reduce the burden a little, experience of applying the Principles to business robustness problems has revealed that the following are more likely to be useful than others:-

10 - Prior Action
('if your system is subjected to harmful factors, create conditions that will protect the system from those harmful factors beforehand')
 3 - Local Quality
(make the system non-uniform, make the environment non-uniform, if multiple functions are to be performed, divide the object into parts according to those functions)
15 - Dynamization
(If a system, or process is rigid or inflexible, make it movable or adaptive)
 2 - Taking Out
(Separate an interfering part or property from a system, or single out the only necessary part (or property).
23 - Feedback
(Introduce feedback (referring back, cross-checking) to improve a process or action)
25 - Self-Service
(Make a system serve itself by performing auxiliary helpful functions)

3) Robustness Check-Lists

In this final section of the chapter, we provide a series of check-lists. Each of the lists is designed for those situations where we are looking to improve the robustness of a given business system using a 'how can we destroy this system?' subversion analysis technique. In order to provide some structure, the lists have been categorized into three focus areas:-

a) lists for when we are analyzing threats emerging from *internal* systems
b) lists for situations when we are looking at *external* threats
c) a more general list for situations in which we are looking to challenge existing norms

Internal Threat Check-List

When we are considering potential threats to robustness emerging from within the organization, the following provides a list of questions designed to help identify where the threats might come from:-

- What's wrong/bad/insufficient/excessive in the organization? (see FAA model) And then; could any of them get worse?
- Could any of them act in combination?
- Are there any self-re-enforcing downward spirals? (Chapter 6)
- What is missing from what we do?
- Is there a unified, over-riding organisational vision and mission?
- Has everyone bought-in to what we are trying to do? Who hasn't? Why haven't they?
- Are we clear about roles and responsibilities?
- What about the overlaps?
- Is there an environment of trust and co-operation?
- Where are the personality conflicts?
- Are people willing to take risks? If not, why not?
- Is there an active suggestion scheme? If not, why not?
- Is the communication between management and staff sufficient? Two-way?
- Is the team under stress? What is causing the stress?
- Is there too much work per person? Are there work balance discrepancies between different roles? Different areas?
- Are there tensions between different areas? Different pay structures?
- Are members of the team happy and involved? Is anyone likely to leave for whatever reason?
- How might home-/tele- working changes affect us?
- How might multiple shift-working patterns affect us? Handover between shifts?
- Is there a succession plan?
- Is there a culture of continuous improvement?
- Are people always encouraged to look for opportunities to improve?
- Are there incentive schemes? Could these turn around and bite us in some way?
- Is enough time allowed for planning?
- Do we review with the team often enough?
- Is initiative fatigue an issue? What are we going to do about it?
- Do we know what skills we will require in the future? Do we know how we will obtain such skills?
- Are there any demographic time-bombs present in the organisation?
- Inventory? Inventory management?
- Cash flow? Working capital?
- Are there any imminent major infra-structure expenditure requirements?
- Is the data we are using accurate, timely and reliable? How do we know?
- Is there anything that we are not measuring that we should be?
- Are there any indicators in place that will let the team know when things are going wrong?
- Are there negative events from the past that may re-emerge and cause problems today?
- Is there any hardware critical to success? Software?
- Are there any emerging changes in pay and conditions expected?
- MRP/ERP – are we working on the right problems?

- Are the shareholders behind us? Hostile/friendly take-over threats?
- Is the trade-union actively engaged in the aims and goals of the work?
- Is the supply chain secure? Where are the weak links? Do we have alternative supplier contingency plans in place?
- Could out-sourced services cause us problems?
- Are suppliers actively engaged in the work? A part of the team?

External Threat Check-List

When we are considering potential threats to robustness emerging from outside the organization, the following provides a list of questions designed to help identify where the threats might come from:-

- Current competitors? How do we discriminate our offering from theirs?
- What are our current competitors doing that is new?
- Are there any emerging competitors in our sector? From other countries?
- In functionally related sectors?
- Any merger or acquisition threats?
- Can anyone outside our industry perform the same functions that we can better than us?
- Do we understand who our 'complementors' are? Are our competitors thinking about complementors?
- Are the channels to the customer stable and secure?
- Do we understand supply-demand elasticity? Are there any cliff-edges we might fall off?
- Are interest rate/exchange rate/tax changes going to affect us?
- Are we too tied to a small number of customers?
- Do we understand our customers fully? Do we visit Gemba?
- Do we understand our competitors' customers? What about non-customers?
- Do we understand how customer requirements may shift in the future?
- Do we take account of religious and cultural differences?
- Would we benefit by importing external knowledge?
- Are there any impending changes in legislation that may affect us? Local? National? Industry?
- How far do people have to travel to get to work? How long does it take them?
- Are there local labour issues that will mean people may leave our organization for another close-by?
- Are we actively involved with the local community?
- What are the ethical and moral issues that may come along and bite us?
- What are we doing about improving environmental and social sustainability?
- Are there likely to be changes in emissions/re-cycling legislation that may affect us?
- Do we have the media on our side? Are there any skeletons in the closet that may re-appear in the future?
- What is our public persona? How might it work against us?
- Possible political threats? Would a change in government affect us?
- Is the education system delivering the people we will need in the future?
- How might future technology shifts affect us?

Challenging Norms

There are many ways to challenge the status quo in systems. We have examined several of them already here. There is a form of subversion analysis technique, however, that is more subtle and difficult to manage than the other forms. This third class involves the words we use as part of every day life that (although we might not be aware of it) are actually very convergent in the way they are interpreted by our brains. Sometimes (most of the time, actually) these convergent words are essential to allow us to select from options and to decide what to do. Convergent thinking is the thing that allows us to get things done. Most of the times this is precisely what we need to do – we don't want to have to think about new ways of brushing our teeth every time we go to the bathroom, for example, we simply want our brain to engage a standard 'teeth-cleaning' programme without the need to consciously think about what we're doing. As most of our lives are about 'getting things done', most of the language we tend to use is convergent in its nature. During the 'divergent' parts of the creative process, however, this naturally 'convergent language' can be more effective idea killers than either psychological inertia or the things we know as 'killer phrases'. More effective because often we don't explicitly think of them as convergent.

Table 21.1 lists some of the main convergent words we use, and, where relevant, their divergent equivalents.

'Convergent' Words	'Divergent' Words
But	And
(this would work, but…)	(this would work, and…)
Either/Or	And
(it's either A or B…)	(A and B…)
The	A/An
(the solution…)	(a solution…)
Is	(Leads) To
(a bottle is…)	(but could lead to…)
Only	A/An
(…is the only way)	(…is a way)
True/False	Often/Maybe
(it is true that…)	(it is often true that…)
Always/Never	Often/Maybe
(we always…)	(maybe we…)
Must/Cannot	Convention/Typically
(we must…)	(conventionally…)
Maximum/Minimum	Convention
(that is the maximum…)	(conventionally…)
Law	Convention
(the law says…)	(conventionally…)

Table 21.1: Convergent and Divergent Words in Language

The table is intended to be used as a check-list of things to try and become conscious of when we are involved in the creatively trying to find ways to destroy systems. Becoming aware of the convergent words being used can in fact open up many new creative opportunities. For example, a long-time systematic innovation user mindset is very much tuned to respond to statements like 'we always…' or 'the solution is' with questions like why? This type of question can be very annoying of course (especially when the person asking the question is thinking divergently and the listener is in (naturally) convergent mode), but it is absolutely fundamental we think to the generation of breakthrough definitions and solutions. The answers to those 'why?' questions may well be the things that our competitors may use to put us out of business.

What Do I Do?

'Robustness' is a very big topic. The database of tools to help do a better job of designing for robustness of business systems is still relatively immature. If you are faced with a 'robustness' problem, however, the recommendation here is:

1) Establish whether or not you can find (or will ever affordably be able to find) the root cause of the problem.

2) If the answer is 'no', or if you establish the existence of a root cause that you have no ability to do anything about, see if you can establish the 'root contradiction' – what is stopping you from improving robustness? Then can you apply the previously described Inventive Principles to derive solution directions? If not, can you formulate a contradiction and use the Business Conflict Matrix or contradiction solution strategies?

3) If not, look at the s-curve progression for design for robustness paradigms (Figure 21.7), see where you are on the trend and then see whether thinking about the next trend along will help you to solve the problem.

4) If it doesn't, or if your answer to the question in 1) was 'yes', then prepare yourself to think about top-down, bottom-up and/or red-team/blue-team subversion analysis techniques as described in Section 2) of this chapter. Keep smiling!

References

1) Utterback, J.M., 'Mastering the Dynamics of Innovation: How Companies Can Seize Opportunities in the Face of Technological Change', Harvard Business School Press, 1996.
2) Tennant, G. 'Six Sigma: SPC and TQM in Manufacturing and Services', Gower Publishing Ltd, November 2000.
3) NASA/MSFC 'Preferred Reliability Practices and Guidelines for Design and Test', web-site, http://msfcsma3.msfc.nasa.gov/tech/practice/prctindx.html

22.
Solution Evaluation

"It is easier to count the bottles than describe the wine."
Thomas Stewart, Fortune

or

"97% of what matters can't be counted."
W.E.Deming

or

"The very essence of the creative is its novelty, and hence we have no standard by which to judge it."
Carl R. Rogers

The final part of the systematic innovation process is the one associated with evaluating the solutions obtained during the previous stages. There are really two tasks to be conducted at this part of the process; the first to identify a 'best' solution from within a range of pre-determined options; and the second to identify whether this solution is 'good enough' to be considered as a final solution. The chapter will examine these two activities separately. In the case of the first – 'best' selection – we will examine two forms of a technique known variously as forced decision making or multi-criteria decision analysis or simply decision analysis. The two forms represent 'simplest' and 'most accurate' capabilities. The second activity under consideration – 'good enough?' – gets us to, first, consider the suggestion that we should always consider 'going around the loop' again, and second presents a series of strategies we can use to help us focus the content of such a loop to best effect.

'Best' Selection?

Multi-Criteria Decision Analysis (MCDA) offers users a systematic method through which it becomes possible to make legitimate 'apples versus oranges' comparisons between different solution options to any complex, multi-dimensional problem. The method also enables multiple people to participate in the process and, perhaps most importantly of all, provides a means of recording the mechanics of the decision process. In its simplest form, MCDA can be conducted using pencil and paper, although for the most part, something like an Excel™ spreadsheet makes a more friendly companion. There are also a number of bespoke software tools (References 22.1, 22.2 and 22.3) to help facilitate the process.

The basic method takes two forms – a 'simple' version based on 'common-sense' calculation procedures, and a more complex form based on the fact that these 'common-sense' based procedures are actually wrong in many situations. We will also examine two extensions, consistent with both procedures, that we can use to obtain the maximum amount of useful information from the decision analysis process.

We will start by examining the simple decision analysis process. This process basically consists of the following steps:

1) The user selects the candidate solutions obtained during the previous 'generate solutions' phase of the systematic innovation process. For the sake of argument, we will label these selected solutions with a unique identifying letter – A, B, C, etc.

2) The user then selects the criteria relevant to the problem and against which each of the solution options will be judged. Typical criteria will be things like the lists provided in Table 22.1. As may be seen from the Table, the evaluation criteria fall into two basic categories; quantitative and qualitative.

Quantitative	Qualitative
Cost/Revenue/Profit/ROI	Aesthetics
Time	Stability
Risk	Durability
Productivity	Transportability
Waste	Convenience
Efficiency/Inefficiency	Adaptability/Flexibility
Robustness	Customisability
Accuracy	Compatibility
Life Expectancy	Controllability
Safety/Liability	Predictability
Environmental Cost	Protectability
	Supportability
	Social Cost

Table 22.1: Typical MCDA Evaluation Criteria
(Notice commonality with Business Conflict Matrix parameters)

3) The user inputs values ('scores') for each of the candidate solutions against each of the evaluation criteria. In the case of 'qualitative' criteria, it is necessary to allocate some form of numerical scoring system. This is done most readily by, first, establishing a numerical range to represent a spectrum from 'worst possible' performance to 'best possible' performance, and then positioning each solution option along the spectrum and allocating an appropriate score. The main things to remember throughout the score allocation process are that the precise numerical value is less important than the relative values between different parameters, and that it is essential to maintain a convention across all of the evaluation criteria of either 'highest score equals best' or 'lowest score equals best'. This is easy to forget, especially when criteria like cost (where higher numerical score value is generally reflective of 'worse') and efficiency (where higher numerical score value is reflective of 'better') are being used in the same analysis – one of the two needs to be inverted (usually using an x/value mathematical operation). If multiple participants are involved in the scoring process, it is useful to collate and average scores, discussing and agreeing any major anomalies that may emerge (preferably before anyone has seen the outcome of the analysis – as it is far more productive to discuss the detailed discrepancies rather than the high-level end result).

4) Next it is necessary to allocate different weighting factors to the evaluation criteria to reflect their different relative importance to the overall outcome. These weightings should again be presented numerically, following appropriate averaging if multiple participants are involved in the process.

5) Having supplied the necessary information, it is now possible to calculate a composite score for each of the candidate solutions. This calculation procedure involves a summation of [score for a given evaluation criterion multiplied by weight of that criterion] for each of the criteria. The candidate solution with the highest (or lowest if that convention is being used) score after the end of the calculation is the 'winner'.

Figure 22.1 below illustrates a set of hypothetical decision analysis data on six candidate solutions (A-F) being ranked against nine different evaluation criteria.

	Price	Op Cost	ROI	MTBF	Life	Performance	Convenience	Ease of Use	Adaptability
A	12000	1200	11	98	400	40	4	4	5
B	11900	1400	10.8	100	430	20	6	6	6
C	10900	1000	9.4	112	450	20	8	8	10
D	10400	1450	11.3	110	400	20	6	6	6
E	10700	1150	10.6	115	400	22	9	8	7
F	11600	1300	9.7	106	360	18	3	6	9
Weight	50	40	10	5	15	10	30	30	40

Figure 22.1: Raw Decision Data For Hypothetical MCDA Analysis

Figure 22.2 below illustrates a sample calculation using this data. A 'highest score equals best' convention has been adopted – note how the price, operating cost and ROI scores have been inverted in order that they remain consistent with this scoring convention. Qualitative criteria like 'convenience' and 'adaptability' have been allocated scores on a 1-10 scale (although any range could have been used). It is recommended that the relative scores for each evaluation criterion are normalised during the calculation procedure in order to maintain consistency. In the calculation process contained in the Figure, all of the evaluation criteria scores have been normalised to a maximum value of 10. The calculation to obtain the Price score for solution A, for example, is [price for A/lowest price (D in this case)]x10. Likewise, A's score for 'ease of use' (where there is already a 'highest is best' scoring scheme) is calculated using [score for A/highest scoring solution (C in this case)]x10.

	Price (N)	Op Cost (N)	ROI (N)	MTBF (N)	Life (N)	Perf (N)	Conv (N)	Use (N)	Adapt (N)	TOTAL
A	8.67	8.33	8.55	8.52	8.89	10	4.44	5	5	1611.35
B	8.74	7.14	8.7	8.7	9.56	5	6.67	7.5	6	1711.6
C	9.54	10	10	9.74	10	5	8.89	10	10	2192.4
D	10	6.9	8.32	9.57	8.89	5	6.67	7.5	6	1755.5
E	9.72	8.7	8.87	10	8.89	5.5	10	10	7	2041.05
F	8.97	7.69	9.69	9.22	8	4.5	3.33	7.5	9	1749
Weight	50	40	10	5	15	10	30	30	40	

Figure 22.2: Sample MCDA Calculation For A Hypothetical Evaluation Activity

The second form of MCDA calculation procedure involves a technique called 'ratio scaling' (Reference 22.4). This technique was developed in response to the recognition that when faced with the above ranking methods, humans all tend to numerically mis-represent the situation. This happens either because by comparing things to a fixed numerical range of score possibilities we fail to adequately measure different parameters relative to each other, or – more seriously – because we fail to capture the true significance of differences. For parameters like perceived value, safety, and risk, for example, humans are generally pretty hopeless in their ability to compare one thing reliably against another. We make the same sorts of errors when we are asked to evaluate qualitative parameters. To give an example here, using an evaluation criterion like 'efficiency' we might identify scores of 98 and 99% for two different solution candidates, but this does not necessarily mean that the difference between them is 1% - indeed if we shift things around to consider the criterion as 'inefficiency, then the 98% efficient solution candidate is actually 200% worse than the 99% efficient candidate. For complex analyses, it is highly likely that the errors introduced by the simplicity of the above calculation procedures will affect the outcome significantly.

The ratio-scaling method seeks to overcome these problems. Although it uses the same basic presentation format as that shown in Figure 22.1, the way in which it acquires the input data is different. The foundations of the enhanced ratio-scaling method involve scoring relative to candidates rather than against an absolute scale. The basic calculation procedure works as follows:-

For each qualitative evaluation criterion:

1) the user selects one of the solution candidates at random. This then becomes the 'datum' for the ratio-scaling analysis. This datum candidate is given a score of, say, 10.
2) The user compares the datum solution candidate and, pairing with each other candidate in turn, asks the question 'how many more times better or worse than the datum is this candidate? There is no limit on the number subsequently supplied. A '1' would signify that the two are equal, a '2' that the new candidate is twice as good, a '0.5' that it is half is good, and so on.
3) After the user has compared all of the other solution candidates against the chosen datum, multiply the resulting comparative scores by the score given to the datum candidate, and then take the logarithm of all the resulting scores. These logarithm scores are the ones that are then used during the decision analysis calculation.

The process is repeated for the criterion weighting factors – a datum criterion being selected, and then the other criteria compared one by one with it.

Note that during this calculation process, some of the scores after the logarithm operation will be negative. If you are using a piece of proprietary software to assist during the analysis, it will normalise results across the different evaluation criteria scores automatically. If you are performing the calculation by hand or using a spreadsheet, you will have to normalise manually.

For each quantitative evaluation criterion:

For quantitative data where it is possible to use the absolute data (e.g. 'price', 'time', 'efficiency', etc) to compare different solution candidates, the only important check to make is to ensure that the scores represent an accurate description of the true differences between different values. The key word here is 'significant', and the key question is 'do the scores truly represent the significance of the differences between different solution candidates?' If the answer is yes they do, then no further action (other than normalising relative to other evaluation criteria) is required. If the answer is no, then some form of mathematical manipulation should be incorporated in order that the significance of differences *is* reflected in the scores.

By way of example, the earlier description of the 98 and 99% efficiency scores may require each value to be subtracted from 100 if it is actually the size of the inefficiency that is important (in terms of lost business, for example, a system achieving 99% customer retention efficiency would have half the level of lost customers of a system achieving 98% retention). The main point here is that the user needs to establish the significance metric on a case-by-case basis.

Figure 22.3 below provides an example ratio-scaling calculation for the analysis previously conducted for Figure 22.1.

	Price (N)	Op Cost (N)	ROI (N)	MTBF (N)	Life (N)	Perf (N)	conv'ce	Conv (C)	Ease Use	Use (C)	Adapt	Adapt (C)	TOTAL
A	8.67	8.33	8.55	8.52	8.89	10	5	5.37	2	2.153	8	6.939	142.3609
B	8.74	7.14	8.7	8.7	9.56	5	10	7.687	10	7.154	10	7.687	150.0861
C	9.54	10	10	9.74	10	5	15	9.039	20	9.307	20	10	175.8654
D	10	6.9	8.32	9.57	8.89	5	10	7.687	10	7.154	10	7.687	155.1836
E	9.72	8.7	8.87	10	8.89	5.5	20	10	25	10	20	10	178.1449
F	8.97	7.69	9.69	9.22	8	4.5	5	5.37	10	7.154	20	10	145.7382
Weight	30	10	4	15	2	10		40		10		2	
Corrected Weight	3.401	2.303	1.386	2.708	0.693	2.303		3.689		2.303		0.693	

Figure 22.3: Repeat of MCDA Calculation for Using Ratio-Scaling Calculation Procedure

To see how an actual calculation is made, take the Convenience assessment criterion and the score for candidate solution A. The highest convenience score is 20 (in row E). Take logs (base e or 10 – we tend to use e) of this value = 2.9957. Then to get this number to equal 10 (so that each column has a common datum level) we need to multiply the ln20 value by 3.338 – which then becomes the multiplication factor applied to all the other parameters. Hence the normalized convenience score for A is calculated as ln(5) x 3.338 = 5.372.

Points to note about this analysis:-

1) Only qualitative parameters – relative evaluation criteria weights and convenience, ease of use and adaptability criteria were subjected to the ratio-scaling calculation as these are the only parameters subject to the previously discussed human errors.

2) In each of these cases, a datum was selected at random and the other values then compared to this value. In the case of the convenience, ease of use and adaptability criteria, solution B was selected as the datum. In the case of the weighting factors, operating cost was selected as the datum. The datum parameters were then given 10 points, and the other solutions or weights were then compared one by one relative to this 10 score. The raw data row and columns reflect the outcome of this comparison exercise.

The basic process worked using a sequence like:-
If solution B scores 10 for comfort, what score would you give A?
If solution B scores 10 for comfort, what score would you give C?
etc

3) The raw scores were then processed by first taking logarithms. In the case of the safety, comfort and appearance columns, these log values were then re-datumed back to a maximum value of 10 in order to maintain parity with the normalised scores for other selection criteria.

Although the case study is obviously hypothetical, it is perhaps interesting to note how the different scoring system has altered the outcome of the analysis. It is unusual for the winner to change when switching from simple to ratio-scaled calculation methods like this, but very common for some order change to take place lower down the ranking list.

Sensitivity Analysis

Occasions when it is possible to supply a single, accurate value for each of the scores and for each of the evaluation criteria weighting factors are rare. This is particularly evident

503

during the scoring of qualitative criteria and the weighting of criteria relative to one when multiple participants are involved in the process. It is often the case in these situations that different opinions will result in potentially considerable differences in scores obtained. In other cases, it may simply not be possible to ascertain or agree any form of 'score' – thus leaving holes in the data.

Sensitivity analyses can help to establish whether these differences and holes are significant or not. They are usually only practical using some kind of automated calculation procedure – either Excel or one of the previously mentioned pieces of proprietary software. A typical sensitivity analysis will take pairs of elements within the calculation grid (i.e. either individual scores or weighting factors) and systematically vary them over a pre-determined range based on the level of uncertainty associated with them. Generally speaking the elements analysed during this activity will be the ones where the level of uncertainty concerning their score is highest. A typical output of this type of paired parameter sensitivity analysis is reproduced in Figure 22.4.

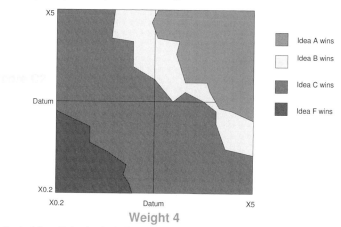

Figure 22.4: Typical Sensitivity Analysis On A Pair Of Uncertain (Or Missing) Scores Or Weights

The figure illustrates how changes in the scores of the uncertain elements of the analysis impact on the ranking of the candidate solutions. In the plot above, only the impact on the winning idea is included, but other forms of presentation may be used to illustrate different phenomena depending on the flexibility of the presentation media.

The main purpose, then, of the sort of picture shown in the figure is to identify how sensitive the 'answer' produced by the analysis is to variation in different elements. In the hypothetical example presented in the plot, the presence of several possible 'best' solutions over the range of the two varied elements suggests that the decision is highly sensitive to variation. On the other hand, a plot that exhibits little or no change in outcome as the two elements are varied is indicative that the sensitivity of the solution to variation is low.

In situations where the sensitivity is shown to be high a useful strategy is to go around the systematic innovation process loop again, looking to establish possible ways of integrating the best features of some or all of the solutions the sensitivity analysis is suggesting are potential winners.

Robustness Analysis

The general idea behind robustness analysis is to identify which of the evaluation criteria scores and weighting factors have the greatest impact on the outcome of the analysis. The analysis is, like the above sensitivity analysis, quite intensive from a calculation intensity perspective, and as such is most practically achieved through a software implementation.

The basic calculation procedure used in this kind of analysis is for each score and each weighting factor to be gradually increased in turn until a change in the candidate solution with the highest score occurs. The calculation sequence is repeated until all scores and weights have been analysed. The changes can be recorded in various ways. Figure 22.5 illustrates a technique using colour change.

The basic idea behind this kind of robustness assessment is to gain a general view across the complete range of variables as to how much of a change needs to occur before the 'answer' produced by the analysis changes. If the analysis indicates that large changes (say 40% or greater) have to take place before any change in outcome occurs, the solution produced is a robust one. If, on the other hand, even small perturbations produce changes in result, it is prudent to consider going around the systematic innovation process loop again, combining the best features from relevant candidate solutions.

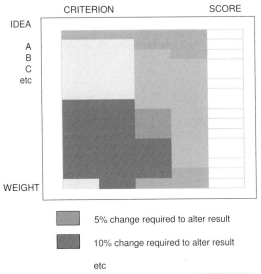

Figure 22.5: Typical Robustness Analysis Output Plotting Format

Good Enough?

Whatever the outcome of the evaluation procedure used to identify the 'best' solution from a range of candidates, the systematic innovation process will recommend that we consider going around the Define-Select-Solve-Evaluate loop at least two times. This is to overcome the psychological inertia problem of our brains entering 'satisfied' mode (Chapter 4) once we have what we think is a good solution. In systematic innovation terms, we can always do better. In practical terms, countless examples – including some described throughout the book – suggest the prudence of going around the loop at least twice.

505

So, how do we decide if our winning solution is 'good enough'?

The simplest way, of course, is to compare the solution to the benefits and 'how will we know when we have got there?' questions we should have answered right at the beginning of the problem/opportunity explorer (Chapter 5) part of the problem definition activity. If the solution meets all of the requirements stated here then we theoretically have good cause to believe we have 'finished'. On the other hand, we would always recommend that you at least briefly explore some of the 'good enough?' tests described below.

We will briefly discuss a number of techniques and tools – some more formal in their approach than others. In all, we will examine four:-
1) Trimming
2) 'The Next Contradiction'
3) Resource Assessment
4) Combinations

Trimming

Although it carries one or two dangers in terms of when it is appropriate to apply it, the Trimming tool (Chapter 18), presents a useful metric concerning the effectiveness and resource efficiency of a system. That metric involves the ratio of useful functions performed by a system per number of elements present. The higher this ratio, the closer to the Ideal Final Result (IFR) end state that a system is likely to be. The ratio is best calculated by, first summing the number of useful functions, and then dividing by the number of elements present. 'Useful functions' here means the functions that are genuinely required – as opposed to, say, functions that are present solely to support other functions that are not being performed well enough, or are there to eliminate harmful side-effects. A ratio of unity represents a good target. When this state has been reached, there is one element per useful function. In many systems, this ratio can be bettered – i.e. elements become capable of performing more than one useful function – but care needs to be taken that the reduction in number of elements has not come at the expense of compromising some other element of the system. In the true IFR state, the ratio will tend to infinity as the useful functions are progressively delivered by fewer and fewer elements.

'The Next Contradiction'

Finding a 'good' unresolved contradiction is an excellent lead into finding a better way of solving a problem. Using the solution that has just emerged as the best from the evaluate part of the systematic innovation process, and seeing if we can spot what the next conflict or contradiction is going to be is an often useful exercise. Imagine the solution in use, the useful functions it delivers and how those functions might be expected to evolve in the future (more? less?). Then try to imagine what in the system will prevent this evolution from taking place. This will then give us a good indication of what the 'next contradiction' will be. Use Chapter 11 or 12 to identify possible means of resolving this contradiction.

Resource Assessment

If looking for the next contradiction is the best way of 'going around the loop again', then identifying resources that we haven't taken advantage of in our chosen solution is not far behind. The key question to be asking here is, did we find a resource (something not being used to its maximum potential) that still is not working as hard as it could? If the answer is 'yes', then explore ways of integrating something from this under-utilised resource into the solution. The evolution potential concept discussed in Chapter 14 offers a means of quantifying the resource effectiveness within system elements. This is possible since it represents a quantifiable scale of global trend discontinuities. Thus, when we examine different systems from the evolutionary potential perspective we are able to compare each against a trend scale uncovered following the study of every available kind of technical or business system. If we take two or more systems that we wish to compare with one another, we then simply have to overlay the radar plot from one on top of the others. An example is provided in Figure 22.6. We usually call this kind of analysis 'global benchmarking' since, not only does it allow comparison of one system with another, but it also allows both to be compared against a global best practice (i.e. the outside perimeter of the radar plot). See also Reference 22.5 for an example of an evolutionary potential *'global-benchmarking'* study.

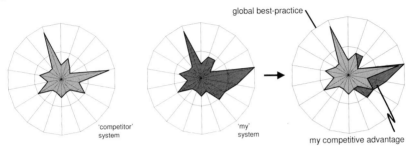

Figure 22.6: Overlaying Of Evolution Potential Plots Offers Global Benchmarking Capability

Combinations

If we see features we like from different solution options, see if there is any way of distilling some of those features into the chosen solution. See Reference 22.6 for more details of formal methods for achieving such integration. If we can see such opportunities, we should take whichever ideas we are looking to combine and feed them into the start of a new iteration of the systematic innovation process. Reference 22.7 describes the very strong correlation between the number of inventive ideas that are combined together and the overall strength of the solution that they produce together.

What Do I Do?

If we are looking to find the 'best' out of a group of solution alternatives, use one of the variations on the multi-criteria decision analysis theme discussed at the beginning of this chapter. If the solution we are looking at represents a relatively simple system and the criteria you are using to evaluate one option against another are few in number (say 5 or less), then a simple ranking or absolute score based evaluation system should be accurate enough. If the solution is complex, and the evaluation criteria many, then you should use the ratio-scaling technique to ensure accurate identification of the winning solution option.

If there is access to a software-based evaluation tool, we would be well advised to conduct sensitivity and robustness analyses in order to satisfy ourselves that the solution we have picked is genuinely the best one for the greatest possible range of circumstances.

In terms of is our solution 'good enough', the systematic innovation process will always encourage us to iterate through at least twice. Use one or more of the techniques identified in the previous section to help clarify the form and direction of that next iteration.

References

1) CREAX Innovation Suite, v3.1 or higher, Multi-Criteria Decision Analysis tool option, www.creax.com.
2) Decision Lab, www.visualdecision.com
3) Analytica, www.lumina.com.
4) Lodge, M., 'Magnitude Scaling – Quantitative Measurement of Opinions', Sage University Papers, Quantitative Applications in the Social Sciences, 1981.
5) Dewulf, S., Ventenat, V., Mann, D.L., 'Case Study In TRIZ: Global Benchmark Evaluation of Thermal Comfort in Sports Equipment', TRIZ Journal, December 2003.
6) Pugh, S. 'Total Design', Prentice Hall, 1991.
7) Mann, D.L., 'Re-Calibrating The Contradiction Matrix, TRIZ Journal, February 2002.

23.
Into The Future

If systematic innovation is so good at predicting the future, then what happens when we apply the method to the method? That is the theme of this chapter.

As we now know, systematic innovation places great importance on the existence of evolutionary s-curves. The first thing to say, then, is that the current level of 'innovation' knowledge and capability does not feel like the 'final s-curve'. There is, in all likelihood, at least one 'higher-level' s-curve still to emerge. In these terms, the difference between the s-curve for systematic innovation (actually, bearing in mind the different variations, such an s-curve should be seen as the average of a cluster of subtly different s-curves) and an equivalent average curve that might be constructed for such a higher-level innovation capability is illustrated in Figure 23.1.

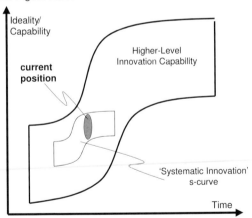

Figure 23.1: Systematic Innovation And A Higher-Level Innovation Capability

The idea that systematic innovation is merely one s-curve (system) inside a bigger system emerges from the concept of recursiveness in systems. The current prevailing view is that recursion will be an important element in the successful realisation of a higher-level s-curve.

This chapter is divided into two unequal parts. The first part describes ongoing work on the development of systematic innovation in which we hope to show that, although the system is relatively mature, there is still scope for significant improvement and extension. The second, longer, part of the paper examines some of the main 'other' creativity tools, methods and philosophies and the role they may be expected to play in the higher-level 'systematic innovation' picture. To varying degrees all of these other tools, methods and philosophies may be represented as systems with their own series of s-curves. Rather than attempt to position such s-curve approximations relative to systematic innovation, we focus only on their role in serving the higher order s-curve development.

Evolving Systematic Innovation

The systematic innovation toolkit in its business and management form is still relatively new. As new inputs and cases are added to the knowledge-base, we have seen fewer and fewer things that have come along and caused us to alter the framework or even the content. As such, we felt that now was an appropriate time to compile and publish this book. That being said, we know – as we have seen with the technical version of the toolkit – that it still has considerable untapped potential. The technical version has the advantage of a much longer pedigree, with nearly sixty calendar years unfolding since the work first began. In that time, we have seen that, for example, the Contradiction Matrix tool published in 1973 is considerably different from the one that we did the research for and published in 2003 (Reference 23.1). We didn't find any new Inventive Principles in this research (although we looked; and we did find a number of important combinations of Principles), but we did find the need to include new parameters in the list that makes up the sides of the Matrix, and we also saw that the Principles being used by 21st Century inventors were often considerably different from their predecessors. There is no reason to assume that the business world will evolve at a pace that is any slower than has happened in the technological one. If anything, the evidence is there to say that it is and will continue to evolve at a somewhat faster rate.

With that thought in mind, we continue to pursue an active programme of business and management research. Among the things we are working on that can be expected to feed into the methodology and future editions of this book are the following:-

- updating the Business Conflict Matrix in terms of both its form (updating the list of 31 parameters for example) and content. Based on the minor shifts that have taken place since the first version of the Matrix published in 2002 and the new version published here, we anticipate that the content will remain stable enough that a revised version will not be necessary until 2008. We will, of course, continue to review the position as new case studies are analysed and conducted.
- identifying new Inventive Principles. Whilst the list of Principles has remained at 40 for some considerable time now, a strong correlation between the number of Inventive Principles used in a given solution and the effectiveness of that solution is emerging. The consequence of this is that we are also seeing the emergence of a number of important Principle combinations – cases where two, three or even four Principles are being combined together commonly enough to merit publishing these combinations.
- identifying the emergence of new trends of evolution. In this regard, we believe that we have already uncovered a host of previously undiscovered discontinuous business trends. We strongly believe that there are more to be uncovered as time progresses.

- identifying the emergence of new Measurement Strategies. Measurement continues to be a significant management activity. We therefore anticipate the possibility that new inventive measurement strategies will emerge in the coming years.
- identifying and incorporating new tools. The speed at which tools outside the current systematic framework will be integrated (or more formally rejected) will largely depend on the demand from the user market. Anyone that is using, and moreover continues to use a tool or strategy that currently resides outside the systematic innovation framework after they have been exposed to it will have found something that we believe has a place in the whole. We continue to actively look for such opportunities. The total presented in this book is the state of the art as we see it so far. I.e. everything we are aware of following our hopefully all-encompassing search has been considered.
- expansion of the knowledge and resources check-lists. In addition to our own in-house team, we have a network of associates and a user-community who will continue to help us to add new entries.
- as the use of semantic tools expands, we anticipate a growing link between them and the thought processes and tools found in the business version of the systematic innovation toolkit.

Evolving The Higher-Level Systematic Innovation Capability

A systematic programme of research to compare and contrast different creativity tools, methods and philosophies in terms of their relevance to business applications (Reference 23.2) has concluded that the current form of the systematic innovation methodology currently offers the most useful foundation for a higher order model. A large part of the justification for this statement comes from the fact that the philosophical pillars of the current system are considerably more developed than for others. Given this foundation, the other available methods that are best able to complement and help deliver the higher order model are those that have also evolved to incorporate elements of a philosophy. In this section we explore the other systems that have evolved to this state and the opportunities that arise when they become integrated with systematic innovation. As shown in Figure 23.2 the current integration opportunities appear to come from Quality Function Deployment (QFD), Six Sigma, Lean and Sustainability.

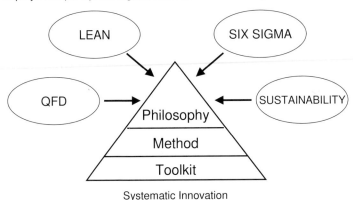

Figure 23.2: Philosophical-Level Integration Opportunities

To varying degrees, all of these additional methods have already been the subject of some form of work to explore the benefits of integration with the systematic innovation framework already. We now briefly review such work with particular reference to integration aspects at the highest philosophical level.

QFD

The integration of the 'holy trinity' of TRIZ, QFD and Taguchi methods was the subject of Reference 23.3. Theoretically, the three complement each other very well; QFD is about capturing the voice of the customer and translating it into design specification; systematic innovation is about generating solutions that fit the specification; and Taguchi/Robust Design tools are about optimising the implementation details of those solutions. The practice is currently seen to be some considerable distance away from the theory for the large majority of users, however.

The biggest problem involves the usual failure of QFD to accurately capture that customer voice. Customers are frequently unable to describe what it is that they want other than in terms of 'better' than the thing they already have. Few if any customers would ask for a digital camera given a conventional film camera and a request for ideas on creating a better solution. This is an area where systematic innovation – and particularly the technology trend prediction elements – is emerging as a more effective start point than QFD. As suggested in Figure 23.3, there are already working processes that are aimed at bringing together the best of each method in order to tackle the customer voice issue.

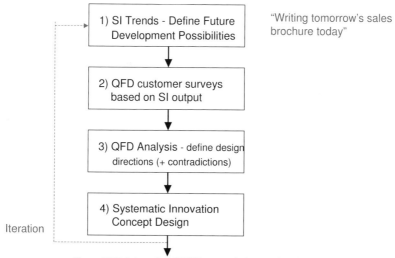

Figure 23.3: Integrated QFD/Systematic Innovation Scheme

Looking beyond this existing integration at the methodological level, it appears clear also that QFD also has something to offer at a philosophical level. Figure 23.4 illustrates a philosophy/method/tool hierarchy for QFD. At the philosophical level, QFD has two main things to offer to systematic innovation; first of all there is the recognition of customer-value as the primary driver of innovation. Actually there is already relatively little distance between the two at this point in time, beyond the fact that the customer is probably viewed as much more a 'way of life' in QFD. It still has something to offer systematic innovation in this regard. The second philosophical connection is the idea of barrier-elimination. This is an area that is emphasised much more explicitly in QFD than it is in systematic innovation. Barrier-elimination in this context is about breaking down the barriers that traditionally exist between customer and provider, 'going to Gemba' is all about intimate observation of what customers *actually* do with the products and services, rather than what we would like them to do.

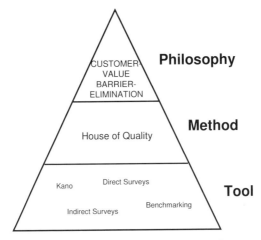

Figure 23.4: QFD Philosophy/Method/Tool Hierarchy

There is believed to still be significant mileage in incorporating the intricate subtleties that emerge from these simple QFD philosophies into the systematic innovation framework.

Six Sigma

Systematic innovation and Six Sigma are becoming more and more intimately connected thanks to a powerful link between the two at the operational level. Whether we are talking about Six Sigma or Design for Six Sigma (DFSS), it is clear that neither is capable of generating the levels of defect-rate reduction that the 3.4 defects per million opportunities target demands in many situations. According to Reference 23.4, very often the limit of capability of the two happens at or around 4.5 Sigma.

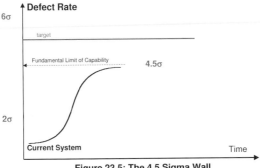

Figure 23.5: The 4.5 Sigma Wall

513

As illustrated in Figure 23.5, when we have a difference between our target and the fundamental limits of a system (the limits in this case often being the human being – which has really not evolved as a 'six sigma animal'), then our only alternative is to do something to change the system. Changing the system, of course, is precisely the area at which systematic innovation excels.

Beyond this – undoubtedly important – working level connection between the two systems, there are many other possibilities for integration between the two. The integration story is really just beginning at this point in time. We focus here on integration possibilities at the philosophical level. One of the reasons that Six Sigma has taken off so extraordinarily well is that companies like GE, Allied-Signal and Motorola have claimed such big savings through their deployment of the method. Another is that, thanks to its longevity (via a number of previous incarnations) it has developed strong philosophical roots.

Figure 23.6 illustrates a philosophy/method/tool hierarchy for Six Sigma. Again we will focus here on the philosophical level possibilities. It is worth noting, however, that the TRIZ version of systematic innovation is already viewed as a tool within the Six Sigma framework by many working in the field.

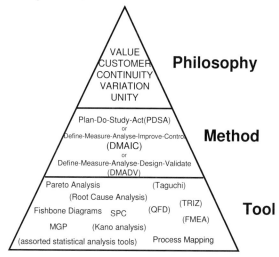

Figure 23.6: Six Sigma Philosophy/Method/Tool Hierarchy

Comparing the philosophy of Six Sigma and the pillars of systematic innovation it is possible to see a number of complementarities and contradictions. The main contradiction – or potential contradiction – involves variation reduction. Variation reduction is one of the fundamental drivers of Six Sigma. Variation reduction is, of course, important. Okay, usually it is – we're probably not too disappointed if the number of fries in our portion doesn't achieve 6σ reliability, but we're probably very, very worried if we think the person who designed the engine that carries us over the Atlantic was thinking in terms less than 8, 9 or maybe even 10 sigma.

The point here is that the 'Define' part of the DMAIC process should be the thing that guides what level of sigma we actually require to achieve. Or rather, does the customer require. Even more important than this is the idea – thinking about the normal curve illustrated in Figure 23.7, below – that it is not just about variation reduction, but also making sure we have identified the right mean value.

Figure 23.7: Defining The Problem And The Normal Curve

Six Sigma, of course, encourages us to think (hard) about customers and what customers want. This means that, hopefully, we stand at least a fair chance that we will pick the 'right' mean. This is a good thing. It could, however, be a much better thing if we begin to integrate some systematic innovation thinking into this Six Sigma philosophy.

We will mention two elements of this kind of systematic innovation/Six-Sigma integration thinking in this discussion:-

a) The first concerns 'function'. Six Sigma will tell us to take into account the wishes of the customer. Unfortunately, customers are often not very good at telling us what they want, and so we have to do things to help elicit the information we need for them. Six Sigma makes no great connection to 'function' since very few customers are explicitly thinking about function either. What systematic innovation will tell us, on the other hand, is that whether they can tell us about it or not, those customers are buying functions from us. So, a very good first step in ensuring we are delivering the 'right' solution – and therefore are working on the 'right' Six Sigma project – is making sure we have understood the function of the thing or service we are working on, and whether our current way of doing things is delivering that function in the most appropriate way.

b) Many of the tools of Six Sigma are concerned with 'optimization'. We have already mentioned the importance of ensuring we are optimizing on the 'right' thing, but there is an even more important point that emerges when we start to bring the systematic innovation ideas on contradiction and contradiction elimination into play. Figure 23.8 presents a hypothetical example of how we might typically use a normal curve to help determine the 'optimum' value of an element of the thing we are designing. This could be 'average' shoe-size, or age of a customer, or operating temperature, or whatever else might be important. As a part of constructing this normal curve we will acquire a bunch of data (which can be very time consuming of course – but not to worry, because, hey, at least we will look and feel busy while we are doing it). Then what do we do? We effectively eliminate anything which lies outside our 6σ range. This is what 'common sense' tells us to do. No problem. Except that we might just have thrown away some very important data. If we think about 'contradictions' then all of the stuff we discard is very definitely important. What about if we could produce a solution that achieved not just the 'average' value, but also achieved the values at the extreme ends? Every thing we say is outside our scope is an either/or decision – you can either have the mean or the extreme. Well, of course, we have selected the mean to include the majority of situations and so why should it matter? It matters because if we can achieve the mean AND the extremes then we have solved a contradiction.

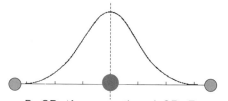

Extreme B   OR   'Average optimum'   OR   Extreme B

Figure 23.8: Every Rejection Of Extreme Values Is A Lost Contradiction Resolution Opportunity

Let's take a trivial example; let's say we're trying to design a computer keyboard, and we're trying to work out the best ('optimum') configuration. One of the things we might look at is the age of the customer that is going to use the keyboard. This is likely to lead us to an average customer age of (say) 25 years. Likely as not, anyone younger than 3, or older than 65 is likely then to be off our design radar screen. Net consequence? Old people and young children are usually disadvantaged when they try and use our keyboard. Probably the marketing department will have done some analysis that shows that neither of these customer types is going to bring us any significant revenue, so, hey, who cares?

How about if we re-think this problem from the perspective of resolving the contradictions present? What about if the keyboard was usable by 2 year-olds *and* the twenty-something hot-shot *and* grandma? Sounds dumb? Let's take the thinking a step further and see:

Grandma is likely to type slowly and uncertainly due to a likely unfamiliarity with the computer. On the other hand, she has probably used a keyboard before and knows what key is where. So she is a user we could classify as 'slow but intelligent'. The two-year-old on the other hand is likely to be 'slow and not so intelligent' – as likely to hit the keyboard with a fist as with a carefully placed finger in fact. What if the keyboard was able to recognize the difference between these two users? Maybe, if we could do this, we would also have a design that could discriminate between a twenty-something able to type with two fingers versus a twenty-something who types with all ten? Or whether a user is relaxed or frustrated (e.g. through the force of key-presses)? Or if the user is dyslexic? The point being that thinking about the extremes of the normal curve gets us to define contradictions that, if we can solve them, make the plotting of the curve completely irrelevant.

Anytime we find ourselves plotting normal curves and trying to find an 'optimum' anything – both things that Six Sigma will encourage us to do – we are missing a potentially very important opportunity to define a better (compromise-eliminating) solution. At the very least, this should be worth a thought during that brief initial planning activity.

Two quotations help us to take this story a little further:-

> *"Normality is the route to nowhere. If we are only willing to behave like all the others, we will see the same things, hear the same things, hire similar people, come up with similar ideas, and develop identical products or services. We will drown in the sea of normality. And Normal Inc. is bankrupt."*[23.5]

and

> *"Mediocrity is the by-product of consistency"*[23.6]

There are elements of Six Sigma and Design For Six Sigma that encourage us to think about the Customer and to use the Customer to help guide you to the best mean, but, the next problem then is that different customers have different ideas about what the mean should be. Some don't even know what mean to ask for. Even fewer are asking you to eliminate it altogether. Take a confectionary manufacturer. The manufacturer wishes to know the 'optimum' size and form of a new cake product. To achieve this they conduct all sorts of customer research, consult dieticians, portion-size experts, psychologists, restaurant owners, the whole shebang, and hey presto, several hundred thousand currency units of consultancy fees later, out comes the magic number. The golden mean. The ultimate cake. And so, happy that they have discovered the ultimate cake, they go into production. As is normal in the food industry there are many uncertainties in the baking and cake making process and so defect rates are inevitably quite high. Obviously the fact that some cakes don't rise as well as others, that some have too much icing one them, that the edges occasionally over-cook means they can't be passed on to the customer – consistency is everything! – and consequently, the rejected cakes cost a lot of lost revenue. So the management embark on a Six Sigma programme with a goal of three defective cakes per million baked. Nine hundred and ninety nine thousand, nine hundred and ninety seven perfect cakes; all the same weight, the same height, the same ratio of sponge to filling to topping. Perfect.

Perfect, except. How many customers decided that that particular combination of weight, height and topping ratio was their own personal definition of perfect? Who, ultimately, wants the compromises that a mean anything ultimately forces on you? Is there really such a thing as an 'optimum' anything?

Answer; yes there is, but only until such times as someone comes along, recognizes that everywhere the words 'optimum' or 'mean' are being used, and says to themselves, 'maybe there is a better way'. Systematic innovation tells us that someone, somewhere already solved our problem. Maybe not in the confectionary business, but someone, somewhere literally has found a way of making things 'heavy and light', 'big and small', 'golden brown and dark brown'. Someone – at the risk of making a very bad pun – literally has already found a way of having their cake and eating it.

The world is increasingly choked with 'optimum' solutions that don't meet the needs of their customer. Next time you are in your local supermarket, take a look at the fruit section. Observe how each of the bananas are the same size and colour, how each bunch looks exactly the same as the next. They got that way because someone decided there was such a thing as the optimum banana and forced a set of inspection criteria on the banana growers; we will only buy your bananas if they conform to these strict size and colour criteria. Result; the six sigma banana. Secondary result; they don't taste anything like as good as they used to and they are rarely as moist, because someone decided that size and colour were more important than taste and texture.

What the supermarkets recognized was that we only taste the banana after we get home; at the point where we decide to buy, we are only able to look, and hence the 'look' is the thing they optimized. Infallible logic. At least until such times as they begin to wonder why bananas aren't selling like they used to.

The main point of this part of the Six Sigma philosophy discussion, though, is to provoke some thinking about how we might go about solving some of these 'having your cake and eating it' contradictions. Let's think, then, about the concepts of common and special cause failures.

The two terms come from the work of Deming during his time thinking about measurement of processes. If we're trying to achieve the 'optimum' (does systematic innovation say that word should always be written in inverted commas?) size of our cake, then we might set up a cake-size survey to present to potential customers. Each customer is asked about their preferred size of cake and their answers are recorded.

If we record this data on a control chart, the first thing that it will (hopefully) show is that our process is 'in control'. That is, we have surveyed enough people to deliver a statistically significant result, with a stable mean value, a standard deviation about that mean, and all of the survey results coming out within plus or minus three standard deviations of the mean. If this were not the case, then we have a problem of the system, or a 'common cause' problem. A 'system problem in this case may mean that we have formulated the survey questions inaccurately, or that different surveyors are interpreting answers in different ways.

But then what happens if a new potential customer has suddenly given us a very different answer to the one the system would have told us to expect. Since we know that our process is 'in control' then we know that this can't happen, that it cannot be a problem of the system. It is, whether we are aiming for Six Sigma understanding of our customer or not, a problem that, therefore, has a 'special cause'.

Deming's main point in discriminating between 'common' and 'special' causes was that each required a different problem solving strategy. Special cause problems are not caused by the system and hence any attempt to resolve them by modifying the system would tend to make the system worse. In this case, worse because it now routinely has to look for a special cause which, by definition of being 'special' is not going to occur again. Conversely, if we treat a common cause problem as a special cause problem, we will miss an opportunity to improve the system.

Another quote from Reference 23.6 to complement the earlier one:-

"The pace of... change is increasing at the same time that we're witnessing a radical contraction in the distance from the Edge to the centre of Social Convention. The result of this acceleration is the Abolition of Context, the disintegration of the social, cultural, and commercial framework. In commercial terms this means that market opportunities are created and disappear with a frequency that can't be monitored by conventional business thinking."

Connection to common cause and special cause problems? Answer; everything is becoming a special cause problem.

In other words, by the time we've worked out what our 'optimum' is, and 'optimized' the system to consistently deliver that optimum, somebody is increasingly likely to have changed the game on us and made that 'optimum' irrelevant.

If this is true, how might that influence the way we think about things? How would we think about our world if we treated everything as a special cause?

The thought is quite probably too radical for many of us to even contemplate. In that sense it is a deliberately provocative suggestion. If we are in charge of a manufacturing operation churning out nuts and bolts then clearly if we are going to continue selling our products in a highly competitive environment, then we absolutely have to have an SPC process in place and be driving towards elimination of defects and waste. But, the big point is that at least *someone* in the organization ought to be taking this 'everything is becoming a special cause' perspective.

The additional thought here is that everything we treat as 'common cause' – everything, in other words, that we treat as an opportunity to improve the current system – is taking us along a well-optimized corridor to a dead-end. This is undoubtedly a philosophical issue that will need to be addressed if Six Sigma and systematic innovation are to be fully integrated with one another.

This is an example of how systematic innovation might alter Six Sigma thinking. There is an influence in the other direction, albeit one that is a little more controversial, when we examine the 'unity' pillar of Six Sigma. Unity is an area that has been one of the great factors behind the success of Six Sigma, since all improvement initiatives require buy-in from everyone involved in the organization. There is no such equivalent in systematic innovation at this point in time. It is difficult to say for certain whether this unity factor explains why Six Sigma has spread so much faster than systematic innovation, but it is something that at least needs to be considered. Based on the number of problem solving jobs we experience with clients, buy-in appears to be a serious issue. This is especially so when thinking about innovation; where, very often, the proposed change is not good news for – or at least is not perceived as such – by significant parts of the organization.

Overall, we expect the links between systematic innovation and Six Sigma to strengthen considerably in the foreseeable future.

Lean

The separate worlds of 'Lean' (Reference 23.7 is a good place to start for newcomers), Six Sigma and systematic innovation appear to be on a convergent path. Like Six Sigma, Lean is rather better known than systematic innovation, thanks in no small part to the successes of Toyota and a large swathe of automotive companies following in their wake. A philosophy/method/tool breakdown of Lean would look something like Figure 23.9.

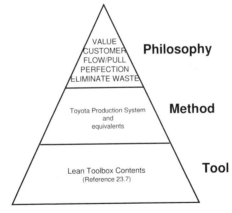

Figure 23.9: Lean Philosophy/Method/Tool Hierarchy

Again, if we focus on the high-level consistencies and contradictions between Lean and systematic innovation, a number of opportunities may be seen to emerge.

On the consistencies side, we may see that the ideas of 'pursuit of perfection' and 'customer value' connect well to the ideality and functionality pillars within systematic innovation. Systematic innovation pushes the perfection idea somewhat further than will be found in Lean, but both are intended to serve the same purpose; encouraging users to take a long term future perspective.

Beyond that, the Lean drive towards a 'pull' based production capability (i.e. things get made only when an order is in place) is again consistent with systematic innovation ideas, except that the idea is less explicit in the latter. 'Pull' is usually connected to the idea of 'flow' in the Lean context. Here we get into an area of potential inconsistency with systematic innovation, as 'flow' is not necessarily viewed as appropriate at all times in an innovation context.

More seriously contradictory is the principal Lean driver – 'waste elimination' – and the equivalent perspective in systematic innovation. The differences here stem mainly from the complexity and emergence perspectives. While 'waste elimination' is generally speaking a good thing to do, according to complexity theory, this is not always the case. This may be a somewhat controversial view to take, since the prevailing management logic would clearly view 'waste' as a bad thing. Indeed, in many instances it is. Natural systems tend towards the same logic. In nature we see the evolutionary pressures of 'survival of the fittest' favour systems that waste less than those around them. But natural systems that optimize themselves too much tend to be the ones that become extinct. Take the dodo – in its original environment, the ability to flight was unnecessary and hence putting energy into flight-worthy wings was 'wasteful' from an evolutionary perspective. Evolution favoured birds that 'spent' their available resources on things other than a flying capability, and over time the whole species became flightless. Fine until a predator appears that is able to run (and shoot!) much faster than the bird is able to do.

Nature has much to teach us about 'waste' elimination. In nature too, evolution favours low waste. But nature also shows how you can waste-eliminate yourself into a cul-de-sac that you will not be able to get out of. Some of the 'waste' in a natural system is the thing that allows life-forms to adapt when their environment changes. In a business world where change has become the only constant, the no-waste companies are increasingly likely to find themselves in a position where they are producing highly efficient, no-waste dodos.

Sustainability

The link between systematic innovation and (environmental) sustainability is still comparatively new. Reference 23.8 presents a state-of-the-art perspective of the working level links currently in place. The pairing is undoubtedly one that looks set to grow in the future, in part due to funding support from the EU (Reference 23.9), but also because there is again a high degree of consistency between the goals of sustainability and the capabilities of systematic innovation.

On some levels, it could be argued that 'sustainability' already fits into the systematic innovation framework. Certainly nothing in any of the systematic innovation tools precludes the incorporation of sustainability issues. It is perfectly possible, for example, to think about and include social and environmental issues when using any of the tools in systematic innovation. The ones where the link is most likely to be made are the situation definition tools concerned with function and attribute analysis and with the Ideal Final Result. At a higher philosophical level, however, 'sustainability' forces a much more holistic emphasis on any innovation activity – with requirements to take account of social and environmental impacts in addition to the economic impacts that are the only normal consideration in most organisations. Figure 23.10 illustrates a philosophy/method/tool hierarchy for 'sustainability' (the word is used in parentheses here since work on sustainability is considerably more fragmented than that found in Lean or Six Sigma or other equivalently sized initiatives).

As with Lean and Six Sigma, the links between systematic innovation and sustainability look set to expand considerably in the coming years.

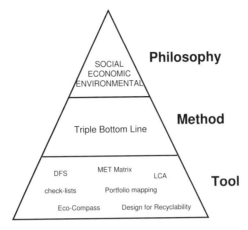

Figure 23.10: Sustainability Philosophy/Method/Tool Hierarchy

In addition to the likely areas of integration discussed above, systematic innovation is also increasingly being used in conjunction with a number of other creativity and innovation systems. Integration here is happening primarily at the tool and method levels:

Theory of Constraints (TOC)
The process of integration of Eli Goldratt's Theory of Constraints into systematic innovation has also begun (Reference 23.10). The Theory of Constraints matches systematic innovation in its recognition of the importance of defining and eliminating contradictions and, while it offers less in terms of strategies to overcome contradictions, it does offer the Evaporating Cloud tool which does offer increased richness in terms of increasing problem understanding and entry points for breaking the contradictions. Related to this, but also a much more important area where TOC can be expected to enhance systematic innovation comes with its emphasis on modelling causes and effects inside systems. Several other important TOC ideas (identification of bottlenecks, strategies for overcoming bottlenecks for example) can be expected to find their way into future systematic innovation models.

NLP
Although instigated more recently than systematic innovation, Neuro-Linguistic Programming has evolved from a very similar philosophical start-point. Both have been built on the study and abstraction of 'excellence'. In the case of systematic innovation, the global scientific, patent and business databases have provided the basis of method development; whereas in the case of NLP it was cognitive science research into linguistics, psychology, cybernetics and anthropology. Both have sought to study 'creativity' from the perspective of modelling known successful creative personalities. Latterly, NLP has drawn additional knowledge from psychotherapy – including Gestalt and Hypnotherapy. Perhaps these latter two extensions have tended to draw NLP away from the mainstream somewhat, and certainly exploitation of NLP in business or scientific practices for example is practically non-existent in most fields of endeavour. This is undoubtedly a pity as NLP offers significantly greater richness than systematic innovation in many areas. Initial research to understand the areas of common ground and opportunities for mutual benefit (Reference 23.11) between the two systems have

521

highlighted a significant number of high level concepts that exist in one or the other but not both.

By way of a simple example, Chapter 4 discusses the 9-window or 'system operator' scheme and how NLP has been used to extend its essentially two-dimensional space and time perspective into a third dimension which might be called 'interface' or relationship. Figure 4.8 illustrates this new three-dimensional operator as an example of a concept that did not exist in either classical TRIZ or NLP, but emerges purely from the integration of the two.

The integration of systematic innovation and NLP tools and methods is still very much at the beginning of what may be expected to be a long and fruitful road. Several important conceptual advances can be expected to emerge. Some of the ones already identified include:-

- strategies emerging from NLP research into application of inventive principles acting in direct combination with one another
- strategies emerging from NLP research into application of inventive principles combinations operating at different hierarchical levels
- explanations of why 'asymmetry' provides such an important inventive strategy
- better understanding of 'inversion' (e.g. Inventive Principle 13) and the importance of 'inversion of inversions'
- identification of how the meta-programmes underlying the way the human brain work and how they in turn determine our behaviours both individually and in groups.
- employing the links between mind-state and parallel physiological phenomena to improve business communications

Kansei

As systematic innovation extends further towards business applications in industrial design, architecture and the arts it becomes apparent that issues like emotion and 'spirituality' are not handled as well as they ought to be by current models. The idea that it is possible to systematise those elements of business design that relate to the things we describe as 'x-factors', 'the mysterious wow', and other labels implying that we don't understand what makes one design better than another one, is positively offensive to some. Kansei engineering on the other hand represents an attempt to achieve exactly this kind of understanding of why people prefer one artefact over another one. Kansei is undoubtedly also at the beginning of its evolutionary potential. It is already possible to embody a number of Kansei principles and strategies into a tool integrated into the systematic innovation framework, but too soon to speculate on whether the integration of the two will create new high level conceptual benefits. All we can say with certainty, is that where systematic innovation is still comparatively weak, Kansei has something of benefit to offer.

Looking Further Ahead

We all have problems to solve, and opportunities we wish to explore in inventive ways right now. Some people may want just a few tools or strategies to help them. Others may be looking for a higher level start-to-finish process. And still others are looking for a higher level creativity philosophy from which they hope everything else might emerge. In other words, we are all different, work in different ways and want different things. There is currently no single 'creativity' entity that will satisfy every individual desire. If there ever is, one thing it will have to encompass is due recognition of individual difference, and (to introduce a systematic innovation concept) be self-adapting to accommodate those differences. At a practical level, this might simply mean that person A likes DeBono, TRIZ and QFD, while person B uses NLP and TOC and doesn't like TRIZ and that both can still work effectively together. The aim of the systematic innovation framework is to achieve this kind of flexibility. As with the higher level 'systematic innovation' s-curve, it is still early days. Our hope is that we've at least realised a framework that offers users the prospect of tangible benefit now.

Beyond the here and now, there are several emerging creativity models that have not so far been explored in the context of their place in a higher level systematic innovation picture. These include game theory, spiral dynamics, general periodicity and quantum psychology/mechanics. Work to explore the relevance and potential benefits of integrating these models into the systematic innovation framework described here (or, indeed, the other way around) has barely begun at this point in time. We expect there to be mutual benefits, and we expect to play a role in exploring what they might be.

What Do I Do?

The systematic innovation methodology is evolving at a steadily increasing rate. If the overall goal is to encapsulate excellence from 'all that is known', then by rights it must be difficult to ignore. Some people will decide that they are happy with just a small element of the enormity of the whole that it offers, others will find themselves wanting not only to expand their knowledge, but also to contribute towards the task of evolving things.

There is still much work to be done to even germinate the seeds of the next generation of capability. It may turn out that the time is not right to do it yet. At this point in time, we cannot know for sure. What is certain, however, is that everyone has some of their own 'excellence' to add to the picture. The next generation of capability will certainly need both bottom-up and top-down inputs. Big-picture thinkers and fine-detail precisionists alike have a part to play.

One of the first big intentions of systematic innovation was that it should be developed by all, for all. It is not clear that the current capitalist-dominated world will allow such a thing to happen. We can but try.

References

1) Mann, D.L., Dewulf, S., Zlotin, B., Zusman, A., 'Matrix 2003: Updating The TRIZ Contradiction Matrix', CREAX Press, June 2003.
2) Mann, D.L., 'Beyond Systematic Innovation (Integration of Emergence and Recursion Concepts into TRIZ and Other Tools)', paper presented at 8th European Conference on Creativity And Innovation, Mainz, Germany, September 2003.
3) Terninko, J., Zusman, A., Zlotin, B., 'Systematic Innovation – An Introduction to TRIZ', St Lucie Press, 1998.
4) Mann, D.L., Domb, E., 'The 4.5 Sigma Wall Using TRIZ to Exceed Fundamental Limits', TRIZCON2003, Philadelphia, April 2003.
5) Ridderstrale, J., Nordstrom, K., 'Funky Business: Talent Makes Capital Dance', Pearson Education Ltd, London, 2000.
6) Mathews, R., Wacker, W., 'The Deviant's Advantage: How Fringe Ideas Create Mass Markets', Random House Business Books, 2003.

7) Bicheno, J., 'The Lean Toolbox', PICSIE Publications, Buckingham, UK, 2001.
8) Mann, D.L., Dekoninck, E. 'Systematic Sustainable Innovation', paper presented at 8th Centre For Sustainable Design conference, Stockholm, October 2003.
9) www.leonardo-support.com
10) Mann, D.L., Stratton, R., 'Physical Contradictions and Evaporating Clouds', TRIZ Journal, April 1999.
11) Bridoux, D., Mann, D.L., 'Evolving TRIZ Using TRIZ and NLP', paper presented at TRIZCON2002, St Louis, April 2002.

Appendix 1
Company Innovation Scan

*"I know that you believe you understand what you think I said, but I'm not sure
you realize that what you heard is not what I meant"*
Richard Nixon

or

*"In a time of drastic change,
it is the learners who inherit the future.
The learned usually find themselves equipped
to live in a world that no longer exists."*
Eric Hoffer

or

"You don't fatten a pig by weighing it"
Anonymous

As managers we are taught to love measuring things. 'To measure is to understand' is a commonly used piece of logic. And of course, up to a point, it is true. One of the main proponents of measuring stuff was quality guru, W. Edwards Deming, but even he said that the most important numbers are unknown and unknowable. So what are we left with? Probably something like; measurement is great if you have no data, but at the end of the day having measured something is only the beginning of the story.

'Innovation' is, for many companies, one area where there is no data. Everyone knows that innovation is important, but few if any know with any kind of objective certainty that they are doing a good job at it.

For us the issue was slightly different. Working with so many different clients in such a wide range of industries and disciplines, and with such diverse skills and capabilities means that everywhere we go we have to tailor what we offer to try and meet the specific needs of the people we are meeting. Trying to work out what modifications were required in which situations was a big problem to us. We could, of course, have simply done what most other companies do and said that we will offer a standard, one-size-fits-all package. There may have been some justification in doing this bearing in mind that one of the big underlying ideas of systematic innovation is that we are all of us solving more or less the same problems at a certain level of abstraction. Try telling a lawyer that your decidedly mechanical-looking contradiction matrix is relevant to his business, however, and you pretty soon get to see that you are not going to make too much progress.

And so we decided that we needed our own measurement 'scan' tool. The big idea then was to distill best innovation practices from wherever we could find them in order to define a global benchmark standard. To do this, we first needed to work out what the right things to be looking for were; what were the parameters that would determine whether a company was 'good' at innovation or not? In the end – two years after beginning to think about the problem – we ended up with 13.

Those 13 stem from the three crucial aspects of innovation that we could see wherever we went. Those three are Action, Knowledge and Creativity. As suggested by Figure A.1, successful innovation requires all three of these elements to happen.

Innovation = DOING THINGS BETTER

Innovation = ACTIONxKNOWLEDGExCREATIVITY

Figure A.1: Three Essential Elements of Innovation

The three elements assume that by 'innovation' we mean that we have actually delivered a new or modified product or service to a customer, that that customer likes, wants to have, and is willing to pay us more than it cost us to produce and deliver it. This is not a definitive definition of 'innovation' of course (something we could argue about for weeks if we wanted to), but it does contain the essence of what we think it is about.

Meanwhile, back to the three core strands of Action, Knowledge and Creativity, it appears clear to us that very few companies have mastered all three. Hence there are very few companies that are indeed 'good' at the job. Many are good at one or two of the three. What the multiplication signs between the three elements try to make clear, however, is that if any one of the three has a value of zero, the end result is zero too. So if your organisation has racks and racks of great ideas that never seem to go anywhere, then your area of weakness is 'Action'. Another common fallacy is that if a company applies enough Knowledge, it can get away with not applying any Creativity. This was a strategy that used to work, but it rarely does any more. Knowing about your customer and technology and all those other things that are needed to understand what it is that you should be doing is not enough, because it is increasingly likely that that information is also available to your competitors. Innovation today needs to take all of the masses of knowledge and work some creative magic on it.

Okay, so now we have 3 main elements that define how good a company is at innovation. In Figure A.2 we expand those three elements into the 13 that we think are necessary to produce a measurement system that will actually produce some meaningful outcomes.

What the figure also shows is the radar plot presentation format we decided to use. This form allows us to summarise a lot of information into a compact and yet hopefully easy to read format. The standard plot offers users an assessment of their capability against each of the 13 assessment criteria, and a 'global average' value. This 'global average' is a constantly moving average that is building and evolving as more and more companies undertake the Scan. In some circumstances, it is also possible to add a third set of data to the plots – what an outsider thinks of your innovation capability. This is a service that several companies have been asking us to provide for some time, and allows them to understand a) how they view their capability, b) how an impartial, knowledgeable outsider views it, and c) how those two compare with a global average. As we've said already, this information does nothing to actually deliver any improvements in the way companies do things, but it does allow them for the first time to objectively see where they are, and what their strengths and weaknesses are.

Figure A.2: Thirteen Elements Of The 'Company Innovation Scan'

Before getting in to the details of how a company can actually begin to access and use the tool, it is worth spending a few moments exploring the meaning of the 13 assessment criteria in a little more detail:

Knowledge Parameters first:-

Internal - how the organisation uses, organises and manages the knowledge contained within the company

Customer - how the organisation extracts knowledge from current and prospective future customers – about what they want and don't want. Includes knowledge of competitors and others in the same field

Intangibles - how the organisation thinks about intangibles within and external to the organisation. Intangibles include skills, experience, alliances, relationships, brand recognition, processes

Global/Env. - how the organisation accesses and utilises global knowledge both in terms of ensuring the business uses the most effective solutions for the job, but also understanding how what the organisation does impacts on the environment. I.e. there is an impact of world on the business and also of the business on the world

Direction - how the organisation manages the fact that knowledge is dynamic and therefore has a characteristic that is constantly changing and evolving.

Creativity:-

Need Aware -   a measure of how aware the organisation is of the importance
of innovation and the culture it contains to ensure that the will,
desire and motivation to be innovative exists and thrives
(similarly, the awareness that there are times in the business
cycle when different types of innovation are required

People -   what is the level of creativity of the people within the organisation
(in effect, this category would be the result of integrating all of the
individual creativity self-assessments for everyone in the company -
such assessments can be performed on-line at www.creax.com/csa)

Tools -   a measure of the number, quality and effective deployment of the
available creativity and innovation tools, techniques and strategies

Action:

Specification -   what the organisation works to produce; the methods of
prototyping, verification and validation and use of physical
resources

Cost Issues -   how well the organisation transforms its financial resources
into useful output ('bang per buck'). Particularly important is the
identification and realisation of win-win opportunities

Time Issues -   how well the organisation utilises its time resources. Again,
identification and realisation of win-win opportunities is important

Risk Mangmt -   how well the organisation understands and accommodates
risk issues into its innovation activities. Use of fall-back models,
understanding of contingency, critical path, 99% complete syndrome
and other issues that result in 90% of projects everywhere finish
either late, over-spent or under-specification

Co-ordination-   how the organisation manages the overall innovation process, both
in terms of action, but also how the other knowledge and creativity
elements are integrated.

The Scan is produced through an on-line questionnaire. You can find this questionnaire at

www.systematic-innovation.com

It takes the form of 101 questions designed to extract the necessary innovation information
required to compare your system with the best-known practices. You will find that the Scan
is context specific in that it will not ask you about manufacture innovation strategies if you
say that you are from a bank (or anywhere else that has no interest in 'making stuff'). It
usually takes around 20 minutes to complete.

All data entered into the system is completely anonymous. There is an option to supply an
e-mail address should you require more information about the Scan or the results that you
obtained. We can even help you to transform your measurement into tangible
improvements if this book hasn't already helped you to make a difference yourself.

Appendix 2
Problem Explorer

In a time of drastic change,
it is the learners who inherit the future.
The learned usually find themselves equipped
to live in a world that no longer exists."

Eric Hoffer

'DEFINE' PACK

This pack offers a series of questions you should be asking during the DEFINE stage of a problem or opportunity.

The main aim is to get you to think about your situation in terms of how it is affected by TIME and SPACE

You may not be able to answer all of the questions and some may not be relevant in your particular situation. The important thing is that you ask them.

Print the sheets out, or fill them in electronically (download available at www.systematic-innovation.com).

If you need more space, make copies or use blank pieces of paper.

Although the pack gives you a structured way of communicating your situation to others it is up to you to use the sheets in a way that best suits the way you work.

Feel free to alter the sequence in which you complete the sheets.

Any time you obtain a new insight into your situation feel free to jump into the Solution Generation toolkit (you can then return to your departure point later on if desired)

Date

Project Title

Project Sponsor

Project Customer

Project Team

Benefits

Where are we trying to get to (what are the goals)?

How will we know when we've got there (measures of success)?

Sponsor

Customer

Team

What Is The Problem?

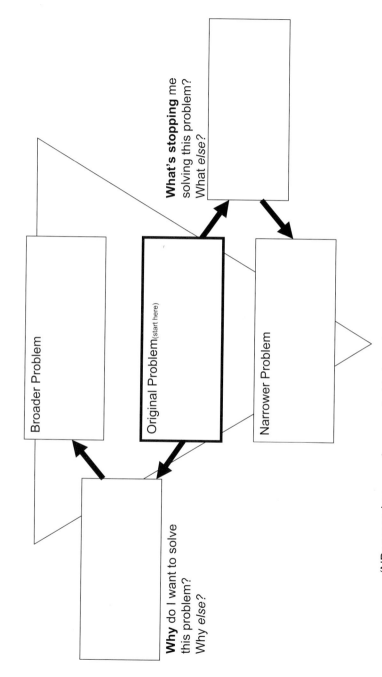

Broader Problem

Original Problem (start here)

Narrower Problem

What's stopping me solving this problem? What *else?*

Why do I want to solve this problem? Why *else?*

(NB: procedure may be repeated to broaden or narrow the problem to more levels)
The aim of this sheet is to get you to think about what your problem is, and at which level you are going to try and solve it

What Is The Current System? (based on the level of problem you decided from the previous sheet)

TYPES OF INTERACTION

Effective _____

Missing ....

Insufficient - - - - →

Excessive ⇒

Harmful ◄〰〰►

(Plot the current components in the system, then identify the positive functional relationships between the components, then identify the negative relationships)

How does TIME affect the system?

(If there is a time either in the past or in the future (or both) where the functionality of the system is different, record those differences here)

(The 'past' or the 'future' may mean less than a second or it might mean more than a decade.')

(Think specifically about times immediately before a problem occurs and/or immediately after)

Future (meaning?)

Past (meaning?)

Perception Mapping? (for situations where different people have different perceptions of a situation)

Question you are trying to answer:

	Perceived Answer	Leads To?	Conflicts ?
A			
B			
C			
D			
E			
F			
G			
H			
I			
J			
K			
L			
M			
N			
O			
P			
Q			
R			
S			
T			
U			
V			
W			
X			

(Suggested minimum number of perceptions: 10)

Perception Map

Look for: - Loops

   - Collector Points

   - Conflict Connector Chains

535

Resources - Technical (Function, Substance, Field) (Pay particular attention to the things that are not being used to their maximum effect, and negative things)

	Past	Present	Future
Around the system			
System			
Within the system			

Resources - Knowledge

	Past	Present	Future
Around the system (SPONSOR)			
System (including CUSTOMER)			
Within the system (TEAM)			

Constraints – Tangible/Technical (Function, Specification, Tools)

	Past	Present	Future
Around the system			
System			
Within the system			

Constraints - Business (Time, Cost, Risk, Process, Skills)

	Past	Present	Future
Around the system (SPONSOR)			
System (including CUSTOMER)			
Within the system (TEAM)			

Sore Point

What are we trying to improve?

What are the things that are stopping us?

Think about time, cost, quality, risk type issues.

Think about the things between the things – relationships, communication links, control links,

Think about where in the value chain the situation exists – pre-production, production, delivery, support

Think about efficiency parameters - waste or loss of all kinds of resources, functions or attributes

Think about all the things that customers are expecting from you - reliability, convenience, price, intangibles
Think also about the things that customers aren't able to described that they want from you.
Think also about the things that your non-customers might expect from you.

Sore Point

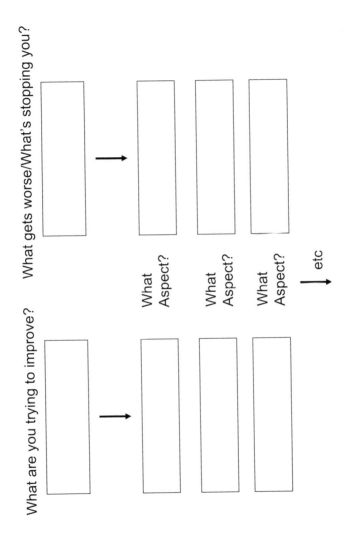

What are you trying to improve?

What gets worse/What's stopping you?

What Aspect?

What Aspect?

What Aspect?

etc

Sore Point - Where/When are the potential or known bottlenecks and contradictions?

	Past	Present	Future
Around the system			
System			
Within the system			

(It may be that the sore point exists in only one of these boxes)

IDEAL FINAL ATTRIBUTES

(Use this template if you wish to make a comprehensive search for conflicts and contradictions in a system)

ATTRIBUTE	CUSTOMER A IFR	CUSTOMER B IFR	PROVIDER IFR	etc →

ATTRIBUTE CONFLICTS

Key questions when looking for conflicts: 'Is there anyone who does not want this IFR?' Why?
'Is there a new attribute we should be thinking about?'

543

IDEALITY

(You should only use this sheet if your constraints allow you the freedom to think of clean-sheet of paper solutions to your problem)

What function are you trying to achieve?

What is the Ideal Final Result (IFR)?
(Achieving the function without any cost or harm.
Think about the system solving the problem by itSELF)

What's stopping you from achieving the IFR?

Why is it stopping you?

How could you make it go away?

How might you work back from the IFR to a practical solution?

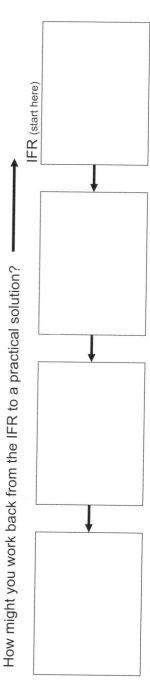

IFR (start here)

(As you work back from the IFR solution, apply minimum compromise at each stage, and concentrate on conceptual solutions rather than specific ideas. The further back from the IFR you go, the more possible concepts there may be.)

544

How Mature Is The Current System?

System

- Retirement
- Maturity
- Growth
- Infancy
- Birth
- Conception

Time

Sub-Systems

Time

Time

Index